REFERENCE

Biography Today

Profiles of People of Interest to Young Readers

Volume 17—2008
Annual Cumulation

Cherie D. Abbey
Managing Editor

South Huntington Pub. Lib.
145 Pidgeon Hill Rd.
Huntington Sta., N.Y. 11746

Omnigraphics

P.O. Box 31-1640
Detroit, MI 48231-1640

Cherie D. Abbey, *Managing Editor*

Peggy Daniels, Laurie DiMauro, Joan Goldsworthy, Jeff Hill, Kevin Hillstrom,
Laurie C. Hillstrom, Eve Nagler, and Diane Telgen, *Sketch Writers*

Allison A. Beckett and Mary Butler, *Research Staff*

* * *

Peter E. Ruffner, *Publisher*
Matthew P. Barbour, *Senior Vice President*

* * *

Elizabeth Collins, *Research and Permissions Coordinator*
Kevin M. Hayes, *Operations Manager*
Cherry Stockdale, *Permissions Assistant*

Shirley Amore, Martha Johns, and Kirk Kauffman, *Administrative Staff*

Copyright © 2008 EBSCO Publishing, Inc.
ISBN 978-0-7808-1021-1

All rights reserved. No part of this publication may be reproduced or transmitted in any form or by any means, electronic or mechanical, including photography, recording, or any other information storage and retrieval system, without permission in writing from the publisher.

The information in this publication was compiled from the sources cited and from other sources considered reliable. While every possible effort has been made to ensure reliability, the publisher will not assume liability for damages caused by inaccuracies in the data, and makes no warranty, express or implied, on the accuracy of the information contained herein.

∞

This book is printed on acid-free paper meeting the ANSI Z39.48 Standard. The infinity symbol that appears above indicates that the paper in this book meets that standard.

Printed in the United States

CMG
INDEXED IN
Children's Magazine Guide

Contents

Preface.. 7

Aly & AJ 11
American Singers and Actresses

Bill Bass 1928- 23
American Forensic Anthropologist and Pioneer in the Study of Human Decomposition

Greta Binford 1965- 39
American Biologist, Arachnologist, and Pioneering Researcher in Spider Venom

Cory Booker 1969- 53
American Political Leader and Mayor of Newark, New Jersey

Sophia Bush 1982- 67
American Actor, Star of the TV Show "One Tree Hill" and the Movies *John Tucker Must Die* and *The Hitcher*

Majora Carter 1966- 79
American Urban Planner, Environmental Activist, and Advocate for Environmental Justice

Anderson Cooper 1967- 91
American Television Journalist and Host of the CNN News Show "Anderson Cooper 360"

Zac Efron 1987-....................................... 107
American Actor, Singer, and Star of *High School Musical* and *Hairspray*

Selena Gomez 1992- 121
American Actor and Star of the Hit TV Show "Wizards of Waverly Place"

Al Gore 1948- 131
    American Political Leader, Environmental Activist, Former Vice
    President of the United States, and Winner of the 2007 Nobel
    Peace Prize

Vanessa Hudgens 1988- 153
    American Actress, Singer, and Star of Disney's *High
    School Musical*

Jennifer Hudson 1981- 165
    American Singer, Actress, and Winner of the 2007 Academy
    Award for *Dreamgirls*

Zach Hunter (Brief Entry) 1991- 179
    American Anti-Slavery Activist and Founder of Loose Change
    to Loosen Chains

Bindi Irwin 1998- 189
    Australian Wildlife Enthusiast and Host of TV Nature Shows

Jonas Brothers 199
    Kevin Jonas, Joseph Jonas, Nick Jonas
    American Rock Band

Lisa Ling 1973- 211
    American TV Journalist and Host of National Geographic's
    "Explorer"

Eli Manning 1981- 225
    American Professional Football Player with the New York
    Giants and Most Valuable Player of the 2008 Super Bowl

Kimmie Meissner 1989- 241
    American Figure Skater and 2006 World Figure Skating
    Champion

Scott Niedermayer 1973- 257
    Canadian Hockey Player with the Anaheim Ducks; All-Star
    Defenseman and 2007 Conn Smythe Trophy Winner

Christina Norman 1963- 271
    American Media Executive and President of MTV

Masi Oka 1974- 285
Japanese-American Actor and Special Effects Artist, Creator of Special Visual Effects for Movies, and Star of the Hit TV Show "Heroes"

Tyler Perry 1969-. 301
American Playwright, Filmmaker, Actor, and Creator of the "Madea" Plays and Movies and the TV Series "House of Payne"

Morgan Pressel 1988- 319
American Professional Golfer, Youngest Woman Ever to Win a Major Golf Championship

Rihanna 1988- 331
Barbadian Singer, Performer of the Hit Songs "Pon de Replay," "S.O.S," and "Umbrella"

John Roberts Jr. 1955- 345
American Lawyer and Chief Justice of the U.S. Supreme Court

J. K. Rowling 1965-. 361
British Children's Writer and Author of the Award-Winning *Harry Potter* Novels

James Stewart Jr. 1985- 383
American Motorcycle Racer and 2008 AMA Motocross Series Champion

Ichiro Suzuki 1973-. 395
Japanese Professional Baseball Player with the Seattle Mariners

Karen P. Tandy 1953-. 415
American Former Administrator of the Federal Drug Enforcement Agency (DEA) and First Woman to Lead the U.S. Battle against Illegal Drugs

Marta Tienda 1950-. 431
American Sociologist and Pioneering Researcher of Ethnic, Economic, and Educational Issues

Justin Timberlake 1981- 447
American Singer, Songwriter, and Six-Time Grammy Award Winner

Lee Wardlaw 1955- 467
  American Writer for Children and Young Adults and Author of
  101 Ways to Bug Your Parents and *101 Ways to Bug Your Teacher*

Photo and Illustration Credits 485

Cumulative General Index 489
  (Includes Names, Occupations, Nationalities, and Ethnic and
  Minority Origins)

Places of Birth Index 541

Birthday Index 557
  (By Month and Day)

The Biography Today General Series 571

Preface

Biography Today is a magazine designed and written for the young reader—ages 9 and above—and covers individuals that librarians and teachers tell us that young people want to know about most: entertainers, athletes, writers, illustrators, cartoonists, and political leaders.

The Plan of the Work

The publication was especially created to appeal to young readers in a format they can enjoy reading and readily understand. Each issue contains approximately 10 sketches arranged alphabetically. Each entry provides at least one picture of the individual profiled, and bold-faced rubrics lead the reader to information on birth, youth, early memories, education, first jobs, marriage and family, career highlights, memorable experiences, hobbies, and honors and awards. Each of the entries ends with a list of easily accessible sources designed to lead the student to further reading on the individual and a current address. Retrospective entries are also included, written to provide a perspective on the individual's entire career.

Biographies are prepared by Omnigraphics editors after extensive research, utilizing the most current materials available. Those sources that are generally available to students appear in the list of further reading at the end of the sketch.

Indexes

Cumulative indexes are an important component of *Biography Today*. Each issue of the *Biography Today* General Series includes a Cumulative Names Index, which comprises all individuals profiled in *Biography Today* since the series began in 1992. In addition, we compile three other indexes: the Cumulative General Index, Places of Birth Index, and Birthday Index. See our web site, www.biographytoday.com, for these three indexes, along with the Names Index. All *Biography Today* indexes are cumulative, including all individuals profiled in both the General Series and the Subject Series.

Our Advisors

This series was reviewed by an Advisory Board comprising librarians, children's literature specialists, and reading instructors to ensure that the concept of this publication—to provide a readable and accessible biographical magazine for young readers—was on target. They evaluated the title as it developed, and their suggestions have proved invaluable. Any errors, however, are ours alone. We'd like to list the Advisory Board members, and to thank them for their efforts.

Gail Beaver
Adjunct Lecturer
University of Michigan
Ann Arbor, MI

Cindy Cares
Youth Services Librarian
Southfield Public Library
Southfield, MI

Carol A. Doll
School of Information Science and Policy
University of Albany, SUNY
Albany, NY

Kathleen Hayes-Parvin
Language Arts Teacher
Birney Middle School
Southfield, MI

Karen Imarisio
Assistant Head of Adult Services
Bloomfield Twp. Public Library
Bloomfield Hills, MI

Rosemary Orlando
Director
St. Clair Shores Public Library
St. Clair Shores, MI

Our Advisory Board stressed to us that we should not shy away from controversial or unconventional people in our profiles, and we have tried to follow their advice. The Advisory Board also mentioned that the sketches might be useful in reluctant reader and adult literacy programs, and we would value any comments librarians might have about the suitability of our magazine for those purposes.

Your Comments Are Welcome

Our goal is to be accurate and up-to-date, to give young readers information they can learn from and enjoy. Now we want to know what you think. Take a look at this issue of *Biography Today*, on approval. Write or call me with your comments. We want to provide an excellent source of biographical information for young people. Let us know how you think we're doing.

                        Cherie Abbey
                        Managing Editor, *Biography Today*
                        Omnigraphics, Inc.
                        P.O. Box 31-1640
                        Detroit, MI 48231-1640

                        editor@biographytoday.com
                        www.biographytoday.com

Congratulations!

Congratulations to the following individuals and libraries, who are receiving a free copy of *Biography Today* for suggesting people who appear in this volume:

Mollie Ballard, Vienna Elementary School, Vienna, WV
Miranda Becker, Danville, ID
Paul Bishette, Silas Bronson Library, Waterbury, CT
Jessica Blanchard, Aboite Elementary, Ft. Wayne, IN
Michael Bosquez, San Saba, TX
Janis Brooks-Owings, Robyler Middle School, El Reno, OK
Amanda Heidecker, Marysville, WA
Mary Louise Helwig-Rodriguez, Little Falls Public Library, Little Falls, NJ
Bershard Horton, Longview, TX
Uzmah Khan, Independence K-8—Elkhorn, Lodi, CA
Hallie Mazzanera, Hartmenie School, Salt Lake City, UT
Alburto McCley, Sulphur Springs, TX
Noel Miranda, Harmon Johnson Elementary School, Sacramento, CA
Randy Olund, Carrington Middle School Media Center, Durham, NC
Alexis Pedretti, Magnolia Elementary, Riverside, CA
Lisa Scharf, Memorial Junior High School and Ridge Junior High School, Mentor, OH
Miranda Trimm, L.E. White Middle School, Allegan, MI
Brianna Watson, Clarksboro, NJ
Tiana Watson, Philadelphia, PA
Diego Yangali, Valley Stream, NY

ALY & AJ
Aly (Alyson Renae Michalka) 1989-
AJ (Amanda Joy Michalka) 1991-
American Singers and Actresses

BIRTH

The singing and acting team of Aly and AJ is made up of two sisters: "Aly" is Alyson Renae Michalka, who was born on March 25, 1989, and "AJ" is Amanda Joy Michalka, who was born on April 10, 1991. Both were born in Torrance, California, and they spent the early years of their life in that city, which is part of the greater Los Angeles area. Their father, Mark Michalka, is a commercial contractor. Their mother, Carrie

Michalka, is a musician who has played in a Christian band and other musical groups and previously worked as a cheerleader for the Los Angeles Raiders football team.

YOUTH

Both Aly and AJ inherited their mother's love of performing, and they took to the stage at a very young age. Their first "shows" took place around the time when Aly was five years old and AJ was three. They put on dance routines for friends and relatives and also sang and appeared in plays at their church. Soon, they began attending acting workshops and studying piano. "It just came naturally to them," their mother said of their musical abilities. "It wasn't forced at all." The girls later took up the guitar and became skilled at that instrument as well. From the beginning, they liked to perform together, which reflects the close relationship they have always enjoyed. Aly and AJ have described themselves as "the first set of twins to be born two years apart," and their bond is a key part of their musical collaboration. "Aly and I are best friends," AJ explained. "Working together means I can basically hang out with my best friend all the time." Aly has agreed with that idea, noting that the few sisterly disagreements they have are short-lived because "we never stay mad at each other for long."

> Aly and AJ have described themselves as "the first set of twins to be born two years apart." As AJ explained, "Aly and I are best friends. Working together means I can basically hang out with my best friend all the time."

The Michalkas moved to Woodinville, Washington, while Aly and AJ were young. It was there that the sisters first began appearing as models for print advertisements and magazine photographs. Those jobs, along with their appearances in plays and musical shows, made it clear that they possessed a great deal of talent and a strong desire to launch serious professional careers. The only holdup was their parents, who worried that the demands of show business might cause the girls to miss out on some important parts of growing up. "They really wanted us to live normal lives," AJ explained in the biography *Amped Up: Aly & AJ*. "That was what they were weird about, in a good way." In the end, however, mom and dad decided to let their daughters pursue their dream.

EDUCATION

Even after becoming professionals, Aly and AJ still had to devote time to their education. They had been home-schooled throughout their lives, however, so they were able to adopt a flexible schedule that helped them to fit their assignments in around their other work. Both girls graduated from an independent-study charter school—Aly in 2006 and AJ in 2007—and were the valedictorians of their respective classes. The sisters are interested in attending college, though they have no definite plans on where or when they will enroll.

CAREER HIGHLIGHTS

Though fans of Aly and AJ's music may think of the girls as an inseparable team, the two started out by pursuing individual modeling and acting careers, and both became successes in those fields before being signed to a record deal. The first to strike gold was AJ, the younger sister, who began modeling around age nine. She landed jobs in print advertisements for Disney and American Girl and also appeared in national television commercials. AJ was eager to take on dramatic roles, and her career got a boost when the Michalkas left Washington and moved back to the Los Angeles area, where many TV shows and movies are produced. She made her breakthrough in 2002, appearing briefly on a daytime drama and then landing the part of the Huntress on the WB series "Birds of Prey," which was cancelled after 13 episodes. Roles in other TV programs followed over the next two years, including a continuing part as Shannon Gressler on the CBS drama "The Guardian."

Meanwhile, Aly was also working hard to establish herself as an actress. In 2004, her efforts paid off big time when she won the leading role on the Disney Channel series, "Phil of the Future." Aly played Keely Teslow, the best friend and love interest of the title character, Phil Diffy. The show proved a huge hit with young viewers and remained on the air for two seasons. "'Phil of the Future' was how I got known," Aly said. "What a way to start out your career, being part of such a great big company that is so successful and is really able to launch you."

Breaking into the Music Business

That "great big company" is Disney, which has helped launch the careers of Hilary Duff, Miley Cyrus, and several other performers, who found stardom as actors and also as recording artists. Aly and AJ were very interested in this kind of dual career because they had continued to work on their music even as they became successful actresses. "Music is what we love the most," Aly declared. "With music, it comes from your heart and soul. It's all you."

BIOGRAPHY TODAY • 2008 Annual Cumulation

Aly & AJ performing onstage at a Christmas concert.

Hoping to land a label contract of their own, the girls recorded a tape of their material and gave it to executives at Hollywood Records, which is part of the Disney Music Group. Both the tape and a live audition wowed company executives, and Aly and AJ were offered a recording contract.

Soon after signing on the dotted line, they entered the studio to record their debut album.

Into the Rush was released in August 2005, when Aly was 16 years old and AJ was 14. The album immediately caught the attention of the so-called 'tween market—young people roughly between the ages of and eight and 14. AJ has described her and Aly's music as "pop with a whole lot of melody," and a catchy, upbeat sound was a big part of the album's appeal. That was especially true of the first single, "Do You Believe in Magic," a tune that originally was a hit 40 years earlier. The duo also won a lot of fans with another "cover" song, "Walking on Sunshine," which was first recorded in the 1980s.

Becoming Songwriters

There was more to Aly and AJ's music than re-recording feel-good numbers that had been written by others, however. They also revealed themselves as prolific songwriters. In fact, the sisters helped write 12 of the 14 songs on *Into the Rush*, collaborating with their mother and other musicians to create the compositions. This kind of hands-on involvement in the creative process is unusual for young artists who are still in their teens, and it helped give the album a personal tone that won the approval of a number of reviewers.

"Music is what we love the most," Aly declared. "With music, it comes from your heart and soul. It's all you."

Even more unusual was the fact that the girls didn't confine themselves to such topics as relationships or enjoying fun times with friends. Instead, they used certain songs to explore more serious topics. "Sticks and Stones" talked about the dangers of bullying, while "I Am One of Them" discussed the topic of kidnapping. "It's not just about boys and having the perfect day," Aly said, commenting on the duo's music. "Sometimes it's nice to listen to a song that makes you think."

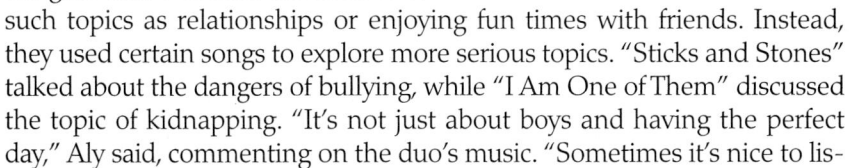

Aly and AJ's mix of infectious music and thoughtful lyrics was a hit, and the CD went gold, meaning that it had sold more than 500,000 copies. They took to the concert stage soon after the album was released and proved that they were accomplished live performers. After a successful 2005 tour opening for the Cheetah Girls, they received top billing for their 2006 performances, and even had the honor of performing an Easter concert at the White House. In the fall of that year, they released the holiday-themed album *Acoustic Hearts of Winter*, which included two original songs along with versions of Christmas favorites.

Following the recipe for success that had been created by other Disney artists, Aly and AJ kept themselves in the spotlight by appearing in TV programs even as they won greater acclaim for their songs and concerts. Aly had a lead role in the Disney made-for-TV movie *Now You See It* in 2005, which featured "Do You Believe in Magic" as part of its soundtrack. Both girls co-starred in the Disney's *Cow Belles* in 2006, where they played two spoiled sisters who are forced to take an active role in running their father's dairy operation.

―――― " ――――

Aly & AJ consider themselves role models for their young fans, and they pick their acting roles accordingly. "We want to make sure it's something we can show our kids when we get older," AJ explained. "We have a standard we want to set—and that means not doing anything we don't believe in."

―――― " ――――

Setting a Good Example

Aly and AJ understand that their fame makes them role models for thousands of young people, and they take that responsibility very seriously. When considering acting roles, they choose projects that they feel send a proper message. "We want to make sure it's something we can show our kids when we get older," AJ explained. "We have a standard we want to set—and that means not doing anything we don't believe in." The sisters followed these guidelines even before they became well known, with AJ once refusing to take part in a scene on the TV show "The Guardian" that she felt was questionable.

The girls' responsible attitude stems from the values they learned in the Christian church that their family attends. While spiritual devotion is central to their lives, the sisters choose not to be overtly religious in their songs. "We don't ever want to preach or shove anything down people's throats," Aly explains. AJ has similar thoughts and adds that too strong of a religious message might alienate some listeners. "We don't want to exclude anybody," she said. "If we have a Muslim fan or an atheist fan, that's their thing—I'm gonna love them no matter what." At the same time, the girls do believe that Christianity has an influence on their art. "There is a sense of unconditional love that AJ and I have," Aly observed. "It helps with our songwriting because there's no pressure—to write a hit or to

Some of their early work—their first CD, Into the Rush, *and a scene from the movie* Cow Belles.

Insomniatic showed the duo's maturing musical tastes.

write certain things. There's a certain calm and peace our faith brings us. We can write about anything."

Using their fame to benefit good causes is another priority for the duo. Their concern about the issue of child abduction led them to become co-chairs of the AmberWatch Foundation, which works to prohibit kidnapping. In addition, they served as the 2007 spokespersons for the Samsung Hope for Education program, which provides technology products to schools.

Insomniatic

When Aly and AJ began work on their third CD, they decided to try a new approach. "On the next album we want to have a little more rock and try to mix things up," AJ said in 2006. By seeking a more powerful sound, they were moving closer to the style of some of their favorite bands, which include two groups that were popular in the 1980s: Heart and The Police.

Once finished, the album *Insomniatic* hit the stores in July 2007. The duo's new direction ended up incorporating not only more rock elements but also a dance-oriented sound, with "Potential Breakup Song" and "Like Whoa" emerging as the initial hit songs. Lyrically, the album focused on romance, exploring both the excitement of new relationships and the disappointment of seeing them end. In both style and subject, the sisters were appealing to an older audience, which was sensible, given that many of the former 'tweens who had bought their first record were now well into their teenage years. Aly put it in simple terms: "We want our fans to grow up with us, not outgrow us." *Insomniatic* received generally positive reviews, and listeners seemed to like what they heard. The album debuted at No. 15 on the national charts, and steady sales will likely make it the sisters' second gold album.

> "There is a sense of unconditional love that AJ and I have," Aly observed. "It helps with our songwriting because there's no pressure— to write a hit or to write certain things. There's a certain calm and peace our faith brings us. We can write about anything."

Several other projects also brought Aly and AJ a lot of publicity. About the time that *Insomniatic* was released, they were also featured in the MTV movie *My Super Sweet 16*, a fictional story inspired by the reality TV show of the same name. In the movie, two best friends since childhood (played by AJ and Regine Nehy) are planning an extravagant, shared sweet-16 party. Then a third girl (played by Aly) steps in and drives them apart, and soon the two former best friends are competing to see who can put on the most outrageous party. Aly and AJ also received a lot of exposure from various promotions and products that were unveiled in the summer of 2007. They appeared on Honeycomb cereal boxes, and their concert tour was sponsored by Sanrio, with the company designing a special "Hello Kitty" tour bus for the occasion. In addition, a long list of Aly and AJ licensed products began to appear on store shelves, including video games, apparel, jewelry, cosmetics, dolls, and more. There is even a book series, Aly & AJ's Rock N Roll Mysteries, which features the young singers' adventures on tour as they solve mysteries. Two volumes have been published to date: *First Stop, New York* and *Mayhem in Miami*.

Aly and AJ have proven themselves to be masters of merchandising and cross promotion. But they find the greatest satisfaction in creating and performing quality music, and they have put a lot of work into achieving that goal. "[Some people] look at our music as some kind of formula. Like we're just actresses trying to be singers," noted Aly. "But we've both loved music since we were little. It's much more than just going up there and singing. It's a lot of blood, sweat, and tears." She also believes that most listeners find real substance and meaning in their songs. "People are starting to realize that we're more than just some pop band," she declared, "[that] we're songwriters with a real message."

HOME AND FAMILY

Aly and AJ reside with their parents in Calabasas, California. They have four dogs, Saint, Bandit, Roadie, and Willow.

HOBBIES AND OTHER INTERESTS

When they're not working, Aly and AJ try to lead fairly quiet lives. "We are normal girls who just happen to act and sing," AJ said. They tend to avoid parties and other high-profile gatherings and instead seek out quiet time away from the celebrity hubbub. "We really value just relaxing," Aly explained. "Every kid—even if you're not in the business—definitely needs to find time to chill and do nothing." Outdoor activities are important to both girls. They spend a lot of their spare time boating, water-skiing, swimming, mountain biking, and riding horses, though they also greatly enjoy the indoor "sport" of shopping.

SELECTED CREDITS

Recordings: Aly and AJ

Into the Rush, 2005
Acoustic Hearts of Winter, 2006
Insomniatic, 2007

Television Programs: AJ

"Birds of Prey," 2002-2003 (TV series)
"The Guardian," 2003-2004 (TV series)
Cow Belles, 2006 (made-for-TV movie)
My Super Sweet 16, 2007 (made-for-TV movie)

Television Programs: Aly

"Phil of the Future," 2004-2006 (TV series)
Now You See It, 2005 (made-for-TV movie)
Cow Belles, 2006 (made-for-TV movie)
My Super Sweet 16, 2007 (made-for-TV movie)

FURTHER READING

Books

Norwich, Grace. *Amped Up: Aly & AJ*, 2007 (juvenile)

Periodicals

Billboard, June 16, 2007, p.7
Girls' Life, Apr./May 2008, p.34
Los Angeles Times, June 23, 2007, p.E16
Today's Christian, Jan./Feb. 2007, p.52
Tulsa World, July 7, 2006
USA Today, July 6, 2007, p.D3

Internet Articles

http://www.billboard.com
 (Billboard, "Aly & AJ Writing New Songs, Plot Films," Jan. 10, 2008)
http://www.discoverygirls.com/entertainment/celebrities/aly-aj-star-sisters
 (Discovery Girls, "Aly & AJ: Star Sisters," no date)

ADDRESS

Aly & AJ
Hollywood Records
500 South Buena Vista Street
Burbank, CA 91521

WORLD WIDE WEB SITES

http://www.alyandaj.com
http://www.myspace.com/alyandaj

Bill Bass 1928-

American Forensic Anthropologist and Author
Pioneer in the Study of Human Decomposition

BIRTH

William Marvin Bass III was born on August 30, 1928, in Staunton, Virginia. His birth father, William Marvin Bass Jr., was a lawyer, and his mother, Jennie Bass, taught home economics.

YOUTH

One of the most important events of Bill Bass's young life occurred when he was very young. When he was just three years old, his father committed suicide, perhaps upset over money-losing investments that he had made for some of his legal clients. "The instant he pulled the trigger, my father slipped from my grasp—slipped away from all of us," Bass later noted in his book *Death's Acre*, "and he remains out of reach to this day."

The loss of his birth father had a lasting influence on Bill. He believed it may have even been a factor in his later decision to choose a career in forensic anthropology. "I deal daily with death," Bass explained about his job, which involves the examination of human remains. "Perhaps when I grasp the bones of the dead, I'm somehow trying to grasp *him*, the one dead man who remains forever elusive." His mother later married his father's brother, Charles Bass, who was a geologist.

> "Bass's father committed suicide when he was very young, which had a profound effect on him. "I deal daily with death," he said about his job, which involves the examination of human remains. "Perhaps when I grasp the bones of the dead, I'm somehow trying to grasp **him**, the one dead man who remains forever elusive."

EDUCATION

Bass lived in Stephens City, Virginia, during his youth and graduated from Stephens City High school in 1946. He earned a bachelor's degree in psychology from the University of Virginia in 1951 and then spent several years as a member of the U.S. Army during the Korean War. After leaving the service in 1953, he began a master's degree program at the University of Kentucky, planning to pursue a career as a college counselor. Bass began to have doubts about his chosen career, however, and came to realize that he "didn't want to talk to people with problems every day." As his interest in counseling faded, he became more interested in anthropology—the study of how humans have lived and developed—and took several classes in the subject.

One aspect of anthropological research involves osteology, the study of human bones, to understand more about the people of the past. These skills can also be used in criminal investigations and legal proceedings, because bone experts are able to obtain important information about a person who has died by looking at skeletal remains. People who specialize in this subject are known as forensic anthropologists. One of the professors

Bass studied with at the University of Kentucky, Dr. Charles E. Snow, was a well-known figure in the field of forensic anthropology.

One day in 1955, Snow asked Bass to assist him as he tried to identify the remains of a person who had been killed in a traffic crash. It was an experience that changed the young student's life. "Right there, I knew: that's what I wanted to do," Bass later explained. "It was fascinating to see the way burned and broken bones could identify a victim, solve a long-standing mystery, close a case. From that moment on, I decided, I would focus on forensics."

Bass received his master's degree in anthropology from the University of Kentucky in 1956 and then enrolled in the doctoral (PhD) program at the University of Pennsylvania. There, he studied with Wilton M. Krogman, a well-known pioneer of forensic anthropology who was known as "the bone detective." Bass graduated with a doctoral degree (PhD) in anthropology in 1961.

CAREER HIGHLIGHTS

Initially, Bass focused on traditional anthropological studies—that is, studying people of the past rather than modern crimes. His first large-scale project grew out of a summer job that he had begun with the Smithsonian Institution in 1956, while he was still a student. That first year, he was based in Washington DC, where he analyzed the bones of Native Americans that had been unearthed from archaeological sites in the western United States. In 1957, he joined other archaeologists at a "dig" or excavation site in South Dakota. He was part of a large team that was working to uncover Native American artifacts before the area was submerged due to the construction of dams on the Missouri River. Bass made important contributions to unearthing historic burial sites in the area, and he continued his summertime work in South Dakota for 14 years.

Bass's career as a college educator began in 1960, when he took a temporary teaching assignment at the University of Nebraska. Later that year, he be-

> "Right there, I knew: that's what I wanted to do," Bass said about the first time he tried to identify someone who had been killed. "It was fascinating to see the way burned and broken bones could identify a victim, solve a long-standing mystery, close a case. From that moment on, I decided, I would focus on forensics."

came a member of the faculty at the University of Kansas and taught in the Department of Anthropology for 11 years. In 1971, he was named the head of the anthropology program at the University of Tennessee in Knoxville.

Forensic Anthropology

Bass began his work in forensic anthropology during his years in Kansas. Law enforcement officers would often contact him after a body had been discovered, and Bass would study the remains to discover important information. "When you examine a body in a forensic case," he explained, "the ultimate goal is to make a positive identification. If possible, you also want to determine the cause of death.... But before you can tell who someone is and how they died—and you won't always be able to tell—you start with the big four: sex, age, race, and stature."

By analyzing bones, a forensic anthropologist can answer these questions in various ways. For instance, the shape of pelvis bones can indicate if a person is male or female. The structure of the teeth and jaw can identify race. The manner in which the bones of the skull are joined indicate age. And the sizes of certain bones, such as the femur or thighbone, allow scientists to estimate the individual's height. In certain cases, more detailed information can be detected from skeletal remains. Damage to the bones may show how the person was killed, and the pattern of cavities in teeth can be matched to dental records to reveal the person's identity.

Bass continued to assist in law enforcement investigations after joining the University of Tennessee faculty. He was named the state forensic anthropologist, and, in that capacity, he frequently worked with police and sheriff's departments all over Tennessee. His expertise yielded useful information in a number of investigations, yet it was a much less satisfying case in 1977 that would inspire him to make an important professional breakthrough.

After examining the body of a man that had been found in the town of Franklin, Bass estimated that the person had died less than a year earlier, and the case became a well-publicized murder investigation. On further study, however, it was found that the body was actually that of a Civil War colonel who had been killed in a battle in 1864 and had been dislodged from his grave by looters. "I only missed it by 113 years!" Bass said of his incorrect estimate. Because the body had been embalmed (not a common practice in the mid-1800s) and well sealed in a cast-iron coffin, it was remarkably well preserved.

The problem was that Bass and other forensic anthropologists knew a lot about bones, but they had relatively little understanding of what happens to a body as it begins to decompose after death. "It made me realize how totally clueless we were about death," he said of the case involving the Civil War corpse. After puzzling over the problem for a time, Bass came up with a simple idea but one that would prove to be extremely important. "The only way to do it," he explained, "was to let a body rot and watch it."

> "When you examine a body in a forensic case, the ultimate goal is to make a positive identification," Bass explained. "If possible, you also want to determine the cause of death.... But before you can tell who someone is and how they died—and you won't always be able to tell—you start with the big four: sex, age, race, and stature."

Creating the "Body Farm"

In May 1981, Dr. Bass and several graduate students retrieved the body of a 73-year-old man who had passed away several days before and whose remains had been donated to the university by his daughter. They took the corpse to a fenced parcel of land on the university campus and laid it on an outdoor concrete pad. Then they closed and locked the gate and left the body to decompose. So began the work of the University of Tennessee An-

Bass studying a body at the Body Farm.

thropology Research Facility, a place that would later become known by a more colorful name: "the Body Farm."

In the years since, hundreds of other corpses have likewise been studied at the site by Bass and his colleagues. Today, more than 25 years after that first study, the Body Farm is still the only facility of its kind in the world.

The idea of a "farm" filled with 20 to 40 decomposing bodies can be an upsetting thought for many people, but it has been a great asset for forensic anthropologists and law enforcement investigators. Determining the precise time that a death took place is extremely important in murder cases because it allows police to better understand what happened and to identify potential suspects. "The crime-scene people find a body in the woods," Bass explained, "and the first thing they want to know is, 'When did he die?'" The studies at the Anthropology Research Facility have provided a great deal of information to answer that crucial question.

To get a better understanding of what happens to human bodies after life has ended, the scientists at the Body Farm conduct carefully controlled experiments. Their findings are helping to create an "atlas of decomposition" that is used to solve cases and convict murderers. The subject is not a simple one. Because bodies are subjected to a wide range of conditions in the real world, the experiments at the Body Farm consider many factors. Corpses are left in car trunks, buried in shallow graves, and submerged in water, to name just a few of the variables that have been studied.

> *Determining the precise time that a death took place is extremely important in murder cases because it allows police to better understand what happened and to identify potential suspects. "The crime-scene people find a body in the woods," Bass explained, "and the first thing they want to know is, 'When did he die?'"*

In addition to being rather smelly and generally unpleasant, the process of decomposition is quite complex. Insects play an important role in the events that take place, and Bass and his fellow researchers have analyzed their activity in great detail. In many cases, blowflies will find their way to an exposed corpse in a matter of minutes. They lay eggs, which soon hatch into maggots that feed on the flesh. Though a body undergoing this process may be a "rotting, maggot-laden mess," to use Bass's own words, it is also loaded with valuable evidence. Because the hatching and growth of maggots follow a predictable timetable, the presence and maturation of the insects allow experts to gauge accurately how much time has passed since the death occurred. The location of maggots on the body can also help investigators determine the cause of death because the insects often mass in an area where the skin has been opened by a wound.

Researchers at the Body Farm have also studied other minute details to aid in criminal investigations. For example, they have analyzed the chemical properties of the residue that is left behind as bodies decompose, documented the effects that fire has on bones, and even classified the precise gases that are emitted by rotting flesh. In addition, the bones of study subjects become part of the school's vast collection of skeletons and are used to train students and to develop powerful new research tools for investigators.

Partly because of the important research carried out at the Body Farm, the University of Tennessee forensic anthropology program has become one of the most respected in the nation. In fact, about one-fourth of the board-certified specialists in that discipline in the United States were educated in Knoxville. In addition, the university operates the National Forensic Academy, which provides specialized training for law enforcement personnel.

The Donation of Bodies

The bodies used by Bass and his colleagues come from two sources. Some are unclaimed corpses contributed by medical examiners. Others are bodies that have been donated for scientific research. As the years have passed, the donations have steadily increased and now make up the majority of the study subjects, with more than 100 arriving each year to begin their eternal rest at the facility. As Bass has joked, "people these days are just dying to get into the Body Farm."

Not surprisingly, the study of the dead at the Anthropology Research Facility has attracted attention, and not all of it has been positive. Some people feel that it is disrespectful to treat human remains in this way. The biggest controversy erupted in the mid-1990s, when local television news stories announced that some of the unclaimed bodies that ended up at the facility were those of military veterans, many of whom had fallen on hard times and had been homeless prior to dying. This led to the introduction of a bill in the Tennessee legislature that would have banned the use of unclaimed bodies for research at the university. Fortunately for Bass, many of the

Law enforcement officers often attend training sessions at the Body Farm, as in this group shown in the distance through the trees.

state's district attorneys valued the research conducted at the Body Farm. They spoke out against the bill, and it failed to become law.

Bass understands the sensitive nature of the subject and has established guidelines and ceremonies that are intended to uphold the dignity of the deceased individuals whose earthly remains are used at the facility. "We do not mistreat the dead," he has stated. "We have yearly a memorial service which is held here." During this gathering, staff and students pay tribute to the late men and women who aid in the university's studies, and family members of the dead, if known, are invited to attend.

Bass is frequently asked about his own plans for his body after death and whether he will donate his remains to the Body Farm. He plans to leave the decision to his survivors and admits that he has mixed feelings about the subject. "The scientist in me wants to sign the donation papers. But the rest of me can't forget how much I hate flies."

On the Case

As one of the most respected forensic anthropologists in the U.S., Bass takes part in criminal investigations all over the country and has worked on more than 3,000 cases in the course of his career. Often, his help is needed in prosecuting suspected murderers. A Mississippi case that he worked on beginning in 1999 provides a good example of the way his expertise can contribute to a conviction.

In this instance, Bass was called in to help determine when three people—a husband and wife and their four-year-old daughter—had been killed. Due to other factors in the case, this question was crucial to the district attorney's prosecution of the suspected murderer, who was the husband of the girl's grandmother. If it could be shown that the victims were killed on or before December 2, 1993, the case against the suspect would be much stronger. Lacking witnesses or other means to pinpoint the time, the prosecutor asked Bass to review the crime scene photos.

> "Bass is frequently asked about his own plans for his body after death and whether he will donate his remains to the Body Farm. He admits that he has mixed feelings about the subject. "The scientist in me wants to sign the donation papers. But the rest of me can't forget how much I hate flies."

The key clue was found in a close-up photo of one of the victims. In it, Bass spotted several tiny brown objects. They were empty pupa casings—the cocoon-like shelters used by maggots as they metamorphose into flies. This was valuable evidence. When a fly lays an egg on a corpse, it takes two weeks until the newly transformed fly leaves its shelter. Thus, the presence of the empty pupa casings in the photo taken on December 16 scientifically proved that the family members were already dead on December 2. Based on Bass's testimony and other evidence, the suspect was convicted of three counts of first-degree murder. It was thought that he killed his relatives in order to collect a $250,000 life insurance policy he had taken out on his step-granddaughter.

Though not every case he works on proves this conclusive, Bass takes great satisfaction from his efforts to secure justice, especially when they help convict individuals such as the murderer in Mississippi. "If my expertise can help put away even one vicious specimen like that," Bass commented in *Death's Acre*, "then all my years of study and research have been well spent."

In another memorable investigation, Bass looked into the reported death of an American citizen in Mexico in 1998. Madison Rutherford was thought to have perished when his rented truck ran off the freeway and burned. He was insured for $7 million, and the insurance companies asked for Bass's input before paying death benefits to his wife. Upon examining the teeth and bones found in the vehicle, Bass concluded that they belonged not to Rutherford, a 34-year-old white man, but to a 50- or 60-year-old man who was probably of Mexican descent. The evidence suggested that Rutherford had placed someone else's body in the truck and then burned it to fake his own death and collect the insurance money. Almost two years later, Bass's findings were proven true, when Madison Rutherford was found alive and well and living under an assumed identity in Massachusetts. After his arrest, it was revealed that he had stolen a corpse from a cemetery mausoleum and placed it in the vehicle.

Bass has also applied his knowledge to clearing up mysteries from the past. In 1982, he analyzed the remains of the so-called Lindbergh baby—the son of famed aviator Charles Lindbergh—who had been kidnapped and killed in 1932. Bruno Hauptman was convicted of the crime and executed. Bass's analysis found no evidence to refute the idea that Hauptman had carried out the kidnapping. In 2007, Bass examined the exhumed body of early rock-n-roll singer J.P. (the Big Bopper) Richardson, who was killed in 1959 plane crash along with several other well-known performers. In this instance, Bass's findings disproved several sensational rumors that surrounded the event, including one that held that Richardson had been to shot prior to the crash.

> *Bass feels that forensic television dramas have created interest in his profession, but he feels that they can sometimes be misleading. "On TV, the police solve the case in an hour," he explained. "The investigators already know the answer to everything—or if they do need to ask a question, they make one phone call and get the answer.... It's not that fast and easy in real life."*

Celebrity Scientist and Author

Though Bass is well known among forensic anthropologists, he has also achieved a certain amount of fame among the general public as well. This began in 1994, when crime novelist Patricia Cornwell published her best-selling fictional book *The Body Farm*, which is partially set at the Anthropology Research Facility. In fact, one of the characters in the book, Dr. Lyall

Death's Acre, which Bass co-wrote with Jon Jefferson, tells stories about his work at the Body Farm.

Shade, is based on Dr. Bass. (Though many people credit Cornwell with creating the "Body Farm" term, it actually predates her book and was coined by an FBI fingerprint expert.) In the years since the novel appeared, Bass and the research facility have frequently been featured in newspaper and magazine articles and in television programs.

In the early 2000s, Bass began working on books of his own. He and his collaborator, Jon Jefferson, have written *Death's Acre* and *Beyond the Body Farm*, which recount some of Bass's professional adventures and major events in his life. The two authors have also produced crime novels that draw on Bass's experiences, publishing them under the pen name Jefferson Bass.

Interest in Bass's work has grown even stronger in recent years due to the popularity of "CSI" and other television dramas that follow the activities of forensic investigators. Bass appreciates the role these programs have played in creating interest in his profession, but he feels that they can sometimes be misleading. "On TV, the police solve the case in an hour," he explained. "The investigators already know the answer to everything—or if they do need to ask a question, they make one phone call and get the answer.... It's not that fast and easy in real life."

Probing the Science of Death

Though he remains involved in activities at the Body Farm, Bass has gradually given up his academic responsibilities over the past 15 years. He retired as a professor in the mid-1990s but remained as the director of the university's forensic anthropology program until 1999. Today, he teaches college courses on occasion and continues to serve on degree committees. "I'm really not retired, I'm just slowly retiring," he told *Tennessee Alumnus Magazine*. In addition, he still consults on forensic cases and is a sought-after public speaker.

Throughout his career, Bass has carried out investigations on dead bodies—work that many people would find too gruesome to endure. Though most of these experiences do not bother him, there are exceptions. "The only forensic cases that give me troubles are the deaths of children," he said, "because here's a life snuffed out early in the game for no reason."

As to the other unfortunate individuals and unpleasant sights he encounters, Bass is able to do his work because he focuses on solving mysteries and is intrigued by the underlying scientific principles that are at play. "I never see a forensic case as death," he said. "You can go out there and that ... individual is dead and in a bad state of repair. But to me, that is a scientific challenge to see if I can figure out who that individual was and what happened to them. And I never see that as death."

Bass also believes that the research he has pioneered sometimes helps others to come to terms with the end of life and that this is part of the reason that the public finds his work so fascinating. "The Body Farm takes what our society often treats as a taboo subject—death—and explores it scientifically," he observed. "We approach death with a combination of objectivity and scientific curiosity, and people seem to find that intriguing, or even comforting. Maybe death isn't so scary after all; maybe it's a natural process, a part of the whole cycle of life."

> "The Body Farm takes what our society often treats as a taboo subject—death—and explores it scientifically," Bass observed. "We approach death with a combination of objectivity and scientific curiosity, and people seem to find that intriguing, or even comforting. Maybe death isn't so scary after all; maybe it's a natural process, a part of the whole cycle of life."

HOME AND FAMILY

Bill Bass and his first wife, Mary Anna Owen, were wed on August 8, 1953. She was an Army dietician at the time and later worked as a nutritionist. The couple had three sons, Charles, William Marvin IV, and James. Mary Anna died of cancer in 1993. Bass married his second wife, Annette Blackbourne, in 1994; she too was diagnosed with cancer, and she passed away in 1996. Two years later, he married Carol Lee Hicks, whom he had known since childhood, and the two continue to reside in Knoxville. In 2002, Bass had his own brush with death when he suffered a serious heart attack, but he has regained his health with the help of a pacemaker.

HOBBIES AND OTHER INTERESTS

Through much of his life, Bass focused most of his attention on his profession. "I never had any hobbies, to be honest," he explained. "I worked 60 to 80 hours a week." Though he still maintains a busy schedule, he enjoys going on trips in his recreational vehicle when time allows.

WRITINGS

Nonfiction

Human Osteology: A Laboratory and Field Manual, 1971

The Leavenworth Site Cemetery: Archaeology and Physical Anthropology, 1971 (with David R. Evans, Richard L. Jantz, and Douglas H. Ubelaker)
Human Evidence in Criminal Justice, 1983 (with Larry Miller and Ramona Miller)
Bodies We've Buried: Inside the National Forensic Academy, the World's Top CSI Training School, 2006 (with Jarrett Hallcox and Amy Welch)

Fiction and Nonfiction, with Jon Jefferson

Death's Acre: Inside the Legendary Forensic Lab, The Body Farm, Where the Dead Do Tell Tales, 2003 (nonfiction)
Carved in Bone, 2006 (fiction, as Jefferson Bass)
Beyond the Body Farm: A Legendary Bone Detective Explores Murders, Mysteries, and the Revolution in Forensic Science, 2007 (nonfiction)
Flesh and Bone, 2007 (fiction, as Jefferson Bass)

HONORS AND AWARDS

Physical Anthropology Award (American Academy of Forensic Sciences): 1985
National Professor of the Year (Council for the Advancement and Support of Education): 1984-1985
Distinguished Fellow (American Academy of Forensic Sciences): 1994

FURTHER READING

Periodicals

Biography, Sep. 2001, p.90
Herald (Glasgow, Scotland), Feb. 17, 2004, p.13
Nashville Tennessean, Jan. 11, 2004
New York Times Magazine, Dec. 3, 2000, p.104
Newsweek, Oct. 23, 2000, p.50
Popular Science, Sep. 1997, p.76

Online Articles

http://news.bbc.co.uk/2/hi/americas/4638835.stm
(BBC News, "Life on Tennessee's 'Body Farm,'" July 3, 2005)
http://www.harpercollins.com/authors/32695/Dr_Bill_Bass/index.aspx
(HarperCollins Author, Dr. Bill Bass, "Interviews: Beyond the Body Farm," undated)
http://www.hbo.com/autopsy/forensic/the_body_farm.html
(HBO, Autopsy, "Forensic Features: Pastoral Putrefaction down on the Body Farm," undated)

http://www.cbsnews.com/stories/2002/03/13/60II/main503634.shtml
   (60 Minutes, "Dead Men Talking," Aug. 14, 2002)
http://pr.tennessee.edu/alumnus/alumarticle.asp?id=668
   (Tennessee Alumnus Magazine, "Questions from the Grave," Spring 2006)

ADDRESS

Bill Bass
Department of Anthropology
250 South Stadium Hall
University of Tennessee
Knoxville, TN 37916

WORLD WIDE WEB SITES

http://www.jeffersonbass.com

Greta Binford 1965-
American Biologist and Arachnologist
Pioneering Researcher in Spider Venom

BIRTH

Greta Binford was born on September 17, 1965, in Crawfordsville, Indiana, a small city some 40 miles northwest of the state capital of Indianapolis. She was the second child of David and Pamela (Crull) Binford. Her parents owned a small farm where they grew corn and soybeans and raised cattle; Pamela Binford also taught elementary school. Binford's older brother, Greg, became an academic researcher, studying soil chemistry as a professor of agronomy at the University of Delaware.

YOUTH

Growing up on a rural farm, Binford lived the life of a "classic tomboy," she recalled. She had hours of unsupervised play time that she often spent by a creek, catching minnows and crawfish. When her father said she could keep a stray cat and its litter of kittens if she fed them herself, "I made a fishing pole and caught chubs to feed the cats." Spending so much time outside, she developed a curiosity about the natural world—including spiders, which were just one of many creatures that she observed. One time, she remembered, "my friend Sheila and I spent hours in search of the 'ancient lost mastodon' and wandered around poking at large piles of cow manure looking for evidence. I guess it's safe to say that I've never been afraid of getting dirty."

> "My friend Sheila and I spent hours in search of the 'ancient lost mastodon' and wandered around poking at large piles of cow manure looking for evidence. I guess it's safe to say that I've never been afraid of getting dirty."

Binford brought energy and enthusiasm to her school activities as well. While attending high school at North Montgomery High School in Crawfordsville, Binford was a versatile athlete, participating in gymnastics, track (as a sprinter), and cheerleading for all four years. She also spent one season diving for her swim team and played trombone in her marching band as a freshman. Although she made the honor society, she confessed that "I was not a super ambitious or driven student," for she had yet to find a subject that kindled any passion. "There were times when I wanted to be a farm wife and have a huge garden, and a lot of dogs and horses," she recalled. "At another extreme, at one point in junior high I wanted to be a disk jockey. In my wildest dreams I wanted a horse ranch somewhere out west."

Biology was a favorite subject in high school, but Binford didn't know how to turn it into a career. When she entered college, she discovered that research could give her those kinds of opportunities, but "at that time the thought of being in school for a long time was not appealing." It was only later she would discover the luxury of being able "to focus and learn deeply about things that you find fundamentally interesting."

EDUCATION

Binford graduated in 1983 from North Montgomery High School and entered Purdue University. She majored in veterinary medicine until she discovered she couldn't overcome feeling "squeamish about sick animals." She then studied psychology until leaving school to get married. In 1987 she began taking classes at a branch of Miami University in Ohio with the hopes of becoming a science teacher. While taking a genetics class there, the professor invited Binford to spend a summer in the Amazon region of South America observing spiders—a summer that changed the course of her life. In 1990 she earned her Bachelor of Arts (BA) degree in zoology, cum laude (with honors), from Miami University. Three years later she received her Master of Science (MS) degree in biology from the University of Utah. In 2000 she completed her doctorate (PhD) in ecology and evolutionary biology at the University of Arizona.

CAREER HIGHLIGHTS

Discovering the Diversity of Spiders

Binford's first expedition awakened an intense scientific curiosity within her. In 1988, while a student at Miami University in Ohio, she traveled with genetics professor Ann Rypstra to the Amazon jungles of Peru. There, she helped Rypstra study an unusual type of spider that created and shared giant webs. Rypstra hoped the observations would help them understand how social behavior developed. She set Binford to observe these social spiders, *Anelosimus eximius,* for hours every morning. The student would sit next to a web—some of them were as large as a semi-trailer—and take notes. "Most of what I'd heard about spiders was nasty, evil stuff—and all I saw was really beautiful," she remembered. The species she studied worked together to build webs, capture large prey such as locusts or even tarantulas, and care for each other's offspring.

When Binford returned home to Ohio she immediately changed her major to zoology. "It was a combination of the biology of that species being cool, and being surrounded by all of the Amazonian diversity that piqued my desire to learn all I could about biodiversity," she recalled. "The realization that I could actually make a contribution to our understanding of the biology of these animals really inspired me." She got divorced around this time, leaving her free to continue her education and perform research wherever she chose.

As Binford studied more about spiders, she discovered diversity in how they capture prey. Spiders can build webs in trees, on the ground, or even in water; others don't build webs, but use silk as weapons or lures; some spiders lie in wait to trap prey, while others attack prey by jumping or spitting. Almost all of the 40,000 known species of spiders, also known as arachnids, have venom. Spider venoms can be very complex, made up of as many as 200 different chemical compounds. While doing research for her doctorate, Binford studied spiders' methods for capturing prey. She became "curious about how venom composition might change as feeding behaviors change," for in studying venom, "the species-level diversity is magnified in the chemical diversity of the venoms."

> "There aren't any spiders for which we know all the chemicals in their venom—none," Binford explained.

Unfortunately, little research had been done on spider venoms. "There aren't any spiders for which we know all the chemicals in their venom—none," Binford explained. After earning her doctorate, she began studying the venom of the brown recluse spider, because "we knew something about the venoms because of their medical effects on humans. This gave me a starting place for studying how the venoms vary among species in the group, and a way to study the venom diversity and evolution." Binford spent over two years in postdoctoral research with Dr. Michael Wells of the Department of Biochemistry and Molecular Biophysics at the University of Arizona, learning to analyze spider venoms of the brown recluse and its relatives, the genus *Loxosceles*.

Because most spider venom targets insects, humans—whose anatomy is completely different—aren't usually affected by spider bites. "If we were wired for spider venoms the way insects are, we'd be screwed," Binford noted. In the United States, only two kinds of spiders produce venom proven to be dangerous to people: the brown recluse and the black widow (genus *Latrodectus*). Black widow venom contains neurotoxins, chemicals that affect nerves and muscles and can cause cramps, spasms, fever, and even death. A cure for black widow venom, known as an *antivenin* or *antivenom*, has been available for decades, and very few people die from black widow bites anymore.

The brown recluse spider and other *Loxosceles* spiders are also known as "fiddleback" spiders because of the violin-shaped marking on their head and thorax. (This marking can be very faint in some species, so the spider's distinctive pattern of three pairs of eyes, rather than the more common four pairs, is a better identifier.) *Loxosceles* spiders produce a different kind of poison than black widows, called a cytotoxin. It kills cells surrounding

SCIENTIFIC CLASSIFICATION

Scientific classification, also called taxonomy, is a method of organizing the millions of earth's living organisms into similar groups. Swedish botanist Carolus Linnaeus was the first to propose this system, in his 1735 text *Systema Naturae*. His work developed into the modern system scientists use to name and catalog everything from bacteria to primates. While biologists sometimes debate the best way to group and place organisms, they all find taxonomy a useful tool for comparing and discussing different creatures.

The largest groupings are called kingdoms. Most commonly, scientists divide life into five different kingdoms: animals, plants, fungi, monera (bacteria and other organisms with simple cells), and protista (protozoa and certain algaes). Kingdoms are divided into phyla (plural for phylum), which in turn are divided into classes, then orders, then families. Finally, an organism is classified into a genus and species, which give it its two-word scientific name. Two creatures are considered members of the same species if a mating would produce fertile offspring.

Scientific names are taken from Latin, to keep them standard throughout the world. They are always italicized; genus names are capitalized and can be abbreviated to a single initial. *Homo sapiens* is the scientific name for humans; *Loxosceles reclusa* is the scientific name for the brown recluse spiders. This is how both species would be classified scientifically:

	Human	**Brown recluse spider**
Kingdom	Animalia	Animalia
Phylum	Chordata (vertebrates and close relatives)	Arthropods (insects, arachnids, crustaceans)
Class	Mammalia (mammals)	Arachnida (8-legged arthropods)
Order	Primata (primates)	Araneae (spiders)
Family	Hominids (upright posture and large brains)	Sicariidae (spiders with cytotoxic poison)
Genus	Homo	Loxosceles
Species	H. sapiens	L. reclusa

the bite area, leaving open wounds that can take weeks to heal. In very rare instances, the venom can affect a person's red blood cells, causing them to burst (a condition called *hemolysis*). *Loxosceles* bites are very rarely fatal; in fact, other conditions are often mistaken for recluse spider bites, including bacterial infections, Lyme disease and other tick-borne illnesses, herpes simplex virus, and other insect or spider bites. In 2001, an infant with anthrax contracted from the attack on NBC News headquarters in New York was misdiagnosed with a brown recluse bite.

> *Recluse spiders fascinate Binford because of the unique way their venom affects people. When it ruptures cells, "the problem that causes the damage in people is an immune reaction ... a complex cascade of immune events that we're still trying to fully understand."*

Recluse spiders fascinate Binford because of the unique way their venom affects people. When it ruptures cells, "the problem that causes the damage in people is an immune reaction ... a complex cascade of immune events that we're still trying to fully understand," she explained. There are around 80 different species of *Loxosceles* in the Americas and over 100 worldwide, including some in Africa, the Caribbean, the Mediterranean, and China. She has traveled as far as Costa Rica, Peru, Argentina, South Africa, and Namibia (in southwest Africa) in search of various recluse specimens. She has also found a transplanted South American relative of the brown recluse, a species called *Loxosceles laeta*, in a Los Angeles Goodwill store. For Binford, field work is "like a scavenger hunt," she explained. "We study old published papers and museum records for locality information, and piece together an itinerary that will take us to as many species in the group as possible." By collecting spiders (including live specimens) and taking them back to her laboratory, she can collect, analyze, and compare different species.

Sharing Her Enthusiasm for Science

Since 2003 Binford has been an assistant professor of biology at Lewis & Clark College in Portland, Oregon. In her lab there, she has a collection of over 600 spiders, both of *Loxosceles* and their closest relatives, the genus *Sicarius*. (This genus includes the six-eyed crab spider and similar desert spiders of Africa and South America.) To figure out how these species are related, Binford and the students under her supervision perform various

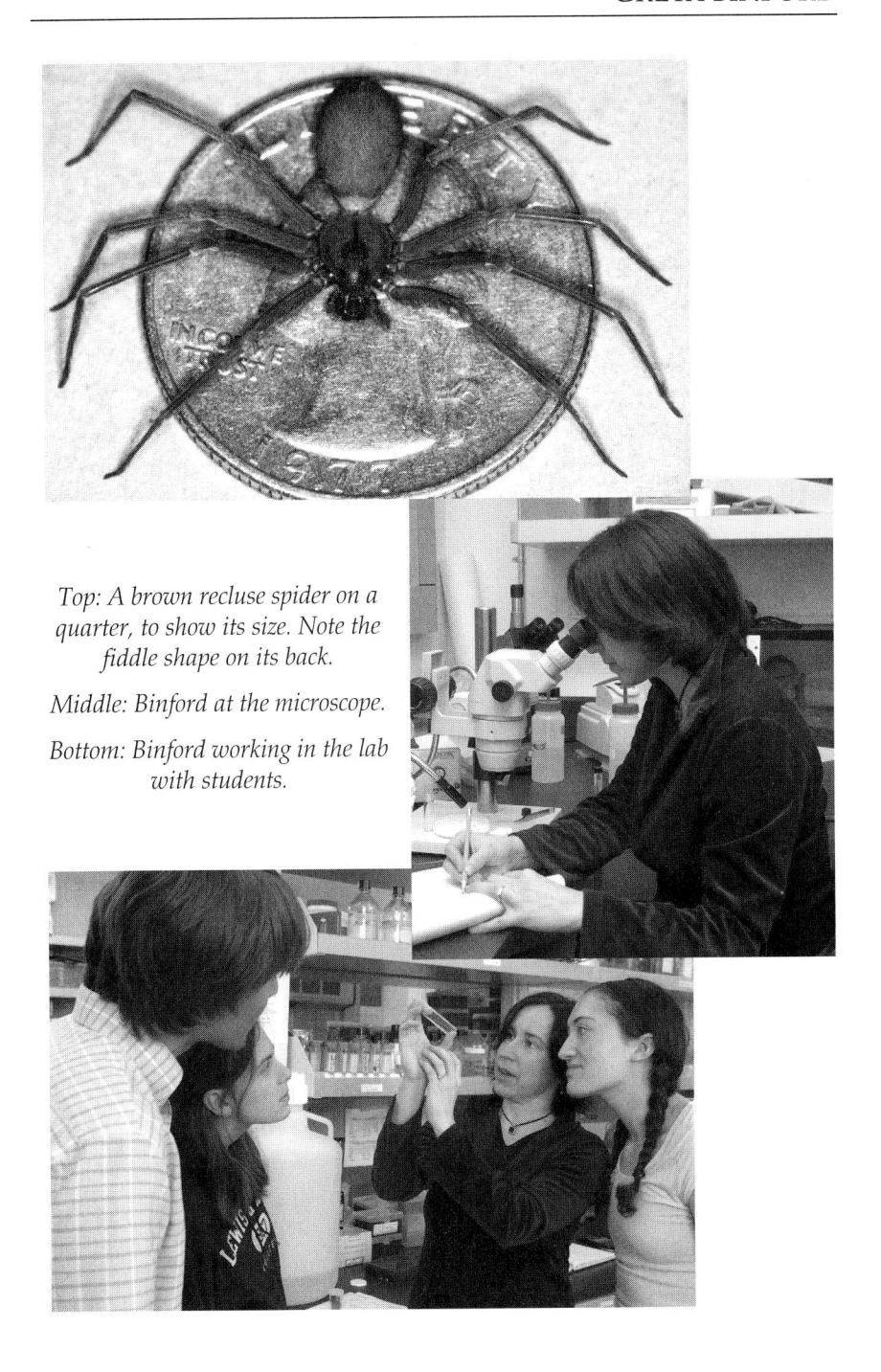

Top: A brown recluse spider on a quarter, to show its size. Note the fiddle shape on its back.

Middle: Binford at the microscope.

Bottom: Binford working in the lab with students.

analyses. They study feeding and mating behavior; they also study the morphology (color and shape) of the spiders to see if they belong to a known species. "Students learn to do basic work that is involved in identifying and describing new species," she related. "So far we have found at least four new species."

Binford's lab also performs more sophisticated studies of the spiders. They get DNA samples by removing legs from spiders (this does no lasting harm to the spiders, and many lab specimens can live as long as five or six years). Using modern techniques of molecular biology, including gene sequencing, they can isolate and reproduce specific genes. "We then analyze these gene sequences using something called phylogenetic analysis and come up with a 'family tree' of species relationships for this group," she explained. Computer programs are an important part of this work as well.

> "I will grab spiders in my hands, but only if I have no other option and I know that the species is harmless. My students and I always capture and transport our toxic spiders by putting them in collecting vials, which does not require physically touching the spider."

Besides studying the biology and genetics of *Sicariidae* spiders, Binford and her students analyze their subjects' venom as well. She collects venom from her spiders in a process known as "milking" the spider. It's a tricky technique, because most *Loxosceles* bodies are only about the size of a toothpaste cap. First, she puts the spiders to sleep with carbon dioxide gas. Using tweezers to handle the spider, she examines it under a microscope and washes its fangs. She gives the spider a small electrical shock to contract its venom glands. She has to be careful when collecting the venom, because the shock also makes the spider vomit and she has to keep the two fluids from mixing.

With pure samples of venom, Binford and her team can test how they work by injecting them into live crickets. "We also isolate and sequence genes that are being expressed in the venoms, which is a way to see what toxins spiders are making and using for prey immobilization," she explained. "For each of these pieces of information we map it on the tree of species and analyze patterns of diversity. This tells us a lot about how the venoms have evolved." Binford encourages her students to participate in all of her research, from the simplest observations to the more complex genetic analyses.

Searching for six-eyed sand spiders in small outcrop caves in Namibia. Binford is to the right; an undergraduate student is in the center; and colleague Pablo Barea Nunez is on the left.

The National Science Foundation has recognized Binford for involving her students in her research. In 2006 they awarded her a five-year CAREER grant worth over $600,000 to help fund her work. "It's an integrative project," she explained, "meaning I do research that's both working with the animals themselves . . . and I'm also doing molecular biology focusing on the toxin." By involving her students in all stages of this research, they learn about the scientific process as well as "a lot about the biodiversity of the spider group." Through these efforts, students can learn "what science is and just how careful you have to be to learn something with confidence," Binford said. "I hope that, fundamentally, my students learn to be creative and critical thinkers, and that if they want to, they too can contribute to our understanding of the natural world." She hopes they will also learn that "we are surrounded by, and dependent upon, a vast diversity of living organisms about which we have much left to learn."

Searching for Practical Research Applications

One of the benefits of performing research into biodiversity is the potential for beneficial practical applications, like medical treatments. As part of her research, Binford has learned more about a specific chemical toxin in *Lox-*

osceles and *Sicarius* venom called sphingomyelinase D (SMD). Working with Matt Cordes, an assistant professor in biochemistry at the University of Arizona, she discovered that SMD is shared with a strain of bacteria, *Corynebacteria*, that infects farm animals. It is a rare instance where genes have been transferred between two completely different species—something especially rare between bacteria and more complex organisms. Binford can't yet prove which species gave the toxin to the other, but suspects the spider is the more likely donor. This discovery is another piece of the puzzle of biological diversity, and may help in developing treatments for both recluse bites and corynebacterial infections.

> "I really liked the spitting spiders and jumping spiders in Eight Legged Freaks. Those are some of my favorite spiders in general and even though they were horrifyingly large in that movie, I liked the fact that they were based on the biological reality of what those spiders do at a microscale."

Already, a Mexican company called Bioclon has used Binford's research to create an antivenom for *Loxosceles* bites. (It is not yet available in the U.S.) In testing, it reduces the pain of the bite and allows lesions to begin healing within a day. Binford hopes that by understanding more about the composition and effects of spider venom, "we will be able to create diagnostics and treatments that will not just work on one species but will work across the entire breadth of species with this toxin, and that includes some pretty unrelated animals." The scientist added: "If you're camping in Peru and you're bitten by something and you have a little antivenom in your pocket, will it work? It's fundamentally an evolutionary question."

In all her years of studying arachnids, however, Binford has only been bitten once: by a social spider during her undergraduate days. "I deserved it (inadvertently smashed it against its cage) and barely felt it," she recalled. Since then she has handled tens of thousands of spiders without incident. Of course, "handling rarely means actually touching them with my hands," she explained. "I will grab spiders in my hands, but only if I have no other option and I know that the species is harmless. My students and I always capture and transport our toxic spiders by putting them in collecting vials, which does not require physically touching the spider." But peo-

*Collecting spiders in Argentina.
Binford is on the left, and an undergraduate student is on the right.*

ple shouldn't be afraid of spiders, she added: "They will only bite if they're in danger of being crushed or in danger themselves. Mostly, they just want to run away and find bugs." Besides, "without spiders there would be a lot more insects and a lot fewer plants." If people would just take the time to watch, she said, spiders "are going about their lives doing very interesting things in your own back yard. Stepping outside and simply watching them can be immensely rewarding."

Unfortunately, popular culture doesn't provide many positive images of spiders. "Outside of *Charlotte's Web*, spiders are nearly universally depicted as objects of horror, evil, and doom—very much unfair," Binford said. She did her part to make spiders appealing by contributing to the 2002 film *Spider-Man*. She served as a consultant to the art department; the lab where Peter Parker is bitten by a spider is very similar to her own. She admitted that "I really liked the spitting spiders and jumping spiders in *Eight Legged Freaks*. Those are some of my favorite spiders in general and even though they were horrifyingly large in that movie, I liked the fact that they were based on the biological reality of what those spiders do at a microscale." Besides the spiders that spit toxic glue to trap prey, other spiders Binford finds fascinating are those that throw a silk string with glue at the tip to catch moths, and brightly colored jumping spiders, which stalk prey like a cat does.

For Binford, it is this variety that makes spider research so intriguing. Besides the 40,000 known species of arachnids, "we know there are at least twice as many that are still undescribed.... There could be tens of thousands still out there we don't know about." No one knows what kinds of treatments might be found in spider venom, although other researchers have discovered potential for heart and diabetes drugs in tarantula venoms. "What's exciting for many people [about spider venom] is that the specificity with which they target the nervous system is really impressive, and we've learned a lot from that specificity, about the diversity of what are called ion channels in the nervous system," Binford said. "And there's a lot of excitement about potential for drugs and insecticides and specific applications of that diversity."

> "I'm happiest in the field, flipping over rocks to see what crawls out," she said. "There's a whole world that lives under rocks and in wood. Being in touch with the natural history of the organism you study is the starting point for any good researcher."

In the meantime, *Loxosceles* still holds endless fascination for Binford—and endless possibilities. "There's an evolutionary puzzle here," she noted. "I'd like to know where SMD originated, how it originated, and what it's doing for the spider." In addition, "there are still big aspects of spider biology that we don't know much about." Spider family trees have been arranged by common physical characteristics (morphology), but she hopes DNA sequencing can provide more definitive answers about the relationship between various species. So she will continue searching for spiders to examine and classify. "I'm happiest in the field, flipping over rocks to see what crawls out," she said. "There's a whole world that lives under rocks and in wood. Being in touch with the natural history of the organism you study is the starting point for any good researcher." Her lab work is just as interesting, she remarked. "It's surprising to me how few of us study spider venom. It's just so cool."

HOME AND FAMILY

Binford was married and divorced while still in college. Currently, she lives in Portland, Oregon, with her fiancé, Dr. Keith Dede, a professor of Chinese linguistics at Lewis & Clark College. They have three pets: a 15-year-old border collie-chow mix named Zoey, and two young cats, Gourgu (Manchu for "beast") and Meme (Chinese for "little beauty").

HOBBIES AND OTHER INTERESTS

Binford enjoys dancing and listening to live music in the alternative country, funk, and bluegrass genres—so much so that she is learning to play the mandolin. She also enjoys outdoor activities like hiking and camping, as well as more homebound pursuits, such as gardening and cooking with her fiancé. When she has spare time, she likes to read fiction.

HONORS AND AWARDS

CAREER Award (National Science Foundation): 2006

FURTHER READING

Periodicals

Lewis & Clark College Chronicle, Summer 2004
New Yorker, Mar. 5, 2007, p.66
Northwest Science & Technology, Fall 2006
Oregonian, July 21, 2007, p.B12
South Bend Tribune, Sep. 24, 2000, p.D7

Online Articles

http://www.orato.com/node/2429
   (Orato, "I'm Spider-Woman," May 17, 2007)

Other

Binford, Greta, e-mail interview for *Biography Today,* Aug. 2007
"The Bliss of the Spider Women," Talk of the Nation: Science Friday
   (transcript), NPR, Mar. 16, 2007

ADDRESS

Greta Binford
Department of Biology
Lewis & Clark College
0615 S.W. Palantine Hill Rd., Mailstop 53
Portland, OR 97219

WORLD WIDE WEB SITE

http://www.lclark.edu

Cory Booker 1969-
American Political Leader
Mayor of Newark, New Jersey

BIRTH

Cory Anthony Booker was born on April 27, 1969, in Washington, DC. He is the son of Cary Booker Sr. and Carolyn Booker. Both of his parents worked for IBM and were among the first African Americans to hold executive positions with the company, with his father specializing in sales and his mother working as personnel director. He has one older brother, Cary Jr.

YOUTH

Cory Booker's parents played an active role in the civil rights movement of the 1960s, and their willingness to directly confront issues of race and discrimination had a strong influence on their children. At about the time that Cory was born, Cary and Carolyn Booker chose to purchase a new home in northern New Jersey and made an offer on a house in the prosperous community of Harrington Park. At that time, the town was almost entirely populated by white residents, and some individuals wanted to prevent minorities from moving into the area. The Bookers were told that the house they wished to purchase had already been sold, but they suspected that this was a lie intended to keep them from living in the city. They sought help from the New Jersey Fair Housing Commission, which secured proof of the realtor's illegal racial discrimination, and the Bookers were soon able to buy the house.

> "They gave me everything I could dream of," Booker said about his parents, "raised me in one of the country's wealthiest suburbs, rooted me in the culture of this country, black culture. I would have betrayed all the opportunities I've had if I didn't give something back."

Cory and Cary Booker had the distinction of being the first African-American students in the local elementary school, and Cory later described his family's presence in Harrington Park as being "like four raisins in a tub of vanilla ice cream." Regardless of whatever awkwardness he may have felt, Cory soon began to impress others with his intelligence and responsible behavior. "He was always so levelheaded," his mother later observed. "Even now it amazes me." Booker has explained that, from an early age, he was encouraged by his parents to work hard in his studies and "to be part of the struggle" for social justice and civil rights. The example set by his mother and father ended up being a big reason why he later sought a career in public service. "They gave me everything I could dream of," he said, "raised me in one of the country's wealthiest suburbs, rooted me in the culture of this country, black culture. I would have betrayed all the opportunities I've had if I didn't give something back."

EDUCATION

Booker excelled as a student, and his outgoing personality made him well known to the students and staff at the schools he attended. "He was the kind of guy who slowed you down when you hung around him," said his longtime friend Chris Magarro, "because he'd say 'hi' to everyone.... The kids, the teachers, the janitors. Everyone." At Northern Valley Regional High School at Old Tappan, he was elected class president in his senior year. He was also an outstanding athlete, earning all-state honors in football prior to his graduation in 1987.

Booker's abilities on the gridiron earned him a football scholarship to Stanford University in Palo Alto, California, where he played tight end for the Cardinals. By the time he reached his senior year, he was being viewed as a prospective NFL player. But football was just one part of his college life. He was equally impressive as a student and volunteer, putting in long hours to master his subjects and also devoting time to tutoring young people and to working at a crisis intervention hotline in Palo Alto. As in high school, he proved himself a leader among his fellow students and was elected president of his senior class. He completed his Bachelor of Arts (BA) degree in political science with honors in 1991. He then undertook an additional year of studies at the university, earning a Master of Arts (MA) degree in sociology and urban affairs.

> "He was the kind of guy who slowed you down when you hung around him," said his longtime friend Chris Magarro, "because he'd say 'hi' to everyone.... The kids, the teachers, the janitors. Everyone."

Wishing to further his education, Booker applied for one of the prestigious Rhodes Scholarships, which allow students from around the world to study at Oxford University in England. The scholarship funds two or three years of study. The program typically selects students who have demonstrated outstanding academic achievement, integrity, concern for others, and leadership ability. In 1992, Booker became one of 32 U.S. students chosen as Rhodes Scholars and spent the next two years studying modern history at the university. During his time in England, he attracted attention for becoming the president of the L'Chaim Society, a Jewish student group at Oxford, even though Booker himself is a Baptist Christian. The study of other religions has continued to be important to him, and he believes that he gains "a deeper reverence for God" by understanding how other people worship.

Booker returned to the U.S. and enrolled at Yale Law School. Upon graduating with a law degree in 1997, he possessed a very impressive education and a reputation as a charming and idealistic young leader. With his cre-

Booker played tight end at Stanford.

dentials and talents, he might have chosen any number of careers, including a high-paying position as an attorney in private practice. Instead, Booker opted to pursue community service work, and this desire led him back to his home state of New Jersey.

CAREER HIGHLIGHTS

Booker moved to the city of Newark in the mid-1990s after receiving a public interest law fellowship. He became a staff attorney for the Urban

Justice Center, where he provided legal assistance to low-income residents in housing cases, and he also worked as a program coordinator for the Newark Youth Project. In some ways, he was on familiar ground in Newark: since his childhood, he had traveled there to visit relatives, and the city is just 25 miles south of his hometown of Harrington Park.

But there is a world of difference between the affluent suburb where Booker grew up and the urban streets of Newark. Home to 273,000 people, Newark is the second-poorest city of its size in the nation, and its history over the past 50 years has not been a happy one. Once a prosperous industrial center, it faced difficulties as its factories began closing down in the decades following World War II. Unemployment and crime began to rise, and in 1967 a deadly race riot erupted in which 23 people were killed. Large numbers of residents moved out of the city in the wake of the riot, and Newark lost nearly half of its population. Though there have been signs of improvement in the decades since, the city continues to struggle with serious problems: one third of its children live in poverty; many of its citizens are unemployed; drug dealing and other crime is widespread; and its school system suffered such acute problems that it is now managed by the State of New Jersey.

> *"You meet real American heroes in these places," he explained, "people that are doing unbelievable things against the odds—not just for themselves and their families, but also for their communities and the children around."*

The difficult conditions did not discourage Booker. In fact, he believed that it was essential to confront the problems of the nation's inner cities, and he felt that his work in Newark was a continuation of the social activism that had been carried out by his parents and others during the Civil Rights movement. "It's just a different set of challenges," he explained. "We have serious urgencies in our cities, . . . and they demand the same kind of sacrifice, the same kind of dedication" as was required of activists in the past. For Booker, this effort was part of the "fight to make America real, to make the promise and the hope of this country fully evident for everyone."

Booker chose to find out about the city's challenges first hand by moving into Brick Towers, a low-income housing project in the city's Central Ward. He soon became familiar with the residents' daily woes, which included a lack of heat and hot water and the presence of drug dealers on nearby sidewalks. Booker helped bring about improvements by filing a lawsuit against the company that managed the housing project and by organizing his neighbors to lobby for better police protection. But beyond the problems, he found life in Brick Towers to be inspiring, and his life there has helped guide his mission as a politician. "You meet real American heroes in these places," he explained, "people that are doing unbelievable things against the odds—not just for themselves and their families, but also for their communities and the children around."

Shaking Up Newark

In 1998, Booker made his entrance into politics by running for a seat on the Newark Municipal Council. His opponent was councilman George Branch, who had been in office for 16 years. Booker was able to raise a large amount of money to finance his campaign, much of it coming from school friends and others who lived outside Newark. He won the May election, and when he took office he was 29 years old—the youngest person to ever serve on the municipal council.

> "I have no disrespect for Sharpe James, but he's been in office as long as I've been alive," Booker said. "After 16 years [as mayor], anything he could have done, he should have done."

Booker's victory was seen as a challenge to the politicians who had led Newark for many years, most of whom had been in office since the 1980s or earlier. The new kid at city hall wasted little time in presenting fresh ideas. He sought to change the way that the city spent taxpayers' money, and he promoted term limits for elected officials and new guidelines on campaign donations. His proposals received little support from other members of the council, however, and were not adopted.

Crime was another major concern for Councilman Booker, and he soon showed that he was prepared to go to great lengths to draw attention to the dangerous conditions that existed in some parts of the city. In August 1999, after a violent incident at a housing complex, he went on a 10-day hunger strike to protest the lack of police protection in the area. To dramatize his action, he moved into a tent outside the project. "It transformed my life," Booker said of the protest, which soon drew in a large group of supporters. "Within 24 hours people were saying, 'You're not sleeping out there alone,' and eventually there were dozens of people sleeping under this huge wedding tent. The first morning of the strike, we had a prayer circle of four people. By the end, there were enough people for us to form a circle around two buildings. Priests, rabbis, Latinos, blacks." The following year, he confronted the city's drug problem by moving into a motor home that he parked on one of the streets where dealers had been doing a booming business. He lived there for five months.

Running for Mayor

As his first term on the municipal council came to a close, Booker set his sights on higher office: he declared himself a candidate for the mayor of Newark in the 2002 election. In doing so, he was taking on the incumbent mayor, Sharpe James, a prominent African-American leader. James had been in the mayor's office since 1986 and had never lost an election of any kind since entering public service in 1970. Considered one of the most powerful politicians in New Jersey, James kept tight control over the city's operations, and this influence helped to assure his reelection every four years. Initially, few observers thought Booker stood much chance of winning the election.

But Booker waged an energetic campaign, going door to door throughout the city and telling voters that Newark needed a new leader to address its problems. "I have no disrespect for Sharpe James, but he's been in office as long as I've been alive," Booker said. "After 16 years [as mayor], anything he could have done, he should have done." In addition, Booker was once again able to attract large campaign donations that totaled more than $3 million, and these funds helped him to finance a range of efforts to reach out to residents.

Sharpe James and his supporters soon realized they were facing a formidable challenger and began to attack Booker in numerous ways. Though both candidates are members of the Democratic Party, James described Booker as a "Republican masquerading as a Democrat." He criticized Booker's support for a voucher system to address problems in public schools as well as the support he received from some prominent Republican politicians.

Focusing on donations to Booker's campaign, Mayor James alleged that the majority of the money came from wealthy people outside the city. James suggested that if Booker were elected, these outsiders would be able to exploit the city's low-income residents. "These wealthy businessmen are investing in an opportunity to take over Newark," the mayor said. In truth, much of Booker's financial support did come from non-residents, including such well-known figures as Stephen Spielberg and Spike Lee. Booker argued that the funds he received came with no strings attached. "I'm blessed with a circle of supporters who donate but don't want anything back," he explained. "They give because they believe in me."

The label of "outsider" was also targeted at Booker himself. The James campaign criticized Booker's prosperous suburban background and noted that he had only been in the city a handful of years. They also hinted that

BIOGRAPHY TODAY • 2008 Annual Cumulation

Booker's mayoral campaign against Sharpe James was documented in the movie Street Fight.

someone educated at such places as Oxford and Yale had little in common with Newark's residents. At times, these attacks veered into the issue of race, even though both men were black. "You have to learn how to be African American," James taunted Booker at one point, "and we don't have time to train you." The mayor even went so far as to make the untrue claim that Booker was Jewish. The increasingly bitter campaign was documented by filmmaker Marshall Curry in the motion picture *Street Fight*, which was nominated for an Academy Award.

Booker was undaunted by the criticism. When Newark voters went to the polls on May 14, 2002, he felt that he was going to emerge the winner. His hopes were dashed when the votes were tallied late that night, and Sharpe James won by the slim margin of 3,494 votes.

Carrying on the Fight

Even as he conceded defeat, Booker vowed that he would be a candidate for mayor again in the 2006 election. Having given up his municipal council seat to run for mayor, he no longer had a voice in city government. Shortly after the election he formed a non-profit group, Newark Now, to aid tenant organizations and neighborhood groups in the city. "Everything we are going to do will be about making Newark a better place," he said of the group's efforts. Over the following years, he worked to strengthen his ties to the city's residents and to overcome the impression that he was an outsider. He also continued his law career, becoming a partner in the firm Booker, Rabinowitz, Trenk, Lubetkin, Tully, DiPasquale and Webster.

Another part of Booker's strategy was to seek a closer relationship with the city's trade unions and churches. Most of these influential groups had backed Sharpe James in the 2002 election, and Booker knew they would play an important part in the next contest. His efforts paid off, and by the time that his second mayoral campaign hit full stride, he had won the allegiance of many union officials and other power brokers.

City residents were expecting an exciting rematch between Booker and James in the May 2006 election, but events took a sudden turn in late March of that year, when Mayor James suddenly announced that he was no longer seeking reelection. The reason he dropped out of the race has never been fully explained, but some observers believe that he was discouraged by the increased support that Booker had gained since 2002 and by opinion polls that showed him trailing his challenger. (In 2007, James would be indicted on corruption charges due to alleged misconduct while mayor.) Another candidate, New Jersey state senator Ronald L. Rice, entered the race after James bowed out, but with less than two months to prepare a campaign and far less money than the $6 million that Booker had raised, Rice stood little chance. On May 9, 2006, Cory Booker was elected by the widest margin of victory ever tallied in a Newark mayoral election and became the chief executive of New Jersey's largest city.

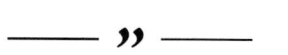

The Burden of Power

> "Everything falls on my shoulders," Booker commented shortly after taking office. "The challenge is to switch from talking about solutions to implementing solutions."

"Everything falls on my shoulders," Booker commented shortly after taking office. "The challenge is to switch from talking about solutions to implementing solutions." He soon discovered the difficulties in taking on that task. Early in his term, auditors found a $44 million shortfall in the city budget that had been created during the administration of Mayor James. As a result, Booker was forced to put through a property-tax increase to cover city expenses, which angered many homeowners. The new mayor also faced some opposition to the person he selected to be the city's new police chief, Garry McCarthy. Booker stood by his choice, however, and McCarthy was approved by the municipal council.

Bringing in a new police chief is part of Booker's focus on reducing crime, which is far and away his biggest priority. "The No. 1 issue, the No. 1 mission, the No. 1 cause for this city is to secure the safety of its citizens," he stated. "I will not stop until confidence is restored to our community." Booker has worked with Chief McCarthy and other officials to put more officers on the street, to install security cameras in the city, and to launch other safety initiatives. His anti-crime image seemed to cause concern among local gang leaders, some of whom issued death threats against Booker at the time he took office.

Many types of crime did decrease during Booker's first year in office, but the murder rate did not. A total of 106 people were killed in the city in 2006, the highest figure since 1995, with many of the murders being linked to the illegal drug trade. Statistics were similarly grim in early 2007, and then on August 4, the news got even worse. That night, four young Newark residents were confronted by a group of gunmen at a school parking lot. In what was apparently a robbery unconnected to drugs, three of the victims were forced to kneel against a wall and were shot dead at point-blank range. The fourth person was badly wounded but survived.

The seemingly random killings shocked the city and became news all across the country. Booker confronted the situation head on, overseeing the police investigation and setting up a command center in his apartment. Six suspects were arrested in the case, with one of them surrendering directly to the mayor. Booker delivered passionate eulogies at the victims' funerals and voiced his hope that the tragic incident would help galvanize the city, stating that "this is a time all Newarkers must pull together and unite around their common challenges."

The new mayor has grappled with other difficulties since 2006, including administrative problems with a city-sponsored youth job program that left workers unpaid. In addition, a vocal group of critics mounted a recall movement to remove him from office. On the plus side, he and his staff scored some significant victories, including the removal of dozens of nonproductive employees from the city payroll and the establishment of programs to help ex-convicts find jobs. Observers also point to other achievements. Crime is down; there have been no scandals among city officials; property taxes have been stabilized; parks are being refurbished, giving youngsters someplace to go; charter schools are being developed; downtown housing is increasing.

In July 2008, at the mid-point of Booker's four-year term as mayor, the *New York Times* published an overview of his time in office. "Mr. Booker is faced—right now, today—with rampant crime, punishing property taxes and a burdensome legacy of municipal corruption," the reporter wrote. "Expectations were high when he came to office, not only because he was an attractive personality but also because his predecessor seemed incurably corrupt. His success depends partly on meeting these expectations. Judging by a recent interview in his spacious City Hall office, in which he exuded a sense of confident serenity, he thinks he can do so. But he says the job has turned out to be every bit as hard as he expected."

Overall, Booker is finding the mayor's job to be a challenging one. "Things come at you 1,000 miles an hour," he explained, "and much of the time you're dealing with chaos. You can easily get distracted by issues that are not central." To help maintain his focus, he frequently makes door-to-door visits throughout the city and also sets aside two days each month to discuss jobs, housing, and other concerns with residents.

Looking Ahead

Even before he became Newark's mayor, Booker was touted as a promising politician who was likely to achieve great things, and he has been recognized as one of the nation's top young leaders by such publications

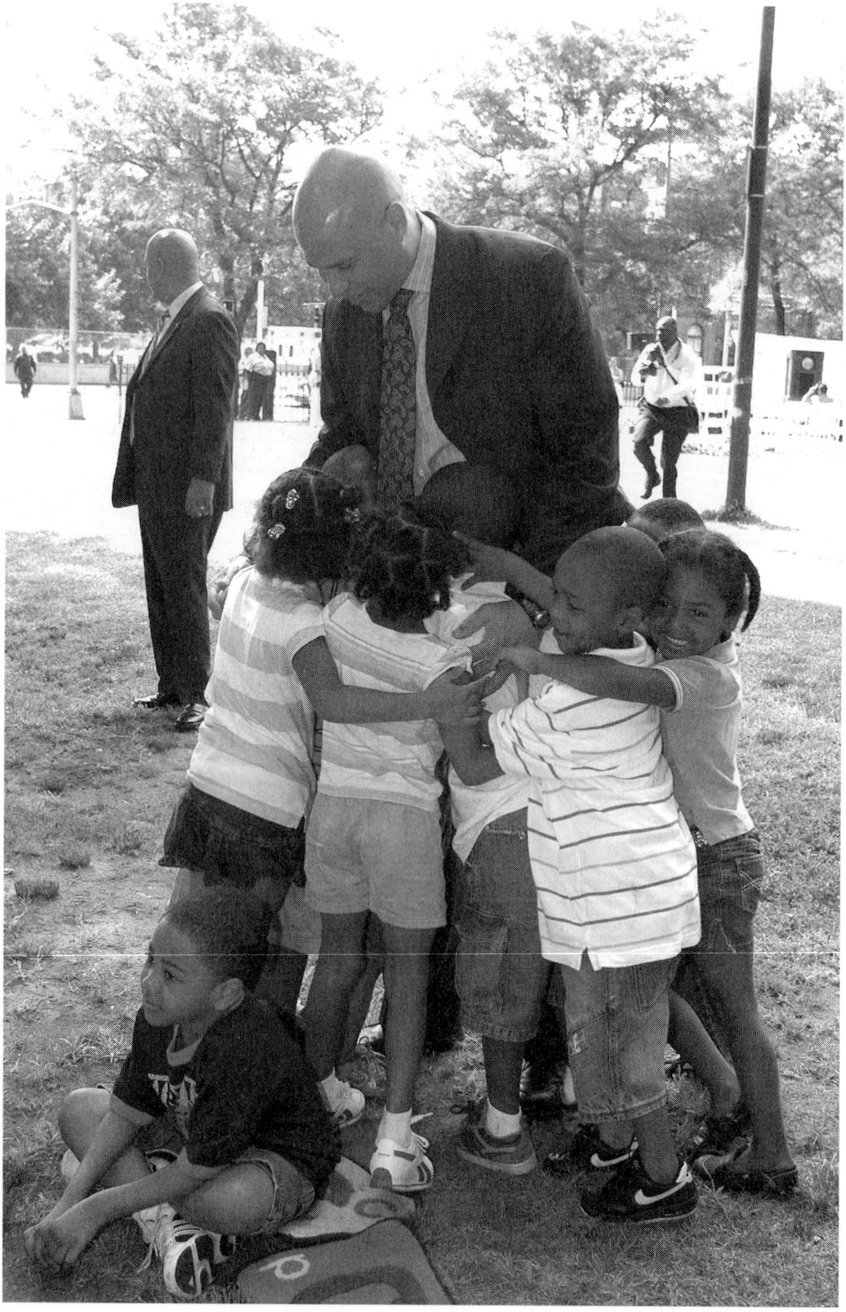

as *Esquire* and *Black Enterprise*. With his youth and charisma, he is often compared to former president Bill Clinton and to Illinois senator and presidential candidate Barack Obama. In fact, more than a few observers have predicted that Booker could one day become the nation's chief executive. This has led to speculation that he will seek other political office in the near future, but Booker denies this. He has said that he plans to focus on Newark for "about a decade" because he believes his work as mayor is of the utmost importance. "My loyalty, my love is here in Newark," he said, "So I'm not going anywhere."

Booker is also viewed as a new style of African-American leader who embodies the idealism of past figures but is also willing to try new approaches to difficult problems. He seems to relish this role, and he believes that the desire to serve the public is widespread among young people today. "We're sort of the hip-hop generation, we are innovators," he told one interviewer. "But that sense of sacrifice is still alive and well, and I see it in my neighborhoods, and I see it in the young activists I'm working with."

Booker refers often to the concept of working for a higher cause and the betterment of his city and nation, and he considers this to be an essential part of his political quest. In talking about his own efforts to become mayor, he described the struggle as a lesson of hope. "If you stay persistent, if you don't give up, if you're unyielding and unhesitating in your values and your principles, you can win. . . . The lesson I took from all that is you can face the darkest of forces or face the most vicious of opposition," he says, "but if your cause is righteous, and if you try to stay worthy of that cause—which is a daily struggle—you can be victorious, you can accomplish your hopes and dreams."

HOME AND FAMILY

Booker is single, and he continues to live in the Brick Towers housing project that he moved into in the 1990s. He remains close with his parents, who assisted in his mayoral campaigns, and with his brother, Cary, who is a professor at Rutgers University.

HOBBIES AND OTHER INTERESTS

Booker is a big fan of science fiction movies and television programs and is especially fond of "Star Trek." He gave up watching television, however, after becoming mayor because he felt it took up too much of his time. A vegetarian, he exercises regularly and is known for going on early-morning runs through the city streets.

FURTHER READING

Periodicals
City Journal, Spring 2007
Current Biography, Feb. 2007
New York Times, Apr. 24, 2002, p.A1; Sep. 26, 2004, Section 14NJ, p.1; Oct. 19, 2006, p.A1; July 3, 2007, p.B1
Newark (NJ) Star Ledger, Apr. 28, 2002, New Jersey section, p.19; July 1, 2007, New Jersey section, p.17; Aug. 28, 2007, p.1
U.S. News & World Report, Apr. 24, 2006, p.35
Washington Post, July 3, 2006, p.C1

Online Articles
http://abcnews.go.com/US/wireStory?id=3496596
   (ABC News/Associated Press, "Shootings Renew Mayor's Sense of Purpose," Aug. 18, 2007)
http://www.city-journal.org/html/17_2_cory_booker.html
   (City Journal, "Cory Booker's Battle for Newark," Spring 2007)
http://www.marshallcurry.com
   (Marshall Curry Productions, "Street Fight," undated)
http://www.npr.org/templates/story/story.php?storyId=5625405
   (National Public Radio Morning Edition, "New Black Leaders Must Innovate," Aug. 8, 2006)
http://www.npr.org/templates/story/story.php?storyId=5446231
   (National Public Radio News & Notes, "Cory Booker Wins Newark's 'Street Fight,'" June 2, 2006)
http://topics.nytimes.com/top/reference/timestopics/people/b/cory_booker/index.html
   (New York Times, "Times Topics: Cory Booker," multiple articles)

ADDRESS
Cory Booker
Mayor's Office
200 City Hall
920 Broad Street
Newark, NJ 07102

WORLD WIDE WEB SITES
http://www.corybooker.com
http://www.ci.newark.nj.us/City_Government/mayor-cory-booker.aspx

Sophia Bush 1982-

American Actor
Star of the Hit TV Show "One Tree Hill" and the Movies *John Tucker Must Die* and *The Hitcher*

BIRTH

Sophia Anna Bush was born on July 8, 1982, in Pasadena, California, a suburb of Los Angeles. Her father, Charles William Bush, worked as a photographer, and her mother, Maureen Bush, was a photography studio manager. Sophia is their only child.

YOUTH

Growing up in Pasadena, Bush liked to have sleepovers with her friends. They would stay up watching scary movies like *Poltergeist*, although no one would be able to sleep afterwards because they would be too frightened.

Bush remembers one of the first people she ever admired was Oprah Winfrey. "When I was a little girl I was obsessed with Oprah.... I just loved her. I loved how powerful she was as a woman.... I think she's amazing!"

EDUCATION

Bush attended Westbridge School for grades seven through 12. The private girls-only school in Los Angeles was small, and there were only 55 girls in her graduating class. Bush flourished in this environment and was a very outgoing and energetic student. "I was a total education geek," she admitted. "I loved school, I loved learning. I loved doing homework." She also enjoyed playing volleyball on her school's team.

> "I was a total education geek," Bush admitted. "I loved school, I loved learning. I loved doing homework."

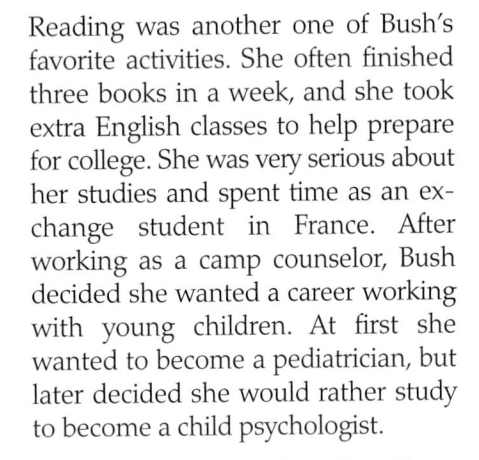

Reading was another one of Bush's favorite activities. She often finished three books in a week, and she took extra English classes to help prepare for college. She was very serious about her studies and spent time as an exchange student in France. After working as a camp counselor, Bush decided she wanted a career working with young children. At first she wanted to become a pediatrician, but later decided she would rather study to become a child psychologist.

Despite growing up so close to Hollywood, Bush never thought of having a career as a performer. She had no desire to be an actor and no interest in the entertainment business. However, her school required all students to participate in a performing arts program, so she had to take part in a play. It was then that she discovered that she loved being onstage, even though it prevented her from playing volleyball. "Part of my school's requirement was to do a play. I was really irritated because I wanted to play volleyball and I had to go and do this play. But there was a moment after the performance when I realized I had gone and been somebody else. I thought, 'If I could do this for the rest of my life, I am set.' It was like love at first sight."

Although acting began as an inconvenient mandatory activity, Bush ended up discovering her dream job. "I decided to follow through with it," she said, "because I never enjoyed anything as much as being up onstage and being someone else." With her parents' support, she decided to pursue a career in acting. "My parents always taught me to believe in myself, and to be true to myself." She went on to act in several plays during high school and began to look for more opportunities to perform.

In 2000, when she was 17 years old, Bush was named the 82nd Rose Queen for the Tournament of Roses in Pasadena. She was chosen from more than 900 other contestants in a selection process that lasted a month. In her yearlong reign as the Rose Queen, Bush appeared at more than 100 community and media functions. Perhaps the most exciting of these was presiding over the Rose Parade and the 2000 Rose Bowl football game.

After graduating from high school, Bush enrolled in the University of Southern California in Los Angeles. She was a member of the Kappa Kappa Gamma sorority and served as the social chairperson. She originally studied for a degree in theater, but changed her major to journalism because she wanted to get a better understanding of the public relations side of the acting business.

> *"Part of my school's requirement was to do a play. I was really irritated because I wanted to play volleyball and I had to go and do this play. But there was a moment after the performance when I realized I had gone and been somebody else. I thought, 'If I could do this for the rest of my life, I am set.' It was like love at first sight."*

CAREER HIGHLIGHTS

Bush began auditioning for roles in movies and on television shows while she was still in college. In 2002, she was cast as the girlfriend of the star of *Terminator 3: Rise of the Machines*. But soon after filming began, the director replaced Bush with another actress because she looked too young for the role. She had minor roles in various television shows and movies throughout 2002-2003. Her first major appearance on television was in a three-episode storyline on the drama "Nip/Tuck."

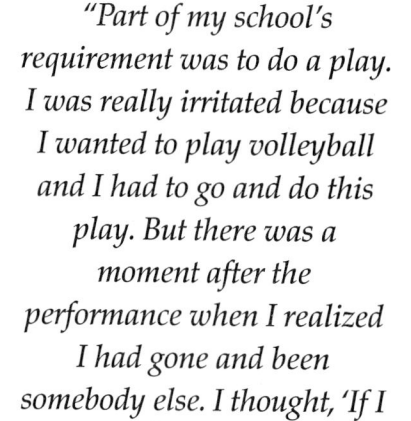

"One Tree Hill"

Bush's big break came in 2003 during her third year of college, when she was 20 years old. She auditioned for a part on a new TV series called "One Tree Hill." After being called back for several auditions and readings, she was offered the role of Brooke Davis, the wild and unpredictable head cheerleader at Tree Hill High. Bush accepted the role, and ten days later she left school in Los Angeles and moved to Wilmington, North Carolina, to begin filming.

The plot of "One Tree Hill" centers on a group of friends who attend high school together in the fictional small town of Tree Hill, North Carolina. Drama unfolds from one episode to the next in ongoing, interconnected stories of friendship, betrayal, romance, heartbreak, rivalry, secrets, lies, deception, and ever-changing alliances among characters. The show started by following the characters through high school but then took a major leap at the start of the 2007-08 season, jumping from the end of high school to the post-college years. "One Tree Hill" became a hit with teen viewers almost immediately and has grown in popularity over the years. Bush was nominated for Teen Choice Awards in 2005 and 2006 for her role as Brooke.

> "What I love about [Brooke] is that she's learning lessons on the show that I had to learn, when I was at that age, or in the last few years. Really starting to realize that you've got to make sure that the people you're giving your heart to are treating it with the respect it deserves. And that's a really valuable life lesson, and that's the reason that I love playing her."

Bush's portrayal of Brooke Davis included the character's growth from a fun-loving party girl to a serious fashion designer. Over the course of the first four years of "One Tree Hill," Brooke deals with the demands of school, cheerleading, friendships, romantic relationships, and family problems. In addition to the everyday worries of high school, Brooke also faces many stressful situations not normally encountered by average teens. "What I love about it is that she's learning lessons on the show that I had to learn, when I was at that age, or in the last few years. Really starting to realize that you've got to make sure that the people you're giving your heart to are treating it with the respect it deserves. And that's a really valuable life lesson, and that's the reason that I love playing her."

Some of the "One Tree Hill" drama spilled over into Bush's life off-screen when she became romantically involved with her costar, Chad Michael Murray. The couple met in 2003 on the set of the show and became friends. A romantic relationship soon developed, and they were married in

SOPHIA BUSH

"One Tree Hill" has been a big hit with teen fans.

2005. However, they separated just a few months later and their marriage ultimately ended in divorce. Bush says of this time in her life, "It devastates me now that I have been reduced to a Hollywood statistic—another joke

71

marriage. I never expected to be married more than once.... But I still believe in love."

After their marriage ended, Bush and Murray were still required to play romantic partners on "One Tree Hill." In 2006, Bush told *CosmoGirl*, "It's not easy for me when the person who Brooke is pining over is someone who I am separating from in real life, and some days are more difficult than others. But I would never disrespect Brooke as a character, my integrity as an actor, and the fans of the show by not giving her my fullest ability just because of something going on in my personal life. I have to check my personal problems at the door. If anything, this is an exercise for my acting ability!" The experience of having her marriage disintegrate in the media spotlight has made Bush cautious about talking publicly about her love life. By January 2007, Bush was refusing to comment on her divorce, saying only, "That's such a dead horse. We just go to work, and that's it. As for me, I'm happier than I've ever been in my life."

Breaking into Movies

While working on "One Tree Hill," Bush continued to audition for roles in movies. Her first major movie part came in 2005 when she played Zoe in the action film *Supercross*, the story of two brothers who compete in motocross. Although the movie was not a commercial success, it quickly gained a following among fans of motorcycle racing. Then in 2006, she starred in the horror thriller *Stay Alive*. She played October, one of a group of teens who must unravel the mystery behind a series of gruesome real-life deaths that mirror those in a strange new video game. *Stay Alive* became a cult hit with teen science fiction fans and video game players alike. Bush enjoyed her role as October, saying, "She's really the mother hen of her group, which is who I have always been. I've always been the mom among all of my buddies and ... definitely the girl who can go hang out with the boys and be comfortable."

Bush's first role in a hit movie came in 2006 when she starred in the teen revenge comedy *John Tucker Must Die*. Three high school girls, played by Bush, Ashanti, and Arielle Kebbel, discover they've all been dating the same guy, John Tucker, played by Jesse Metcalfe. Smooth and charming, Tucker seems to be able to get any girl he wants. At first they blame themselves, but after coming to terms with their discovery they turn their anger toward Tucker. The girls decide to band together to get revenge with the help of a new girl who just transferred to their school, played by Brittany Snow. They give the new student a makeover designed to attract the attention of their target. John Tucker falls for her, and their plot for revenge soon

Bush played Zoe Lang and Steve Howey played KC Carlyle in Supercross.

unfolds. The movie was an instant hit with teens, particularly with teen girls, and Bush won a 2007 Teen Choice Award for her role.

The Hitcher

In 2007 Bush starred in *The Hitcher*, an updated remake of the 1986 film of the same name. The plot of this thriller blends action, horror, and suspense in the frightening story of two college students who decide to pick up a hitchhiker while on a cross-country drive. Bush plays Grace Andrews, part of the unfortunate couple who is being terrorized by "the hitcher." As the story unfolds, Grace must summon the strength to fight off the hitcher's increasingly dangerous attacks. Although the movie was generally panned by critics, it became a hit with teen horror fans. Bush received two Teen Choice Awards in 2007 for her performance as Grace.

The role was Bush's most physically challenging performance, and she did many of her own stunts. Preparing for the stunts required her to be in excellent physical condition, which required a lot of training. "I did about 90 percent of my own stunts.... I started with a trainer and started working really hard back home just to get to a point where my body would be prepared to take the beatings every day and prepared to run through the desert all day on some days and ... dive into and under things and be manhandled and thrown into rooms by large men in the cast.... It was definitely something I had to discipline for and decide to go the extra mile."

> *Filming some of the action scenes in* The Hitcher *was extremely dangerous. "There was one moment where I was in a harness, hanging out the window of a car, going 70 miles per hour down a highway," Bush recalled. "I thought, 'If we get in an accident, I'll be severed in half.'"*

Filming some of the action scenes was extremely dangerous. "There was one moment where I was in a harness, hanging out the window of a car, going 70 miles per hour down a highway," Bush recalled. "I thought, 'If we get in an accident, I'll be severed in half.'" In spite of the danger, she thoroughly enjoyed the role. "I will hold this as the best experience I've ever had. A movie of that scale, with suspense, drama, adrenaline, fear; it is a film that's all across the board for me as an actor."

The success of Bush's performances in "One Tree Hill," *John Tucker Must Die*, and *The Hitcher* has earned her numerous awards. In 2007 she won the most individual Teen Choice Awards, taking home three life-sized surfboard awards in the categories of "Choice Movie Actress-Comedy" (for *John Tucker Must Die*) and "Choice Movie Actress-Horror/Thriller" and "Choice Movie-Breakout Female," both for *The Hitcher*. Bush also won the 2007 Rising Star Award at the Vail Film Festival.

Living With Fame

Starring in a successful TV series and two hit movies has cemented Bush's status as a celebrity. Yet despite all the attention from the media and fans, Bush has said that her life is not that different from what it was before she became a star. "I can go to the mall alone. I can put on a hat and put my hair in a ponytail and go out in jeans and a T-shirt with no makeup on and people almost don't notice me. So life for me is what it used to be, only now I get to do what I love every day. I get to crawl into somebody else's head, and I love that."

John Tucker Must Die *was Bush's first big movie success.*

Bush has preferred to downplay her fame, saying, "I work on a TV show so I'm notable for the TV show, but I'm not a celebrity. I don't call myself a celebrity. I'm an actor." She has been described as a much more thoughtful and smart person than the high school or college students she typically portrays on screen. "People are generally astounded that I'm intelligent or educated or socially conscious or grounded, which is a nice change for me because I'm not a ditzy cheerleader—I wasn't even a cheerleader in high school—I just play one on television."

MARRIAGE AND FAMILY

Bush married Chad Michael Murray in April 2005. The marriage lasted just five months, and the couple separated in September 2005. Their divorce was finalized in January 2007.

Bush lives in the house she owns in Wilmington, North Carolina, the town where "One Tree Hill" is filmed. "I love being in North Carolina but it's a struggle being away from home. Even though I'm on this hit show, I still have my best girlfriends who I grew up with and who I went to college with.... The most important thing you have is your relationship with your friends. And it doesn't need to be defined by a clique or defined by your stereotype, it needs to be defined by girls that you love and that you laugh with, and that you get along with. And those are the people that are going to be in your life forever."

> "The most important thing you have is your relationship with your friends. And it doesn't need to be defined by a clique or defined by your stereotype, it needs to be defined by girls that you love and that you laugh with, and that you get along with."

HOBBIES AND OTHER INTERESTS

Bush enjoys photography, watching movies, spending time with her friends, and playing with her dogs. She has a mastiff, a one-eyed pit bull, and a pomeranian. "I bring my dogs to work every day.... When I have my lunch break and between scenes, I walk them around the lot and play." Reading is still one of her passions. "I was such a bookworm in school and I still am. Everyone on set makes fun of me because I'm always reading, and I still underline things and make notes in the margins."

SELECTED CREDITS

"Nip/Tuck," 2003 (TV series)
"One Tree Hill," 2003- (TV series)
Supercross, 2005 (movie)

Stay Alive, 2006 (movie)
John Tucker Must Die, 2006 (movie)
The Hitcher, 2007 (movie)

HONORS AND AWARDS

Rising Star Award (Vail Film Festival): 2007
Teen Choice Awards: 2007 (three awards), Choice Movie Actress-Comedy, for *John Tucker Must Die*; Choice Movie Actress-Horror/Thriller, for *The Hitcher*; and Choice Movie Breakout-Female, for *The Hitcher*

FURTHER READING

Periodicals

Chicago Sun Times, Jan. 14, 2007, p.D3
CosmoGirl!, Feb. 2006, p.98
Los Angeles Times, Oct. 27, 1999, p.B1
Teen People, Sep. 1, 2005, p.142; Dec. 1, 2005, p.102
USA Today, July 14, 2004, p.D3

Online Articles

http://www.thecinemasource.com/celebrity/interviews/Sophia-Bush-Not-Beating-Around-the-Bush-interview-332-0.html
(TheCinemaSource.com, "Spotlight on Sophia Bush," undated)

http://www.horror.com/php/article-1485-1.html
(Horror.com, "Sophia Bush—Interview with The Hitcher Actor," Dec. 27, 2006)

http://movies.ign.com/articles/721/721026p1.html
(IGN.com, "Interview: Sophia Bush, One of the Stars of *John Tucker Must Die*," July 26, 2006)

http://movies.ign.com/articles/698/698234p1.html
(IGN.com, "Interview: Sophia Bush, 'One Tree Hill' Star Talks *Stay Alive*," Mar. 24, 2006)

http://www.snmag.com/content/view/146/
(Saturday Night Magazine, "Sophia Bush Interview," Jan. 30, 2007)

http://www.ugo.com/channels/filmTv/features/interactivehorror/stayalive_sophia.asp
(UnderGroundOnline, "Sophia Bush of Stay Alive," undated)

ADDRESS

Sophia Bush
The CW Television Network
4000 Warner Boulevard
Burbank, CA 91522

WORLD WIDE WEB SITES

http://www.cwtv.com/shows/one-tree-hill
http://www.myspace.com/johntucker
http://www.neverpickupstrangers.com

Majora Carter 1966-
American Urban Planner, Environmental Activist, and Advocate for Environmental Justice
Founder and Executive Director of Sustainable South Bronx

BIRTH
Majora Carter was born on October 27, 1966, in New York City. She was the youngest of ten children born to her parents, Major and Tinnie Carter.

YOUTH
In the 1940s, Carter's parents moved to the New York City neighborhood known as the South Bronx and began raising a

family there. As the years passed, though, the South Bronx underwent a grim transformation. "When my parents moved there in the '40s," Carter explained, "it was this mostly white working class community and this was [my parents'] first step up the economic ladder." In the 1950s and 1960s, however, many white families moved to the suburbs. Banks and other financial institutions also abandoned the neighborhood. The poor residents who were left—mostly African-American and Latino families—had little economic or political power. As a result, their neighborhood became an industrial dumping ground. By the 1970s, the South Bronx was lined with abandoned factories, crumbling warehouses, and waste treatment plants. Its streets were mostly used by drug dealers, prostitutes, and diesel-powered trucks that polluted the neighborhood air.

It was hard for Carter and her older siblings to grow up in this setting. "I watched half of the buildings in my neighborhood burn down," she recalled. "My brother Lenny fought in Vietnam only to come home and be gunned down a few blocks from our home. I grew up with a crack house across the street. Yes, I'm a poor black child from the ghetto."

——— " ———

"I watched half of the buildings in my neighborhood burn down," Carter recalled. "My brother Lenny fought in Vietnam only to come home and be gunned down a few blocks from our home. I grew up with a crack house across the street. Yes, I'm a poor black child from the ghetto."

——— " ———

As she grew older, the misery and poverty that surrounded Carter also took a toll on her self-image. "When everything you see is dirty and ugly, it's hard not to have it reflect on you," she explained. "As a kid, you never fully understand what makes that sort of thing happen, but it teaches you that you're probably not worth much."

Fortunately, Carter had a strong foundation of support to lean on during her childhood years. As she later said, she was able to lift herself to a better life thanks to the "love inside [her] home" and the "encouragement of teachers, mentors, and friends along the way." Still, when she left her neighborhood to attend college, Carter felt grateful at the thought of leaving the South Bronx behind. "I left and vowed never to return," she admitted. "It did not seem to present any kind of livable opportunities."

EDUCATION

Carter attended elementary school in the South Bronx. She earned excellent grades, which enabled her to gain admission into the Bronx High School of Science, one of the best public schools in the city. She graduated from the school in the spring of 1984.

A few months later, Carter enrolled at Wesleyan University in Middletown, Connecticut. "The older folks were just pleased as punch and super proud that I was in college, period, that I didn't become a statistic, that I wasn't pregnant at 14 the way many of my friends were," she said. Carter made many friends at Wesleyan, but she admits that few of her friends knew much about her background. Since she was ashamed of her old neighborhood, she always spoke vaguely when friends asked her about her childhood. "The South Bronx was the poster child for urban blight for many, many years and I hated it," she said.

After graduating from Wesleyan with a bachelor's degree in cinema studies in 1988, Carter spent the next few years trying to decide what she wanted to do with her life. She eventually settled on the idea of going back to school. She returned to New York City, and in 1997 she earned a master's degree in English from New York University.

CAREER HIGHLIGHTS

In order to obtain her master's degree, Carter did something that she had vowed that she would never do: she moved back into her childhood home in the South Bronx. She intended to stay only a short time. Carter reasoned that temporarily moving in with her parents would enable her to save enough money to finish graduate school. She also thought that her parents' loving presence might help her deal with the emotional bruises she had acquired from a very brief marriage that had just ended in divorce. "I returned because there was nowhere else to go," she later acknowledged.

During her first weeks back in the South Bronx, Carter felt moments of great regret. The grim warehouses, trash-strewn lots, and dangerous alleyways depressed her, as did the roaring parade of diesel trucks and the stink of the sewage treatment plants. But little by little, her feelings of hopelessness gave way to anger about living conditions in the community. With a growing sense of duty to her old neighborhood, she became a program director for a small arts-related community development organization.

A short time later, Carter made her first forays into political activism. "One day I heard about the mayor's plan to privatize waste handling in the city," she recalled. "They were going to shut down the Staten Island landfill

Carter has long been involved in public outreach, talking to community members about social issues.

without any environmental review and divert the waste handling to our neighborhood. I thought, 'Wait, we already handle 40 percent of the city's commercial waste, and that would bring in another 40 percent of the city's municipal waste.' As I researched, I began to realize that if we're not actively meeting the environment needs of our community, then all the art in the world isn't gonna help."

It was around this time that Carter decided to take action. She did not want to see the next generation of South Bronx kids "grow up in such a toxic environment," so she decided "I would like to be part of something that actually makes life better for people as opposed to doing nothing." With that in mind, she launched a grassroots campaign to derail the city's plan to build yet another waste facility in the South Bronx.

"Mobilizing the community wasn't easy," Carter admitted. "I think we had been so demoralized and dejected—people knew that this was a forgotten place—that it was hard at first to inspire interest and hope." But Carter did not give up. Instead, she patiently approached community groups, church organizations, and ordinary residents and asked them to join the fight. The people of the South Bronx rallied to her side, and in 2000 more than 700 of them showed up at a public hearing to register their objections to the city's plan. A short time later, city officials quietly dropped the idea.

Reclaiming the Riverfront

Carter's next crusade was triggered by the curiosity of a stray dog that she had rescued from the streets of the South Bronx. After finding the dog on the street, she took it home and named it Xena, after the television series about a warrior princess. Before long the two were fast friends. Carter even took the dog along for companionship when she went jogging. On one of these morning excursions, Xena made an amazing discovery. "She pulled me into what I thought was another illegal dump," Carter recalled. "She kept dragging me through weeds and other garbage ... and lo and behold at the end of that lot was the [Bronx] river. I knew this forgotten street end, just like my abandoned dog that brought me there, was worth saving. And just like my new dog, this idea got bigger than I had ever imagined."

> "Mobilizing the community wasn't easy," Carter admitted. "I think we had been so demoralized and dejected—people knew that this was a forgotten place—that it was hard at first to inspire interest and hope."

The sight of the river reminded Carter how warehouses, waste facilities, and other industrial buildings had transformed the South Bronx over the previous decades. Like many other residents, Carter had practically forgotten that the Bronx River even ran past her neighborhood. But after she and Xena returned home later that morning, she began thinking about ways to re-establish the neighborhood's relationship with the river.

Carter decided that the answer was a new riverfront park. She knew that the cost of buying property, removing garbage and abandoned buildings, and building a park would be enormous. But she did not let these obstacles stop her. Instead, she lobbied tirelessly for private donations and grants from nonprofit organizations and government agencies. Little by little, Carter found the necessary money, and in April 1999 the Hunts Point Riverside Park opened to the public. "People were out on the water in canoes and kayaks," she recalled. "They were saying, 'Wow, oh my gosh, there's water here.' It was a very beautiful moment."

Carter and local young people at the opening of the Riverside Park.

According to Carter, the opening of the park also triggered an important change in community attitudes. "It was one of those life-changing moments," she said. "We asked, 'What do you want to see within your community?' It was very empowering to folks who had never been asked what they wanted."

Sustainable South Bronx

The triumphant opening of Hunts Point Riverside Park launched Carter down a new career path as an urban planner. Inspired by her success with the park, she established a nonprofit organization called Sustainable South Bronx in 2001. The goal of this organization, she explained, was to further improve the lives of the people of the South Bronx by creating jobs, reducing local pollution, and expanding "green space"—trees, parks, and other natural surroundings—within the city. "Poor communities of color are just as deserving of clean air, clean water, and open space as wealthier ones," she declared.

Over the next few years, Carter launched a wide range of SSBx projects to help the people of the South Bronx. She designed a community waste reduction program and sponsored "Greening for Breathing," a neighborhood-wide effort to plant trees and other greenery. Carter even collaborated with Columbia University and the City University of New York (CUNY) on an air quality study of the neighborhood. This study confirmed that the South Bronx was saddled with very high levels of local air pollution, which has been widely blamed for causing high rates of asthma among South Bronx children.

In addition, Carter established a successful job training project for the community called the Bronx Environmental Stewardship Training (BEST) Program. The BEST program takes area residents and trains them for careers that protect and restore the urban environment in which they live. "We recruit folks, almost exclusively from the neighborhood," Carter said. "I'd say 95 percent have been on public assistance, and most just received their GEDs [high school General Equivalency Diplomas]. The ages range from about 20 to 45 and we train them in everything from landscaping and green-roof installation to brownfield remediation [cleaning up urban areas contaminated by pollution]." According to Carter, most graduates of the BEST program immediately move into paying jobs.

> "Poor communities of color are just as deserving of clean air, clean water, and open space as wealthier ones," Carter declared.

Carter is especially excited about so-called "green-roof installations" as an environmentally smart job creator. She even launched a company, SmartRoof, to install and maintain green roofs around the city. Green roofs are not a reference to color, but rather to their environmental character. These flat roofs are covered with thin beds of soil that sustain wild flowers, native grasses, and strawberry and blueberry plants. Green roofs provide additional insulation for buildings, which cuts energy use. They also absorb rainwater, which reduces the volume of runoff that city sewage plants must process. Finally, they provide welcome sanctuaries of color and life in this urban setting.

Champion of Environmental Justice

All of the Sustainable South Bronx programs that Carter has launched over the years reflect her deep belief in "environmental justice." According to Carter, this term means that "environmental benefits and burdens [should be] equally distributed among all people, and ... not determined by race or class." As she noted in a 2007 speech, though, the United States is far away

Carter at the installation of a green roof, an environmentally friendly approach to building construction.

from reaching this goal: "Right now, it is race and class that are excellent indicators of where you will find the good stuff like parks and trees and where you'll find the bad stuff like waste facilities and power plants and dead-end jobs that degrade the environment and, by the way, lead to such things as really high asthma rates and obesity and diabetes."

According to Carter, the path to greater environmental justice lies in "creating opportunities for people to enjoy the environment around them, which means the environment needs to be something that can *be* enjoyed. It needs to be supportive of people's health and their economic quality of life." She also believes that environmental justice is only possible if all people—not just the wealthy or politically connected—are given a voice in shaping the world around them.

Many people in the South Bronx report that Carter's voice has already made a big difference in their lives. "The neighborhood has done a 180-degree turn," said one resident. "Trees are coming in, people are keeping the streets cleaner. There are new stores—all these things have made living here a lot better." Another resident who works for SSBx declared that the foundation's success in greening the community "gives me hope for the future."

A National Leader

The efforts of Carter and her Sustainable South Bronx organization have attracted national attention as well. In 2005 she received one of the most famous awards in the United States—a MacArthur Fellowship, also known as a "genius" grant. These awards are given annually by the John D. and Catherine T. MacArthur Foundation, an organization that is "dedicated to helping groups and individuals foster lasting improvement in the human condition." To do this, they identify individuals whose creativity and past accomplishment suggest a successful future. The foundation praised Carter as a "relentless and charismatic urban strategist" who is "profoundly transforming the quality of life for South Bronx residents." The award includes a grant of $500,000 over five years, enough to allow the winners the financial independence to pursue further creativity.

Carter's public profile has risen in other areas as well. She has played a leadership role on a number of New York state environmental councils, and she was keynote speaker at the 2006 National Business for Social Responsibility Conference. Carter is also a member of The Clinton Global Initiative's Poverty Alleviation Panel, a philanthropic organization founded by ex-president Bill Clinton. Her work has been praised by such diverse magazines as *Newsweek,* which named her to its 2007 list of 25 to Watch, and *Essence,* which named her to its list of the country's 25 Most Influential African Americans. Finally, Carter has received prestigious awards from such respected environmental organizations as the National Audubon Society and the Natural Resources Defense Council.

> "The neighborhood has done a 180-degree turn," said one South Bronx resident. "Trees are coming in, people are keeping the streets cleaner. There are new stores—all these things have made living here a lot better."

The effective work carried out by SSBx is the most obvious reason for Carter's meteoric rise to prominence. Close observers say that the accomplishments of Sustainable South Bronx are a direct result of her bold personality. Carter refused to be intimidated by corporate lawyers, city bureaucrats, powerful lawmakers, or wealthy philanthropists. Instead, she showed spirit, determination, and confidence in her dealings

Carter at her desk at Sustainable South Bronx.

with everyone she came across. "She is as comfortable chatting with world leaders as she is training single mothers and returning felons who are reentering society to care for shade trees or build green roofs on energy-efficient buildings," concluded Bracken Hendricks in *Apollo's Fire.*

Carter has also refused to let the awards and attention distract her from her goals. In 2008, in fact, she achieved a long-time SSBx priority when the city of New York began construction of the South Bronx Greenway. When completed, this Greenway will include 11 miles of cycling and walking paths extending from the heart of the South Bronx community to the Bronx River waterfront. And Carter continues to raise millions of dollars to clean up areas of blight in the South Bronx—and block other polluting businesses and facilities from entering the community.

Urging Others to Get Involved

In her travels around the United States, Carter often speaks with journalists, lawmakers, and community organizers. But she also makes a special effort to reach people who are living in depressed urban surroundings. "My dream is that others will do what we've done in their own communities," she observed. "Do something that gives back to your community, whether it's writing to your representative in Congress about an environmental issue or volunteering at a neighborhood park clean-up." Carter believes that once people get involved in community issues, they often discover leadership skills that they did not even know they had. "A successful leader is somebody who follows the needs represented by the population," she stated. "Everybody has the capacity to be a leader. It's just stepping up to the plate when something has to be done."

Carter also urges people who live in comfortable suburban homes and neighborhoods to show greater compassion for those who are less fortunate. "I see so many women getting worked up about polar bears, when in reality every city has its own South Bronx, where greenhouse-gas sources have been affecting people for decades," she said.

MARRIAGE AND FAMILY

Carter was briefly married in the mid-1990s, but that marriage ended in divorce. She then remained single until October 2006, when she married James Burling Chase, a communications specialist. The couple exchanged wedding vows at Hunts Point Riverside Park. "He's one of the most stabilizing and funny forces in my life," said Carter.

HOBBIES AND OTHER INTERESTS

Carter's work with Sustainable South Bronx keeps her very busy, but when she does get a break she likes to go camping, snorkeling, and roller-skating. She also enjoys reading and home renovation. "One day I'd like to write a screenplay for a movie," she adds, "but I don't have the time now."

SELECTED HONORS AND AWARDS

Environmental Quality Award (U.S. Environmental Protection Agency): 1999
Union Square Award (Fund for the City of New York): 2002
Women's History Month Pacesetter Award (New York City Council): 2004
MacArthur Fellowship (John D. and Catherine T. MacArthur Foundation): 2005
Earth Day Environmental Advocates' Award for Achievements in Community Development (Natural Resources Defense Council): 2006
Rachel Carson Women in Conservation Award (National Audubon Society): 2007
Martin Luther King Jr. Award for Humanitarian Service (New York University): 2007

FURTHER READING

Books

Inslee, Jay, and Bracken Hendricks. *Apollo's Fire: Igniting America's Clean-Energy Economy,* 2008

Kerry, John, and Teresa Heinz Kerry. *This Moment on Earth: Today's New Environmentalists and Their Vision for the Future,* 2007

Periodicals

Chicago Tribune, Nov. 12, 2007
Christian Science Monitor, Oct. 31, 2007, p.13
Chronicle of Philanthropy, Oct. 27, 2005, p.44
Essence, Jan. 2005, p.24; Dec. 2007, p.207
Jet, Oct. 10, 2005, p.36
New York, Feb. 26, 2007, p.26
New York Times, Dec. 3, 2000, p.C1; Aug. 15, 2001, p.B2
Newsweek, Dec. 25, 2006, p.68
PCMA Convene, Dec. 2006, p.79
Shape, Nov. 2007, p.168

Online Articles

http://www.outside.com
 (*Outside,* "Green All Stars: Community Leader," Apr. 2007)
http://www.plentymag.com
 (*Plenty Magazine,* "A Bronx Tale," Feb. 13, 2007)
http://www.quickandsimple.com
 (Quickandsimple.com, "The Queen of Green," undated)
http://www.vibe.com
 (*Vibe,* "Majora Carter: The Green Thumb," Aug. 8, 2007)
http://www.grist.org
 (*Weekly Grist,* "Majora League," Sep. 28, 2006)

ADDRESS

Majora Carter
Sustainable South Bronx
890 Garrison Ave., 4th Floor
The Bronx, NY 10474

WORLD WIDE WEB SITE

http://www.ssbx.org

Anderson Cooper 1967-

American Television Journalist
Host of the CNN News Show "Anderson Cooper 360"

BIRTH

Anderson Hays Cooper was born on June 3, 1967, in New York City, New York. His father was Wyatt Emory Cooper, a screenwriter who hailed from a poor farming family in Mississippi. His mother was Gloria Morgan Vanderbilt, a famous socialite and fashion designer. She was an heiress to the family fortune built by her great-grandfather, railroad tycoon Cornelius Vanderbilt. Cooper had one older brother, Carter, who committed suicide in 1988.

YOUTH

Cooper grew up in a luxury apartment building in Manhattan, in New York City. Such famous individuals as Andy Warhol, Charlie Chaplin, and Truman Capote were frequent dinner guests. According to Cooper, though, his parents created a home environment that kept him from becoming spoiled or snobbish. "Neither of my parents believed in joining clubs or being involved in anything that reeked of elitism or exclusiveness," he recalled. "Growing up, 'elitist' was the worst thing you could say about someone."

Instead, Cooper's parents encouraged him to be independent and curious about the world around him. "What was cool about my parents was, my brother and I were expected to sit at the adult table," he said. "There was never a kids' table. To me, the greatest privilege of the way I grew up was realizing at a very young age that these [famous] people are just as unhappy as everyone else. Once you realize that, it frees you up from believing that fame or riches are going to bring you happiness. I think it takes a lot of people a long time to figure that one out." These conversations also helped him understand that successful people did not have all the answers when they were young, either. "It was comforting to me when I figured out that you don't have to know what you want to do with your life; you just have to take a few steps in one direction, and other opportunities will open up."

> "Neither of my parents believed in joining clubs or being involved in anything that reeked of elitism or exclusiveness," he recalled. "Growing up, 'elitist' was the worst thing you could say about someone."

In other respects, Cooper had a normal childhood. He spent countless hours playing with his brother, who was two years older. "He created giant battlefields for war games with our toy soldiers," Cooper remembered. "The rules were too intricate for me to follow, but I loved to sit and watch him direct armies across the sweeping plains of our bedroom floor."

Like countless other youngsters, Cooper also loved watching television. "I've been addicted to TV since I emerged from the womb," he admitted in a 2006 interview. "I recently found a schedule I made for myself in fourth grade, which was all blocked out based on the TV schedule.... I think I allotted 15 minutes for dinner, and homework was done in front of the tele-

ANDERSON COOPER

Anderson Cooper (left) running down a street in New York City with his mother, Gloria Vanderbilt, and his brother, Carter Vanderbilt Cooper.

vision. News was always on the schedule as well. I had a reading problem when I was a kid, so writing came a little slow."

In fact, Cooper had dyslexia, an inherited neurological condition in which the reader's brain has difficulty processing letters and words in the proper order. People with dyslexia have trouble recognizing and decoding words, which can make reading and spelling difficult. As a result, they often have trouble with reading comprehension. Cooper's parents hired a special reading instructor to help him deal with it. The instructor's guidance was an important factor in his ability to deal with his disability. "One way she helped was to encourage me to find books that I was really passionate about," he recalled. "I remember reading a biography of Helen Keller and a book about people who chose to live in the woods. Eventually, I read *Heart of Darkness* [by Joseph Conrad]. That novel, in particular, sparked an interest in seeing what happens to society when everything is stripped away, when you're living without the niceties of modern culture."

> "To me, the greatest privilege of the way I grew up was realizing at a very young age that these [famous] people are just as unhappy as everyone else. Once you realize that, it frees you up from believing that fame or riches are going to bring you happiness. I think it takes a lot of people a long time to figure that one out."

Cooper's curiosity also extended to other, distant parts of the world. As a child, he kept by his bedside a miniature globe that had been given to the family by Isak Dinesen, author of *Out of Africa*. "When I couldn't sleep I'd touch the globe, trace the contours of the continents in the dark," he wrote in his autobiography, *Dispatches from the Edge*. "Some nights my small fingers would hike the ridges of Everest, or struggle to reach the summit of Kilimanjaro. Many times, I rounded the Horn of Africa, more than once my ship foundering on rocks off the Cape of Good Hope. The globe was covered with names of nations that no longer exist: Tanganyika, Siam, the Belgian Congo, Ceylon. I dreamed of traveling to them all."

Death in the Family

Cooper's comfortable childhood was shattered in January 1978, when his father died while undergoing heart bypass surgery. The shock of this sudden loss triggered major changes in Cooper's emotional make-up.

"For years, I tried to swaddle the pain, encase the feelings," he admitted in his autobiography. "I boxed them up along with my father's papers, stored them away, promising one day to sort them all out. All I managed to do was deaden myself to them, detach myself from life. That works for only so long."

The death of their father also opened an emotional divide between Cooper and his brother. "After the funeral, both of us retreated into separate parts of ourselves, and I don't think we ever truly reached out to each other again," he later acknowledged.

After his father's death, Cooper became even more determined to find his own path. At age 11 he worked briefly as a model, and as a teenager he spent several of his summer vacations waiting tables at a New York City restaurant. These jobs gave him a feeling of independence and illustrated his growing resolve to succeed in life without depending on his family's wealth or influence.

EDUCATION

Cooper attended private schools in Manhattan during his childhood, including an arts-oriented high school called the Dalton School. During his years at Dalton, he signed up for a number of survival courses during summer breaks, ranging from sea kayaking excursions in Mexico to mountaineering expeditions in the Rockies. "I needed to prove to myself that I could survive on my own," he later explained.

After graduating from Dalton one semester early in 1985, Cooper organized a solo trip for himself through portions of southern and central Africa. He spent several months in Africa, traveling on foot or by truck or bus before returning home. "I knew it was in his nature to take risks, live on the edge," his mother said. "He got malaria and was in a hospital in Kenya, and he never told me about this until he came home safe."

After returning to the United States, Cooper enrolled at Yale University in New Haven, Connecticut, where he studied political science. He also served as the coxswain on the university's crew team. In crew, teams of rowers work together, while the coxswain instructs the rowers and steers the boat during competitions. But on July 22, 1988, as Cooper was preparing for his senior year at Yale, his brother Carter committed suicide by jumping from the balcony of the family's apartment in front of their mother's horrified eyes.

Television, magazine, and newspaper reporters swarmed around the family for the next few weeks, drawn by Gloria Vanderbilt's fame and wealth.

Cooper was disgusted by the callous behavior of many of these journalists. "It certainly makes me more sensitive now about how I cover tragedies," he asserted. "I've never asked somebody how they feel after they've lost a member of their family. I would never use that word. How do you feel? You see that a lot on TV. It's a terrible question. The response is, 'How do you think I feel?'"

When Cooper returned to the Yale campus a few weeks later, he went to classes in a kind of daze. "I spent most of my time trying to understand what had happened,"

Cooper in his yearbook photo from Yale University.

he said in *Dispatches from the Edge*. "Many times that year, I wished I had a mark, a scar, a missing limb, something children could have pointed at, at which adults could tell them not to stare. At least then they would have seen, would have known. I wouldn't have been expected to smile and mingle, meet and greet."

Cooper graduated from Yale in 1989 with a bachelor's degree. A year later, he continued his education, but under unusual circumstances. He took several months of Vietnamese language lessons at the University of Hanoi in Vietnam. But by that time, he was already making his first early forays into the world of television journalism.

CAREER HIGHLIGHTS

After leaving Yale, Cooper applied for an entry-level job at ABC News. He refused to use his family connections to launch his career, though, so he failed to even land an interview at ABC. He finally got a job as a fact-checker at Channel One, a company that broadcasts a 12-minute daily news program to thousands of high schools throughout the United States. After several months at Channel One, according to Cooper, "I came up with a plan to become a foreign correspondent. It was very simple, and monumentally stupid. I figured if I went places that were dangerous or exotic, I wouldn't have much competition, and if my stories were interesting and inexpensive, Channel One might broadcast them."

Armed with a video camera and a forged press pass, Cooper left the United States in 1991 for the Southeast Asian nation of Burma (now known as

Myanmar). He spent several weeks covering the country's growing violence between Burma's repressive military government and pro-democracy students. After Channel One bought his Burma footage, Cooper moved on to other Southeast Asian nations, including Cambodia, Thailand, and Vietnam. He spent most of his time—nearly six months—in Hanoi, the capital of Vietnam. It was during this period that he took language classes at the University of Hanoi.

In September 1992 Cooper moved on to Somalia, a civil war-torn country that sits on the coastal edge of the Horn of Africa. His coverage of the violence in Somalia was snapped up by Channel One, and in 1993 Channel One hired him as its chief international correspondent. Over the next two years, Cooper traveled all over the globe for Channel One, visiting one troubled place after another. The list of countries that he reported from included Bosnia, Croatia, Russia, Ukraine, Georgia, Israel, Cambodia, Haiti, Indonesia, South Africa, and Rwanda.

> *"I came up with a plan to become a foreign correspondent. It was very simple, and monumentally stupid. I figured if I went places that were dangerous or exotic, I wouldn't have much competition, and if my stories were interesting and inexpensive, Channel One might broadcast them."*

Covering Wars

In most of these places, the threat of violence was a daily fact of life. And in some of them, brutal war had shattered cities and villages alike. "Anyone who tells you they aren't scared in a war zone is a fool or a liar, and probably both," Cooper wrote in *Dispatches from the Edge*. "The more places you've been, the more you know just how easy it is to get killed. It's not like in the movies. There are no slow-motion falls, no crying out the names of your loved ones. People die, and the world keeps spinning."

Cooper initially thought that he could report from these war zones without suffering any emotional damage to himself. "I thought I could get away unscathed, unchanged," he wrote. "The truth was I hadn't gotten out at all. It's impossible to block out what you see, what you hear. Even if you stop listening, the pain gets inside, seeps through the cracks you can't close up. You can't fake your way through it. I know that now. You have to absorb it all. You owe them that. You owe it to yourself as well."

After a while, Cooper realized that the things that he had seen made it difficult for him to live a "normal" life. When he returned to the United States between assignments, he discovered that he had a great deal of difficulty adjusting to the sights and sounds of a functioning society. "Coming home meant coming down," he wrote. "I'd return home to piles of bills and an empty refrigerator. Buying groceries, I'd get lost—too many aisles, too many choices; cool mist blowing over fresh fruit; paper or plastic; cash back in return? ... The more I was away, the worse it got. I'd come back and couldn't speak the language. Out there the pain was palpable; you breathed it in the air. Back here, no one talked about life and death."

> "Anyone who tells you they aren't scared in a war zone is a fool or a liar, and probably both," Cooper wrote. "The more places you've been, the more you know just how easy it is to get killed. It's not like in the movies. There are no slow-motion falls, no crying out the names of your loved ones. People die, and the world keeps spinning."

Covering the News at ABC and CNN

In 1995 Cooper left Channel One and took a job at ABC News, where he became the youngest correspondent at the network. Over the next three years he kept a very busy schedule, working as a field reporter and as co-anchor of "World News Now," an ABC late-night news program. In 1998 ABC named him a contributor to their newsmagazines "20/20" and "20/20 Downtown" in addition to his other duties. Cooper contributed a number of well-received reports over the ensuing months, but he also became unhappy with his grueling schedule and some of his assignments.

In 2000 Cooper left ABC for USA Networks, which wanted him to host and produce a new weekly documentary series. Six months later, the series was cancelled and ABC Entertainment approached him about serving as the host of "The Mole," a new reality series. Cooper accepted the offer against the advice of news industry insiders who said the job would destroy his credibility as a journalist. "The Mole" was popular in its first season, but it struggled with poor ratings in its second season.

In January 2002 Cooper left his hosting duties with "The Mole" for a position on the news staff of the cable news network CNN. Defying critics who thought that his time with "The Mole" would kill his journalism career, he

Cooper on the set of his CNN news program, "Anderson Cooper 360."

quickly became a high-profile member of the CNN news team. During 2002 Cooper served as a field reporter, weekend anchor, and substitute host on various CNN programs. In March 2003 he was named co-host of a morning news show with Paula Zahn, and six months later he was given his own nightly show, "Anderson Cooper 360." When the new program was unveiled, he explained the reasoning behind the show's name. "It's 360 degrees in terms of the scope of what we're talking about, whether it's foreign policy, political events, or pop culture things."

> "Here, you grow up believing there's a safety net, that things can never completely fall apart," Cooper wrote. "Katrina showed us all that's not true. For all the money spent on homeland security, all the preparations that have allegedly been made, we are not ready, not even for a disaster we know is coming. We can't take care of our own."

Cooper loved hosting the show, which blended coverage of breaking news with special feature stories. "In the past, I'd make fun of anchors, but I've learned it's actually really stimulating," he said. "It's a mental exercise that I equate to running along the edge of a sand cliff that's collapsing underneath you: It's very easy for everything to go wrong and for you to fall, but if you can keep yourself upright and moving forward, it can be exhilarating. Every night it's about learning and synthesizing, being able to formulate thought and come up with questions, all in real time. It's a challenge that I really enjoy."

Hosting a high-profile news program also gave Cooper additional opportunities to travel around the world. In January 2005, for example, he gave a series of reports from Sri Lanka, where a horrible tsunami had devastated the country. He also carried out broadcasts from Iraq, the Vatican (for the April 2005 funeral of Pope John Paul II), and Florida after Hurricane Dennis hit the state in July 2005.

Reporting on Hurricane Katrina

Cooper's most notable journalistic efforts on "Anderson Cooper 360," though, came in the late summer of 2005, when Hurricane Katrina roared into the Gulf of Mexico and devastated New Orleans and many smaller communities along the Louisiana and Mississippi coastlines. The response

ANDERSON COOPER

Cooper returned to New Orleans one year after Hurricane Katrina to report on progress. Here, he's shown at The Musician's Village, a housing project under construction by Habitat for Humanity to house musicians and artists.

to this natural disaster from state and federal authorities was woefully slow and incompetent. Thousands of desperate residents of New Orleans and other communities were left to fend for themselves for several days under nightmarish circumstances before the first help arrived. But in the first few days after Katrina reached the mainland on August 29, most lawmakers and government officials were acting as if the rescue and recovery efforts were going well.

Cooper witnessed the death and destruction in Katrina firsthand. On September 1 his frustration and anger with the terrible governmental response to the disaster finally boiled over. That anger surfaced during a televised interview with U.S. Senator Mary L. Landrieu of Louisiana.

At the beginning of the interview, Landrieu started thanking various state and federal officials for their recovery efforts. Cooper listened for a moment, then he interrupted her to declare that "for the last four days I've been seeing dead bodies in the streets.... And to listen to politicians thanking each other and congratulating each other—you know, I've got to tell you, there are a lot of people here who are very upset, and very angry, and very frustrated."

Cooper's words forced Landrieu to agree that the response had been inadequate. Other journalists also began asking tougher questions about the government's performance during this period. Within a matter of days, even government officials and lawmakers were apologizing for the fumbling response to Katrina.

Cooper's coverage of Hurricane Katrina brought him a flood of viewers who had never tuned in to his program before. According to many critics, these viewers were drawn by the sense that he was one of them. "He reacted the way any of us might have—raging against government officials when help didn't come fast enough, and weeping when it all got to be too much," wrote Jonathan Van Meter in *New York*. "But it wasn't just his raw emotion that set him apart ... it was his honest humanity.... He connected to those in the hurricane's path, and to the people watching at home."

For his part, Cooper believed that Hurricane Katrina changed his perception of America forever. "Here, you grow up believing there's a safety net, that things can never completely fall apart," he wrote. "Katrina showed us all that's not true. For all the money spent on homeland security, all the preparations that have allegedly been made, we are not ready, not even for a disaster we know is coming. We can't take care of our own. The world can break apart in our own backyard, and when it does many of us will simply fall off."

Dispatches from the Edge

One month after Cooper gave his dramatic, popular reports from the Gulf Coast disaster zone, CNN announced that it was expanding "Anderson Cooper 360" to two hours and moving it to 10:00 p.m. In May 2006, CBS announced that it had added Cooper to its list of contributors to "60 Minutes," the most famous newsmagazine on television.

Also in May 2006, Cooper's long-awaited autobiography was published. *Dispatches from the Edge: A Memoir of War, Disasters, and Survival* reported his experiences as a correspondent for CNN, in covering tragedies both in the United States and around the world. But it also offered a candid look at some of the tragedies in own life, showing how all of these crises affected him. *Dispatches from the Edge* immediately jumped to the top of various bestseller lists. It also received strong reviews from critics. A reviewer for the *Saturday Evening Post* called it a compelling memoir that "serves as a refreshing reminder of the power of the written word." As a writer for *Booklist* described it, "In straightforward yet passionate prose, the author recounts his experiences not only in Louisiana and Mississippi but also in sniper-riddled Sarajevo, famine-plagued Niger, tsunami-destroyed South-

Cooper's autobiography combined his professional experience covering tragedies around the world as well as his personal experience with tragedy.

east Asia, and civil-war-ravaged Somalia. At the same time, Cooper takes a look inward, at his motivations in gravitating to dangerous adventures, and at his family history and his relations to his late father and brother and his famous mother.... He scrutinizes how those relations helped formulate his life view and compelled him to follow his dreams and desires. Cooper is both respected and popular; expect the same attitude toward his book."

Throughout 2007, Cooper traveled around the world for *Planet in Peril*, which he co-hosted with chief medical correspondent Dr. Sanjay Gupta and Animal Planet host Jeff Corwin. This four-hour documentary explored issues that threaten the planet and its inhabitants. It featured places around the world where environmental change has created environmental crises, exploring such topics as global warming, species loss, habitat loss, and overpopulation. After the documentary, Cooper continued with its theme, incorporating segments devoted to environmental issues into "Anderson Cooper 360." These segments culminated in a new program in fall 2008 called *Planet in Peril: Battle Lines*, co-hosted by Cooper, Gupta, and National Geographic host Lisa Ling. (For more information on Ling, see page 211.)

> "I love what I'm doing," Cooper said. "CNN is a cool place to work because I'm able to anchor and still do a lot of field reporting. But I've never hung anything on the walls in the offices I've had because nothing seems to last very long in TV. Who knows what will happen down the road?"

In 2007, Cooper also moderated the presidential debates sponsored by CNN and YouTube. For the Democratic debate, the presidential candidates spoke at The Citadel in Charleston, South Carolina; for the Republican debate, the presidential candidates spoke in St. Petersburg, Florida.

Cooper's autobiography, combined with his continued work as a TV reporter and anchor, has made him one of CNN's best-known journalists. He appreciates the role that he has been able to carve out with the network. "I love what I'm doing," he said. "CNN is a cool place to work because I'm able to anchor and still do a lot of field reporting. But I've never hung anything on the walls in the offices I've had because nothing seems to last very long in TV. Who knows what will happen down the road?"

HOME AND FAMILY

Cooper is single and lives in a loft in downtown Manhattan. He routinely turns aside questions about his personal life. "I understand why people might be interested," he admitted. "But I just don't talk about my personal life. The whole thing about being a reporter is that you're supposed to be an observer and to be able to adapt with any group you're in, and I don't want to do anything that threatens that."

HOBBIES AND OTHER INTERESTS

Cooper admits that he still relaxes by watching quite a bit of television. He relies on TiVo to keep up with "jaw-dropping and mind-numbing" programs like MTV's "My Super Sweet 16" and "Tiara Girls."

SELECTED WRITINGS

Dispatches from the Edge: A Memoir of War, Disasters, and Survival, 2006

HONORS AND AWARDS

Silver Plaque (Chicago International Film Festival): for reporting from Sarajevo on the Bosnian civil war
Bronze Award (National Educational Film and Video Festival): for report on political Islam
GLAAD (Gay and Lesbian Alliance Against Defamation) Media Award for Outstanding Journalism: 1999
Emmy Award: 2006 (two), to "Anderson Cooper 360" for "outstanding live coverage of a breaking news event" and "outstanding feature story"

FURTHER READING

Books

Cooper, Anderson. *Dispatches from the Edge: A Memoir of War, Disasters, and Survival,* 2006

Periodicals

Booklist, June 1, 2006, p.4
Boston Globe, Sep. 8, 2003, p.B5
Current Biography Yearbook, 2006
Entertainment Weekly, June 2, 2006, p.26
Interview, Oct. 2004, p.122
Maclean's, June 5, 2006
New York, Sep. 19, 2005

New York Times, Feb. 11, 1996, sec. 2, p.32; Sep. 12, 2005, p.E6
Newsweek, Dec. 26, 2005, p.22
O, The Oprah Magazine, July 2005, p.130
People, May 6, 1996, p.54; Jan. 15, 2001, p.77; Dec. 2, 2002, p.102
Saturday Evening Post, Sep.-Oct. 2006, p.24
Time, June 19, 2006, p.19
USA Today, June 4, 1993, p.D3
Variety, Jan. 9, 2006, p.24

Online Articles

http://www.cbsnews.com
   (*CBS News Online,* "Anderson Cooper: Coping with Grief," May 25, 2006
http://www.salon.com
   (*Salon.com,* "Method Anchor," Aug. 23, 2006)

ADDRESS

Anderson Cooper
"Anderson Cooper 360"
One CNN Center
Atlanta, GA 30303

WORLD WIDE WEB SITES

http://www.cnn.com/CNN/Programs/anderson.cooper.360

Zac Efron 1987-

American Actor and Singer
Star of the Disney *High School Musical* Movies and
the Feature Film *Hairspray*

BIRTH

Zachary David Alexander Efron was born on October 18, 1987, in San Luis Obispo, California. He is the son of David Efron, an engineer at a power plant, and Starla Efron, a secretary at the same plant. Efron has one younger brother, Dylan.

YOUTH AND EDUCATION

Efron grew up in Arroyo Grande, a suburban town north of Los Angeles on the Pacific Coast. "I grew up in California completely ignorant of the entertainment industry," he said. "I grew up as a regular guy with a regular life. I went to school and got good grades. I have the most normal family in the world."

One of his parents was always at home when Efron got home from school, and they always made sure he did his homework. "My parents were very strict," he said. If he play-wrestled too roughly with his little brother, which he often did, he was grounded. Once he was grounded for a week after he cut his hair and then lied about it.

Mostly, Efron recalls a happy childhood in which he often burst into song or dance. "When Zac was a toddler, after watching *The Wizard of Oz,* we found him emulating the Tin Man dance," his father told *Rolling Stone*. "Over time we noticed that he had an uncanny ability to listen to a song on the radio, memorize the lyrics, and sing it back a capella with the correct rhythm and pitch."

> "I grew up in California completely ignorant of the entertainment industry," Efron said. "I grew up as a regular guy with a regular life. I went to school and got good grades. I have the most normal family in the world."

In elementary school, Efron liked playing sports, especially baseball. But he was small and didn't play that well. Meanwhile, his musical talents were blossoming. When he was 11 years old, he told his parents that he didn't want to play baseball anymore. They suggested that he take piano lessons. Reluctant at first, Efron eventually agreed. He began taking lessons with Jeremy Mann, who also worked for a company that staged musicals. Efron's upbeat personality charmed Mann immediately. "The first time I met him," Mann remarked, "I said to myself,'This kid's going to grow up to be Brad Pitt.' He's probably the most charismatic little kid I've ever met."

Becoming an Actor

Mann thought Efron would be a natural performer. He encouraged the 11-year-old to audition for *Gypsy*, which was being staged by the Pacific Conservatory of the Performing Arts. Efron needed a big push from his father to show up for the tryouts. "I went into this audition kicking and scream-

Efron appearing on "The Suite Life of Zack and Cody" with Brenda Song (left) and Ashley Tisdale (right).

ing, and little did I know my dad had just showed me the coolest thing on earth," he said. He got a small part as a newsboy and appeared in more than 70 performances of *Gypsy*. "From day one, I got addicted to being on stage and getting the applause and laughter," he said.

After *Gypsy*, Efron said, "[I] started auditioning for every single play that was in our area. Luckily, I booked some of the roles and started doing very well." His favorite role was as Wendy's brother John in *Peter Pan*. "That was a really fun part because I got to fly around on a 'fly' wire," he said. "I was hovering over people in the audience. I actually knocked off a guy's toupee once." A lot of the fun came from the friendships he made with other young actors. Many of them appeared in the same plays, and they liked to hang out together backstage.

In middle school, Efron took drama classes to learn more about his craft and be with students who shared his passion for performing. When he was 14, his drama teacher recognized his talent and arranged an audition for him. His mother drove him three hours to Los Angeles, where his successful reading landed him an agent.

For the next few months, mother and son repeated the trek to Los Angeles. Efron auditioned for television and film roles, but was repeatedly rejected. Tired of the long commute, his mother told him that unless he got some jobs within the next year, she was through being the chauffeur. Before her deadline, Efron landed a few small television roles and commercials. In 2003 he appeared in the TV drama "ER," playing a young teenager who got caught in gang crossfire and died on the operating table. After that, he landed TV guest spots more regularly. A big break came in 2004, when he co-starred in the made-for-TV movie *Miracle Run* as a developmentally disabled teenager. The movie, including Efron's performance, was well received.

Between acting jobs, Efron attended his hometown high school and worked hard to keep up his grades. English was his favorite subject, and chemistry was his least favorite, although he got straight A's in the class. Acting jobs kept him too busy to play sports or participate in after-school clubs or high-school theater. Eventually, Efron found it hard to keep up with his classes, and he left school in the middle of 10th grade. "I enrolled in junior college courses—that's how I graduated," he said.

CAREER HIGHLIGHTS

Efron's first consistent acting job came in 2004. It started with "Summerland," a TV series about a career woman, played by Lori Loughlin, who was left to raise her sister's three children after a fatal car crash. Efron appeared as Cameron Bale, a 14-year-old neighbor who became involved with one of the children, played by Kay Panabaker. His performance impressed the producers so much that he was hired to be a regular member of the cast. "I really got to see what acting was like," he said of his "Summerland" experience. "It was a big break in the business." Unfortunately, "Summerland" was cancelled after a single season. Efron was disappointed at the time, but his career was about to skyrocket.

High School Musical

In 2005 the Disney Channel began casting for an original film about teenagers who get together to put on a musical in their high school. *High School Musical* begins as two teens on vacation at a ski resort are forced to sing karaoke together at a New Year's Eve party. Athletic Troy Bolton (played by Efron) and brainy Gabriella Montez (played by Vanessa Hudgens) enjoy their duet, although neither has done much singing before. When Gabriella transfers to Troy's high school, the two of them end up in their own cliques. They think about trying out for the school musical, although their friends disapprove and their musical rivals, twins Sharpay and Ryan, scheme to stop them. Troy and Gabriella have to withstand the disapproval of their

Efron in scenes from High School Musical *and* High School Musical 2.

friends to be together, a theme that the creators of the movie acknowledge is reminiscent of the Broadway musicals *West Side Story* and *Grease*.

Efron was one of many teenage actors to audition for the film, and the competition was fierce. He had to go through several rounds of tryouts. "They would send you to these rooms to learn the songs and the dances," he said. "Then you would rehearse. You would audition and then all you would hear was, 'OK, we'll call you.' It was nerve wracking. I mean, you never know what's going on in a director's head."

Efron's background in local musical theater productions gave him an edge and the stamina to make it through the marathon auditions. "I had it easier than some of the guys.... Some of them were passing out!" he said. "It was Broadway-style, seven-and-a-half hours of singing, acting, and dancing. And then we had to play basketball. I was probably weakest at that."

> "I went into this audition kicking and screaming, and little did I know my dad had just showed me the coolest thing on earth," he said. "From day one, I got addicted to being on stage and getting the applause and laughter."

Some of the male and female aspirants were asked to audition together. Efron was asked to sing with Vanessa Anne Hudgens, who was trying out for the role of Gabriella. "It was fun; we were put together from the beginning," he said. "And to some degree, I think that helped us out because we really got to know each other." At the end of the tryouts, it was Efron, along with Hudgens, who landed the starring roles. Efron called Troy a "dream character to play. He's kind of like Danny Zuko in *Grease* [played by John Travolta in the movie version of the musical]. I think that every guy would like being more like Troy when they were in high school. I wish I was more like him because he's so good. He's so good at basketball."

It took just six weeks to make *High School Musical*. For the first two weeks the cast was put through day-long rehearsals at the southwest Utah film site. After Efron went over the singing and dancing routines, he went to basketball practice with his fellow *Musical* teammates. Then came four weeks of filming. Despite the hectic schedule, the young actors enjoyed being with each other during the production. "The whole cast would hang out after every day of shooting," Efron said. "We'd go and eat dinner and we just did fun stuff together and it made being on the set a lot more fun."

High School Musical Becomes a Hit

High School Musical proved to be a blockbuster for Disney. The January 2006 television premiere averaged almost 7.7 million viewers, and repeat telecasts drew many millions more. The show won an Emmy for Outstanding Children's Program as well as a 2006 Teen Choice Award for Choice Comedy/Musical Program. Disney has aired several different versions of the musical, including a sing-along version with song lyrics; a dance-along version, in which cast members show the audience footwork routines; and a pop-up version, which includes information about the making of the movie. It also produced nationwide concert tours and even ice shows.

The soundtrack of the movie was in the Top 10 on the Billboard charts for over five months and became the biggest selling CD of 2006, with more than four million in sales. For Efron, the music in *High School Musical* is a bit of an embarrassment. "I didn't sing on the first album," he admitted. "It wasn't my voice in the movie. Even though I wanted to do it." The DVD, which included the original and sing-along versions, broke sales records in 2006 when 1.2 million copies were sold in its first six days, making it the fastest-selling TV movie of all time.

> *"The whole cast would hang out after every day of shooting,"* Efron said about making *High School Musical*. *"We'd go and eat dinner and we just did fun stuff together and it made being on the set a lot more fun."*

After the success of *High School Musical*, producers of an earlier Efron movie moved to capitalize on his fame. Efron had filmed *The Derby Stallion* before *High School Musical*, but it wasn't released right away; instead, it went straight to DVD in 2007. *Stallion* is the story of a conflicted 15-year-old boy (played by Efron) who hooks up with an elderly horseman and ends up training for the Derby Cup. Efron spent weeks learning how to ride a horse in order to play the part. Beth Johnson of *Entertainment Weekly* wrote that although the film is "full of cliches," the "relationship between boy and mentor is touching, Efron is adorable, family values are applauded and, well, you have the satisfaction of knowing how it will all turn out."

Hairspray

In the winter of 2007, the cast of *High School Musical* began a 40-city concert tour without Efron, who was busy filming the big-screen musical

Link Larkin (Efron) and Tracy Turnblad (Nikki Blonsky) share a moment in Hairspray.

Hairspray. The movie tells the story of Tracy Turnblad (played by Nikki Blonsky), a bubbly, overweight Baltimore teenager who longs to sing and dance on a local TV show. Efron landed the role of slick-haired Link Larkin, the heartthrob of the dance show and Tracy's love interest. John Travolta, dressed in drag, plays Tracy's mother.

Efron almost blew his initial audition for Link. "I saw this sweet, goofy kid," Adam Shankman, the director and choreographer of *Hairspray*, told *USA Today*. "I thought he was too light. Link is more cool. Then my sister, Jennifer, one of the executive producers, said to me, 'You passed on him? Are you out of your mind? He's the biggest star on the planet to anyone under 15.'" Shankman called Efron back, gave him more specific directions about Link's character, and was impressed enough by Efron's second audition to hire him. Nikki Blonsky thought Efron nailed the part. "He just jumps off the screen and right into every girl's heart," she said.

For Efron, working in a major Hollywood production was a dream come true. "I sat down to a table read, and I was next to Michelle Pfeiffer, and on the other side of me was Amanda Bynes and across from me were John Travolta and Chris Walken," he said. "It was such a star-studded cast, I couldn't believe I was sharing a table—let alone working in the same movie as them." Sharing the screen with Travolta was a special thrill for Efron, who has idolized the actor since seeing him in the 1978 movie *Grease*. "I remember thinking musicals were cool all because of John," he said.

> *According to Adam Shankman, the director of* **Hairspray,** *Efron almost blew his initial audition for Link. "I saw this sweet, goofy kid," Shankman said. "I thought he was too light. Link is more cool. Then my sister, Jennifer, one of the executive producers, said to me, 'You passed on him? Are you out of your mind? He's the biggest star on the planet to anyone under 15.'"*

Hairspray was filmed in Toronto, Canada, which marked the first time Efron had ever lived on his own. "Toronto was where I grew up, and it happened quick," he said. "I was self-sufficient in a matter of weeks. It was great, but then I started clinging to the people I was working with. I would come to the set and just observe, even if I wasn't working that day."

Hairspray opened in July 2007 to mostly good reviews. Susan Wloszczyna of *USA Today* noted that the part of Link Larkin allowed Efron to escape from the "squeaky-clean confines" of *High School Musical*. "He lets loose with a lusty yelp during a solo number, 'Ladies Choice,' which finally showcases his inviting baritone in all its unadulterated glory," Wloszczyna wrote.

High School Musical 2

Soon after he finished work on *Hairspray*, Efron reunited with the original *High School Musical* cast and the director, Kenny Ortega, to film the movie's sequel. *High School Musical 2* focuses on a scheme by Sharpay to woo Troy away from Gabriella. School has let out for summer vacation, leading up to senior year. The East High classmates all have summer jobs at a country club controlled by Sharpay's wealthy family. But things become tense as Sharpay schemes to break up Gabriella and Troy. Troy must decide whether to pursue the advantages that are available from Sharpay's wealthy family—even if it means neglecting Gabriella and his friends. It's a difficult summer, but all is resolved as the group participates in the country club's annual talent show, an opportunity for more great song-and-dance numbers from the cast.

> *According to Efron,* High School Musical 2 *offered new insight into his character. "Troy is balancing a lot of temptations," he said. "He's very goal-oriented, almost to a fault. It was fun to play the other side of him. He gets lured to the dark side."*

According to Efron, *High School Musical 2* offered new insight into his character. "Troy is balancing a lot of temptations," he said. "He's very goal-oriented, almost to a fault. It was fun to play the other side of him. He gets lured to the dark side."

High School Musical 2 was eagerly anticipated by the first movie's many fans. More than 17 million people watched its premiere on the Disney Channel on August 17, 2007, making the sequel the most watched basic cable telecast in history. The movie generated mostly positive reviews. Robert Bianco of *USA Today* called the sequel "a first-rate family film: sweet, smart, bursting with talent and energy, and awash in innocence." At the 2007 Teen Choice Awards, *High School Musical 2* won the award for Choice TV Movie, and Efron won the award for Choice Male Hottie. Efron sang all of his character's songs in the sequel, although he acknowledged that none of the actors have control over the finished product. "Once it's edited, the people in this cast sound like Mariah Carey," he said. "There's skill involved [but] with computers these days, you never know."

The dancing and singing scenes are part of what makes High School Musical 2 *so much fun.*

Future Plans

As one of the hottest young actors in Hollywood, Efron is sifting through many offers. Currently, he has two film projects in development. One is tentatively called *Seventeen*, which has been described as a reverse of the 1988 Tom Hanks film *Big*. Instead of a kid turning into an adult overnight, it's about an adult who turns into a kid. Efron described his starring character as a man who "wishes he could go back to high school again, and sure enough, he wakes up and he is young again, he is 17 again." Another project in development is a new musical version of the 1984 movie *Footloose*, which originally starred Kevin Bacon. Efron would star in the new film, which would be directed and choreographed by Kenny Ortega.

Then there's the *High School Musical* franchise, which is slated to go from TV to a big-screen production. "I would love to do a third *High School Musical*," Efron said, "to finish off on the silver screen would be a great legacy for the *High School Musical* series to leave." Efron got his wish, as Disney made plans for a theatrical release of *High School Musical 3: Senior Year* in fall 2008.

HOME AND FAMILY

Efron lives in an apartment in North Hollywood, but he often visits his parents and younger brother in Arroyo Grande. When in Los Angeles, he likes to hang out with his childhood friends who live in the area. "These are the friends I used to do theater with," he said. Staying close to old friends helps Efron keep his teen-idol stardom in perspective. "I could show you 500 kids in L.A. who are my height, weight, hair color, and age," he said. "We're a dime a dozen. Why did I get the parts I did? Who knows? But the minute I start thinking it's because I was special, that's when I know I'm in trouble."

Efron has been linked romantically to his *High School Musical* co-star Vanessa Anne Hudgens. While calling her an "amazing girl," Efron has downplayed their relationship and expressed frustration at the paparazzi—photographers who snap celebrity pictures for sale—who are always pointing cameras in their faces when they go out. "I never in a million years saw myself as dealing with the paparazzi," he said. "It seems it wouldn't be that big of an issue, but there are personal things you don't want captured on camera."

SELECTED CREDITS

Miracle Run, 2004 (TV movie)
"Summerland," 2004-05 (TV series)
High School Musical, 2006 (TV movie)
The Derby Stallion, 2007 (movie released on DVD)
Hairspray, 2007 (movie)
High School Musical 2, 2007 (TV movie)

HONORS AND AWARDS

Teen Choice Award: 2006 (two awards), TV-Choice Breakout Star and Choice Chemistry for *High School Musical* (with Vanessa Hudgens); 2007, Choice Male Hottie
Hollywood Film Award: 2007, Ensemble Acting (with the cast of *Hairspray*)

FURTHER READING

Books

Norwich, Grace. *Zac Attack: An Unauthorized Biography*, 2006 (juvenile)

Periodicals

Chicago Sun Times, Aug. 19, 2007, p.D2
Entertainment Weekly, Aug. 31, 2007, p.34
Los Angeles Times, Aug. 27, 2007, p.E1
New York Times, Mar. 11, 2007, Arts and Leisure section, p.1
People, Sep. 3, 2007, p.62

Rolling Stone, Aug. 23, 2007, p.38
Time, Aug. 27, 2007, p.9
USA Today, July 20, 2007, p.D1

Online Articles

http://www.movieweb.com/dvd/news/56/12756.php
   (Movieweb.com, "Zac Efron and Vanessa Anne Hudgens Sing Their Praises for *High School Musical*," May 22, 2006)
http://pbskids.org/itsmylife/celebs/interviews/zac.html
   (PBSKids.org, "Zac Efron," undated)
http://sanluisobispo.com/ticket/story/95872.html
   (SanLuisObispo.com, "A Rising Star," July 19, 2007)
http://content.scholastic.com/browse
   (Scholastic, "Zac Efron Talks Troy," Aug. 22, 2007)
http://www.timeforkids.com/TFK/kidscoops/story/0,14989,1169108,00.html
   (Time for Kids, "The Scoop on High School Musical," Mar. 2, 2006)
http://www.thestar.com/entertainment/article/242589
   (Toronto Star, "Zac Efron: The High School Hunk," Aug. 4, 2007)
http://www.usatoday.com/life/television/reviews/2007-08-16-hsm2_n.htm
   (USAToday, "*High School Musical* Sequel Holds onto Note of Innocence," Aug. 16, 2007)

ADDRESS

Zac Efron
Disney Channel
3800 West Alameda Avenue
Burbank, CA 91505

WORLD WIDE WEB SITES

http://tv.disney.go.com/disneychannel/originalmovies/highschoolmusical/index.html

Selena Gomez 1992-
American Actor
Star of the Hit TV Show "Wizards of Waverly Place"

BIRTH

Selena Gomez was born on July 22, 1992, in Grand Prairie, Texas, a suburban city located between Dallas and Fort Worth. Gomez was born when her mother, Mandy Teefy, was 16 years old. Her young parents did not stay together, and she was raised by her mother. She has no brothers or sisters. Her father is of Mexican descent, and she was named after his favorite performer, the popular Tejano singer Selena.

YOUTH

Growing up in Grand Prairie, Gomez enjoyed spending time with her friends, hanging out at the lake near her home, and going to the mall, skate parks, or the movies. One of her favorite things to do was to go on long walks around the neighborhood with her friends. Gomez recalled, "I used to walk barefoot around my neighborhood without worrying about anything. It's nice and peaceful. We could walk in the middle of the street, and there would be no cars coming at all."

> "I wanted to be just like my friends. I hung out with girls who had blue eyes and blonde hair and I thought, 'I want to look like them!'" But when Gomez started acting, she realized that her Mexican heritage set her apart in a good way. "When I went on auditions, I'd be in a room with a lot of blonde girls, and I always stood out. It actually helped that I looked different. It got me to where I am today!"

Although Gomez had a large group of friends, her Mexican heritage often made her feel left out. She remembered, "I wanted to be just like my friends. I hung out with girls who had blue eyes and blonde hair and I thought, 'I want to look like them!'" Once she started acting, however, Gomez realized that her Mexican heritage set her apart in a good way. "When I went on auditions, I'd be in a room with a lot of blonde girls, and I always stood out. It actually helped that I looked different. It got me to where I am today!"

EDUCATION

Gomez initially attended elementary school in Grand Prairie, but soon began homeschooling. After moving to Los Angeles in 2006, she studied with a tutor, usually together with the other young actors on the set of her current television show or movie.

CAREER HIGHLIGHTS

Starting Out

Gomez knew from a very young age that she wanted to become an actor. Her mother had some experience acting with local theaters in Dallas, and Gomez decided when she was six years old that she wanted to try acting too. On her seventh birthday, Gomez joined 1,400 other hopeful young ac-

Gomez appeared on "Barney & Friends" when she was only seven years old.

tors in an audition for the PBS children's television show "Barney & Friends." She won the role of Gianna, one of the children who sang and danced with Barney the purple dinosaur. Because the show was filmed about 20 minutes from Gomez's home, she was able to continue living at home and going to school as usual. She was featured in many episodes during the two years she appeared on "Barney."

This early experience helped to prepare Gomez for her acting career. As she later recalled, "I learned everything from 'Barney.' Stage directions, camera angles.... I even learned good manners." After "Barney & Friends," Gomez went on to play small roles in the 2003 movie *Spy Kids 3-D: Game Over* and the 2005 television movie *Walker, Texas Ranger: Trial by Fire*.

The Disney Channel

In 2004, when she was 12 years old, Gomez auditioned at an open casting call for The Disney Channel in Austin, Texas. She did so well at that audition that, two weeks later, she and her mother were asked to travel to Hollywood for more auditions. Disney wanted Gomez to try out for the lead role in a new TV series called "Stevie Sanchez," a spinoff of the popular "Lizzie McGuire" series. She recalls being very nervous about auditioning in Hollywood. "It was definitely scary. I was in this room full of executives and I was testing against girls who have done movies." She got the part, but Disney later decided not to produce the series.

When plans for the Disney series fell through, Gomez decided to audition for roles with other studios. She auditioned for parts in a television series and a movie to be produced by Nickelodeon. Although she had no contract with Disney at that point, she already felt some loyalty to The Disney Channel for giving her so many opportunities. She described her Nickelodeon auditions as "uncomfortable, like I was cheating on Disney." Gomez decided to wait and see if Disney had any parts for her.

"*I learned everything from 'Barney,'*" Gomez later recalled. "*Stage directions, camera angles.... I even learned good manners.*"

Her loyalty paid off, and Disney soon offered Gomez roles in two TV series pilots, "House Broken" and "The Amazing O'Malleys." She was cast in both shows, although Disney planned to produce only one of the two shows for the 2006 TV season. She and her mother moved from Texas to Los Angeles to prepare for filming to begin. "It was hard," Gomez admitted. "It was almost a test of how badly I really wanted to pursue acting.... It was really tough to leave my friends behind." Then Disney decided not to make either of the shows after all. But she wasn't out of work for long. Disney gave her a guest role in a 2006 episode of the hit show "The Suite Life of Zack and Cody."

Then in 2007, on her 15th birthday, Gomez filmed a guest role on "Hannah Montana," Disney's most popular TV show. She played the recurring character of Mikayla, Hannah Montana's rival, a part that allowed her to do her own singing. This set off a flurry of publicity and attention, as fans hotly debated the relative talent and merits of Hannah Montana star Miley Cyrus versus newcomer Gomez. Gomez's success quickly led Disney to cast her in a starring role on a new TV series, "Wizards of Waverly Place."

"Wizards of Waverly Place"

"Wizards of Waverly Place" premiered on The Disney Channel in 2007. The story focuses on the adventures of a New York City family of wizards who live a double life as they try to keep their magical powers a secret. The three Russo siblings get magic lessons from their wizard father, who teaches them spells and charms in a magical laboratory hidden behind a secret door in the family's sandwich shop. As the stories unfold, viewers find that such typical teenage issues as sibling rivalry, competition with schoolmates, schoolwork, dating, and popularity are all made more complicated with the addition of magic.

Gomez plays Alex Russo, the tomboy middle sister who is always getting herself into trouble with magic. Alex and her two brothers (played by David Henrie and Jake T. Austin) often work together to get each other into—and out of—sticky situations. The three are not allowed to use magic when their parents are not around, and they quickly learn the consequences of bending that rule. In one episode, Alex magically duplicates herself so that she can be in two places at once, only to find it difficult to control both versions of herself. In another episode, she tries to sneak into a theater to see an R-rated movie, but only succeeds in getting herself trapped in the movie itself.

Although she has enjoyed playing the role of a young wizard, Gomez revealed that before "Wizards of Waverly Place," she was not particularly drawn to other popular magical characters. "I've never actually gotten into Harry Potter, but I love the special effects of the movies. They are so cool and I love magic. All of my friends are into it.…I'm happy that I'm working on a magic show."

> *One of the things Gomez has enjoyed the most about playing Alex is her TV family, especially her two television brothers. "My mom laughs at me all the time because we're constantly in touch with one another off the set, we're always calling.… I don't have any real-life siblings so this way I can have brothers."*

One of the things Gomez has enjoyed the most about playing Alex is her TV family. She has forged close relationships with the actors who play her two television brothers. She counts her costars among her closest friends, explaining, "My mom laughs at me all the time because we're constantly in touch with one another off the set, we're always calling.…I don't have any real-life siblings so this way I can have brothers." The wizarding Russos are also a bicultural family, with a Mexican-American mother and an Italian-American father. This reflection of Gomez's real life family has been a bonus. "I don't know if I would've had the opportunity to be on 'Wizards of Waverly Place' if it weren't for my heritage."

"Wizards of Waverly Place" is Gomez's first big TV series.

Gomez's favorite scenes to film are those that include the whole Russo family. "Whether it's a funny or dramatic scene, whether we're trying to solve a problem or doing magic or turning my brother invisible, it comes off best when we're with the whole family.... I think when we're all together, the show is at its strongest point. And I love being with the entire cast in a scene."

"Wizards of Waverly Place" became an instant hit with TV critics and viewers alike. Critics praised the show for its portrayal of family relationships and called the silly jokes and visual comedy entertaining for all ages. Gomez has her own explanation for the show's popularity: "The reason why it's so successful, and especially for young kids, is because kids wish they could be invisible and kids wish they could rewind time. And we bring that on screen. I know I wished that when I was younger."

Movies and Music

Along with starring in a hit TV show, Gomez has expanded her performing credits to include movies. For the 2008 animated film *Horton Hears a Who*, she provided the voices for Helga and many of the other 95 daughters of the Mayor of Whoville. "I had to change up my voice to do higher voices, and then bring it down to do lower voices. All of the Mayor's daughters look different, so I play many different characters." She appeared in the 2008 musical romantic comedy *Another Cinderella Story*, a modern retelling of the classic fairy tale co-starring Drew Seeley. He played Joey Parker, a wealthy teen who is a senior at Beverly Hills High. She played Mary Santiago, a poor girl who is forced to work for her evil guardian. The movie includes many singing and dancing numbers, which allowed the co-stars to show their talents.

Also in 2008, Gomez appeared in *Princess Protection Program*, a Disney Channel original TV movie. Princess Rosaline (played by Demi Lovato) is threatened by an evil dictator, so the Princess Protection Program, a secret agency, steps in to save her. Mason, an agent with the program, hides the princess in his own home. His daughter, Carter (played by Gomez), helps

> *Gomez enjoys singing and would like to record more music. "I think you can be more of yourself when you're singing," she explained. "You can have a little bit more control over it. It's a different process, with going into the studio and not having to worry about what you look like on camera."*

In the animated movie Horton Hears a Who, *Gomez provided the voices for many of the Mayor's daughters, including these two getting ready for school.*

Rosie (as the princess is called) learn how to act like an ordinary girl, and Rosie helps Carter feel more confident—and more like a princess herself.

Gomez has also expanded her repertoire to include music. She performed the "Wizards of Waverly Place" theme song "Everything Is Not What It Seems." She also recorded the "Cruella De Vil" song for the *101 Dalmatians: Platinum Edition* DVD release. Disney produced a music video for the song, which has been playing regularly on The Disney Channel. In addition, she can be heard on the soundtrack for *Another Cinderella Story*, which includes several tracks by Gomez as well as duets with Seeley. Gomez enjoys singing and would like to record more music. "I think you can be more of yourself when you're singing," she explained. "You can have a little bit more control over it. It's a different process, with going into the studio and not having to worry about what you look like on camera."

HOME AND FAMILY

Gomez lives in Los Angeles, California, with her mother, her stepfather Brian, and her four dogs.

HOBBIES AND OTHER INTERESTS

Although Gomez became a Disney star almost overnight, she describes her life as normal. She does chores at home, including taking care of her own laundry, washing dishes, and cleaning her room. She enjoys surfing, cooking, photography, singing karaoke, and going to the movies. She likes to play basketball and watch basketball games, and her favorite team is the San Antonio Spurs. One of her most prized possessions is her large collection of Converse sneakers, which she wears as often as she can.

SELECTED CREDITS

"Barney & Friends," 1999-2000 (TV series)
"Wizards of Waverly Place," 2007- (TV series)
Horton Hears a Who!, 2008 (movie)
Another Cinderella Story, 2008 (movie)
Princess Protection Program, 2008 (movie)

FURTHER READING

Periodicals

Entertainment Weekly, July 20, 2007, p.46
Girls' Life, Feb./Mar. 2008, p.40
Twist Magazine, Mar. 2008, p.11, p.23, p.36, p.67
Variety, Oct. 4, 2007, p.A46
Washington Post, Oct. 19, 2007, p.C7

Online Articles

http://www.discoverygirls.com/node/414
  (Discovery Girls, "Selena Gomez's Star Power," undated)
http://www.discoverygirls.com/node/455
  (Discovery Girls, "Selena Gomez Talks to DG," Oct. 12, 2007)
http://pbskids.org/itsmylife/celebs/interviews/selena.html
  (PBSkids.org, "It's My Life: Selena Gomez," undated)
http://www.teenmag.com
  (TeenMag.com, "Getting to Know: Selena Gomez," undated)
http://www.timeforkids.com
  (Time for Kids, "10 Questions for Selena Gomez," archived story, Oct. 15, 2007)

ADDRESS

Selena Gomez
Disney Channel
Attn: Fan Mail Dept.
3800 West Alameda Avenue
Burbank, CA 91505

WORLD WIDE WEB SITE

http://tv.disney.go.com/disneychannel/wizardsofwaverlyplace

Al Gore 1948-

American Political Leader and Environmental Activist Former Vice President of the United States, Author of *An Inconvenient Truth*, and Winner of the 2007 Nobel Peace Prize

BIRTH

Albert Arnold Gore Jr. was born on March 31, 1948, in Washington DC. His father, Albert Arnold Gore Sr., was a former member of the U.S. Congress from Tennessee who served 14 years in the House of Representatives and 18 years in the Senate. His mother, Pauline (LaFon) Gore, was the first woman to graduate from Vanderbilt University Law School in

Tennessee. She worked as an attorney before giving up her practice to support her husband's political career. Gore's only sibling was his older sister, Nancy, who died in 1984.

YOUTH

Gore spent his first few years in Tennessee. But after that, he divided his time between two very different worlds: Washington DC, and Carthage, Tennessee. He lived part of each year with his parents and sister at the Fairfax Hotel in Washington DC. The Fairfax was an exclusive residential hotel on Embassy Row, where many of the foreign embassies are located. But at that point his family wasn't wealthy—they lived there because it was owned by a relative. His parents were very frugal, although they did pay for private education. When Gore was in Washington, he was surrounded by adults in the politically charged atmosphere of the U.S. capitol, and he was exposed there to his parents' passion for politics. But there wasn't much for a boy to do, living in a hotel.

> "Even though I spent more time each year in Washington, Tennessee was home," Gore later recalled. "Now I'm sure that part of that was me, as a kid, absorbing my parents' insistence on the political reality of their lives, that they were representing Tennessee in Washington. I'm sure I picked up a lot of that as a child. But it was more than that." For Gore, Tennessee was where "the human relationships were much warmer."

Gore spent the remainder of his time on his family's farm in Carthage, Tennessee. In Tennessee, he was often left in the care of the Thompson family, who were tenant farmers. According to the *New York Times*, "[Gore] lived in two worlds that could hardly have been more different.... [He] essentially adopted the Thompsons as a second family... Their home became a kind of emotional citadel, a refuge from the larger world, where great expectations awaited him." There he swam in the Caney Fork River and worked alongside the hired hands. The natural, casual environment of his time on the farm stood in sharp contrast to the setting of wealth and power he experienced in Washington.

"Even though I spent more time each year in Washington, Tennessee was home," Gore later recalled. "Now I'm sure that part of that was me, as a kid, absorbing my parents' insistence on the political reality of their lives, that they were representing Tennessee in Washington. I'm sure I picked up a lot of that as a child. But it was more than that." For Gore, Tennessee was where he had close friends and where "the human relationships were much warmer."

But life in Tennessee wasn't all fun and games. Gore's father was determined that Al would develop a strong work ethic, and he'd wake his son at 6:00 a.m. to join the workers in the field. The younger Gore would bale hay, cut tobacco, clear fields, clean the hogs' pens, or whatever the farm hands were doing. In fact, his father usually assigned the worst tasks to his son.

The Gores were a family of high achievers, and expectations were especially high for young Al. His father was strict and taught Gore from an early age to work hard in preparation for a bright future. As a Congress member's son, he was encouraged to pursue a career in politics. Being somewhat in the public eye because of his father's position in Congress, Gore developed an early sense of reserve and caution that made him seem more adult than his peers.

EDUCATION

In Washington DC, Gore attended St. Alban's Episcopal School for Boys, a highly competitive and elite private school modeled after British schools. He was an honor student and captain of the football team. In his high school yearbook, Gore was called the model of the all-American young man.

Gore entered Harvard University in 1965. In addition to his studies, he was president of the freshman council and worked as a messenger for the *New York Times*, where he ran errands in the newspaper's offices. During his last summer before graduation, he was the chairman of Tennessee Youth for McCarthy, an organization working on Eugene McCarthy's 1968 presidential campaign. Gore graduated from Harvard *cum laude* (with distinction) in 1969, earning a bachelor's degree in government.

FIRST JOBS

After graduating from Harvard, Gore found himself in a painful and confusing situation. The Vietnam War was in full swing, thousands of young men were being drafted into military service, and war protestors were holding demonstrations all across the country. Meanwhile, Gore's father was in a tight race for re-election to the Senate. As an outspoken critic of U.S. military involvement in Vietnam, the senior Gore was being called unfit to rep-

From 1969 to 1971, during the Vietnam War, Gore served in the U.S. Army; he was assigned to be a reporter and was stationed in Vietnam.

resent the people of Tennessee. Considering all of this, his son realized that he had an important decision to make about what he would do next.

Like many other young men of his generation, Gore opposed the war in Vietnam and seriously considered resisting the draft. But he chose to volunteer for enlistment in the U.S. Army so that his actions would not reflect poorly on his father. Gore's family did not pressure him to enlist—they urged him to follow his conscience, and his mother even offered to flee with him to Canada if he decided to avoid military service. Gore made his decision to enlist both as a point of personal honor and as a political sacrifice. From 1969 to 1971, he served in the U.S. Army in Vietnam, working as a reporter with the 20th Engineering Battalion outside Saigon.

Serving as an army reporter in Vietnam led Gore to a career in journalism when he returned to the U.S. From 1971 to 1976, he worked for the *Tennessean* in Nashville, first as a reporter and later as an editorial writer. During the same time, he also enrolled in the School of Religion at Vanderbilt University. He decided to attend divinity school, he said, not to become a minister but instead "to study the spiritual issues that were most important to me at the time ... to find some answers." Gore transferred to Vanderbilt's law school in 1974. He planned to use the degree in tandem with his already budding career in journalism. In addition to studying and working for the *Tennessean*, Gore also worked as a real estate developer and livestock and tobacco farmer. He insisted that he was not interested in a career in politics, although that soon changed.

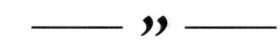

> *Years of writing about local government for the* Tennessean *rekindled Gore's interest in politics. "I felt intensely frustrated about policies and decisions I was writing about because I felt they were often dead wrong," he recalled. "But as a journalist I could do nothing to change them."*

CAREER HIGHLIGHTS

Entering Congress

In 1976, when Gore was 28 years old, he received the unexpected news that the U.S. Representative from his home district had decided to retire. Despite his earlier objections to a career in politics, Gore now found that years of writing about local government for the *Tennessean* had rekindled his interest in public service. "I felt intensely frustrated about policies and decisions I was writing about because I felt they were often dead wrong," he recalled. "But as a journalist I could do nothing to change them." Gore entered the Democratic primaries, winning his party's nomination by a narrow margin. He went on to win the general

Gore speaking with potential voters in 1976, before his election to the U.S. House of Representatives.

election, and in 1977 he moved to Washington DC, to take his place in the U.S. House of Representatives.

In Washington, Gore quickly gained a reputation as a tough investigator and a thorough researcher—skills he had learned in his work as a reporter. He involved himself in a variety of issues, ranging from organ transplants, to housing for the poor, to the economic development of the Tennessee River and surrounding areas. During his time in the House of Representatives, Gore also began focusing on health-related environmental issues. He held the first Congressional hearing on toxic waste, bringing national attention to the damage caused by toxic waste dumping near Memphis, Tennessee and the Love Canal neighborhood near Niagara Falls, New York. He also played an important role in the passage of the "Superfund" bill in 1980, which provided money to clean up chemical spills and toxic waste dumps.

Becoming a Senator

In 1983, after serving four terms in the House of Representatives, Gore decided to run for the U.S. Senate. He ran a hard campaign and won easily, but a cloud fell over the victory. His sister Nancy, a tireless worker through the years on her brother's behalf, died of lung cancer before the 1984 election, without ever knowing that he had won.

In the Senate, Gore continued to earn his reputation as a workhorse. While he served on a number of committees with diverse interests, he was by this time mainly concerned with environmental topics and nuclear arms control. He looked for a balance, he said, between "national power and security on the one hand, and long-term human survival on the other." Gore diligently studied complex issues, talked with experts, and impressed his peers with his uncanny ability to absorb and process the most scientific details of new technologies. He was recognized as an authority in his special areas of interest.

Based on his successes in Congress, Gore declared his intent to run for president in early 1987. Many observers said that his driving ambition pushed him to seek the highest level of government. But he was unable to adequately define his policies or himself as a candidate, and he ultimately withdrew from the presidential race. He returned to his seat in the Senate and focused on furthering his work there.

> *Gore's work as a legislator helped pave the way for the development of the Internet. According to former Republican House Speaker Newt Gingrich. "Gore is the person who, in the Congress, most systematically worked to make sure that we got to an Internet."*

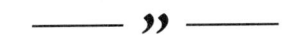

Gore became the chairperson of the Senate Subcommittee on Science, Technology, and Space. In this position, he focused on issues related to space exploration, environmental protection, and linking the nation via supercomputers—a project that would prove to be the foundation of the Internet and World Wide Web. In the 1970s, the Internet was a closed system that was limited to the Pentagon and a few universities. It was mainly used for research by scientists. In the late 1980s, Gore sponsored two bills that turned the fledgling computer network into a true "information superhighway," a term he popularized to describe the proposed new system that would be accessible to everyone. According to former Republican House Speaker Newt Gingrich. "Gore is the person who, in the Congress, most systematically worked to make sure that we got to an Internet."

Tragedy Strikes

By 1989, Gore was married with four children. That year, the family suffered a tragic accident. Gore's son Albert III, then six years old, had darted in front of a car and was thrown 30 feet into the air and dragged across the

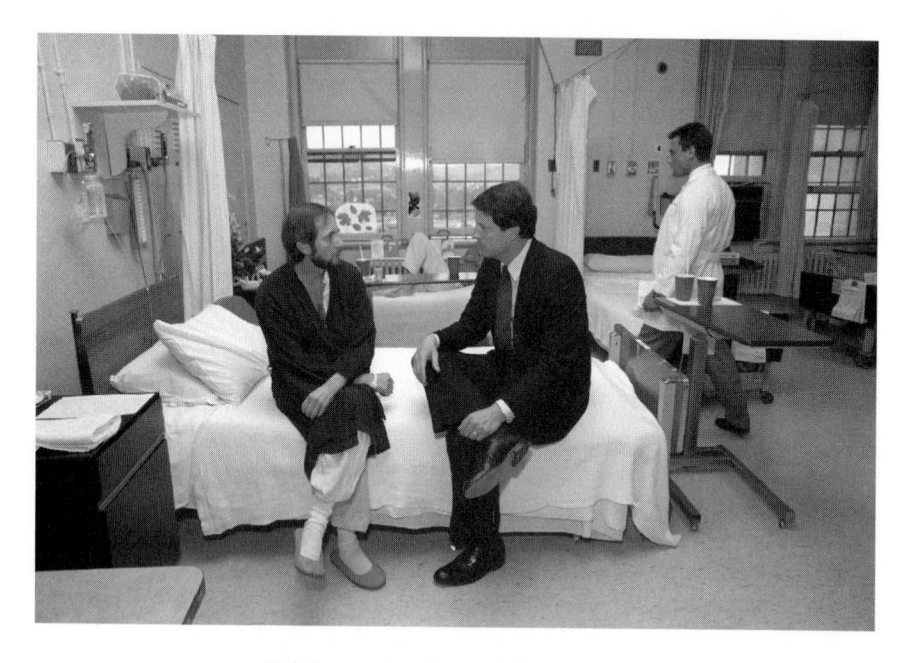

*While running for president in 1987,
Gore visited with this AIDS patient in Los Angeles.*

pavement before his horror-stricken father's eyes. He lay in the gutter, recalled Gore, with his eyes open in an "empty stare of death." After extensive surgery, a lengthy hospital stay, and a long period of recuperation, the boy eventually made a full recovery. Gore has said that the traumatic accident that almost took his son's life led him to "confront some difficult and painful questions about what I am really seeking in my own life, and why."

Earth in the Balance

While his son recovered from the accident, Gore realized that he wanted to "reevaluate serious issues." He wondered if he had done enough to ensure his children's future. He saw a connection between "the global environmental crisis and [his own] inner crisis that is, for lack of a better word, spiritual." Gore began to consider the effect an environmentally unstable world would have on his four children.

Gore began writing his book *Earth in the Balance: Ecology and the Human Spirit* during his son's 1989 hospital stay. The book is divided into two main sections. The first section includes a complete explanation of the worldwide environmental crisis, covering issues such as global warming, acid rain, deforestation, and overpopulation. The second section provides a series of recommended steps to fix the problems, such as the creation of an international environmental council to monitor activities that damage the environment.

The book attracted a lot of attention from the media and critics because it discussed complicated environmental issues and solutions in terms that everyone could understand. Some people criticized Gore's ideas as "unworkable" and said that his proposed solutions would result in too much harm to the U.S. economy. The book received the harshest criticism from members of the Republican Party, which published a statement that said, "Earth in the Balance is plagued by a combination of liberalism, elitism, hypocrisy, and hyperbole, punctuated by an unhealthy extremism." Meanwhile, environmental activists praised Gore for presenting complex scientific issues in language that was easy to understand. A reviewer writing in Business Week called the book "a useful primer on the world's environmental problems." The New York Times Book Review said that Gore's writing was "fresh and compelling." And Time praised Gore as an "intellectual politician who is more committed to important issues than most of his colleagues."

> In reviewing Earth in the Balance, Gore's first book on environmental issues, Time magazine praised him as an "intellectual politician who is more committed to important issues than most of his colleagues."

Although Gore had been working on environmental issues for many years already, the 1992 publication of Earth in the Balance gave him a public reputation as an environmental pioneer. In that same year, he served as an official U.S. representative to the Earth Summit held in Rio de Janeiro, Brazil. The Earth Summit was a conference held by the United Nations to focus on global environmental issues. The largest environmental conference held up to that time, it was attended by representatives of the governments of more than 170 nations.

Becoming Vice President

Gore was offered another major opportunity in 1992—the chance to become Vice President of the United States. When Bill Clinton secured the Democratic Party's nomination in the presidential elections that year, he asked Gore to be his running mate. Balancing one another's strengths and

As vice president, Gore met in the Oval Office with President Bill Clinton and Chief of Staff Erskine Bowles.

weaknesses, the two men pooled their considerable resources for a campaign that ultimately led to victory.

Clinton was an expert on domestic and economic issues, and Gore was knowledgeable about foreign affairs. The president-elect had avoided the draft, but his running mate was a Vietnam veteran. Clinton's experience was limited to state administration, while Gore knew his way around the nation's capital. Clinton had been publicly accused of infidelity, while the Gore marriage stood up to scrutiny. The governor of Arkansas was an exuberant man of the people, but the senator from Tennessee was less comfortable in public.

In November 1992, the Clinton-Gore ticket beat their Republican opponents, President George H.W. Bush and Vice President Dan Quayle. Gore was inaugurated as the 45th Vice President of the United States on January 20, 1993. President Clinton and Vice President Gore were re-elected to a second term in 1996, and Gore was sworn in again on January 20, 1997.

During his two terms as vice president (1993-2001), Gore served as an advisor to President Clinton and as the President of the U.S. Senate, a member of the National Security Council, and the head of a wide range of Administration initiatives. Because of his close relationship with President

Clinton, and his involvement in so many critical issues of the time, Gore has been called one of the most influential vice presidents in U.S. history.

As vice president, Gore continued to focus attention on environmental issues on a worldwide scale. He worked tirelessly to raise awareness of the growing environmental problems caused by such human factors as automobile exhaust and toxic waste. In December 1997, against the objections of many top U.S. government officials, Gore attended an international environmental issues meeting in Kyoto, Japan. The goal of the meeting was to create the Kyoto Accords—a worldwide strategy to reduce global warming. The governments of European countries wanted the U.S. government to reduce the amount of air pollution produced by Americans. Although the U.S. government ultimately did not sign the Kyoto Accords, Gore's presence and diplomatic negotiation ensured that nearly all of the other attending governments signed on to reduce the amount of air pollution they produced.

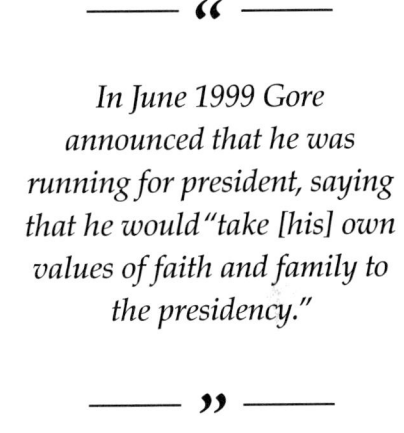

> *In June 1999 Gore announced that he was running for president, saying that he would "take [his] own values of faith and family to the presidency."*

Running for President

With President Clinton's second term in office coming to a close, Gore decided that he would run for president himself in the 2000 election. He announced his candidacy in June 1999, saying that he would "take [his] own values of faith and family to the presidency." In August 2000, Gore won the Democratic Party's nomination for president. He campaigned against George W. Bush, the son of the previous president, George H.W. Bush.

The race between Gore and George W. Bush was close from the very beginning of the campaign. In polls conducted during the summer of 2000, the two candidates were separated by only 10% of potential voters. In such a heated contest, not even the three televised debates between Gore and Bush could produce a clear winner. During the debates, the candidates answered questions about their ideas for education, foreign policy, and other important issues. Opinion polls conducted after the debates showed that voters were still almost evenly divided between Gore and Bush.

Indeed, the 2000 presidential election proved to be one of the closest—and strangest—elections in U.S. history. After the voting took place on

November 7, and after most of the votes were counted, it became clear that the outcome of the election would depend entirely on the votes of the state of Florida. A great controversy then developed over the manner in which Florida votes had been collected and counted. There were accusations that ballots were misleading, causing people to vote for a different candidate than the one they intended. More accusations claimed that ballots were tampered with or even thrown away without being counted. Inconsistent election rules also seemed to have prevented many people from voting at all.

In the midst of all the confusion and suspicion, a preliminary total of Florida votes indicated that Gore had slightly more votes than Bush, although less than one half of one percent of votes separated the two candidates. It was an extremely close result—so close, in fact, that a mandatory automatic recount of votes was required by law.

Counting the Votes

The first recount of votes was done by machine. The machine recount revealed further problems with the punch-card ballots used by some Florida voting precincts. Many ballots were rejected—and therefore not counted—by the machines. After the recount by machine, Bush emerged slightly ahead of Gore. But due to the large number of rejected ballots, Gore and the Democratic Party demanded a second recount to be done by hand.

An investigation into the accusations of ballot-tampering and the problems with rejected ballots revealed that many of the punch-card ballots were torn. Tiny slips of paper, called chads, were supposed to be punched out from the ballot to indicate which candidate received a vote. The problem was that some of the chads were not fully detached from the ballot, and were hanging by one or two corners, while other chads were only indented and not punched out at all. The inconsistent punches and torn slips of paper were what had caused so many problems with the vote counting machines.

The torn ballots caused even more problems during the hand recount. A heated argument developed between voting officials and officials from the Republican and Democratic Parties about how to interpret the torn ballots. The outcome of the election depended entirely upon how the voter's intention was interpreted, based on the appearance of the hanging or indented chad. Using one interpretation, Bush would win by more than 1,700 votes. But using another interpretation, Gore would win by fewer than 200 votes. The debate raged on for weeks, as Americans waited to learn who the new president would be.

Gore at a rally during the 2000 presidential campaign, flanked by his wife, Tipper Gore, and President Bill Clinton.

The recount by hand proved to be the most controversial issue. When the results of a partial hand recount indicated that Bush would be the winner, Gore and the Democrats challenged the decision in court. The case went all the way to the U.S. Supreme Court, which eventually issued a historic 5-to-4 ruling (in itself a very close decision) that any further recounting would be unconstitutional. When this decision was made, Bush was ahead by slightly more than 500 votes—a very small number considering the overall total number of votes.

All of the confusion had been focused on Florida's popular vote—the votes cast by the citizens of Florida. U.S. Presidential elections are determined by the votes of the Electoral College, whose votes are generally given to the candidate who receives the most popular votes in a particular state. In order to win a presidential election, a candidate must have a minimum of 270 of the total 538 available electoral votes. Because the electoral votes of most states are awarded by a strict majority, and not based on population or total number of votes cast, it is possible for a candidate to receive the most popular votes nationwide and yet not gain enough electoral votes to win the election.

And that is what happened in the 2000 election. When the Florida vote-counting crisis occurred, 99% of all the popular votes in the nation had been counted. Gore had been awarded 255 electoral votes and Bush had received 246. Although Gore had almost a half million more popular votes when the Supreme Court stopped the recounts, Florida's 25 electoral votes went to Bush, making him the winner with a total of 271 electoral votes. This was the first time since 1888 that the candidate with the most popular votes did not win the election.

> "Let there be no doubt: While I strongly disagree with the court's decision, I accept it," Gore said after the Supreme Court decision that led to Bush's presidential win. "And tonight for the sake of our unity as a people and the strength of our democracy, I offer my concession." Gore emphasized the need for unity and reconciliation and called on Americans to support the new president. "We are a nation of laws and the presidential election of 2000 is over."

Once the Supreme Court decision was made and Bush was declared the winner, Gore conceded defeat. On December 13, more than one month after the November 7 election, he said, "Let there be no doubt: While I strongly disagree with the court's decision, I accept it.... And tonight for the sake of our unity as a people and the strength of our democracy, I offer my concession." Gore emphasized the need for unity and reconciliation after the bitterness of the vote-counting crisis and called on Americans to support the new president. "We are a nation of laws and the presidential election of 2000 is over."

Leaving Politics

After suffering the devastating loss of the 2000 presidential election, and wanting to get away from any further controversy, Gore withdrew from public life. He moved to Nashville and concentrated on building a new life as a private citizen. He had served 25 years in federal government and needed to decide what to do next. Recalling the weeks just after the election, Gore said, "That was a hard blow, but what do you do? You make the best of it." He spent time with his family and went on a vacation with his wife. He accepted a visiting professorship and taught journalism classes at universities around the country. He even considered running for president again in 2004, but changed his mind after the terrorist attacks of September 11, 2001. Believing that the U.S. again needed unity, Gore used the occasion that he had planned to announce his candidacy to publicly call for Americans to support President Bush.

An Inconvenient Truth

While Gore was struggling to find a new purpose for his work, his wife Tipper suggested that he return to the issue that had been most important to him for many years—the environment. She encouraged him to put together an updated version of a slideshow he had once created to teach people about global warming. The first time he used the presentation was in 1989, when he was writing *Earth in the Balance*. Gore had carried an easel to a dinner party and stood on a chair to display a large chart that he drew, showing the rise of air pollution.

The slideshow presentation focused on the same issues that Gore had been talking about since the 1970s. He converted his old slides to a computerized presentation and began giving his lecture anywhere he could find an audience. Recalling those early lectures, Tipper Gore said to *Time*, "We were on tour, doing the slide show, and men and women would come up to Al after, silently weeping." Gore's presentation was striking a chord with many who were deeply affected by what he had to say. This was the beginning of *An Inconvenient Truth*, which would soon become an Academy Award-winning documentary film with several companion books.

The central message of *An Inconvenient Truth* is that global warming threatens all life on earth, and a solution must be found quickly in order to avoid the worst consequences. "We have become capable of doing catastrophic damage without realizing it," Gore explained. "We've quadrupled the population in less than a century, amplified the power of technology many thousands of times over, and we haven't matched those changes with a shift in our thinking that lets us take into account the long-term consequences of our actions." But in addition to raising awareness of the problem, Gore also offered hope for a realistic solution. "I believe this is the rare crisis that requires a fundamental shift in public opinion at the grass-roots level.... The path to a solution lies through changing the minds of the American people.... It is very possible to start leveling it out within the next five years.... I'm trying to say to you, be a part of the change. No one

An Inconvenient Truth *has taken many forms: it has been a lecture, a documentary film, a book for adults, and a book for young adults, as shown here.*

else is going to do it. The politicians are paralyzed. The people have to do it for themselves!"

As Gore traveled around the country to present his lecture, he spoke to a group in Hollywood, California. Afterwards, he was approached by movie producers who wanted to make a documentary film version to bring the message to more people. At first, he later said, "I was dubious that anyone would be willing to make a movie with so much science in it." Despite his doubts, the movie came together very quickly and was released in 2006. It became an unexpected success, both in theaters and in sales of the DVD version. *An Inconvenient Truth* won two Academy Awards in 2007, for Best Documentary Feature and Best Original Song. Companion books have been published for adult and young adult readers, with translations into 28 languages for worldwide distribution.

The documentary and book have received overwhelmingly positive reviews. Gore's presentation has been called "scarily persuasive" and a "case for immediate action." *Booklist* praised the young adult version of the book, saying "few, if any, books for youth offer such a dynamic look at the climate issues threatening our planet." There has been some criticism of *An Inconvenient Truth*, which has focused on the idea that Gore exaggerated the seriousness of the problem.

In spite of this criticism, *An Inconvenient Truth* helped to energize the "green" environmental movement that subsequently swept the nation. A movie critic writing for *Time* said, "Gore's film helped trigger one of the most dramatic opinion shifts in history as Americans suddenly realized they must change the way they live." The movie has inspired thousands of people to get involved in environmental activism. Gore has trained more than 1,000 volunteers from all walks of life to give his lecture and also train others to do so. The list of trained speakers includes such celebrities as actress Cameron Diaz and Philadelphia Eagles linebacker Dhani Jones. On July 7, 2007, the Live Earth global music festival, inspired by *An Inconvenient Truth*, was televised around the world, with performances on all seven continents. The festival was designed to increase awareness of and involvement in environmental causes.

> "We have become capable of doing catastrophic damage without realizing it," Gore explained. "We've quadrupled the population in less than a century, amplified the power of technology many thousands of times over, and we haven't matched those changes with a shift in our thinking that lets us take into account the long-term consequences of our actions."

The Nobel Peace Prize

In 2007, Gore was awarded the Nobel Peace Prize for his work raising public awareness of global warming and climate change. He shared the

> *"We, the human species, are confronting a planetary emergency—a threat to the survival of our civilization.... The future is knocking at our door right now.... [The] next generation will ask us one of two questions. Either they will ask, 'What were you thinking; why didn't you act?' Or they will ask instead: 'How did you find the moral courage to rise and successfully resolve a crisis that so many said was impossible to solve?'"*

prestigious award with the Intergovernmental Panel on Climate Change, a United Nations network of scientists. In its formal citation, the Nobel committee honored Gore for his work "to build up and disseminate greater knowledge about man-made climate change." The committee also called Gore "the single individual who has done most to create greater worldwide understanding of the measures needed to be adopted."

In accepting the Peace Prize, Gore said this: "We, the human species, are confronting a planetary emergency—a threat to the survival of our civilization that is gathering ominous and destructive potential even as we gather here. But there is hopeful news as well: we have the ability to solve this crisis and avoid the worst—though not all—of its consequences, if we act boldly, decisively, and quickly.... The future is knocking at our door right now. Make no mistake, the next generation will ask us one of two questions. Either they will ask, 'What were you thinking; why didn't you act?' Or they will ask instead: 'How did you find the moral courage to rise and successfully resolve a crisis that so many said was impossible to solve?'"

MARRIAGE AND FAMILY

Al Gore has been married since May 19, 1970, to Mary Elizabeth Aitcheson, known as Tipper, a childhood nickname taken from a favorite nursery rhyme. The couple met at a high school dance and, after only a few dates, knew that they would one day marry. Tipper holds undergraduate and graduate degrees in psychology and has worked as a professional photographer. She is well known for her controversial campaign against profanity and violence in rock music and for her success in forcing record companies to attach warning labels to albums with explicit lyrics.

AL GORE

Gore won the 2007 Nobel Peace Prize for his environmental work. He shared the prize with the Intergovernmental Panel on Climate Change, a United Nations group of scientists represented by Rajendra Pachauri. Gore and Pachauri are shown here receiving their Nobel medals and diplomas.

The Gores have four children—Karenna, Kristin, Sarah, and Albert III—all now grown. They also have two grandchildren, Wyatt Gore Schiff and Anna Hunger Schiff.

The Gores live in Nashville, Tennessee, in a 1915 mansion that has been remodeled to be as energy efficient as possible. They also own a farm in Tennessee, located across the Caney Fork River from Gore's parents' farm. In addition, the Gores have homes in California and Virginia.

SELECTED CREDITS

Earth in the Balance: Ecology and the Human Spirit, 1992 (book)
An Inconvenient Truth, 2006 (film)
An Inconvenient Truth: The Planetary Emergency of Global Warming and What We Can Do About It, 2006 (book)
An Inconvenient Truth: The Crisis of Global Warming, 2007 (juvenile book)
The Assault on Reason, 2007 (book)

HONORS AND AWARDS

One of Ten Outstanding Young Americans (Jaycees): 1980
Humanitas Prize, Special Award: 2006, for *An Inconvenient Truth* film
Quill Award in History/Current Events/Politics: 2006, for *An Inconvenient Truth*; 2007, for *The Assault on Reason*
Academy Awards (Academy of Motion Picture Arts and Sciences): 2007 (two awards), Best Documentary Feature and Best Original Song, for *An Inconvenient Truth*
Nobel Peace Prize: 2007

FURTHER READING

Books

Hillstrom, Kevin. *People in the News: Al Gore,* 2008 (juvenile)
Jeffrey, Laura S. *Al Gore: Leader for the New Millennium,* 1999 (juvenile)
Maraniss, David. *The Prince of Tennessee: The Rise of Al Gore,* 2000
Sapet, Kerrily. *Political Profiles: Al Gore,* 2008 (juvenile)
Sergis, Diana K. *Bush v. Gore: Controversial Political Election Case, Landmark Supreme Court Cases Series,* 2003 (juvenile)
Turque, Bill. *Inventing Al Gore,* 2000

Periodicals

Current Biography Yearbook, 2001
New York Times, Oct. 13, 2007

New York Times Magazine, Oct 25, 1992, p.40; May 20, 2007, p.42
Time, Aug. 8, 2005, p.32; June 5, 2006, p.24; May 28, 2007, p.30; Dec. 31, 2007-Jan. 7, 2008, p.98
USA Today, Apr. 25, 2007, p.D1
Vanity Fair, Oct. 2007
Washington Post, Oct. 3, 1999, p.A1; Oct. 10, 1999, p.A1; Dec. 11, 2007, p.A14
Wired, May 2006

Online Articles

http://www.nytimes.com/library/politics/camp/052200wh-dem-gore.html
 (New York Times, "Al Gore's Journey: A Boyhood Divided—A Boy's Life In and Out of the Family Script," May 22, 2000)
http://www.nytimes.com/2007/10/13/world/13nobel.html
 (New York Times, "Gore Shares Peace Prize for Climate Change Work," Oct. 13, 2007)
http://www.pbs.org/wgbh/pages/frontline/shows/choice2000/gore/
 (PBS, "The Choice 2000: Al Gore," no date)
http://www.rollingstone.com/news/story/10688399/al_gore_30
 (Rolling Stone, "Al Gore 3.0," June 28, 2006)
http://www.vanityfair.com/politics/features/2007/10/gore200710
 (Vanity Fair, "Going After Gore," Oct. 2007)
http://www.washingtonpost.com/wp-srv/politics/campaigns/wh2000/stories/gore101099a.htm
 (Washington Post, "Al Gore: Growing Up in Two Worlds," Oct. 10, 1999)
http://www.wired.com/wired/archive/14.05/gore_pr.html
 (Wired, "The Resurrection of Al Gore," May 2006)

ADDRESS

Al Gore
2100 West End Avenue
Suite 620
Nashville, TN 37203

WORLD WIDE WEB SITES

http://www.algore.com
http://www.wecansolveit.org

Vanessa Hudgens 1988-

American Actress and Singer
Star of Disney's *High School Musical* Movies

BIRTH

Vanessa Anne Hudgens was born on December 14, 1988, in Salinas, California. She was the first child of Greg Hudgens and Gina Guangco, who manage her career. Her sister, Stella, is six years younger and is also pursuing acting. Her family background helped set Hudgens up for stardom: her grandparents were big band musicians, so she became interested in singing at a young age. Her striking good looks come from her parents' multiethnic background—her mother is Filipino, Chinese, and Hispanic, while her father is Irish and Native American.

YOUTH

Hudgens spent her early childhood in a small town in Oregon. Because she demonstrated a talent for performing, her family moved to San Diego, California, so the eight-year-old Vanessa could take lessons in singing, dancing, acting, and piano. She earned several roles in local community theater productions, including performances of *Cinderella, The King and I, The Music Man,* and *The Wizard of Oz*. The experience convinced her she wanted to become an entertainer. "It wasn't that my parents were pushy or anything," Hudgens recalled. "They were actually the ones going, 'Are you sure you want to do this?' because they knew this was a tough business, and they were afraid I'd get hurt. So I was the one pushing them."

A chance audition landed the aspiring actress her first television commercial; a good friend was too sick to attend, so Hudgens took her place. Afterwards, her parents moved the family to Los Angeles to bring them closer to more acting opportunities. By the time she entered her teens she was making guest appearances on popular television series; at 14 she appeared in her first film. This led to her first leading role, in Disney's *High School Musical,* which established her as a young star to watch.

> "It wasn't that my parents were pushy or anything," Hudgens recalled. "They were actually the ones going, 'Are you sure you want to do this?' because they knew this was a tough business, and they were afraid I'd get hurt. So I was the one pushing them."

EDUCATION

As a working child actor, Hudgens stopped attending school after seventh grade so that she would have the flexibility to pursue acting jobs. Instead, she was home-schooled by her mother, who also teaches her younger sister. Hudgens earned her high school equivalency in 2007, shortly after turning 18. She has stated that some day she would like to go to college, but she hasn't yet chosen a college or a date to begin her studies.

CAREER HIGHLIGHTS

Starting Out in Supporting Roles

In 2002 Hudgens earned a couple of one-episode guest appearances on the CBS shows "Still Standing" and "Robbery Homicide Division." The following year she won her first film role, playing a small supporting part in *Thirteen*. This hard-hitting drama focused on 13-year-old Tracy, played by Evan Rachel Wood, who falls into shoplifting and other risky behaviors. It also featured an Oscar-nominated performance by Holly Hunter. Hudgens played Noel, the wholesome friend whom Tracy shuns after getting in with the "cool" crowd. While the film didn't perform well at the box office, it did earn awards at several film festivals and gave Hudgens her first experience with film.

In 2004, Hudgens earned a larger role in *Thunderbirds*, a kids' action movie based on the classic British television show. Alan Tracy is the youngest member of a wealthy family that uses their spectacular vehicles, the Thunderbirds, to respond to disasters all over the world. Alan wants to be part of the International Rescue team, but his father thinks he is too young. When a villain traps the older Tracys on their space station, it's up to Alan and his two friends, Fermat and Tintin (played by Hudgens) to thwart his plans. A *Hollywood Reporter* critic called the three young actors "all appealing," and found the film "a piece of whiz-bang children's entertainment that could appeal to the family market far and wide."

Hudgens continued finding steady work with guest appearances on television. In 2005 she appeared on the Fox sitcom "Quintuplets," while in 2006 she appeared in an episode of Nickelodeon's "Drake and Josh." She also found work on the Disney Channel, with a recurring guest role on "The Suite Life of Zack and Cody." In this comedy about twin brothers living in a luxury hotel, Hudgens appeared as part of their circle of friends.

During this time, Hudgens got the opportunity to audition for an upcoming Disney Channel movie that would revive the classic musical genre. When she read the script, the actress recalled, she got "crazy excited because it was everything I loved in one movie." After gaining the role, she and her co-stars spent months practicing their dance steps and recording vocals. "We all lived in each other's pockets for the whole year, and we be-

> *While filming* **High School Musical,** *the cast spent months practicing their dance steps and recording vocals. "We all lived in each other's pockets for the whole year," Hudgens recalled, "and we became a sort of family."*

came a sort of family." Their hard work and closeness paid off when the film, *High School Musical,* debuted in January 2006.

The *High School Musical* Phenomenon

High School Musical begins as two teens on vacation are forced to sing karaoke together at a New Year's Eve party. Bookish Gabriella Montez (played by Hudgens) and athletic Troy Bolton (played by Zac Efron) enjoy their duet, although neither has done much singing before. When Gabriella transfers to Troy's high school, the two of them think about trying out for the school musical, although this goes against their friends' expectations. When their musical rivals, twins Sharpay and Ryan, scheme to get Troy's big basketball game and Gabriella's scholastic decathlon scheduled for the same time as the musical callbacks, their friends come together to get them to the theater on time.

> "I think young people are deprived of musicals they can relate to," Hudgens said to explain the popularity of High School Musical. "When I was growing up I'd watch them all the time, but now there are very few out there for kids, and I'm just glad we brought the genre back in the way that we did."

The premiere of *High School Musical* in January 2006 was an instant success; it brought a then-record 7.7 million viewers for a Disney Channel movie and was the highest non-sports cable broadcast of the month. Later airings brought in nearly 20 million more viewers in the U.S. alone. Worldwide it has been shown in over 100 countries, drawing over 170 million fans. In addition, the DVD of the film sold nearly eight million copies.

High School Musical also found unprecedented success on the music charts. The soundtrack hit No. 1, with over four million copies sold in the U.S., and was the top-selling CD in 2006. The soundtrack spawned several hit singles; the best-performing was a duet between Hudgens and Efron, "Breaking Free," which hit No. 4 on the Billboard Hot 100 and was the fastest moving single on the chart in 48 years. Another duet, "Start of Something New," hit No. 28, while her solo, "When There Was Me and You," charted at No. 71.

The show won several awards, including an Emmy for Outstanding Children's Program and a Teen Choice Award for Choice Comedy/Musical

High School Musical *was a huge hit on DVD.*

Program. Hudgens's turn as Gabriella Montez brought her recognition as well. She was nominated for a Teen Choice Award for TV Breakout Star, but lost to costar Efron; the two of them earned the Teen Choice Award for TV Chemistry. She was also nominated for best television actress by the Imagen Awards, which celebrate positive portrayals of Latinos.

> "Just being on the tour bus is like a school field trip—when you're on the school bus and you're heading there and everybody is just having a blast, singing songs and everything."

Hudgens was amazed by the runaway success of *High School Musical*. "I had no idea that [it] was going to be so huge," she said. When asked to explain it, she remarked, "I think young people are deprived of musicals they can relate to. When I was growing up I'd watch them all the time, but now there are very few out there for kids, and I'm just glad we brought the genre back in the way that we did." She and her co-stars also brought the musical to their fans in person. They sold out a concert tour of over 40 North American cities, with over 620,000 tickets sold. A DVD of the Houston show also became a hot seller. Hudgens not only got to re-create her numbers from *High School Musical*, she got a chance to showcase herself as a solo artist. "Her powerful vocals and magnetic smile set the crowd screaming," observed a reporter from the *San Jose Mercury News*.

Launching a Solo Album

Hudgens also used her popularity from *High School Musical* to begin building a recording career. She had offers from several companies, but chose to sign with Hollywood Records, a division of the Disney Company. It took her less than two months to record her first solo album, *V*. "The songs were already there, so I just went with the flow," she explained. *V*—the title refers to both "Vanessa" and "variety"—debuted in September 2006 and contained a mix of pop, rock, dance, and R&B songs. She sold 34,000 copies the first week, earning a respectable debut at No. 24 on the Billboard 200 album chart. Her first single, "Come Back to Me," debuted on MTV's "TRL" program and hit No. 18 on Billboard's Top 40 Mainstream chart. A second single, "Say OK," hit No. 47 on the Pop 100 chart. The album's combination of strong beats and teen-appropriate lyrics led some critics to call Hudgens a "baby J.Lo." By July 2007, *V* had been certified gold, with over 500,000 albums sold. The

vanessa HUDGENS

Hudgens's first solo CD.

album also earned her a 2007 Teen Choice Award for Choice Music Breakout Artist: Female.

That fall and winter Hudgens went on tour in support of her album, performing concerts with the Cheetah Girls, a singing group with their own Disney Channel movies. Although traveling around the country and performing in a different place every night can be exhausting, she enjoyed the camaraderie with her fellow performers. "Just being on the tour bus is like a school field trip—when you're on the school bus and you're heading there and everybody is just having a blast, singing songs and everything."

High School Musical 2

After she finished touring, Hudgens rejoined the cast of *High School Musical* to film the sequel, *High School Musical 2*. With a bigger budget, the director and cast wanted to feature even more elaborate musical numbers. Luckily, the actress enjoys the dance numbers, although she admits dancing in heels can leave her feet aching. The set of *High School Musical 2* "was so crazy," Hudgens recalled. "Everything was way more chaotic because we really stepped it up."

In this sequel, school has let out for summer vacation, leading up to senior year. Troy and Gabriella get summer jobs working at the country club controlled by Sharpay's wealthy family. But things become tense as Sharpay schemes to break up Gabriella and Troy. Troy must decide whether to pursue the advantages that are available from Sharpay's wealthy family—even if it means neglecting Gabriella and his friends. It's a difficult summer, especially for Gabriella, but all is resolved as the group participates in the country club's annual talent show. The club's talent show provides a crucial decision for Troy—as well as the opportunity for more great song-and-dance numbers from the cast.

When the sequel aired in August 2007, its success showed the *High School Musical* phenomenon was still going strong. The first airing set a record as the most-watched basic cable telecast of all time, with over 17 million viewers. (Since many families held viewing parties, the actual number of viewers was most likely even higher.) It had more viewers than any broadcast program that week—in fact, it was the most-watched program on cable or broadcast television during the summer season.

The soundtrack *High School Musical 2* also fared well on the music charts. The soundtrack debuted at No. 1 on Billboard's Album chart, with 625,000 copies sold the first week alone. Its first single, the group number "What Time Is It," hit No. 6 on the Billboard Hot 100 chart. Three duets between Hudgens and Zac Efron also had strong single debuts: "You Are the Music in Me" was No. 9 on "Hot Digital Tracks" and debuted at No. 29 on the Pop 100; "Gotta Go My Own Way" placed on those same charts at No. 19 and No. 44; and "Everyday" reached No. 30 and No. 55.

Disney is already preparing for another sequel, this time as a motion picture, with plans to present *High School Musical 3: Senior Year* in theaters in fall 2008. Hudgens will reprise her most famous role: "Gabriella is such a good role model that I'm not going to put her down in any way," the actress said. "[She is] a smart girl and she's into her studies, and yet she still gets the guy." It has also enabled Hudgens to reach a level of success that led *Forbes* magazine to place her in their Top 10 list of "Young Hollywood's Top-Earning Stars," with an estimated $2 million in earnings for 2006 alone.

VANESSA HUDGENS

Scenes from High School Musical 2.

In addition to *High School Musical 3*, Hudgens has plenty to keep her occupied. She's already planning to record her second solo album and perhaps write some songs for it. "I figured my first album I'll leave to the professionals," she said. "Once I know the process, I'll get my creative juices flowing." She also wouldn't mind taking on a more adult acting role, she says, "something more edgy that would be fulfilling as an actor." Her dream role would be to play and sing the part of Maria in the classic musical *West Side Story*, just as her idol, the late actress Natalie Wood, did in 1961.

Hudgens is conscious that she has many young fans watching her future career. "Kids look up to the wrong people these days, not knowing right from wrong," she said. "I am honored to know kids are looking up to me." To those interested in following her into the entertainment business, she recommended, "Do all the school plays that you can, like theater and musicals. . . . It's good experience!" Entertainment is "a hard business and there is a lot of rejection involved. But if you really want to do it, I'd say don't let anyone stop you!" Nevertheless, the actress admitted, "at times I wish I was a normal teenager. I never went to a real high school, to prom, or a high school football game." In the end, the hard work and sacrifice has been worth it, she said. "I gave it all up for my career, and it's going better than I could have wished. I made the right decision."

> "At times I wish I was a normal teenager. I never went to a real high school, to prom, or a high school football game,"Hudgens said. But she also felt that the hard work and sacrifice has been worth it."I gave it all up for my career, and it's going better than I could have wished. I made the right decision."

HOME AND FAMILY

Hudgens lives in Los Angeles with her family, which includes a toy poodle and other pets. She has been seen dating Zac Efron, her *High School Musical* co-star.

HOBBIES AND OTHER INTERESTS

Like any other teenager, Hudgens enjoys spending time with friends talking, shopping, or going to amusement parks. She also likes outdoor activities, such as hiking and camping. "I'm totally fine with not doing my hair or makeup, not taking a shower, and just hiking," she noted. Nevertheless, Hudgens knows how to take care of her appearance, and in 2007 she earned a contract as a celebrity spokesmodel for Neutrogena skin care products.

CREDITS

Film and Television
Thirteen, 2003
Thunderbirds, 2004
High School Musical, 2006 (TV movie)
High School Musical 2, 2007 (TV movie)

Recordings
High School Musical Soundtrack, 2006
V, 2006
High School Musical 2 Soundtrack, 2007

HONORS AND AWARDS
Teen Choice Awards: 2006, for TV Choice Chemistry for *High School Musical* (with Zac Efron); 2007, for Choice Music Breakout Artist-Female

FURTHER READING

Periodicals
Mail on Sunday (London), Dec. 3, 2006, p.46
Minneapolis Star-Tribune, Nov. 10, 2006, p.F1
New York Times, Mar. 11, 2007, sec.2, p.1
People, Summer 2007 (HSM2 Special), p.24; July 27, 2007, p. 8
San Jose Mercury News, Dec. 2. 2006
USA Today, Feb. 28, 2006, p.D4
Washington Post, Aug. 20, 2007, p.C1

Online Articles
http://www.hollywoodreporter.com
   (Hollywood Reporter, review of *Thunderbirds,* July 20, 2004; "'High School Musical 2' Upstages TV Records," Aug. 19, 2007)
http://www.timeforkids.com
   (Time for Kids, "Vanessa Hudgens Goes Solo," Nov. 7, 2006)

ADDRESS

Vanessa Hudgens
Hollywood Records
500 South Buena Vista Street
Burbank, CA 91521

WORLD WIDE WEB SITES

http://hollywoodrecords.go.com/vanessahudgens
http://www.disney.go.com/disneychannel
http://www.myspace.com/vanessahudgens

Jennifer Hudson 1981-
American Singer and Actress
Winner of the 2007 Best Supporting Actress
Academy Award for *Dreamgirls*

BIRTH

Jennifer Kate Hudson was born on September 12, 1981, in Chicago, Illinois. Her mother, Darnell Hudson, is a secretary. The name of Hudson's father, who worked as a bus driver, is unclear; various sources have listed him as Samuel Simpson and Samuel Samson. The youngest of three children, Hudson has a brother, Jason, and a sister, Julia.

YOUTH

Hudson grew up in Englewood, on the southwest side of Chicago. "We were poor, but we weren't that poor—the house I grew up in had nine bedrooms," she said. In fact, she added, "we thought we were rich because we had everything we needed. My mother made sure we all did extracurricular activities to keep us busy. My brother James took piano lessons and I did ballet and modeled for the Sears catalogue when I was five."

An important part of their family life was worship at Pleasant Gift Missionary Baptist Church in Chicago, where Hudson developed her love of music. "I've known I wanted to sing since I was seven," she said. That was the age when she joined the church choir, singing alongside her sister Julia. "She liked it, I didn't," Julia Hudson recalled in an interview with *Vogue*. "When we were little girls, I was the tomboy, but she wanted style. When we could afford it, our mother took us to buy clothes and let us pick. I wanted pants. Jennifer always wanted the frilly skirt."

> "I'd ask for solos in church and they'd give me the runaround," she said. "I remember sitting in the bathroom of my house at seven years old crying and saying, 'Nobody will listen to me, so I'll listen to myself sing.'"

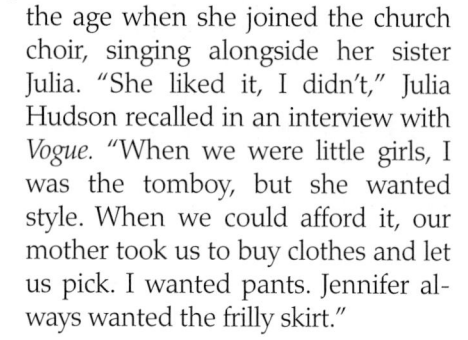

Not only did Hudson love to sing, she also craved an audience. "I'd ask for solos in church and they'd give me the runaround," she said. "I remember sitting in the bathroom of my house at seven years old crying and saying, 'Nobody will listen to me, so I'll listen to myself sing.'" But eventually, people did listen. One of the first people to notice and nurture her vocal talent was her maternal grandmother, Julia Kate Hudson, who was a prominent and inspirational singer at the Pleasant Gift Church. "They say I got my voice from my grandmother," Hudson recalled. "She just wanted to sing for the Lord in church. That's part of where I got my emotion from. I would hear her voice singing, 'How Great Thou Art.'"

It wasn't long before Hudson did get solos in church, giving rousing renditions that often brought the worshipers to tears. While still in elementary school, she was often asked to sing at family and friends' weddings and baptisms. She also performed in school musicals and talent shows, where audiences were astounded by her vocal range of six octaves.

Hudson attended Paul Laurence Dunbar Vocational Career Academy, a public high school in Chicago that offers students specialized career training in 22 vocations, including music. She was active in the school's chorus, which was directed by Richard Nunley. "[Hudson is] also a great classical singer and a lot of people don't know that," Nunley told the *Chicago Sun-Times*. "I wanted her to learn classical technique and develop a good instrument so she could be prepared to sing whatever music she wanted. She was crazy about Whitney Houston, Gladys Knight, Aretha Franklin—old school. She'd always say, 'Mr. Nunley, I'm going to make you proud of me. I'm going to be a famous singer.'" In city and state school singing competitions, Hudson always earned "superior" ratings.

At age 16, Hudson got a job at a local Burger King. She didn't stay there very long, as she preferred standing in the drive-thru practicing her singing rather than working on orders. Her last two years in high school were emotionally difficult, as she mourned the loss of her grandmother, Julia Kate Hudson, in 1998, and her father the following year.

Hudson graduated in 1999 from Paul Laurence Dunbar Vocational Career Academy, where she was voted "most talented" by the senior class. She enrolled in Langston University, in Langston, Oklahoma. But she left after a single semester, unhappy with the weather and homesick for Chicago. She then signed up for classes at Kennedy-King College, a community college in Chicago, and resumed singing with the Pleasant Gift choir.

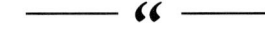

> *After Hudson's daily performance on stage in* Big River, *"there wouldn't be a dry eye in the house," said fellow performer Norissa Pearson. "Every night people cried, including the other actors."*

EARLY CAREER

Hudson's professional career began in 2001 with the help of her music teacher at Kennedy-King, who arranged an audition for her at a local production of *Big River*, a musical based on *The Adventures of Huckleberry Finn* by Mark Twain. Hudson's vocal skills at the audition were so impressive that she was hired on the spot. She didn't receive a speaking part, but she did get to showcase her talent by singing a solo, "How Blest We Are." After Hudson's daily performance on stage, "there wouldn't be a dry eye in the house," fellow performer Norissa Pearson told *Jet*. "Every night people cried, including the other actors."

Hudson's next job was on a Disney cruise ship, the *Disney Wonder*. She was the singing narrator of the musical *Hercules*, the story of the strong-man hero of Greek mythology. The production ran five or six days a week from February through August 2003. A self-described homebody, Hudson considered it a huge milestone in her life that she lived on a ship away from her family for almost seven months. "To be able to sing for 8,000 people a week is amazing," she said. "It's like, are you serious? You're paying me to do this? It was very exciting."

CAREER HIGHLIGHTS

"American Idol"

While Hudson was working on the cruise ship, her mother saw an advertisement that auditions were being held for the Fox network TV reality series "American Idol: Season 3." Darnell Hudson knew that her daughter dreamed about auditioning for the show, which gives aspiring singers a chance to sing on national television and jumpstart a singing career. At that point, in the summer of 2003, Hudson had a big decision to make: should she renew her contract with Disney Cruise Ships or should she leave and audition for "American Idol"? She decided on "Idol."

Hudson flew to Atlanta, Georgia, one of six cities in the U.S. where auditions were being held. After hours of waiting in line, it was finally her turn. She sang the Aretha Franklin hit "Share Your Love with Me," which was later shown on "Idol" in February 2004. The television judges—Paula Abdul, Simon Cowell, and Randy Jackson—all praised her voice. Jackson was the most enthusiastic, calling Hudson's rendition of the song "absolutely brilliant."

Once picked for the first round of semi-finals, Hudson flew to Hollywood, California, to continue in the competition. She sang "Imagine," by John Lennon, which the judges seemed to like, although they clearly weren't as bowled over as they were by her initial appearance. On the next night's results show, Hudson was not selected for the next round.

A Second Chance on "American Idol"

Hudson's stint on "Idol" would have been brief and forgotten by many if not for the Wild Card Round. For this part of "Idol," the judges Abdul,

Cowell, and Jackson each select a rejected contestant to bring back for another chance, with a fourth singer selected by popular vote. Hudson was Randy Jackson's Wild Card choice. Thrilled to be back on the show weeks after she was initially booted off, Hudson sang the Whitney Houston hit, "I Believe in You and Me." While Hudson had to endure some biting criticism from the notoriously tough judge Cowell about her choice of clothing, all the judges liked her vocal performance and she made it to the next round.

Over the next several weeks, the "American Idol" contestants prepared a different song from a specific musical genre for each week's show. Hudson continued to impress just about everyone but Cowell. After her rendition of "Baby I Love You" by Aretha Franklin for Soul Week, Cowell told Hudson he thought that the song was a bad choice and criticized her for "oversinging" it. Abdul and Jackson disagreed, and both warmly praised Hudson's performance. For Country Week, Hudson chose "No One Else on Earth" by Wynonna Judd, and Cowell's criticism was even more caustic: "Let me sum this up for you. I think you are out of your depth in this competition." The studio audience booed Cowell's remarks, and Abdul and Jackson came to Hudson's defense yet again, praising her ability to belt out a song.

Despite Cowell's lack of enthusiasm, Hudson stayed in the competition with her performances of "No One Else on Earth" by Wynonna Judd for Country Week, and "(Love Is Like a) Heat Wave," made famous by Martha and the Vandellas, for Motown Week. One of Hudson's most memorable performances was her version of "Circle of Life," by Elton John. "Jennifer Hudson blew me away," said John, a guest judge that evening, after listening to all the contestants sing his compositions. "She sent chills up my spine. It was my favorite performance of the whole lot.... That voice is astonishing."

Hudson's rendition of the Whitney Houston hit "I Have Nothing" from the movie *The Bodyguard* for Movie Theme Week impressed the guest

Hudson competing during "American Idol."

judge, the director Quentin Tarantino. "Hudson takes on Houston and wins!" Tarantino declared. By that point in the competition, even Cowell was coming around, telling Hudson, "You could be a front-runner."

On the episode aired on April 20, 2004, Hudson was one of seven singers left in the competition. She sang "Weekend in New England" by Barry Manilow. A guest judge on the show, Manilow told Hudson, "You took it all the way, sweetie. I loved it." Abdul, Cowell, and Jackson all agreed that she was becoming more confident with each song. Thrilled by her success, Hudson told Cowell, "I feel like I'm getting to be me now. This is Jenny's world."

Voted off "American Idol"

But the next night, the three singers with the least votes from television viewers were Hudson, Fantasia Barrino, and La Toya London. Many people were surprised and angry by this result, since these three women were widely considered to be the most talented contestants. The fact that all three are African American spurred some people, including an outraged Elton John, to dub the vote "incredibly racist." In the end, it was Hudson who was voted off the show.

> One of Hudson's most memorable performances was her version of "Circle of Life," by Elton John. "Jennifer Hudson blew me away," said John, a guest judge that evening, after listening to all the contestants. "She sent chills up my spine. It was my favorite performance of the whole lot.... That voice is astonishing."

A possible factor in Hudson's ouster was a Midwest storm that knocked out power to 15,000 homes in the Chicago area the night she was voted off "American Idol." Hudson was a favorite in her hometown, and many of her fans didn't see the show because of the outage. Ryan Seacrest, the show's host, had another theory—most people thought Hudson was such a shoo-in that they didn't bother to vote. After the final tally was announced, Seacrest reminded television viewers that they had to vote for their favorites every week. "You cannot let talent like this slip through the cracks," he said. A short time later, Fantasia Barrino ultimately won the competition.

Hudson has been asked many times how she felt about her loss on "American Idol." "I never felt it had anything to do with racism because I

Contestents performing on the "American Idol" grand finale (from left): Hudson, Fantasia Barrino, La Toya London, and Diana DeGarmo.

don't feel like I have a color," she reflected in an interview two years later. "Of course I was hurt. Oh, I cried. But clearly God had a greater plan for me."

As for Cowell, Hudson professed no hard feelings about his comments. Several years later, after she was nominated for an Academy Award for *Dreamgirls*, she had this to say. "I like Simon, he was always my favorite judge," she said. "He never criticized my weight, just my wardrobe. And looking back, I'm glad I was eliminated, because I don't think I'd be here if I had been the 'American Idol.' But I did tell Simon then that it wasn't over and I'd be back, so maybe now I could say, 'I told you so.'"

Dreamgirls

After the finale of "American Idol: Season 3," the 10 finalists, including Hudson, went on a 48-city tour. She was a guest star on the TV show "On Air with Ryan Seacrest," singing a duet with Barry Manilow, and she performed at several benefit concerts. Then, in May 2005, Hudson got a call at her Chicago home asking her to audition for the role of Effie in the movie version of the Broadway musical *Dreamgirls*.

Dreamgirls is the story of a singing group formed in the 1960s by Effie White, the lead singer, and her best friends Deena Jones and Lorrell Robinson. They meet Curtis Taylor Jr. at a local talent show. He becomes their manager and arranges for them to be a backup act for James "Thunder" Early, a rhythm and blues star. Eventually, Taylor turns the Dreamettes into the Dreams, a pop music act, with Deena as the lead singer. Deena, who is slender, also replaces Effie, who is heavier, as Taylor's love interest. Effie quits the group and ends up as a single mother trying to survive on her own. She tries to make a comeback years later, recording a song written by her brother. But Taylor attempts to stymie her success by arranging for Deena to record the same song. In the end, Deena sees through Taylor's manipulations, and she and Effie are finally reconciled.

> "I like Simon, he was always my favorite judge," she said. "He never criticized my weight, just my wardrobe. And looking back, I'm glad I was eliminated, because I don't think I'd be here if I had been the 'American Idol.' But I did tell Simon then that it wasn't over and I'd be back, so maybe now I could say, 'I told you so.'"

Dreamgirls opened on Broadway in 1981 and was a smash hit. The show won six Tony Awards, including Best Actress in a Musical for Jennifer Holliday, whose portrayal of Effie was widely acclaimed. Many people who saw the show thought the role of Effie was based on the singer Florence Ballard, who started the real-life 1960s trio called the Supremes. Ballard was eventually fired from the group and replaced as lead singer by Diana Ross. Ross went on to have a successful career as a solo singer and actress, while Ballard became impoverished and died of a heart attack at age 32. The creators of *Dreamgirls* have said that the story is fictional, and Ross has angrily denied in interviews she was in any way like the character of Deena.

For the new movie version of *Dreamgirls,* almost 800 young women tried out for the role of Effie, including Fantasia Barrino, winner of "American Idol: Season 3." "The casting of Effie was crucial," said Bill Condon, the director and screenwriter of *Dreamgirls*. "If we had made a mistake, it would have been impossible to overcome." Hudson actually had three auditions

JENNIFER HUDSON

Hudson in scenes from Dreamgirls: with Jamie Foxx (top); with Beyoncé Knowles (center); and with Eddie Murphy, Beyoncé Knowles, and Anika Noni Rose (bottom).

173

for the role over a six-month period. Condon and the movie's producers were concerned about her lack of acting experience. Her final on-camera screen test, however, proved to be convincing. Condon called her to say, "Congratulations, you're our Effie White." Recalling that moment, Hudson said, "I shouted, I hit the floor, I thanked Jesus. I celebrated for ten minutes, then I said,'I got to focus.'"

The other lead roles in *Dreamgirls* were played by Jamie Foxx as Curtis Taylor, Beyoncé Knowles as Deena, Eddie Murphy as James "Thunder" Early, and Danny Glover as Marty Madison—all established movie stars and seasoned performers. Meeting them for the first time, at a read-through of the script, made Hudson feel nervous. "I was afraid they were all thinking, 'How is this little girl gonna play this role? She's not experienced like we are,'" Hudson recalled. "But it wasn't like that at all. They were very supportive and patient and helpful."

> "The casting of Effie was crucial," said Bill Condon, the director and screenwriter of Dreamgirls. "If we had made a mistake, it would have been impossible to overcome."

Becoming Effie

Hudson was instructed to pack on extra weight to play Effie, which she did by eating cookies, cakes, and pies. She went from a size 12 to a size 16. Gaining 25 pounds wasn't nearly as hard for Hudson as Condon's requirement that she become temperamental and isolate herself from the other actors in order to better portray Effie's tough nature. Condon's "Diva 101 course," as Hudson put it, "took some getting adjusted to, but it was part of Effie that was needed, that he felt I didn't have and that I needed to tap into."

Another hurdle for Hudson was preparing herself for her love scenes with Jamie Foxx, not all of which were included in the final cut of the movie. Playing Curtis Taylor, Foxx tried his best to make her feel comfortable, and Hudson got over her jitters by letting the action in the movie take over. "After a while it became Effie and Curtis, not Jennifer and Jamie," she said. As the story of *Dreamgirls* progresses, Effie faces the rejection of Curtis as well as her singing group. That's when Effie belts out "And I Am Telling You I'm Not Going," a highly emotional and defiant response to being cast aside. The song is the linchpin of the movie, and Hudson said she thought of Florence Ballard, the rejected, real-life Supreme, when she sang the song. "In reading [about Ballard] I got angry for Florence," Hudson said. "Like highly upset. Like, oooh, and I felt like her voice."

Hudson could identify with Effie because of her experience on "American Idol." "Effie was told that she was no good and couldn't make it either," she said. "She was cast aside. But in the end we both prevail. I like that."

Dreamgirls opened in December 2006 to mostly excellent reviews. Many of the critics singled out Hudson for praise. "The film is worth seeing simply for the on-screen splendor of Hudson, a losing contestant on TV's 'American Idol,'" Claudia Puig wrote in *USA Today*. "She's a natural—musically and theatrically—and delivers a tour-de-force performance." Another great review appeared in the *New York Times*. "The dramatic and musical peak of *Dreamgirls*—the showstopper, the main reason to see the movie—comes around midpoint, when Jennifer Hudson, playing Effie White, sings 'And I Am Telling You I'm Not Going,'" wrote reviewer A.O. Scott. "That song has been this musical's calling card since the first Broadway production 25 years ago, but to see Ms. Hudson tear into it on screen nonetheless brings the goose-bumped thrill of witnessing something new, even historic."

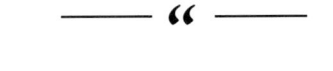

> *Hudson could identify with Effie because of her experience on "American Idol." "Effie was told that she was no good and couldn't make it either," she said. "She was cast aside. But in the end we both prevail. I like that."*

Winning the Golden Globe and the Oscar

Not long after the film opened, the nominations for the 2007 Golden Globe awards were announced, and Hudson's name was on the list for the award for Best Supporting Actress. She won, and made a tearful acceptance speech in which she said, "I had always dreamed, but I never dreamed this big. This goes far beyond anything I could ever have imagined." But for Hudson, the dreams got even bigger. She was also nominated for an Academy Award (Oscar), and at the awards ceremony in February 2007 she heard her name called as the winner of the award for Best Supporting Actress. A visibly shaken Hudson asked the audience for a moment so she could compose herself. "I didn't think I was going to win but, wow, if my grandmother was here to see me now," she said. "She was my biggest inspiration for everything because she was a singer and she

*Winning the Academy Award for
Best Supporting Actress was a wonderful shock for Hudson.*

had the passion for it but she never had the chance. And that was the thing that pushed me forward to continue."

In October 2006, Hudson signed a record deal with the veteran musical producer Clive Davis. She spent six months recording songs for her debut album, which will appear on J Records, a division of Arista. Hudson has also pursued her acting career, working with fellow Oscar winner Forest Whitaker in the film *Winged Creatures*, due to be released in 2008. "I don't want to do just musicals," she remarked. "I want to experiment and do different things and exercise that acting muscle. I'm a firm believer in using what God gives you to make your living. Singing is Number 1, and now it's singing and acting."

HOME AND FAMILY

Hudson lives in a four-bedroom co-op in Hyde Park, a neighborhood of Chicago. "I've always wanted to live in Hyde Park, so that's where I'm going to be," she said. "Of course they're like, 'You should move to L.A., New York,' but I want my first place to be here at home in Chicago. There's no other place in the world like it. It's where my family is." Hudson met her boyfriend, James Payton, a maintenance engineer, in Chicago when she was 13, and they've been together ever since. "He was my brother's best friend," she said.

HOBBIES AND OTHER INTERESTS

> *Hudson is proud of her body size. "Why should I feel like the minority when the majority of America is a size 12?" she remarked. "Plus a lot of singers don't sound the same when they lose weight. . . . Hey, somebody has to represent the big girls. Why not me?"*

Hudson likes to draw in her spare time. She enjoys going to church, which is still her favorite place to sing. She is proud of her clean-cut image. "I don't smoke and I don't do drugs," she said. "I never have and I never plan on it." She is also proud of her body size. "Why should I feel like the minority when the majority of America is a size 12?" she remarked. "Plus a lot of singers don't sound the same when they lose weight. I have a little singer's pouch, and that's where my voice comes from, so you're all just going to have to get used to my jelly. Hey, somebody has to represent the big girls. Why not me?"

CREDITS

Dreamgirls, 2006 (movie)
Dreamgirls, 2006 (soundtrack)

HONORS AND AWARDS

National Board of Review Awards: 2006, Breakthrough Performance (Female), for *Dreamgirls*
New York Film Critics Circle Awards: 2006, Best Supporting Actress, for *Dreamgirls*
ShoWest Awards: 2006, Female Star of Tomorrow
Academy Awards: 2007, Best Supporting Actress, for *Dreamgirls*

British Academy of Film and Television Arts Awards (BAFTA): 2007, Best Actress in a Supporting Role, for *Dreamgirls*
BET Awards: 2007 (2 awards), Best New Artist and Best Actress, for *Dreamgirls*
Broadcast Film Critics Association Awards: 2007, Best Supporting Actress, for *Dreamgirls*
Golden Globe Awards: 2007, Best Supporting Actress, for *Dreamgirls*
Screen Actors Guild Awards: Outstanding Performance by a Female Actor in a Supporting Role, for *Dreamgirls:* 2007
Teen Choice Awards: 2007, Choice Movie Actress-Drama, for *Dreamgirls*

FURTHER READING

Books

West, Betsy. *Jennifer Hudson American Dream Girl: An Unauthorized Biography,* 2007

Periodicals

Chicago Sun Times, Dec. 17, 2006, p.D1
Chicago Tribune, Dec. 17, 2006, p.C1
Essence, Mar. 2007, p.129
Evening Standard (London), Jan. 25, 2007, p.32
Los Angeles Times, Dec. 4, 2006, p.E1
Minneapolis Star Tribune, Apr. 29, 2007, p.F1
New York Post, Feb. 25, 2007, p.38
New York Times, Dec. 15, 2006, p.E1
Newsweek, Dec. 11, 2006, p.96
San Francisco Chronicle, Dec. 10, 2006, Sunday Datebook, p.19
Toronto Star, Dec. 24, 2006, p.S10
USA Today, Dec. 15, 2006, p.D1
Vogue, Mar. 2007, p.542

ADDRESS

Jennifer Hudson
J Records
745 Fifth Avenue
New York, NY 10151

WORLD WIDE WEB SITES

http://www.myspace.com/jenniferhudson
http://www.hollywood.com/celebrity/Jennifer_Hudson/1745865
http://www.dreamgirlsmovie.com

BRIEF ENTRY
Zach Hunter 1991-
American Anti-Slavery Activist
Founder of Loose Change to Loosen Chains and
Author of *Be the Change*

EARLY YEARS
Zach Hunter was born in 1991 in Washington State. His parents are Gregg and Penny Hunter. His father is the vice president of public affairs for a non-profit organization. His mother is a marketing consultant. Zach has one sibling, Nate, who is seven years younger. Zach attended the Christian Fellowship

School in Ashburn, Virginia, but later transferred to the Providence Christian Academy in Lilburn, Georgia, located in suburban Atlanta. He lives in Suwanee, another suburb of Atlanta. In fall 2007, he entered the tenth grade. He has been a good student in school, getting mostly A's and B's. He enjoys playing tennis, listening to music, and reading.

MAJOR ACCOMPLISHMENTS

Twenty-First Century Slavery

Zach was 12 years old and in the seventh grade when he learned that even though slavery has long been outlawed, the modern world still supports the business of buying and selling human beings. He first became aware of this during Black History Month (February), when his school curriculum included information about the history of slavery. He learned about William Wilberforce, a member of the British Parliament during the 1800s who, although he had once been a slave trader, later fought long and hard to abolish slavery in England. He learned about Harriet Tubman, a former slave who led hundreds of people on a dangerous flight from slavery in the American South to freedom in the North and in Canada. He learned about Frederick Douglass, an African American who was born into slavery. Douglass later became one of the driving forces behind the American abolitionist movement of the 1800s, which sought to wipe out slavery and slave trade. One of Zach's favorite books is *The Diary of Frederick Douglass.*

>> *According to statistics from the United Nations, about 27 million people now live as slaves worldwide, with some 200,000 of them held captive in the United States. Roughly half of those counted as slaves are children.* <<

Zach was inspired by these heroes and felt that if he had been alive during the 1800s, he would certainly have joined them in their fight against slavery. Then he learned that slavery still exists and is even thriving in the modern world. The trans-Atlantic slave trade was abolished in 1807, and slavery was outlawed in the United States in 1865 and declared illegal worldwide by the United Nations in 1948. Yet, the proportion of the world's people who live as slaves today is actually higher than it was in the days of legal enslavement. According to statistics from the United Nations, about 27 million people now live as slaves worldwide, with some 200,000 of them held captive in the United States. Roughly half of those counted as slaves are children.

Although their bondage has no legal basis, these people are physically imprisoned or held by threats of violence against themselves or their family members. They are often tricked by false information about good jobs in faraway locations. Then when they travel long distances in search of these jobs, they are kidnapped or trapped. Their official identification papers may be taken from them, and they are then forced to work for the benefit of others, with no pay or other benefit to themselves. They may be told that they will be allowed to return home someday, but only after they have "earned" the freedom that was stolen from them. In some places, entire families are enslaved by unfair lending practices that force generations into unpaid work in order to pay off a debt. The jobs they must do are frequently dangerous, and they work long hours in conditions that are inhumane. Slaves are often imprisoned and used until they can no longer be productively exploited, then simply abandoned, or are forced to work until they die.

> "It's sickening that people are still owning other people and using them to do their work," he said. "It made me feel bad. But I didn't think it was enough just to feel bad. If I just had those emotions and didn't do anything with them then they would pretty much be worthless."

Zach was shocked to learn the truth about modern slavery. "It's sickening that people are still owning other people and using them to do their work," he said. "It made me feel bad. But I didn't think it was enough just to feel bad. If I just had those emotions and didn't do anything with them then they would pretty much be worthless."

Loose Change to Loosen Chains

Zach pondered what one teenager could do about the huge problem of global slavery. In a way the problem is harder to fight now than it was in the 1800s, because slavery is illegal and thus is more hidden from view. For help he turned to his mother, Penny Hunter, who then worked for the International Justice Mission (IJM), an organization that fights slavery as part of its overall mission to protect basic human rights around the world. Zach learned that in addition to the IJM, there are other modern organizations like Free the Slaves, Rugmark, and others that work to ex-

Students working to raise money for Loose Change to Loosen Chains. (Photo Credit: Ted Haddock/International Justice Mission®)

pose and smash slavery rings. He wanted to do whatever he could to support the work of these anti-slavery organizations, and most importantly, he wanted to alert other people to the reality that slavery does exist in the world today.

Zach hoped to accomplish both these goals with a program called Loose Change to Loosen Chains (LC2LC). According to *Real Simple* magazine, there may be as much as $10.5 billion lying around American homes in the form of loose change. Zach asked his classmates at the Christian Fellowship School in Ashburn, Virginia, to search their homes for loose change and bring it in to a fundraising drive at school. By doing so, they would raise money to donate to anti-slavery activist groups, and they would also raise awareness of this terrible problem. His initial drive was a success, bringing in more than $8,500 in just a little more than a month.

Zach wanted to do much more. He widened the scope of LC2LC by inviting other students around the world to set up similar drives in their schools, churches, and youth groups, using simple plastic cups to collect the change. He kept things simple and local. He provided those who wanted to help with the information they needed, entrusted them with the responsibility of handling the funds they collected, and let them decide which activist group would receive the cash they raised. Because of this approach, it is difficult to say how much LC2LC fundraising has now contributed toward the cause of abolishing slavery, but Zach has personally raised more than $20,000.

Talking about the success of LC2LC, Zach reflected, "I decided to take something as underestimated as loose change [and] as underestimated as the teenage years, [and] put them together. This is an important issue for my generation. Thanks to the media we have seen suffering up close and many of us feel compelled to do something about it. The main plan is to abolish slavery within my lifetime and I really believe that that can happen. This Loose Change to Loosen Chains campaign is really in my heart. It is something I am passionate about. People my age can really change things. It is sort of my dream for my generation."

Becoming a Public Speaker

Zach's commitment to fighting slavery didn't end with his creation of LC2LC. At about the same time as Zach was starting his abolitionist efforts, the life story of the British abolitionist William Wilberforce was released as the film *Amazing Grace*. The film led to several anti-slavery actions, including The Amazing Change Campaign and The Better Hour—both movements designed to raise awareness about modern slavery and bring it to an end. Hunter became the youth spokesman for both The Amazing Change Campaign and The Better Hour. With The Amazing Change Campaign, he became an energetic promoter of their anti-slavery petition and presented it at a White House Policy Roundtable on Human Trafficking. There were more than 100,000 signatures on the petition, mostly those of students like Zach.

> "I decided to take something as underestimated as loose change [and] as underestimated as the teenage years, [and] put them together. This is an important issue for my generation. Thanks to the media we have seen suffering up close and many of us feel compelled to do something about it."

Just a few years before he founded LC2LC, Zach had been considered a shy child. "I was deathly afraid to get up in front of a class and do a book report," he recalled. He had even struggled with an anxiety disorder that sometimes left him feeling weak and nauseated. Taking his message about slavery to the world, Zach now speaks to groups ranging from school assemblies to huge crowds at music festivals and other events. He

Hunter speaking to students at a music festival in Wisconsin. (Photo Credit: Ted Haddock/International Justice Mission®)

has even appeared on national television several times and has been honored as a modern day hero by CNN. A Christian, he gives God credit for his newfound self-confidence. He recalled one incident where he felt very afraid to get up before the crowd he was supposed to address, and his mother told him that it was okay to back out of the commitment. He considered doing so for a moment, then realized that if he gave in to his nervousness, the message that slavery needs to be fought would fail to reach the people in that large audience. Zach went on stage. Now, he said, "I don't usually get nervous speaking," and he has spoken to hundreds of thousands of people.

Graphic Stories about Slavery

When Zach gives a speech, he tries to reach the hearts of his listeners. He holds up a pair of small shackles designed to be locked around the ankles of a child who might be no more than five years old. These are not historical artifacts from a museum, but real tools used to enslave people today, he points out. "What if it were you, or your best friend, or your brother, or your mom?" he asks. "What if your feet were shackled together all day long as you sit on a dirt floor rolling cigarettes? What if you had to dive down to the bottom of the river to untangle your masters' fishing nets, after your best friend had just drowned the day before doing the same thing?"

Zach often tells the story of Rakesh, an Indian boy who was kept captive in a rug factory. Rakesh and other children were kept from school and forced to work on the looms, which have strings stretched so tight that the workers' fingers are frequently cut and bloody from working with them. Thanks to the efforts of modern abolitionists, Rakesh and his fellow child-slaves were freed. Zach tells of children enslaved because their parents were too poor to feed them or were in debt. He tells of entire families who work all day long crushing boulders into gravel or making bricks in red-hot kilns. He tells of the many children who are forced to work as servants, soldiers, and even prostitutes.

> *"What if it were you, or your best friend, or your brother, or your mom?"* Hunter asked. *"What if your feet were shackled together all day long as you sit on a dirt floor rolling cigarettes? What if you had to dive down to the bottom of the river to untangle your masters' fishing nets, after your best friend had just drowned the day before doing the same thing?"*

His busy public speaking schedule means that Zach sometimes has to miss school. While some of his teachers are supportive, it can still be very difficult to keep up, so his parents have tried to limit his travel to weekends and summers. He works hard to balance his priorities at school with his desire to change the world.

Zach's Book: *Be the Change*

Trying to extend the reach of his message even further, Zach published a book in 2007. *Be the Change: Your Guide to Freeing Slaves and Changing the World* is full of facts, short entries about inspirational people from the past and present, and large and small ideas for making positive changes in the world. Quotes from Wilberforce and other early abolitionists are side-by-side with narratives from people who have escaped modern-day slavery, and there is also material that is not specifically about slavery, but simply about using passion to do great things.

"It's about world-changers . . . people who have really made a difference," Zach said of his book. "It's to inspire kids to get involved. I have questions at the end and personal reflections about it. Each of the chapters has a theme like courage or influence or compassion. It's geared toward teens but I'd be glad to have anyone read it." Zach is also working on his second book, *Generation: Change,* which is scheduled to come out in 2008. In addition, he blogs for *Breakaway Magazine.*

> *Hunter passionately hopes that many people will get involved in spreading the message about modern slavery. "Just get educated," he urged. "Tell everyone you know about it. Information is one of the most powerful tools against slavery."*

Future Plans

In addition to carrying on with school, his public speaking, and his work with LC2LC, Zach hopes to travel to India or Africa soon and also to film a documentary. He passionately hopes that many people will get involved in spreading the message about modern slavery. "Just get educated," he urged. "Tell everyone you know about it. Information is one of the most powerful tools against slavery." Although the issue of slavery is the most important one to him, he knows that it is vital for people to work on other issues as well. "There are so many great things out there, but I usually encourage people to just get involved with one specific thing. It can be very overwhelming to take on a lot of causes at once. I encourage people to find one cause they are passionate about and dedicate their lives to that."

Zach has great faith in the ability of teenagers to get things done. "I believe that we can be written about in the history books as a generation that put ourselves behind and thought of other people instead of ourselves," he stated. Sometimes the special power of young people comes directly from their lack of experience, he explained: "As you get older, you become more familiar with reality, and it just doesn't seem realistic that you can abolish slavery." Creating LC2LC as a student-led movement was, in part, because "adults, as nice as they are, can sometimes be wet blankets. But since students are resource-poor and have passion, and adults are often passion-poor and have resources, together we can be a deadly combination."

Zach's book is a guide for others interested in learning more about slavery and abolition.

WRITINGS

Be the Change: Your Guide to Freeing Slaves and Changing the World, 2007

FURTHER READING

Books

Hunter, Zach. *Be the Change: Your Guide to Freeing Slaves and Changing the World,* 2007

Periodicals

Atlanta Journal-Constitution, Feb. 25, 2007
Christian Science Monitor, Feb. 21, 2007

Online Articles

http://www.abcnews.go.com
   (ABC News, transcript of interview with Zach Hunter from *Good Morning America,* Mar. 15, 2007)
http://www.christiantoday.com
   (Christian Today, "Meet Zach Hunter—The Teenage Abolitionist," Feb. 22, 2007)
http://www.cnn.com/SPECIALS/2007/cnn.heroes
   (CNN.com, "CNN Heroes Gallery: Young Wonder," no date)
http://www.publishersweekly.com
   (Publishers Weekly Online, "Abolitionist Teen Speaks out against Modern-Day Slavery," Feb. 21, 2007)

ADDRESS

Zach Hunter
Zondervan Publishing
5300 Patterson Avenue SE
Grand Rapids, MI 49530

WORLD WIDE WEB SITES

http://www.myspace.com/lc2lc
http://www.lc2lc.com

Bindi Irwin 1998-

Australian Wildlife Enthusiast
Host of the TV Series "Bindi the Jungle Girl" and
"Planet's Best with Terri and Bindi"

BIRTH

Bindi Sue Irwin was born on July 24, 1998, in Queensland, Australia. Her father, Steve Irwin, was an Australian-born animal expert. He was best known for his television program, "The Crocodile Hunter," an internationally broadcast wildlife documentary series. Steve Irwin co-hosted the program with Bindi's mother, Terri Raines Irwin, an American-born conservationist. The couple owned and operated the Australia Zoo, a giant wildlife park. Terri Irwin has continued to run the zoo since Steve Irwin's death in 2005. Bindi has a younger brother, Robert.

Bindi's name means "young girl" in the language spoken by Aborigines, the indigenous people of Australia. Steve Irwin once named a female crocodile "Bindi" that he caught in Aboriginal territory. He moved the crocodile to the zoo for its protection. Years later, when his daughter was born, "he saw how tiny and sweet and special she was," Terri Irwin recalled, "and [he] said, 'I have to name her Bindi after my favorite crocodile.'" Bindi's middle name, Sue, was also inspired by an animal—her father's pet dog, Suey.

EARLY CHILDHOOD

Bindi has been around cameras since her birth. Determined not to be absentee parents, Steve and Terri Irwin made a point of bringing Bindi along on their many field trips for "The Crocodile Hunter" and other wildlife projects. Six days after she was born, the Irwins took Bindi to Fraser Island, off the coast of Australia, where they were filming a documentary about wildlife. By the time she was a year old, Bindi had made 110 airplane trips, including 10 visits to the United States. "It's exciting doing things with Bindi because you can experience things through a child's eyes," Terri Irwin said.

> "She is remarkably gifted with animals," Terri Irwin said when Bindi was only two years old. "Her dad's got the gift and she's got the same gift—whether it's koalas, camels, or crocodiles."

Steve Irwin was famous for capturing crocodiles and many other endangered species in order to save them from poachers (people who illegally kill wildlife for profit). "My daughter is going to grow up doing this," Irwin said, when Bindi was just a toddler. "There's this shot of me with Bindi and a big croc, and he's all teeth.... She's like 'Oooh!' It's sure to make some mothers cringe." In fact, several years later, Steve Irwin was criticized in the media for holding Bindi's little brother, Robert, too close to a crocodile. But Irwin insisted that he only brought his children into controlled situations and would never put them in danger.

Irwin brought many of the animals he captured to the Australian Zoo. As directors of the zoo, Steve and Terri Irwin tried to duplicate the animals'

BINDI IRWIN

Bindi at age four with her parents, Terri and Steve Irwin.

natural habitats as much as possible, without the use of cages or pens. Visitors to the zoo can mingle with koala bears, feed the kangaroos, and pet the non-poisonous snakes. Bindi has grown up surrounded by the zoo's wildlife, which became her earliest playmates. "She is remarkably gifted with animals," Terri Irwin said when Bindi was only two years old. "Her dad's got the gift and she's got the same gift—whether it's koalas, camels, or crocodiles."

One of Bindi's first pets was a small carpet python, which she liked to cuddle and kiss. One day the snake bit her nose. "She just looked very surprised," her mother recalled. "Then she kissed it again and it bit her lip. She learned a valuable lesson, that some snakes bite." To Bindi's parents, learning to handle animals with respect was very important. Her father often told her "to treat animals as you would like to be treated."

When Bindi was three years old, her father built her a two-story treehouse. As Bindi has grown, she has spent more and more time there. "I love it in my treehouse," she said. "It's the best place to be, pretty much. I just go there to sleep over sometimes. My little brother comes to visit me for a little sleepover as well." Many of Bindi's pets spend time with her in the treehouse, too. "I have Blackie, my black-headed python," Bindi said. "I also have Cornie the snake. He sleeps with me at night. I also have Jaffa, my koala (bear), and Ocker, my favorite cockatoo. And I have other birds that stay with me. And Candy, my pet rat, sometimes stays with me."

EDUCATION

Bindi is home-schooled by a teacher on the zoo grounds. When she is traveling for wildlife filming, the teacher accompanies her. Her favorite subject is creative writing. By the time she was six, she was writing a journal of her adventures called "Bindi's Say," which her father posted on his web site.

In addition to her schoolwork, Bindi has daily chores when she's at home on the zoo grounds. She checks on many of the animals, including the shingle-back skinks, the large lizards that are among her favorite animals at the zoo. To make sure all the skinks are accounted for in their enclosure, she digs up sand, lifts rocks, and moves small logs.

CAREER HIGHLIGHTS

By the time she was seven, Bindi was no longer just watching her father interact with animals during his film shoots—she was often an active participant. She was such a natural presence on camera, and so fearless around the wildlife, that her parents decided that she ought to have a television series of her own. Steve Irwin negotiated a deal with the Discovery Channel for a show, and filming for "Bindi the Jungle Girl" began in 2005.

The premise of the series is to show children how animals live around the world and describe the efforts of wildlife lovers to protect them. "I get to grow up with animals," Bindi said. "I can teach people. I'm not an actor, I'm a teacher. I can teach people about animals."

The Death of Steve Irwin

Before "Jungle Girl" ever aired, however, Bindi's father was killed. On September 4, 2005, Steve Irwin and a cameraman were filming dangerous sea creatures in the waters off Queensland, Australia. A 220-pound stingray suddenly became defensive and thrust the 8-inch poisonous barb on its tail upward, striking Irwin in the heart. Irwin pulled the barb out, but the damage was too great, and he soon died.

At the time of the accident, Bindi was in Tasmania, the island-state off Australia, with her mother and brother. Devastated by her father's death, Bindi nonetheless found the courage to speak at his funeral. "My daddy was my hero," she said. "He was always there for me when I needed him. He listened to me and taught me to do many things. But most of all he was fun. I know that daddy had an important job. He was working to change the world so that everyone would love wildlife like he did.... I don't want daddy's passion to ever end. I want to help endangered wildlife just like he did."

Deciding to Continue with "Jungle Girl"

Bindi, like her mother, believed the death of her father was a freak accident and the animal was not to blame. But the question of whether to continue filming "Jungle Girl" remained. Terri Irwin said that she discussed it with Bindi before coming to a decision. "Grief is a road every individual travels in their own way," she told the *Times* of London. "Bindi said that she wanted to get back to filming right away. We wanted to get right back out there and stand proud."

Over the next year, preparation for Bindi's show continued. A two-level treehouse, based on the treehouse built by her father, was assembled as the main "Jungle Girl" set. It features tree branches and bushes, along with a bedroom, a long wooden table with a computer, bean bag chairs, and a play area. "All of her animal friends, from iguana and snakes and wombats—everything comes to visit her," her mother said.

> "My daddy was my hero," Bindi said. "He was always there for me when I needed him. He listened to me and taught me to do many things. But most of all he was fun."

"Bindi the Jungle Girl" debuted on the Discovery Kids cable channel in July 2007. A good deal of the program is devoted to film of animals in the wild, including whales, elephants, lions, tigers, orangutans, big birds like macaws, and small lizards like the gecko. Steve Irwin is featured in early episodes, filmed prior to his death, doing things like helping an injured lion and climbing trees to visit the nests of endangered orangutans. Continuing the family tradition, Bindi and her mother also travel around the globe to show viewers wildlife in its natural habitat. In those settings, Bindi says she always follows her father's words of caution: "if it's out in the wilderness, like snakes, leave it alone, and just look at it. Don't touch it."

Bindi also narrates many stories close to home, such as animal dental care at the Australia Zoo. "I'm trying to get across the message that 'don't be

Bindi with the Crocmen, the backup band for her Discovery Kids TV show.

afraid of animals,'" she said. "Some people think that I would be afraid of them, but I'm never ever afraid of an animal. I just get excited."

In each "Jungle Girl" episode, Bindi sings and dances to animal-themed songs with the show's backup band, called the Crocmen. Another program feature is "Bindi's Video Blog," in which she answers email questions sent to her at discovery.com. Bindi works hard on "Jungle Girl," but she does not mind the effort. "I love it!" she said about her TV show. "Animals are my friends, and this means I get to be with all my friends."

In his enthusiastic review in the *Chicago Sun Times*, Doug Elfman wrote, "'Jungle Girl' moves fast, as you'd expect of a kid's show, but it's smooth, sleek, stylish, and mesmerizing. Like 'The Crocodile Hunter,' it's environmentally conscious education completely disguised as amazing, upbeat entertainment."

Other Projects

Bindi hosted a television special called "My Daddy the Crocodile Hunter," which aired in June 2007 on the Animal Planet cable channel. The program featured family video clips of Steve Irwin and his family interacting with animals and teaching Bindi and her brother how to care for wildlife habitats. There was also film of Bindi assisting her father on his last crocodile research adventure in August 2006.

Also in June 2007, Animal Planet began featuring Bindi and her mother as co-hosts of "Planet's Best with Bindi and Terri." On this Sunday evening program, the Irwins introduce documentaries and specials about wildlife and the people who work with them. The films, which come from Animal Planet's extensive library of previously seen shows, span the globe. Bindi and her mother discuss the films from their home at the Australia Zoo. They also give viewers a glimpse of the many animals on the zoo property and answer questions people send in about wildlife issues.

In August 2007 Bindi introduced a new children's clothing line called Bindi Wear International, which is sold online at the Australia Zoo web site. All profits from the clothing go to support the zoo's conservation programs. "My daddy was working to change the world so everyone would love wildlife like he did," Bindi said. "Now it's our turn to help." The clothing line is designed by Pamela DiStasi, an Irwin family friend. The clothes feature animal prints and themes and include messages about wildlife and environmental conservation written in Bindi's handwriting.

In addition to appearing on TV, Bindi has also appeared with her backup band, the Crocmen, in a live stage show. The first performances were staged in 2007 in Australia and the United States. Bindi sang and danced in the show, which had an animal theme. "I just like the feeling of all the people actually cheering for me and saying, 'Bindi, Bindi.' ... I just feel like I've got a place there," she said. "It feels really good when I get on stage." The shows have included appearances by her mother, who brings animals on stage to show the audiences, and by the Australian musical groups the Wiggles and the Qantas Choir.

> *According to reviewer Doug Elfman, "'Jungle Girl' moves fast, as you'd expect of a kid's show, but it's smooth, sleek, stylish and mesmerizing. Like 'The Crocodile Hunter,' it's environmentally conscious education completely disguised as amazing, upbeat entertainment."*

Bindi's stage shows in the United States were scheduled around speaking appearances that she did on behalf of the Australian tourism board, to attract American visitors to Australia. She also spoke as an advocate of wildlife preservation. The youngest person ever to speak to the National Press Club in Washington DC, Bindi told the assembled reporters, "It is very sad that in my lifetime a lot of wildlife could disappear. We could lose tigers and gorillas and even my favorite koalas. We need to help my daddy's work and make this world a perfect place for animals."

Is It Too Much?

The adults who help guide Bindi's career have faced criticism that she is working too hard and that she is being denied a normal childhood. According to Catherine Dawson March, a columnist for the Canadian newspaper the *Globe and Mail*, "Bindi Irwin, the nine-year-old daughter of crocodile hunter Steve Irwin, seems a little too 'on' for her age, a little too ebullient, and isn't it a little early to be hosting your own wildlife series when your dad's been dead only a year?" Other critics have speculated that Bindi has been pushed into several projects at once as a way to continue Steve Irwin's money-making wildlife activities. John Stainton, the family's career manager, dismisses the criticism as unfounded, saying that she has been eager to spread her father's conservation message. "I think they (critics) don't understand that this little girl is very much enjoying what she is doing. She is in control," Stainton told the *Gold Coast Bulletin*.

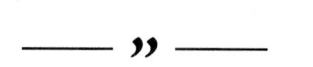

> "It is very sad that in my lifetime a lot of wildlife could disappear. We could lose tigers and gorillas and even my favorite koalas. We need to help my daddy's work and make this world a perfect place for animals."

Terri Irwin has also weighed in on this issue, telling the *Times* of London, "I think Bindi's schedule is a lot easier than a lot of children's. There's a lot of kids who have soccer practices, dance lessons, and parents start feeling like a chauffeur and kids start to feel overwhelmed. Bindi is certainly not like that."

For her part, Bindi insists that she enjoys working with animals and traveling with her mother and brother to different parts of the world. "I just love this life so much!" she said. "I couldn't stand it if I was in an apartment with a goldfish!"

When asked what she wants do when she grows up, Bindi didn't hesitate. "Exactly what I am doing now," she said. "I want to be what my dad was. I want to do wildlife stuff, pretty much."

HOME AND FAMILY

Bindi lives with her mother and brother, Robert, in a house on the grounds of the Australia Zoo, a neighborhood that Bindi loves. "Every morning I wake up to elephants screeching and tigers chuffing—they don't roar, they chuff," she said. "As soon as you walk outside the front door, you've got the whole zoo, which is very nice." Bindi and Robert watch a video of their father every day while they eat breakfast. "We've got so much terrific footage of Steve, that he'll be part of our conservation work forever," Terri Irwin said. "And it's great to know, for kids particularly, that when your hero dies, everything he stood for lives on." During her spare time, Bindi takes piano lessons and martial arts lessons, and she is also learning how to surf.

SELECTED CREDITS

Bindi Kidfitness, 2006 (DVD)
"Bindi the Jungle Girl," 2007- present (TV series)
"Animal Planet's Best with Bindi and Terri," 2007- present (TV series)
"My Daddy the Crocodile Hunter," 2007 (TV special)

FURTHER READING

Periodicals

Chicago Sun Times, June 6, 2007, p.43
Daily Telegraph (Australia), Sep. 9, 2000, p. 120; Sep. 21, 2006, p.2; July 18, 2007, p.6
Globe and Mail (Toronto), Sep. 28, 2007, p.R39
Gold Coast Bulletin (Australia), Sep. 12, 2002; Oct. 17, 2006, p.3
New York Post, Sep. 5, 2006, p.2
People, Oct. 16, 2000, p.93; Oct. 30, 2006, p.72; June 18, 2007, p.133
Pretoria News (South Africa), July 4, 2007, p.6
Times (London), Jan. 20, 2007, p.50
Women's Wear Daily, Aug. 14, 2007, p.14

ADDRESS

Bindi Irwin
Discovery Kids
7700 Wisconsin Avenue
Bethesda, MD 20814

WORLD WIDE WEB SITES

http://www.australiazoo.com
http://kids.discovery.com/tv/bindi
http://animal.discovery.com/tv/planets-best/planets-best.html
http://www.crocodilehunter.com.au/crocodile_hunter/about_steve_terri/bindi_say.html

JONAS BROTHERS
Kevin Jonas 1987-
Joseph Jonas 1989-
Nick Jonas 1992-
American Rock Band

BIRTH

The Jonas Brothers band includes three members: Paul Kevin Jonas, known as Kevin, was born on November 5, 1987, in Teaneck, New Jersey; Joseph Adam Jonas was born on August 15, 1989, in Casa Grande, Arizona; and Nicholas Jerry Jonas, known as Nick, was born on September 16, 1992, in Dallas, Texas. They also have a younger brother, Frankie, whom they call "the bonus Jonas." Frankie is eight years younger than

Nick. Their father, Kevin Jonas, is an evangelical minister. He was the co-founder of Christ for the Nations Music and also served as a worship leader for that organization in Dallas. He was later pastor of an Assembly of God church in Wyckoff, New Jersey. Their mother, Denise Jonas, is a sign-language teacher.

YOUTH

The Jonas family lived in Wyckoff, New Jersey, for some years before the boys started their band. Wyckoff is close to New York City, where they spent a lot of time. Music has always been important in the Jonas family. Both parents sang church music, and the boys' father co-founded a Christian music ministry. Each of the brothers recalls feeling strongly drawn to performance at an early age. Kevin, the trio's lead guitarist, remembers being home sick from school, finding a guitar and a how-to-play book, and learning the basic chords after about three days of practicing. "The moment I picked up a guitar," he said, "that was the minute I knew I wanted to do this for the rest of my life." Nick says that from the time he was about two years old, he would wake up in the morning and start singing for the rest of the day. "I'd watch *Peter Pan*, the VHS of the Broadway version, and I'd have a temper tantrum if anybody turned it off," he said.

> "The moment I picked up a guitar," Kevin said, "that was the minute I knew I wanted to do this for the rest of my life."

EDUCATION

Before becoming a touring act, the Jonas Brothers attended the East Christian School in North Haledon, New Jersey. After they formed the band and became a touring act, they were homeschooled. Using curriculum from Accelerated Christian Education, they study with parents and tutors, juggling coursework with touring and rehearsing. Kevin, the eldest, has earned his diploma. Balancing the demand of performing with the demands of school is hard, said Nick, "but we find a way to get it done. You have to be really disciplined (about school work). We remember we have to get it done, but have a big opportunity, too, with music."

FIRST JOBS

Nick Jonas was at the barber for a haircut one day, and as usual, he was singing a song. Another customer at the shop heard him and was so impressed with his voice that she referred him to a talent manager. It wasn't long before Nick was landing roles in Broadway productions. Joseph Jonas, the middle brother, had aspired to be a member of a comedy troupe, but after seeing his younger brother in a Broadway musical, he decided to audition for stage roles, too. He soon won a part in Baz Luhrmann's Broadway production of the opera *La Boheme*. The Jonas brothers also worked together in television commercials, including advertisements for Burger King, Clorox bleach, LEGO toys, and Battle Bots.

Nick's strong vocal skills earned him roles in the casts of several Broadway shows, including *Annie Get Your Gun, Beauty and the Beast, A Christmas Carol,* and *Les Miserables*. It was his singing on a cast album of *Beauty and the Beast* that brought him to the attention of Johnny Wright, the man who had also created the pop bands Backstreet Boys and *N Sync. Soon after that his solo demo CD landed on the desk of Steve Greenberg, the new president of Columbia Records.

Columbia signed Nick to a contract and began planning an album for this new talent. After hearing some songs Nick had written with Joseph and Kevin, record company representatives asked all three brothers to come for an audition. In the end, they signed a group contract. "I didn't like the record he'd made," Greenberg said about Nick's initial solo demo. "But his voice stuck out, so I met with him and found out he had two brothers." Greenberg had discovered Hanson, so he knew how to handle a family act. "I liked the idea of putting together this little garage-rock band and making a record that nodded to the Ramones and '70s punk. So Michael Mangini and I went into the studio with the Jonas Brothers and did it."

> *Balancing the demand of performing with the demands of school is hard,* said Nick, *"but we find a way to get it done. You have to be really disciplined (about school work). We remember we have to get it done, but have a big opportunity, too, with music."*

CAREER HIGHLIGHTS

In July 2005, the Jonas Brothers began performing as a band. Even though Nick and Joe had already faced major audiences on Broadway, performing in a rock band was a very different experience. They broke in their act with short sets at the Bloomfield Avenue Café in Montclair, New Jersey, and played their first full-length concert in Acton, Massachusetts. They also

BIOGRAPHY TODAY • 2008 Annual Cumulation

Kevin, Nick, and Joe at the 2007 Teen Choice Awards.

toured and made appearances with other musical acts during the summer of 2005, including Jesse McCartney, Aly & AJ, the Veronicas, the Backstreet Boys, and the Click Five.

The boys' good looks undoubtedly won them some fans, but they also showed that they had legitimate musical talent from the start. They wrote their own songs, played their own instruments, and sang their own lyrics. The result was a high-energy sound that had a grunge/garage-band edge, with powerful guitar work from Kevin, catchy hooks, and strong harmonies. Lead vocals were shared by Nicholas and Joseph, while Kevin contributed backup.

The Jonas Brothers were very busy in 2006. In April, they released their first album, titled *It's About Time.* They also participated in the government campaign "What's Your Anti-Drug?" which took them to schools around the country. Late in the summer, they made an appearance at the Revelation Generation Christian Rock Festival in Frenchtown, New Jersey. In December, they went to Germany as part of a USO tour designed to reach children of military personnel, educating them about the music business and encouraging them to pursue their dreams. In addition, their music was featured in the made-for-TV Nickelodeon movie *Zoey 101: Spring Break-up.*

It's About Time

The Jonas Brothers' first CD, *It's About Time,* was released in 2006. They wrote about 60 songs before settling on the seven that, along with four tunes not written by them, made the final cut. Several of the songs had a time-related theme. For example, "7:05" is about the way the exact moment of meeting someone special might be etched in your mind. "Time for Me to Fly" celebrates reaching the moment when dreams come true. "Year 3000" is about meeting a time traveler, and "6 Minutes" reflects on the range of emotions that a person can go through in a very short time when attracted to somebody new. Other songs on the album included "Underdog," about an unpopular girl who will eventually go on to do great things in the world; "Dear God," a plea for guidance in life; and "Mandy," a tribute to a girl the boys knew in real life. Mandy had been Nick's best friend when they were younger and had dated Joe for a while. They made three different videos to support the hard-driving song, and the real Mandy even made an appearance.

Reviewing *It's About Time* for the *Virginian-Pilot,* Hilary Saunders called it "a surprisingly impressive debut" considering the young ages of the band members. Another reviewer, Angelique Moon, wrote in *Soundings:* "With its upbeat, catchy vibe, vocal harmonies, and mature, thought-provoking lyrics, it's a great choice to introduce listeners to this up-and-coming pop punk rock band. It'll be hard to not want to listen to the blend between Nick's strong powerhouse voice, Joseph's cooler, smooth rock pipes, and Kevin's killer guitar handlings."

> As reviewer Angelique Moon wrote in **Soundings:** "With its upbeat, catchy vibe, vocal harmonies, and mature, thought-provoking lyrics, it's a great choice to introduce listeners to this up-and-coming pop punk rock band. It'll be hard to not want to listen to the blend between Nick's strong powerhouse voice, Joseph's cooler, smooth rock pipes, and Kevin's killer guitar handlings."

Despite the band's solid appeal and growing fan base, *It's About Time* didn't sell particularly well. Steve Greenberg, the executive at Columbia Records who had taken an interest in the band, had left the company. After that, there was little in the way of traditional promotion or radio airplay for the album. Only about 62,000 copies were sold, and *It's About Time* went out of print when the boys left Columbia to sign with Hollywood Records in 2007.

Disney Connection

Hollywood Records, the band's new home, is owned by Disney, a company that has proven its skill at promoting young stars. Raven-Symone, Miley Cyrus, and the Cheetah Girls are some of the company's success stories. The first project they worked on with Hollywood Records was "Kids of the Future," a remake of the song "Kids of America." It was to be used on the soundtrack for the Disney film *Meet the Robinsons*. According to Joe, making the video to go with that song "was cool because we shot the whole thing in front of a greenscreen and they added the futuristic things behind us [later]."

Until then, the Jonas Brothers had received almost no airplay on traditional radio. Now, their music began to be heavily rotated on the satellite music channel, Radio Disney, and in videos featured on the Disney Channel. They also had a guest appearance on the popular Disney television program "Hannah Montana."

Jonas Brothers

In addition to being strongly promoted by Disney, the Jonas Brothers got even more publicity when it signed a multimillion-dollar deal to endorse

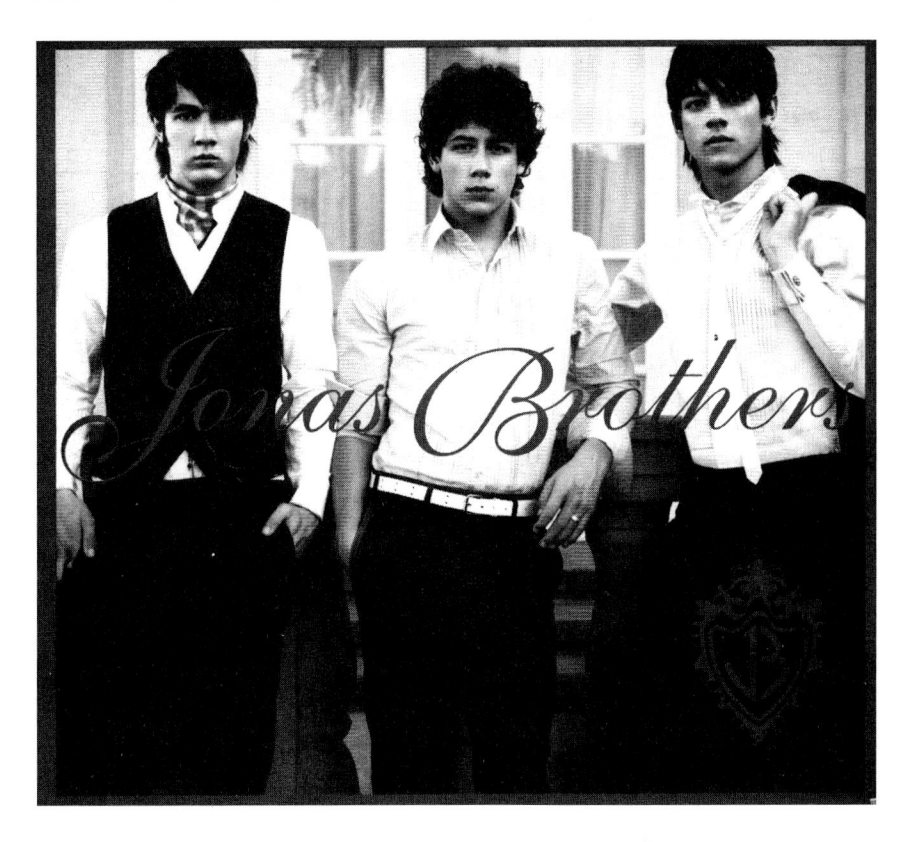

Their second CD, Jonas Brothers, *was a hit with fans and critics when released in 2007.*

the popular candy, Baby Bottle Pop. The band appeared in television commercials for the candy and in special videos and downloads available on the Baby Bottle Pop web site. The company also sponsored the band's 2007 "Invasion" tour, which featured songs from their first album from Hollywood Records, *Jonas Brothers.*

Unlike their debut album, *Jonas Brothers* was put together relatively quickly—in about a month's time. The CD was released on August 7, 2007, and debuted at No. 5 on the Billboard 200 list, with two hit singles—"Hold On" and "S.O.S."—leading the way. The album contains a mix of power pop and ballads that showed the band was just on the verge of stardom, according to many observers. *Los Angeles Times* writer Mikael Wood called the band "Green Day minus curse words," while a *USA Today* critic described their music as "pure power-pop ear candy." Another reviewer, Jay Lustig, commented in the *Newark Star-Ledger:* "Like a lot of their peers, they have grown up amid the ubiquity of boy-band pop and emo-punk. And they see no reason not to combine the two. Their sound is glossy but not sappy, and their vocals can be sweet or snarling."

Writing about the hit song "S.O.S." in *Billboard* magazine, critic Chuck Taylor summed up the band's appeal like this: "With its manic faux-wave beat, storytelling lyric about a broken heart primed for healing, and ready-made teen idol vocals from 17-year-old Joe Jonas, the latter song's appeal is just opening the door for the phenom in store for the sibling threesome. These dudes have it all: versatility, youth, looks, and hooks. Truly a match made in pop heaven."

Stage Presence

Two years after putting their act together, the Jonas Brothers are now confident and happy performing as a rock band. Their shows are high-energy events. "I'm pretty much stationary," Kevin said, "just singing and playing my guitar. But Joseph and Nick, they run and do a ton. They jump around all over the place. Sometimes, if someone in the front row isn't paying attention, Joseph will run over and tap her on the shoulder and just start singing in her face. . . . It's a way to get everyone involved."

> "Joseph just has this really cool, smooth rock voice," Nick said. "He really knows how to get the crowd going. Kevin is the one that holds us all together. Joseph and I are the singers and we take turns on keyboards and percussion, but Kevin mostly plays the guitar and that's the part of the group that we need—he's the glue that keeps it together."

Nick offered his analysis of the group's appeal: "Joseph just has this really cool, smooth rock voice. . . . He really knows how to get the crowd going. Kevin is the one that holds us all together. Joseph and I are the singers and we take turns on keyboards and percussion, but Kevin mostly plays the guitar and that's the part of the group that we need—he's the glue that keeps it together."

Thanks to their good looks, the boys do have some girls who follow them from show to show, but they aren't too comfortable with attention for their looks. "We wear rings on our fingers that are purity rings, so we stay pure until marriage," Joe pointed out. He also noted that their appeal isn't limited to girls. "Guys will always come up to us after a show and say, 'Dude—

Performing onstage at Six Flags—Magic Mountain.

you rock,' which is great." Above all, he said, "We want to be a good influence.... We want people to have a good time with our music."

While the brothers' Christian faith is not at the forefront of their lyrics, it is definitely an influence on their overall tone and is a vital part of their daily lives and their performances. Although their songs thus far haven't been particularly religious, Kevin has said that "we hope to break into the Christian market after we've had success in the pop market." Joe said that before every show, "We pray that the sound is fine, that we have the right energy." They call the last 45 minutes before show time "lockdown," and as Joe explained, "It's just us and no one comes in and no one goes out. It's a cool time to get focused and we just get psyched and really excited about the show."

Future Plans

The future for the Jonas Brothers looks very positive, as Disney continues to give the band strong support. A TV special, *Jonas Brothers in Concert,* premiered in late 2007. A series pilot has been filmed for a television show called "J.O.N.A.S.," an acronym for Junior Operatives Networking As

Spies. This comedy/spy series will feature their music as well as funny and exciting adventures involving their work as espionage agents. In addition, the band is slated to star in *Camp Rock*, a Disney Channel original musical movie that is planned for 2008.

The brothers are enjoying their growing success and continue to appreciate it on a daily basis. "We wake up every day and we freak out," admitted Joseph. "You can't wake up and say, 'Oh, another show in front of fans.' We don't take any of this for granted. It's such a blessing. It's seriously our dream come true."

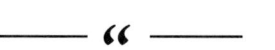

> "We wake up every day and we freak out," admitted Joseph. "You can't wake up and say, 'Oh, another show in front of fans.' We don't take any of this for granted. It's such a blessing. It's seriously our dream come true."

HOME AND FAMILY

The Jonases still own their home in Wyckoff, but since the boys' career has taken off, the family has moved their home base to Los Angeles, California. "We're still New Jersey boys at heart," Nick commented.

The Jonas family is close-knit. One parent usually travels with the boys as they tour, and their tour manager is an uncle. Although their music has a punk sound, Nick says that on the whole, the boys are "good about not getting into trouble—we don't see the point." Their parents don't hesitate to discipline them, according to Nick. "They do not mind grounding us from our cell phones and TV—not me too much, because I'm a good kid—but Kevin and Joe get their cell phones grounded almost every day, just for being stupid, I guess, not taking out the trash or washing dishes."

The brothers are happy to perform together, because as family members, according to Nick, "You have a security that everything is going to be okay, even when you mess up." Kevin said that "It feels like the most natural thing we could be doing. When we write a song we get in a triangle. I start playing the chords that we've chosen over and over and then we'll keep going around in a circle until we have figured out the lyrics for our song." Joseph offered his perspective: "We're brothers so it's not like if we got upset at each other that we can be like, 'well I quit.' They're still my brothers. We love to do this and we know we're going to keep doing it for a very long time."

"I think we definitely fit in because we're different," Nick reflected. "We're not trying to be the next somebody. We're trying to be the Jonas brothers, and people enjoy that. There's nothing like us out there, and they appreciate our creativeness."

MEMORABLE EXPERIENCES

In November, 2005, Nick was diagnosed with Type 1 diabetes. Diabetes is a medical condition that occurs when the body does not produce enough insulin, a substance that is needed to convert sugar into energy the body can use. Before his diagnosis, Nick had the classic symptoms of the disorder: rapid weight loss (15 pounds in two weeks), extreme thirst (he was drinking 20 to 30 bottles of water a day), and extreme irritability. Nick was scared by his diagnosis, wondering if diabetes could even cause him to die.

He was admitted to the hospital to learn about his condition and how to control it. At first, he was required to give himself as many as ten insulin injections a day. Later, he switched to the use of an Omni Pod, a "smart pump" device that is worn as a patch on the skin. Controlled by a handheld, wireless device that looks something like an iPod, the Omni Pod can monitor blood sugar levels and deliver the correct dosages of insulin automatically, without the need for injections.

> "At first, I was worried that diabetes would keep me from performing and recording and doing everything a teenager likes to do, but, my career is really ramping up," Nick said. "I want to let kids know that it doesn't have to be so hard. The most important thing is to never ever let yourself get down about having diabetes, because you can live a really great life as a kid with diabetes."

Nick went public with his condition in March 2007, while playing at the Diabetes Research Institute's Carnival for a Cure, held in New York City. Asking for a show of hands from people in the audience who had diabetes, he then surprised the crowd by raising his own hand. "At first, I was worried that diabetes would keep me from performing and recording and doing everything a teenager likes to do, but, my career is really ramping up," Nick said. "I want to let kids know that it doesn't have to be so hard. The most important thing is to never ever let yourself get down about having diabetes, because you can live a really great life as a kid with diabetes."

FAVORITE MUSIC

The Jonas brothers enjoy a wide range of music, including Weird Al Yankovic, Backstreet Boys, My Chemical Romance, Stevie Wonder, Sham '69, the Ramones, Switchfoot, Coldplay, Fall Out Boy, Motion City Soundtrack, and Jack's Mannequin.

HOBBIES AND OTHER INTERESTS

When they aren't busy with music, the boys enjoy playing Xbox 360, basketball and other sports, and making movies.

SELECTED RECORDINGS

It's About Time, 2006
Zoey 101: Music Mix, 2006 (contributor)
Jonas Brothers, 2007
Meet the Robinsons, 2007 (soundtrack; contributor)

FURTHER READING

Periodicals

Billboard, Feb. 24, 2007, p.57; Nov. 3, 2007, p.53
Kansas City Star, Feb. 9, 2006
New Haven (CT) Register, Feb. 16, 2006
New York Times, June 18, 2006, p.11
Newark (NJ) Star-Ledger, Apr. 24, 2007, p.19
People, Aug. 27, 2007, p.79
Village Voice, May 3, 2006
Wall Street Journal, July 19, 2007

Online Articles

http://www.ym.com
   (YM.com, "Meet the Jonas Brothers," June 14, 2007)

ADDRESS

Jonas Brothers
Hollywood Records
500 South Buena Vista Street
Burbank, CA 91521

WORLD WIDE WEB SITES

http://www.jonasbrothers.com
http://www.kenphillipsgroup.com/Phillips/jonasbrothers.htm

Lisa Ling 1973-
American Journalist
Host of the National Geographic Television Show "Explorer"

BIRTH

Lisa Ling was born on August 30, 1973, in Sacramento, California. Her parents are Douglas Ling, an aviation administrator, and Mary Ling, the owner of an import-export company. Both of her parents are of Chinese descent. She has one younger sister, Laura.

YOUTH AND EDUCATION

Ling was raised near the McClellan Air Force Base outside of Sacramento, where her father worked. Her parents divorced when she was seven years old. Ling and her younger sister lived with their father, but their mother was a constant, reassuring presence as the two siblings went through childhood and adolescence. "Even though I didn't grow up with her, she was a very integral part of my life," said Ling.

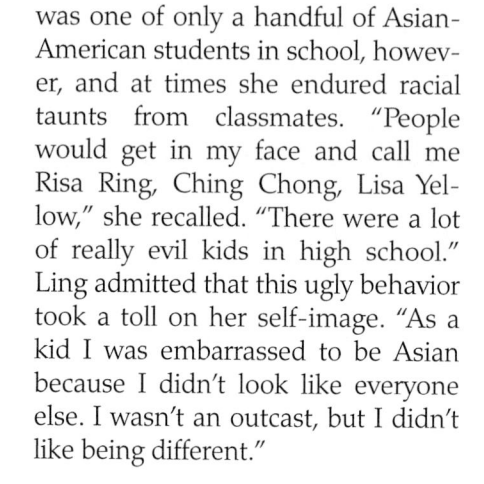

Ling was a good student, and she participated in debate and other extracurricular activities at school. She was one of only a handful of Asian-American students in school, however, and at times she endured racial taunts from classmates. "People would get in my face and call me Risa Ring, Ching Chong, Lisa Yellow," she recalled. "There were a lot of really evil kids in high school." Ling admitted that this ugly behavior took a toll on her self-image. "As a kid I was embarrassed to be Asian because I didn't look like everyone else. I wasn't an outcast, but I didn't like being different."

> "People would get in my face and call me Risa Ring, Ching Chong, Lisa Yellow. There were a lot of really evil kids in high school," Ling recalled. "As a kid I was embarrassed to be Asian because I didn't look like everyone else. I wasn't an outcast, but I didn't like being different."

Ling graduated from high school in 1990. Two years later, in 1992, she enrolled at the University of Southern California (USC) in Los Angeles. She studied history at USC and even made the dean's list as a freshman. But Ling left college before graduating because she decided to devote all her attention to her television career—a career that began back when she was in high school.

CAREER HIGHLIGHTS

Ling's rise to television stardom began at age 16, when she was still in high school. Her speech class teacher (who was also her debate team coach) announced that a new local television show targeted at teens was holding auditions at a nearby mall. Ling went to the mall after school and videotaped a short audition. Soon after, she was stunned to learn that the show's producers wanted to talk to her about serving as one of the show's four teen hosts. After a quick flurry of meetings, Ling found herself appearing on TV every week as a host of "Scratch," a teen magazine program that was syndicated to stations around the country. She co-hosted the show from 1989 to 1991.

The demands of Ling's work schedule for "Scratch" left her with little time to engage in the usual pastimes of high school. Her hosting duties required her to travel constantly, and she admitted that she sometimes missed just hanging out with friends, going to high school sporting events, and other "normal" activities. "I sacrificed my whole junior and senior years," she acknowledged. "I mean, I still had a good time ... but at the same time, I missed a lot of school." But Ling also was quick to add that her early experiences with "Scratch" provided her with a foundation for much of her later success. "I learned to perform in front of the camera [on "Scratch"], and I was able to gain a lot of confidence from that," she said.

After graduating from high school in 1990, Ling continued to work on "Scratch." But a year later—having worked on the program for three years by that point—she made plans to leave the show and resume her education at Boston University. A few months before classes began, however, she received an intriguing phone call from New York City. The caller was a producer for Channel One, a satellite news service that broadcasts a daily news program to thousands of middle schools and high schools across the United States. The producer asked Ling if she was interested in auditioning for a reporter position with the channel.

> "There was a time when I wanted to do the whole acting thing, but then I started to get educated," Ling said. "I just decided that I wanted to pursue a career that will allow me to really utilize my mind.... I can't believe that I'm actually getting paid for getting fed knowledge. I'm learning so much every day, and I actually get paid for it."

Making Her Mark at Channel One

Ling turned in a terrific audition, and the Channel One producers offered her the opportunity to become the network's youngest news reporter. She quickly accepted, working at Channel One from 1991 to 1998. Ling spent seven years there delivering news stories that reached an estimated eight million student viewers on a daily basis. The experience convinced her to explore a career in journalism. "There was a time when I wanted to do the whole acting thing, but then I started to get educated," she said. "I just decided that I wanted to pursue a career that will allow me to really utilize my mind.... I can't believe that I'm actually getting paid for getting fed knowledge. I'm learning so much every day, and I actually get paid for it."

During her years at Channel One, Ling delivered reports from more than two dozen countries, including Vietnam, China, India, Iran, Iraq, and Japan. Some of these assignments, such as ones that had her report on drug cartels in Colombia and civil war in Afghanistan, placed her in personal danger. "I saw boys who looked about ten years old carrying weapons larger than they were," she recalled about her time in Afghanistan. "They had no light in their eyes; they looked like they could shoot me right then and there with no remorse whatsoever."

Carrying out these assignments would have exhausted most young reporters, but Ling's ambition, enthusiasm, and energy drove her to take on other challenges as well. For example, she took history classes at USC during her first few years at Channel One. She also found the time to help make eight documentary films with the local Public Broadcasting System (PBS) affiliate in Los Angeles during the 1990s. Ling admitted that managing her obligations as a student, reporter, and documentary filmmaker was "incredibly difficult. I'm up all the time till two in the morning doing papers. I rarely, rarely go out. I've almost completely eliminated my social life. But I have a really good time at work. It's fun. I don't think I'll regret anything because I don't think I've sacrificed anything. I can party all I want when I finish school.... I know that sounds weird that I actually like being at work. I really do."

Joining "The View"

In 1997 Ling entered an exciting new phase of her career when she reached an agreement with ABC News to deliver ten news feature stories for broadcast on national television. The work that she turned in for ABC over the next several months deeply impressed veteran ABC news journalist Barbara Walters. Intrigued by the smart but approachable image that the young journalist projected in her reports, Walters asked Ling if she would be interested in joining "The View," one of the nation's top-rated daytime talk shows. "The View" uses a format in which five women of different ages and backgrounds, led by Walters, informally discuss everything from breaking news stories to lighthearted family topics and celebrity gossip.

Walters explained that the show's producers wanted to find a fresh face to represent the perspective of America's "20-something" generation of

LISA LING

Ling on the set of Channel One in 1997. Her reports from around the world drew enthusiastic letters from students who were eager to learn about current events.

women. The woman they chose would join the other "View" hosts—Walters, Meredith Vieira, Star Jones, and Joy Behar—on broadcasts into American living rooms five days a week. The 25-year-old Ling jumped at

Ling and her co-hosts from "The View" appearing at an awards show. From left: Star Jones, Joy Behar, Barbara Walters, Ling, and Meredith Vieira.

the invitation to audition, and she beat out more than 12,000 applicants for the job. According to the other hosts of "The View," selecting Ling was an easy decision. "She was very likable and she was smart but also adorable," said Vieira. "She wasn't a know-it-all but she knows a lot. She had it all and we just immediately clicked." Walters also sang her praises. "The number one thing was chemistry," she explained. "Lisa just seemed to fit with all of us ... but she's also able to give her opinions. And she has opinions based on fact."

After joining "The View" in May 1999, Ling's public profile increased enormously. Ratings for the show soared, and television critics praised her friendly personality and her ability to stand her ground without offending her opinionated co-hosts. In 2000 she agreed to be a spokesperson in Old Navy television commercials, and she also became a regular contributor to the *USA Today* weekend magazine and the *New York Times* wire service.

Growing Restless

In 2000 Ling filled breaks in the taping schedule of "The View" with work on the College Television Network, a satellite television channel that reached an estimated two million students at colleges and universities all across the United States. She worked for the network as its senior political correspondent for the 2000 elections.

The excitement of reporting on important presidential and congressional elections reminded Ling of her journalistic experiences during her Channel One days. She realized that she missed the adventurous lifestyle of the international news reporter. Ling still enjoyed her work on "The View," but as the months passed she became increasingly restless. Her restlessness became even greater after the September 11, 2001, terrorist attacks on New York City and Washington DC. "That was really a pivotal moment that really propelled me to just want to get back in the world," she recalled. "I just felt like there weren't enough people asking why this happened."

In 2002 Ling's growing desire to find a new challenge led her to apply for the job of host of "National Geographic Ultimate Explorer," a program that appeared on Sunday nights on the MSNBC cable network. As host, she would get the opportunity to travel to exotic and fascinating places around the world and "cover the world and all that's in it," in the words of Alexander Graham Bell, one of the founders of the National Geographic Society.

According to the other hosts of "The View," selecting Ling was an easy decision. "The number one thing was chemistry," Walters explained. "Lisa just seemed to fit with all of us ... but she's also able to give her opinions. And she has opinions based on fact."

Ling was awarded the job, and she made her last hosting appearance on "The View" on December 5, 2002. All of her colleagues wished her well, and she expressed appreciation to them for being both friends and mentors to her. Looking back, though, Ling had no regrets about the decision. "['The View'] raised my profile a lot," she admitted, "but it's not where you want to spend the rest of your career."

Exploring the Globe

Ling approached her new job as host of "National Geographic Ultimate Explorer" with a tremendous feeling of excitement and anticipation. She knew that it was a once-in-a-lifetime opportunity. "I'm not married and I don't have kids," she said. "If I don't do this now, I don't know if I could do it in a couple of years." Ling's first reports began airing in May 2003. Over

BIOGRAPHY TODAY • 2008 Annual Cumulation

On "China's Lost Girls," an episode in the series "National Geographic Ultimate Explorer," Ling examined the issues surrounding the country's one-child policy and its impact on Chinese society—especially on girls.

the next several months, viewers watched her report on topics ranging from the black market trade in Tibetan antelope hides to the violence and looting that wracked Baghdad following the 2003 U.S.-led invasion of Iraq.

Ling also confirmed that she had made the right choice in leaving "The View" and joining "National Geographic Ultimate Explorer." "Here, we work weeks—if not months—exploring one topic," she explained. "Having a discussion about Tom Cruise's backside versus jumping out of cranes and rolling around on the ground in the middle of forest fires—while both are thoroughly engaging, there's no question which story is meatier." She also claimed that her hosting job was more rewarding than those offered by more powerful and famous news organizations. "Network news covers international stories when there is catastrophe or war, but there are so many other rich, appealing stories out there," Ling stated. "One reason I love National Geographic so much is that they take a risk. They cover stories not because they think it will rate hugely but because they really are compelling, interesting, educational stories."

In January 2005 Ling's program was renamed "Explorer" and made the centerpiece of the new National Geographic Channel. These changes did not alter the show's emphasis on world exploration, though. "Before I got the job at "Explorer," I was living in New York seven days a week," stated Ling. "Now I'm out of the country every month: I was in China in February, Mexico in March, Japan and Korea in April, and Israel and Russia in May and June."

In addition, Ling's assignments remained just as exciting and unpredictable as ever. The show has taken her to Colombia, where she reported on that country's problems with violent drug cartels. She also went to China to examine that country's controversial "one-child" family planning policy, which has resulted in countless unwanted female babies since Chinese culture values male children more. She also traveled to Chechnya and

> "Network news covers international stories when there is catastrophe or war, but there are so many other rich, appealing stories out there," Ling stated. "One reason I love National Geographic so much is that they take a risk. They cover stories not because they think it will rate hugely but because they really are compelling, interesting, educational stories."

the Middle East to report on female suicide bombers. In addition, Ling also explored the dangerous culture inside American prisons and the vicious behavior of El Salvador street gangs. She even used a medical technician disguise to record and smuggle footage out of the secretive Communist country of North Korea.

Special Correspondent for "Oprah"

In keeping with her history, though, Ling did not permit her hectic "Explorer" schedule to keep her from pursuing other interests. For example, she dedicated much of her rare free time to an intensive study of her family's genealogy or family tree. "Looking back at my heritage, I've learned that the values that my family lived by have become a part of me," she said. "And their struggles as immigrants taught me to appreciate what it means to be American, without forgetting what it means to be Chinese." Ling's interest in genealogy even led her to write the 2005 book, *Mother, Daughter, Sister, Bride: Rituals of Womanhood*, in which she blends an account of her family's history with discussions of the rites of passage experienced by women all around the world.

> "Looking back at my heritage, I've learned that the values that my family lived by have become a part of me," Ling said. "And their struggles as immigrants taught me to appreciate what it means to be American, without forgetting what it means to be Chinese."

In 2005 Ling also began working as a special correspondent for "The Oprah Winfrey Show." This arrangement has given her the opportunity to put together detailed reports on such troubling subjects as the toll of AIDS and civil war in various parts of Africa. Ling has acknowledged that some of the stories are grim and depressing, but she thinks that people have to become more emotionally engaged about the suffering and injustice that surrounds them. "I've been so disenchanted with the apathy amongst young people for what's going on around the world," she said. "Our generation will inevitably assume the problems our country is faced with, and we are so ill-equipped to do so. My hope is that I can somehow raise the level of consciousness about world events."

To this end, in 2007 Ling launched a documentary series called "Who Cares about Girls?" on the Oxygen cable television network. The individ-

On a report in the documentary series "Who Cares about Girls," Ling drew attention to the many poor girls in India who are forced into prostitution to earn money for their families.

ual reports in this series all share the same basic goal: to educate viewers about the different challenges confronting women in America and around the world. One early report in the series, for example, looked at women in the U.S. prison system, showing the difficulties that imprisoned mothers have maintaining relationships with their children on the outside. Another story concerned the thousands of poor girls in India who are forced into prostitution to support their families.

Ling hopes that American families will gather together to watch the reports that she prepares for National Geographic, Oxygen, and "The Oprah Winfrey Show." "These are real stories about real people, and I think kids should be exposed to it, especially American kids who are, in many cases, very entitled and impervious to what happens in the world," she explained. "Honestly, there's a lot of stuff on TV, people have a lot of options, but I truly hope that people watch and respond to this, because only if people watch and respond will we be able to continue doing these stories. Otherwise, the little voice I'm giving them will disappear."

No Plans to Slow Down

Ling has occasionally taken a break from her more serious work to take on fun, glamorous jobs such as interviewing celebrities at the Academy Awards. "I am very proud that most of my work is very serious," she said. "But you know, I'm a girl and I sometimes like to ask girlie things, and I don't think that jeopardizes my ability to do quality journalism at all."

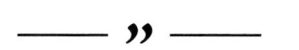

Ling insists that she will never waste her time and talent reporting on the tabloid trials and celebrity scandals that major news media outlets cover so heavily. "We have soldiers dying every day," she declared. "[Excessive coverage of those kinds of stories] doesn't sit well with me. I also don't want to sound like this nerdy activist. But to me it's just sort of a sad commentary on the culture."

> "I love what I'm doing now," Ling revealed. "And I've never been this way before. I've always wanted to figure out what the next step should be, what ladder to climb and to what end. Now I love what I do and I'm praying to God it doesn't go away soon."

With this in mind, Ling has said that she hopes to continue hosting "Explorer" and working on other noteworthy projects for years to come. "I love what I'm doing now," she revealed. "And I've never been this way before. I've always wanted to figure out what the next step should be, what ladder to climb and to what end. Now I love what I do and I'm praying to God it doesn't go away soon."

MARRIAGE AND FAMILY

Ling married Paul Song, a doctor who specializes in the treatment of cancerous tumors, in Los Angeles, California, on May 26, 2007.

HOBBIES AND OTHER INTERESTS

Despite her busy and successful career, Ling has always remembered the things in life that are of lasting importance, such as family ties. In April 2001, for example, she decided to race in the Boston Marathon as part of an effort to raise money and awareness for the Ali & Dad's Army Foundation. This pediatric cancer research foundation had been founded in memory of Ling's cousin, Ali Pierce, who died of liver cancer at age 13. A short time after founding the charity, though, Ali's father (and Ling's uncle) died of a heart attack while running a mini-marathon. Ling decided to run the Boston Marathon as a way to honor her uncle, her cousin, and the good work of the charity. Even though she had only had a few short months to train, Ling managed to finish the 26-mile marathon in four hours and 34 minutes.

When enjoying one of her rare breaks from her work on "Explorer" and other programs, Ling likes to read, listen to music, and practice yoga.

SELECTED CREDITS

Television

"Scratch," 1989-1991
"Channel One," 1991-1998
"The View," 1999-2002
"National Geographic Ultimate Explorer," 2002-present (renamed "Explorer" in 2005)

WRITINGS

Mother, Daughter, Sister, Bride: Rituals of Womanhood, 2005 (with Joanne Eicher)

FURTHER READING

Books

Ling, Lisa, with Joanne Eicher. *Mother, Daughter, Sister, Bride: Rituals of Womanhood,* 2005

Periodicals

Daily News of Los Angeles, Mar. 22, 2007, p.U7
In Style, Mar. 2001, p.470
Los Angeles Times, Nov. 13, 1997, p.F50; Mar. 5, 2007, p.E3
New York Daily News, May 25, 1999; May 26, 1999
New York Post, Aug. 8, 1999, p.110
People, May 24, 1999; Dec. 2, 2002, p. 24; Aug. 25, 2003, p.79
Philadelphia Daily News, Aug. 2, 1999, p.39
Psychology Today, Jan. 1, 2003, p.37
Television Week, Jan. 5, 2004, p.7
Time, May 22, 2000, p.126
Transpacific, June 1994, p.18

Online Articles

http://www.nationalgeographic.com/adventure/0412/excerpt5.html
 (National Geographic Adventure Magazine, "Lisa Ling Changes Channels," Dec. 2004/Jan. 2005)

ADDRESS

Lisa Ling
National Geographic Society
P.O. Box 98199
Washington, DC 20090-8199

WORLD WIDE WEB SITES

http://www.abc.com/theview/hosts/ling.html
http://www.channel.nationalgeographic.com/channel/explorer

Eli Manning 1981-

American Professional Football Player with the New York Giants
Most Valuable Player of the 2008 Super Bowl

BIRTH

Elisha "Eli" Nelson Manning was born on January 3, 1981, in New Orleans, Louisiana. His father, Archie Manning, was a legendary quarterback who starred in college for the University of Mississippi (known as Ole Miss), then went on to play 14 seasons in the National Football League (NFL). He spent most of his professional career, which spanned from 1971 to 1984, as the starting quarterback for the New Orleans Saints.

Archie Manning met Eli's mother, Olivia Manning, at Ole Miss, where she was homecoming queen as a senior.

Eli Manning has two older brothers, Cooper and Peyton. Cooper, who is five years older than Eli, was a star football player in high school, but a spinal injury forced him to give up the game before college. Peyton, who is two years older than Eli, enjoyed a tremendous college career with the University of Tennessee Volunteers. He then went on to become one of the top quarterbacks in the NFL.

YOUTH

Manning grew up in a family whose activities revolved around sports. His older brothers often went with their father to team practices, where they were treated as lovable mascots by Archie's massive teammates. They even got their little ankles taped once in a while by team trainers, just like their dad. These experiences instilled in both Cooper and Peyton a deep love for football. Eli, on the other hand, was only three years old when his father retired from the NFL, so he never had the opportunity to watch his dad practice or play in an actual NFL game.

> *Eli Manning sometimes found himself the target of unwanted attention from his older siblings. "I got pounded on a little bit," he admitted. "Cooper was two years older than Peyton, so he used to be able to pick on him a little bit. All of a sudden I come along, and I'm five years younger, and Peyton needs someone to beat on a little bit, and I took a pounding. At the time I didn't really enjoy it, but it made me tough."*

As he grew older, Eli sometimes felt overshadowed by his older brothers. They were big strapping boys who loved nothing more than to play sports and quiz their father about his NFL playing days. The three of them usually dominated dinner table conversations while Eli, who was naturally shy, listened quietly. At other times, he sometimes found himself the target of unwanted attention from his older siblings. "I got pounded on a little bit," he admitted. "Cooper was two years older than Peyton, so he used to be able to pick on him a little bit. All of a sudden I come along, and I'm five years younger, and Peyton needs someone to beat on a little bit, and I took a pounding. At the time I didn't really enjoy it, but it made me tough."

Eli also toughened up in the intense backyard football games that his brothers often organized. He did the dirty work of snapping the ball and

*Eli (center) with his brothers, Peyton and Cooper,
at Ole Miss, his father's alma mater.*

blocking for the older boys, who did most of the passing and receiving. When Peyton grew into a highly touted high school quarterback, Eli spent hours in the yard catching passes from his rifle-armed brother. He got so many bruises on his arms from catching these hard-thrown balls that Peyton finally invented some homemade padding for him. "I got him a great big T-shirt, a triple-X T-shirt, and stuffed it full of pillows and put towels in the sleeves," recalled Peyton. "He looked like the Stay-Puft Marshmallow Man."

As the years passed by, though, Eli grew to be the same size as his brothers. He remembered one occasion when this reality hit home for Peyton. Throughout Eli's youth, he had always lost to Peyton at whatever sport they played, from football to ping pong. But this losing streak came to an end during a one-on-one basketball game when Peyton was visiting from college. "I was about 17, 18 years old," Eli recalled. "It was in the backyard.... Neither one of us has a great shot, so we'd back each other in, and you're getting fouled.... We both had cuts, and it was a brutal game." A short time later, Peyton challenged his little brother to a rematch. But their father took the backboard down first. "Dad got a little worried about one of us getting hurt or something, so that ended our basketball game," said Eli. "We haven't played since."

Eli's home environment became quieter as his brothers grew older. Cooper and Peyton spent a lot of time at sporting and other school events, and after they graduated from high school they moved on to college. During these years Eli's close relationship with his mother became even stronger. They established a routine of going out to eat at least once a week, and she took Eli with her on so many shopping trips for antiques that he developed a taste for antiques himself. "They have that special bond that you see between mamas and their baby boys," his father explained.

For his part, Eli declared that his mother was the cornerstone of the Manning household. "Growing up, we would have been lost and clueless without her," he said. "She ran the household and was our biggest supporter." Friends of the Manning family, meanwhile, praised both parents for creating a loving and supportive home environment. "They were taught to respect adults and have the right manners," said Billy Van Devender, who was best man at their wedding. "All Archie and Olivia wanted was for their kids to be normal. You don't see them flaunting their success. The whole family is warm and generous, a joy to be around."

EDUCATION

Manning had trouble learning to read in his first years at school. "As a child, it's embarrassing and frustrating," he remembered. "They call on students to read out loud in class and it's one of those deals where you're praying the whole time that they don't call on you." His mother, though, helped him get through his early struggles and develop into a top student. "She worked with me and stayed patient," Eli said. "Her laid-back attitude and her soft Southern drawl helped me keep calm about it. She's the one who kept telling me it would all work out and it did."

Like his brothers, Manning attended Isidore Newman High School in New Orleans. And like Peyton, Eli was a star quarterback on the school's football team. By the time he graduated from high school in 1999, the youngest Manning boy was being recruited by major college programs across the country. "Eli has everything Peyton had when he was here, a strong arm, good size, and excellent leadership ability," said Isidore Newman Head Coach Frank Gendusa. "He could eventually be as attractive to the pros as Peyton and Archie."

Manning eventually decided to play football for the Ole Miss Rebels, the same program that had made his father a star. In fact, Archie Manning enjoys such legendary status at the school that the campus speed limit is 18 miles per hour, in honor of his jersey number. Peyton had decided to attend the University of Tennessee in part because of the huge pressure that he would have felt to duplicate his father's career at Ole Miss. Eli agreed that going to Ole Miss would put additional pressure on him, but he decided that it was still the right school for him.

Eli Manning played football at Ole Miss, but he also excelled in the classroom throughout his years there. His name regularly appeared on various academic honor rolls, and he even won a postgraduate academic scholarship. He graduated from the University of Mississippi in December 2003 with a bachelor's degree in marketing.

> *Manning had trouble learning to read. "As a child, it's embarrassing and frustrating. They call on students to read out loud in class and it's one of those deals where you're praying the whole time that they don't call on you," he remembered. "My mother worked with me and stayed patient. Her laid-back attitude and her soft Southern drawl helped me keep calm about it. She's the one who kept telling me it would all work out and it did."*

CAREER HIGHLIGHTS

College—University of Mississippi Rebels

Manning made an even bigger impact on the Ole Miss football field. When he first enrolled at his father's alma mater, he admitted that he did not know whether he could be as successful as Peyton, who was already tearing up the college football world at Tennessee. "I was nervous and scared when I went to school because I didn't know if I could complete a pass in college," he admitted. "Forget about trying to be like Peyton."

Manning redshirted as a freshman (a "redshirt" is a college player who practices with the team but does not play in games so that he can preserve four years of eligibility). He did not play much the following season. But he was the starting quarterback for Ole Miss the next three seasons, and during that time he lived up to the legendary Manning name. Torching some of the best defenses in all of college football with his throwing arm, Eli guided Ole Miss to three consecutive winning seasons.

> *The transition from high school to college football was tough for Manning. "I was nervous and scared when I went to school because I didn't know if I could complete a pass in college," he admitted. "Forget about trying to be like Peyton."*

Manning could have entered the NFL draft after his junior year, but instead he returned to Ole Miss for his senior season in 2003. "I felt like I needed to come back to become a better player," he explained. By season's end, he was very happy with his decision. He guided the Rebels to a 10-win season that was capped by a 31-28 Cotton Bowl victory over Oklahoma State on New Year's Day. "Everything about this year has been great," he said afterward. "That's the way it has been, the way the seniors stepped up and really played well together. To come to the Cotton Bowl and have your last game with all of those guys and get a win—it has been a great run."

Manning also received several prestigious awards at season's end, including the Maxwell Award, given to the nation's best all-around college football player, and the Johnny Unitas Golden Arm Award, which goes to the best quarterback. Manning also finished third in the voting for the Heisman Trophy, the best-known award in college football.

Manning finished his career at Ole Miss with 86 touchdowns and more than 10,000 passing yards. Only four other quarterbacks in conference history had broken the 10,000-yard mark in career passing yards before him. In addition, he set 47 different school records (game, season, and career) at Ole Miss.

Manning's exploits made him a sure-fire top pick in the 2004 NFL draft. Many coaches and scouts thought that Eli might have even more poten-

ELI MANNING

Manning became a star quarterback at Ole Miss, with 86 touchdowns and more than 10,000 passing yards.

> *Manning's exploits made him a top pick in the 2004 NFL draft. According to New York Giants General Manager Ernie Accorsi, "He elevates the play of the people around him. The majority of the teams Mississippi plays in the SEC have far better talent, but Mississippi still won 10 games [in 2003]. He makes people better."*

tial than Peyton, who had emerged as a star quarterback with the Indianapolis Colts. "At this stage, Eli is much further along than Peyton," said former Mississippi State Coach Jackie Sherrill. "There is not another quarterback in the nation as good as him." New York Giants General Manager Ernie Accorsi agreed: "He elevates the play of the people around him. The majority of the teams Mississippi plays in the SEC have far better talent, but Mississippi still won 10 games [in 2003]. He makes people better."

NFL-New York Giants

As expected, the San Diego Chargers selected Manning first overall in the 2004 NFL draft. But Manning refused to play for the Chargers, a losing team with controversial ownership. The young quarterback praised the city and its fans, but most observers believe that the team's struggles convinced him that he should begin his career elsewhere. "I didn't think San Diego was the place for me to go," he said. "It was my decision, and I felt strongly about it. I knew I was going to get criticized and harassed about it, and I was willing to go through that."

A few days after the draft, the Chargers traded Manning to the New York Giants. In return, the Giants gave the Chargers quarterback Philip Rivers, who had been selected fourth overall in the draft, and three other high draft picks. The high price paid for Manning, along with his brother Peyton's success in Indianapolis, led many New York fans to demand immediate results from the rookie quarterback.

Unfortunately, Manning's rookie season with the Giants was a disappointment, both for him and for fans. He started the season on the bench so that he could watch and learn the pro game from Kurt Warner, a veteran quarterback who had won a Super Bowl a few years earlier with the St. Louis Rams. When Warner struggled at midseason, Head Coach Tom Coughlin benched him and put Manning in his place. But the quarterback switch failed to spark the team. Instead, New York lost the first six games

ELI MANNING

Manning's rookie season in the NFL was disappointing—to Manning himself, as well as to New York Giants' fans.

Manning started. He did not earn his first NFL victory until the last game of the season, and he finished his rookie year with more interceptions (9) than touchdowns (6).

Manning's difficult introduction to the NFL was made even harder by the fact that he was compared unfavorably to big brother Peyton, who fired a then-NFL record 49 touchdown passes in 2004. After the season ended, Manning admitted that he had a lot to learn. "I looked at film [of my rookie season], and I said, 'That's not me,'" he recalled. "That's not the way I've played before. That's not the way I practiced. I didn't have the answer for what was going on and why." In a smart move, Manning turned to his older brother for advice and support. "It's rare to have a best friend who is also your brother and also an NFL football player," Eli explained, "and he knows exactly what I'm talking about."

Manning studied and practiced hard in the offseason. As the 2005 season approached, he felt a renewed sense of confidence in his abilities. "I feel I know what I'm doing," he said. "It's just a matter of actually doing it." Other observers, though, wondered if the pressure of living up to the Manning name and playing in the biggest city in the country would get to him. "I cannot imagine what it's like to be Eli Manning," wrote sportscaster Joe Buck in *Sporting News* in 2005. "Can it be any fun? Think of the pressure this guy is under every time he steps on the field. Being a member of the NFL's royal family has to make each mistake hurt just a little bit more. Not only was his father a beloved figure, but his brother is now the golden boy of the league."

>
> "I cannot imagine what it's like to be Eli Manning," wrote sportscaster Joe Buck. "Can it be any fun? Think of the pressure this guy is under every time he steps on the field. Being a member of the NFL's royal family has to make each mistake hurt just a little bit more. Not only was his father a beloved figure, but his brother is now the golden boy of the league."

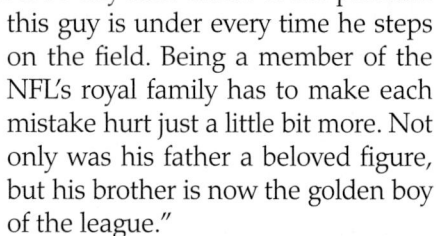

Fighting Through Difficult Years

In 2005 Manning showed off the talent that had convinced the Giants to trade for him. He passed for 3,762 yards and 24 touchdowns to help lift the Giants to an 11-5 record and the NFL East division title. But Manning also threw 17 interceptions, and he suffered through a nightmarish game in his first playoff start. Facing the Carolina Panthers, he threw 3 interceptions, lost a fumble, and was sacked 4 times in a 23-0 loss. Up to that game, even the most demanding Giants fans had acknowledged that the young quarterback was learning on the job. But after the Carolina drubbing, some fans declared that New York would never win a Super Bowl with Manning at the helm.

The 2006 season started off with a bang, as Eli and the Giants faced big brother Peyton and the Colts in the season opener for both teams. Eli and Peyton thus became the first brothers ever to start at quarterback for opposing teams in an NFL game. The Giants lost the game by a 26-21 score, though, and the team struggled to get untracked all season long. New York finished with a disappointing 8-8 record, which was not good enough for a playoff berth. Once again, fans and sports media placed much of the blame squarely on Manning. Dismissing his 24 touchdown passes and his career-best completion percentage (57.7 percent), they dwelled on his 18 interceptions. They also charged that he was so soft-spoken and mild-mannered that he could not be an effective team leader.

This criticism of Manning became even greater during the lead up to the 2007 season. Tiki Barber, a star running back for the Giants who had retired after the 2006 campaign, openly questioned Manning's ability to inspire his teammates. Barber said that the quarterback's motivational speeches were "almost comical" and suggested that he did not command respect from his teammates in the huddle.

Manning's coaches and teammates defended him, and the quarterback himself tried not to let Barber's comments bother him. "You just have to learn to accept [criticism]," he stated. "You never know when it is going to happen or what is going to cause it or what strikes it up. But it is out there, and you can't let it affect your personality or the way you are in the locker room or your approach. You have to stay the same and have a good attitude about everything and show everybody that it doesn't bother you and doesn't affect you and you are going to go out there and still practice hard and perform hard."

> "You just have to learn to accept [criticism]," Manning stated. "You never know when it is going to happen or what is going to cause it or what strikes it up. But it is out there, and you can't let it affect your personality or the way you are in the locker room or your approach. You have to stay the same and have a good attitude about everything and show everybody that it doesn't bother you and doesn't affect you and you are going to go out there and still practice hard and perform hard."

Proving His Doubters Wrong

As the 2007 season unfolded, Manning's doubters continued to criticize him. He finished the season with 20 interceptions, tied for most in the league. Critics claimed that high interception total showed that he was not maturing into a top quarterback, and they continued to question his leadership skills.

But Manning's teammates, coaches, and other supporters defended the young signal-caller. They noted that he also threw for 3,336 yards and 23 touchdown passes in 2007, even though his receivers struggled with injuries and dropped passes all season long. In addition, he did manage to

In the 2008 Super Bowl, Manning scrambles away from the Patriots' defense to fire a fourth-quarter pass to David Tyree, leading to the New York Giants 17-14 victory.

lead the Giants to a 10-6 record and a wild card spot in the 2007 NFL playoffs. They also reminded critics that in the final game of the season against the unbeaten New England Patriots, Manning's four touchdown passes almost enabled New York to pull off a massive upset.

Manning and the Giants entered the playoffs knowing that as a wild card entry, they would have to win three playoff games on the road just to reach the Super Bowl. Their first foe was the Tampa Bay Buccaneers. Manning turned in a terrific performance, completing 20 of 27 passes for 185 yards and two touchdowns, as the Giants cruised to a 24-14 victory. The Giants then moved on to play the Dallas Cowboys, who had beaten New York twice during the regular season. Once again, though, Manning's steady play helped lift the Giants to victory. He completed 12 of 18 passes for 163 yards and two touchdowns in a 21-17 victory.

The victory over Dallas put the Giants in the National Football Conference (NFC) Championship game against the Hall of Fame quarterback Brett Favre and the Green Bay Packers. The winner of this game would earn the right to play in Super Bowl XLII. At game time, most people thought the

ELI MANNING

Packers would win. The weather conditions were terrible, with heavy snow, extreme cold, and high winds out on the field, and Favre was famous for performing well in those situations. But as the game unfolded, it was Manning who seemed immune to the frigid cold and arctic winds. He outplayed Favre from beginning to end, throwing for 251 yards and rallying his team to an exciting 23-20 overtime win.

Super Bowl Champion

New York's opponent in the Super Bowl was the New England Patriots. Led by star quarterback Tom Brady, the Patriots entered the game with an 18-0 record (16 regular season wins and 2 playoff victories). Most experts expected Brady and the Patriots to beat the Giants and complete the first undefeated NFL season since the Miami Dolphins went 17-0 in 1972.

> *"This [victory] is about this team, about the players, the coaches, everybody who has believed in us," Manning declared. "It's not about proving anything to anybody. It is just about doing it for yourself, doing it for your teammates."*

When the game actually started, though, it became clear that the Giants intended to give the mighty Patriots all they could handle. The New York defense held Brady and the explosive Patriots offense in check, in part because Manning and his offensive teammates mounted time-consuming drives. Late in the fourth quarter, though, Brady guided New England to a touchdown that gave the Patriots a 14-10 lead.

The Giants received the ball with less than three minutes to go in the game. As Manning joined his teammates in the huddle, he spoke confidently about their chances of pulling out a victory. "I said [to the team], 'This is where you want to be,'" he recalled. "I've talked to Tom [Coughlin] before and with Peyton, and ... this is the situation you want to be in. You want to be down by four at the end of the game where you kind of have to score a touchdown."

As the stadium crowd screamed, Manning calmly moved his team down the field. The drive almost stalled at mid-field, but the Giants kept it going with one of the most miraculous plays in Super Bowl history. Dropping back to pass, Manning was swarmed by New England tacklers. But he somehow wriggled free and fired a pass far downfield to receiver David

Holding his Vince Lombardi trophy for Most Valuable Player, Manning celebrates during a Super Bowl parade in New York.

Tyree. The Giants receiver outjumped a New England defender for the ball, then trapped the football against his helmet with one hand. Tyree then somehow kept possession of the ball as he and the Patriot defender fell in a heap. "I knew people were grabbing me, but I knew I wasn't getting pulled down," Manning recalled. "I was trying to make a play, trying to avoid the sack. I saw [Tyree] in the middle, and the ball just hung up there forever. It was an unbelievable catch."

A few plays later, Manning fired a touchdown pass in the game's closing seconds to clinch a pulse-pounding 17-14 victory for the Giants. Fans and reporters alike immediately began debating whether the New York triumph ranked as the biggest upset in NFL history.

Manning's gutsy performance made him the obvious choice for the Super Bowl Most Valuable Player Award. He had played well all game long, completing 19 of 34 passes for 255 yards. But it was in the fourth quarter—with the game on the line—that Manning had really shined. He completed 9 of 14 passes for 152 yards and 2 touchdowns, including the game winner. "He not only made plays, he made spectacular plays," said broadcaster and Hall of Fame quarterback Terry Bradshaw.

Manning's amazing 2007 playoff run silenced all of his critics. But the young quarterback insisted that he did not spend a lot of time thinking about that. "This [victory] is about this team, about the players, the coaches, everybody who has believed in us," he declared. "It's not about proving anything to anybody. It is just about doing it for yourself, doing it for your teammates."

> "When I call him on Tuesdays, on his off day, he is always at the facility lifting weights or studying film," said his brother Peyton. "When I call him on Wednesday nights or Thursday nights, what is he doing? He is always studying film. As a quarterback, I just can't tell you how much I appreciate that kind of work ethic, because I'm very much in the same mode."

MARRIAGE AND FAMILY

Manning married his college girlfriend, Abbey McGrew, in Mexico on April 19, 2008. They live in Hoboken, New Jersey, during the football season.

HOBBIES AND OTHER INTERESTS

Manning loves to shop for antiques, but does not have time for a lot of other hobbies during football season. "When I call him on Tuesdays, on his off day, he is always at the facility lifting weights or studying film," said his brother Peyton. "When I call him on Wednesday nights or Thursday nights, what is he doing? He is always studying film. As a quarterback, I just can't tell you how much I appreciate that kind of work ethic, because I'm very much in the same mode."

Manning also lends his time and money to a variety of charitable organizations. He and Peyton were particularly active in helping the people of

New Orleans after Hurricane Katrina struck the city in 2005. They even sent an airplane full of food, clothing, and other supplies to New Orleans. "It's hard to watch what's happened to the city, people with no place to go, up to their waists in water," Eli recalled. "We just wanted to do something extra, so we set up this plan to help some of these people."

SELECTED HONORS AND AWARDS

Conorly Trophy (Mississippi Sports Hall of Fame): 2001, 2003
All-SEC First Team (Associated Press): 2003
College Hall of Fame Scholar Athlete Award: 2003
Johnny Unitas Golden Arm Award (Unitas Golden Arm Foundation): 2003
Maxwell Award (Maxwell Football Club): 2003
Player of the Year (Southeastern Conference): 2003
Most Valuable Player, Super Bowl XLII: 2008

FURTHER READING

Periodicals

Boys' Life, Aug. 1998, p.24
Football Digest, Dec. 2001, p.34; Summer 2004, p.30
New York Times, Oct. 14, 2001, p.S5; Jan. 29, 2008, Sports section, p.1
Sporting News, Sep. 30, 2002, p.30; Mar. 22, 2004, p.12; Dec. 23, 2005, p.10
Sports Illustrated, Nov. 12, 2001, p.46; May 3, 2004, p.50; Sep. 5, 2005, p.130; Jan. 14, 2008, p.52; Feb. 13, 2008, p.66
Sports Illustrated for Kids, Aug. 2003, p.T7; Nov. 2003, p.82; Nov. 2006, p.25
Time, Dec. 5, 2005, p.95
USA Today, Sep. 23, 2005, p.C1; Sep. 6, 2006, p.A1; Feb. 1, 2008, p.C1; Feb. 4, 2008, p.C9; Feb. 5, 2008, p.C4

ADDRESS

Eli Manning
New York Football Giants
Giants Stadium
East Rutherford, NJ 07073

WORLD WIDE WEB SITES

http://www.giants.com
http://www.nfl.com
http://sports.espn.com

Kimmie Meissner 1989-

American Figure Skater
2006 World Figure Skating Champion

BIRTH

Kimberly Claire Meissner, who goes by the nickname Kimmie, was born on October 4, 1989, in Baltimore, Maryland. She grew up in nearby Bel Air, Maryland. Her mother is Judy Meissner; her father is Paul Meissner, a podiatrist, or doctor specializing in treatment of the feet. Kimmie has three older brothers: Nate, Adam, and Luke.

YOUTH

Meissner's three older brothers "probably helped shape her competitive force," said the skater's long-time coach, Pam Gregory. "She competed with them in everything." It was Nate, Adam, and Luke who first got Kimmie up on skates in 1994, after a sudden winter storm left the family's backyard coated in ice. The boys were all hockey players, so they put on their skates and started an impromptu game. They also put a pair of old hockey skates on their little sister and dragged her outside to join them. She loved it.

Before long, Meissner was taking part in the U.S. Figure Skating Basic Skills Program, which uses a carefully designed curriculum to help young skaters build strength, coordination, and technique. She started private lessons with Gregory when she was about eight years old. About two years later, Gregory became Meissner's coach, working with her five times a week at the Ice Skating Science Development Center at the University of Delaware.

> "She always wanted to go more," her mother said about Kimmie's early days in skating. "Even when we left the rink here, as we were walking out the door, she would go up to one of the coaches and say, 'Watch my spin.' She just could never have enough of it."

The skating center was about an hour drive from Meissner's home, but her parents didn't mind putting in the time and effort to get her there. They knew that their daughter had a lot of talent, and, even more important, that she loved skating. Her mother, who usually did the driving, often took a book and read during the long hours that Meissner spent training. "She always wanted to go more," her mother said about Kimmie's early days in skating. "Even when we left the rink here, as we were walking out the door, she would go up to one of the coaches and say, 'Watch my spin.' She just could never have enough of it." Still, Judy Meissner regarded skating as something that her daughter would probably only do for a few years, perhaps until she reached high school. She never imagined that Meissner's high school years would include a trip to the Olympics as part of the U.S. figure skating team.

EDUCATION

Meissner remained in public school until she was 18. She attended Hickory Elementary School and, later, Fallston High School in Bel Air,

Maryland. The demands of her skating schedule meant that she could not be in the classroom full-time, however. Between the hour-long drive each way and the time on the ice, training took up about eight hours of a typical weekday, and competitions often took her away from school for days at a time. Many young skaters are home-schooled or tutored to meet their educational requirements, but Meissner and her parents both felt that it was important for her to stay enrolled at Fallston. They wanted her to have a life that was as normal as possible, despite her skating commitments. "My family and I purposely made sure that I stayed in school," Meissner said. "I loved school. I was always happy to have that separate outlet. I wasn't just skating all the time."

Staying in school required a lot of effort and dedication. Meissner would arrive before normal class hours to work privately with some of her teachers, then spend time in regular classes with the other students. By noon, she would leave school for the day to head to Delaware for her session with Gregory. She made up for her shortened school hours with additional tutoring and online work, and she often did her homework in the car on the way to Delaware or back. When she had extended absences because of competitions, her teachers offered to tutor her in the evenings to help her catch up. She always kept her grades up, consistently getting A's and B's.

> "My family and I purposely made sure that I stayed in school," Meissner said. "I loved school. I was always happy to have that separate outlet. I wasn't just skating all the time."

Meissner graduated from Fallston High School in 2007. Later that year, she enrolled as a freshman at the University of Delaware, taking classes in English, psychology, and philosophy. She had been skating at the university's ice center for more than 10 years, so the campus was already like a second home to her. She was happy to take classes there so that she could continue her established routine, commuting back and forth between her parents' home and the university and rink. "It really helps after a day of skating to go back with my parents," she said. "I can just relax, unwind, and talk to them about everything." Skating commitments made keeping up with college a challenge, but the flexibility of online coursework helped her manage her schedule in her freshman year.

CAREER HIGHLIGHTS

International Competitor

When Meissner first began training with Pam Gregory, she disliked the coach's emphasis on mastering the basics. "She had me do edges and stroking. No jumps. I didn't like it, not at all. I was like, 'Let's jump,' and she would shake her head no and say, 'I need to see crossovers in a circle,'" Meissner remembered. "Now, I'm really glad I got that training, because that's what you rely on when you're out there on the ice all by yourself."

> "She had me do edges and stroking. No jumps," Meissner said about her coach, Pam Gregory. "I didn't like it, not at all. I was like, 'Let's jump,' and she would shake her head no and say, 'I need to see crossovers in a circle.' Now, I'm really glad I got that training, because that's what you rely on when you're out there on the ice all by yourself."

Under Gregory's guidance, she progressed well and eventually began entering figure skating competitions. In 2003, Meissner accomplished one of her first major skating goals—making it to the U.S. Championships. Just reaching that level of competition would have been quite an achievement, but she did more—she won the ladies' novice title.

Meissner's success at the national level spurred her on to new goals. "From there I wanted to get to Junior Worlds and then it kind of progressively got bigger," she said. Her drive to achieve paid off in the next season. She won two Junior Grand Prix medals and placed fifth at the Junior Grand Prix Final. At the U.S. Figure Skating Championships in Atlanta, she skated to the junior title. Following that triumph, she went on to the 2004 World Junior Championships, held in The Hague, Netherlands. There she landed her first triple lutz-triple toe combination jump in competition and won the silver medal, finishing second to Miki Ando of Japan.

An Incredible Jump

In the 2004-2005 skating season, Meissner moved up to the senior level of competition in the United States, but she was too young to qualify for senior status on the international level. In the Junior Grand Prix skating series that season, she won silver medals at competitions in Courchevel, France,

Meissner placed third at the 2005 U.S. Figure Skating Championships, when she was only 15.

and Long Beach, California. At the Junior Grand Prix Finals in Helsinki, Sweden, in December 2004, she took the bronze medal for third place.

In January 2005, she competed in the U.S. Figure Skating Championship. Although she was only 15 years old, she placed third in the women's over-

Skating isn't as glamorous as it looks in competition; in fact, most of the sport is spent in practice sessions.

all standings. That accomplishment alone was outstanding, but her performance that year was especially memorable because she executed the demanding and difficult triple Axel jump during her program. The triple Axel requires the skater to kick off on the left foot, do three and a half rotations in the air, and land on the right foot. Only one other U.S. female skater had ever successfully done this in competition before—Tonya Harding, in 1991. "I was really excited to land that jump," Meissner remembered. "I was just doing them really well at that competition in practices, so I kind of threw it in and happened to land it." After the U.S. Championships, Meissner finished fourth at the Junior World Championships held that year at Kichener, Ontario, Canada.

2006 Winter Olympics

During the next season, Meissner turned 16 years old and became eligible to compete as a senior skater at the international level. From these ranks, Olympic team members are selected. Meissner hoped that she might make it to the Olympic Games by 2010. Her 2005-2006 season began well; she competed at two Grand Prix competitions, the NHK Trophy and the Trophee Eric Bompard, and took fifth place at both. Her performances continued to be strong as the season went on, including winning the silver medal at the 2006 U.S. Championships. Her first year in senior-level international competition had been so outstanding that Meissner was selected to be part of the Olympic team sent to the 2006 Winter Olympics in Turin, Italy.

Meissner had already done quite a bit of travel in the course of her career, but going to the Olympics was a thrill unlike any she had experienced before. Thinking back to her early years in figure skating, she recalled, "I set goals like, 'I want to go to the Olympics,' but it is different when you are actually there. Then it is like, 'Wait a minute!' You kind of do a double take. It is strange." Coach Pam Gregory noted that Meissner was excited about everything she encountered on the trip to Turin: "Every five feet, there's something about the Olympics—the rings or something. Every single thing has impressed her, from flying into town, the big welcome, the Olympic Village, going through processing to get her U.S. team gear." Meissner was probably also excited to hear that her teachers had decided to give her a three-week reprieve from homework while she was at the Olympics, so she could concentrate on her performance. In the short program part of the competition, she landed a triple lutz-triple toe jump and placed fifth; in the free skate portion, she placed sixth. Meissner came in sixth overall in the women's figure skating standings at the 2006 Winter Olympics.

2006 World Champion

As the Olympics drew to a close, Meissner came down with an illness that left her head very congested. On the flight home to the United States, the air pressure in the plane caused a complete rupture of one of her eardrums, and a partial rupture of the other. Her ears did eventually heal, but for a time, the ruptures had a negative effect on her performance. Her sense of balance was off, making it hard to spin, and she had a tough time hearing what her coach was saying to her as she skated. Nevertheless, she kept working, getting ready for her first year of competition at the senior level at the World Championships, held in Calgary that year. Her performance at Calgary was outstanding; in her free skate, she landed seven triple jumps, including two triple-triples. She was awarded the gold medal and named World Champion. Her performance at the 2006 World Championships impressed David Raith, the executive director of U.S. Figure Skating. "She had the skate of her life at the World Championships," Raith commented. "She has a great attitude and always looks for the next opportunity to show what she can do."

Being an Olympic competitor and a world champion all in one season was "awesome," Meissner said. "It was one big thing after another," It changed her life in many ways. She had a chance to throw out the opening pitch at baseball games with the Baltimore Orioles and, later, the Philadelphia Phillies. She took a televised ride with NASCAR driver Wally Dallenbach and visited the White House to read stories to children and take part in the annual Easter Egg Roll. A street in her hometown was renamed "Kimmie Way" in her honor. She signed national endorsement deals with Subway, Under Armor, and Visa, as well as a local endorsement agreement with a BMW car dealership near her home. The dealership even gave her a car of her own, but Meissner had been too busy with her skating career to learn how to drive.

High Expectations

Meissner was on top of the world, and yet, her new level of success brought new challenges. "When I won Worlds, I went from being the underdog to people expecting me to win everything I did after that," she said. The pressure to maintain her extremely high level of performance was intense. "I think that was the roughest part for me, just that year afterwards. That whole year was difficult, going after every competition. I wanted to do really well, but it was just hard."

As the 2006-2007 season began, Meissner's first event was Skate America, where she competed against two young Japanese skating stars, Mao Asada and Miki Ando. Like Meissner, Asada had successfully landed a triple Axel in competition. Media coverage tried to build up the idea of a rivalry between the two young skaters because they were both noted for making the tough jump. According to Meissner, however, their relationship is amicable. "Mao and I are actually pretty good friends.... We did juniors together so if we go to [the same] competitions we always have fun together. I think we both push each other." Meissner won the silver medal at Skate America, behind Ando and in front of Asada.

> "When I won Worlds, I went from being the underdog to people expecting me to win everything I did after that," Meissner said. The pressure to maintain her extremely high level of performance was intense. "I think that was the roughest part for me, just that year afterwards. That whole year was difficult, going after every competition. I wanted to do really well, but it was just hard."

KIMMIE MEISSNER

The year 2006 was exciting for Meissner—she skated in the Olympics and won first place at the World Figure Skating Championship (shown here).

The media's emphasis on the triple Axel was another challenge Meissner had to face. She was frequently asked when, or if, she would incorporate it into her programs. It was a difficult jump that she was not consistently able to do. When she landed it at the 2005 Worlds, it was something she had impulsively added to her program. Since then, the interpretation of the scoring system had become more strict, and the more stringent style of judging makes it "kind of hard to throw in a jump," Meissner said. "If you are going to take that risk, you have to know that you are going to do it. It was different under the old system. Now you have to be pretty sure of yourself."

> According to Coach Gregory, Meissner has a good personality for dealing with the stress of international competition."For a teenage girl, she is pretty even keel," said Gregory. "One of the reasons Meissner has had so much success is that even on frustrating days, she gets through problems much faster than if she were an emotional mess out there."

In trying to manage the intense pressure that top-level competition can bring, Meissner said she tries to avoid any feeling that the other skaters are her rivals. "I try and compete to beat my own scores.... I try not to look at it like, 'I have to beat this person or I have to be ahead of her.' That doesn't work for me." Coach Gregory commented that Meissner has a good personality for dealing with the stress of international competition. "For a teenage girl, she is pretty even keel," said Gregory. "One of the reasons Meissner has had so much success is that even on frustrating days, she gets through problems much faster than if she were an emotional mess out there."

Meissner felt the 2006-2007 season was a tough one, but she nevertheless won gold medals at the 2007 U.S. Championships and the Four Continents competition. At the World Championships, she placed fourth, placing behind Ando, Asada, and Yu-Na Kim from Korea. She also got her driver's license that year and achieved her personal goal of driving her BMW to Fallston High, just a couple of weeks before she graduated. While remaining a student there, she had traveled around the world to compete, visiting France, Italy, Slovenia, Bulgaria, Japan, and many other countries. "I've been balancing school and skating pretty much my whole life," said Meissner of her busy schedule. "It gets to be a lot and sometimes it's overwhelming because of how much work I have off the ice and then how much work I have to do on the ice." Nevertheless, she chose to continue her education along with her skating, enrolling as a freshman at the University of Delaware in autumn 2007.

A Slump in Performance

Meissner started the 2007-2008 season in good form, winning the gold medal at the Skate America competition in Reading, Pennsylvania. Soon, however, things began to unravel for her. In November, she sprained her ankle. She continued to train as best she could, but the injury certainly had an effect on her practice and her performances. At the Grand Prix Final in December 2007, she fell three times and finished last. She also had three falls at the 2008 Annual Cumulation Nationals, where she placed seventh. Some of the up-and-coming skaters who defeated her were Mirai Nagasu, Rachael Flatt, and Caroline Zhang, all just 14 and 15 years old.

Meissner on the winners' podium at the 2007 U.S. Championships; she took first and Emily Hughes (left) took second.

In addition to her injury, the very fact of growing up presents a physical challenge to any young skater, especially a female skater. Experts say that balance and confidence can be greatly affected when the body starts to reach physical maturity. Weight distribution changes, and the body resists spinning in the way it formerly did, because its mass is not packed so tightly around its center. Skaters can try to compensate by working on more powerful launches, or by squeezing in their arms to pull their body mass closer to its center, but in any case, the female skater needs to relearn a lot of things once her body develops. "Growing up is hard," said Michelle Kwan, a former Olympic skating champion. "You're a little off-balance. Your speed and your timing may be off. When you're at that age, you're not that confident with your body. It's an instrument, and you have to fine-tune it."

The Jump Doctor

Despite her substandard performances at the Grand Prix Final and the Nationals, U.S. skating officials selected Meissner as part of the team for the World Championships to be held in March 2008 at Gothenburg, Sweden. Her confidence was shaken from her series of falls in competition, and she actually considered turning down the opportunity to be part of the team. Instead, she took another drastic step. Many figure skaters change trainers fairly frequently, but Meissner had trained with Pam Gregory since she was a young child—for most of her life, in fact. Gregory was known as a fine coach, and had been named Coach of the Year by the Professional Skaters Association in 2006. Still, Meissner decided it was time for a change, at least temporarily. About five weeks before the Worlds, she left her Delaware skating base to go to Coral Springs, Florida, and work intensively with Richard Callaghan, a former Olympic skater himself and a trainer noted for his emphasis on the technical aspects of skating. "It was hard to say goodbye for now. Pam and I have been together forever. This is only through Worlds. After that, I don't know," Meissner said at the time. "But clearly something had to change. I couldn't go on like that."

In Florida, Meissner trained at Incredible Ice, the facility used by the NHL's Florida Panthers. Incredible Ice was also the home base for Callaghan, who had been a competitor in singles, pairs, and ice dancing during the early 1960s. In 1965, at the age of 19, Callaghan placed in the top 10 at Nationals. After he retired from competition, he spent seven years on the road with ice shows, then became a coach. One of his best skaters had been Todd Eldredge, a six-time United States champion; he had also coached top skaters Nicole Bobek, Tara Lipinski, and Shizuka Arakawa. Eldredge came to join Meissner and Callaghan for a few days of intensive work.

Eldredge and Callaghan worked on Meissner's jumps and her showmanship, but most of all, they hoped to restore her bruised confidence in herself. "It wasn't like boot camp," Meissner said of the experience. "I was working harder than I ever had, but I was having fun." The sessions included "a lot of positive reinforcement and just, you know, feeling good every day." She noted, "I got to the practice rink just wanting to skate and not feeling like I had to be perfect." The change in routine did Meissner a lot of good. At the Worlds, she took ninth place. It wasn't a gold medal, but she stayed on her feet the whole time and skated confidently. "I was happy, because it was the best that I could do and I did it," she said. "It just feels great to come back after hard performances and do something well." She wrapped up the 2007-2008 season with a strong performance at the Japan Open in 2008 Annual Cumulation at the Saitama Super Arena, where she took fourth place in the Ladies' Free Skate. Meissner then joined the cast of the touring show Smucker's Stars on Ice.

Meissner's goals for the future include developing more emotion in her skating, to bring maturity to the simple, athletic, technically excellent style that has taken her to the top. She hopes to be part of the U.S. team at the 2010 Winter Olympics in Vancouver, Canada, and perhaps to skate in more touring shows after that. "I am going to try and skate as long as I can," she declared. "But my family has instilled in me that there has to be something after skating. Skating is what I do for fun but I also need to have something that will be like a job." With that in mind, she may study sports medicine or physical therapy.

> "I am going to try and skate as long as I can," Meissner declared. "But my family has instilled in me that there has to be something after skating. Skating is what I do for fun but I also need to have something that will be like a job."

HOME AND FAMILY

Meissner's family is very important to her. Like her long-time coach, Pam Gregory, she believes that her siblings helped to propel her to skating success. "From growing up with three brothers, I am a tomboy," she claimed. "I challenge them to do everything and they are always challenging me to these big races on the ice. But, they never actually put their skates on the ice. They are too scared."

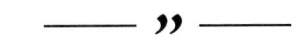

Meissner is especially close to her parents. "I can't be away from my parents too much because I love them too much," she once stated. "It makes me sad to be away from them." The 2007-2008 skating season was the first time she had traveled without one of her parents accompanying her. Meissner's parents helped her to succeed by making sacrifices to ensure that she got the coaching she needed and by giving her strong emotional support. Figure skating is a demanding sport, but her parents never pressured her to be perfect. As her long-time coach Pam Gregory summed it up, "I've come across a lot of different kinds of skating parents, and I think sometimes when people are too intense they want a return at the end.... Meissner's parents just want the return to be her happiness."

Meissner has been actively involved with Cool Kids, a group that helps young cancer patients. Among other activities, they provide supplies for kids going into the hospital, including such fun stuff as art supplies and iPods. Photo Credit: Cool Kids Campaign/Mitch Stringer.

HOBBIES AND OTHER INTERESTS

When she isn't busy practicing or competing, Meissner enjoys keeping active in other ways, including running, biking, tennis, and horseback riding. She loves animals and has several pets, including a cat and a few dogs. She enjoys drawing, reading, and shopping with her friends. While traveling, she has collected charms from various countries, putting them on a necklace she likes to wear when skating. When putting on her skates, she always puts the left one on first, but when taking them off, she always takes the right one off first.

In 2006, after losing two friends to cancer, Meissner became involved with the Cool Kids Campaign, an organization based in Baltimore, Maryland. Cool Kids raises money to help support young cancer patients who are in treatment at the University of Maryland Medical Center and nearby Johns Hopkins Hospital, as well as other hospitals around the country. The organization gives financial help to families of patients if they need it. It hosts special outings for patients and their families. When children come in for treatment, Cool Kids supplies them with a bag containing pajamas, a journal, art supplies, an iPod or GameBoy, and other fun items. Meissner acts as a spokesperson for the organization. She has hosted a skating party for the kids in treatment at the medical centers and has put on special skating performances for them. She also designed a wrist band with the words "Cool Kids" on one side and "Triumph" on the other; it is sold to raise funds for the organization.

SELECTED HONORS AND AWARDS

State Farm U.S. Championships: 2003, Gold Medal for novice
Triglav Trophy: 2003, Bronze Medal for novice
Junior Grand Prix, Sofia: 2003, Silver Medal
Junior Grand Prix, Slovenia: 2003, Gold Medal
State Farm U.S. Junior Championships: 2004, Gold Medal
World Junior Championships: 2004, Silver Medal
Junior Grand Prix, Courchevel: 2004, Silver Medal
Junior Grand Prix, Long Beach: 2004, Silver Medal
Junior Grand Prix Final: 2004, Bronze Medal
State Farm U.S. Championships: 2005, Bronze Medal
International Figure Skating Classic: 2005, Silver Medal
Campbell's Classic: 2005, Silver Medal
State Farm U.S. Championships: 2006, Silver Medal
Olympic Winter Games: 2006, 6th place
World Figure Skating Championships: 2006, Gold Medal
Campbell's Cup: 2006, Silver Medal
Skate America: 2006, Silver Medal
Trophee Eric Bompard: 2006, Bronze Medal
Readers' Choice Award (*Skating* magazine): 2006, for skater of the year
State Farm U.S. Championships: 2007, Gold Medal
Four Continents: 2007, Gold Medal
Skate America: 2007, Gold Medal
Trophee Eric Bompard: 2007, Silver Medal

FURTHER READING

Periodicals

Baltimore Sun, Feb. 19, 2006; Mar. 26, 2006; June 15, 2006; Oct. 22, 2006; Jan. 31, 2007; Feb. 5, 2008; Mar.18, 2007; Oct. 24, 2007; Oct. 29, 2007; Feb. 5, 2008; Feb. 10, 2008; Mar. 20, 2008; Apr. 2, 2008
Chicago Tribune, Oct. 26, 2006; Jan. 21, 2007
International Figure Skating, Feb. 2007, p.11; Apr. 2007, p.18; Feb. 2008, p.32

Los Angeles Times, Oct. 27, 2006, p.D10; Jan. 24, 2007, p.D1
Philadelphia Inquirer, Jan. 30, 2006; Feb. 20, 2006; Oct. 28, 2006; Jan. 22, 2007; Jan. 23, 2007; Jan. 28, 2007
Seattle Times, Jan. 28, 2007, p.C1
Sports Illustrated, Jan. 24, 2005, p.52
Sports Illustrated for Kids, June, 2006, p.2
USA Today, Feb. 24, 2005, p.C6; Feb. 21, 2006, p.C1
Washington Post, Jan. 8, 2005, p.D1

Online Articles

http://www.baltimoresun.com/news/local/harford/bal-te.sp.meissner19feb19,0,6606769.story
(Baltimore Sun, "Nice on Ice: Kimmie Meissner of Bel Air Typically Approaches Skating with a Positive Spin," Feb. 19, 2006)

http://sports.espn.go.com/oly/columns/story?id=2391509
(ESPN, "Unlike Other 'Shock' Stars, Meissner Here for Long Haul," Mar. 31, 2006)

http://www.ifsmagazine.com/archive/2008/JANUARY/INDEX.PHP
(International Figure Skating, "Kimmie Meissner: America's Newest Golden Girl," Jan. 2008)

ADDRESSES

Kimmie Meissner
U.S. Figure Skating Headquarters
20 First Street
Colorado Springs, CO 80906

Kimmie Meissner
Cool Kids Campaign
9711 Monroe Street
Cockeysville, MD 21030

WORLD WIDE WEB SITES

http://usfigureskating.org
http://www.bfpf.org/cool-kids-campaign
http://www.starsonice.com

Scott Niedermayer 1973-

Canadian Hockey Player with the Anaheim Ducks All-Star Defenseman and 2007 Conn Smythe Trophy Winner

BIRTH

Scott Niedermayer (pronounced *NEE dur MY ur*) was born on August 31, 1973, in Edmonton, Alberta, Canada. His mother, Carol, was a schoolteacher, and his father, Bob, was a surgeon. Scott has one brother, Rob, who is 18 months younger. Their parents divorced when the boys were both in their teens.

YOUTH AND EDUCATION

Scott and his brother Rob were raised in Cranbrook, British Columbia, a town of about 20,000 people nestled on the western edge of the Canadian Rockies. Cranbrook is a community in which outdoor activities like skiing, fishing, and hockey are enormously popular, and the Niedermayer boys enthusiastically participated in these and other activities. Over time, however, hockey became their primary focus.

Carol Niedermayer provided valuable coaching to both of her sons during their youths. A power skating instructor, she was able to carve out free ice time at the local rink for her and her boys. During the school year, she regularly picked them up at lunch time, gave them skating lessons at the arena, then delivered them back to school before their classes resumed. These lessons gave Scott and Rob a valuable boost over other players their age. By the time they were 10 or 11 years old, they were known as two of the top young players in the region.

> "They're good kids, but they were typical boys growing up," recalled Carol Niedermayer. "Believe me, they got into plenty of mischief."

Scott and Rob shared a passion for hockey, but they still engaged in the usual brotherly quarrels. "They're good kids, but they were typical boys growing up," recalled Carol Niedermayer. "Believe me, they got into plenty of mischief." As the older brother, Scott had admitted that he did his share of picking on his smaller sibling when they were kids. But when Rob experienced a growth spurt in his mid-teens, Scott sensibly curtailed his teasing. "He was a lot smaller until he was 14 or 15," he recalled. "Then we stopped fighting."

At age 15 Scott left home to play for a junior hockey team in nearby Kamloops. He spent the rest of his teen years tearing up the Western Hockey League (WHL) as a member of the Kamloops Blazers. Rob also joined a junior hockey club at age 15, but he played for a team in Medicine Hat. Both boys showed a lot of promise, but Scott was clearly the greater star of the two. In 1991 he helped lift Team Canada to a gold medal finish in the 1991 World Junior Hockey Championships. One year later, he led Kamloops to the WHL championship, earning league most valuable player honors in the process.

SCOTT NIEDERMAYER

Niedermayer during his rookie season with the Devils, playing at Madison Square Garden in New York. Teammate Doug Brown is behind him.

CAREER HIGHLIGHTS

Niedermayer's exploits in the WHL caught the attention of scouts from all across the National Hockey League (NHL). In the 1991 NHL Draft, the New Jersey Devils selected him with the third overall pick. Niedermayer's lifelong dream of playing professional hockey was about to come true.

Joining the New Jersey Devils

During his first few seasons with the Devils, Niedermayer experienced both exciting triumphs and disappointing setbacks. He earned a spot on the NHL All-Rookie Team in 1992-93 as a defenseman, and the following year he played an important role as the team cruised to its best-ever regular season record. But the Devils continued to fall short in their efforts to reach the Stanley Cup Finals. In addition, Niedermayer became frustrated at times with the defensive philosophy of Head Coach Jacques Lemaire, a conservative coach who preached positioning and conservative play to his defensemen. Niedermayer understood Lemaire's philosophy, but he felt that it did not take full advantage of his fluid skating style and offensive skills.

> "I love the offensive part of the game—I like to rush, and I love to score. But Jacques' system has worked—you can't argue with that. We won the Cup. Someday I'll get the chance to play a more open style, but for now I'm happy here."

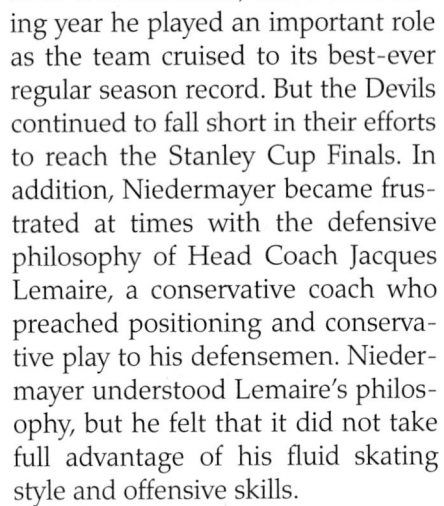

In the 1994-95 season, though, Niedermayer and the Devils finally broke through to claim the franchise's first-ever Stanley Cup. After New Jersey swept the Detroit Red Wings in four games to claim the 1995 Cup, Niedermayer expressed satisfaction with his career and his progress as a player. "I love the offensive part of the game—I like to rush, and I love to score. But Jacques' system has worked—you can't argue with that. We won the Cup. Someday I'll get the chance to play a more open style, but for now I'm happy here."

Niedermayer continued to hone his game over the next several years, both in the NHL and in international competition. In 1996 he was named to Team Canada for the 1996 World Cup of Hockey. This prestigious event, which was known as the Canada Cup until the early 1990s, brings together the top hockey-playing nations around the globe. Canada advanced to the finals, but was relegated to the silver medal when it fell one goal short against the gold-medal winning United States.

On Top of the World

Back in the NHL, Niedermayer continued his steady ascent into the front ranks of league defensemen. In both 1996-97 and 1997-98, New Jersey allowed the fewest goals in the entire league, and Niedermayer's play was an important factor in this achievement. At the same time, the swift skater became increasingly known for his offensive production. In the 1997-98 season, for example, Niedermayer led the Devils in three offensive categories—assists (43), power-play goals (11), and power-play points (29). In recognition of his growing value on both ends of the rink, he was named an all-star for the first time in 1998.

The Devils won a number of division and conference titles during these years, but their quest for a second Stanley Cup went unfulfilled until the 1999-2000 season. Niedermayer led New Jersey's defensemen in scoring for the fifth straight campaign that year, and his steady play in the defensive zone was instrumental in getting the team back to the Finals. The Devils and Head Coach Larry Robinson then knocked off the Dallas Stars in six hard-fought games.

With the season behind him, Niedermayer celebrated his second Stanley Cup in an unusual fashion. According to NHL tradition, each player and coach on the winning team is permitted to keep the Cup for a 24-hour period during the offseason, before the trophy is returned to its regular home at the Hockey Hall of Fame in Toronto in Ontario, Canada. Most players and coaches take the Cup to their hometowns or other places that are important to them for parties with family and friends. Niedermayer, though, took the Cup with him and his family on a helicopter ride to the summit of Fisher Peak, one of the highest peaks in all of British Columbia. He then posed for a photo session for *Canadian Geographic* as his family looked on. His brother Rob joined the fun, but he kept his vow that he would not touch the trophy until he earned a championship himself.

A Family Affair

In 2001-02, the Devils limped to a disappointing third-place finish in the Atlantic Division and a first-round loss in the playoffs. The high point of the season for Niedermayer was actually a mid-season break so that NHL players could participate in the 2002 Winter Olympics in Salt Lake City, Utah. He was a member of the Team Canada squad that defeated the United States 5-2 to claim Olympic gold.

Niedermayer hoisting the Stanley Cup on the top of Fisher Peak, near his hometown of Cranbrook, British Columbia.

New Jersey rebounded from its shaky 2001-02 season one year later, thanks in large part to Niedermayer's steady defensive play and stellar special teams work. After claiming the Atlantic Division crown, the Devils cruised through the opening rounds of the playoffs to reach the Stanley Cup Finals once again. Their foe in the 2003 Stanley Cup championship was the Anaheim Ducks—the team for which Rob Niedermayer played.

The prospect of brothers playing on opposing teams for the first time in Stanley Cup history attracted plenty of attention. Carol Niedermayer further stirred the publicity pot when she admitted that she would be rooting for the Ducks since Rob had not yet won an NHL championship. Scott took the news in stride, assuring everyone that he understood his mother's perspective on the series.

As it turned out, Scott and his Devils teammates disappointed Carol Niedermayer by earning a third Stanley Cup in a tense and exciting seven-game series. Scott was thrilled to win the Cup once again, but he freely admitted afterward that he felt bad for his younger brother. "I was disappointed for him," he said. "To put that much time and sacrifice and commitment to get there . . . to be that close and all of a sudden nothing, it's a pretty devastating feeling."

> "I was disappointed for him," Scott said. "To put that much time and sacrifice and commitment to get there . . . to be that close and all of a sudden nothing, it's a pretty devastating feeling."

One month after their Stanley Cup showdown, the Niedermayer brothers flew to Prague, the capital city of the Czech Republic, to train with Team Canada for the upcoming 2004 World Ice Hockey Championships. The experience was a tremendous one for both men. Not only did Canada win the gold medal with a 5-3 victory over Sweden in the final, the tournament gave them a rare opportunity to play hockey together. "It was new for us," Rob said afterward. "It got us thinking that before both of us retired, we wanted to play on the same team together."

Moving to the Anaheim Ducks

Scott Niedermayer returned to the international stage with Team Canada in the fall of 2004, at the World Cup of Hockey. Once again his cool approach and graceful skating proved vital to the team's success. Anchored by the steady play of Niedermayer and other veteran stars, Team Canada beat the Czech Republic in the semifinals and then claimed the gold medal with a 3-2 victory over Finland in the finals.

Niedermayer returned to North America to prepare for the upcoming NHL season, but the entire 2004-05 season was cancelled due to a bitter labor dispute between players and team owners. In July 2005 the two sides finally agreed on a new long-term contract to get the NHL up and running

Niedermayer was happy to be able to play alongside his brother Rob on the Anaheim Ducks.

again. Niedermayer's contract with the Devils had expired during the dispute, however, making him a free agent for the upcoming season.

New Jersey wanted to re-sign their star defenseman, and several other NHL teams courted him as well. But his brother Rob's team, the Anaheim Ducks, offered him a four-year, $27 million contract. Given the chance to play side-by-side with his brother, Niedermayer quickly signed up.

As the 2005-06 NHL campaign got underway, Niedermayer knew that he had made the right decision. For one thing, he loved being united with his brother. "It's just little things," he explained. "You go to practice, he's there every day. On the road, maybe we go out for dinner. Not every day. But it's always there. We're competing together for our team, trying to help us win. It's a lot of fun. It's something we'll remember forever."

Making Waves

In addition, the Ducks coaching staff turned Niedermayer loose, giving him greater freedom to rush into the offensive zone. As a result, he tallied a career-best 63 points (13 goals and 50 assists) in 2005-06 without losing any of his effectiveness on the defensive end of the ice. The Ducks were thrilled with Niedermayer's instant impact on the team. "Ask anyone who works here, they will tell you they were amazed at how good Scotty was," said General Manager Brian Burke. "We knew he was a great player, but it isn't until you see him every day that you realize how much he dominates games. Then there is the side the public doesn't see—the quiet, effective leadership side."

Niedermayer and a core group of talented young players helped drive Anaheim deep into the 2005-06 playoffs. The Ducks knocked off the heavily favored Calgary Flames in seven games, then swept the Colorado Avalanche before being sidelined by the Edmonton Oilers in the Western Conference Finals.

Prior to the 2006 season, the Ducks signed star defenseman Chris Pronger, giving the club two of the finest defensive players in the entire NHL. Pronger's tough, intimidating presence made Anaheim even more formidable, but Niedermayer remained the undisputed team leader "A lot of the guys in this [locker] room look to Scotty for that leadership," said Ducks center Andy McDonald. "He has an even-keel outlook. He doesn't get too high or too low. That kind of attitude is contagious. You see it rubbing off on the younger guys." Ducks right wing Teemu Selanne voiced similar sentiments. "Everybody respects him so much. He's not the most vocal guy, but the way he leads by example and how he approaches things, it's just unbelievable."

> *Niedermayer loved being united with his brother on the Anaheim Ducks. "It's just little things," he explained. "You go to practice, he's there every day. On the road, maybe we go out for dinner. Not every day. But it's always there. We're competing together for our team, trying to help us win. It's a lot of fun. It's something we'll remember forever."*

Head Coach Randy Carlyle also sang Niedermayer's praises. He noted that "a player of that caliber has the ability to play the huge minutes," but he indicated that the veteran defenseman's leadership qualities were even more important to the team. "I think the one thing you can say about Scott Niedermayer is he has a calming effect on your group. When things get a little hairy, and they always do at certain times, he has the ability to just slow down the tempo or speed up the tempo at the right time. . . . He's very unassuming in the way he handles himself. But I would say that the

No. 1 asset for him as a person is his ability to calm things down and calm people down in tense situations."

Winning another Stanley Cup

The Ducks roared out of the gate at the beginning of the 2006-07 season and never looked back. Anaheim posted the second-best regular season record in the Western Conference, in part because Niedermayer posted his best ever offensive season with 69 points (15 goals and 54 assists). In the playoffs, he seemed to provide a goal whenever the team needed it most. He scored a series-clinching double overtime goal over Vancouver in the second round of the playoffs. Then, in a pivotal Game Two conference final contest against the Detroit Red Wings, he once again scored an overtime game-winner. Three games later against the Wings, he scored a goal in the final minute of regulation to force overtime in a crucial 2-1 Anaheim victory.

> "A lot of the guys in this [locker] room look to Scotty for that leadership," said Ducks center Andy McDonald. "He has an even-keel outlook. He doesn't get too high or too low. That kind of attitude is contagious. You see it rubbing off on the younger guys."

Thanks in part to Niedermayer's heroics, Anaheim was able to slip past Detroit in six games to advance to the Stanley Cup Finals. The last obstacle to a Stanley Cup championship was the Ottawa Senators, the Eastern Conference champ. But the series proved to be a lopsided one, with the Ducks cruising to victory in five games. After Anaheim won Game Five by a 6-2 score to earn the franchise's first NHL championship, Niedermayer was the first Duck to hoist the Stanley Cup above his head and skate around the rink. When he was done celebrating, he handed the Cup over to his brother Rob, who then got to hold the Cup for the first time in his career. For his outstanding performance in the playoffs, Scott Niedermayer was named the series MVP, winning the Conn Smythe Trophy.

Anaheim's Stanley Cup triumph marked the first time since the 1982-83 season that brothers were on the same Cup-winning team. Since the formation of the NHL in 1918, 15 sets of brothers have shared the Stanley Cup. The most recent set was Brent and Duane Sutter of the 1983 New York Islanders.

SCOTT NIEDERMAYER

Rob and Scott Niedermayer pose with Scott's sons, Logan, Jackson, and Josh, after winning the 2007 Stanley Cup.

Afterwards, Scott said he treasures all four of his Stanley Cup championship teams. But he acknowledged that winning the fourth one with his brother had added significance for him. "It hits pretty hard right in the heart," Niedermayer declared. "Our names will be side-by-side forever, on the Cup, in the Hall of Fame. That's pretty special."

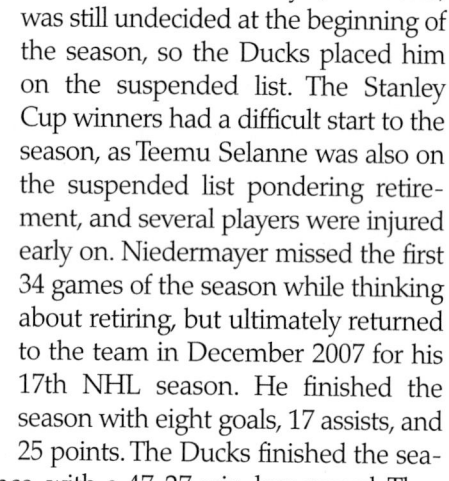

As the 2007-08 NHL season approached, many hockey observers speculated that Niedermayer might decide to retire, after winning a Stanley Cup with his brother. Niedermayer, however, was still undecided at the beginning of the season, so the Ducks placed him on the suspended list. The Stanley Cup winners had a difficult start to the season, as Teemu Selanne was also on the suspended list pondering retirement, and several players were injured early on. Niedermayer missed the first 34 games of the season while thinking about retiring, but ultimately returned to the team in December 2007 for his 17th NHL season. He finished the season with eight goals, 17 assists, and 25 points. The Ducks finished the season fourth in the Western Conference, with a 47-27 win-loss record. They clinched a playoff spot, facing the Dallas Stars in the conference quarterfinals, the first round of the Stanley Cup Playoffs. During the series, Niedermayer scored no goals but had two assists, and Anaheim lost to Dallas 4-2. As of September 2008, Niedermayer had ruled out retirement and planned to return to play in the 2008-09 season for the Anaheim Ducks.

> "It hits pretty hard right in the heart," Niedermayer declared. "Our names will be side-by-side forever, on the Cup, in the Hall of Fame. That's pretty special."

MARRIAGE AND FAMILY

Niedermayer and his wife Lisa have three sons, Logan, Jackson, and Joshua. The family divides its time between Anaheim and Niedermayer's hometown of Cranbrook, British Columbia.

HOBBIES AND OTHER INTERESTS

The Niedermayer brothers run a youth hockey camp in Cranbrook every summer.

HONORS AND AWARDS

Scholastic Player of the Year (Canadian Major Junior League): 1990-91

World Junior Championships: 1991, gold medal
Memorial Cup: 1992, gold medal
Stafford Smythe Memorial Trophy (Western Hockey League): 1991-92
NHL All-Rookie Team: 1992-93
World Cup of Hockey: 1996, silver medal; 2004, gold medal
NHL All-Star Team: 1997-98, 2000-01, 2003-04
Olympic Men's Hockey: 2002, gold medal
Norris Trophy (NHL Defensive Player of the Year): 2003-04
NHL First All-Star Team: 2003-04, 2006-07
World Ice Hockey Championships: 2004, gold medal
Mark Messier Leadership Award: 2006
Conn Smythe Trophy (NHL Playoffs Most Valuable Player): 2007

FURTHER READING

Periodicals

Canadian Geographic, Nov. 2000, p.23
Los Angeles Times, Sep. 1, 2005, p.D1; July 2, 2007, p.D1
New York Times, Feb. 2, 1998, p.C3; May 26, 2003, p.D1; Aug. 5, 2005, p.D7; Dec. 15, 2005, p.D6
Newark (NJ) Star-Ledger, May 28, 2007, p.37
Orange County (CA) Register, Apr. 13, 2006, SPORTS; June 6, 2007, p.C1
San Diego Union-Tribune, June 8, 2003, p.C8
Sports Illustrated, Jan. 8, 1996, p.46; Oct. 3, 2005, p.77; June 18, 2007, p.50
Sports Illustrated for Kids, Aug. 2007, p. 11
USA Today, June 2, 2003, p.C3; June 7, 2007, p.C10

ADDRESS

Scott Niedermayer
Anaheim Ducks
2695 East Katella Avenue
Anaheim, CA 92806

WORLD WIDE WEB SITES

http://ducks.nhl.com
http://www.nhl.com
http://www.nhlpa.com

Christina Norman 1963-

American Media Executive
President of MTV

BIRTH

Christina Norman was born on July 30, 1963, in New York, New York. She was raised by her father and her mother, and she has one brother. Her family is Hispanic and African American.

YOUTH

Norman grew up in working-class neighborhoods in the South Bronx and Queens, two sections of New York City. Her father was passionate about music, spending a lot of his free time listening to jazz and classical recordings. Her parents were serious enough about music to invest in a piano and send both their children to piano lessons. Sometimes her mother would take Christina along to the office building where she worked as an administrative assistant. Through such outings, Norman remembered, "I learned how to carry myself in a corporate setting." She also watched a lot of television during the 1970s and 1980s, something that would serve her well later in life.

EDUCATION

Asked to give one word to describe herself in high school, Norman said: "Goofy." At the time, according to Norman, "I thought I would have some sort of creative pursuit. I didn't know *how* I'd do that exactly but I knew I wanted to contribute something in that way." After graduating from high school, she attended Boston University, where she earned a degree in film production during the mid-1980s.

> *In high school, according to Norman, "I thought I would have some sort of creative pursuit. I didn't know* **how** *I'd do that exactly but I knew I wanted to contribute something in that way."*

FIRST JOBS

In 1985, after graduating from college, Norman took a job in the Boston area with a small company that produced television commercials. She was hired as a production assistant, and her specialty was the "tabletop shot," in which the camera focuses exclusively on the product that is the subject of the advertisement. As simple as that sounds, it can be very difficult to do properly. Even though the tabletop shot is recognized as a vitally important part of a successful advertisement, it is one of the least creative parts of the entire commercial production. Setting up the tabletop shot and making it look just right requires a great deal of time and patience.

Her job had its tedious moments, but Norman liked it, especially when she compared it to the corporate jobs many of her friends were taking. "It was really freeing," she said. "A lot of my friends were going to work for Raytheon and Digital Equipment and those kinds of tech companies. I was, like, this is much better than having to do that." She also found working in media quite unusual compared to the role models she had when growing up. "A good job was a teacher, a nurse and, if you were lucky, a lawyer. But television was not a career choice in those days."

Still, she admitted that at times the boring aspects of her job did bother her. "I still remember my last spot," Norman recalled. "It was for Tylenol Allergy Sinus. It was all night shooting because the pill was the wrong color and we were using a motion control camera, which takes forever to set up." For a while, she thought about going into the film industry and making movies instead of advertisements. Eventually she decided against it. Instead, she moved from Boston back to New York City, where she continued doing production work on a freelance basis.

During the late 1980s, Norman heard of a job opening at MTV. Debuting in 1981, MTV was a cable television network broadcasting music videos, which were still a relatively new phenomenon at that time. Norman eagerly interviewed for a staff position at the network. She did not get the job, but she soon had a chance to do some work for the company as a freelance production coordinator. This gave her the opportunity to prove her skills and competence to those in charge at MTV. They continued to use Norman for freelance work until 1991, when she was hired as a full-time staff member. In her new position as a production manager, she worked on promotional material related to MTV and its programming.

> *According to Tom Freston, chairman and chief executive officer of MTV Networks, "Christina is a most gifted, creative executive and has helped make MTV just about the smartest and most distinctive network out there."*

CAREER HIGHLIGHTS

"Beavis and Butt-Head" Provides Norman's First Big Break

In 1993, Norman's supervisor at MTV came through the office asking if anyone there had any experience with animation. Employees were being recruited to work on a new animated series. Norman immediately volunteered, even though she had no previous experience with animation at all. "I can figure anything out," she thought at the time. Her confidence paid off. The new program was "Beavis and Butt-Head," which focused on two teenaged boys, their crude humor, and their relentless ridiculing of old MTV videos. The show was heavily promoted through the advertising campaign

Norman's promotional campaign for "Beavis and Butt-Head" was her first big success.

Norman helped design, and once it began airing, "Beavis and Butt-Head" became a huge success. It was one of the top-rated programs on MTV and gave rise to "Beavis and Butt-Head" clothing, toys, games, and more.

Following her triumph with "Beavis and Butt-Head," Norman rose steadily through the ranks at MTV. She became supervising producer of on-air promotions, director of on-air promotions, senior vice-president of promotions, and finally in 1999, senior vice-president of marketing and on-air promotions. In 2002, she was in charge of the marketing campaign for "The Osbournes," a quirky reality show featuring the life of aging rocker Ozzy Osbourne (from the band Black Sabbath) and his offbeat family. "The Osbournes" was another big success, attracting an audience far beyond MTV's usual viewers. During its first season, "The Osbournes" won the highest television ratings of any show ever aired on the MTV network.

Jump-Starting VH1

During the 1990s, Norman had proven her leadership ability. Under her direction, MTV won many awards for its advertising, promotion, and design. She had shown she was able to be creative, to inspire creativity in those working for her, and to lead and guide her employees to work together as a team. Her success caught the attention of Judy McGrath, who was then president of MTV Networks Music Group and was later promoted to chief executive officer of MTV Networks. McGrath decided that Norman's strengths were needed at MTV's sister network, Video Hits 1 (VH1). (For more information on Judy McGrath, see *Biography Today Business Leaders*, Vol. 1.)

VH1 had been founded in 1985, four years after MTV's debut. While MTV was aimed primarily at a teen audience, VH1 was designed for those in an older age bracket. Instead of the cutting-edge image of MTV, VH1 featured softer pop sounds from established adult-contemporary artists. "Behind the Music," a documentary series, gave in-depth looks at the stories behind the popular artists and bands featured on the network. VH1 was a great success for its first several years, but in 2000, ratings for the music network began a nosedive. The decline continued until 2002, leaving VH1 trailing far behind MTV in popularity.

McGrath wanted to turn that situation around. She created a new position, that of general manager of VH1, and offered it to Norman, who accepted it. In announcing Norman's new position, McGrath said, "Christina is a tremendously creative executive who has a great strategic understanding for connecting with consumers, combined with a great feel for how to brand and position a network. In her 11 years at MTV, she's proven to be a fantastic leader of creative people—cultivating an environment where they

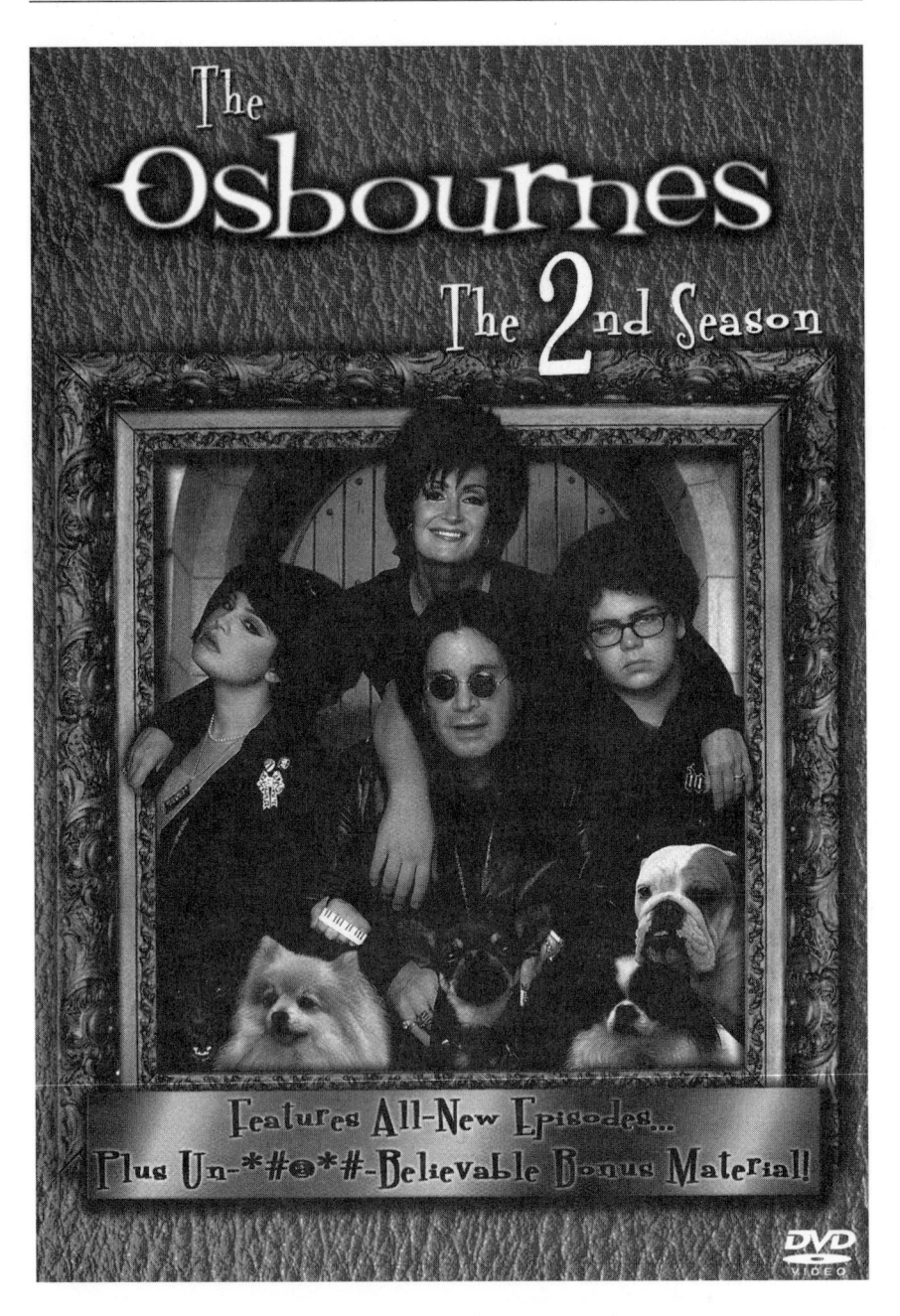

"The Osbournes" was another big success for Norman.

can produce their absolute best work." Praise also came from Tom Freston, chairman and chief executive officer of MTV Networks. He commented, "I can't think of a better choice to lead VH1 into the future. Christina is a most gifted, creative executive and has helped make MTV just about the smartest and most distinctive network out there."

Norman's first move was to spend some time with her executive team discussing the challenges facing VH1. They identified a few problems that were hurting the cable channel. The network had been relying too much on old material like "Behind the Music," which had grown stale. At the same time, there was an atmosphere in the VH1 offices that discouraged new ideas. "Morale was really down. Everyone was waiting around for permission," Norman said. "The VH1 team had become a little discouraged during a tough time. They really just needed to sort of regain their footing and work together in a new way than they had. Once they trusted themselves again, great ideas could bubble up and make it successful again." Norman encouraged everyone at VH1 to take risks and throw out all the new ideas they could, as they sought ways to make the network feel fresh and exciting again. "For me, it was all about making VH1 live," she said.

> *"Music education isn't just important to VH1," Norman said. "It should be important to everyone. Studies have shown that music education builds brain-power. We feel that restoring music programs in public schools across the country is helping kids do better in school."*

While trying to dispel the image of the network as a dry, dull music archive, Norman also made it clear from the start that she and VH1 were committed to music education. The network's Save the Music campaign utilized fund-raising concerts and public-service announcements to support music programs in public schools. "Music education isn't just important to VH1," she said. "It should be important to everyone. Studies have shown that music education builds brain-power. We feel that restoring music programs in public schools across the country is helping kids do better in school."

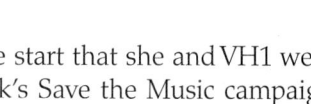

New Energy and New Ideas

VH1's makeover included new on-air graphics, new set designs, new programming, and new advertising. A Pop-Art style was adopted, based on the work of artists from the 1950s and 1960s. Probably the best-known artist in the Pop movement was Andy Warhol. He and others in the Pop Art school used images from popular culture and advertising in their works, rather than images from religion or nature, which had inspired the art of earlier eras. Andy Warhol's repeating patterns of soup cans, or his silkscreen prints of famous faces, are among the best-known examples of Pop Art. At VH1, the Pop Art style showed a new willingness to be playful rather than stuffy and self-important.

The network extended this fun, fresh feeling with new programs that focused on nostalgia for the recent past. "I Love the '80s" was a fast-paced program featuring clips from music and TV from the 1980s, mixed with footage of contemporary interviews with the stars of that time. "Bands Reunited" brought together members of defunct bands in an interview format. A comedy show, "Best Week Ever," gave various comedians a chance to comment on the newsworthy events of the preceding week. Other new shows included "Driven," which exposed the ambitions of stars, and "Inside Out," a reality show that exposed the everyday lives of musicians. "I Love the '80s" gave rise to successful spinoffs, "I Love the '70s" and "I Love the '90s."

Not every program started during this period was a success. "Music Behind Bars," a reality show about rock bands formed by prison inmates, was canceled after complaints from the families of crime victims. Another highly-publicized reality show was developed to give an inside look into the celebrity marriage of Liza Minnelli and David Gest, but the couple broke up before the show could be produced.

Despite those failed programs, Norman's changes were overwhelmingly effective. VH1 became very popular once again. In fact, under Norman's leadership, ratings for the network increased by 80 percent, climbing to the highest levels VH1 had ever reached. Her success led to her being honored as one of *Ebony* magazine's Top 10 African-Americans in Television for 2002. In 2003 she was recognized by *Crain's New York Business* as one of the Top 40 under 40 Businesspeople in New York, and by *Hollywood Reporter* as one of the Power 100 Women in Entertainment. In January 2004, McGrath promoted Norman to the position of president of VH1. As she took on her new job, Norman became one of the most influential women of color in the television industry.

Leading MTV into the 21st Century

Norman's term of service at VH1 was significant, but short. In 2005, McGrath asked her to come back to MTV, this time as the network's president.

As president of MTV, Norman often meets with music celebrities, including (from left) T.I., Beyoncé, and Justin Timberlake.

MTV had changed drastically since it was founded in 1981. By this time the main cable channel was focused more on original programming than music videos. Yet MTV had become much more than merely a single cable channel. The network now had many faces, based on evolving technologies. MTV was available not only on cable television networks, but also on the Internet and wireless mobile platforms. It had developed numerous ways to fine-tune and deliver its product, and McGrath wanted someone in charge who would strengthen and continue MTV's progressive growth.

As president, Norman took over a wide range of responsibilities. They included overseeing business development, research, communications, marketing, and finance. She was responsible for guiding not only MTV but many of its offshoots, which include MTV2, which plays more music than the original station; MTV Tr3s, designed to reach a young Hispanic audience; MTVu, a college service; and other MTV offshoots such as MTV Chi, MTVK, and MTV Desi, which are available online and are designed to appeal to Chinese Americans, Koreans, and South Asians. As she told an interviewer, "Reaching out to multicultural audiences, I believe, will be a hallmark of the Christina Norman era."

In addition to fine-tuning these specialized offerings, Norman also supervised the digital networks MTV Hits and MTV Jams, as well as the popular

MTV.com and MTV Overdrive broadband service. Overall, the MTV brand has grown to include more than 50 television channels in 28 languages, seen in 168 countries. When all its applications are considered, MTV reaches into 88 million homes in the United States and 442 million homes around the globe.

The MTV empire is vast, but Norman proved she had the vision necessary to manage it. In 2006, she announced that MTV would be restructured into two units or "ecosystems." One would focus on short-form content to be broadcast on television, on-line, and mobile sources. The other would be devoted to producing long-form entertainment, such as reality television shows. Remarking on the fast-changing technological possibilities, Norman said, "I think there's a lot of experimentation, which is a good thing because I think that's what fuels MTV and will continue to fuel MTV."

> "Every generation of young people has chafed against the world they've inherited.... It's our mission at MTV and our privilege to focus that revolutionary energy and to build tomorrow's leaders. Now, we do it all through a three-step mantra: engage, educate, and empower."

Also in 2006, Norman announced MTV's new social awareness program, Break the Addiction. This public-service effort encourages young people to combat global warming by using less oil. "The spirit of rebellion is part of our rock and roll DNA," she announced. "Every generation of young people has chafed against the world they've inherited.... It's our mission at MTV and our privilege to focus that revolutionary energy and to build tomorrow's leaders. Now, we do it all through a three-step mantra: engage, educate, and empower. Engage young people on the issues they care about. Educate them about those issues. And empower them to take action that's going to make a difference."

New Opportunities

Despite all her corporate responsibilities, Norman still makes sure to stay in touch with MTV's primary audience. "We spend a lot of time talking to young people on-line, in person—it's what we do," she said. "[It's] our mission." She also emphasizes that in the 21st century, "MTV is not a cable network." With cable being just one of its methods of delivering its content, new ways of reaching and serving audiences continue to evolve as technology expands. Norman is committed to making the best use of new technologies and making sure that MTV stays up-to-the-minute. In England, MTV is experimenting with new ideas such as Flux, an online application that combines traditional MTV content with features from other popular online sites like YouTube and MySpace.

Reflecting on the future of MTV, Norman said, "We've got this incredible collection of assets, starting with the big channel of MTV and going down to mobile and MTV2 and all the new channels. How are we going to make sure that all of those are presenting and creating a unique experience for the audience? That's job one every day: making sure the audience is connected to the music and the artists and the shows that they love."

Norman remains committed to helping educate, as well as entertain, young people. She is active in PENCIL (Public Education Needs Civic Involvement in Learning), an organization that gets the business world involved in public school education. PENCIL generates millions of dollars in donations to public schools each year. It also sponsors the Principal for a Day program, in which business executives come to public schools and act as principals for one day. Norman has taken her turn as Principal for a Day and strongly supports the program.

Norman gave part of the credit for her success to the cable television industry. "The cable industry is friendly to women, probably I would assume because in its infancy it paid less and jobs were plentiful. And that I think attracted more women to it," she said. "Throughout this whole organization, not just MTV, but Viacom, there's a lot of women in charge." Referring to Judy McGrath, Norman added, "I came here when Judy was president, and that was definitely one of the things that kept me here.... It was inspiring and motivating.... She was very who she was, and that sort of makes you comfortable being who you are. And know that you can succeed."

> "We've got this incredible collection of assets, starting with the big channel of MTV and going down to mobile and MTV2 and all the new channels. How are we going to make sure that all of those are presenting and creating a unique experience for the audience? That's job one every day: making sure the audience is connected to the music and the artists and the shows that they love."

When MTV and MySpace hosted the "Presidential Dialogue Series" with Barack Obama, Norman posed with Obama (center), Ian Rowe from MTV (left), and Jeff Berman and Liba Rubenstein from MySpace (right).

Norman urged young women to take themselves seriously. "Speak up for yourself because you *are* valid. Your needs are valid, what you want is valid, and what you give is valid. You've got to find a way to use your voice to get what you need. But it's not just running off at the mouth. A lot of people talk but don't have anything to contribute. So learn when to listen and when to talk.... There are interns who say they want to be me. But I'm like, 'Be great at *you* first. Then you can be somebody else.' You have to be the best *you* you can be."

MARRIAGE AND FAMILY

Christina Norman is married to Charles Hunt, and the couple has two daughters, Zoe and Asha. The family lives in Brooklyn, New York. "I love spending time with my family," Norman said. "Outside of work, my complete and total devotion is to them."

HOBBIES AND OTHER INTERESTS

Norman loves to cook, ice skate, and go in-line skating.

HONORS AND AWARDS

One of the Top 10 African-Americans in Television (*Ebony*): 2002
Emmy Award for National Public Service: 2002
One of the Top 40 under 40 Businesspeople in New York (*Crain's New York Business*): 2003
One of the Power 100 Women in Entertainment (*Hollywood Reporter*): 2003
Quasar Vision Award (National Association for Multi-Ethnicity in Communications): 2003
Diversity List of Most Powerful Businesspeople of Color (*Fortune*): 2005
Entertainment Marketing Award (*Ebony* magazine): 2005
One of Cable Television's Most Powerful Women (*Cableworld*): 2006
One of the Top 25 New York Latino Movers and Shakers (*New York Post*): 2006

FURTHER READING

Periodicals

Billboard, Aug. 27, 2005, p.23
Broadcasting & Cable, June 16, 2003, p.42; Mar. 14, 2005, p.7; May 16, 2005, p.4
CosmoGIRL!, June 1, 2006, p.122
Current Biography Yearbook, 2007
Daily Variety, Apr. 19, 2002, p.1
Miami Herald, Aug. 27, 2005
Multichannel News, Jan. 30, 2006, p.A20

Online Articles

http://www.hollywoodreporter.com
  (Hollywood Reporter, "Rock Chick-MTV at 25," June 2, 2006)
http://www.npr.org,
  (National Public Radio, "From Upstart to Parent Network," Aug. 1, 2006)

ADDRESS

Christina Norman
MTV
1515 Broadway
23rd Floor
New York, NY 10036

WORLD WIDE WEB SITES

http://www.mtv.com

Masi Oka 1974-

Japanese-American Actor and Special Effects Artist
Star of the Hit TV Show "Heroes"
Creator of Special Visual Effects for Movies, including
The Perfect Storm, Star Wars: Episodes I, II, and *III,* and
Pirates of the Caribbean: Dead Man's Chest

BIRTH

Masayori (Masi) Oka was born on December 27, 1974, in Tokyo, Japan. His parents divorced when he was only one month old, and he never met his father. He was raised by his mother, Setsuko Oka. He has no siblings.

YOUTH

In 1980, when Oka was six years old, he and his mother moved from Japan to Los Angeles, California. One of his earliest memories of being in the United States was his first trip to a pizzeria. He was eager to try what he thought was typical American food. "I had never had pizza before, and I was like, 'I'm in America, must get pizza!'" Oka was so excited that he didn't pay attention to where he was going in the restaurant. As he ran to a table, he bumped into a sharp corner and cut himself so badly that he needed stitches. When he and his mother got home from the hospital emergency room, Oka finally got his pizza. His mother had saved the pizza he ordered at the restaurant—one slice of cheese pizza and one slice of pepperoni.

> *Oka values his heritage and is proud of being Japanese, but he is also grateful to his mother for making the decision to move to the United States. "Coming to America alone to raise a kid, she gave up everything for me. I owe her a lot."*

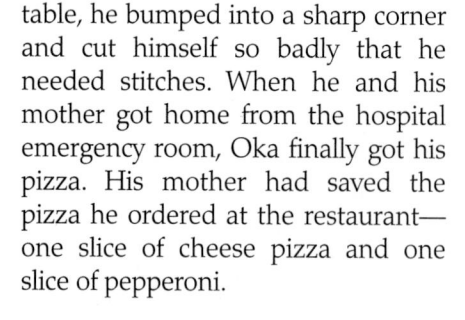

Oka has lived in the U.S. for most of his life, but he has kept his Japanese citizenship. While he was growing up, he stayed connected to Japanese culture by reading Japanese anime and manga comic books, particularly the *Dragonball* series. His grandmother regularly sent him videotapes of everyday life in Japan, and Oka attended Japanese language school on weekends. Oka values his heritage and is proud of being Japanese, but he is also grateful to his mother for making the decision to move to the United States. "Coming to America alone to raise a kid, she gave up everything for me. I owe her a lot."

EDUCATION

As a child in Japan, Oka had performed very well on an intelligence test and he had been given a high Intelligence Quotient (IQ) score. An IQ score is a number intended to represent a person's mental abilities compared to others of the same age. Generally, a person with a high IQ score is thought to be smarter than the average person. The test is often used to predict a person's ability to learn, to do well in school, or to develop special talents. Some have felt that relying on a single test to predict a person's future is too limiting, and the accuracy and fairness of IQ tests are now questioned by some educators.

Oka's IQ has been reported as 180, which is considered genius. Because of his high IQ score, his mother decided to move to the United States so that he could go to American schools. She believed that in the U.S. he would get a more personalized education that would help to bring out any special talents he might have. Oka explained that when he was young, schools in Japan did not provide opportunities for individual students to excel. "So my mother made a conscious choice that we're going to go to America where you can go to a school where they're going to let your scientific skills, your mathematical skills, blossom. That's why she actually took that trip and made that jump to come to America."

Although the media has focused attention on his high IQ score, Oka himself prefers to downplay his reported intelligence. He has said in numerous interviews that he wished his IQ score had not become a topic for public discussion. "I'm just book smart. But definitely not street smart. . . . I would rather kind of lower everyone's expectations. I'd rather be kind of dumb and exceed peoples' expectations rather than . . . raise the bar and not be able to meet it."

> "I'm just book smart. But definitely not street smart. . . . I would rather kind of lower everyone's expectations. I'd rather be kind of dumb and exceed peoples' expectations rather than . . . raise the bar and not be able to meet it."

Oka attended Harvard Westlake School in Los Angeles, an independent college preparatory school for grades 7-12. His favorite subjects in school were those that involved computers. "I've been programming computers since elementary school, where they taught us, and I stuck with computer science through high school and college. . . . I've always loved problem-solving and the computers kind of help you do that." Oka graduated from high school in 1992. After graduation, he worked at the 1992 Summer Olympics in Barcelona, Spain, as an English, Japanese, and Spanish translator.

Oka then attended Brown University in Providence, Rhode Island. He always knew that he wanted to study computer programming, but he was also interested in acting. Not wanting to limit himself to only one area of study, Oka chose to attend Brown instead of a more technical university so that he could get a well-rounded education. "I thought, 'You know what, college is a place where I need to grow as a human being.' I wanted to learn more about myself and get a social education, not just an academic one. I could always go to Harvard or MIT for graduate school." In 1997, Oka received a Bachelor of Science (BS) degree in computer science and mathematics with a minor in theater arts from Brown University.

CAREER HIGHLIGHTS

After college, Oka went to work for Industrial Light & Magic (ILM), the visual effects studio founded by filmmaker George Lucas, who also created the *Star Wars* movies. "ILM offered me an entry-level position . . . but they refused to fly me out for the job interview. Fortunately, Microsoft also was interested in hiring me and they flew me out to Seattle, then down to San Francisco and back to Providence." Oka was offered a job at Microsoft, but took a job at ILM instead because the position there would allow him to combine his love of computers with his interest in movies and acting.

Pioneering Special Effects

Oka became a digital artist and technical director at ILM. His work there allowed him to write computer programs that were used to create special effects for many popular movies. He contributed to important scenes in many films, including all of the *Star Wars* prequels, *Episode I—The Phantom Menace* (1999), *Episode II—Attack of the Clones* (2002), and *Episode III—Revenge of the Sith* (2006), as well as *The Perfect Storm* (2000), *Terminator 3: Rise of the Machines* (2003), *Hulk* (2003), *War of the Worlds* (2005), and *Pirates of the Caribbean: Dead Man's Chest* (2006). Many of Oka's computer programs supported the creation of new and unique special effects, allowing ILM's artists to expand the range of possibilities for the digital movie effects known as CG (computer graphics).

One of the first large projects that Oka worked on was the 1999 *Star Wars* prequel *Episode I—The Phantom Menace*. For this movie, he created new computer software that allowed digital artists to produce any kind of solid-material explosion that they wanted. "With *Star Wars* there was a whole explosion effect of Obi Wan Kenobi's chase sequence through the asteroids and they wanted a way to destroy the asteroids. So they came up with different shots, to blow up the asteroid in a million pieces, but they didn't have the software. . . . I'd come up with software, and write the tools to create that explosion and I would teach it to the artists and they would adjust it and tweak it to get the image they wanted."

Oka's reputation as a talented programmer grew because of his cutting-edge CG work for the 2000 movie *The Perfect Storm*. Telling the dramatic story of a fishing boat stranded in the Atlantic Ocean during a severe storm, the movie presented many special effects challenges. At that time,

Oka designed software to create special effects for many popular movies, including the storm scenes in The Perfect Storm.

creating realistic simulated water effects was one of the most difficult things to do with computer graphics. As part of the largest ILM team ever assembled for a non-science-fiction movie, Oka designed innovative new software that revolutionized the creation of computerized water effects. His work allowed ILM's digital artists to create the impressive ocean storm scenes that were the focal point of the movie.

Although the movie itself received mixed reviews, critics and film industry professionals praised *The Perfect Storm* for its breakthrough special effects technology. The movie was nominated for many awards, including an Academy Award for Best Effects/Best Visual Effects and a Saturn Award for Best Special Effects from the Academy of Science Fiction, Fantasy & Horror Films. All of the water effects in *The Perfect Storm* were produced using computer programs that Oka wrote. His programs have been used in many movies since then, including *Pirates of the Caribbean: Dead Man's Chest* (2006).

> "With *Star Wars* there was a whole explosion effect of Obi Wan Kenobi's chase sequence through the asteroids.... They came up with different shots, to blow up the asteroid in a million pieces, but they didn't have the software.... I'd come up with software, and write the tools to create that explosion and I would teach it to the artists and they would adjust it and tweak it to get the image they wanted."

"For *Pirates of the Caribbean [Dead Man's Chest]* they used a lot of the water stuff I wrote for *The Perfect Storm*," Oka said. "You know, lots of particles of water stuff, and their interactions. Most of the stuff in *Pirates* was Davey Jones and the water dripping off him, and being able to control the drip. So they can say at this frame I want four drips, or streams down his face, and we could do that.... Of course, you can't time that in the practical world. But with CG you can do all that."

Taking a Chance on Acting

After finishing work on *The Perfect Storm*, Oka needed a break from special effects. While he thoroughly enjoyed his job at ILM, he still wanted to be an actor. By 2001, he had already become a member of the Screen Actors Guild by appearing in various technical training films in the San Francisco area. Oka felt it was time to pursue larger roles, and so he decided to move to Los Angeles to look for parts in television and movies.

ILM allowed Oka to transfer temporarily to their office in Los Angeles on one condition: he had to get a part in either a movie or a television series within one year. If he could not find any acting jobs, he would have to return to his job in San Francisco or leave ILM. Oka signed a contract with ILM agreeing to these terms, and he moved to Los Angeles. "I only gave myself a year to make it, which of course is very naïve," he recalled. "Because anyone who's trying to pursue a career in the entertainment industry knows that it's a marathon, not a sprint. But I made a bet with ILM that was signed into my contract, that if I didn't get a recurring role in a pilot or a supporting role in a film during my first year in L.A., then I'd go back to San Francisco full time."

Within a short time, Oka landed a part in the pilot episode of a television series called "Straight White Male." The show was never aired on television, but his role in the pilot meant that he'd fulfilled his contract and could stay in Los Angeles. While Oka continued to work on various projects for ILM, he also performed improvisational comedy and managed to get small roles in movies and television shows. He appeared in episodes of the TV shows "Without A Trace," "Sabrina the Teenage Witch," "Reba," "Reno 911!," "Gilmore Girls," "Dharma & Greg," and "Punk'd," and he also appeared in small parts in the movies *Austin Powers: Goldmember*, *Legally Blonde 2*, and *Along Came Polly*. In his first recurring role in a television series, Oka played Franklyn the lab technician on "Scrubs" (2002-2004). Throughout this time, he also worked with several improvisation groups such as Second City, ImprovOlympics, TheatreSports, and The Groundlings.

> "To be honest ... it's much easier to break into roles. There's less competition ... and the producers are more open to changing smaller, one-line roles into bigger roles," he explained. "The hard part is to sustain a career. How many visible Asian actors are out there? When you compare the number to the total population it's significantly lower."

Oka realized that finding so many roles so quickly is unusual for an aspiring actor. He believed that being Japanese helped him get more acting

Oka in season one of "Heroes," backstage in Las Vegas among the show girls.

work during his first few years in Los Angeles. "To be honest . . . it's much easier to break into roles. There's less competition . . . and the producers are more open to changing smaller, one-line roles into bigger roles," he explained. "The hard part is to sustain a career. How many visible Asian actors are out there? When you compare the number to the total population it's significantly lower."

"Heroes"

Oka continued to get small roles regularly, but by 2005 he was almost ready to give up hope of landing larger parts. He decided to try one last season of auditions for TV series pilots. If he wasn't offered any substantial acting work, he intended to focus on screenwriting and producing his ideas for TV shows and movies while continuing to work for ILM.

The first role that Oka auditioned for that year was one that he completely identified with. The character was a Japanese computer programmer who loved comic books, and the show's producers were looking for a Japanese-speaking Asian actor with comedy experience. The role seemed almost as if it had been created especially for Oka, and he won the part of Hiro Nakamura in the pilot episode of a television show called "Heroes."

"Heroes" was not only Oka's first pilot to be made into a television series, it was an instant hit and became the most popular new television show of 2006. The comic-book style series follows the adventures of a group of people as they each discover that they have extraordinary and mysterious superpowers. Hiro is one of several characters whose intersecting stories gradually reveal that they must all work together to save the world. In its first broadcast season, the show regularly attracted more than 15 million viewers each week, placing it consistently among the top 20 most-watched programs.

On "Heroes," Oka plays Hiro Nakamura, an office worker who loves comics and videogames and who suddenly realizes that he has the ability to manipulate time and space through sheer will power. Hiro can stop time, travel instantly to another place, and travel back and forth through time to visit the past or the future. Because of his love of comic books and superheroes, Hiro is excited to have these powers and knows exactly what he wants to do with them. Unlike the other "Heroes" characters, Hiro enjoys being a superhero. The character was an afterthought that was added to the pilot at the last minute after it was observed that none of the other characters were happy to be superheroes.

Hiro was originally intended to simply be one of many characters on the show. Everyone, including Oka, was surprised when Hiro became the breakout star of the series. "He was comedic relief and he embraced being a superhero. But from my perspective, he was a foreign character who doesn't speak any English and he's a geek. I wasn't sure how much the audience would be able to relate to him." In attempting to explain his character's wide appeal, Oka said, "He's basically a wide-eyed kid full of wonder. He's the kind of person so many of us want to be, but we lose much of that wonder as we grow up and grapple with societal pressures."

> "He was comedic relief and he embraced being a superhero," Oka said about his character, Hiro. "But from my perspective, he was a foreign character who doesn't speak any English and he's a geek. I wasn't sure how much the audience would be able to relate to him."

Oka puts a lot of himself into his portrayal of Hiro, and the "Heroes" writers have also included his personality and some of his talents in the role. Oka's lifelong love of science fiction, anime, and comics helps him to bring genuine enthusiasm and excitement to the character. Because he has practiced the Japanese art of Kendo swordfighting his whole life, he is able to realistically perform Hiro's swordfighting scenes. Oka also translates all of Hiro's scripted dialog into Japanese, a process which takes him only about an hour per episode and helps him to memorize his lines.

Critics have praised Oka's Hiro as a refreshing, childlike character who is full of joy and spirit. *Wired* magazine called his portrayal of Hiro endearing and said that Hiro's geekiness gives him an edge in popularity over the other characters on the show. *Wired* also praised his acting, saying, "In an ensemble cast that features solid acting all around, Oka steals the show every time he's on the screen." An *Entertainment Weekly* critic applauded his "gleeful cheer" in the role of Hiro and credited Oka for keeping fans riveted to the show. A reviewer writing for msnbc.com called Oka's portrayal of Hiro "brilliantly crafted" and stated that "Masi Oka is so cool, he should get an award just for being Masi Oka."

Oka was nominated for many awards in 2007 for his role on "Heroes," including a Golden Globe Award for Best Performance by an Actor in a Supporting Role in a Series, Mini-Series or Motion Picture Made for Television; an Emmy Award for Outstanding Supporting Actor in a Drama Series; and a Teen Choice Award. He received a 2007 Saturn Award for Best Supporting Actor in a Television Program from the Academy of Science Fiction,

Scenes from "Heroes," seasons one and two.

Fantasy & Horror Films. He also won a 2007 Future Classic Award from TV Land and a 2007 Asian Excellence Award for Outstanding Actor in Television from AZN Television. Oka was also named one of *Wired* magazine's Rave Award winners in 2007.

The second season of "Heroes" was a disappointment to many fans. Some of the initial excitement of the show's unusual premise had worn off. New characters and new story lines were introduced, some of which didn't appeal to the show's viewers. To make matters worse, a strike by the writers' union delayed the creation of new scripts and interrupted the season. The show returned for a third season in September 2008, with all involved promising that the new episodes would be as thrilling as the first season. Excitement was also generated by the NBC web site, which featured graphic novels, online novels, fan art, webisodes with all-new scenes, and other related materials adding to fans' anticipation of the new season.

> "Laughter is kind of a symbolism of peace. It's easy to cry, but it's so hard to laugh.... Love and laughter are universal. Romantic comedies are my specialty, because they transcend the beliefs you have, your religion, your ethnicity, your cultural background. That's a direction I would love to go."

Looking to the Future

Oka's success on "Heroes" has resulted in new opportunities in movies. In 2007, he appeared in the table-tennis themed comedy *Balls of Fury*, and in 2008 he appeared with Steve Carell and Anne Hathaway in the secret agent comedy *Get Smart*. In addition to acting, Oka sees his career eventually growing to include directing, particularly comedies. "Laughter is kind of a symbolism of peace. It's easy to cry, but it's so hard to laugh.... Love and laughter are universal. Romantic comedies are my specialty, because they transcend the beliefs you have, your religion, your ethnicity, your cultural background. That's a direction I would love to go."

His current filming schedule keeps him very busy, but Oka continues to work part-time for ILM as a consultant. He is only able to work on ILM projects for the equivalent of about three days each week. Working for ILM allows Oka to achieve the goals he set as a child, when he was determined to embrace all of his interests and be successful in more than one kind of job. As he explained, "I always dreamed of winning two Oscars—one technical, one creative."

Oka has also remained philosophical about being categorized by the media as a nerdy geek. "Being a geek is a great thing. I think we're all geeks. Being a geek means you're passionate about something and that defines your uniqueness. I would rather be passionate about something than be apathetic about everything."

HOME AND FAMILY

Oka is single and lives in Los Angeles. He still has a close relationship with his mother, who he says is his real-life superhero. "Anyone who raises a child as a single mother is a hero." He credits her support for his success both behind the scenes and in front of the camera. "She's told me, 'Do what you want to do. Live a life that you don't regret. No matter what happens, make sure that's what you want to do. Just be happy with it and don't have regrets.'"

HOBBIES AND OTHER INTERESTS

Oka speaks English, Japanese, and Spanish. His hobbies include practicing the Kendo style of Japanese swordfighting, playing video games, playing the piano, and singing. He enjoys reading Japanese manga comics, especially those of his favorite author Naoki Urasawa. Oka also writes romantic comedy screenplays. His favorite romantic comedies are *When Harry Met Sally, The Princess Bride, Serendipity,* and *Notting Hill.*

SELECTED CREDITS

Acting

"Scrubs," 2002-04 (TV series)
"Heroes," 2006- (TV series)

Special Effects

Star Wars: Episode I—The Phantom Menace, 1999 (visual effects producer, technical support worker)
The Perfect Storm, 2000 (digital artist)
Star Wars: Episode II—Attack of the Clones, 2002 (digital effects artist)
Hulk, 2003 (technical director)
Terminator 3: Rise of the Machines, 2003 (computer graphics artist)
Star Wars: Episode III—Revenge of the Sith, 2005 (digital artist)
War of the Worlds, 2005 (digital artist)
Pirates of the Caribbean: Dead Man's Chest, 2006 (digital artist)

Writing

Chester's Big Night, 2004 (short film screenplay)

HONORS AND AWARDS

Saturn Award (Academy of Science Fiction, Fantasy & Horror Films, USA): 2007, Best Supporting Actor in a Television Program, for "Heroes"
Future Classic Award (TV Land Awards): 2007, for "Heroes"
AZN Asian Excellence Award (AZN Television): 2007, Outstanding Actor—Television, for "Heroes"
Rave Award (*Wired* magazine): 2007, for "Heroes"

FURTHER READING

Books

Contemporary Theatre, Film, and Television, 2007

Periodicals

Boston Herald, May 7, 2007, p.031
Entertainment Weekly, Nov. 10, 2006, p.30; May 11, 2007, p.H17
Los Angeles Times, Oct. 29, 2006, p.E20
New York Times, Dec. 4, 2006, p.E3
San Francisco Chronicle, Apr. 23, 2007, p.C1
Seattle Times, May 14, 2007
USA Today, Nov. 19, 2006
Wired, Oct. 2006; May 2007, p.130

Online Articles

http://www.comic-con.org/cci/cci07prog_oka.shtml
   (Comic-Con 2007, "Extended Interview with Masi Oka," undated)
http://www.ifmagazine.com/feature.asp?article=2001
   (iF Magazine, "Exclusive Interview: Heroes Star Masi Oka Looks to the Future," Apr. 2, 2007)
http://www.msnbc.msn.com/id/16756741
   (MSNBC.com, "Super Hero: Japanese Nerd Is Hit of 'Heroes,'" Apr. 26, 2007)
http://www.mtv.com/ontv/dyn/trl/interviews.jhtml?interviewId=1560069
   (MTV.com, "TRL Interview: Masi Oka," undated)
http://www.wired.com/entertainment/hollywood/news/2007/04/magkring
   (Wired.com, "Behind the Scenes With 'Heroes' Creator Tim Kring and 'Hiro' Masi Oka, Apr. 23, 2007)
http://www.wired.com/culture/lifestyle/news/2006/10/71984
   (Wired.com, "Masi Oka: Coder, Actor, Hero," Oct. 25, 2006)

ADDRESS

Masi Oka
"Heroes," NBC
30 Rockefeller Plaza
New York, NY 10112

WORLD WIDE WEB SITE

http://www.nbc.com/Heroes/bios/hiro.shtml

Tyler Perry 1969-

American Playwright, Filmmaker, and Actor
Creator of the "Madea" Plays and Movies and the TV Series "House of Payne"

BIRTH

Tyler Perry was born Emmitt Perry Jr. on September 14, 1969, in New Orleans, Louisiana. His father, Emmitt Perry Sr. was a carpenter and contractor. His mother, Maxine Perry, was a preschool teacher. Tyler was the third of four children; he has two older sisters and one younger brother.

YOUTH

Perry grew up in New Orleans in a working-class neighborhood. Two blocks north, there were mansions; two blocks south, there were gang-filled housing projects. Living between the extremes of wealth and poverty "became my metaphor for life," he later noted. Perry faced some significant challenges growing up. Although he was a tall child, he was also sick fairly often, due to asthma. When he joined his father on a worksite, the sawdust would bring on coughing fits. He would rather play quietly at home than run around outside; reading, writing, and drawing were his preferred activities. His father, an orphan who had begun doing manual labor as a child, "understood only the physical," Perry later recalled. "He thought he could beat the softness out of me and make me hard like him." Physical abuse became a regular part of his childhood. He was harmed further when a neighbor molested him.

At school, Perry hid his pain by becoming a class clown. He expressed himself through drawing. He liked to imagine other worlds, "worlds in which I didn't worry about being poor, in which I was someone else's child, a child who lived in a mansion and had a dog." Still, he found it difficult to cope. In his early teens, he slashed his wrists, a half-hearted suicide attempt which was really "a cry for attention," he later recalled. At age 16, Perry's resentment of his father led him to change his first name to Tyler, rather than share the name of the man who beat him. Although he had big dreams, there were few people who supported them. "Where I come from, you can have your dream, but keep it private," he related. "Don't share it with anybody, because they'll try to take it from you and snuff it out. That was the mentality of a lot of people I grew up around."

> "Where I come from, you can have your dream, but keep it private," Perry related. "Don't share it with anybody, because they'll try to take it from you and snuff it out. That was the mentality of a lot of people I grew up around."

EDUCATION

An unhappy teenager, Perry dropped out of high school before graduating. He later earned his General Equivalency Diploma (GED), a certification in which students must pass several exams to demonstrate knowledge equal to a high-school graduate.

CAREER HIGHLIGHTS

Discovering the Healing Power of Writing

After leaving school, Perry tried various occupations. He became a carpenter's apprentice and also worked as a car salesman and a bill collector. In 1990 he moved to Atlanta, Georgia, encouraged by the city's large community of upwardly mobile African Americans. Still, happiness kept eluding him. "The things that I went through as a kid were horrendous. And I carried that into my adult life," Perry said. "I didn't have a catharsis for my childhood pain, most of us don't, and until I learned how to forgive those people and let it go, I was unhappy." One day he was watching Oprah Winfrey's daytime talk show and heard her talk about the power of writing to help heal old hurts. He was inspired to write a journal, but because he didn't want anyone to discover he was writing about himself, he invented characters to relate his story. "That's how my first play started, which features a character who confronts an abuser, forgives him, and moves on," the writer explained.

> "The things that I went through as a kid were horrendous. And I carried that into my adult life," Perry said. "I didn't have a catharsis for my childhood pain, most of us don't, and until I learned how to forgive those people and let it go, I was unhappy."

That first play, *I Know I've Been Changed*, is about two victims of childhood abuse whose faith leads them to overcome their past. In 1992 Perry spent his entire life savings of $12,000 to rent a theater, produce the play, and act in it. It was a dismal failure, drawing only 30 people during a weekend run. One of those audience members invested in the show, however, which allowed Perry to continue pursuing his dream. The aspiring playwright worked at odd jobs over the next six years as he tried to make it in the theater. He had little success, and at times was forced to sell his belongings and live in his car. His financial troubles led to arguments with his family; during one such conflict he yelled back at his father, letting out all the feelings of anger and resentment he had kept inside for so long. The experience led him to forgive his father; "slowly but surely, I began to fuel my days with joy instead of fury," he recalled.

In 1998, Perry resolved to give himself one last chance to succeed and decided to stage his play at Atlanta's House of Blues. On opening night,

Tyler Perry as himself.

putting on his makeup in a freezing room, he felt like giving up—until he looked out the window and saw a line of theatergoers stretched around the block. "God said, 'I tell you when it's over, you don't tell me,'" Perry related. "From that moment on I've been going 100 percent. It sold out everywhere." The playwright toured with his play for the next year, performing in New York, Chicago, Philadelphia, Miami, Dallas, and Washington DC. In each city, *I Know I've Been Changed* played to sellout crowds of mostly African-American audiences.

The success of *I Know I've Been Changed* led to new opportunities for Perry. In 1999, Perry met with Dallas pastor Bishop T.D. Jakes. (For more information on Jakes, see *Biography Today,* Jan. 2005). He asked Perry to help adapt his best-selling book *Woman, Thou Art Loosed* for the stage. Perry asked for creative control, and Jakes allowed him to rewrite the play as well as produce and direct it. The play explored the conflicts between a single mother and her teenage daughter and the abuse that both must confront. The play, featuring numerous gospel numbers, earned some $5 million over a five-month tour in 1999. It made Perry a full-fledged star on the urban theater circuit, sometimes called the "chitlin circuit." This circuit refers to touring performances at theaters that cater primarily to African Americans. Historically, segregation limited black performers to such theaters, because they were banned from performing at many others. "When African Americans couldn't play certain venues, they would play this mar-

TYLER PERRY

Tyler Perry as Madea, his signature character.

ket and do extremely well from the support of the African-American community," Perry explained. "It's the children and grandchildren of those same people that will come out for you."

These first two works show just how unusual Perry is in the world of entertainment. Most entertainers hope to do just one or two things well—for example, they might act, or act and write, or act and direct. But Perry has done it all. While he started out as a playwright, he has also directed, produced, and acted in his own plays; adapted another writer's plays; adapted his own plays into films; directed, produced, and acted in his own films; written a book; and created a TV series. It's a diverse and impressive string of accomplishments.

Creating His Signature Character

Although Perry was pleased with his newfound success, he wanted to move away from issue-oriented drama and include more comedy in his work. He achieved this in his next play, *I Can Do Bad All by Myself* (2000). The play introduced the character of Mable Simmons, also known as "Madea." (Madea, a contraction of "Mother Dear," is an affectionate nickname for grandmother in some African-American communities.) Played by Perry in drag, Madea is a tough grandmother who is never afraid to speak her mind. "We watch with nostalgia when we think about this type of grandmother," he explained. "When she was around, everybody's kid belonged to her.... She kept the entire neighborhood straight.... She doesn't care what you think about her. She's going to tell the truth." The character was inspired by the strong women in Perry's life: his mother, Maxine; his father's mother, who shared wisdom from the Bible; and an aunt from Houston, who was rumored to carry a gun in her purse.

In *I Can Do Bad All by Myself,* straight-talking Madea has plenty to say about the love triangle between Vianne, her husband, and her sister, and the dark family secret they must overcome. Perry, who stands six feet six inches tall, had no doubts about playing the larger-than-life Madea himself. "Men watch women all the time. We sleep with you, we love you, we talk to you, we watch you shower," he explained. "I don't know if it's a Virgo thing, but I'm tuned in." Theater professionals in the Washington DC area found Perry's portrayal of Madea believable, nominating his performance for a Helen Hayes Award for Outstanding Lead Actor in a non-resident production. It was the first time this traditional Washington theater award had recognized a play staged on the urban theater circuit. With Madea's crowd-pleasing character, the play became a hit in theaters all over the U.S.

In this play, Perry established the distinctive style that has marked all his works: a mixture of comedy and melodrama, often dealing with difficult life issues, spiced with musical numbers and presented with professional production values, all communicating a message of Christian faith and forgiveness. In the character of Madea, Perry created a recurring iconic character that has appeared in many of his works, sometimes in the foreground as the main character and sometimes in the background as a subsidiary character—although Madea always manages to make herself heard. In many of his works, Madea is surrounded by her eccentric family members.

Perry continued producing a new play every year, touring to sell-out crowds all over the country. His next three plays also featured Madea, a crowd favorite. In *Diary of a Mad Black Woman* (2001), which opened in his hometown of New Orleans, the play's ending could change every night. The title character is Helen, whose husband of 18 years announces he wants a divorce so he can be with another woman—a woman who has already borne him a child. Helen gives up her middle-class comforts, moves in with her grandmother, Madea, takes a job as a waitress, and learns to move on and find love. In *Madea's Family Reunion* (2002), Madea deals with a funeral, a wedding, and a family reunion all on the same weekend.

The following year, in *Madea's Class Reunion*, Madea meets up with old friends 50 years after graduating from high school. With these plays, Perry was not only earning record box office receipts, but also millions in DVD sales. By marketing his DVDs to small urban stores, Perry found he could increase his audience. "People could see that if they spent their hard-earned money to go to my shows, they were going to have a good time."

Although Madea is a fun role to play, it can be a challenge. "I have to talk high for two hours," Perry remarked, "and the costume is really, really, really hot. I'm soaking wet under there." For his next two works, the playwright remained behind the scenes as director and producer. *Why Did I Get Married?* (2004) tells the story of several couples struggling with issues related to maintaining their relationships, while *Meet the Browns* (2005) shows a dysfunctional family trying to cope after the death of a family member. Both films found loyal audiences. In late 2005 Perry produced *Madea Goes to Jail*, in which the law finally catches up with the outrageous character. For this production he returned to the stage as Madea, but since then he has had little time for touring. He still writes and produces plays, but allows other actors to bring life to his distinctive mixes of comedy, drama, and music. In *What's Done in the Dark* (2006), Mr. Brown visits the emergency room, where staff and patients deal with various emotional problems. In *The Marriage Counselor* (2008), the title character has plenty of advice for her patients, but has trouble fixing her own troubled relationships.

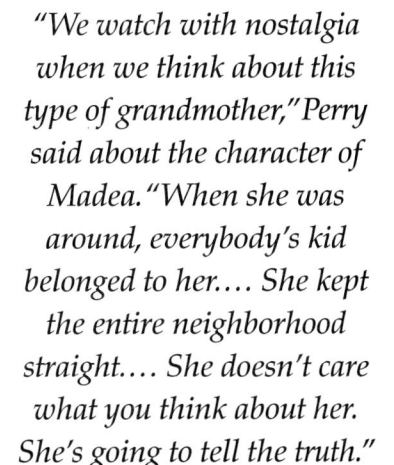

> "We watch with nostalgia when we think about this type of grandmother," Perry said about the character of Madea. "When she was around, everybody's kid belonged to her.... She kept the entire neighborhood straight.... She doesn't care what you think about her. She's going to tell the truth."

Critics have given mixed reviews to Perry's plays, sometimes faulting the comedy as overly broad and the characters as stereotypes. But the author doesn't let negative reviews bother him. He was encouraged by the late African-American playwright August Wilson, author of such Pulitzer Prize-winning dramas as *The Piano Lesson* and *Fences*. "He said, 'If that's your gift, then that's what you do and do it.' Those words stuck with me." According to Perry, his theatrical specialty is "to build a bridge that marries what's deemed 'legitimate theater' and so-called 'chitlin' circuit theater,' and

I think I've done pretty well with that." His popularity and financial success as a playwright are undeniable. In 10 years, his 12 touring stage plays earned more than $150 million at the box office. Perry uses his website, more than half a million subscribers strong, to keep bringing his audience to the theater. They have also purchased more than 15 million DVDs of his plays and films.

Surprising Hollywood with Film Success

Perry's success in theater brought him to the attention of several Hollywood studios. They offered to turn his plays into movies, but only one, Lions Gate, agreed to give him complete creative control. Lions Gate, along with the BET cable channel, financed the adaptation of *Diary of a Mad Black Woman*. Perry did not direct, but he did put up some of his own money to produce the film. "This was the story I wanted to tell most because it's about infidelity, because it's about people learning how to forgive," the writer said. "It's a movie for everyone who needs information on faith, karma, and what goes around comes around. It spoke to so many situations. This is the one I wanted to be my first." *Diary of a Mad Black Woman* (2005) surprised industry experts by earning $22 million in its opening weekend, making it the No. 1 film of the week. Perry wasn't surprised by the film's performance, however. His audience, he explained, were "people who were underserved [by Hollywood], who wanted films with no gratuitous sex, no profanity, no extreme violence."

Perry made his debut as a director with his second film, an adaptation of *Madea's Family Reunion* (2006). He also played three roles in the film: Madea, her grumpy brother Joe, and her upstanding nephew, Brian. The story focuses on two of Madea's nieces, who are dealing with relationships and family expectations. For the film version, "I'm not changing anything or trying to make anything more mainstream," Perry explained. "I'm staying true to the gift God has given to me and I want to give it to people that way." Mindful that more young viewers were watching, however, he did take Madea's guns out of the story. When the film hit theaters in 2006, it scored $30 million in its opening weekend and was No. 1 at the box office for two weeks. Overall, Perry's first two films cost only $11 million to make, yet they grossed nearly $110 million in box office—a financial success that made Hollywood take notice.

For his next film, Perry produced his first original screenplay. *Daddy's Little Girls* (2007) tells the story of a mechanic who falls in love with the lawyer who is helping him fight for custody of his three daughters. Perry remained behind the camera for the film, leaving the acting to Idris Elba,

Scenes from Diary of a Mad Black Woman, *the first of Perry's plays to be made into a movie.*

Gabrielle Union, and Oscar-winner Louis Gossett Jr. *Daddy's Little Girls* earned a respectable $31 million in total box office, and several critics remarked that Perry's skills as a filmmaker were improving. A *Variety* writer observed that "Perry gets better at directing every time he tries" and that his "storytelling is best when it defies convention."

Perry adapted another play for his next film, *Why Did I Get Married?* (2007). This drama about four married couples on a retreat to work on their relationships featured singer-actress Janet Jackson. Perry played the part of a pediatrician married to a busy lawyer. When it opened in 2007, it gave the writer-director another No. 1 hit, earning $21 million in its opening weekend. Because the film didn't feature his signature character, Madea, the film's success again confounded Hollywood's expectations. During its opening weekend, more people went to see *Why Did I Get Married?* than more mainstream Hollywood films starring George Clooney, Mark Wahlberg, and Cate Blanchett.

> "I look at movies where there are no African Americans at all and I go, 'Where in the world is this place where there are no black people?' I want ... people who have been ignored by Hollywood for years to get great entertainment that they can share with their families."

Perry followed that up with another successful adaptation, *Meet the Browns* (2008). There is only a brief appearance by Madea in this movie, which is a family drama and romance. Oscar nominee Angela Bassett starred as a single mother who travels to Georgia for the funeral of her estranged father and meets the family she never knew. The film became one of the all-time top 5 Easter weekend openings, earning $20 million in its first weekend of release. Perry hoped to expand his audiences with his next two films, both based on original screenplays. *The Family That Preys,* scheduled for fall 2008, features award-winning actresses Kathy Bates and Alfre Woodard in the story of a friendship between a wealthy white socialite and a working-class African-American woman. *A Jazz Man's Blues,* scheduled for 2009, is a drama set in the days of segregation.

With total box office grosses for his first five films at $242 million and growing, Hollywood is now well aware of the Tyler Perry phenomenon. In 2007 *Entertainment Weekly* ranked him No. 7 on their list of the "smartest

Perry directing and acting in Madea's Family Reunion *(top),*
Why Did I Get Married? *(middle), and* Daddy's Little Girls *(bottom).*

people in Hollywood." Having proven himself in independent films, Perry believed he was ready to achieve success in a more mainstream film, if he could get the opportunity. He made a start when he earned a role as the head of Starfleet Academy in the 11th *Star Trek* film, expected to be one of the biggest blockbusters of 2009.

Expanding into Other Areas

After his success with plays and movies, Perry was ready to expand into new areas. He decided to branch out and write a book as Madea, which created a bidding war among book publishers. *Don't Make a Black Woman Take off Her Earrings: Madea's Uninhibited Commentaries on Love and Life* is filled with all sorts of common-sense advice. The subjects range from love and marriage to success and politics, with opinions told in Madea's unmistakable voice. It appeared in 2006 and debuted at No. 1 on the *New York Times* bestsellers list, eventually selling more than 400,000 copies. It earned two Quill Awards, which promote literacy and reading, for Book of the Year and Best Humor Book. Perry's profile also increased in 2006 when he won the NAACP Theatre Awards'Trailblazer Award.

Perry next turned his attention to television. He created a sitcom, "House of Payne," and financed the initial run of 10 episodes himself. The story follows Curtis "Pops" Payne, a fire chief whose nephew and children move in after the nephew's drug-addicted wife burns down their house. Their clashes over the best way to raise the children provide most of the comedy. Perry cited classic 1970s sitcoms "Sanford and Son" and "The Jeffersons," both family comedies featuring African Americans, as inspirations for his show. "I want a show that really has heart, deals with life issues, and still makes you laugh," he said. When the initial run was successful, Perry signed an unprecedented deal with cable station TBS. They ordered 100 episodes of the sitcom—the equivalent of four full network seasons—for an amazing $200 million. In 2008, Perry won an NAACP Image Award for Outstanding Comedy Series for "House of Payne."

In addition, Perry has plans for a possible TV series based on his plays *Why Did I Get Married?* and *Meet the Browns*. He has also signed a deal to produce 22 episodes of an animated series to feature his character Madea, targeted to a younger audience. In the long run, he aspires to own his own television network. Tyler Perry's channel, he explained, would be "a network where you can turn it on with your family all day long and get positive reinforcement."

Becoming an Entertainment Mogul

It's unusual to find both creative talent and business savvy in the same person, but Perry seems to have plenty of both. While developing a career as a playwright, actor, and filmmaker, he has made a series of smart business decisions that have earned him a reputation as one of the savviest people in Hollywood. One of his smart decisions was that he has retained ownership of all his work. "I haven't sold one thing, from day one—not one song, not one show, not one script—nothing," Perry said, "and I will not sell a thing. I

A cast shot from "House of Payne."

want to leave all of this to my children." By keeping control of his work, he gains a greater percentage of its profits. This has given him the money and the clout to build his own entertainment production facility in Atlanta. In 2006 he designed and opened his first facility, Tyler Perry Studios (TPS), one of the country's first studios owned by an African American. It had 75,000 square feet, with three soundstages for filming, a 300-seat theater, and enough room to house an acting school and a theater company. By 2008, already needing to expand, he purchased the former world headquarters of Delta Airlines. This new 30-acre studio has 200,000 square feet of space, five soundstages, and a five-acre pond with ducks and geese.

Another smart business decision was the way Perry set out to create a brand for his work, from the very beginning of his career. "If you remember when I started doing plays, there was a 'Mama-I'm-Going-To-The-Store play every week," he explained. "So I started to have them put my name on the marquee and on the ticket so that people would know this play is different from the other shows. I was building the brand, and it started to work. With film, I knew other movies would come along and try to duplicate what I was doing. That's why my name is in front of my movies." In fact, the titles of each of Perry's creations—plays, movies, a book, a TV show—begin with his name. In that way, his many fans can always recognize his works.

> "People need laughter. They need a way to feel better," Perry explained. "I want my work to be a mirror to motivate and inspire."

Despite the financial rewards his career has brought him, Perry stated that "I don't want to just do entertainment to do entertainment. I've never chased money. It's always been about what I can do to motivate and inspire people." If he can reach people who don't ordinarily see themselves in popular entertainment, that's a bonus, he added. "I look at movies where there are no African Americans at all and I go, 'Where in the world is this place where there are no black people?' I want . . . people who have been ignored by Hollywood for years to get great entertainment that they can share with their families." He attributes his success to keeping true to his beliefs and emotions. "I come from a real place, and I come from the realness in my heart," the filmmaker explained. "People can connect to what they know, and I feel like people think they know me and I feel like I know them." In the end, Perry said, "people need laughter. They need a way to feel better. I want my work to be a mirror to motivate and inspire." He concluded: "I'm so glad that God knows what is around the corner, even when we lose hope and lose faith."

HOME AND FAMILY

Perry designed and built his own 16,000-square-foot home on a 12-acre estate outside Atlanta, Georgia. "I wanted this house to be vast. I wanted to make a statement, not in any grand or boastful way, but to let people know what God can do when you believe." He also started a company, Tyler Perry Construction, to build several other homes in the neighborhood, all worth over $1 million. After zealous fans broke into his original home, he began building another Atlanta-area mansion planned to be almost 30,000 square feet in size.

Perry is single but hopes to have a family someday. He looks at the 40-year-plus marriage of his parents—with whom he has reconciled—and knows he needs to have time to devote to a family. "I want to see this time of my life through first, because when I get to [raising children], it will become more important," he said. "When you've been through what I have, you want to know where your kids are. I want to know they're either with me or with their mama."

HOBBIES AND OTHER INTERESTS

After spending years performing his plays on the road and expanding his career into film and television, Perry has had little spare time to devote to hobbies. Even his efforts in designing his own home turned into a side business. He does enjoy spreading the wealth his hard work and success have brought him. After Hurricane Katrina hit his hometown of New Orleans in 2005, he donated $1 million to Oprah's Angel Network, to build new homes for displaced people. He also gave $500,000 to help rebuild Great St. Stephen Full Gospel Baptist Church, which was ruined by flooding.

CREDITS

Plays; Writer, Producer, and Director

I Know I've Been Changed, 1998 (and actor)
Woman, Thou Art Loosed, 1999 (author, with T.D. Jakes)
I Can Do Bad All by Myself, 2000 (and actor)
Behind Closed Doors, 2000 (author, with T.D. Jakes)
Diary of a Mad Black Woman, 2001 (and actor)
Madea's Family Reunion, 2002 (and actor)
Madea's Class Reunion, 2003 (and actor)
Why Did I Get Married?, 2004
Meet the Browns, 2004
Madea Goes to Jail, 2005 (and actor)
What's Done in the Dark, 2006
The Marriage Counselor, 2008

Movies; Writer and Producer

Diary of a Mad Black Woman, 2005 (and actor)

Madea's Family Reunion, 2006 (and director and actor)
Daddy's Little Girls, 2007 (and director)
Why Did I Get Married?, 2007 (and director and actor)
Madea Goes to Jail, 2008 (and director and actor)
Meet the Browns, 2008 (and director and actor)
The Family That Preys, 2008 (and director and actor)

Other

Don't Make a Black Woman Take off Her Earrings: Madea's Uninhibited Commentaries of Love and Life, 2006 (book)
"House of Payne," 2007- (television series; producer, writer, director)

HONORS AND AWARDS

Helen Hayes Award: 2001, for excellence in theater
BET Comedy Award (BET Networks): 2005 (two awards), Outstanding Lead Actor and Outstanding Writing in a Theatrical Film, for *Diary of a Mad Black Woman*
Black Movie Award (Film Life): 2005, Outstanding Achievement in Writing, for *Diary of a Mad Black Woman*
NAACP Theatre Awards (Beverly Hills/Hollywood NAACP): 2006, Trailblazer Award
Quill Awards (Quills Literacy Foundation): 2006 (two awards), Book of the Year and Best Humor Book, for *Don't Make a Black Woman Take off Her Earrings: Madea's Uninhibited Commentaries on Love and Life*
Image Award (NAACP): 2008, Outstanding Comedy Series, for "House of Payne"

FURTHER READING

Periodicals

Current Biography Yearbook, 2005
Ebony, Jan. 2004, p.86; Oct. 2008, p. 72.
Entertainment Weekly, Mar. 3, 2006, p.70; Oct. 12, 2007, p.23; Oct. 26, 2007, p.9
Essence, Mar. 2006, p.120; July 2006, p.70; Aug. 2007, p.96
Forbes, Sep. 15, 2005, p.75
Fortune, Feb. 19, 2007, p.76
Hollywood Reporter, Mar. 31, 2008
Jet, Dec. 1, 2003, p.60; Feb. 28, 2005, p.51; Feb. 27, 2006, p.32
New York Times, July 8, 2004
USA Today, Mar. 2, 2005, p.10D
Variety, Feb. 19, 2007, p.41

Online Articles

http://money.cnn.com/magazines/fortune/fortune_archive/2007/02/19/8400222/index.htm
 (Fortune, "Diary of a Mad Businessman," Feb. 14, 2007)
http://www.oprah.com/rys/omag/rys_omag_200603_aha_c.jhtml
 (Oprah.com, "Tyler Perry's Aha! Moment," 2006)

ADDRESS

Tyler Perry
Tyler Perry Studios (TPS)
541 10th Box Street
Atlanta, GA 30318

WORLD WIDE WEB SITES

http://www.tylerperry.com

Morgan Pressel 1988-

American Professional Golfer
Youngest Woman Ever to Win a Major
Golf Championship

BIRTH

Morgan Pressel was born in Tampa, Florida, on May 23, 1988, the oldest child of Mike and Kathy (Krickstein) Pressel. Her parents owned a real estate business, and her mother was also a professional tennis coach. Pressel has a younger sister, Madison, and a younger brother, Mitchell. Both siblings are following their sister onto the junior golf circuit.

YOUTH

Pressel was born into a very athletic family. Her father played hockey in high school, while her mother won a Big Ten title in tennis at the University of Michigan. Her uncle, Aaron Krickstein, was only 16 when he became the youngest man ever to win a Grand Prix Championship on the Association of Tennis Professionals (ATP) Circuit. He was also the youngest to earn a top 20 world ranking. Pressel showed athletic talent at a young age, able to turn cartwheels at age two. She tried tennis, but her grandfather, Herb Krickstein, felt she wasn't quick enough to become an elite player. He did notice she had great hand-eye coordination, and when she was eight he took her to the driving range. After seeing her natural golf swing, Pressel recalled, "he said, 'that's it, no more tennis.'"

Her parents left Morgan's training up to "Papa" Krickstein, a retired doctor who had experience managing his own kids to athletic success. He enlisted Martin Hall, who had worked with golf greats like Jack Nicklaus, to coach his granddaughter's swing. She practiced regularly, both at home in Florida and summers at her grandparents' home in Michigan. By age 11, Pressel had broken par for an 18-hole course, and by age 12, she was competing against adults—and beating them—in organized tournaments.

> *Pressel was only 15 when her mother died in 2003. "I grew up in a hurry," she recalled. "I've been through a lot. It was the toughest time in my life, and I miss her every day. I know my mother is always with me. She pops into my mind all the time."*

Pressel was finding increasing success in golf, but athletics weren't the defining experience of her teen years. Her mother was diagnosed with breast cancer when Morgan was just 11. Despite going through surgery and chemotherapy, Kathy Pressel was able to support her daughter by attending tournaments. "She was always telling me to be dedicated and determined and competitive, because she was very competitive herself," Morgan remembered. Kathy Pressel fought hard, but her cancer recurred. She died in September 2003 at the age of 43. Morgan was only 15, and the loss devastated her. "I grew up in a hurry," she recalled. "I've been through a lot. It was the toughest time in my life, and I miss her every day. I know my mother is always with me. She pops into my mind all the time." Her mother's fighting spirit would serve as an inspiration to the young golfer.

GOLF SCORING

Golf scoring can be complicated to learn. Players keep track of how many "strokes" it takes them to hit the ball from the tee to the cup; the fewer strokes, the better. "Par" refers to the standard number of strokes it should take a player to complete each hole. For example, most golf courses include short holes, which are usually designated as "par 3," as well as longer holes, which are designated as "par 5." On a regulation, 18-hole golf course, par for all holes will add up to 72. Depending on the number of strokes taken on a given hole, a player can shoot par, a birdie (one under par), an eagle (two under par), a bogey (one over par), a double bogey (two over par), etc.

On the professional golf circuit, most tournaments take place over four days. Each day, all the players shoot one "round" of 18 holes. After the first two rounds, they often cut the field to the top 60 or 70 golfers (players either "make" or "miss the cut"). After all four rounds, the scores are totaled and the player with the lowest score wins the tournament. This format is called "stroke play." There are many tournaments on the women's professional golf tour, but the most prestigious are the four major or "Grand Slam" events: the British Open, the Kraft Nabisco Championship, the U.S. Women's Open, and the McDonald's LPGA Championship.

Many amateur tournaments and team tournaments (like the Solheim Cup) use a different scoring system, called "match play." In this system, golfers play one-on-one over 18 holes. Whoever takes the fewest strokes on a hole scores a single point; if the two golfers tie, they split the point. They keep a running tally of holes; if Player A has won 5 holes and Player B has won 3 holes, Player A is considered "2 up." A match can end before 18 holes if one player mathematically eliminates the other. In this case, the final score is listed as two numbers: the first indicating how many up the winner was, the second showing how many holes were left over. The highest winning score in match play is thus "10-and-8," meaning the winner won the first 10 holes, so they did not need to play the last eight. If a round of 18 holes ends in a tie, the match goes to "sudden death" on extra holes—meaning that the first player to win a hole wins the match.

EDUCATION

Pressel attended St. Andrew's High School of Boca Raton, Florida. As a freshman, she placed second in the state golf finals; her last three years she won the state competition, setting records for both one-day and total scores. Her low scores also helped her team to state championships in 2002 and 2003. She graduated from St. Andrew's in 2006, earning a 3.9 grade point average with a schedule that included Advanced Placement classes. She scored well enough on the SAT (including 790 out of 800 on the math portion) to qualify for Duke University, which offered her a golf scholarship. She decided to forego college, however, to begin her career as a professional golfer.

CAREER HIGHLIGHTS

Enjoying a Brilliant Amateur Career

Pressel first garnered national attention for her golf game when she was only 12 years old. In 2001 she won a qualifying tournament for the U.S. Women's Open by shooting two under par, setting a record (later broken) as the youngest player ever to qualify for an LPGA event. At the Open (one of golf's four major championships), she played two rounds of 77 and missed the cut to play the final two rounds. Still, it was a respectable performance for someone so young—better than 19 pros scored that year—and it brought her national media attention. "I had so much fun that week, I knew I wanted to be a professional golfer," Pressel remembered. The competition "was a wakeup call, too," she added. "I saw how good these players were, how much I needed to improve, but I knew this is where I wanted to be every week."

Although Pressel gained attention by qualifying for professional tournaments at such a young age, she felt she could best develop her skills by competing in amateur events. She entered tournaments sponsored by the American Junior Golf Association (AJGA); by playing against golfers her own age, she learned to hone her game under pressure. Pressel also increased her practice time, devoting hours after school and on weekends to improving her game. In 2002 she participated in the PING Junior Solheim Cup, a team match-play competition between the top 12 girl golfers from the U.S. and Europe. She went undefeated in her matches to help the U.S. win the Cup. She also had at least three top-20 finishes at AJGA events that year, including a third-place tie at the Thunderbird International Junior.

In 2003 Pressel qualified for the U.S. Women's Open again. This time she made the cut and finished 52nd with an average of 76. She earned a fourth-place finish in the Rolex Girls Junior Championship and had a 12-stroke victory at the Buick Junior Open. She was again named to the PING Junior Solheim Cup team, but was unable to travel to Europe with the team because of her mother's illness, which also forced her to pull out of three tournaments that summer. Despite her up-and-down year, Pressel earned her first appearance on the Junior All-American First Team in 2003. After her mother's death, she found some solace on the golf course and in the knowledge that her mother would have wanted her to keep pursuing her dream.

In 2004, Pressel began achieving more consistent results in her tournaments. She tied for second at the Rolex Girls Junior Championship and tied for fourth at McDonald's Betsy Rawls Girls Championship. She also began a phenomenal run of victories in AJGA invitational events, winning the Rolex Tournament of Champions in July; the Polo Golf Junior Classic in November; the Thunderbird International Junior in May 2005; the Rolex Girls Junior Championship in June 2005; and finally the McDonald's Betsy Rawls Girls Championship in July 2005. This accomplishment made her one of only two players to ever win the "Career AJGA Slam." She also helped the U.S. to another victory at the 2005 PING Junior Solheim Cup. Overall, she won 11 AJGA tournaments, including all five she entered in 2005. She set a record for largest margin of victory (16 strokes) in an AJGA tournament and was named AJGA Player of the Year in 2005.

Pressel at age 12, when she qualified for the 2002 Women's Open Tournament. She was the youngest player ever to qualify for an LPGA event.

Besides dominating AJGA events, Pressel was also having success in adult events, both amateur and professional. By early 2005 she was the nation's number one-ranked female amateur. She won the 2004 North and South Women's Amateur Golf Championship (their youngest champion ever) and the 2005 Women's Amateur Golf Championship—the latter by a dominating score of 9-and-8. Most impressive, she was the runner-up at the 2005 U.S. Women's Open. Going into the last hole, she was tied for the lead with Birdie Kim—until Kim hit a phenomenal shot out of a sand bunker and scored a birdie. "When her shot went in, it felt like someone smacking me on the head with a two-by-four," Pressel recalled. "Oh, no, somebody pinch me. That didn't just happen. I knew how tough it was to make birdie on that hole and that I'd probably just lost. But I gave it my best shot."

« *At the 2005 U.S. Women's Open, Pressel was tied for the lead with Birdie Kim on the last hole—until Kim hit a phenomenal shot out of a sand bunker and scored a birdie. "When her shot went in, it felt like someone smacking me on the head with a two-by-four," Pressel recalled. "Oh, no, somebody pinch me. That didn't just happen. I knew how tough it was to make birdie on that hole and that I'd probably just lost. But I gave it my best shot."* »

During 2005 Pressel competed in seven LPGA events, making all seven cuts and never finishing below 25th place. She capped off her amateur career by winning the 2006 Nancy Lopez Award as the year's outstanding female amateur golfer. "I got a little taste of winning, and I want a whole lot more," Pressel stated of her amateur career. "AJGA golf was a great experience for me. I made a lot of friends, and I played well, and I competed against the toughest fields in junior golf for four years."

Turning Pro at 17

With her success on both the amateur and LPGA levels, Pressel decided she was ready to turn professional. LPGA rules state that a player must be 18 to apply for membership, but those between the ages of 15 and 18 can ask for an exception to the rule. She asked for, and was granted, permission to try to qualify for the LPGA tour. She attended LPGA "Qualifying School"—a five-round competition—and tied for sixth. This earned her "exempt" status for future LPGA events, meaning she could bypass qualifying. Based on this finish, she asked the LPGA to allow her to join the tour at the beginning of 2006, instead of having to wait for her birthday at the end of May. When the tour granted her request, Pressel called it "a dream come true."

Pressel reacts to a missed birdie putt during the 2005 U.S. Women's Open.

Although she was now competing as a professional, Pressel didn't try to change her game. "I don't think it's going to be that much different, I'm still out there trying to win tournaments and play my best," she said. "The only thing that has changed is the level of competition and hopefully my ability." The young golfer made the most of her new status on the LPGA tour. She earned nine top-10 finishes in 2006, including a third place at the Longs Drugs Challenge and three fifth-place ties. She competed in all the major tournaments, including her first McDonald's LPGA and British Open Championships; her best finish was a tie for 13th at the Kraft Nabisco Championship. In the 2006 season, she finished third in the rookie of the year race, with total winnings of $465,685. At the end of the year she was in 21st place in the Rolex Women's World Golf Rankings, and she was selected for the 16-member Team International for the Lexus Cup.

Although this was a promising start for a pro golfer, Pressel wasn't satisfied. "I didn't play as well as I would have liked," she later observed. So to get ready for 2007, "I worked really hard in the off season, worked hard in the gym, worked hard on my swing with my coach, Martin Hall, and I came out a little bit more prepared to play well this year. And I got a lot of experience last year. And I was certainly ready to compete and ready to win." She began the 2007 season with some promising performances. She tied for fourth at the SBS Open at Turtle Bay; the following week she tied for third at the Fields Open in Hawaii.

> "I love to compete," Pressel noted. "I love the search for perfection. I'm constantly refining things, trying to be as perfect a player as I can be."

Entering the first major tournament of the 2007 season, the Kraft Nabisco Championship at Mission Hills Country Club in Rancho Mirage, California, Pressel had the same confidence and high hopes she has brought to all her tournaments. She played most of the tournament behind the leaders, starting the final round of 18 four strokes behind. But Pressel played the last 24 holes of the tournament without a single bogey, finishing three under par overall. Then she had to wait for the last golfers to finish their rounds. As she watched, the leader bogeyed four holes in a row and then missed a birdie on 18, leaving Pressel alone in the lead. As winner of the 2007 Kraft Nabisco Championship, Pressel became the youngest woman ever to win an LPGA major. The win also vaulted her into the top five of the Rolex World Rankings and qualified her for the ADT Championship, the final event of the LPGA season, which earns $1 million for the winner. "[It] seems like it's been forever" since her first LPGA appearance, Pressel told the media after her win. "I've always had high hopes and dreams. This is exciting."

Two months later, Pressel broke the $1 million career earnings mark at the McDonald's LPGA Championship, finishing 14th. Through her first 18 tournaments of the 2007 season, she missed the cut only twice and finished in the top 10 seven times. This included a tie for 10th at the U.S. Women's Open and a second-place finish at the Jamie Farr Owens Corning Classic. In the latter tournament, Pressel recorded her first hole-in-one as a professional—the only one shot during the competition's four rounds. By the end of August 2007 she had earned a place on the 2007 Solheim Cup team, as one of 12 golfers to represent the U.S. in competition against Europe. In all, she had eight finishes in the top 10, with total season winnings of $1.8 million.

Pressel with the trophy from her first major win—the Dinah Shore Trophy from the 2007 LPGA Kraft Nabisco Championship.

Pressel's performance starting the 2008 season was good, although not spectacular. As of August 2008, she had played in 19 tournaments, earning almost half a million dollars. She didn't win any of those events, but she had four finishes in the top 10: in March at the HSBC Women's Champions (tied for eighth place); in May at the Sybase Classic (tied for second place, her highest finish that season); in June at the McDonald's LPGA Championship (tied for sixth place); and also in June at the Wegman's LPGA (tied for tenth). As of this writing, the season had several months left to go, so her ultimate finish was unclear.

Building a Pro Career

Pressel believes that, with hard work and determination, she can have a long career as a professional golfer. "I love to compete," she noted. "I love the search for perfection. I'm constantly refining things, trying to be as perfect a player as I can be." For instance, she admitted that "putting is what I need to practice the most," so she set up a track and practiced 100 putts in a row. Strength and flexibility training are also important parts of her regimen.

Although Pressel is full of focus and control when it comes to her golf game, she is not always so reserved when it comes to her emotions. She cried tears of happiness during her victory at the Kraft Nabisco Championship and tears of frustration when she double-bogeyed her final hole at the 2007 U.S. Women's to finish a 6-over-par round. Although tradition dictates that golf players should be more restrained on the course, "I don't think it's a bad thing at all, not only in my playing, but in relating to fans," Pressel said. "I don't think I'm going to change anytime soon." Her emotional style certainly hasn't hurt her appeal with fans, or her ability to win lucrative endorsements. In 2007 she had deals with Callaway Golf, Polo Ralph Lauren (their first American female athlete), Oakley sunglasses, and Gemisis cultured diamonds.

> "I know my mom wants me to keep chasing my dream and to be happy," Pressel said. "I'm where I want to be. And she's with me every day."

Pressel has also earned a reputation as a player who is not afraid to speak her mind. She gained a lot of publicity for her remarks about Michelle Wie, the sometimes controversial teen sensation who has played in men's PGA tournaments. Although Wie has millions of dollars in endorsements, she has yet to win a professional tournament. Pressel observed, "Michelle hasn't played a lot of junior golf, so she hasn't learned how to finish tournaments. She's obviously more interested in making cuts. But if you keep playing against players you can't beat, how are you going to learn to win?" When asked if she thought her comments were controversial, she responded that "people always have their own opinions and say what they want. Whether it's unfair or not, I don't know. That's just the way I am. I'm just being myself. I'm not going to hide anything because I have nothing to hide. I'm not going to sugarcoat it, that's for sure." (For more information on Wie, see *Biography Today*, Sep. 2004).

Pressel hasn't focused on Wie more than any other competitor. "We have an on-course rivalry, but are friendly both on and off the course," she explained in her blog. "Any comments I have made in the past about her were always about a general situation, never anything personal. But, if the media wants to build it up, it is probably a good thing for the LPGA Tour."

Besides Pressel and Wie, there are several golfers in their teens and early 20s who are becoming prominent on the tour. "Everyone has their time, and our time is now," Pressel said. "We're bringing a lot of interest to the game. The ratings [for the Open] were way up. I just think it's fantastic for the game."

Professional golf is a game Pressel hopes to both dominate and champion in the future. "I want to be the best player in the world, definitely Hall of Fame, and see where it takes me," she has said. "I want to be influential, maybe help change the game a little bit, help change the face of the game: [make it] a little more popular, maybe raise prize money." At a petite 5'5" tall, Pressel doesn't have the power to drive the ball as far as some of her competitors. She makes up for it with precision drives, a superb short game, and careful putting—in short, she finds the greens and makes birdies. With the hard work and determination her family has inspired in her, she is likely to meet her goal. "I know my mom wants me to keep chasing my dream and to be happy," Pressel said. "I'm where I want to be. And she's with me every day."

HOME AND FAMILY

When not on tour, Pressel lives in her home town of Boca Raton, Florida, with her grandparents, Herb and Evelyn Krickstein. She has lived with them since her mother's death in 2003; they accompany her when she is traveling on the LPGA Tour, while her father takes care of her two younger siblings. While at home, she spends time with friends and her younger siblings. She and her family also attend services at a local Jewish synagogue, where Pressel made her bat mitzvah.

HOBBIES AND OTHER INTERESTS

Pressel enjoys photography, computers, and using the newest electronic gadgets (such as her Blackberry) to keep in touch with friends. She loves music and enjoys alternative bands such as her favorite, Fall Out Boy, as well as the occasional top-40 and hip hop artist. Pressel is involved with breast and ovarian cancer charities, including the Florida Hospital Cancer Institute's Kathryn Krickstein Pressel Memorial Fund, which is named after her late mother. In late 2005 she received the CoURagE Award from fellow golfer Cristie Kerr's charity Birdies for Breast Cancer. Pressel has also stated her intent to create her own charity golf event, perhaps as soon as 2008.

HONORS AND AWARDS

Junior All-American First Team: 2003, 2004, 2005

Girls Rolex Junior Player of the Year (American Junior Golf Association): 2005
Nancy Lopez Award (American Junior Golf Association): 2006
Kraft Nabisco Championship: 2007

FURTHER READING

Periodicals

Baltimore Sun, Feb. 16, 2006, p.E9
Detroit Free Press, July 6, 2005
Golf Digest, Feb. 2006, p.83
New York Times, June 6, 2007, p.D1
Palm Beach Post, Aug. 14, 2005
Philadelphia Inquirer, June 2, 2006
South Florida Sun-Sentinel, Nov. 8, 2004, p.A1; Aug. 8, 2005, p.C1; June 24, 2007
Sports Illustrated, May 28, 2001, p.G11; Aug. 8, 2005, p.52
Sports Illustrated for Kids, July 2007, p.42
USA Today, May 16, 2001, p.C3; Aug. 7, 2005; June 27, 2007, p.C3

Online Articles

http://sports.espn.go.com
 (ESPN, "Pressel Survives, Becomes Youngest to Win LPGA Major," Apr. 1, 2007)
http://www.golfdigest.com
 (GolfWorld News & Tours, "Continuing Education," Feb. 3, 2006)
http://www.jewishtimes.com
 (Jewish Times, "They Punch, Putt, Dribble, Tackle and Skate and They're All Jewish," Mar. 16, 2007)

ADDRESS

Morgan Pressel
Ladies Professional Golf Association
100 International Golf Drive
Daytona Beach, FL. 32124-1092

WORLD WIDE WEB SITES

http://www.LPGA.com
http://www.callawaygolf.com

Rihanna 1988-

Barbadian Singer
Performer of the Hit Songs "Pon de Replay,"
"S.O.S." and "Umbrella"

BIRTH

Rihanna was born Robyn Rihanna Fenty in St. Michael, Barbados, on February 20, 1988 (some sources say February 18). Barbados is an island nation located in the southeastern Caribbean region with strong ties to Great Britain. Rihanna is of mixed Irish and Guyanese ancestry, with a black mother and a biracial father. Her mother, Monica Fenty, worked as an accountant and now owns a clothing store. Her father, Ronald

Fenty, is employed by a clothing manufacturer. Rihanna has two younger brothers, Rajad and Rorrey.

YOUTH

Rihanna has said that her early life was often troubled by unhappy incidents associated with her father's substance abuse problems. He has since recovered. At the time, however, his use of alcohol, crack cocaine, and marijuana disrupted the household and caused problems for the family. Rihanna experienced severe headaches that persisted until her parents divorced when she was 14 years old.

Still, during her free time Rihanna enjoyed island life. She played with her brothers and their friends more than with dolls or other girls. According to Rihanna, "I was more of a tomboy, so I'd climb trees and come home all scratched up." She loved singing and dancing, too. She recalled, "I just knew that I loved music, and I developed a passion for it. I really, really wanted to become a singer from a very young age." However, she only sang in the shower or in front of a mirror in her bedroom. "I would hold a broom like a mike stand.... My neighbors would complain—they always knew when I was home." Rihanna first performed publicly in 2004, when she appeared in a high school talent show. She sang Mariah Carey's "Hero" in the school competition and won. At about the same time she won a local beauty contest and formed a trio with two of her friends.

————— " —————

From an early age, Rihanna recalled, "I just knew that I loved music, and I developed a passion for it. I really, really wanted to become a singer from a very young age."

————— " —————

EDUCATION

Rihanna attended Charles F. Broome Memorial elementary school and Combermere secondary school, which is equivalent to high school in the United States. She left school before graduating in order to pursue her singing career. After that, she was home schooled to complete her education.

CAREER HIGHLIGHTS

In December 2003, when Rihanna was 15 years old, a friend introduced her to record producer Evan Rogers, who had worked with such recording artists as Christina Aguilera, Kelly Clarkson, and Jessica Simpson. Rogers was vacationing in Barbados with his wife, a native of the island, when Rihanna auditioned for him at the hotel where he was staying. Based on that performance, Rogers introduced her to Carl Sturken, his partner in the production company SRP Records. The pair invited her to record with them in New York. During breaks from school Rihanna traveled to the United States and began working on recordings for a demo CD. Among the songs on the disc was the original version of "Pon de Replay," which would become her first international hit.

As soon as Rihanna completed the demo recording, she returned to Barbados. In the meantime Rogers sent the disc to several record companies. Def Jam Recordings was the first to call him—the very next day—to set up a live audition for Rihanna with Def Jam president Jay-Z (Shawn Carter). Rihanna flew back to the United States and within 24 hours was in Jay-Z's office in New York performing for him and a small group of record company executives and lawyers. She later recalled the whirlwind speed of the event. "I left to go back to Barbados from New York on the Monday. The demo was sent in on Wednesday, Def Jam called back Thursday, and the producers went over for a meeting, so I had to come back on Friday evening. I was supposed to come back on my next school holiday in February but the guys over at Def Jam said, 'Why do you have to wait?' That's when I knew it was serious."

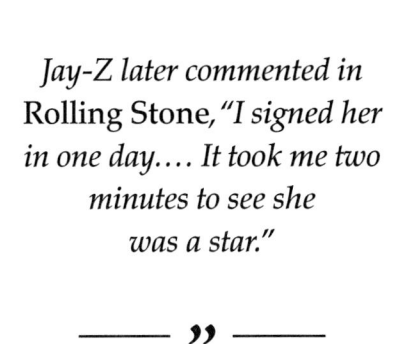

> *Jay-Z later commented in* Rolling Stone, *"I signed her in one day.... It took me two minutes to see she was a star."*

The audition so impressed Jay-Z and Def Jam that they told Rihanna's representatives to cancel her auditions for other companies, and they worked out an agreement on the spot. That same night, Rihanna signed a contract to record six CDs for the label. She was just 16 years old. Jay-Z later commented in *Rolling Stone*, "I signed her in one day.... It took me two minutes to see she was a star."

Music of the Sun

Rihanna's first album, *Music of the Sun* (2005), combines urban dance pop, rhythm and blues, and reggae with straightforward pop ballads that showcase her vocal talents and her island charm. The biggest hit on the album was the dance anthem "Pon de Replay," cowritten by Rogers and Sturken,

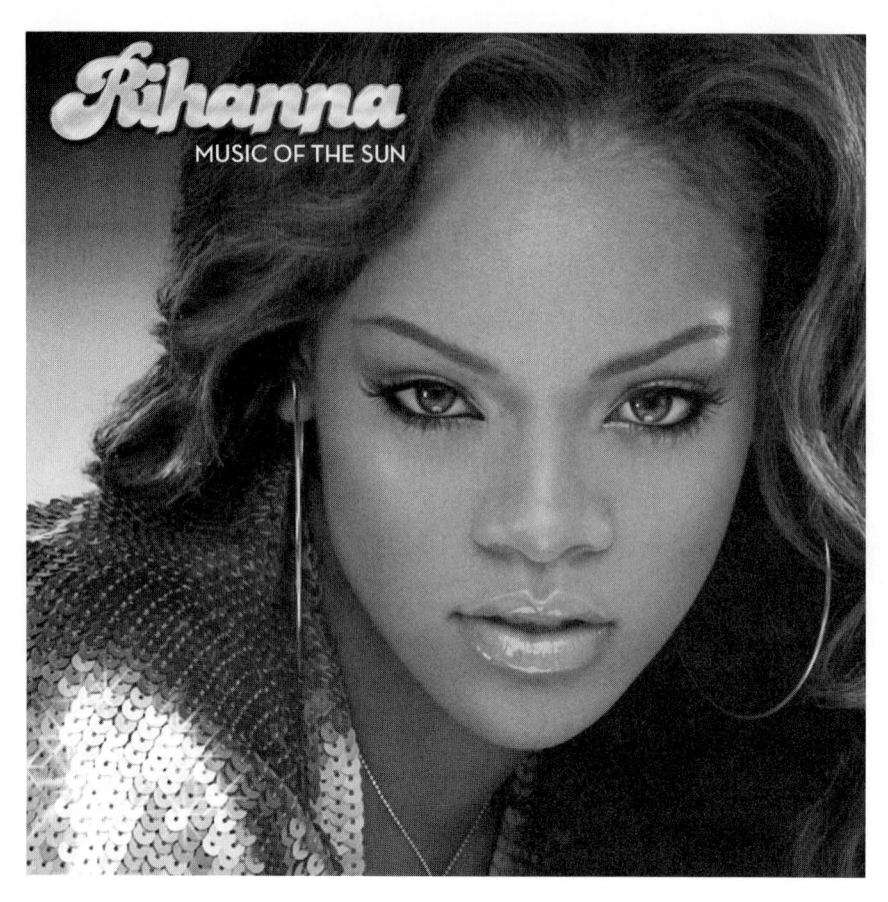

Rihanna released her first CD, Music of the Sun, *when she was just 17.*

along with Vada Nobles and Alisha Brooks. Released as a single in June 2005, "Pon de Replay" became a chart-topping international hit that summer. It was the first song of her own that Rihanna ever heard on the radio. She recalled, "My mom and I were in a mall. The deejay had given me a heads-up that he was going to play it, so I bought a handheld radio, and I was listening to it all day. When it came on, I just started screaming with my mom."

"Pon de replay" is a Barbadian dialect phrase meaning "play it again." She explained the expression, saying, "It's just language that we speak in Barbados. It's broken English. Pon is *on*, De means *the*, so it's just basically telling the DJ to put my song on the replay." In the song Rihanna repeatedly urges a deejay to "turn the music up." *People* reviewer Chuck Arnold noted that with "its infectious, hand-clapping dancehall groove, Rihanna's smash 'Pon de Replay' has indeed had deejays turning the music up, over and over." Mark Medina, the program director of a radio station in Phoenix, Arizona, called "Pon de Replay" "a good summer song.... You kind of get into the rhythm of it and it jumps off the dial."

With the worldwide success of her first release, Rihanna embarked on a concert tour as the opening act for singer Gwen Stefani. Initially, some critics believed that Rihanna would not be able to sustain the level of success that she attained with her first album. Others compared her to the American pop and R&B superstar Beyoncé Knowles, who rose to fame in the 1990s as the lead singer of the group Destiny's Child. Rihanna found the comparison flattering at first because she was a fan of Beyoncé, but it became frustrating as she struggled to create her own musical identity. As she later said, "it does get a little upsetting when people say I copy her."

> *The first time Rihanna heard one of her songs on the radio, "My mom and I were in a mall. The deejay had given me a heads-up that he was going to play it, so I bought a handheld radio, and I was listening to it all day. When it came on, I just started screaming with my mom."*

Before long Rihanna was in the studio again, working on her second album, *A Girl Like Me* (2006). By summer she had another international success with the single "S.O.S." from her new album. "S.O.S." grabs listeners' attention with the repeated use of a sampled beat from the 1981 megahit "Tainted Love" by the British duo Soft Cell. In the song Rihanna fuses a Caribbean dance groove with 1980s power pop. "'S.O.S.' talks about being rescued from a crazy feeling, calling out for help," she explained. "You know like when you have a huge crush on a guy, come rescue me from feeling this crazy." The single topped the *Billboard* Pop, Dance, and Hot 100 charts in the United States, surpassing the earlier success of "Pon de Replay."

In support of *A Girl Like Me,* Rihanna toured during 2006 with such acts as Jay-Z and Ne-Yo in Australia and with the Pussycat Dolls in the United Kingdom. She soon released a second single from the album, the ballad "Unfaithful," a song written by her friend Ne-Yo. "Unfaithful" tells the story of a woman who regrets cheating on a good man. Critics noted that the song showcased a different aspect of Rihanna as a performer who could sing with emotion rather than just produce danceable pop tunes. Reviewer Clover Hope commented in *Billboard* that "['Unfaithful'] ultimately reveals a promising young vocalist growing into her own."

For the third single from *A Girl Like Me*, Rihanna chose "We Ride." The song tells a story very different from the one in "Unfaithful." According to Rihanna, "'We Ride' is about this guy saying over and over again, 'When we ride, we ride, we're gonna be together until the day that we die'—promising all these things.... And then it turns out he broke all of his promises."

Good Girl Gone Bad

Rihanna's third album, *Good Girl Gone Bad*, was released in June 2007, less than two years after her first CD. The rapid pace with which she produced new recordings drew comments from music writers, who noted that artists often wait two to three years between CDs in order to maximize sales. But Rihanna confessed to having workaholic tendencies. "I just love making music and the label loves to put me in the studio, so that always works great together." Antonio "L.A." Reid, chairman of the Island Def Jam Music Group, characterized Rihanna as an exceptionally dedicated performer. He told *Jet*, "Since the day that Rihanna was signed to the label, I don't recall her ever not working.... I don't recall her ever taking time off for anything, whether it is personal or whatever. We've always had scheduling nightmares because this woman works so hard. She's absolutely one of the hardest-working artists I've ever met or been involved with at any level."

Good Girl Gone Bad presented Rihanna as a more mature, edgy artist. She explained the title as referring to attitude, not behavior. In order to emphasize the break with her previous records, she transformed her appearance for the promotional tour introducing the record. She wore black leather clothing, dyed her hair black, and had her hair cut in a short, jagged bob. According to Rihanna, "My new look is purposely adult.... I wanted to show growth as a person and artist. But for me, 'bad girl' does not mean 'wild girl.' It's more about taking chances, trying new things—visually and musically."

In spring 2007 Rihanna had her biggest success yet with the release of "Umbrella," the lead single from *Good Girl Gone Bad*. The song reached No. 1 on the charts in numerous countries around the world, including the United States, United Kingdom, Canada, and Australia. The song was cowritten and produced by Jay-Z, who also performed on the song. "'Umbrella' is about being there for the ones you love," Rihanna said, "whether it is a friend, family, or a boyfriend, the song is basically saying no matter what, I'll be there for you. We all have and need those friends in our lives!" In December 2007 the song was nominated for two Grammy Awards, for song of the year and for record of the year.

Rihanna had a string of hits with her third release, Good Girl Gone Bad.

In addition to collaborating with Jay-Z and Ne-Yo on the album, Rihanna also worked with Justin Timberlake, who cowrote the ballad "Rehab," and with Timbaland (Timothy Z. Mosley), who performed with Rihanna on that track. As Timberlake told *Entertainment Weekly,* "[Rihanna is] a young artist stepping into the adult world.... To me, that song is the bridge for her to be accepted as an adult in the music industry."

The single "Shut Up and Drive," written by Rogers and Sturken, was released in June 2007. In the accompanying video Rihanna was shown working in an all-female auto shop and waving the checkered flag to start a race between two rival drivers. In *Billboard* Chuck Taylor asserted that with such hits "Rihanna and an able collaborative stable have catapulted a potential one-trick dancehall diva to the most dexterous singer of the decade's second half."

Several songs on *Good Girl Gone Bad* describe relationship troubles, including the title track "Good Girl Gone Bad" and "Let Me Get That."

"Breaking Dishes" is a revenge song sung by a woman waiting for an unfaithful man to come home. It includes the lines, "I am killing time, you know bleaching your clothes / I am roasting marshmallows on the fire / And what I am burning is your attire." But there are also danceable club hits, such as "Don't Stop the Music," a song about meeting a new guy at a disco. The song samples Michael Jackson's "Wanna Be Startin' Somethin'" (1982) with Rihanna repeating the African chant made famous by Jackson: "Mama-se, mama-sa, ma-ma-koo-sa." "Don't Stop the Music" was nominated for a Grammy Award as the best dance recording of 2007. Rihanna related her ability to create hit dance music to her own love of dance. "I love to dance and love seeing people dance. I'm from Barbados—it's all about rhythm and groove."

> "Since the day that Rihanna was signed to the label, I don't recall her ever not working," said L.A. Reid, chairman of the Island Def Jam Music Group. "I don't recall her ever taking time off for anything.... We've always had scheduling nightmares because this woman works so hard. She's absolutely one of the hardest-working artists I've ever met or been involved with at any level."

In fall 2007 Rihanna and Ne-Yo scored a hit together with their duet "Hate That I Love You," cowritten by Ne-Yo. The song relates the feeling of an overwhelming romantic relationship that leaves each partner feeling vulnerable. Reaching the top ten on the American pop charts, the song was also nominated for two Grammy Awards, as the best R&B performance by a duo or group and as the best R&B song of the year. The pair performed "Hate That I Love You" on the telecast of the American Music Awards in November 2007, where Rihanna was named Favorite Female Soul/R&B Artist of the year.

With hit after hit, *Good Girl Gone Bad* elevated Rihanna to a new level of global stardom in 2007 and enhanced her reputation as a singer who could delve into a broader range of subjects and genres. In a review of the album in *Entertainment Weekly*, Neil Drumming noted that "Rihanna's at her best when she's brash and unpredictable and summoning the spirit of years past." Zac Soto gave an enthusiastic review in *Giant*, calling *Good Girl Gone Bad* "one of the most daring albums in the recent history of mainstream music. To say that this album exceeds expectations would be an understatement; it changes the way we should view Rihanna as an artist from now on."

Spokesperson for Beauty and Fitness Lines

With youth, beauty, charisma, and a global audience, Rihanna was quickly identified as a fashion trendsetter who would appeal to young consumers worldwide. By 2006 she had signed a number of product endorsement deals. Her image and music were used to promote tourism in Barbados and to market such well-known brands as Nike, JCPenney, CoverGirl, and Fuzed. For the cosmetics line Clinique, Rihanna recorded "Just Be Happy," a jazzy, upbeat pop song to be used in promotion of the Happy fragrance. The CoverGirl campaign featured her in ads for lip products and included life-size Rihanna stand-up cut outs in stores. Because she is young, she has maintained a special connection with teenaged fans. "I'm at the age where you start to cross over into young womanhood, but I'm still a teen and I love being a teen. I like to read magazines. I like to go shopping. I love using the telephone."

A scene with Rihanna and Ne-Yo from the video for "Hate That I Love You."

Rihanna has described herself as a "very fun-loving person" and a risk-taker. "I like to be adventurous in everything," she once said. "I like things that are cool. I hate the typical. I like to go bowling. I love going to the movies. That's just who I am." While her success in the music industry has transformed her life, as of 2007 she was still getting used to the idea of international celebrity. "Star-studded events kind of weird me out," she confided. "I'm scared to talk to anybody so I just stand in the corner!" She hopes to avoid the distractions that have landed some other young stars in jail or rehab and sees herself as a role model for other teens. "I'm very aware of the impact I have on people's lives … so I only wanna make positive ones. Why not help? Be that example they can follow. I always wanted to make a difference in the world. I was always trying to figure out how can I change the world."

BIOGRAPHY TODAY • 2008 Annual Cumulation

Rihanna performing live on "The Today Show."

Rihanna remains humbled by the success she has achieved during her teen years. "It's definitely a fairytale, and I wake up every day so thankful," she revealed "It's just proof to everyone out there that no matter where you're from, if you work really hard and believe in your dreams they can come true."

HOME AND FAMILY

When she first traveled to the United States to work, Rihanna lived in Connecticut in the home of her music producer, Evan Rogers, and his wife, Jackie. In 2007 Rihanna moved into her own apartment in Los Angeles, California.

FAVORITE MUSIC

Rihanna lists the pop and R&B singers Mariah Carey, Whitney Houston, Brandy, and Beyoncé as particular influences. When recording *Good Girl Gone Bad*, she says, she listened to the Brandy album *Afrodisiac* and "admired that every song was a great song." Coming from the Caribbean, she also names several reggae artists among her influences: "Of course Bob Marley. I love Sean Paul. I love Beenie Man. Bounty Killer is still one of my favorites. Vybz Kartel. 'Redemption Song' is my all time favorite."

> "It's definitely a fairytale, and I wake up every day so thankful," Rihanna revealed "It's just proof to everyone out there that no matter where you're from, if you work really hard and believe in your dreams they can come true."

HOBBIES AND OTHER INTERESTS

Rihanna founded the medical charity Believe, whose "goal is to assist children with life-threatening diseases," including AIDS, leukemia, and cancer, among others. An international organization, Believe raises money for medical research and funds medical care for those in need. In addition, Rihanna performed in a special benefit concert in May 2007 in New York City in support of the organ donation network DKMS and the Bone Marrow Association, and she also performed in the Live Earth concert in July 2007 in Tokyo, Japan.

SELECTED RECORDINGS

Music of the Sun, 2005
A Girl Like Me, 2006
Good Girl Gone Bad, 2007

SELECTED FILMS

Bring It On: All or Nothing, 2006

HONORS AND AWARDS

Billboard Music Awards: 2006 (three awards), Female Artist of the Year, Female Hot 100 Artist of the Year, Pop 100 Artist of the Year
MTV Video Awards: 2006, Best New Artist Video; 2007 (two awards; with Jay-Z) Monster Single of the Year and Video of the Year, both for "Umbrella"
MuchMusic Video Awards: 2006, Best International Artist
Music of Black Origin (MOBO) Awards: 2006, Best R&B
Teen Choice Awards: 2006, Choice Music-R&B Artist; 2007, Choice Music-R&B Artist
American Music Awards: 2007, Favorite Soul/R&B Female Artist
World Music Awards: 2007, Female Entertainer of the Year

FURTHER READING

Periodicals

Billboard, Aug. 13, 2005; Mar. 18, 2006, p.18; Apr. 29, 2006, p.39; Apr. 28, 2007; p.36; May 12, 2007, p.24; June 9, 2007, p.63; June 16, 2007, p.36; Sep. 8, 2007, p.52
CosmoGirl!, June/July 2007, p.53
Entertainment Weekly, May 19, 2006, p.29; June 8, 2007, p.79; June 29, 2007, p.80
Essence, June 2007, p.154
Giant, June/July 2007, p.76
Girls' Life, Aug. 1, 2006, p.40
Guardian (London), Nov. 25, 2005, p.9
Interview, Oct. 1, 2005, p.88
Jet, May 22, 2006, p.35; June 11, 2007, p.54
People, Aug. 29, 2005, p.49; Sep. 5, 2005, p.48
Teen Vogue, Nov. 2006, p.107
USA Today, Aug. 2, 2005, p.D3

Online Articles

http://www.eveningtimes.co.uk/timesout/display.var.1882868.0.music
_rihannas_fairytale_dreams_come_true.php
(Evening Times Scotland, "Rihanna's Fairy Tale Dreams Come True," Dec. 5, 2007)

http://www.giantmag.com/content.php?cid=135
  (Giant, "Good Girl Gone Great," June 5, 2007)
http://www.mtv.com/news/articles/1535606/20060705/rihanna.jhtml?headlines=true
  (MTV.com, "Rihanna Lets Fans Be Her Guide, Selects Summer Jam 'We Ride' as Next Single," June 6, 2006)
http://observer.guardian.co.uk/magazine/story/0,,2153857,00.html
  (Observer/Guardian Online, "Singing in the Rain," Aug. 26, 2007)
http://www.rollingstone.com/artists/beyonce/articles/story/7567167/rihanna_brings_riddims
  (Rolling Stone, "Rihanna Brings Riddims," Aug. 18, 2005)

ADDRESS

Rihanna
Def Jam Recordings
825 Eighth Avenue
New York, NY 10019

WORLD WIDE WEB SITES

http://www.defjam.com
http://www.rihannanow.com
http://www.srprecords.com

John Roberts Jr. 1955-

American Lawyer
Chief Justice of the U.S. Supreme Court

BIRTH

John G. Roberts Jr. was born in Buffalo, New York, on January 27, 1955. His parents were John G. Roberts Sr., an executive with the Bethlehem Steel company, and Rosemary (Podrasky) Roberts, a homemaker. Roberts has three sisters, Kathy, Peggy, and Barbara.

YOUTH AND EDUCATION

Roberts spent most of his childhood in northwestern Indiana, where his family moved after his father accepted a job at a local steel plant. He grew up in Long Beach, a prosperous Indiana town not far from Chicago, Illinois. His childhood was a happy one, full of bike rides around the neighborhood and evening games of Monopoly and Scrabble with his sisters. Roberts also possessed a natural curiosity about the world around him that was nurtured by his parents. "We were very concerned about the news and everything," recalled his mother. "We have always been a family that was interested in things other than ourselves."

Roberts attended Catholic schools for both his elementary and high school education. He was self-motivated and smart, and he excelled in his studies. He did not just bury himself in books, however. During his four years at La Lumiere High School, an all-boys Catholic boarding school in LaPorte, Indiana, Roberts also immersed himself in a wide range of extracurricular activities. He wrestled, sang in the school choir, co-edited the school newspaper, served on the student council, and was chosen captain of the varsity football team his senior year. He even played the role of Peppermint Patty in an all-male school production of the musical *You're a Good Man, Charlie Brown*.

> "It became very, very clear and evident when he first came here," remembered one high school teacher, "that he was a person who was destined to do big things."

Despite his popularity and school spirit, though, Roberts remained best known for his intelligence, his maturity, and his conservative outlook on issues and events. When the administration at La Lumiere High School acknowledged that it was considering opening enrollment to girls, for example, Roberts promptly published an editorial in the school newspaper that strongly objected to the idea. "It became very, very clear and evident when he first came here," remembered one teacher in an interview with the *New York Times*, "that he was a person who was destined to do big things."

Attending Harvard

Roberts graduated first in his high school class of 25 students in 1973. He then enrolled at Harvard College, one of the most prestigious undergraduate schools in the world. He spent the next three academic years on the Harvard campus in Cambridge, Massachusetts, working on a history major. During each summer, though, he returned home to Indiana and worked at a steel mill to earn money for his tuition. "John was a serious student," recalled one of his roommates in an interview

The 1979 yearbook photo of the Harvard Law Review. *Roberts is in the third row from the front, the ninth person from the left.*

with the *Harvard Crimson.* "There were no parties, but John did have a social life."

Roberts earned a bachelor's degree in history *summa cum laude* (with highest honors) from Harvard College in 1976, finishing in only three years (instead of the usual four years). He then opted to continue his education at Harvard University Law School. A top student, he also found time to work as managing editor of the *Harvard Law Review,* a student-run journal that publishes articles on legal issues. It's a prestigious publication, and being one of its editors is a significant achievement. Roberts graduated *magna cum laude* (with high honors) from Harvard Law School in 1979.

Despite these accomplishments, Roberts was always modest about his intellectual abilities. "He was somebody who got along with everyone, who was obviously very bright but not aggressive," recalled a fellow editor in an interview with the *Harvard Crimson.* "He had a Midwestern reserve about not showing off how smart he was." Other college friends remembered him for his easygoing, friendly manner as well. "John and I probably spent several hundred hours debating every issue known to humankind, coming from very different perspectives on many issues," recalled one liberal Harvard classmate in the *New York Times.* "He's the type of person you could debate any issue with, and you could sometimes change his mind and sometimes he would change yours.... He was someone who's just soft-spoken and brilliant, but yet very interested in what other people had to say."

CAREER HIGHLIGHTS

After finishing law school, Roberts began a wide-ranging and impressive law career, working in many different types of legal positions. He started as a law clerk for Henry J. Friendly, one of the most influential and respected judges in the entire U.S. Court of Appeals. The federal judicial system, where Roberts clerked for Judge Friendly, is composed of three different levels. The lower courts, the level at which most cases are originally tried, include 94 district courts. After a case is tried, the loser has the option of "appealing" the verdict (an appeal is a request to have a higher court hear the case in hopes that it will make a different ruling). Then the case would go to the next level, the court of appeals. There are 12 courts of appeals (also called circuit courts), organized geographically, that cover the 50 states and the District of Columbia. When a case is appealed, the appeals (or appellate) court judge reviews the lower court's decision and either sustains it (agrees) or overturns it (disagrees). After that step, the case could be taken to the Supreme Court, the highest court in the land and the final authority on American law. At all three levels in the U.S. judicial system, federal judges are nominated by the president, confirmed by the Senate, and serve for life.

"He was somebody who got along with everyone, who was obviously very bright but not aggressive," recalled a fellow law student. "He had a Midwestern reserve about not showing off how smart he was."

As a law clerk for Judge Friendly, Roberts researched legal issues and also wrote judicial positions on the cases before the judge. After one year with Friendly, Roberts joined the staff of U.S. Supreme Court Justice William Rehnquist in 1980. He spent the next year as a law clerk for Rehnquist. In early 1981 he was named a special assistant to the Office of the U.S. Attorney General, which is responsible for overseeing the U.S. Department of Justice. Roberts spent the next year lending his legal expertise to the administration of Republican President Ronald Reagan. He reviewed presidential speeches, laws that had been proposed, and positions taken by the White House to make sure that they were legally sound.

Triumphs and Setbacks

In 1982 Roberts moved from the Department of Justice to the Office of White House Counsel. This office is an important one, for its staff serves as top advisors to the president of the United States on all legal issues concerning the White House. Roberts spent the next four years as an associate counsel. He then accepted a position at Hogan & Hartson, one of the most prestigious law firms in Washington DC, and worked there from 1986 to 1989. During this period he became known as one of the firm's most effective specialists in federal appellate law—the stage of the American legal process in which people, companies, or organizations unhappy with a trial verdict can appeal the verdict to an appeals court or to the U.S. Supreme Court.

In 1989 Roberts returned to governmental service, taking a position as principal deputy solicitor general with the U.S. Department of Justice. The solicitor general is the federal government's legal representative in all cases that come before the U.S. Supreme Court. This new job, then, gave Roberts lots of exposure to the Supreme Court and the individual justices who sat on the Court. On several occasions, he even argued cases before the Court.

In January 1992 Republican President George H.W. Bush nominated Roberts to fill a vacancy on the U.S. Court of Appeals for the Washington DC circuit. Roberts was extremely excited at the prospect of becoming a federal judge, but his nomination quickly became mired in politics. The U.S. Senate must confirm all federal judicial nominations, but the Democratic leadership of the Senate refused to bring his nomination up for a vote. The Democrats worried that his conservative view of the law would lead him to make rulings that ran counter to Democratic positions on civil rights, abortion rights, environmental protection, and other issues. The Democrats thus decided to block his nomination until the 1992 presidential election. They hoped that their party's presidential nominee, Bill Clinton, would win the upcoming election and replace Roberts with a nominee they considered more attractive.

The Democratic strategy worked. When Clinton defeated Bush to win the presidential election in November 1992, Roberts knew that his appeals court nomination was doomed. He refused to complain publicly about this setback, but friends and family members say that he was bitterly disappointed. Roberts returned to Hogan & Hartson in early 1993. He spent the next several years arguing dozens of cases before the U.S. Supreme

Court—and earning an annual salary of more than $1 million. In most of these cases, he represented "conservative" clients. On several occasions, though, he used his courtroom skills on behalf of "liberal" clients such as a group of environmentalists locked in a legal battle to preserve wilderness around Lake Tahoe—a famous outdoor destination on the California-Nevada border—and protect it from developers.

> "John and I probably spent several hundred hours debating every issue known to humankind, coming from very different perspectives on many issues," recalled one Harvard classmate. "He's the type of person you could debate any issue with, and you could sometimes change his mind and sometimes he would change yours.... He was someone who's just soft-spoken and brilliant, but yet very interested in what other people had to say."

A New President and a Nomination

In November 2000 Roberts became involved in the disputed presidential election between Democratic candidate Al Gore and Republican candidate George W. Bush (son of President George H.W. Bush). On election night, the vote count was so close that the winner of Florida would win the election and become president. But the vote count in Florida became a matter of tremendous controversy because of problems with ballot cards and voting machines.

In the days following the election, both campaigns mounted fierce legal efforts to place their candidate in the White House. During this legal battle, Roberts traveled to Florida to provide legal assistance to the Bush campaign. The Gore campaign turned to the U.S. court system to demand a recount of the Florida vote, and the issue quickly ended up in the U.S. Supreme Court. The conservative majority on the Supreme Court refused to approve the Gore campaign's demand for a recount, the Bush campaign prevailed, and George W. Bush became president.

A few months later, in early 2001, President Bush nominated Roberts to fill an open seat on the federal circuit court for Washington DC—the same seat for which he had been nominated eight years earlier by Bush's father, President George H.W. Bush. Once again, politics interfered with the nomination. Organizations devoted to preserving abortion rights were convinced that Roberts was hostile to their position, and they and other

President George W. Bush nominating Roberts for the Supreme Court. Roberts is accompanied by his family: (left to right) John, Jane, and Josephine.

progressive groups managed to convince their Senate allies to block his nomination for two years. In June 2003, however, his nomination finally came up for a vote. First his nomination was approved by the Senate Judiciary Committee by a 16-3 margin. This vote brought his nomination before the full Senate, which gave final approval to the nomination. A full decade after his first nomination, Roberts was finally a federal appeals court judge. He served in this capacity for the next two years.

Nominated to the U.S. Supreme Court

On July 19, 2005, Roberts once again returned to the public spotlight when President George W. Bush nominated him to fill a vacancy on the U.S. Supreme Court left by the retirement of Sandra Day O'Connor. "He has the qualities Americans expect in a judge: experience, wisdom, fairness, and civility," stated Bush in announcing his nomination.

Many Americans recognized that this nomination was an extremely important one for the future of the Supreme Court. Over the previous several years, the nine-member Court had been closely divided on a wide range of issues, including abortion. O'Connor had been the deciding fifth vote in favor of preserving abortion rights in several high-profile cases. Conservative and liberal observers alike believed that if she was replaced with a judge who opposed abortion rights, then legal access to abortion might be outlawed in the future.

Debate about Roberts's nomination was fierce. On one side were pro-choice organizations and other liberal advocacy groups that disagreed with his conservative legal philosophy, and they urged the U.S. Senate to defeat his nomination. On the other side were opponents of abortion rights and other conservative voices, and they declared their support for his nomination. A *Wall Street Journal* editorial, for example, declared that his record as an appeals judge showed that Roberts would be a superb Supreme Court justice: "His opinions are meticulous and circumspect. He avoids sweeping pronouncements and bold strokes, and instead pays close attention to the legal material at hand. He is undoubtedly conservative. But ideology has played only a modest role in his judicial work."

> "His opinions are meticulous and circumspect," declared a **Wall Street Journal** editorial. "He avoids sweeping pronouncements and bold strokes, and instead pays close attention to the legal material at hand. He is undoubtedly conservative. But ideology has played only a modest role in his judicial work."

In September 2005 the controversy surrounding Roberts took an unusual turn when Supreme Court Chief Justice William Rehnquist—for whom Roberts had clerked two decades earlier—died of thyroid cancer. Bush quickly withdrew Roberts's nomination for O'Connor's seat and instead recommended him to take Rehnquist's place as chief justice.

Becoming the Chief Justice of the Supreme Court

Senate Judiciary Committee hearings on the Roberts nomination opened on September 12, 2005, and continued for the next three days. During these hearings, many Democratic senators on the committee voiced concern about his record as a judge and as an attorney for two Republican administrations. They argued that the evidence showed that Roberts would be unfriendly to civil rights, voting rights, abortion rights, the separation of church and state, environmental protection, and other ideas that they supported. Republicans on the committee, meanwhile, praised him as a brilliant jurist who was dedicated to upholding basic constitutional principles.

Roberts being sworn in as Chief Justice of the U.S. Supreme Court by Justice John Paul Stevens, the senior justice on the court.

For his part, Roberts used his appearance before the committee to try to reassure doubters. "Judges and justices are servants of the law, not the other way around," he stated. "Judges are like umpires. Umpires don't make the rules; they apply them. The role of an umpire and a judge is critical. They make sure everybody plays by the rules. But it is a limited role. Nobody ever went to a ball game to see the umpire."

Roberts performed well throughout the hearings. Some Democratic senators voiced frustration with some of his answers, in which he avoided expressing personal views about abortion and other issues. But other Democrats expressed admiration for his legal mind, and Republicans were united in expressing support for his nomination. When the hearings concluded, his nomination was approved by the committee by a 13-5 vote. It was then approved by a 78-22 vote by the full Senate.

Roberts was sworn in as the 17th chief justice of the U.S. Supreme Court on September 29, 2005. He was sworn in by Justice John Paul Stevens, the most senior justice on the Supreme Court. Roberts thus became the first justice to join the Court in more than 11 years—the longest stretch without a new member since 1823. He also became the youngest chief justice—50 years old—since his idol John Marshall took the same role in 1801 at the age of 45. Four months later, Samuel Alito replaced O'Connor to bring the Court up to its full nine members.

The Role of the Supreme Court

As chief justice, Roberts presides over America's judicial branch, one of the three branches of the U.S. government. The other two branches are the legislative branch (Congress) and the executive branch (the Presidency). Each of these branches has clearly defined responsibilities. The legislative branch makes laws, the executive branch carries out laws, and the judicial branch interprets the laws, making sure that they do not violate the U.S. Constitution. The U.S. Supreme Court is the ultimate authority on American law; once the Supreme Court rules on a case, the decision is final.

> "Judges and justices are servants of the law, not the other way around," Roberts stated. "Judges are like umpires. Umpires don't make the rules; they apply them. The role of an umpire and a judge is critical. They make sure everybody plays by the rules. But it is a limited role. Nobody ever went to a ball game to see the umpire."

In joining the Supreme Court, Roberts became one of nine judges—one chief justice and eight associate justices—on the highest court in the country. The Supreme Court decides whether the laws made by all levels of government—federal, state, and local—follow the Constitution. The Court accomplishes this by interpreting the provisions of the Constitution and applying its rules to specific legal cases. Because the Constitution lays out general rules, the Court tries to determine their meaning and figure out how to apply them to modern situations. After the justices select a case for review—and they accept fewer than about 100 of the 6,000 cases presented to them each year—they first will hear arguments by the two opposing sides. They begin discussing the case, take a preliminary vote, and then one justice from the majority is assigned to write up the Court's opinion. Drafting an opinion is complex and time-consuming, and the whole process can take over a year. The Court's final opinion has tremendous importance, setting out a precedent that all lower courts and all levels of government throughout the United States are required to follow. The reasoning given in the opinion is also important, because it helps people understand the basis for the decision and how the ruling might apply to other cases in the future.

As Roberts shouldered the challenge of leading the Court, many people expressed confidence in his abilities. Justice Stevens, perhaps the most liberal member of the Court, publicly declared that he already had the trust of the other justices. Sandra Day O'Connor also spoke in glowing terms about his capacity to lead the Court. "As Justice Byron White used to say, the arrival of a new justice creates an entirely new court," she wrote in *Time* magazine in early 2006. "This is particularly true when the new justice is also the new chief justice. The new chief can bring tremendous changes in the operations of the court, from the way cases are discussed and opinions written to the very guiding ethos and atmosphere. Few have made the transition as seamlessly and effectively as Roberts. He knew our traditions well, as he had clerked in 1980 for then Associate Justice Rehnquist. His sense of humor and articulate nature and calm demeanor combine to make him a very effective chief. I'm certain he will serve a long tenure in the role and be an effective leader not only for the Supreme Court but for all the federal courts in the nation."

For his part, Roberts spoke about the need to seek common ground among the members of the Court. In 2006 he asserted that "working toward broader agreement should be one of the shared aims" of all Court justices, and in 2007 he stated that "the Court functions most effectively as a judicial institution saying what the law is when it can deliver one clear and focused opinion of the Court." As time passed, however, Roberts frequently found himself presiding over a bitterly divided Court.

Areas of Unity and Division

During the first two Supreme Court terms with Roberts as chief justice, he has achieved mixed results in efforts to unify the Court on legal issues facing the nation. On the one hand, legal observers point out that under his leadership, the percentage of unanimous Supreme Court decisions in 2006 and 2007 was actually higher than it had been in the final years of the Rehnquist-led Court. The Roberts Court also had a lower percentage of total cases decided by a 5-4 vote. A writer for the conservative *Weekly Standard* applauded these trends and proposed that "over time, the Roberts effect may produce not only larger majorities and more stable rulings but also a Court that ... pays more attention to working out the relevant law and less to mere politics.... The prospect of the continuing advancement of that philosophy is a happy one, and a reason to say hail to this particular chief."

As Chief Justice, Roberts has tried to unite the Supreme Court, shown here in 2006.

Roberts told *Atlantic Monthly* that his previous career experiences have helped him enormously as chief justice. "I do think it's extremely valuable for people to be on both sides, and I mean being in private practice and being in government, arguing against the government and for the government. It does give you a perspective that you just can't get any other way, in terms of what the concerns of the other side are. And it also gives you an added credibility, and that's very, very important."

Other Court watchers, though, have pointed out that Roberts's own voting record since joining the Supreme Court is a very conservative one. They also claim that the addition of Roberts and Alito has swung the balance of power on the Court toward conservatives in a number of major policy areas. These observers note that by 5-4 votes, the Supreme Court in 2006-07 issued rulings that weakened abortion rights, struck down campaign finance laws, and limited the ability of school boards to adopt voluntary desegregation plans that use race as a factor in enrollment. All of these rulings, which reversed earlier legal precedents, were hailed by conservatives and condemned by liberals.

In some of these cases, the liberal justices on the Supreme Court have voiced clear anger with Roberts and his conservative allies on the bench. These justices have issued a string of harshly worded dissents. Justice Stephen Breyer, a liberal, even declared that in the entire history of the United States, rarely have "so few so quickly changed so much" in American law.

Roberts has been critical of the media coverage of the Supreme Court. He has acknowledged that the members of the Court have disagreed strongly on several important cases and that the liberal justices have become frustrated in some instances. But he also expressed his belief that media coverage of the Court has not paid enough attention to the large number of unanimous decisions that the justices have handed down since he came on board. He also pointed out in a 2007 interview with *Atlantic Monthly* that "a chief justice has the same vote that everyone else has.... [His] authority is really quite limited, and the dynamic among all the justices is going to affect whether he can accomplish much or not."

In July 2007 Roberts suffered a seizure while vacationing in Maine. This seizure, which was similar to one that he experienced in 1993, led doctors to wonder whether he might have a mild form of epilepsy. Epilepsy is a physical disorder in which the electrical activity of the brain is interrupted for brief periods of time. In severe cases, this interruption can result in loss of consciousness or uncontrolled muscle spasms. Roberts was released after a brief hospital stay, and reporters openly wondered whether doctors might put him on medication to prevent future seizures. Even if Roberts is formally diagnosed with epilepsy, however, the disorder is not expected to interfere with his duties as chief justice.

> "Few have made the transition as seamlessly and effectively as Roberts," said Associate Justice Sandra Day O'Connor. "His sense of humor and articulate nature and calm demeanor combine to make him a very effective chief. I'm certain he will serve a long tenure in the role and be an effective leader not only for the Supreme Court but for all the federal courts in the nation."

The 2007-08 Supreme Court term had fewer 5-4 decisions than the previous term, but observers also claimed there was less unanimity on the Court, with fewer than 30 percent of the cases decided without dissent. Two major decisions were marked by sharp 5-4 divisions: a decision that overturned a ban on handguns in the District of Columbia, and a decision that those who have been detained at Guantanamo Bay and who are terrorism suspects have a constitutional right to access to federal courts to challenge their detention. The Chief Justice seemed to have a strong influence on the Court: he was on the majority side of the opinion in 90 percent of the cases, more than any other justice. But his future influence is less clear. Court watchers are waiting to see who will win the 2008 presidential election. The new president is expected to nominate at least one or maybe more justices to the Court, since five of the current justices are age 70 or older. With the Supreme Court so evenly divided, a new justice could have a profound effect on the future direction of the Court.

MARRIAGE AND FAMILY

Roberts married Jane Marie Sullivan, a fellow lawyer, in 1996. They live in the wealthy suburb of Chevy Chase, Maryland, outside Washington DC. They have two children, Josephine and John.

HOBBIES AND OTHER INTERESTS

Roberts enjoys playing golf and listening to the opera. He also enjoys reading and playing with his young children.

FURTHER READING

Books

McElroy, Lisa Tucker. *John Roberts Jr.: Chief Justice,* 2006 (juvenile)
Toobin, Jeffrey. *The Nine: Inside the Secret World of the Supreme Court,* 2007

Periodicals

Atlantic Monthly, Jan./Feb. 2007, p.110
Current Biography Yearbook, 2006
Economist, July 23, 2005; Sep. 10, 2005
New York Times, July 21, 2005, p.A1; June 28, 2007, p.A1; Aug. 1, 2007, p.A1
New Yorker, June 25, 2007, p.35
Newsweek, Aug. 1, 2005, p.22; Aug. 15, 2005, p.23; Jan. 30, 2006, p.68; Mar. 6, 2006, p.44
People, Sep. 12, 2005, p.109
Time, Aug. 1, 2005, p.30; Sep. 5, 2005, p.28; Apr. 30, 2006; July 10, 2006, p.26; Feb. 26, 2007, p.44; Oct. 22, 2007, p.40
U.S. News and World Report, Oct. 1, 2007
USA Today, Aug. 31, 2005, p.A13; Dec. 28, 2005, p.A4; June 26, 2006, p.A4; July 6, 2006, p.A11; Apr. 10, 2007, p.A1; June 29, 2007, p.A8

Washington Post, Sep. 14, 2005, p.A1; Sep. 30, 2005, p.A1
Weekly Standard, Mar. 20, 2006

Online Articles

http://supreme.lp/findlaw.com/supreme_court/justices/roberts.html
  (FindLaw Online, "John G. Roberts," undated)
http://www.thecrimson.com/article.aspx?ref=508284
  (Harvard Crimson Online, "Alum Picked as Court Nominee," July 22, 2005)

ADDRESS

John Roberts
U.S. Supreme Court
Supreme Court Bldg.
1 First Street NE
Washington, DC 20543

WORLD WIDE WEB SITES

http://www.oyez.org
http://www.supremecourtus.gov
http://www.uscourts.gov/index.html

J. K. Rowling 1965-
British Children's Writer
Author of the Award-Winning *Harry Potter* Novels

[Editor's Note: J.K. Rowling was first profiled in Biography Today *in September 1999, after the publication of* Harry Potter and the Prisoner of Azkaban *and before the release of any of the movies. A lot has happened since then—in Rowling's life, and in Harry's—which is covered in this entry.]*

BIRTH

Joanne Kathleen (J. K.) Rowling (pronounced "rolling") was born on July 31, 1965, in Chipping Sodbury, a small town in

South Gloucestershire, England. Her parents, Peter and Anne Rowling, met on a train when they were both 18 years old and on their way to join the British Navy. Peter worked as an aircraft factory manager, and Anne was a lab technician. Rowling's birth name was simply Joanne; she added the name of her favorite grandmother, Kathleen, as her middle name later in life when her publisher wanted her to have another initial. Rowling has one younger sister, Dianne.

YOUTH

In describing her childhood, Rowling compares herself to one of the characters in her popular *Harry Potter* books. "By nature I am most like Hermione ... or at least I was when I was younger." Rowling was considered "the smart one" while her sister was "the pretty one." As children, they were best friends even though they fought a lot.

> *In describing her childhood, Rowling compares herself to one of the characters in her popular* **Harry Potter** *books. "By nature I am most like Hermione ... or at least I was when I was younger."*

When Rowling was four years old her family moved to the town of Winterbourne just outside Bristol, England. There she had lots of friends in the neighborhood, including a brother and sister whose surname was Potter, a name that Rowling liked. As a young child, she began making up elaborate stories and plays starring herself, her sister, and their friends. She first began writing stories around age six. Most of the stories she wrote at that time featured rabbits, because she wanted a rabbit as a pet.

When Rowling was nine years old, her family moved again. Her parents wanted to live farther out in the countryside, so they settled in the village of Tutshill, near Chepstow in Wales. Wales is one of the four countries that make up the United Kingdom, along with England, Scotland, and Northern Ireland. Wales is known for its 400 castles, its ancient legends, and its tongue-twisting place names. Rowling would later draw on her experiences growing up in Wales when creating the magical world of Harry Potter.

EDUCATION

Rowling enjoyed going to school and generally did well as a student, except for a period in elementary school. The elementary school where she started out, in Winterbourne, did not prepare her for her new school in Tutshill. On Rowling's first day in her new school, her teacher gave her a math test to determine where to place her in the class. Rowling got every question wrong because she did not know anything about fractions. The teacher placed her at a desk as far away from her own as possible. Rowling spent that year primarily focused on carving a hole in the wooden desktop with the point of her geometry compass.

Things improved greatly when Rowling was 11 years old and was able to attend Wyedean Comprehensive School in Chepstow. There she struck up a friendship with Sean Harris, who was the first person with whom she shared her dream of becoming a writer and also the person who most believed that she could achieve that goal. When Harris learned to drive, he often took Rowling for rides in his Ford Anglia. "That turquoise and white car meant freedom. . . . Some of the happiest memories of my teenage years involve zooming off into the darkness in Sean's car." Her second book, *Harry Potter and the Chamber of Secrets,* is dedicated to him.

> "I think most people believe, deep down, that their mothers are indestructible; it was a terrible shock to hear that she had an incurable illness, but even then, I did not fully realize what the diagnosis might mean."

By this time in her life, Rowling loved writing more than anything else. During lunchtime at school, she entertained her friends by telling stories starring themselves as the courageous heroes of dangerous—and sometimes silly—adventures. But Rowling still didn't show anyone most of the things she had written. She remembers being too shy to let anyone see her work.

In 1980, when Rowling was 15 years old, her mother, Anne Rowling, became very ill and was diagnosed with multiple sclerosis. Multiple sclerosis (MS) is an incurable disease of the central nervous system that affects the brain and spinal cord. It can eventually result in numbness and loss of muscle control, balance, and vision. Some people with MS have periods of time during which the disease stops getting worse, but Anne Rowling gradually became weaker and more seriously ill. Her illness had a huge impact on Rowling. "I think most people believe, deep down, that their mothers are indestructible; it was a terrible shock to hear that she had an incurable illness, but even then, I did not fully realize what the diagnosis might mean."

Rowling finished secondary school in 1983 and went on to study at the University of Exeter in southern England. She wanted to study English literature, but took her parents' advice and studied French instead. Although she later said that choice was a mistake, it did provide her with the opportunity to live in Paris for one year. She received a Bachelor of Arts (BA) degree in French from the University of Exeter in 1987.

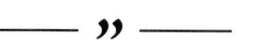

CAREER HIGHLIGHTS

After college, Rowling continued to write stories and also began writing two novels while working a series of different jobs in London, England. The longest job she held was as a secretary with the international human rights organization Amnesty International. Rowling has described herself as "the worst secretary ever." She recalled not paying very much attention in business meetings because she was too busy making notes of her story ideas. "This is a problem when you are supposed to be taking the minutes of the meeting. . . . I'm not proud of that. I don't think it's charming and eccentric. I really should have been better at it, but I really am just all over the place when it comes to organizing myself."

> "On a crowded train, the character of Harry Potter "simply fell into my head," Rowling said. "I didn't have a functioning pen with me, and I was too shy to ask anybody if I could borrow one. . . . I simply sat and thought, for four hours, and all the details bubbled up in my brain, and this scrawny, black-haired, bespectacled boy who didn't know he was a wizard became more and more real to me."

Creating Harry Potter

In 1990, Rowling decided to move to the city of Manchester, England. On a crowded train back to London after a weekend spent looking for a place to live, the character of Harry Potter "simply fell into my head." In her web site biography, she wrote, "I didn't have a functioning pen with me, and I was too shy to ask anybody if I could borrow one. . . . I simply sat and thought, for four hours, and all the details bubbled up in my brain, and this scrawny, black-haired, bespectacled boy who didn't know he was a wizard became more and more real to me." When she got home that evening, Rowling began to write *Harry Potter and the*

Rowling with Daniel Radcliffe, who would bring her creation to life.

Philosopher's Stone (published in the United States as *Harry Potter and the Sorcerer's Stone*).

Rowling's story of Harry Potter focuses on a young orphan who learns on his 11th birthday that he has a magical legacy and must attend a special school for wizards. From the very beginning, Rowling imagined a series of seven books that would follow the life and adventures of Harry from age 11 to age 18. During those years, he would discover many things about himself. In between the challenges of schoolwork and sports, Harry and his friends Ron and Hermione would fight monsters and evil wizards, prevent magical disasters, and survive many narrow escapes while saving the wizarding world from the fearsome Voldemort.

By the end of 1990, Rowling had made significant progress on the first Harry Potter book. She had a good start on the story and lots of ideas for the books that would follow. Then on December 30, 1990, her mother died.

Rowling was devastated. Her mother was only 45 years old, and Rowling never thought she would die so young. "It was a terrible time.... I remember feeling as though there was a paving slab pressing down upon my chest, a literal pain in my heart."

In 1991 Rowling was still struggling with grief over her mother's death. Wanting to get away, she took a job teaching English in Portugal and continued working on her book. The storyline had changed since her mother's death and now included much more detail about Harry's feelings for his own parents. In Portugal, Rowling wrote her favorite chapter of the book, "The Mirror of Erised," in which Harry discovers images of his long-dead parents.

> "From that very first idea, I [envisioned] a series of seven books—each one charting a year of Harry's life whilst he is a student at Hogwarts School of Witchcraft and Wizardry," Rowling explained. "And I wanted to fully sketch the plots of all the stories and get the essential characteristics of my principal characters before I actually started writing the books in detail."

Also during this time, Rowling was briefly married to a Portuguese man and gave birth to her daughter Jessica. When the marriage ended in divorce in 1994, Rowling moved with her daughter to Edinburgh, Scotland, to live near her sister. She had accepted a teaching position and wanted to finish writing the book before her new job began. She was afraid that once she started working full-time again, she wouldn't have enough time for writing. "And so I set to work in a kind of frenzy, determined to finish the book and at least try and get it published. Whenever Jessica fell asleep in her pushchair [stroller] I would dash to the nearest café and write like mad. I wrote nearly every evening. Then I had to type the whole thing out myself. Sometimes I actually hated the book, even while I loved it."

From her first thought of Harry while riding the train to London to the last bit of writing in Edinburgh, it ultimately took Rowling five years to finish the book. "The reason so much time slipped by was because, from that very first idea, I [envisioned] a series of seven books—each one charting a year of Harry's life whilst he is a student at Hogwarts School of Witchcraft and Wizardry," she explained. "And I wanted to fully sketch the plots of all the stories and get the essential characteristics of my principal characters before I actually started writing the books in detail." Because Rowling always knew how the story of Harry Potter would end, she never thought of them as children's books.

Once Rowling found a literary agent to help her, it took over a year of rejections before she was offered a publishing contract. In August 1996, she signed an agreement with a British publisher. "The moment I found out that Harry would be published was one of the best of my life." Her excitement could not be diminished, not even by the career advice she got from her first editor. The editor warned Rowling that she wouldn't make any money by writing children's books, so she should get a regular job and not try to depend on Harry Potter to earn her living.

But just a few months after her book was accepted for publication in England, a U.S. publisher also bought the publishing rights. Rowling was offered $100,000 for the rights to publish the first Harry Potter book in the United States. This was the highest fee ever paid for a first novel by a children's book author, and it allowed Rowling to quit her teaching job to concentrate on writing Harry's story full time. And so Harry Potter began breaking publishing records before the first copies of the first book were even printed.

Book 1: *Harry Potter and the Sorcerer's Stone*

Harry Potter and the Philosopher's Stone was released in England in 1997 and followed by the U.S. version, *Harry Potter and the Sorcerer's Stone,* in 1998. In this first Harry Potter book, readers are introduced to an unlikely hero. Harry is an orphan boy who lives in a closet under the stairs in the home of his mean-spirited aunt and uncle who only reluctantly took him in. He leads a completely miserable life in which he is constantly bullied by his cousin Dudley and treated as a servant by his aunt and uncle. The only remarkable thing about Harry is the mysterious lightning bolt scar on his forehead.

Then, on his 11th birthday, Harry receives a letter that sets off a chain of events leading to the revelation that he is, in fact, a wizard. His parents were not killed in a car accident as he had been told. They were murdered by an evil wizard named Voldemort. Harry himself is a legend among wizards because he is the only person ever to have survived a direct attack by Voldemort. With this new information, Harry's life is changed forever. He is whisked away on a flying motorcycle to Hogwarts School of Witchcraft and Wizardry, where he studies charms, potions, and the history of magic. He forms friendships with Ron and Hermione, and together they investigate the many forbidden secrets of Hogwarts, play Quidditch, battle evil

The first book in the saga of Harry Potter.

forces, and uncover the secret of the sorcerer's stone. In another series of revelations, Harry discovers the true meaning of his scar.

Rowling's first book became a runaway bestseller. Harry Potter was met with rave reviews by book critics in England as well as in the U.S. A reviewer for the *Times* of London praised Rowling as "a sparkling new author brimming with delicious ideas, glorious characters, and witty dialogue," while the *Sunday Times* called the novel a "very funny, imaginative, magical story, for anyone from ten to adulthood." American book reviewers called Rowling's writing "charming, readable, delightful" and "brilliantly imagined and written." *Harry Potter and the Sorcerer's Stone* was a spectacular beginning to what would become a huge international publishing sensation.

> *When Rowling saw the first movie, "it was really like walking into my own head, it was a very peculiar experience.... I mean there are obviously things that are not the same as the books but that is because if you did every scene in the book and translated that into films, the films would be about 24 hours each."*

The movie version of *Harry Potter and the Sorcerer's Stone* was released in 2001, bringing the world of Harry Potter to life on the screen. Although initially reluctant to allow her books to be made into movies, Rowling is happy with the films. "It was really like walking into my own head, it was a very peculiar experience.... I mean there are obviously things that are not the same as the books but that is because if you did every scene in the book and translated that into films, the films would be about 24 hours each.... By and large they meet my expectations."

Book 2: *Harry Potter and the Chamber of Secrets*

Harry Potter and the Chamber of Secrets was published in 1998, and the movie version of the book was released in 2002. Detailing Harry's exploits during his second year at Hogwarts, the storyline centers on a terrible monster that has escaped from the Chamber of Secrets and is turning Hogwarts students to stone. While dealing with flying cars, angry willow trees, various bullies and ghosts, and the suspicions of many Hogwarts students that he is to blame for the escaped monster, Harry must confront the evil Voldemort and solve the mystery. Harry's adventures and mishaps along the way prompt Hogwarts Headmaster Dumbledore to offer the advice that gives a hint of our hero's future: "It is our choices, Harry, that show what we truly are, far more than our abilities."

Proving just as popular as the first book, *Harry Potter and the Chamber of Secrets* became the best-selling book in the U.S. as soon as it was released. *Publisher's Weekly* called the book "even more inventive than *Harry Potter and the Sorcerer's Stone.*" Readers and critics alike praised Rowling's story as imaginative, funny, suspenseful, and truly magical.

Book 3: *Harry Potter and the Prisoner of Azkaban*

Harry Potter and the Prisoner of Azkaban, released in 1999 with the movie version following in 2004, is the third installment in the series. In this story, Harry learns about the wizard prison called Azkaban, which is guarded by the frightening and ghoulish Dementors. Harry's godfather Sirius Black, who is believed to have helped Voldemort murder Harry's parents, escapes from prison and is looking for Harry. Harry and his friends study Defense Against the Dark Arts and learn how to perform the difficult Patronus charm. As the story unfolds, Harry learns more about his parents while encountering werewolves, mysterious disappearances, daring rescues, and surprising friendships. Harry must also once again confront the power of evil.

By the time the third Harry Potter book was published, the series had attracted readers of all ages, all of whom expressed delight with the newest story. The book was greeted by critics as an enthralling, thrilling addition to the series. And Harry Potter fans were already looking forward to more from Rowling, who said in 1999, "I've actually got the final chapter of book seven written, just for my own satisfaction so I know where I'm going."

Book 4: *Harry Potter and the Goblet of Fire*

Harry Potter and the Goblet of Fire, released in 2000 with the movie version following in 2005, chronicles Harry's fourth year at Hogwarts. The school is hosting the Triwizard Tournament, and although he is technically too young to participate, Harry is drawn into the competition. The tournament events place competitors in grave danger, and advanced magical skills are required to escape injury. Readers are also introduced to the Quidditch World Cup, magical transportation by portkey, and the terrible Death Eaters. The story rushes toward a shocking conclusion in which Harry again confronts Voldemort in battle, and an important character is killed. Rowling has admitted to crying while writing the death scene, but she persevered because she felt the death was critical to the storyline.

J. K. ROWLING

Top: Harry with the Dursleys, as he learns he is going to Hogwarts.

Center: Hermione, Harry, and Ron, with Scabbers.

Bottom: Harry and the sorting hat.

Rowling struggled with the process of writing *Harry Potter and the Goblet of Fire,* particularly Chapter 9, "The Dark Mark," which introduces the Death Eaters. "The worst ever was 13 different versions. . . . I hated that chapter so much; at one point, I thought of missing it out altogether and just putting in a page saying 'Chapter 9 was too difficult' and going straight to Chapter 10." Her hard work paid off, and the book received glowing reviews. A *Newsweek* book reviewer called the book astonishing and "the best Potter book yet." The book was also praised as complex, finely plotted, and suspenseful but funny.

> *Rowling said in 1999, "I've actually got the final chapter of book seven written, just for my own satisfaction so I know where I'm going."*

The phenomenon of midnight bookstore release parties began with the publication of *Harry Potter and the Goblet of Fire.* Eager fans waited in line for hours to get their copies of the latest Harry Potter book at the stroke of midnight. The book sold an unprecedented three million copies in the first 48 hours of release. *Harry Potter and the Goblet of Fire* became the fastest-selling book in history, a distinction that was later eclipsed by sales of subsequent Harry Potter titles.

Quidditch Through the Ages and *Fantastic Beasts and Where to Find Them*

In 2001, Rowling published a special supplement to the Harry Potter series as a fundraiser for the charitable organization Comic Relief U.K. *Quidditch Through the Ages* was written by Rowling under the pen name Kennilworthy Whisp, while *Fantastic Beasts and Where to Find Them,* also written by Rowling, was published under the pen name Newt Scamander. The two books were designed to look like Hogwarts textbooks. The titles were a huge hit with fans who by now wanted to know every detail of Harry's life and the magical world of wizards.

Book 5: *Harry Potter and the Order of the Phoenix*

Harry Potter and the Order of the Phoenix details Harry's fifth year at Hogwarts and was released in 2003, with the movie version following in 2006. As Harry grows into adolescence, he becomes more serious and angry. Dementors attack Harry and his cousin Dudley, and Harry is suspended from Hogwarts and must undergo a disciplinary hearing at the Ministry of Magic. He begins having horrible nightmares that he doesn't understand.

J. K. ROWLING

Top: A pensive Dumbledore.

Middle: Snape in his classroom, with wand at the ready.

Bottom: Harry, Hermione, and Ron, with the golden egg.

Harry learns about the Order of the Phoenix, a group working against Voldemort, and gets more information about his parents, who were early members of the Order. New characters are introduced, and Hogwarts comes under the control of the spiteful Professor Umbridge. A battle with the Death Eaters ensues, and another important character is killed. Harry learns of a prophecy made before he was born, and the stage is set for the final two books of the series.

Anticipation of *Harry Potter and the Order of the Phoenix* had reached fever pitch by the time the book was released. One reviewer writing for *January* magazine noted that "this novel is no longer children's literature" and continued that the book was "written on several levels for a wide variety of readers." Rowling's work in creating the Harry Potter series was also praised as a richly realized universe that became more complex with each book.

Book 6: *Harry Potter and the Half-Blood Prince*

Harry Potter and the Half-Blood Prince was released in 2005 and immediately called "the darkest and most unsettling installment yet" by the *New York Times*. In this story, Harry learns of the existence of the half-blood prince through a mysterious book that helps him pass his Hogwarts exams. Voldemort and the Death Eaters commit a string of heinous murders and the full-blown wizard war causes several disasters in the Muggle world. Dumbledore tells Harry about the horcruxes, which if destroyed will also kill Voldemort. The book's tragic and shocking ending leads Harry to finally understand his life's destiny.

With the publication of the sixth book, critics continued to rave about the Harry Potter series. A *National Review* critic called the book a "breathless story of heroism, intrigue, and cowardly villainy" and praised the intricate storyline, engaging mystery, and suspense. A reviewer for *Booklist* praised Rowling as a writer who "blends literature, mythology, folklore, and religion into a delectable stew." The publication of *Harry Potter and the Half-Blood Prince* set a new world record for the number of copies ordered for the first printing of a book. But that record would ultimately be broken by the final book in the series.

Book 7: *Harry Potter and the Deathly Hallows*

The final installment of the Harry Potter series, *Harry Potter and the Deathly Hallows*, was the most highly anticipated book in history by the time it was released in 2007. The story opens with a raging war in the wizarding world. Voldemort is gaining control of the Ministry of Magic and hunting Muggles and half-blood wizards. Harry is named "Undesirable Number One" and goes into hiding along with Ron and Hermione. Together they search for the mysterious horcruxes in an attempt to defeat Voldemort once and for all. They also try to find the Hallows, a legendary collection of items that will make whoever possesses them the master of death. Mayhem, betrayal, mistrust, reversals of alliance, and bitter clashes unfold. Beloved characters die, but Harry learns that love can triumph over death—although the cost is sometimes high.

The public frenzy surrounding the publication of the final Harry Potter book required an elaborate secrecy campaign to prevent spoilers—advance information about how the story would end. *Harry Potter and the Deathly Hallows* had the largest first printing of any book in history, and the more copies of a book that are printed, the greater the risk of spoilers. Everyone who came into contact with the book before its release date of July 21, 2007, was legally bound to secrecy. Only a limited number of people were granted access to the manuscript during the editing process. When Rowling finished her final revisions to the book, the editor assigned to deliver the manuscript to the publisher sat on it during the long flight from London to New York. As copies of the books were printed, they were automatically wrapped in black plastic and loaded onto locked trucks with electronic devices that tracked their location at all times. Libraries and bookstore managers who received the advance shipments of books were required to sign a security agreement as well as provide their names and contact information. Many bookstores and libraries that received their copies days in advance hid the books to prevent them from being stolen.

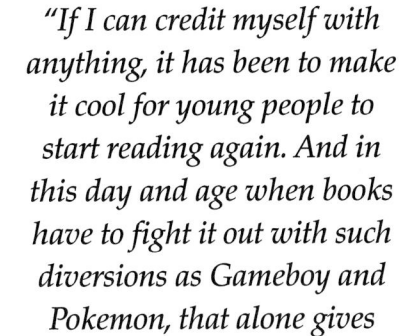

> "If I can credit myself with anything, it has been to make it cool for young people to start reading again. And in this day and age when books have to fight it out with such diversions as Gameboy and Pokemon, that alone gives me more pleasure than anything."

When readers and critics finally had access to the book, they were not disappointed. The *Washington Post* called the series finale "exhilarating but also exhausting . . . spectacularly complex." A *Chicago Tribune* reviewer described the story as "dark, rich, sophisticated, packed with action." Fans all over the world celebrated the seventh and final book—and immediately began guessing what Rowling would write next. Rowling addressed that

The publication of the last book was a moment of great joy and sadness for Rowling's fans, who were excited to read the story but sorry to have it end.

question by saying, "I definitely have thought about it, but I've made no decisions at all. I will definitely be writing. I literally don't quite feel right if I haven't written for awhile. A week is about as long as I can go without getting extremely edgy.... It really is a compulsion. Yeah, so I have ideas, but they could all be rubbish."

Rowling's Harry Potter books have been translated into more than 60 languages and distributed in 200 countries around the world. More than a quarter of a billion copies have been sold, and the characters have been licensed for use in hundreds of toys and video games. Although the final book has already been published, Harry Potter's popularity shows no signs of waning as fans anticipate the release of the movie versions of the last two books.

Time magazine called Harry Potter the most popular children's series ever written and said that Rowling "gets everything right, writes as though she knows what it is to be 13 years old and anxious or shocked at discovering what you can actually do if you try." One Time book reviewer observed, "Parents report reading levels jumping by four grades in two years. They cannot quite believe this gift, that for an entire generation of children, the most powerful entertainment experience of their lives comes not on a screen or a monitor or a disc but on a page." Rowling responded by saying, "If I can credit myself with anything, it has been to make it cool for young people to start reading again. And in this day and age when books have to fight it out with such diversions as Gameboy and Pokemon, that alone gives me more pleasure than anything."

> "I don't think there's any subject matter that can't be explored in literature. Any subject matter at all. I really hate censorship. People have the right to decide what they want their children to read, but in my opinion they do not have the right to tell other people's children what they should read."

Responding to Controversy

In spite of the worldwide Harry Potter phenomenon, not everyone is happy with Rowling's creation. The American Library Association reports that the Harry Potter books are the most challenged books in the United States, meaning that many people have requested that the books be banned from libraries and schools. Some religious organizations believe the books promote witchcraft and Satanism. One mother told a reporter that the Potter books have "an anti-Christian agenda." "My prayer is that parents would wake up, that the subtle way this is presented as harmless fantasy would be exposed for what it really is—a subtle indoctrination into anti-Christian values," she said. "The kids are being introduced to a cult and witchcraft practices."

> "The Potter books in general are a prolonged argument for tolerance, a prolonged plea for an end to bigotry, and I think it's one of the reasons that some people don't like the books, but I think that it's a very healthy message to pass on to younger people."

Rowling responds to the accusations by saying, "These extreme religious folk have just missed the point so spectacularly. I think the Harry books are actually very moral, but some people just object to witchcraft being mentioned in a children's book. Unfortunately, if such extremist views were to prevail, we would have to lose a lot of classic children's fiction. . . . I don't think there's any subject matter that can't be explored in literature. Any subject matter at all. I really hate censorship. People have the right to decide what they want their children to read, but in my opinion they do not have the right to tell other people's children what they should read."

An additional subject of controversy came up in late 2007, when Rowling appeared at Carnegie Hall in New York City. She read from *Harry Potter and the Deathly Hallows* and answered questions from the audience. She revealed several interesting tidbits about the characters—that Neville Longbottom married Hufflepuff Hannah Abbott, who became the landlady at the Leaky Cauldron pub; that Hagrid never married, since it was so difficult for him to meet women his size; and that Professor Dumbledore was gay and that the great love of his life had been his friend Grindelwald. The revelation about Dumbledore excited and intrigued many of her fans, but angered and inflamed those who object to her works. For Rowling, however, it was never an issue. "The Potter books in general are a prolonged argument for tolerance, a prolonged plea for an end to bigotry, and I think it's one of the reasons that some people don't like the books, but I think that it's a very healthy message to pass on to younger people." As Dumbledore himself said, "Differences of habit and language are nothing at all if our aims are identical and our hearts are open."

Rowling signing a copy of Harry Potter and the Deathly Hallows *for a student in New Orleans.*

Living with Fame

Thanks to Harry Potter, Rowling has become one of the wealthiest women in the world. She is the first person ever to become a billionaire by writing books. She has given countless interviews and appeared on television and radio programs around the world. For an entire decade Rowling was Amazon.com's No. 1 Top Selling Author. In spite of her fame, however, Rowling is almost unrecognizable in public.

"It's really the exception rather than the norm that anyone would approach me.... There was a phase when I had journalists at my front door quite a lot, and that was quite horrible. That was not something that I ever anticipated happening to me, and it's not pleasant, whoever you are. But I don't want to whine, because this was my life's ambition, and I've overshot the mark so hugely.... I am an extraordinarily lucky person, doing what I love best in the world."

At one time Rowling was too shy to show her writing to even one person, but that has now become her favorite part of being a published author. "I have found readings to be the most fantastic experience. I think part of that satisfaction comes from the fact that I was writing the books in secret for so long that I never talked to anyone about them. For five years I was the only person who had read a word of Harry Potter, and the only person who knew all these things about Harry's world and his friends. So the novelty of sitting in front of all these hundreds of people in bookshops all over the world and hearing them laugh, answering their questions and discussing my characters still hasn't worn off."

MARRIAGE AND FAMILY

Rowling married Jorge Aranes on October 16, 1992. They had one daughter, Jessica. The marriage ended in divorce on November 30, 1993. On December 26, 2001, Rowling married Neil Murray. They have a son, David, and a daughter, Mackenzie. Rowling lives with her husband and three children near the small town of Aberfeldy, Scotland.

WRITINGS

Harry Potter and the Philosopher's Stone, 1997 (British title)
Harry Potter and the Sorcerer's Stone, 1998 (U.S. title)
Harry Potter and the Chamber of Secrets, 1998
Harry Potter and the Prisoner of Azkaban, 1999
Harry Potter and the Goblet of Fire, 2000
Quidditch Through the Ages, 2001 (under name Kennilworthy Whisp)
Fantastic Beasts and Where to Find Them, 2001 (under name Newt Scamander)
Harry Potter and the Order of the Phoenix, 2003
Harry Potter and the Half-Blood Prince, 2005
Harry Potter and the Deathly Hallows, 2007

HONORS AND AWARDS

Children's Book of the Year (British Book Awards): 1997, for *Harry Potter and the Philosopher's Stone*

Gold Winner, Nestle Book Prize (Nestle): 1997, for *Harry Potter and the Philosopher's Stone;* 1998, for *Harry Potter and the Chamber of Secrets;* 1999, for *Harry Potter and the Prisoner of Azkaban*

Carnegie Medal: 1997, for *Harry Potter and the Philosopher's Stone*

Anne Spencer Lindbergh Prize in Children's Literature: 1997-98, for *Harry Potter and the Sorcerer's Stone*

Best Book designation (*Publisher's Weekly*): 1998, for *Harry Potter and the Sorcerer's Stone*

Editor's Choice designation (*Booklist*): 1998, for *Harry Potter and the Sorcerer's Stone;* 1999, for *Harry Potter and the Chamber of Secrets;* 1999, for *Harry Potter and the Prisoner of Azkaban*

Notable Book designation (American Library Association): 1998, for *Harry Potter and the Sorcerer's Stone*

Best Book of the Year (New York Public Library): 1998, for *Harry Potter and the Sorcerer's Stone*

Best Book for Young Adults (American Library Association): 1999, for *Harry Potter and the Chamber of Secrets*

Best Book of the Year (*School Library Journal*): 1999, for *Harry Potter and the Chamber of Secrets*

Whitbread Prize for Children's Literature: 1999, for *Harry Potter and the Prisoner of Azkaban*

W.H. Smith Children's Book of the Year Award: 2000, for *Harry Potter and the Goblet of Fire*

Hugo Award (World Science Fiction Society): 2001, Best Novel, for *Harry Potter and the Goblet of Fire*

Officer of the Most Excellent Order of the British Empire (O.B.E.) (Charles, Prince of Wales): 2001, for services to children's literature

Scottish Arts Council Book Award: 2001, for *Harry Potter and the Goblet of Fire*

Rebecca Caudill Young Reader's Award: 2001, for *Harry Potter and the Sorcerer's Stone*

Bram Stoker Award: 2003, Young Readers Category, for *Harry Potter and the Order of the Phoenix*

W.H. Smith Book Award: 2004, fiction category, for *Harry Potter and the Order of the Phoenix*

Book of the Year (Quill Book Awards): 2006, for *Harry Potter and the Half-Blood Prince*

Book of the Year (British Book Awards): 2006, for *Harry Potter and the Half-Blood Prince*

Best Book Award (Kids' Choice Awards): 2006, for the *Harry Potter* series

Rave Award (*Wired*): 2007

FURTHER READING

Books
Authors and Artists for Young Adults, Vol. 34, 2000
Major Authors and Illustrators for Children and Young Adults, 2002
Who's Who in America, 2007

Periodicals
Chicago Tribune, July 22, 2007, p.C1
Entertainment Weekly, Nov. 22, 2002, p.49; June 11, 2004, p.93; Nov. 11, 2005, p.22; July 20, 2007, p.30; Nov. 2, 2007, p.72; Nov. 30, 2007, p. 34
New York Times, July 10, 2007, p.E1
Newsweek, July 10, 2000, p.56; June 30, 2003, p.50
Time, Apr. 12, 1999, p.86; Sep. 20, 1999, p.66; July 17, 2000, p.70; Oct. 30, 2000, p.108; Dec. 25, 2000, p.116; June 23, 2003, p.60; June 30, 2003, p.60; June 7, 2004, p.117; July 25, 2005, p.60; July 9, 2007
Toronto Star, Nov. 3, 2001, p.A31
USA Today, July 7, 2005; July 10, 2007, p.D2
Washington Post, July 22, 2007, p.D1

Online Articles
http://www.januarymagazine.com/kidsbooks/potter5.html
   (January magazine, "Growing Up With Harry," July 2003)
http://www.msnbc.msn.com/id/20026225
   (MSNBC.com, "Rowling: I Wanted to Kill Parents," July 29, 2007)
http://today.msnbc.msn.com/id/19991430
   (MSNBC.com, "Rowling Regret: Never Told Mom About *Potter,*" July 27, 2007)

ADDRESS

J.K. Rowling
Scholastic
555 Broadway
New York, NY 10012

WORLD WIDE WEB SITES

http://www.jkrowling.com
http://www.scholastic.com/harrypotter/books/author
http://www.bloomsbury.com/authors

James Stewart Jr. 1985-

American Motorcycle Racer
2008 AMA Motocross Series Champion

BIRTH

James Stewart Jr., known to race fans as "Bubba," was born on December 21, 1985, in Bartow, Florida. His father, James Sr., worked as a supervisor at a Coca-Cola bottling plant before becoming his son's full-time riding coach. His mother, Sonya, also helps manage their son's business affairs. James Jr. has one younger brother, Malcolm.

YOUTH

Ever since he was a toddler, Stewart has been passionate about motorcycles. He loved going to local dirt tracks to watch his father, who was an amateur rider. Before long, he was constantly badgering his parents for his own little motorbike. "Little James, he wanted to ride from the time he was in diapers," his mother recalled. "We'd come home from work and Little James would just beg us to take him riding. We'd say, 'We're tired!' but he was like, 'I want to go!' So if he wants to do it, you continue to do it. And that's what made him better."

According to Stewart, racing appealed to his competitive nature. "In school I raced kids [during tests] to finish first," he said. "I slammed the pencil down so that everybody knew I was done. 'Done!'" His love for motorbike racing, though, was so great that other competitive sports never really interested him. "I never played much football or baseball," Stewart admitted. "I just wanted to be a bike racer."

> *Stewart's love for motorbike racing was so great that other competitive sports never really interested him. "I never played much football or baseball," he admitted. "I just wanted to be a bike racer."*

"Boogie," as he was known within his family, started racing 50cc (cubic centimeters) motorbikes at age four. He won his first national junior AMA (American Motorcycle Association) title when he was seven years old. (These events are officially called amateur events, but junior is the term by which they're usually known.) As he grew older, he also frequently went with his father to professional AMA events. These weekends exposed him to the best riders in both supercross and motocross, which are the two main types of competitive dirt-track motorcycle racing in the United States. Supercross races are held inside arenas and stadiums from January through May, taking place on shorter but more treacherous man-made dirt tracks. Motocross races are held outdoors from May through September, taking place on outdoor dirt tracks on natural terrain. For both, the riders participate in events over the course of the season, and the winner is determined by the number of wins during the season.

During race weekends, it was not unusual for Stewart and members of his family to be the only African Americans in attendance. According to Stewart, skin color was never an issue for him or other riders. "When I came in it I was such a young kid. I was so small and so young, I never really

JAMES STEWART JR.

Stewart in his garage on his family's farm in Haines City, Florida, showing off some of his motorcycles. The family gradually built up the property with a practice track, outdoor lighting for night riding, a motorcycle garage that holds Stewart's three dozen motorcycles, and multiple buildings for the family's fleet of vehicles.

thought about it," he explained. "And then once I realized everything—oh, there's not a lot of 'me' out there—I was already used to it."

EARLY INFLUENCES

Stewart credits his father's guidance and racing smarts for his early success. "My dad has had more of an impact in my career than anyone could ever imagine," he declared. "He has always pushed me and saw things in me that I didn't know I had. He helped me pull things out such as heart, courage, and a strong mind."

Stewart's mother also played an important role in his racing career. "My mom's the backbone of the family," he explained. "My dad comes to the races with me on the weekend, and my mom's back doing the tickets, going to the races with my brother, making dinner and stuff like that. She's keeping us in line."

Another important influence in Stewart's young life was Tony Haynes, who was one of the few other junior African-American motocross riders in America when Stewart was growing up. Stewart and his father even shared quarters with Haynes and his father when the two young riders were competing at the same track on racing weekends. In 1992, however, Haynes suffered a terrible crash on the track that left him paralyzed from the waist down. A short time later, Stewart asked his injured friend if he could wear the number 259—Haynes's number—in future competitions. Touched by Stewart's efforts to pay tribute to him, Haynes agreed. Stewart wore the number 259 jersey for the next 13 years, and he and Haynes remain close friends.

> "My dad has had more of an impact in my career than anyone could ever imagine," Stewart declared. "He has always pushed me and saw things in me that I didn't know I had. He helped me pull things out such as heart, courage, and a strong mind."

Riding with the number 259 on his back, Stewart spent the rest of the 1990s building a legendary reputation in the world of junior motorcycle racing. He became the rider to beat in every age category through which he passed, but few competitors were able to challenge him.

Stewart's dominance became even greater after 1998, when his family moved to a 40-acre parcel of land in Haines City, Florida, and built a practice dirtbike track for him. The young racing wizard spent hours on the track every day, honing his skills and practicing new moves to shave valuable seconds off his time. By 2001 "Bubba" Stewart, as he was known throughout the sport, had recorded an amazing 47 race victories in junior AMA competition and 11 AMA national junior titles.

EDUCATION

Stewart attended public school in Florida until middle school, when his race schedule became so demanding that his parents decided to home-school him. Stewart has acknowledged that he missed out on some of the pleasures of traditional school experiences. "I kind of wish I went to a prom," he once said. "Sometimes, it bums me out when people go: 'I got Homecoming this weekend; I'm taking so-and-so.'" Ultimately, however, Stewart believes that his decision to focus on his racing career was the correct one.

CAREER HIGHLIGHTS

In 2001, after years on the junior circuit, the 16-year-old Stewart made the leap to professional motorcycle racing. He started out in the 125 class, the

JAMES STEWART JR.

Stewart made this jump in 2002, while still a rookie.

lower class or level of professional motocross and supercross. The name comes from the 125cc bikes used by riders in the lower class at that time. In the early 2000s, though, the class transitioned to more powerful 250cc four-stroke models, and in 2005 the division formally changed its name to Lites Class. As it turned out, it did not matter what sort of motorcycle Stewart rode. He dominated the field in race after race throughout his four years in the Lites Class, earning Lites Motocross Championship titles in both 2002 and 2004.

As usual, Stewart was often the only African-American rider in the field. But he never let this fact become a distraction. "Sometimes it's hard, when you look around and don't see any other African Americans racing," he admitted. "But you have more [African Americans] coming to the races to watch and if I'm bringing them in, that's cool. It does feel good to be the first ever, but I honestly don't sit here and think about it a lot. With a helmet on, we all look the same anyway."

> "Sometimes it's hard, when you look around and don't see any other African Americans racing," Stewart admitted. "But you have more [African Americans] coming to the races to watch and if I'm bringing them in, that's cool. It does feel good to be the first ever, but I honestly don't sit here and think about it a lot. With a helmet on, we all look the same anyway."

Stewart preferred to focus his attention on the sheer thrill of riding. Whether soaring airborne over hills, tearing down beaten-up straightaways, or flying through hairpin turns, the young star enjoyed every minute of every race. "It's kind of like the same feeling you get on a roller coaster ride!" he said.

During this period, Stewart became particularly famous for a riding stunt known as the Bubba Scrub, in which he tilts his motorcycle sideways in midair on steep jumps so that he can return to the ground sooner than other riders. "It's mind-boggling to see it," one racing journalist told *Sports Illustrated*. "He's doing things on a motorcycle that other people haven't considered."

Achieving Fame

By 2004 Stewart was earning more than $3 million a year in prize money and endorsements from such companies as Kawasaki (his motorcycle sponsor) and Oakley sunglasses. These earnings enabled the Stewart family to make major investments in their Haines City property, from building a new motorcycle garage to installing a bank of towering field lights along the practice track so that Stewart and his friends could ride at night. Stewart and his father also used the earnings to indulge their love of four-wheeled vehicles. By 2004 the family had a fleet of trucks, SUVs, and vintage cars tucked away in the various buildings on their property.

During this same period, Stewart became so famous that such professional sports stars as baseball players Barry Larkin and Ken Griffey Jr. regularly dropped in to ride with him. Both Larkin and Griffey bought several motorcycles for their families and kept them at the Stewart home. Stewart also became friendly with basketball legend Michael Jordan. "He was the first person I was ever nervous to meet," he admitted. "Now I talk to him all the time."

Stewart's racing exploits also led to interest from major media magazines and newspapers. He was featured in stories in *Sports Illustrated*, *Rolling Stone*, the *Washington Post*, *USA Today*, and the *New York Times*. In 2003 *Teen People* even named him as one of 20 teens "who will change the world." Despite all this attention, though, Stewart has said that he is just an ordinary guy who likes to race motorcycles. "I may have cars and money now, but I'm the same person I was before," he said. "If I worked at McDonald's, I'd be the same person."

Joining the Heavyweights

In January 2005 Stewart made his long-awaited move up into the premier class, the highest class of professional dirt-bike racing. By moving up into the supercross and motocross field, he would be riding bigger and more powerful 450cc motorbikes. He would also be competing against top riders like Ricky Carmichael, who had been the king of professional motorcycle racing for several years. "It's more pressure now," Stewart said. "People expect me to win. There are greater expectations, and my job is to make sure people believe."

Motorcycling fans all across America were thrilled at the prospect of watching a season's worth of showdowns between Stewart and Carmichael. But Stewart broke his arm during a practice session before the second race of the 2005 supercross season (which runs from January through May). He missed nearly half of the season before he was able to return to competition. When he did climb back aboard his Kawasaki, though, he showed that he would be a force to be reckoned with. In his second race after his return, at a supercross event in Dallas, Stewart led all

Stewart leading Travis Pastrana during a round of the 2006 AMA Supercross Series.

20 laps of the final and crossed under the checkered flag five seconds before Carmichael. "I'm so happy," he said afterward. "I have one [Supercross victory] under my belt, and now I know how it feels."

Stewart finished his rookie year in supercross with three victories and managed to climb to tenth place in the season-ending standings. He then turned his attention to the upcoming outdoor motocross season (which runs from May through September). Unfortunately, a serious bacterial infection bothered him for much of the outdoor season, and he was unable to make a major impact. "You have to learn to deal with the positives and the negatives," he later said. "I think champions are built when they overcome adversity and shine even better the next time. Some of the races I lost, I felt like I came back stronger the next weekend."

Winning the Championship

In 2006 Stewart retired his legendary 259 jersey and started wearing the number 7. He explained that he had taken the 259 number to the top of the Lites world, but that he was ready for a change as he set out on the next phase of his career. As the 2006 campaign unfolded, Stewart proved that he had put the injuries and illness that marred his rookie year behind him. In the AMA Supercross Series, he raced to eight wins and finished second in the year-end standings. he posted another three victories in the AMA Motocross Championship, which lifted him to fourth place in the final standings.

> "I've always felt that the passing of the torch is not a passing of the torch until you earn it. Now I feel like I've earned [the reputation as the country's top rider]. A lot of people were trying to hand it to me before I won a championship, and that's not for me."

In 2007 Stewart finally claimed the ultimate championship of his sport. He utterly dominated the year's supercross circuit, winning 13 of the 16 races in which he competed. "It feels great," he declared. "I've always felt that the passing of the torch is not a passing of the torch until you earn it. Now I feel like I've earned [the reputation as the country's top rider]. A lot of people were trying to hand it to me before I won a championship, and that's not for me." His favorite race of the season was one that took place in Indianapolis, when he rocketed from far back in the pack to win the 20-lap final. "That might be one of the best races of my career," he said. "Like an NFL team in the Super Bowl, I was pulling out every trick play in the book to win that one."

By capturing the 2007 AMA Supercross Championship in the 450cc Division, Stewart became the first ever African-American AMA champion. As the 2007 motocross season got underway, he was poised to claim that championship as well. He was the season's points leader as the riders headed into Washougal, Washington, in late July for the eighth race in the season's 12-race schedule. But Stewart injured his knee in Washougal and was forced to sit out the rest of the season, so he slid to seventh in the final standings. "I was bummed because I love racing for my fans and I wanted to win that other title," he said. "[But] it gave me a well-needed break. I haven't had a break since the 2005 season. I have been grinding it out a long time and I think it's good to give my body a break and a chance to heal up. It gets me really motivated for the upcoming season. When you keep racing all the time it starts to get old but now it's like a slap in the face which really motivates me."

> *Motorcycle racing legend Jeremy McGrath claimed that "Stewart can do things on a bike that nobody ever has.... He is a student, he watches tapes of myself and other people, and he has taken his skills one step further. He sees the little things, the things an average fan, even an average rider, might not see. Just amazing."*

In 2008, Stewart led throughout the 15-week motocross season. Although he had just had knee surgery four months earlier, he dominated at each of the 12 events during the season. In fact, he registered a perfect 24-0 record. With that achievement, he joined Ricky Carmichael, a 10-time AMA motocross champion, to become one of only two riders to achieve a perfect season. In addition, Stewart led for 369 out of 382 laps during the season, and at eight events he led the pack for every lap during the entire event. As of 2008, he is tied for fifth on the AMA motocross career wins list, with 16 wins.

At this point, no one in the world of professional dirt-bike racing doubts that Stewart is the best rider in the sport. "I don't think anyone is on his level right now," said Carmichael. "There really is no one in his league." Another motorcycle racing legend, Jeremy McGrath, claimed that "Stewart can do things on a bike that nobody ever has.... He is a student, he watches tapes of myself and other people, and he has taken his skills one

Stewart winning his 13th race of 2007 in this season finale in Las Vegas, where he clinched the 2007 AMA National Supercross Championship.

step further. He sees the little things, the things an average fan, even an average rider, might not see. Just amazing."

HOME AND FAMILY

Stewart lives and practices at his family's compound in Haines City, Florida. One of the buildings on the property houses the three dozen or so motorcycles that Stewart has ridden over the years, from the little 50cc bikes he rode as a youngster to the monster 450cc Kawasaki models he races today. Another building contains the hundreds of trophies that he has earned over the years. "I have to put them out there because I don't have enough room in the house," said his mother. "It's crazy!"

HOBBIES AND OTHER INTERESTS

Stewart enjoys relaxing with music and video games in his spare time.

HONORS AND AWARDS

AMA Amateur National Championship: 11 titles from 1993-2001
AMA Rookie of the Year: 2002
AMA Lites National Motocross Championship: 2002, 2004
AMA Lites West Supercross Championship: 2003

AMA Lites East Supercross Championship: 2004
AMA National Supercross Championship: 2007
AMA National Motocross Championship: 2008

FURTHER READING

Books

Amick, Bill. *Motocross America*, 2005
Savage, Jeff. *James Stewart*, 2007 (juvenile)

Periodicals

Cincinnati Post, Apr. 13, 2002, p.B2
Detroit Free Press, Apr. 2, 2004, p.H4
Detroit News, Apr. 20, 2007, p.E8
Hartford (CT) Courant, June 7, 2002, p.A1
Los Angeles Times, Jan. 8, 2005, p.D1
Orlando Sentinel, Mar. 8, 2003, p.E1
Sacramento (CA) Observer, May 19, 2004, p.3
San Jose (CA) Mercury News, Jan. 28, 2006, p.3
Sports Illustrated, Apr. 29, 2002, p.A35; Apr. 11, 2005, p.Z8
Sports Illustrated for Kids, Mar. 2004, p.34; July 2007, p.36
St. Petersburg (FL) Times, Dec. 18, 2004, p.C1
USA Today, Apr. 30, 2003, p.C6; Nov. 30, 2005, p.C2; May 4, 2007, p.C7
Washington Post, July 23, 2004, p.A1

Online Articles

http://www.dirtbikemagazine.com
(Dirt Bike Magazine, "James Stewart: The Future of MX," Nov. 9, 2000)

ADDRESS

James Stewart
Kawasaki Motors Corp., USA
9950 Jeronimo Road
Irvine, CA 92618

WORLD WIDE WEB SITES

http://www.jamesstewartonline.com
http://www.amamotocross.com
http://www.kawasaki.com
http://www.racerxonline.com
http://www.supercrossonline.com
http://www.amaproracing.com

Ichiro Suzuki 1973-

Japanese Professional Baseball Player with the Seattle Mariners
First Japanese Position Player in American Major League Baseball

BIRTH

Ichiro Suzuki (pronounced *EE-chee-row suh-ZOO-ki*) was born on October 22, 1973, in Kasugai, a city in the Aichi prefecture (a regional government) of Japan. The name "Ichiro" is generally given to the first son in a family, but Ichiro was the second son of Nobuyuki Suzuki, a businessman who owned a mechanical parts plant, and his wife Yoshie. Ichiro's older brother,

Kazuyasu Suzuki, is a fashion designer in Japan who specializes in hip-hop style clothing.

YOUTH

Suzuki grew up in Nagoya, the capital of the Aichi prefecture, a city located about 160 miles from Tokyo, the Japanese capital. Baseball has always been part of his life, and one of his earliest memories involved receiving a bat and glove at age three. "The glove wasn't a toy, but a real glove made of red leather," he recalled. "I was so excited about getting it I carried it everywhere." Suzuki's father was a big baseball fan who played the sport in high school. He also coached the local little league team, which young Ichiro convinced him to let him join at age six, two years early. Because the team only practiced on Sundays, his father helped him practice hitting and catching during the week. After work, the elder Suzuki devoted time every day to helping young Ichiro improve his game. He would also take his son to games played by Nagoya's home team, the Chinuchi Dragons of the Central League.

His father was very strict in training Ichiro, forbidding junk food and limiting television time. "Sometimes it was pretty hard to take," the athlete recalled. "It bordered on hazing. I suffered a lot." Still, he admitted, "once I started training again I'd enjoy it," and all the practice paid off. The naturally right-handed Ichiro learned to bat left-handed, bringing him a couple steps closer to first base. He became so skilled at hitting that by the time he was 10, his father's pitches didn't provide enough of a challenge. They would go to a local batting center, where Ichiro would hit 60-mile-an-hour pitches, as many as 250 every night. By the time Suzuki reached junior high, the center had to install a special spring on the batting machine so that it would shoot out 80-mile-an-hour pitches. His pitching arm was also outstanding, and he helped his junior high team place third in a national tournament.

EDUCATION

Suzuki was a good student in junior high, earning A's and B's. After taking his high school entrance exams, he enrolled in the Aiko-dai Meiden High School in Nagoya, a school that had a rich baseball tradition. It was too far for him to commute, so he stayed in a dormitory on campus and worked hard on his training. Suzuki became a standout pitcher for the Aiko-dai team, with a 93-mph fastball. After a bike accident left him on crutches for six weeks, he lost some of his pitching form and began to focus more on fielding and batting.

During Suzuki's sophomore and junior years, his team qualified to attend the Koshien, Japan's National High School Baseball Tournament. Only 50 of more than 3,000 high school baseball teams qualify each year. Unfortunately, Suzuki's team lost in the first round each time. His team failed to qualify for the Koshien during his senior year, but his performance in the regional tournament—batting .643—made professional scouts take notice. He graduated from high school in 1991 and entered the draft for Nippon Professional Baseball (NPB). Selected in the fourth round by the Orix Blue Wave, he decided to begin his professional baseball career rather than attend college. Suzuki believed baseball was his future. "If I wasn't going to be a ballplayer, I [couldn't] think of anything else."

CAREER HIGHLIGHTS

Beginning His Pro Career in Japan

Suzuki signed a contract with the Orix Blue Wave, which played in the port city of Kobe, 100 miles away from his hometown. His team didn't expect much of him at first. At 5'9" and only 150 pounds, he was considered too small to handle the demands of being a major league pitcher. Instead, his fielding and hitting skills gave him potential as an outfielder. He began playing in 1992 with Orix's minor league affiliate, and in 58 games he batted .366 and led the minors in stolen bases.

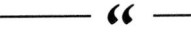

> *One of Suzuki's earliest memories involved receiving a bat and glove at age three. "The glove wasn't a toy, but a real glove made of red leather," he recalled. "I was so excited about getting it I carried it everywhere."*

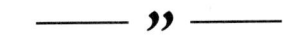

Called up to the Blue Wave for their final 40 games of the season, Suzuki hit a respectable .253. He began the 1993 season back down in the minors, where he hit a blistering .371. When he returned to the Blue Wave, however, the manager tried to force him to change his unconventional batting stance. At the time, Suzuki kicked up his front leg before hitting the ball, using its downward motion to add to his swing's power. Under pressure to change his stance, the outfielder hit only .188 during his 43 major-league games in 1993. During those first two partial seasons in the majors, however, he didn't make a single error in the outfield.

Suzuki's luck turned in 1994, when Orix changed managers. Akira Ohgi had seen the outfielder play in a winter league in Hawaii, where his .311 batting average helped his team win the league. Ohgi was willing to let him keep his unconventional batting style, as long as he worked hard and

Baseball in Japan

Baseball was introduced to Japan in about 1872 by Horace Wilson, a Civil War veteran from Maine. Wilson was teaching at the Kaisei Gakko School in Tokyo when he decided his students needed a break from studying. The students were intrigued by this simple game involving hitting a ball with a stick, throwing, catching, and running. They called it *yakyu*, or "field ball." As the sport grew in popularity throughout the country, the first organized team formed around 1883 and the game spread to high school and college campuses throughout Japan. A national high school baseball tournament, the Koshien, was founded in 1915. Today, the Koshien is one of Japan's most popular sporting events.

The first Japanese professional baseball team, the Shibaura Club, appeared in the early 1920s, but the sport didn't take off until seven teams created the Japan Baseball League in 1936. These teams were founded by newspaper and train companies that hoped to boost sales. The teams were named after their companies, not their home cities, a tradition that continues today. During Japan's involvement in World War II, between 1940 and 1945, many baseball teams ceased playing or even dissolved. After Japan's surrender to the United States in 1945, however, the sport returned. American soldiers helped the Japanese rebuild playing fields, and in 1950 the Japan Baseball League reorganized into Nippon Professional Baseball (NPB).

The NPB structure includes 12 teams split into two leagues. The Central League consists of the Chunichi Dragons, the Hanshin Tigers, the Hiroshima Carp, the Yakult Swallows, the Yokohama Bay Stars, and the Yomiuri Giants. The Pacific League consists of the Chiba Lotte Marines, the Nippon Ham Fighters, the Orix Buffaloes (formerly the Blue Wave, Ichiro Suzuki's team), the Rakuten Golden Eagles, the Seibu Lions, and the Softbank Hawks. After a season, which lasts between 130 and 140 games, the two league champions meet in the Japan Series. Japanese professional baseball has most of the same rules as American baseball, except that games can end in a tie after 12 innings. Japanese teams also put much less emphasis on home runs than do American teams.

Some observers have wondered whether the NPB will suffer now that many of their biggest stars have left to play in America, but Suzuki has suggested that "the more that Japanese players go to the big leagues to play and succeed, the more that will serve to inspire young kids in Japan to want to become baseball players." With more potential players, plus Japanese major leaguers bringing their skills back to Japan, he added, "in the long run, it will be a plus."

ICHIRO SUZUKI

supported the team. He put Suzuki on his roster for the beginning of the season and made a unique suggestion: that his outfielder use his first name on his jersey instead of "Suzuki," which is one of the most common surnames in Japan. Suzuki resisted at first—no other player had ever gone by his first name—but Ohgi insisted it would bring good luck. Thus "Ichiro" debuted in the Orix outfield in the spring of 1994.

It didn't take long for Japanese baseball fans to take notice of Ichiro. During the first 17 games of the season, he hit nearly .400 with four home runs. His hitting streak of 69 games between May and August set a Japanese record. The Blue Wave was in the pennant race for most of the season, while fans all over the country watched Suzuki chase the 200-hit mark, a number no Japanese player had ever reached. He ended the 130-game season with 210 hits, a .385 batting average, and 29 stolen bases. He earned a Gold Glove for fielding and was named to the Best Nine, Japan's equivalent of the All-Star Team. He topped it off by being named the Pacific League's Most Valuable Player, even though his team finished second in the league.

The 1995 season began under a dark cloud for the Orix Blue Wave. On January 17, their home city of Kobe had been hit by a major earthquake that measured 7.2 on the Richter scale. More than 6,300 people died, and more than 7,000 buildings were damaged or destroyed. As the baseball season started, there were city-wide efforts to rebuild and boost morale, and the Blue Wave became part of that effort. Suzuki was inspired that Kobe fans continued to come out for games. "They'd gone through much and you'd think baseball wasn't much of a priority, but they still came to cheer us on," he commented. "That encouraged us a lot, and we did our best to live up to their expectations." That year he led the league in batting average (.358), RBIs (80), hits (179), and stolen bases (49), helping his team win the Pacific League pennant. Although the Blue Wave lost the Japan Series, Suzuki earned another Gold Glove, Best Nine, and MVP award.

Suzuki had another standout year in 1996. He led the Pacific League with a .356 batting average and 193 hits on the way to a third consecutive MVP citation. He also earned Gold Glove and Best Nine citations. Even better, the Blue Wave won the Pacific League pennant. In the Japan Series, they faced the Yomiuri Giants, Japan's most successful franchise, which had 18 previous Japan Series titles. The first game went into extra innings when the teams were tied 3-3 after the first nine. In the tenth inning, Suzuki hit a homer off pitcher Hirofumi Kono to score the winning run. The Blue Wave went on to win the Series four games to one.

BIOGRAPHY TODAY • 2008 Annual Cumulation

Suzuki blasting a homer to score the winning run against the Yomiuri Giants in October 1996. The game went into extra innings when the teams were tied at the bottom of the 9th. With Suzuki's home run in the 10th inning, the Blue Wave won the first game of the 1996 Japan Series and went on to win the Series 4-1.

Becoming a Japanese Superstar

Suzuki's success with the Orix Blue Wave made him an extremely popular figure in Japan. Reporters began following his every move and fans crowded around him in public, even in public restrooms. He was known by a single name—Ichiro—and one survey showed he was more famous than the Japanese emperor. For a young man still in his early 20s, this kind of attention was head-turning. "I was flattered and I wanted to see what they were saying about me, to read it every day," he admitted. "But I realized I should not have those kinds of feelings. It showed there was something wrong inside me." He turned back to baseball and focused on improving his skills. He had a new ambition: to play in the American major leagues. In late 1996 a team of American All-Stars had come to Japan, and Suzuki had performed well against them, getting seven hits in 11 at-bats during eight exhibition games. "I saw these good American players and I wanted to play against them," he recalled. Unfortunately, his contract tied him to the Orix Blue Wave through the 2001 season, and the team would not release its star player, who drew thousands of fans to the stadium.

Suzuki didn't let his disappointment affect his play. In 1997 he had another stellar season, leading the league with 185 hits and a .345 batting average. He also set a Japanese record with 216 consecutive at-bats without a strikeout. He earned a fourth consecutive Gold Glove, committing only two errors in 135 games, and another Best Nine citation. He achieved similar success in the 1998 season, leading the league with 181 hits and a .358 batting average. Because he recorded only 11 stolen bases, his career low for a full season, some people speculated that he had lost enthusiasm for the game. "I didn't lose my desire to play in Japan," he later admitted, "but it wasn't interesting to me anymore."

To help provide their star player with a challenge, the Blue Wave sent Suzuki to participate in the 1999 spring training camp with the Seattle Mariners. Suzuki thoroughly enjoyed his time at their facility in Peoria, Arizona. He asked the other players about the strategies they used against major-league pitchers, hoping that he might compete against them some day. He participated in a couple of exhibition games and learned some American slang. Best of all, he enjoyed everyday life in a place where he wasn't famous. He returned to Japan feeling invigorated and confident that Major League Baseball was in his future.

> "I was flattered and I wanted to see what they were saying about me, to read it every day," Suzuki said about the publicity he received early in his career. "But I realized I should not have those kinds of feelings. It showed there was something wrong inside me."

The Blue Wave wanted to keep their star player happy playing in the NPB, so they signed Suzuki to a record-setting contract during 1999. His one-year deal earned him 500 million yen, or almost $4.15 million dollars. Nevertheless, he started the season with a bit of a hitting slump. "When I went after a pitch, just before I hit it I couldn't follow it with my eyes," Suzuki recalled. During this bad streak, a simple groundout provided the mental image he needed to fix his problem. He adjusted the angle of his front foot so that he made contact with the ball at the correct angle. Soon after making this adjustment, he hit his 1,000th career hit, setting a Japanese record by reaching the milestone in only 757 games. By the time an errant pitch broke his wrist and ended his season five weeks early, Suzuki had 141 hits and led the league with a .343 batting average.

Although Suzuki still yearned for the challenge of playing in America, his loyalty to his manager, Akira Ohgi, kept him in Japan for the 2000 season. During the season he came close to his goal of hitting .400, but another injury, this time a rib muscle strain, ended his season in August. He finished with an average of .387, the second-best in NPB history, and earned his seventh consecutive Best Nine and Gold Glove citations. Although he still had one season left before he became a free agent, the Blue Wave allowed him to "post" with Major League Baseball. In the posting system, Japanese clubs auction off the rights to a player to a Major League team, earning a fee for trading their player. Several teams bid for the rights to Suzuki, including the New York Mets and the Los Angeles Dodgers. The Seattle Mariners won the auction with a bid of $13.1 million and offered the outfielder a three-year contract worth more than $15 million. Suzuki was thrilled. "I needed something more for my own love of the game and also to make my fans happy," he explained. "The decision to come to the United States was a natural one so that I could challenge the best in the world."

> "Compared to the pressures I had in the past, this pressure is nothing. When I play in Japan, people expect me to be the leading hitter every year," Suzuki explained. "Even if there are things that become stressful, I think they're interesting. Isn't it because of those things that I am to be struck by the significance of being alive?"

Joining the Seattle Mariners

Suzuki's contract with Seattle made him the first Japanese position player (non-pitcher) to join a Major League Baseball (MLB) franchise. Although his lifetime stats in Japan were impressive—a .353 batting average, with 1278 hits and 199 stolen bases—there were many in the United States who doubted he could make much of an impact with Seattle. They argued that American pitching was far superior to Japanese pitching and that, at just 5'9" and 160 pounds, he was too small to hit well in larger American

Suzuki during his first season with the Mariners, 2001.

ballparks. Suzuki didn't listen to naysayers; instead he studied tapes of American pitchers, learned to work with his teammates, and perfected his technique. "Compared to the pressures I had in the past, this pressure is nothing. When I play in Japan, people expect me to be the leading hitter every year," he explained. "Even if there are things that become stressful, I think they're interesting. Isn't it because of those things that I am to be struck by the significance of being alive?"

Suzuki was still the focus of the Japanese media, despite the move to Seattle. Over 150 reporters followed him to America, and his games—even preseason ones—were broadcast live in Japan. Nevertheless, the move meant he could get his hair cut or take his wife out to eat without attracting a crowd.

Suzuki began proving his worth early in the 2001 season. By the end of April, he was batting .333 and the Mariners had set a major-league record by winning 20 games for the month. His teammates nicknamed him "the Wizard" for his speed and skills, while American fans were now the ones shouting "Ichiro" from the stands. He had a 23-game hitting streak during May and June; in July he became the first rookie to lead all players in All-Star voting. He earned a record 3.3 million votes, including half a million internet votes from Japan. Suzuki didn't let up for the rest of the year. He led the league with a batting average of .350 and 56 stolen bases, the first player to lead both categories since Jackie Robinson in 1949. His 242 hits

Suzuki's batting skill continued unabated after he joined the Mariners.

set a new record for a rookie and also made him the first player since 1930 to have more than 240 hits in a season. Suzuki was named American League Rookie of the Year and Most Valuable Player, only the second player ever to earn both accolades in the same year. He also earned a Gold Glove for fielding, committing just one error during 152 games in the outfield.

Aided by Suzuki's incredible rookie performance in 2001, Seattle tied the MLB record for wins in a season with 116 and was headed for the playoffs. In the division series against the Cleveland Indians, Suzuki hit .600, going 12-for-20 as Seattle took three of five games. The Mariners then had to face the New York Yankees in the American League Championship. The Mariners folded against Yankees pitching, and Suzuki's .222 average for the series contributed to the team-wide batting slump as they lost the series four games to one. Although he found it painful to watch the Yankees in the World Series, Suzuki said that "I and my teammates gave it everything we had. We showed our best. Because of this I didn't anguish over the loss for a long period of time." Still, despite his magical rookie season he felt he had more to prove. "[Am I] satisfied? That is a difficult word," he said. "In some aspects of the game, I still have things to do."

In the 2002 season Suzuki started strong, carrying a .384 average into June. At mid-season he again led the majors in All-Star voting with 2.5 million votes. Although he suffered a bit of a slump in September, he still finished the year with a .321 average and 208 hits, second-best in the league. He earned his second consecutive Gold Glove, making only three errors in the outfield. Although Seattle missed the playoffs, in November Suzuki led the MLB All-Stars to victory over the Japanese All-Stars, hitting 4-for-4.

In 2003, his third major league season, Suzuki proved he was just as dependable as he had been in Japan. He played in all but three of 162 games. His 2.1 million All-Star votes led the majors for the third season in a row. Although his season average dipped to .312, that still placed him in the top 20 players in the league. In addition, his 212 hits placed him second in the league, and his two fielding errors earned him a third Gold Glove. And he was still drawing the fans to Seattle's stadium, including thousands of Japanese tourists. Well aware of his value, the Mariners signed him to a contract extension at the end of the year, worth $44 million over four years.

Breaking Batting Records

Suzuki entered the 2004 season feeling he still had something to prove to himself and his fans. He started slowly, taking until mid-May to keep his batting average above .300, and then he became unstoppable. He collected at least 50 hits in the months of July, August, and September, becoming the

Suzuki had a stupendous season at the plate in 2004, including this at-bat on October 1. He's about to get his 258th hit of the season, breaking the previous record by George Sisler of the St. Louis Browns, set in 1920.

first MLB player to ever have three consecutive 50-hit months. By the end of August he had already reached 200 hits, the fastest pace in 35 years. People began talking about the possibility that Suzuki could break one of baseball's oldest records: George Sisler's single-season hits record of 257, set in 1920. Ichiro passed the mark on October 1 and finished the season with a new record of 262 hits. That total included 225 singles, which broke Willie Keeler's major league record from 1898. Suzuki won the 2004 batting title with an average of .372, which set a Mariners team record. As the first player to record 200 hits in his first four seasons, Suzuki also set an all-time major league record for the most hits—924—for a player's first four years, or for any four-year span.

It is difficult for any athlete to follow up a record-breaking season, and 2005 was no exception for Suzuki. While his 206 total hits were second-best in the American League, his season batting average was .303, his lowest yet. Suzuki had hoped to perform better, but he had learned a lesson after his record-breaking run of hits in 2004. "I realized it was impossible to please [everyone]. I discovered I needed to do what I needed to, [and] if people like it, that's good. I became more confident. And that Ichiro became a part of me, instead of me chasing after him," he said. "When people get placed upon a pedestal—when they start chasing after that person on the pedestal—they become mannequin-like. People striving for approval from others become phony. You should seek approval from yourself." Despite the dip in his statistics, Suzuki still became the first player in the majors to record at least 200 hits in his first five seasons.

> "I realized it was impossible to please [everyone]. I discovered I needed to do what I needed to, [and] if people like it, that's good. I became more confident," Suzuki clarified. "When people get placed upon a pedestal—when they start chasing after that person on the pedestal—they become mannequin-like. People striving for approval from others become phony. You should seek approval from yourself."

Suzuki returned to form in spring 2006, when he competed for Japan in the first ever World Baseball Classic (WBC). A 16-team tournament featuring the best players from leagues all around the world, the WBC was the first international tournament to include MLB players. Suzuki helped Team

Japan reach the championship game, which they won 10-6 over Cuba. The outfielder was named to the all-tournament team with a batting average of .364; he hit safely in all eight games and got 12 hits in 33 at-bats. He was thrilled to compete for his home country in the tournament. "Apart from the Olympics, I really wanted this WBC tournament to be the event that decides the true world champions, so that's why I participated in this event," he said. "And at the end, I was able to be on the championship team, and this is probably the biggest moment of my baseball career."

Suzuki had little time to rest before the 2006 MLB season began. He had another good year, leading the league with 224 hits and posting a respectable .322 average. He set both Mariners and American League records by stealing 39 bases in a row. Nevertheless, the outfielder felt somewhat discouraged that 2006 was Seattle's third year in a row finishing last in their division. "We've had three years here where we haven't won. It's definitely been hard on me mentally to spend so much time with us losing," he said. There was talk about his contract expiring after the next season and whether he might jump to a team with better prospects. But Suzuki wasn't eager to leave, noting that "Seattle is a special city to me…. I want to be a player who is wanted and needed for the team and for the fans. The fans have always been behind me, and I thank them and appreciate them."

Suzuki and the Mariners were back in form during 2007. In mid-season he signed a contract extension that kept him in Seattle. The five-year contract was worth around $18 million a season, making him one of baseball's top earners. With questions about his contract behind him, Suzuki could focus on performing. In his seventh consecutive All-Star Game, he was named MVP after going 3-for-3 and hitting the first inside-the-park home run in the game's history. Shortly after, he earned his 1500th major league hit. He finished the season with a .351 average, second best in the majors, and led the league with 238 hits, 203 singles (the third highest singles mark in league history), and 44 infield hits. Suzuki hadn't lost his step in the outfield, either, with only one error in 155 games—even though he had switched from right field to center field. He earned his seventh consecutive Gold Glove for fielding excellence and a Silver Slugger award for batting.

Fans' high hopes for the Mariners' 2008 season were quickly dashed, however. As of September 2008, the team was dead last in the American League Western Conference, with a .396 win-loss percentage. Ichiro's batting average of .313 with 190 hits and 39 RBIs wasn't enough to stop the team's serious skid.

Suzuki's fielding skills are one of the reasons he is considered a superlative player. In his first seven seasons in the major leagues, he played nearly 9,400 innings but only made 15 errors.

Striving for Excellence

A number of elements, both physical and mental, have contributed to Suzuki's triumphs as a baseball player. His success at hitting is a matter of talent and skill, developed through hard work. His opponents marvel at the hand-eye coordination that allows him to consistently put the fat part of the bat on the ball. Infielders respect his speed—half a second faster to first base than the average major leaguer—which forces them to play closer to home plate and allows him to lob more singles past their positions. "The ability to make contact is just how I learned to hit," he explained. "That's been a focus ever since I was a little player. That was important, and so I worked on it." He carefully considers his opponent up on the pitching mound. "When I get up [to bat], I feel and get a sense of the pitcher. I analyze what he might throw me, then I trust my sense of the pitcher and make the adjustment." During games, if he does not place the ball exactly where he planned, he will sometimes watch himself on video replays and then make corrections.

But hitting and offense are only part of Suzuki's skill as a ballplayer. "I cannot be the player I am without defense and speed," he noted. "I cannot impress you only with hitting. Defense and running make me a good player." With his strong defensive skills, opponents rarely try to take an extra base when a ball is hit to him in the field, for fear his rifle-fast arm will throw them out. In addition, he has only 15 errors for his major league career, although he has spent nearly 9,400 innings in the outfield.

> "You don't turn in a spectacular performance because you happen to be in supreme condition that day," Suzuki argued. "It's the times when you're in a normal mental state that you have a chance to turn in a great performance. If you allow yourself to drift out of normalcy because of pressure or frustration or some other factor, that's when things can go wrong."

Conditioning is also an important part of his game. Suzuki is noted for performing an elaborate stretching routine before every at-bat, and sometimes during downtime in the outfield. He pays attention to fitness during the off-season as well. One year he regularly ran up and down stairs for 90 minutes, logging more than 25,000 steps over 2.5 months. "Actually, I don't know if I'm that disciplined," he remarked. "I only do what my body asks me to—not what my head tells me to do. If I start doing things I don't like, baseball won't be fun anymore."

Although he makes the most of his physical skills, Suzuki has said that the mental aspect is the most important part of his game. "You don't turn in a spectacular performance because you happen to be in supreme condition that day," he argued. "It's the times when you're in a normal mental state that you have a chance to turn in a great performance. If you allow yourself to drift out of normalcy because of pressure or frustration or some other factor, that's when things can go wrong." He focuses on specific points in a ballpark before each at-bat in order to "achieve mental control." Then, after a game is finished, he oils and maintains his own glove, which is custom-made in Japan, before storing it in a special cotton bag. "This is not only baseball equipment to me, but they are part of me. You know, parts of my body," he explained. "The goal is to be as close [to perfect] as possible. In order to achieve that, it is imperative to set aside a period of self-reflection daily. That's what the time with my glove represents for me."

With his new, long-term contract in Seattle, Suzuki feels he can be the type of player who has "the security he needs to settle down and devote himself entirely to the game.... As long as I can enjoy playing ball I hope to keep playing the way I have been." But he'll continue to try to perfect his game. "I'm surprised at the things I still don't know, which makes me want to keep on playing."

MARRIAGE AND FAMILY

Suzuki began dating television broadcaster Yumiko Fukishima in late 1997, and they married on December 3, 1999. "If it weren't for her there wouldn't be an Ichiro of the Mariners," he said. "My wife's the one who helped make my dreams come true." The two of them live in Seattle with Ikky, their pet Shiba Inu (a Japanese breed of small dog). They reportedly have homes in Los Angeles and Arizona, near the Mariners' spring training camp.

HOBBIES AND OTHER INTERESTS

Suzuki enjoys playing Go, a strategic board game that originated in Asia. He also collects coins, paintings, and exotic Japanese custom cars, and he practices the traditional Japanese art of bonsai, or growing miniature trees. In 2006 he began taping his own Japanese television show, "Ichiro Versus." The program pits him against a prominent figure from another field, such as science, law, fashion, or entertainment, as they talk one-on-one and participate in a psychological test. His favorite part of the program is the word-association game, in which each person says the first thing that comes to mind after hearing a word or phrase. Suzuki enjoys talking with different types of people. "I think it's important to come in contact with people from as many different walks of life as possible. Otherwise, you limit what you can experience and you end up stifling your growth potential."

Suzuki earns about $10 million a year in endorsement deals, including agreements with companies related to sports gear, financial services, oil, drugs, and mobile phones. Although he doesn't often publicize his efforts, he is also very involved with various charities. In Japan he has been involved with the Make-a-Wish Foundation, which helps grant wishes to seriously ill children.

WRITINGS

Ichiro on Ichiro: Conversations with Narumi Komatsu, 2004 (translated by Philip Gabriel)

HONORS AND AWARDS

Most Valuable Player, Pacific League (Nippon Professional Baseball): 1994-1996
Best Nine (Nippon Professional Baseball): 1994-2000
Gold Glove (Nippon Professional Baseball): 1994-2000
Most Valuable Player, American League (Baseball Writers Association of America): 2001
Rookie of the Year, American League (Baseball Writers Association of America): 2001
All-Star Team (Major League Baseball): 2001-2007
Gold Glove, American League (Rawlings): 2001-2007
Silver Slugger Award, American League (Hillerich & Bradsby): 2001, 2007
Players Choice Award (MLB Players Association): 2001, for Outstanding Rookie, American League, and 2004, for Outstanding Player, American League
Commissioner's Historic Achievement Award (Major League Baseball): 2005, for setting single-season hits record
All-Tournament Team, World Baseball Classic: 2006
Most Valuable Player, All-Star Game (Major League Baseball): 2007

FURTHER READING

Books

Leigh, David S. *Ichiro Suzuki,* 2004 (juvenile)
Levin, Judith. *Ichiro Suzuki,* 2007 (juvenile)
Suzuki, Ichiro. *Ichiro on Ichiro: Conversations with Narumi Komatsu,* 2004 (translated by Philip Gabriel)

Periodicals

Baseball Digest, Dec. 2001, p.40; Nov. 2002, p.22; Dec. 2004, p.20
Chicago Sun-Times, May 13, 2001, p.126
Current Biography Yearbook, 2002
Fort Lauderdale (FL) Sun-Sentinel, July 9, 2001, p.C1

Los Angeles Times, Mar. 9, 2001, p.D13
New York Times, May 21, 2001, p.D4; June 9, 2002, p.SP3; Sep. 14, 2004, p.D1; Sep. 5, 2007, p.D4
New York Times Magazine, Sep. 16, 2001, p.50
Seattle Post-Intelligencer, Sep. 29, 2006, p.C1
Seattle Times, Mar. 30, 2007
Sporting News, Mar. 19, 2001, p.12; May 21, 2001, p.22; Mar. 10, 2003, p.10; May 20, 2005, p.14
Sports Illustrated, Dec. 4, 2000, p.68; Apr. 23, 2001, p.36; May 28, 2001, p.34; July 8, 2002, p.50
Sports Illustrated for Kids, Apr. 2002, p.29; Dec. 1, 2004, p.15
St. Louis Post-Dispatch, June 10, 2001, p.F9
Tacoma (WA) News Tribune, July 14, 2007
USA Today, Feb. 21, 2001, p.8C; May 15, 2007, p.C1
Washington Post, May 24, 2005, p.D1

ADDRESS

Ichiro Suzuki
Seattle Mariners
SAFECO Field
1250 1st Avenue South
Seattle, WA 98134

WORLD WIDE WEB SITES

http://seattle.mariners.mlb.com

Karen P. Tandy 1953-

American Former Administrator of the Federal
Drug Enforcement Agency (DEA)
First Woman to Lead the U.S. Battle against
Illegal Drugs

BIRTH

Karen Patrice Tandy was born on October 24, 1953, in Fort Worth, Texas, to William C. Tandy Jr., a communications technician for Southern Bell Telephone Co., and Juanita Jo Tandy, a secretary. She has a sister, Pamela.

YOUTH AND EDUCATION

Tandy grew up in Hurst, Texas. Years later, she said that her parents worked hard so "my sister and I achieved the higher education that eluded them." She described her father as "a blue collar worker" and her mother as "a hero and a role model of her own, for she was a working mother at a time when society frowned on working mothers."

Tandy attended Lawrence Dale Bell High School (better known as L.D. Bell) in Hurst, where she was a member of the National Honor Society and voted Miss L.D. Bell. After graduating from high school in 1971, she attended Texas Tech University in Lubbock, Texas. Tandy earned a Bachelor of Science (BS) degree in education in 1971. She continued her education at Texas Tech's School of Law, where she became president of the student bar association. Her election to that prestigious college position "reflected the respect and confidence that the rest of us had in Karen, and her willingness to step up and be a leader," said a former classmate, Walter Dean, who is dean of the Texas Tech Law School. Tandy received her law degree in 1977.

——— " ———

Tandy described her mother as "a hero and a role model of her own, for she was a working mother at a time when society frowned on working mothers."

——— " ———

FIRST JOBS

Tandy began her legal career by serving as a judicial clerk for a federal judge in Texas. Judicial clerks typically assist judges by researching the legal backgrounds of pending cases. During her time as a clerk, Tandy came into contact with the assistant district attorneys who were prosecuting criminals, and she became interested in their work. "I decided that is what I wanted to do with my life," she said. "I had thought I would stay in Texas, but one of the potential employers I interviewed with told me that women didn't have the killer instinct to be criminal prosecutors. That caused me to look to the Department of Justice and move to Washington."

CAREER HIGHLIGHTS

In 1979, Tandy began working for the Department of Justice. The DOJ is the nation's highest law-enforcement agency, responsible for enforcing federal laws. Many separate agencies make up the DOJ, including the

Drug Enforcement Administration (DEA), the Federal Bureau of Investigation (FBI), the U.S. Marshals, and others. Agencies in the DOJ both investigate crimes and prosecute criminals in court.

At the Department of Justice, Tandy's first assignment was as an assistant United States attorney in the Eastern District of Virginia and in the Western District of Washington, DC. She worked on the prosecution of cases involving illegal drugs and violent crimes. She soon began her steady movement up the ranks, earning many promotions. Over the next 11 years, Tandy held several leadership positions, including Chief of the Narcotics Division and Lead Attorney for the Organized Crime Drug Enforcement Task Forces.

When she moved to the Justice Department's Criminal Division in 1990, Tandy broadened her work in drug-related prosecutions. She became an expert in forfeiture law, which is the government's right to seize property gained by, or connected to, illegal activity. She was named Deputy Chief of the Narcotics and Dangerous Drug Section, and her duties included supervising narcotic prosecutions and drug wiretap investigations nationwide. During this time, Tandy developed a reputation for taking a hard-line approach against drug users and sellers. In 2001, she was named Associate Deputy Attorney General, a position that gave her responsibility for developing anti-drug enforcement policies across the country.

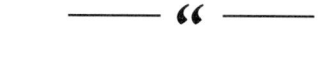

> *Tandy first became interested in becoming a prosecutor while working as a law clerk. "I had thought I would stay in Texas, but one of the potential employers I interviewed with told me that women didn't have the killer instinct to be criminal prosecutors. That caused me to look to the Department of Justice and move to Washington."*

Nomination by President Bush

Tandy's biggest promotion came in 2003, when President George W. Bush nominated her to be the Administrator of the Drug Enforcement Agency (DEA). The DEA was created in 1973 to coordinate enforcement of federal drug laws. The Agency is a division of the Justice Department and has an annual budget of $2.2 billion, employs approximately 11,000 people, and has 237 offices throughout the U.S. as well as 80 offices in 58 foreign countries.

Tandy with her husband, Steve Pomerantz, during her swearing-in ceremony as the new adminstrator for the DEA.

Becoming the head of a federal agency requires confirmation by the U.S. Senate. Tandy was questioned first by the members of the U.S. Senate Judiciary Committee, who had to approve her nomination before the full Senate could vote on it. Tandy said that a major focus of her leadership at the DEA would be to fight international drug traffickers, many of whom smuggle drugs into the United States. "A key piece in this is developing our partnerships overseas, so we can work together hand and glove," she said.

Tandy's appearance before the committee prompted a discussion about the controversial issue of medical marijuana. Many patients who suffer from such chronic or life-threatening illnesses as cancer, multiple sclerosis, and glaucoma say that smoking marijuana helps ease their severe pain. These patients are able to obtain marijuana by getting a medical prescription from their doctor. As a result, nine states—Alaska, California, Colorado, Hawaii, Maine, Maryland, Nevada, Oregon, and Washington—either do not arrest patients or providers of medical marijuana, or just impose a small fine for violations.

But since the law banning the use of marijuana is a federal statute, the DEA has continued to make arrests for medical-marijuana possession or its sale, even in the nine states with lenient laws. Two Democratic senators on the Judiciary Committee—Dianne Feinstein of California and Dick Durbin of Illinois—wanted to know if Tandy supported this policy. Tandy stated emphatically that she did. In a written statement to the committee, she said, "If I am confirmed as administrator of the DEA, it will be my duty to see the uniform enforcement of federal law. I do not believe that it would be consistent with that duty for me to support a moratorium on enforcement of this law, or any law, in selected areas of the country."

In her Senate testimony, Tandy disputed the position that marijuana is medically beneficial. The active ingredient in marijuana, tetrahydrocannabinol (THC), has been proven effective when processed into a federally approved pill called Marinol, she stated. But "marijuana itself, however, has not been shown to have medical benefits," Tandy argued. Senators Feinstein and Durbin disagreed and submitted several published studies showing the medical benefits of marijuana into the Judiciary Committee's official record.

> "I am committed to devoting all of my energy to do whatever it takes to remove drugs as a threat to the security and the future of our great country," Tandy said.

Tandy's nomination was ultimately approved by the committee, and its chairman, Sen. Orrin G. Hatch, R-Utah, praised her "long and impressive 25-year career with the Department of Justice."

Becoming DEA Administrator

On August 2, 2003, Tandy was confirmed as DEA Administrator without dissent by the entire Senate. She promised "proactive and bold leadership" in the fight to eliminate drug-smuggling operations. "I am committed to devoting all of my energy to do whatever it takes to remove drugs as a threat to the security and the future of our great country," she said.

As DEA Administrator, Tandy was charged with enforcing the laws related to drugs and other controlled substances. She was also responsible for bringing to the criminal justice system any individuals or organizations involved in growing, manufacturing, or distributing drugs. In addition, she was charged with investigating and prosecuting any violators of controlled substance laws, including criminals and drug gangs; running a national drug intelligence program, in conjunction with other agencies; seizing assets from drug trafficking; coordinating with other U.S. law enforcement agencies, as well as foreign governments, to enforce drug laws and reduce drug availability; and working with such international organizations as Interpol and the United Nations on drug-control programs.

The War against Methamphetamine

The increase in the use of methamphetamine (commonly called meth) is one of the most significant challenges facing the DEA and other law enforcement agencies around the U.S. Meth can be smoked, snorted, injected, or taken orally. It comes in the form of crystal-like powder or rock-like chunks. It can be made in a fairly simple lab, and labs have even been set up in people's homes. Before it is sold, the drug is mixed with a number of ingredients, most often the decongestant agents pseudophedrine or ephedrine—but in some cases with household-cleaning ingredients or even battery acid. Meth has many street names, including "speed," "Tina," "crystal," and "chalk."

The use of methamphetamine is extremely dangerous. Meth is one of the most addictive illegal substances, according to the National Institute on Drug Abuse (NIDA). Meth releases high levels of dopamine into the brain and acts as a mood enhancer, providing the user with a rush, with a false sense of ecstasy and control. This extra sense of pleasure is followed by a crash that impairs the user and leads to more craving. The immediate side effects can include convulsions, dangerous fevers, strokes, heart irregularities, stomach cramps, and shaking.

The long-term effects of using methamphetamine are even more devastating. The user builds up tolerance, so it takes more meth to get that rush. Users don't eat or sleep while they're looking for drugs, obsessed with trying to repeat that initial rush. After they don't sleep for days, they become exhausted, paranoid, and angry. Their teeth become rotten. They smell like chemicals, including cat urine. Many feels like bugs are crawling under their skin, and they scratch so hard that they develop ugly and infected open sores. Meth can also cause cardiovascular damage and brain damage.

The use of methamphetamine presents a danger to all users, but it presents an even greater danger to children. Meth use has risen in recent years among teens, who are often introduced to the drug at a party. Some users, particularly teenage girls, use the drug as a weight-loss aid. According to the DEA, one out of five people who enter treatment for meth addiction is

DEA agents making an arrest in California during Operation Wildfire, an attack on meth manufacturing and distribution networks.

under the age of 18. "Meth has spread like wildfire across the United States," Tandy said. "It has burned out communities, scorched childhoods, and charred once happy and productive lives beyond recognition."

The DEA has focused significant attention on methamphetamine. Cracking down on meth use is especially difficult because the drug is "homemade, cheap, and readily available," Tandy explained. In 2005 the DEA launched a sweep called Operation Wildfire, which was intended to strike all levels of meth manufacturing and distribution in the U.S. Coordinating with partners from state and local law enforcement agencies, the DEA arrested 400 people in 200 U.S. cities for producing and selling meth. The DEA also seized more than 200 pounds of meth and closed 56 labs that made it. Some of the labs were small operations, such as one found in a hotel room in Minneapolis. They also seized 28 vehicles and 123 weapons, and removed 30 children from dangerous environments.

"The consequences of meth are undeniable—for the abuser, for the trafficker, for the environment, for communities, and for the innocent children who live in filth and neglect," Tandy said. "Methamphetamine abuse has ruined families, destroyed neighborhoods, put a tremendous strain on all levels of law enforcement and social services. This historic enforcement effort illustrates our commitment to extinguishing this plague and protecting innocent Americans from the harmful ripple effects meth leaves behind."

The War against Drugs Worldwide

As head of the DEA, Tandy's job is not limited to battling drug trafficking in the U.S. She is also responsible for the coordination of efforts by DEA agents with officials from other countries to combat international drug smuggling into the U.S. Less than three weeks after assuming the DEA leadership, Tandy traveled to Mexico for the first of many trips to try and strengthen international ties in the war against drugs. Tandy praised the joint U.S.-Mexican operation in July 2003 that led to the arrest of 240 drug-smuggling suspects on both sides of the border. Mexico and the U.S. "are committed to the same goals of ensuring that we protect national security in both countries from the evils of drug trafficking," she said.

"*The consequences of meth are undeniable—for the abuser, for the trafficker, for the environment, for communities, and for the innocent children who live in filth and neglect,*"*Tandy said.* "*Methamphetamine abuse has ruined families, destroyed neighborhoods, put a tremendous strain on all levels of law enforcement and social services.*"

But preventing drugs from other countries, including Mexico, from reaching the U.S. continues to be a serious problem. Government officials estimate that two-thirds of the methamphetamine that reaches the U.S. comes from Mexico. During Tandy's tenure as DEA Administrator, the agency also participated in anti-drug operations in Canada, Colombia, the Dominican Republic, Panama, Jamaica, Afghanistan, and the Bahamas, among others. In one internationally coordinated sting in 2005, Operation Three Hour Tour, suspects were arrested in Colombia and the Dominican Republic the same day as their associates were arrested in California, New York, Connecticut, and Iowa. The arrests destroyed three major drug transportation rings that together smuggled the following into the United States each month: 4,000 pounds of cocaine, 20-30 pounds of heroin, and more than 50 pounds of meth. Thousands of pounds of illegal drugs and millions of dollars were seized, including 3,163 pounds of cocaine, 216 pounds of marijuana, 55

DEA agents and police officers ready to strike in Operation Mallorca, an attack on money-laundering activities by Colombian drug lords and U.S. criminal organizations.

pounds of meth, 15 pounds of heroin, 10,000 doses of ecstasy, $5.5 million in cash, 58 vehicles, and 52 firearms.

Since becoming the DEA administrator, Tandy has made use of her expertise in forfeiture law. She has focused on seizing drug merchants' assets, which have included airplanes, boats, houses, jewelry, and furs. "When I came through the door, I made money the No.1 priority," she said. In her first three years as administrator, the value of goods seized by the DEA more than quadrupled, to $1.9 billion annually.

One such operation was Operation Mallorca. This was a 27-month investigation into the money-laundering activities of several Colombian-based brokers who used drug proceeds to buy other goods. Money laundering means using a series of financial transactions to conceal the source or destination of funds—for example, taking drug money and moving it from one account to another, many times, so that the final placement of the funds can't be traced to the original drug money. The operation resulted in 36 arrests, including 13 traffickers who had handled $12 million in drug money and laundered it through 300 wire transfers to 200 bank accounts in 16 cities and 13 foreign countries. "DEA is targeting the financial networks of drug cartels like never before to bankrupt traffickers and money launderers," Tandy explained. "In Operation Mallorca, we followed the money around the globe and into the hands of three Colombian drug traffickers.... DEA showed today that traffickers can move their money around the world, but we will track it down."

The War against Internet Drug Crime

The DEA has also investigated drug crimes involving the Internet, both in the U.S. and overseas. In July 2004, in Operation Web Tryp, DEA agents arrested 10 people in five states and targeted 10 web sites that distributed drug analogues (copies of drugs that are designed to look real) to unsuspecting customers. Two young men, one 18 and the other 22, died after ingesting chemicals purchased from two of the sites. "The formulation of analogues is like a drug dealer's magic trick meant to fool law enforcement," Tandy said. "They didn't fool us and we must educate our children so they are not fooled either."

In 2005 the DEA created a new Virtual Enforcement Initiative to prevent drug criminals from using modern technology to spread drug use. The first drug sting was Operation Cyber Chase in April 2005. This investigation resulted in 20 arrests in eight U.S. cities and four foreign countries. This operation targeted major traffickers who sold narcotics, amphetamines, and anabolic steroids directly to buyers of all ages without a prescription from a doctor. "In this first major international enforcement action against on-line rogue pharmacies and their sources of supply," said Tandy, "we've logged these traffickers off the Internet."

Another 2005 sting targeting illegal Internet drugs, Operation Gear Grinder, was a 21-month investigation into eight major steroid manufacturing companies, as well as their owners. "Steroid traffickers market their product by luring young people with promises of enhanced performance and appearance," Tandy said, "but what they don't say is the illicit use of these harmful drugs can destroy the very bodies that they are supposed to improve. Drug traffickers prey on the belief that steroids enhance ability, but steroids only rob that ability, as we have seen so often from the affected lives of too many youth and professional athletes."

Creating a Web Site for Young People

A cornerstone of Tandy's work at the DEA has been her determination to steer young people away from drug use. "It is every parent's worst nightmare," she said. "I have two teenaged daughters and I'm no different than any other parent—I worry about my kids. They are great kids, but peer pressure can be a big issue."

Tandy decided that the best way to reach young people is through the Internet. In 2005 she authorized and helped develop www.justthinktwice.com, a web site designed to show teenagers the consequences of illegal drug use. The site, which includes animation, colorful graphics, and videos of former drug users, has been praised by teenagers, school officials, and parents for its ease of use and wealth of information. The "DEA is providing primary source information to help teens make good decisions," said Tandy. "We're taking them directly to the data and objective sources of medical, scientific and legal information."

The web site is divided into several sections, each of which discusses the dangers of specific drugs, including cough syrup, marijuana, methamphetamine, heroin, and steroids. Clicking on the cough-syrup link, for example, pulls up an animated character that yawns, burps, and scratches his belly-all while pointing to a second link that asks: "What's the big deal about DMX (dextromethorphan) anyway?" The potential serious side effects of vomiting, cardiac arrest, muscle spasms, and delirium are shown in a cartoon with the same animated character.

Not all of the links are entertaining. The site features pictures of drug users' rotting teeth, for example, and the disturbing before and after pictures of methamphetamine users. There are also short videos of young people talking about their negative experiences with drugs, as well as a link for treatment options and counseling centers for people who need help. "There is no more powerful message for teens than hearing from their peers about the impact that drugs had on other young lives," said Tandy.

For young people who have questions about drugs that they are reluctant to ask adults, the web site features a "Teens Ask Teens" option. Six teenage volunteers from the Drug Abuse Resistance Education (DARE) Advisory

> *Tandy is determined to steer young people away from drug use. "It is every parent's worst nightmare," she said. "I have two teenaged daughters and I'm no different than any other parent—I worry about my kids. They are great kids, but peer pressure can be a big issue."*

*Tandy announcing the successful results of an
Internet trafficking case, Operation Cyber Chase.*

Committee are profiled and are available to answer questions through an e-mail link.

The justthinktwice web site also focuses on the dangers of ordering prescription drugs, particularly Vicodin and Xanax, from the Internet. Drug transactions without a prescription are illegal, and doing so can lead to fatal consequences, as it did for two teenagers whose stories are told on the site. "The Internet has become the street corner for many of the drug users and traffickers," Tandy said. "These dealers now enter the privacy of our homes to entice and sell destruction to our children veiled under the illusion of being safe and legal."

Stumbleweed

The justthinktwice web site also includes an on-line magazine, *Stumbleweed*, which highlights the potential dangers of using marijuana. Readers can click on four articles: "Hey Dude, Where Did My Future Go"; "Totally Lame (and Dangerous and Illegal) Things to Do on Pot"; "Rx Pot: A Prescription for Disaster"; and "It's Just a Plant: How Could It Be Bad for Me?" Like the rest of the DEA site, *Stumbleweed* uses appealing graphics and cartoons in addition to providing a lot of informational text and a strong anti-drug message.

Tandy's strong stand against marijuana, even for medical uses, has been criticized by advocates who favor decriminalizing the substance. But Tandy has said that her concern about children is an important reason for her hard line. "We have more teens in (counseling) for marijuana than for all other drugs combined, including alcohol," she said.

> "[The] DEA is reminding kids to 'just think twice' about what they hear about marijuana from their friends, popular culture, and adults," Tandy said. "Think about the harm drugs cause to families, the environment, to innocent bystanders. Think about how drugs will impact your future: your health, your chances for a good job, your eligibility for student loans."

Stumbleweed argues that marijuana is not just a harmless plant. It's the active chemical ingredient in marijuana, THC, that makes people high. Marijuana with more THC is more potent and more likely to cause short-term memory loss, poor judgment, and impaired driving ability. "[The] DEA is reminding kids to 'just think twice' about what they hear about marijuana from their friends, popular culture, and adults," Tandy said. "Think about the harm drugs cause to families, the environment, to innocent bystanders. Think about how drugs will impact your future: your health, your chances for a good job, your eligibility for student loans."

In addition to its efforts in the area of education, the DEA sponsors programs for teenagers who are interested in a career in law enforcement and participating in drug prevention activities. One such program, the Law Enforcement Explorers, has posts across the country, and focuses on career development, leadership, citizenship and life skills. Another program, Teens in Prevention (TIP), focuses on mobilizing positive peer interactions and community support to reduce drug abuse and violence. More information on both programs is available on the justthinktwice web site.

> "It just doesn't get any better than this—leading 11,000 extraordinarily gifted people in DEA around the world who sacrifice everything to live our dangerous mission 24-7, every day of the year, in order to protect America's children and communities."

Leaving the DEA

Tandy racked up some impressive accomplishments during her tenure at the DEA. As DEA administrator, she directed investigations that resulted in criminal charges against 87 percent of the most wanted drug trafficking leaders. She aggressively seized drug proceeds and assets, with $3.75 billion in seized drug assets from 2004 to 2006. She led DEA initiatives to wipe out meth labs. She worked to strengthen the DEA's partnerships around the world. She met with heads of state from many different countries and initiated intelligence-sharing agreements with China and Russia. She deployed teams of DEA agents to conduct operations in Afghanistan against Taliban-connected drug lords, resulting in the seizure of opium, heroin, and drug labs.

By late 2007, Tandy was ready for a change. After more than 30 years of public service, she announced she was retiring from the DEA. "It just doesn't get any better than this—leading 11,000 extraordinarily gifted people in DEA around the world who sacrifice everything to live our dangerous mission 24-7, every day of the year, in order to protect America's children and communities," she said. "I will forever remain grateful to President Bush for this opportunity."

In October 2007, Tandy joined Motorola as the Senior Vice President of the Global Government Relations and Public Policy Division. In this position, she will be the company's top spokesperson on issues related to global telecom policy, trade, regulation, and related matters. She will be working on policy issues both within the United States and around the world. Gene Delaney, a Motorola executive, was enthusiastic about her role with the company. "Karen's substantial international relations and government affairs experience, as well as her policy understanding, make her an ideal and logical fit to lead our government and policy team," Delaney said. "We are confident that she will play an integral role in Motorola's continued success both in North America and around the world."

MARRIAGE AND FAMILY

Tandy lives in Virginia with her husband, Steven Pomerantz, a retired FBI agent, and their two daughters, Lauren and Kimberly. In her spare time, she serves as a Girl Scout leader and helps organize food drives for homeless children.

HONORS AND AWARDS

Attorney General's Award for Distinguished Service
Department of Justice Award for Extraordinary Achievement
United States Attorney Director's Award for Superior Service
Women in Federal Law Enforcement Director's Award: 2004
Texas Tech University School of Law Distinguished Alumna Award: 2004
Public Service Award from the Drug Abuse Resistance Education (DARE) Program: 2005

FURTHER READING

Books

Who's Who in America, 2007

Periodicals

Fort Worth Star Telegram, June 26, 2003, p.A1; July 11, 2004, p.A5
Houston Chronicle, Aug. 2, 2003, p.A8; Sept. 28, 2003, pp.A1 and A33; May 21, 2006, p.A12
New York Times, Aug. 31, 2005, p.A16
Washington Post, Aug. 31, 2005, p.A2

ADDRESS

Karen P. Tandy
Motorola Inc.
1301 East Algonquin Road
Schaumberg, IL 60196

WORLD WIDE WEB SITES

http://www.usdoj.gov/dea/index.htm
http://www.justthinktwice.com
http://www.motorola.com

Marta Tienda 1950-

American Sociologist
Pioneering Researcher of Ethnic, Economic, and Educational Issues

BIRTH

Marta Tienda was born August 10, 1950, in Edcouch, Texas. Her parents were Toribio "Toby" Tienda, a steelworker, and his wife Azucena Tienda, a homemaker. Marta was the second of their five children. The family also included older sister Maggie, younger brother Juan Luis, and younger sisters Irene and Gloria. After his first wife's early death, Toby Tienda remarried and added another brother, Reynaldo, to the family.

YOUTH

As a teenager, Toby Tienda had come to Texas from Mexico in search of the American dream: a better life. Azucena Tienda was born in the United States, the child of Mexican migrant workers. They were willing to work hard and travel far in order to improve life for their family. Marta was just a toddler when they moved the family to Detroit, Michigan, in search of a better job. When Marta began kindergarten, she was still learning English, and she felt out of place among her mostly white classmates. Still, she tried her best to learn because her parents expected her and her siblings to make the most of their education. By the time the family bought their own house in the working-class suburb of Lincoln Park, Marta was learning to read in English.

> *The Tienda family went through some rough times. After Marta's mother died and her father lost his job, the entire family was forced to work for two summers as migrant workers. Marta and her older sister were expected to pick 20 pecks (about 40 gallons) of tomatoes every day. After working in the fields, they returned to a shack with no running water and no kitchen.*

Tragedy struck the family in 1957 when Azucena Tienda died after suffering complications during surgery. Marta was only six and never got to say goodbye to her mother; her family tried to protect the children by not telling them of their mother's death until after the funeral. Marta and her siblings returned to Texas with her maternal grandmother, but the arrangement didn't work out. Their father came for them at the end of the year, taking them to visit relatives in Mexico before they went back home. Even at a young age, Marta could see that life was much harder for her Mexican cousins. She was happy to return to Michigan with her father and siblings.

The Tienda family went through some rough times after Azucena Tienda's death. They often depended on charity for food and clothing. When Toby Tienda had trouble keeping a regular babysitter, child protection services threatened to split up the family. His marriage in 1959 seemed to solve child-care issues, but the following year he lost his steelworker job because of a strike. The entire family was forced to work the next two summers as migrant workers. Marta and her older sister were expected to pick 20 pecks (about 40 gallons) of tomatoes every day. After working in the fields, they

Mexicans who work as migrant workers, as the Tienda family did for two summers, often are forced to live in substandard, dilapidated housing with no running water or electricity.

returned to a shack with no running water and no kitchen. The summer work allowed them to keep their house in Lincoln Park, however, and the children returned to school in the fall.

School provided Tienda with both stimulation and refuge. Because her father emphasized the importance of education, she worked hard and excelled in her classes. She especially enjoyed math and science, finding excitement in solving problems. Her teachers' encouragement was a satisfying contrast to the constant disapproval of her stepmother, who was very strict and expected Marta and her siblings to do most of the housework. When she was in middle school, one of her teachers planted the idea of going to college in her young student. "It was such a riveting moment for me that I even remember what the teacher was wearing that day. Until then, I thought that college was only for rich people." Before that day, Marta had planned on becoming a beautician, but her teacher's suggestion led her to develop bigger dreams. She resolved to become the first person in her family to go to college.

EDUCATION

At Lincoln Park High School, Tienda was an excellent student and an enthusiastic athlete. She was a member of the National Honor Society and was elected president of the Girls' Athletic Association. Despite working several jobs during her high school years, she graduated in 1968, finishing third in her class of nearly 600 students.

Tienda earned a full scholarship to Michigan State University, where she studied Spanish literature with the intent of becoming a high school teacher. She hoped to return home to Lincoln Park to teach with a passion for the subject some of her own teachers had lacked. During her student teaching assignment, however, she discovered that creative teaching methods were discouraged. She earned her bachelor's degree in Spanish in 1972, graduating *magna cum laude* (with high honors). Unsure what career would suit her best, she decided to continue her studies.

> *When Tienda was in middle school, one of her teachers planted the idea of going to college in her young student. "It was such a riveting moment for me that I even remember what the teacher was wearing that day. Until then, I thought that college was only for rich people."*

Tienda earned a Ford Foundation scholarship that paid for graduate school and elected to attend the University of Texas in Austin. While there she discovered sociology, the study of social groups and how they behave. The field often uses math and statistics to explore important issues, such as the relationship between education and income. Although she had to take additional undergraduate classes to complete some of the requirements for the field, she earned her master's degree in sociology in 1975. She remained at Texas to work toward her PhD (doctorate or doctoral degree).

During her graduate studies, Tienda focused on the branch of sociology called demography, which explores human populations, what they're made of, and how they change. She analyzed data from government censuses, official surveys of a country's population. She explored such questions as how women who work outside the home affect the economy, or whether larger families are necessarily poorer than smaller ones. She was determined to avoid being stereotyped as a "minority" sociologist, so she made sure her studies were not focused on racial issues. She also strove to produce research and writing of the highest quality. She was proud when she earned her PhD degree in 1977 and was offered a teaching job at the University of Wisconsin.

WHO ARE HISPANIC AMERICANS?

Several different terms are used to describe people from Spanish-speaking countries. The term *Hispanic*, from the Latin word for "Spain," is the most broad; it refers to a person living in the U.S. from any of the countries where Spanish is the primary language. The terms *Latino* (masculine) and *Latina* (feminine) refer to a person of Latin-American descent who is living in the United States. Latin America includes all of Mexico as well as other Central and South American countries where Spanish or Portuguese is the national language. The terms *Chicano* (masculine) and *Chicana* (feminine) refer to a person who comes from Mexico or is of Mexican descent. The term comes from the Mexican Spanish word *mexicano*, meaning "Mexican." A person of Mexican descent who is a resident or citizen of the United States is often referred to as a *Mexican-American*.

According to the U.S. Census, Hispanic Americans are those citizens who define their origin or descent as coming from Mexico, Puerto Rico, Cuba, Spain, or any of the Spanish-speaking countries in Central America, South America, or the Caribbean. Hispanic Americans, sometimes also called Latinos, can be of any race. Some trace their ancestors to Western Europe; some to the native peoples of Latin America; some to Africans brought to the region as slaves; and some to combinations of these groups.

In the government's population survey of 2006, 44.3 million Americans, or 14.8% of the population, identified themselves as Hispanic. The majority of that group, 28.3 million, was of Mexican heritage. Puerto Ricans made up the second largest group, at almost 4 million, with another 1.5 million identifying themselves as Cuban and 1.2 million as Dominican. While 25 years ago the majority of Hispanic Americans lived in the West, in the 2000s the Southeast and Midwest saw the greatest growth rates in Latino population. By 2050, the U.S. Census estimates, nearly one in every four Americans will be of Hispanic origin.

CHOOSING A CAREER

Tienda had two pivotal experiences that affected her choice of career. The first was during college, when she got a summer job working for the state of Michigan. In northern Michigan she interviewed migrant workers to see if they qualified for food stamps, a form of government assistance. On her own time, she visited the workers in their homes, witnessing the sub-standard living conditions many migrant workers endured. She also visited the farm owners, and she was surprised to see that the growers she had considered wealthy when she was working in the fields were actually struggling to make ends meet. She discovered that an "us vs. them" mentality between growers and workers didn't help solve problems; instead, both groups needed each other. She organized a meeting between growers and workers and helped establish a day-care center for parents who worked in the fields. The experience left her determined to find a career that would allow her to find helpful solutions to everyday problems.

> *Tienda vowed to look for ways to help Hispanic Americans improve their lives."Becoming a sociologist would give me that opportunity," she explained. "When you know the stories behind the numbers, then you can find ways to help people. I wanted to make a difference in people's lives by changing the rules and policies that govern them."*

The second experience was more tragic, occurring shortly after she finished her graduate studies and received her doctorate. Just before she was to begin her career as a professor at the University of Wisconsin, a family tragedy struck. Her brother Juan Luis, visiting Texas for her wedding, was killed in a car accident. Only one year younger than Marta, Juan Luis had always been very close to his sister. His death cut short a promising career. He had served in the army, earned his bachelor's degree in three years, and was studying law at the University of Michigan. He was active in trying to bring more Hispanic students and professors to the university, and he also offered legal help to local migrant workers. Upon his death, Marta Tienda vowed to continue his work and look for ways to help Hispanic Americans improve their lives. "Becoming a sociologist would give me that opportunity," she explained. "When you know the stories behind the numbers, then you can find ways to help people. I wanted to make a difference in people's lives by changing the rules and policies that govern them."

CAREER HIGHLIGHTS

Helping Create a Definitive Study of Hispanics

Tienda began her career at the University of Wisconsin in 1976, starting out as an assistant professor of sociology. She had not held the position

Tienda's demographic research with Frank Bean resulted in their collaboration on The Hispanic Population of the United States, *considered a landmark reference on the subject.*

long when a group of sociologists asked her to serve as an advisor on their first-ever survey of the Mexican-American population. She helped analyze the questions they were going to ask, to make sure they were appropriate and that they would produce testable data. Her contributions to this survey helped her earn a government grant from the U.S. Department of Labor.

Tienda used the grant to analyze a new survey of the Hispanic-American population. It was the first to study all groups of Hispanics (Chicanos, Puerto Ricans, Cubans, etc.) across the country, instead of just a single group or a single area. Tienda used computers to analyze the data and compare the groups. She looked at levels of education, employment, annual income, poverty rates, and household composition (the numbers and relationship of people living together). The report she prepared set a new standard for studying Latinos and helped establish her as a talented voice in the field. She was promoted to associate professor in 1980 and to full professor in 1983.

After the government's official census in 1980, Tienda performed a similar analysis of Hispanic Americans. She worked with Frank Bean, her former professor at the University of Texas. They performed *quantitative analysis*, or performing analysis, comparisons, and interpretations of numerical data. Using quantitative analysis, they compared the 1980 data to that from previous censuses. The result was the 1987 book *The Hispanic Population of the United States*. It was the first in-depth scientific analysis of America's Hispanic population, and it is still considered a landmark reference. The book looked at differences within the Hispanic population, as well as differences between Hispanics and Anglos (whites). Unfortunately, their study showed that Hispanic Americans were falling behind Anglos in terms of schooling, jobs, and income.

At Wisconsin, Tienda continued this research using quantitative analysis. By studying census data, she could compare one moment in time to another, measuring changes in populations over time. This led her to discover that, among Hispanics, economic conditions between 1970 and 1980 improved the most for Cubans. They improved to a lesser degree for those of Mexican heritage, while conditions for those of Puerto Rican heritage actually declined. This was useful information, but she wanted to explore why this had happened. In 1987 she took a position at the University of Chicago, a private university with a world-class reputation. Chicago, as the university is known, is one of the top schools in the country.

Looking for Reasons Behind the Statistics

At the University of Chicago, Tienda had the opportunity to do more in-depth research on the Hispanic experience. Because the Chicago area has

Tienda in her college office, surrounded by just a few of the many books she uses in her research. Photo Credit: Susan R. Geller, Office of Communications, Princeton University (1998).

a large local population of Hispanics, she could perform *longitudinal analysis,* or studying the same group of people over time. In this way she could explore why economic conditions varied between groups. She could also perform *qualitative analysis,* or conducting actual interviews with people. At Chicago, she began research to explore how different ethnic groups—white, black, and Hispanic—moved from school to work. She

> "Tienda earned a reputation as a challenging teacher who gets the best out of students by showing them how to use criticism to improve their work—even in her freshman classes. "I deliberately mixed reading materials from political interest groups, academic publications, and various types of journalism to make the point about the need to require standards of evidence to support claims."

discovered that Hispanics often dropped out to get jobs, which improved earnings at first but cost them in the long term. African Americans tended to stay in school longer than Hispanics, but discrimination often impeded their job search. This meant they often had lower incomes than whites with the same amount of education. On average, she found whites spent longer in school, but since they found jobs sooner, they earned more money over time.

Tienda also explored what role families played in the educational success of immigrants. She looked at groups of Hispanics, Asians, and African Americans. She discovered that first-generation immigrants, the ones who move to the U.S., get less education because of language and financial barriers. Their U.S.-born children, the second generation (like Tienda herself), often did best, because foreign-born parents emphasize education as the way to succeed. The next generation, however, didn't always perform as well. This seemed to happen in all groups; Tienda speculated it might be because they assimilated into American culture so well that there was less drive to succeed.

Tienda continued producing interesting work at the University of Chicago and was eventually chosen to chair the department of sociology. She took her role as teacher very seriously as well. In 1994, for instance, she went to Israel with a former student while they worked on a book. Tienda and her children lived in Tel Aviv for a few months, having their own immigrant experiences in a country where they didn't speak the language. The book was based on the Urban Poverty and Family Life Survey, which Tienda helped design and lead. The survey started with Chicago neighborhoods that had at least a 20% poverty rate; then they divided the subjects into black, white, Mexican, and Puerto Rican groups; finally, they chose randomly among the groups until they had 2,500 people. The survey was a landmark in studying poverty, for they actually went into high-poverty and high-crime neighborhoods and asked questions face-to-face.

Tienda teaching a class for graduate students on the subject of population changes in developing countries.

Tienda's work with Haya Stier analyzing this survey resulted in their 2001 book titled *The Color of Opportunity: Pathways to Family, Welfare, and Work.* They tried to answer whether poor people who live in inner-city ghettos are different from other poor families in the way they start families, receive government welfare, and find and keep jobs. In the end, they found there wasn't much difference between poor people who live in ghettos and those who live elsewhere. In general, the continuing disadvantages of poverty—lack of opportunities for good education and good jobs—make it hard for them to compete with the non-poor. The key to breaking the cycle of poverty, Tienda observed, lay in education.

Exploring Opportunities in Education

In 1997 Tienda left the University of Chicago for Princeton University, one of the country's oldest and most prestigious universities. She taught sociology and also served as a research associate at Princeton's Office of Population Research, which she headed as director from 1998 to 2002. She earned a reputation as a challenging teacher who got the best out of students by showing them how to use criticism to improve their work. In her freshman seminar, she explained, "I deliberately mixed reading materials from political interest groups, academic publications, and various types of journalism to make the point about the need to require standards of evidence to support claims." Since 1999, when she was named Maurice P. During '22 Professor in Demographic Studies, she has focused her research on college admissions and affirmative action.

In education, "affirmative action" is the name given to policies that attempt to increase minority enrollment in university programs. The Supreme Court has struck down quotas that guarantee a certain number of spaces for minorities as unconstitutional. Universities have struggled to find ways to maintain a diverse population within their student body. To explore this issue, Tienda has studied Texas's "Top 10 Percent Law," which was enacted in 1997. The law guarantees any Texas student who graduates in the top 10% of his or her high school class admission into any of the state's public universities. While this increased opportunities for students from poorer, presumably minority-heavy schools, some worried it might harm excellent students who placed just outside the top 10%.

> "I'm not a woman, I'm not Mexican; I'm just a sociologist. Having said that, I am also someone who was given an opportunity through ... a doctoral fellowship targeted at Mexican Americans and Puerto Ricans. I would never have gone to graduate school without that. And I think opening those opportunities, those doors, is really what we should strive for."

Tienda designed questionnaires for Texas high school seniors to explore how the new law affected them. She also studied data about how minority enrollment changed after the law was enacted. Her analysis showed that the Top 10% Law did give more opportunity to kids from schools that don't usually send many students to college; in addition, it didn't force those just outside the top 10% to schools out of state (her study showed they were likely to leave anyway). However, neither did the law raise minority enrollment back to levels where it had been during affirmative action days. The results surprised her somewhat. At first she had thought her study would show that affirmative action isn't the best way to promote diversity. But "when I began to look at the evidence, the possibilities and alternatives that were 'race neutral' in a society that in many ways had become race stratified, there didn't seem to be answers," she explained. "After studying the data, I concluded that there was simply no hope that an individual could break the chains of educational inequality without affirmative action." She knows there is no single solution to increasing diversity, but she is strongly against using standardized test scores, which many researchers believe tend to be racially biased and fail to predict future academic success.

Tienda's work on issues of diversity, education, poverty, and their effects on American society have brought her international recognition. She has been elected to several prestigious scientific societies and has served as president of the Population Association of America. In 2003 the University of Texas named her an Outstanding Alumna and also awarded a fellowship in her honor. She has served on boards of numerous charitable foundations and research councils, including the RAND Corporation (a nonprofit public policy research company) and the Jacobs Foundation (an international nonprofit that supports youth development). She considers her work with these foundations essential, since "they can afford to take risks as well as trail blaze, set standards, and study issues in ways that our government, for instance, cannot."

Tienda continues research that emphasizes the importance of education for minorities. She notes that the increasing education gap between whites and Hispanics will become more important as Hispanic population increases. While Hispanics have the highest high school dropout rate in the 2000s, they are also one of the youngest segments of American society. "Hispanics are coming of age in an aging society. Education is the bottom line," Tienda said, if they are to find good jobs to keep the economy growing. "It would be nice if we could be a color-blind society." When she thinks of herself, "I'm not a woman, I'm not Mexican; I'm just a sociologist. Having said that, I am also someone who was given an opportunity through … a doctoral fellowship targeted at Mexican Americans and Puerto Ricans. I would never have gone to graduate school without that. And I think opening those opportunities, those doors, is really what we should strive for."

HOME AND FAMILY

Tienda met Wence Lanz, a native Venezuelan, while at graduate school in Texas. They married on August 20, 1976. Their first child, Luis Gabriel, was born in 1982, while a second son, Carlos, arrived in 1989. Tienda and her husband separated and divorced in the mid-1990s; he died of cancer in 2001. With her children now grown, Tienda lives in Princeton, New Jersey, with a dog named Sancho Panza.

HOBBIES AND OTHER INTERESTS

Between research, teaching, and serving on the boards of research foundations, Tienda has little time for hobbies. She enjoys reading and names

Tienda with her two sons, Luis Gabriel and Carlos.

Nobel Prize-winner Gabriel García Márquez of Colombia as her favorite author. She also has a love of fashionable shoes that she traces to her childhood, when necessity forced her to wear ugly saddle shoes instead of shiny patent-leather styles. She likes to demonstrate that a scholar can be stylish as well as smart.

SELECTED WRITINGS

The Hispanic Population of the United States, 1987 (with Frank Bean)
Divided Opportunities: Minorities, Poverty and Social Policy, 1988 (editor, with Gary D. Sandefur)
The Color of Opportunity: Pathways to Family, Welfare, and Work, 2001 (with Haya Stier)
Youth in Cities: A Cross-National Perspective, 2002 (editor, with William J. Wilson)
Multiple Origins, Uncertain Destinies: Hispanics and the American Future, 2006 (editor, with Faith Mitchell)
Coeditor of other academic volumes and reports; author of over 100 journal articles; editor, *American Journal of Sociology,* 1991-95.

HONORS AND AWARDS

Outstanding Young Scholar Recognition Award (American Association of University Women): 1984-85

Lifetime Achievement Award (Hispanic Business Inc.): 2004
Outstanding Latina Faculty in Higher Education Award in Research and
   Teaching (American Association of Hispanics in Higher Education): 2006

FURTHER READING

Books

O'Connell, Diane. *People Person: The Story of Sociologist Marta Tienda,* 2005

Periodicals

Carnegie Reporter, Spring 2004
Hispanic Business, Apr. 2003
Princeton Alumni Weekly, Mar. 12, 2003
Princeton Weekly Bulletin, Nov. 7, 2005
USA Today, Mar. 2, 2006, p.A3

Online Articles

http://www.princeton.edu/~paw/archive_old/PAW98-99
   (Princeton Alumni Weekly, "Color and Opportunity," Mar. 10, 1999)

ADDRESS

Marta Tienda
Office of Population Research
Princeton University
Wallace Hall
Princeton NJ 08544-2091

WORLD WIDE WEB SITES

http://www.iwaswondering.org/marta_homepage.html
http://theop.princeton.edu/
http://opr.princeton.edu/faculty/page.asp?id=tienda

Justin Timberlake 1981-

American Singer and Songwriter
Six-Time Grammy Award Winner

BIRTH

Justin Randall Timberlake was born on January 31, 1981, in Memphis, Tennessee, and grew up in Millington, a town just north of Memphis. His father, Randy, played bass and sang harmonies in a bluegrass band. His mother, Lynn, was the sister of one of the other band members. Justin's parents split up when he was just a toddler, and they both remarried. Justin was primarily raised by his mother and her second husband, a banker named Paul Harless. Justin developed a very close relationship with his stepfather, but he also maintained contact with his father, who now works as a building contractor. Justin enjoys being the older sibling to Jonathan and Steven, his half-brothers from his father's marriage to his second wife, Lisa. Justin also had a half-sister, Laura Katherine, who died shortly after she was born.

YOUTH

Lynn Timberlake was fairly young when her son was born, just 20 years old. Both mother and son say they did a lot of growing up together, and they remain very close. According to Lynn, her son always responded enthusiastically to music. "When Justin was a little-bitty baby, like three or four months old, we'd sit him in those seats, like a car seat, on the kitchen counter. He'd kick his legs to the beat of the music. We'd change the music and he'd kick his legs to the new beat. We'd say to our friends, 'Dude! Look at this!' He was like a little toy," she remembered. When he was just two years old, he harmonized with music he heard on the radio.

> "When Justin was a little-bitty baby, like three or four months old, we'd sit him in those seats, like a car seat, on the kitchen counter," his mother recalled. "He'd kick his legs to the beat of the music. We'd change the music and he'd kick his legs to the new beat. We'd say to our friends, 'Dude! Look at this!' He was like a little toy."

As he got older, Timberlake took singing lessons and sang in the church choir in Millington. The experience showed him how much he enjoyed singing in front of people. When he was in middle school, he and some friends entered a talent show, dressing like the popular group New Kids on the Block and singing one of their songs. The audience, composed of his classmates, chased him down the hallways, giving him his first taste of being pursued by adoring fans.

EDUCATION

Timberlake attended school in the Memphis area. He started high school there, but finished his education through a correspondence course after his career began to require frequent travel

FIRST JOBS

Timberlake began performing early in life, with his mother managing his career. He was only 10 years old when he sang at the Grand Ole Opry, a world-famous country music show in Nashville. He also won the Preteen Mr. America contest at about that time. The following year, in 1992, he was on the national TV talent show "Star Search." Performing under the name Justin Randall and wearing a cowboy outfit, he sang a country song and came in second.

The Mouseketeer Years

While taping "Star Search," Timberlake and his mother heard that auditions were going to be held across the nation to choose cast members for a television show, "The All New Mickey Mouse Club." This was an update of a popular program first produced by the Walt Disney Studios in the 1950s. In the original program, which aired every weekday, the cast wore special outfits and mouse-ear hats, sang songs, danced, and acted in skits. Cartoons and continuing adventure series were also part of the show. Each day of the week had a special theme, and adult "Mouseketeers" were there to guide the younger cast members and offer advice about life.

The "Mickey Mouse Club" was so popular that it was shown in reruns for years after the original run ended. In 1977, it was revived with a new cast as the "All New Mickey Mouse Club," but it wasn't very successful and was cancelled in 1979. Ten years later, Disney tried again. The 1989 version was officially titled "The All New Mickey Mouse Club" but was usually called MMC."

"MMC" was filmed at the Disney-MGM complex in Orlando, Florida. Featuring a talented cast of teenagers, it was made up of comedy skits, live music performed for a studio audience, pre-recorded videos by the cast, and a continuing serial called "Emerald Cove." In the original "Mickey Mouse Club," older cast members were replaced by younger ones as they became too mature to fit the show's image. The same formula was followed with "MMC," which was successful enough to stay in production for several years. During the year Timberlake auditioned to become one of the new cast members, he was one of 30,000 kids who tried out for the show. Out of all those auditions, only seven new cast members were chosen—and 12-year-old Justin was one of them. He and his mother moved to Orlando, where the show was filmed. He was part of the "MMC" cast from 1993 to 1995.

With the MGM/Disney studio, Nickelodeon studios, and many theme parks all located in the Orlando area, it was an intense place for young, tal-

A cast shot from "MMC," including Timberlake (back row, right), Christina Aguilera (middle row, right), and Britney Spears (front row, right).

ented people to meet and make connections. Timberlake's fellow "MMC" cast members included many who would go on to stardom, including singers Christina Aguilera and Britney Spears; actor Keri Russell, who starred in the television show "Felicity"; actor Ryan Gosling, who was later nominated for Academy and Golden Globe Awards; and singer J.C. Chasez, who, along with Timberlake, would become part of the sensationally successful singing group *N Sync.

CAREER HIGHLIGHTS

Forming *N Sync

Once "MMC" was cancelled, Timberlake and his mother headed back to the Memphis area, where he returned to his high school. He wasn't happy about going back to normal life, but it didn't last for long. He and fellow Mouseketeer J.C. Chasez had been working on some demo recordings. Eventually, Timberlake returned to Orlando to record solo material and try to make a deal for a recording contract. As he was working on that project, though, he and Chasez were recruited to be part of an all-male singing group that was being developed at that time.

*N Sync was no overnight sensation, but the product of a lot of hard work and planning. The other members were mostly drawn from the big pool of young talent that congregated in Florida. The band included Justin Timberlake, Christopher Alan Kirkpatrick (Chris), Joseph Anthony Fatone Jr. (Joey), James Lance Bass (Lance), and Joshua Scott Chasez (JC). The name *N Sync was created by Timberlake's mother, by using the last letters of each band member's first name. But the band name was created before Lance replaced an earlier group member named Jason. Since they liked the name, they hired Lance but jokingly referred to him as Lansten so the name would still make sense.

With Lynn Timberlake acting as their manager, the members of *N Sync began to work on their choreography and harmonies. Using an empty warehouse as a studio, they would practice for hours. In the fall of 1995, they had their first gig, at a nightclub located in Walt Disney World. A friend who had worked as a cameraman on "MMC" taped their performance, and they used that recording as a demo to send out to agents and recording companies. In 1996, the tape came to the attention of Louis J. Pearlman, a business manager with Trans Continental Records. His clients included the Backstreet Boys, a hugely successful singing group at that time. Pearlman mentioned *N Sync to an associate, Johnny Wright, who also worked with the Backstreet Boys and had previously managed another singing sensation, New Kids on the Block.

> *The year Timberlake auditioned to become one of the new "MMC" cast members, he was one of 30,000 kids who tried out for the show. Out of all those auditions, only seven new cast members were chosen—and 12-year-old Justin was one of them.*

At first, Wright felt that he didn't want to take on another group, one that seemed to have a lot of similarities to the Backstreet Boys. When he saw them in person, however, he changed his mind. "They could really sing," he said. "They had a chemistry—an aura about them. When they talked to

*The members of *N Sync (clockwise from upper left): Timberlake, JC Chasez, Chris Kirkpatrick, Joey Fatone, and Lance Bass (center).*

me they talked to me as a group, as a unit, rather than five individuals trying to pitch themselves to me—they weren't selfish." Wright and Pearlman agreed to sign *N Sync to a record deal with the BMG recording company.

Record company executives began looking for new music to expand the group's sound, and they decided to follow the same course with *N Sync that they had used to bring the Backstreet Boys to the peak of success. This involved taking the band to Europe for extensive on-the-road experience. They could work out any kinks in their performance, build up a European following, and bring them back to the United States to debut as a polished act. When their music was released overseas, the singles "I Want You Back" and "Tearin' Up My Heart" immediately went platinum, and their first album quickly rose to the top spot on the record charts. As the five boys took their show through Mexico, Africa, Asia, Europe, and Canada, they were playing to sell-out crowds. But when the tour ended in 1998, they returned to the United States still virtually unknown in their own country.

> "They could really sing," manager Johnny Wright said about *N Sync. "They had a chemistry—an aura about them. When they talked to me they talked to me as a group, as a unit, rather than five individuals trying to pitch themselves to me—they weren't selfish."

*N Sync Hits the U.S.

Their first U.S. album, titled *N Sync*, was released in spring 1998. It included "Tearin' Up My Heart" and "I Want You Back," already hits overseas. In the United States, though, the boys had to work hard to get recognition. They made appearances at radio stations, record stores, and even shopping malls to draw attention to their music. They got a big break in July of that year, when the Backstreet Boys were unable to fulfill a commitment they had made to sing for an "In Concert" special to be filmed at Disney World for the Disney Channel. *N Sync filled in for the Backstreet Boys in a show that featured their music as well as interviews with group members and footage of them enjoying Disney World with their families.

The "In Concert" special was rerun frequently on the Disney Channel after its initial airing, which gave *N Sync a lot of exposure and built up their popularity. Fans started calling radio stations requesting their music, asking for their videos to be shown on MTV, and begging for articles to be written about them in teen magazines. They began to get bookings for major television appearances, such as "The Tonight Show," "Live with Regis and Kathie Lee," and the Miss Teen USA Pageant. They were featured performers in the Macy's Thanksgiving Day Parade in New York City, and they served as the opening act for Janet Jackson on her sold-out "Velvet Rope" tour.

Their first CD confirmed the band was a hit, selling more than 10 million copies.

After a somewhat slow start, the *N Sync album built to a huge success. It had four No. 1 singles and sold more than 10 million copies. The group quickly followed up on their wave of popularity by releasing Home for Christmas in November 1998. This album featured new music written just for the group as well as some traditional holiday favorites.

*N Sync's appeal rested on many factors. The members were all solid performers, and the group featured tight harmonies and a wide vocal range and variety of singing styles. They could perform high-powered dance music but also be convincing in slow ballads. Their well-practiced choreography was just one aspect of an exciting stage show that included lots of special effects, costume changes, acrobatics, and a spectacular light show. The boys' good looks didn't hurt the band's appeal, while they also seemed like ordinary guys. As Timberlake said at the time, "I think there's a sense of reality that surrounds us. We don't try to make ourselves do cute, we just are who we are. We're boys. We burp and fart, just like boys."

Timberlake was the youngest member of the group. At the time he went by several nicknames including Baby, Curly, and Mr. Smooth. He has admitted that fame changed him—and not always in good ways. "I thought I was the coolest guy," he said of the period after he first signed his recording contract. "You couldn't talk to me. Nobody could tell me anything." Once *N Sync's fame was firmly established, he realized how much influence he had over other people. "We were playing stadiums, and I could say, 'Hey, we should fly down!' and suddenly people are building rigs for us to fly down on. We had a blast doing it, but I was really a perfectionist."

Taking Control: *No Strings Attached*

*N Sync was selling millions of albums and making a tremendous amount of money. But when band member Chris Kirkpatrick asked their managers for more of his share, he was informed that, in fact, he owed money to the management. That announcement sparked the group to review the agreements they had signed with Pearlman and Trans Continental Records. The group discovered that the contract granted Pearlman control of the band's name, 75 percent of all record royalties, 100 percent of music publishing royalties, 80 percent of all merchandising revenue, and 55 percent of earnings from celebrity endorsements and touring revenue. After Pearlman took his share, the remaining earnings were supposed to pay for the band's expenses before being split among the five of them.

> *"I think there's a sense of reality that surrounds us,"* Timberlake said at the time. *"We don't try to make ourselves do cute, we just are who we are. We're boys. We burp and fart, just like boys."*

In September 1999, the band told Pearlman that the contract was unfair and they wanted to change it. The agent's response was to file a lawsuit against them for $150 million. The band fought back with a $25 million countersuit. In December, a settlement was reached that terminated Pearlman's control over the band while granting him a share in their future profits. They were allowed to continue using the name *N Sync, but they moved to a new record label, Jive Records. They were also granted much more creative control over their music.

> "Timberlake has admitted that fame changed him—and not always in good ways. "I thought I was the coolest guy," he said of the period after he first signed his recording contract. "You couldn't talk to me. Nobody could tell me anything."

In 2000, they released the album *No Strings Attached*. *N Sync was so hot at the time that the record sold two million copies in its first week of sales. The title of the album expressed their feeling of freedom after escaping Pearlman's control. It also poked fun at a criticism sometimes expressed about the band: that they were over-managed and overproduced, and really not much more than a collection of pretty faces.

In the stage show for *No Strings Attached*, the boys descended from above the stage on puppet strings, which they then struggled to break. The album again contained a mix of danceable tunes and ballads, but it had a more urban feel and showed a broader range of influences, including hip-hop and old-school R&B. The *No Strings Attached* tour was a sellout in every venue, with more than a million tickets sold in six months. In 2001, the band released *Celebrity*, which didn't quite reach the heights of *No Strings Attached*, but still sold 1.8 million copies in its first week of sales. *Celebrity* was the last CD released by the group. In total, *N Sync has sold more than 27 million records.

Developing a Solo Career: *Justified*

In 2002 Timberlake branched out on a solo career, although *N Sync never officially broke up. At the MTV Video Music Awards in August 2002, he danced his way out of a gigantic boom box to sing "Like I Love You." The style of the song, his dance moves, and even the fedora hat he wore strongly suggested the influence of Michael Jackson, whose music Timberlake has acknowledged as a major inspiration.

In his solo work, Timberlake was reaching for a more mature sound that featured urban and R&B influences. He got help from the music producers Timbaland and the Neptunes. In late 2002, he released a solo album, *Justified*, to mixed reviews. Some critics dismissed it as lightweight pop, while others were impressed with Timberlake's development of an edgier sound. Fans expressed their support by buying more than three million copies of the album and flocking to see Timberlake on the *Justified and Stripped* tour,

Timberlake's appearance at the 2002 MTV Video Music Awards marked his debut as a solo artist.

which put him on a double bill with his former "MMC" co-star, Christina Aguilera. Timberlake eventually won two Grammy awards for his work on *Justified,* one for Best Pop Vocal Album and one for Best Pop Vocal Performance, for the single "Cry Me a River."

Controversy and Negative Publicity

> "Artie's sort of a nerd," Timberlake commented about his **Shrek** character. "He is told his whole life that he's a loser, so he doesn't believe in himself, doesn't believe he can be the king. He's got to get confidence. He's not cool, you know?"

The year 2002 was a pivotal point in Timberlake's music career and in his personal life. During this period—in fact, ever since he first became famous—Timberlake has had to deal with tremendous public fascination with his personal life. He was involved in several events around this time that contributed to a wave of negative publicity. One cause was his relationship with Britney Spears. He had known Spears for about 10 years, since they had worked together on "MMC." In addition to being friends, the two of them were romantically involved for quite a while, although they had kept it out of the public eye as much as possible. In 2002, their long-standing relationship ended amid a swirl of nasty rumors. Timberlake refused to say much about his relationship with Spears or what had ended it, although "Cry Me a River" is widely thought to be about their breakup.

After Timberlake and Spears split up, he got a lot of publicity for a series of brief relationships with high-profile women, whom he usually refrained from discussing. He also got some bad publicity from the MTV show "Punk'd," in which the host, Ashton Kutcher, played elaborate pranks on people. In 2003, "Punk'd" filmed men going to Timberlake's house dressed as federal agents. They told the singer that he owed the government hundreds of thousands of dollars in taxes. Timberlake was completely taken in by the prank and was visibly fighting back tears.

More negative publicity came from the events at the Super Bowl in February 2004, when Timberlake performed at half-time with Janet Jackson. In a choreographed move, he tore at Jackson's costume and a whole section of her costume came off to reveal her breast. Many viewers were deeply offended by what appeared to be a flagrant act, although all involved swore that it was an accident. Timberlake issued a public apology for his part in

Timberlake voiced the character of Artie in Shrek 3.

the show. Jackson later suggested that the stunt had been intentional, but Timberlake maintained he hadn't known anything about it in advance. The incident led to a record fine of $550,000 from the FCC against CBS, the network that broadcast the Super Bowl.

More trouble came in November 2004. At the time, Timberlake was in a romantic relationship with actress Cameron Diaz, which he hadn't tried to keep secret. They were often followed by paparazzi (photographers who try to get candid shots of celebrities). One night while they were still a couple, Timberlake and Diaz were surprised by two photographers. There was a scuffle, Timberlake got physical, and the photographers ended up suing the two stars. The case was eventually settled out of court.

Commenting on the relentless public interest in his life, Timberlake said: "I've run the gamut with how I feel about it. I had the confrontation, where I slapped a paparazzo, and that was bad. I had to go meet the district attorney, who slapped the back of my hand and said I shouldn't retaliate with violence. I was like, 'Of course. You're right.' We live in an interesting time where everybody and everything is completely accessible. And I love what I do, but I also love my life and my privacy."

A Change in Direction

By 2004, Timberlake's career had been in high gear for several years. His father advised him to take some time off, and he agreed. "This is what

> "I write about what I know, but I also write about things that are just fantasies in my head," he said. "I don't really think I brought sexy back. It just seemed like something catchy to say. I don't really think of myself that way. It's just fun. It's like acting, because you create a character in your mind, and you run with it."

the world looks like at a regular pace," he observed then. "That was amazing for me. Just the little things, like sitting home on the weekend or making a Sunday tee time. Play golf, then come back home, have a beer and call it a day."

Timberlake took some time to branch out into acting. Besides his skit work on "MMC," he had already played small roles in a few television programs, including "Switch," "Touched by an Angel," "Longshot," and hosting "Saturday Night Live." In 2000, he played opposite Kathie Lee Gifford in the made-for-television movie *Model Behavior.* He worked with top stars Kevin Spacey and Morgan Freeman in *Edison Force,* playing the part of an investigative reporter. After premiering at the Toronto Film Festival in September 2005, the film got mediocre reviews and went straight to DVD. Timberlake won praise for his work in *Black Snake Moan* (2006), in which he portrayed a soldier who suffers from panic attacks, and in *Alpha Dog* (2006), in which he played a dim-witted thug who helps a drug dealer kidnap a customer's brother in order to force payment of a debt.

Timberlake added a major hit movie to his resume when he joined the cast of *Shrek the Third,* in which he played the young King Arthur, or Artie. "Artie's sort of a nerd," Timberlake commented about his *Shrek* character. "He is told his whole life that he's a loser, so he doesn't believe in himself, doesn't believe he can be the king. He's got to get confidence. He's not cool, you know?" Even though Timberlake might seem to some people to define the word "cool," he said that he could definitely understand Artie's character. "I have my moments," he said. "We can all relate to adolescence, when nobody's cool. I used to get picked on all the time. I had terrible acne, weird hair. My arms were too long."

FutureSex/LoveSounds

During this time off, Timberlake was also working on music. In May 2004, he had surgery to remove some nodules from his vocal chords. By the end of 2004 he began working on his next album, which wasn't released until

On FutureSex/LoveSounds, *Timberlake worked with a wide array of noted producers who helped him stretch his musical boundaries.*

September 2006. He also collaborated on projects with other musicians, including Snoop Dog and 50 Cent, did backup vocals for Charlie Wilson and Black Eyed Peas, and appeared in videos by Johnny Cash and Nelly Furtado. He wrote the songs "Okay" and "Get Out" for Macy Gray, "Rehab" for Rihanna, and collaborated on "The Only Promise That Remains" with country singer Reba McEntire.

In July 2006, Timberlake released "SexyBack," the first single from his second solo album, titled *FutureSex/LoveSounds*. Like the other tracks on the album, it had grown out of his collaboration with Timbaland, who co-produced it with Timberlake and with Nate "Danja" Hills. *FutureSex/LoveSounds*, released in full in September 2006, continued to expand Timberlake's musical boundaries. Even more than *Justified,* it featured an urban sound, with a lot of techno beats and little of his famous high falsetto. "It didn't sound like Justin vocally," admitted Barry Weiss, head of Jive Records. "It was a bit of a risk for all of us. But it was a risk that clearly paid off."

At the 2006 Grammy Awards, Timberlake won two awards, for Best Rap/Sung Collaboration (with T.I.), for "My Love," and for Best Dance Recording, for "SexyBack." He followed that up at the 2007 Grammy Awards with two more awards, for Best Male Pop Vocal Performance, for "What Goes Around … Comes Around," and Best Dance Recording, for "LoveStoned/I Think She Knows." As of late 2007, the album had sold more than eight million copies, boosting Timberlake's total album sales as a solo artist to well over 15 million.

After the release of *FutureSex/LoveSounds,* Timberlake toured extensively to support the new record, appearing in concert around the world in 2007 and 2008. He also found time to collaborate with Madonna on the single "4 Minutes" and to make an appearance in the 2008 movie *The Love Guru,* starring Mike Myers.

Discussing his lyrics and his music in general, Timberlake said that it isn't all a direct reflection of his life, and that it has to be looked at light-heartedly. "I write about what I know, but I also write about things that are just fantasies in my head," he said. "I don't really think I brought sexy back. It just seemed like something catchy to say. I don't really think of myself that way. It's just fun. It's like acting, because you create a character in your mind, and you run with it." Trying to describe how he really sees himself, he offered: "I think my style is kind of a cross between a skater hippie and an R&B singer."

New Ventures

At an age when some people still haven't decided on a career, Timberlake has already had a long one. His success has been great, but there have been low points, too. While show business has provided him with many incredible experiences, he doesn't see it as something he wants to stick with forever. He has spent so much time in the spotlight that he doesn't really crave it any more. "Ten years from now," he commented, "I don't want to be jumping around onstage. I've been in this business for 15 years—which is kinda creepy—and I'm interested in other things."

In the future, Timberlake sees himself writing more music for other performers, which he views as a means of expressing himself more fully, using

Timberlake and Timbaland in a sizzling performance of "SexyBack" at the MTV Video Music Awards.

others' voices. "I want to write country music, because that's where I grew up—Tennessee. Soul music.... I want to be involved in hip-hop. And sometimes I feel the only way to really express all those different sides, even just for myself, is [by writing songs for] different people."

HOME AND FAMILY

Timberlake, who is single, has homes in Orlando and in the Hollywood Hills. He remains close with his family, especially his mother. He enjoys going home to Tennessee and having his grandmother cook for him.

FAVORITE MUSIC

Some of the musicians who have most influenced Timberlake include Michael Jackson, Stevie Wonder, Donnie Hathaway, Al Green, Marvin Gaye, the Eagles, and the Beatles. His favorite newer artists include Bjork, Avril Lavigne, John Mayer, the Strokes, the Killers, Arcade Fire, Radiohead, and Coldplay.

HOBBIES AND OTHER INTERESTS

Timberlake enjoys a variety of sports, including playing basketball, snowboarding, and surfing. He collects sports jerseys and enjoys owning several cars, motorcycles, and jet skis. He is involved with charitable activities, too. In 2000, he founded the Justin Timberlake Foundation, a music education program serving needy children. He loves playing golf, and in 2008 he began a five-year stint hosting a PGA charity tournament in Las Vegas, the Justin Timberlake Shriners Hospital for Children Open.

Timberlake has also started up a few business ventures. Tennman Records is his own production company. He has opened several restaurants, including one in Manhattan called Southern Hospitality. It features barbeque and other down-home recipes, including some from Timberlake's grandmother, Sadie Bomar. One of the singer's partners in that restaurant is Trace Ayala, a friend since childhood. Ayala designed costumes for *N Sync, and he is also one of Timberlake's partners in a line of designer clothing called William Rast, featured at upscale department stores.

SELECTED CREDITS

Recordings with *N Sync

*N Sync, 1998
Home for Christmas, 1998
No Strings Attached, 2000
Celebrity, 2001

Solo Recordings

Justified, 2002
FutureSex/LoveSounds, 2006

Television

The All New Mickey Mouse Club, 1993-1994
Model Behavior, 2000

Films

Edison Force, 2005
Black Snake Moan, 2006
Alpha Dog, 2006
Southland Tales, 2006
Shrek the Third, 2007
The Love Guru, 2008

SELECTED HONORS AND AWARDS

American Music Awards: 2003, Favorite Pop/Rock Album, for *Justified*; 2007 (two awards), Favorite Male Artist; Favorite R & B/Soul Album, for *FutureSex/LoveSounds*

BRIT Awards: 2004 (two awards), Best International Male Artist, Best International Album, for *Justified*; 2007, Best International Male Artist

Grammy Awards: 2004 (two awards), Best Pop Vocal Album, for *Justified*; Best Male Pop Vocal Performance, for "Cry Me a River"; 2007 (two awards), Best Dance Recording (with Timbaland), for "SexyBack"; Best Rap/Sung Collaboration (with T.I.), for "My Love"; 2008 (two awards), Best Male Pop Vocal Performance, for "What Goes Around ... Comes Around," and Best Dance Recording, for "LoveStoned/I Think She Knows"

Emmy Award: 2007, outstanding original music and lyrics, for "Dick in a Box"

Teen Choice Awards: 2007 (two awards), Choice Music-Male Artist; Choice Music-Payback Track

FURTHER READING

Books

Biography Today, 2001 (entry on *N Sync)

Periodicals

Entertainment Weekly, Sep. 20, 2002, p.36; Feb. 9, 2007, p.32
Fort Worth Star-Telegram, Mar. 2, 2007, p.32
New York Post, Jan. 7, 2007, p.36
New York Times, Oct. 22, 2006, section 9, p.1; Dec. 23, 2006, p.B11
Newsweek, Apr. 5, 2004, p.56
People, Feb. 8, 1999, p.93; June 24, 2002, p.58; Nov.11, 2002, p.73; Aug. 6, 2007, p.70
Teen People, Dec.1, 2002 p.92
USA Today, May 1, 2007, p.D1
WWD, Aug. 22, 2005, p.8

ADDRESS

Justin Timberlake
Jive Records
137 West 25th Street
New York, NY 10001-7200

WORLD WIDE WEB SITES

http://www.justintimberlake.com
http://www.tennmanrecords.com

Lee Wardlaw 1955-

American Writer for Children and Young Adults
Author of *101 Ways to Bug Your Parents* and *101 Ways to Bug Your Teacher*

BIRTH

Lee Wardlaw was born Lee Anna Wardlaw on November 20, 1955, at the Smoky Hill Air Force Base Hospital in Salina, Kansas. Her father, Joseph Patterson Wardlaw, was a captain in the Air Force and a professional photographer who ran the photo lab on the base. He and her mother, Margaret Laux Wardlaw, had degrees in business from Ohio University. Lee remembers her father proudly saying that her birth "only cost him and my mother $7.62, as the rest of the tab was picked up by the United States Air Force." She has two younger brothers, Scott and John. Her married name is Lee Wardlaw Jaffurs, but she uses Lee Wardlaw for her pen name.

YOUTH

Wardlaw moved with her parents to Erie, Pennsylvania, when she was less then a year old. Her parents owned and operated WLEU, a radio station there. In 1960, they purchased another station, KIST radio in Santa Barbara, California, where Wardlaw grew up.

> "You could almost always find me holed up in my room with paper and pencil," Wardlaw said. "All through elementary school and high school I wrote poems, songs, stories, even my own magazine—complete with articles, ads, and an advice column. I also wrote a silly soap opera with multiple daily episodes that I secretly passed to my best friend during class."

Writing Her First Book

Wardlaw wrote her first book as a seven-year-old second grader for her school's spring art festival. The book was called *Teena Bell*, about a little girl who was only one-inch high. Wardlaw modeled the character after Tinkerbell from *Peter Pan* and Thumbelina from a story by Hans Christian Anderson. Teena Bell "looked just like me—skinny, brownish hair, crooked smile—only shorter," Wardlaw wrote on her website, www.leewardlaw. com. She has also said that "One of the reasons I made Teena Bell so small was because I wanted to grow up to look like Tinkerbell and I wanted to marry Peter Pan. I had a mad crush on him!" Teena had a grasshopper for a best friend and 14 baby brothers and 14 baby sisters, all of whom were still in diapers. "My brother John had just been born, so I was expected to do a lot of diaper duty. Ha!" she wrote. Her mother typed up the book and bound it in a bright red report cover.

After she finished *Teena Bell*, Wardlaw continued to write. As a third grader, she created a play about an 11-year-old girl who meets the Beatles and then gets to join the band. She was taking guitar lessons at the time, which inspired the story. When Wardlaw turned 11 herself, her parents got a di-

Wardlaw enjoying a book at an early age.

vorce, which she described on her website as the worst thing that has ever happened to her. In the sixth grade, she and three girlfriends formed a rock band called the Shooting Stars. She played the guitar and wrote many of the songs that the band performed.

Wardlaw kept herself busy through good and bad times by writing. "You could almost always find me holed up in my room with paper and pencil," she said. "All through elementary school and high school I wrote poems, songs, stories, even my own magazine—complete with articles, ads, and an advice column. I also wrote a silly soap opera with multiple daily episodes that I secretly passed to my best friend during class."

EDUCATION

Wardlaw attended Santa Barbara High School, where she contributed to the literary magazine and was captain of the drill team. After graduation, she enrolled in California Polytechnic State University in San Luis Obispo, California. She earned a Bachelor of Arts (BA) degree in elementary education, also earning her teaching credential. She graduated with honors from Cal Poly in 1977.

Losing Her Childhood Home to Fire

Wardlaw experienced a personal trauma during the summer before she graduated from college when her family's home in Santa Barbara burned down. It started after a kite became entangled in some power lines, sending sparks into the dry weeds below. Despite the best efforts of firefighters, the resulting blaze burned for more than 24 hours and destroyed 200 homes. "My family's home was one of those that burned to the ground," Wardlaw recalled. "We lost everything—including my cat. Days later, while sifting through the wreckage and ash, I found only two recognizable items: a blackened baby spoon and our front door knob! I kept both as souvenirs of what I call the 'before time.'" Years later, Wardlaw used her memories of the blaze in her novel, *Corey's Fire*.

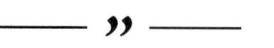

FIRST JOBS

Wardlaw began her teaching career at the Los Ninos Head Start early education program in Santa Barbara, California. She continued teaching for the next five years, first at the pre-school and then at an elementary school in Santa Barbara. She also worked as a tutor and served as the "tooth fairy" for a dental foundation. "There was no magic wand or tutu," Wardlaw remarked. "I drove the Brush Bus—a mobile dental education classroom." She drove the bus to area schools and gave 30-minute lessons on tooth care in the bus. She had to quit when her dentist said she was wearing away the enamel on her teeth from giving tooth-brushing demonstrations all day.

During her years as a teacher, Wardlaw continued to write in her spare time. She often watched the clock all day, she once admitted, waiting for the time when she could go home and resume writing. She knew she wanted to be a children's author, she explained, because "I have total recall of my childhood, not just what I did, but the emotions I felt. Childhood is a series of firsts and the wonder, the embarrassments, the traumas, and the tribulations are timeless. If you can remember what it felt like when you were a kid, you can connect with the kids of today."

CAREER HIGHLIGHTS

Becoming an Author

Wardlaw's path to becoming an author took some twists and turns, and she wrote for many years before she became successful. Her first published book was *Me + Math = Headache* (1986), a beginning chapter book that she started writing when she was a 19-year-old college student. The first sentence of the book is "I flunked another math test today." Those very words were "something my mother heard a lot from me when I was in elementary school, junior high school, high school," Wardlaw recalled. The manuscript was rejected by many publishers before it was finally published in 1986.

Since that time, Wardlaw has continued to write in a wide variety of forms. She has written for children of all ages, including picture books for the youngest children, easy readers and beginning chapter books for those just beginning to read independently, and novels for middle-grade readers and young adults. In addition, she has written several non-fiction books for this older age group as well. Many of these books show the humor in growing up, both in funny and in more difficult situations, and they often feature determined, goal-driven characters that work hard to achieve their goals.

> *"[Corey's Fire] took nine months to write and three years to sell," Wardlaw later recalled. "And that was fast. They say it can take seven years to break into the children's book market."*

Corey's Fire

Wardlaw's first full-length novel for middle-grade readers and young adults was *Corey's Fire,* a story based on the fire at her childhood home. To prepare to write the novel, she did research by interviewing family and friends and reading many news accounts. "Reliving the fire was painful," she said, "so painful that I was unable to begin writing the book until March of 1982, five years after the disaster." She quit teaching to finish the book.

After finishing the novel, she went looking for a publisher. "The book took nine months to write and three years to sell," Wardlaw later recalled. "And that was fast. They say it can take seven years to break into the children's book market." Still, her struggle wasn't over. She hoped the book would be published in 1987, which was the 10th anniversary of the fire. But the pub-

BIOGRAPHY TODAY • 2008 Annual Cumulation

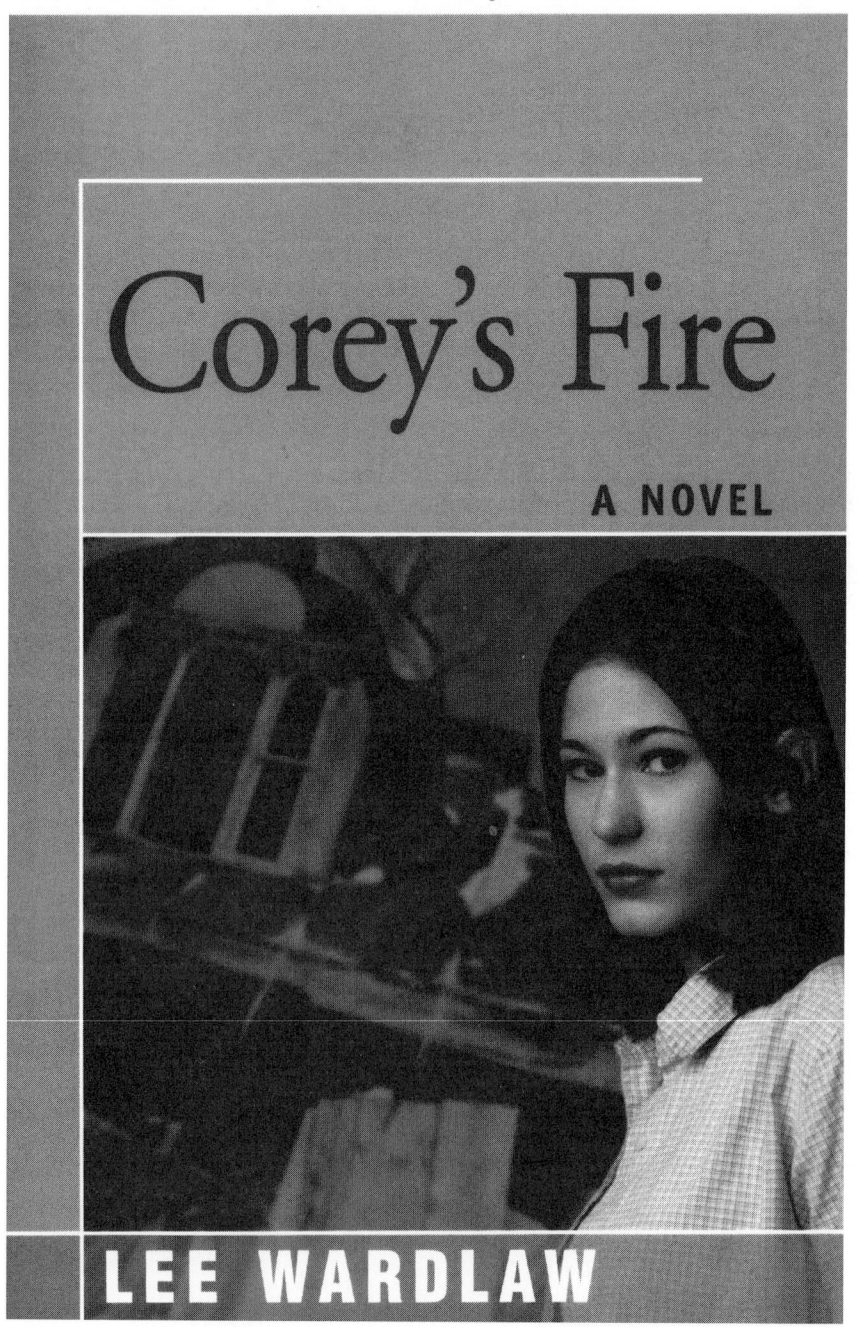

Corey's Fire *was Wardlaw's first young adult novel.*

lishing company appointed a new editor for the project, and the editor hated it. Wardlaw had to find a new publisher, and the book didn't come out until 1990.

Corey's Fire (1990) tells the story of an immature 14-year-old girl who thinks no one understands her problems. Her deepening relationship with a neighbor, Christopher (Topher), is the center of the novel. At first, she can't stand him. Topher is sarcastic and likes to chase Corey's cat with his motorcycle. After her house burns down in a fire, however, it is Topher who helps her look for her cat and work through her problems. Another neighbor, Ericka, is also sympathetic, and eventually Corey begins to think about people other than herself. "It's not the disaster that changes Corey," Wardlaw explained. "She chooses to change. That's her first step to becoming an independent young woman."

Corey's Fire is dedicated to Wardlaw's mother and two brothers, who lived through the Santa Barbara fire with her. The book was well received by *Publishers Weekly*, where a critic wrote: "In this refreshing twist on the standard love story, romantic problems are upstaged by a natural disaster.... Corey finds the strength to rebuild her home and her life. The author's unflinching realism in describing the fire and its aftermath adds sizzle to an already appealing romance."

Other Fiction for Young Adults and Middle-Grade Readers

Wardlaw's writing career took off as she published book after book for various age groups. These included two novels for young adults: *Alley Cat* (1987) and *Don't Look Back* (1993). In *Alley Cat*, she relies on her own teenage experiences to tell the story of Allison Blake. Though initially awkward, Allison wins respect through her job as a weekend disk jockey at a radio station. In *Don't Look Back*, Wardlaw tells the story of 17-year-old Drew. Her father abandoned her and her mother and moved to Hawaii, for which she has never forgiven him. Now Drew is gong to spend the summer in Hawaii with him and his friend Jane. According to *Publishers Weekly*, "Drew has been afraid of flying, heights, and romantic relationships ever since her doctor father walked out on her family to start a new life in Hawaii. The unhappy girl must face her phobias when she spends the summer with the man she has grown to despise.... [Wardlaw] once again combines coming-of-age struggles with a predictable but pleasing romance."

Wardlaw has also written several books for middle-grade readers, including *Seventh Grade Weirdo*, published in 1992 and later released as *My Life as a Weirdo*. This novel tells the story of Christopher "Rob" Robin, whose family causes him major embarrassments. His mother, a Winnie-the-Pooh fanatic, drives around in a shocking pink van with Pooh characters on it; his father is an ex-surfer who likes to talk "surfer dude" slang around Rob's friends; and his sister, Winnie, is a six-year-old genius who is famous for inventing a board game. Rob wants nothing more than to be considered normal when he starts junior high school. But, of course, his "weird" family interferes with his plan, and Rob has the additional problem of dealing with a school bully. According to a reviewer for *VOYA (Voice of Youth Advocates)*, *Seventh Grade Weirdo* "humorously recounts the trials and tribulations of Rob's first year in junior high.... Wardlaw unerringly hits upon one of the chief fears of this age group: to be thought weird by their peers. Her light touch keeps a smile on your lips as you read. Sections cry out to be read aloud to classes, especially at the beginning of a new school year." The reviewer for the *Houston Chronicle* specifically recommended the book "for those entering the cutthroat social whirl of middle school or junior high."

> *Wardlaw knew she wanted to be a children's author, she explained, because "I have total recall of my childhood, not just what I did, but the emotions I felt. Childhood is a series of firsts and the wonder, the embarrassments, the traumas, and the tribulations are timeless. If you can remember what it felt like when you were a kid, you can connect with the kids of today."*

Non-Fiction Books

Wardlaw has also written several non-fiction books for middle-grade and young adult readers. *Cowabunga! The Complete Book of Surfing* (1991) tells the history of surfing, recounts how the different kinds of surfboards were developed, and describes the movies, music, and slang associated with the sport. The book does not offer an instructional guide for beginners who want to learn to surf. "I'm not a great surfer," Wardlaw said. "I didn't feel I should teach kids how to do it." But there is a chapter on avoiding shark attacks, which includes this tip: paint two mean-looking eyes on the bottom of the board.

Bubblemania: The Chewy History of Bubble Gum (1997) is full of facts and off-beat trivia about bubble gum. It includes tips on how to blow huge gum bubbles, as well as a gum recipe suitable for an entire class to try. There is also a section on what Wardlaw calls "damage control: how to get gum off clothes, furniture, and hair—and how not to get it stuck there in the first place!"

Wardlaw and her pet cockroach, Toto, encourage kids to "catch the reading bug" at a presentation to young readers.

We All Scream for Ice Cream! The Scoop on America's Favorite Dessert (2000) is another favorite. To research and write the book, Wardlaw toured a dairy farm and two ice cream factories, interviewed taste testers, took scoop lessons, made ice cream, cones, and chocolate sauces in her kitchen, and gained six pounds tasting every brand of ice cream she could find. The result is a jam-packed book full of ice cream history, lore, licking tips, recipes, and more.

101 Ways to Bug Your Parents

One of Wardlaw's best-loved books is the middle-grade novel *101 Ways to Bug Your Parents* (1996). She got the idea for the book when a local California newspaper featured a story about a third grade teacher who gave her students an offbeat assignment—write down 10 things you've done that have really bugged your parents. The children began writing copiously, compiled a long list of their favorites, and wrote them on the blackboard. A teacher's aide thought the list was funny, and she copied it and sent it to the newspaper.

101 Ways to Bug Your Parents has been a big hit with middle-school readers.

Intrigued by the story, Wardlaw arranged to meet the California teacher, Nancy Revlin, and her class. Revlin was a first-year teacher who was worried that she would be fired due to the publicity from the news story and the negative letters the newspaper later received from irate parents. However, the principal saw the humor in the situation and supported her. But the incident tweaked Wardlaw's imagination, and she began to develop characters and a fictional storyline to go along with the list.

101 Ways to Bug Your Parents tells the story of Sneeze (Steve) Wyatt, a 12-year-old inventor whose latest invention is the Nice Alarm, which taps a person awake gently—when it works properly. Sneeze has written to a manufacturing company about his gadget, and the president of the company offers to meet him during the annual Invention Convention in July. He figures he'll be able to keep the appointment during his family's summer vacation, which is near the convention. But then his parents, unaware of his plans, cancel the vacation at the last minute and sign him up for a summer school creative-writing class. Frustrated and disappointed, Sneeze starts making a list of ways to annoy his parents. Some of his friends hear about the list, think he's writing a book on the subject, and want to buy copies.

> *"I think the parents who complained [about* **101 Ways to Bug Your Parents***] don't have much of a sense of humor, which is something you need today if you're going to raise children,"* Wardlaw said. *"Of course, none of these parents actually took the time to read the book. If they had, they would've seen that the book is actually very pro-parent."*

Steve compiles his list gradually as the novel progresses, but the full list of 101 ways to bug your parents is included at the end. The "suggestions" include such annoyances as: chew with your mouth open, turn on the hot water when your dad's in the shower, give your brother or sister a haircut, lose french fries under the car seat, repeat everything your parents say, make your parents come to school with the homework you "forgot," put clean clothes back in the hamper, don't flush the toilet, and say to your mom: "that's a woman's job."

101 Ways to Bug Your Parents found an enthusiastic audience among middle school readers, many of whom continue to write to Wardlaw with suggested additions to the list. The book was also well received by the literary press. A critic for *School Library Journal* called the book "a fast, fun read. The humor and depth of the characters are reminiscent of Louis Sachar's *There's a Boy in the Girls' Bathroom*. Readers will hope for further adventures of Sneeze and his friends." According to a reviewer for *Booklist*, "Wardlaw has written a funny story with more substance than is evident initially. The death of a parent, job insecurity, gifted children, teacher respect, true friendship, and even intellectual freedom all find play here. Although adults may find Sneeze's suggestions predictable and overdone—after all, we've weighed in on both sides of this issue—children will probably continue to turn the pages just to see whether they've overlooked even one idea." *101 Ways to Bug Your Parents* was a great success: it won several awards, became a perennial favorite among readers, and was optioned for a movie on the Disney Channel.

101 Ways to Bug Your Parents sparked some controversy, however, especially among parents who worried their children would take the book to heart and use it as an instructional manual. Parents in two school districts in Texas and Oklahoma went so far as to challenge the book and ask that it be removed from school shelves. They felt the book undermined parental authority and encouraged children to disobey. In both cases, members of the school board read the book and then denied the requests.

"I think the parents who complained don't have much of a sense of humor, which is something you need today if you're going to raise children," Wardlaw said. "Of course, none of these parents actually took the time to read the book. If they had, they would've seen that the book is actually very pro-parent, and that Sneeze learns that bugging your parents not only gets you into real trouble, but that it's an ineffective and improper means of communicating with your mom and dad."

101 Ways to Bug Your Teacher

Several years later, Wardlaw followed up with the sequel, *101 Ways to Bug Your Teacher* (2004). This book features the same main characters, Sneeze Wyatt and his friends at Jefferson Middle School. This time Sneeze's problem is his parents' desire for him to take advanced math and science classes. They want him to skip a grade and go straight into high school at the end of seventh grade. Sneeze is horrified by the idea of skipping eighth grade, mostly because he'd miss his friends. So he sets out to prove that he's not high-school material by becoming disruptive in his classes. He makes a list of 101 ways to bug his teachers, with the hope that they will recommend that he stay in middle school.

Most of the ideas on the list were contributed by real students, with others added by Wardlaw, drawing on her days as a teacher. "Number 13 and 33 [on the list] used to drive me crazy!" she said. Number 13: "While the teacher is talking, get up to grind your pencil. Grind loudly." And Number 33: "When a teacher asks a question, wave your arm like a palm tree in a hurricane and say: 'Pick me! Pick me!' When the teacher calls on you, say: 'Never mind.'"

> *Wardlaw has said that these two suggestions from* **101 Ways to Bug Your Teachers** *used to drive her crazy. Number 13: "While the teacher is talking, get up to grind your pencil. Grind loudly." And Number 33: "When a teacher asks a question, wave your arm like a palm tree in a hurricane and say: 'Pick me! Pick me!' When the teacher calls on you, say: 'Never mind.'"*

101 Ways to Bug Your Teacher has several subplots, including the pregnancy of Sneeze's mother and his friend Hayley's difficulties with the woman dating her widowed father. There is also a story line about the group project that Sneeze and his friends have to prepare for their class in ancient Egyptian history. After some initial reluctance, the group decides to go ahead with Sneeze's idea to make a mummy out of a chicken. Wardlaw ends *101 Ways to Bug Your Teacher* with a three-page, 21-step recipe for making a mummy out of a store-bought chicken!

Most reviewers of *101 Ways to Bug Your Teacher* praised the book, including this comment in *School Library Journal:* "References are made to the first book, but this one can stand alone. In spite of the title, the characters show respect for their teachers and parents, and for one another. A delightful read." A *Booklist* reviewer agreed. "Sneeze is an appealing, dimensional character whose first-person narrative is bound to entertain. The story is both comical and compassionate as it highlights the challenges of living up to expectations and the rewards of trying your best."

Wardlaw has been working on two additional sequels to the series, tentatively titled *101 Ways to Bug Your Brother or Sister* and *101 Ways to Bug Your Friends and Enemies.* She invites her readers to offer suggestions on their "bugging" techniques by clicking on the "Just for Kids" icon on her website.

Wardlaw plans to continue to write because "It's fun.... First and foremost, I write to entertain myself. But I also write to show my readers a world they can delight in, a world of wonder and awe, a world where so much is possible. Around any bend, at any moment, might come Mystery! Adventure! Romance!"

> *Wardlaw plans to continue to write because "It's fun.... First and foremost, I write to entertain myself. But I also write to show my readers a world they can delight in, a world of wonder and awe, a world where so much is possible. Around any bend, at any moment, might come Mystery! Adventure! Romance!"*

MARRIAGE AND FAMILY

Wardlaw married Craig Jaffurs in 1983. They are the co-owners of Jaffurs Wine Cellars, which makes about 5,000 cases of wine a year from grapes purchased from vineyards in Santa Barbara, California. The couple lives in Santa Barbara with their son, Patterson, who was born in 1996. The family has two cats.

HOBBIES AND OTHER INTERESTS

When she's not writing, Wardlaw has many favorite activities, which she listed on her website as: "crossword puzzles; reading history (American Revolutionary and Civil War eras); body-surfing; hanging out with my son;

baking (and eating) anything with dark chocolate; shopping with friends; blowing bubble gum bubbles; collecting beach glass; and visiting schools to talk to kids about writing." In addition to her work with children, she also teaches workshops for adult writers, parents, librarians, and teachers. Wardlaw writes daily blogs on her lively and kid-friendly website.

SELECTED WRITINGS

Fiction for Young Adults

Alley Cat, 1987
Don't Look Back, 1993
See You in September, 1995 (collection of stories by Wardlaw and three other authors)

Fiction for Middle-Grade Readers

Corey's Fire, 1990
Operation Rhinoceros, 1992
Seventh Grade Weirdo, 1992; later released as *My Life as a Weirdo*
101 Ways to Bug Your Parents, 1996
101 Ways to Bug Your Teacher, 2004
Tripping Over the Lunch Lady and Other School Stories, 2004 (collection of stories by Wardlaw and nine other authors)

Non-Fiction

Cowabunga! The Complete Book of Surfing, 1991
Bubblemania: The Chewy History of Bubble Gum, 1997
We All Scream for Ice Cream! The Scoop on America's Favorite Dessert, 2000

Easy Readers and Beginning Chapter Books

Me + Math = Headache, 1986
The Eye and I, 1988
The Ghoul Brothers, 1996
Dinosaur Pizza, 1998
Hector's Hiccups, 1999

Picture Books

The Tales of Grandpa Cat, 1994
Punia and the King of Sharks: A Hawaiian Folktale, 1997

An illustration of Wardlaw by Cathi Mingus.

Bow-Wow Birthday, 1998
First Steps, 1999
Saturday Night Jamboree, 2000
The Chair Where Bear Sits, 2001
Peek-a-Book: A Lift-the-Flap Bedtime Rhyme, 2003

SELECTED HONORS AND AWARDS

Reluctant Young Adult Reader Award (American Library Association): 1991, for *Corey's Fire;* 1992, for *Cowabunga!*
Children's Choice Award (International Reading Association/Children's Book Council): 1991, for *Corey's Fire;* 2005 (two awards), for *101 Ways to Bug Your Teacher* and *Tripping Over the Lunch Lady and Other School Stories*
Santa Barbara High School Distinguished Alumni Award: 1993, for success as a children's book author
Pick of the Lists Award (American Booksellers): 1994, for *The Tales of Grandpa Cat;* 1996, for *101 Ways to Bug Your Parents*
Best Books for the Teen Age Award (New York Public Library): 1996, for *See You in September*
Notable Children's Book in the Field of Social Studies (Children's Book Council/National Council for the Social Studies): 1998, for *Punia and the King of Sharks*
100 of the Decade's Best Multi-Cultural Read Alouds (Reading Is Fundamental): 1998, for *Punia and the King of Sharks*
Best Children's Books of the Year Award (Bank Street College): 2000, for *First Steps;* 2001, for *Saturday Night Jamboree*
Best Humorous Books of the Year Award (Bank Street College): 2001, for *101 Ways to Bug Your Parents*
International School Librarians Recommended Reading List: 2004, for *101 Ways to Bug Your Parents*
Shojai Mentor Award (International Cat Writers' Association): 2005

On her web site, Wardlaw encourages readers to "Catch the reading bug!" Illustration by Cathi Mingus.

FURTHER READING

Periodicals

Daily Oklahoman, May 10, 2000, Community section, p.1
Fresno (CA) Bee, Mar. 19, 1995, p.J8

Los Angeles Times, Aug. 1, 1991, p.J14; July 6, 2000, p.B9; June 25, 2003, Food section, p.7

New England Reading Association Journal, Vol.37, No.3, 2001, p.14

Santa Barbara News-Press, Dec. 10, 2003

Online Articles

http://www.californiareaders.org/interviews/wardlaw_lee.php
(*California Readers*, "Meet Lee Wardlaw," no date)

http://patriciamnewman.com/wardlaw.html
(*Patricia M. Newman*, "Who Wrote That? Featuring Lee Wardlaw," originally published in *California Kids!* June 2002)

ADDRESS

Lee Wardlaw
c/o Ms. Ginger Knowlton
Curtis Brown, Ltd.
Ten Astor Place
New York, NY 10003
Email: author@leewardlaw.com

WORLD WIDE WEB SITE

http://www.leewardlaw.com

Photo and Illustration Credits

Front Cover: Majora Carter: James Burling Chase, courtesy of Sustainable South Bronx; Al Gore: Courtesy, Office of Al and Tipper Gore; Jennifer Hudgens: Jennifer Graylock/Associated Press; James Stewart Jr.: Brian Myrick/Associated Press.

Aly & AJ: Todd Williamson/WireImage for Elizabeth Glaser Pediatric AIDS (p. 11); John M. Heller/Getty Images (p. 14); CD: INTO THE RUSH. Copyright © (p) 2005 Hollywood Records, Inc. All rights reserved. Photo by Keith Munyan. (p. 17 top); DVD: COW BELLES © Disney. All rights reserved. (p. 17 bottom); CD: INSOMNIATIC. Copyright © (p) 2007 Hollywood Records, Inc. All rights reserved. (p. 18).

Bill Bass: Rich Cooley/Northern Virginia Daily/Associated Press (p. 23); University of Tennessee Video and Photography Center (pp. 26, 31); John Sommers II/Reuters (p. 28); DEATH'S ACRE: Inside the Legendary Forensic Lab—the Body Farm—Where the Dead Do Tell Tales. Copyright © 2003 by Dr. Bill Bass and Jon Jefferson. All rights reserved. Jacket design and front jacket photograph by Andrea Ho. Published by G. P. Putnam's Sons/Penguin Group (USA) Inc. (p. 34).

Greta Binford: Courtesy Lewis & Clark College (pp. 39, 45 center, bottom); Jim Kalisch/University of Nebraska Department of Entomology (p. 45 top); Courtesy Greta Binford/Lewis & Clark College (pp. 47, 49).

Cory Booker: Courtesy Mayor's Office, Newark, New Jersey (pp. 53, 64); Tim Davis/Stanford Athletics (p. 56); DVD: STREET FIGHT © 2005 Marshall Curry Productions, LLC. Package design © Genius Products, LLC. All Rights Reserved. Photographs © The Star Ledger, Newark, NJ. (p. 60).

Sophia Bush: USA Network Photo/NBC Universal, Inc. (p. 67); DVD: ONE TREE HILL: The Complete First Season. Copyright © 2003, 2004, 2005 Warner Bros. Entertainment Inc. All rights reserved. (p. 71); SUPERCROSS. Photo by Ron Batzdorff. Copyright © 2005 TAG Entertainment, Inc. All rights reserved. (p. 73); DVD: JOHN TUCKER MUST DIE. Copyright © 2006 Twentieth Century Fox Film Corporation and Dune Entertainment LLC. All Rights Reserved. (p. 75).

Majora Carter: MacArthur Foundation (pp. 79, 82); James Burling Chase (pp. 84, 86, 88). All photos are courtesy of Sustainable South Bronx.

Anderson Cooper: Jason Kempin/WireImage (p. 91); Susan Wood/Getty Images (p. 93); Courtesy, Yale University (p. 96); lm1/Zuma Press/Newscom (p. 99); Charlie Varley/Sipa Press/Newscom (p. 101); DISPATCHES FROM THE EDGE © 2006 by Anderson Cooper. All rights reserved. Published by HarperCollins. Photograph by Brent Stirton/Getty Images for CNN; jacket design by Chip Kidd (p. 103).

Zac Efron: Francis Specker/Landov (p. 107); DVD: SUITE LIFE OF ZACK AND CODY: TAKING OVER THE TIPTON. Copyright © Disney. All rights reserved. (p. 109); Copyright © Disney. All rights reserved. (p. 111 top, bottom); DVD: HIGH SCHOOL MUSICAL 2: Extended Edition. Copyright © Disney 2007. All rights reserved. (pp. 111 center, 117); HAIRSPRAY. Copyright © 2007 David James/ New Line Cinema (p. 114).

Selena Gomez: Fitzroy Barrett/Landov (p. 121); BARNEY & FRIENDS. HIT Entertainment, The Lyons Group/Connecticut Public Television. All rights reserved. (p. 123); DVD: WIZARDS OF WAVERLY PLACE: WIZARD SCHOOL © Disney. All rights reserved. (p. 126); DR. SEUSS' HORTON HEARS A WHO! TM © 2008 Twentieth Century Fox Film Corporation. Photo by Blue Sky Studios. Dr. Seuss, Horton Hears a Who! and Dr. Seuss Characters TM & © 1954, 2008 Dr. Seuss Enterprises, L.P. All rights reserved. (p. 128).

Al Gore: Junko Kimura/Getty Images (p. 131); AP Photo (p. 134); Jeffrey Markowitz/Sygma/Corbis (p. 136); Marilyn Weiss/AP Photo (p. 138); William J. Clinton Presidential Library (p. 140); Luke Frazza/AFP/Getty Images (p. 143); AN INCONVENIENT TRUTH by Al Gore, © Al Gore, 2006, 2007. Adapted for young readers by Jane O'Connor. Published by Viking/Penguin/Rodale, Inc. Photo of Al Gore © Eric Lee/Renewable Films, front cover photo courtesy of NASA, jacket design by Jim Hoover. (p. 146); Daniel Sannum Lauten/AFP/Getty Images (p. 149).

Vanessa Hudgens: Jesse Grant/WireImage/Getty (p. 153); DVD cover: HIGH SCHOOL MUSICAL: ENCORE EDITION copyright © Disney. All Rights Reserved. (p. 157); CD: VANESSA HUDGENS V © (p) 2006 Hollywood Records, Inc. All Rights Reserved. Photo by Andrew MacPherson. Art direction and design by Enny Joo. Creative director: David Snow. (p. 159); Copyright © Disney. All Rights Reserved. (p. 161).

Jennifer Hudson: Marcel Thomas/FilmMagic/Getty (p. 165); AMERICAN IDOL. Logo. ™ ©2006 FOX BROADCASTING CR:FOX (p. 168); Ray Mickshaw/WireImage/Getty (p. 169); Frank Micelotta/Getty Images (p. 171); David James/copyright © 2006 Dreamworks LLC and Paramount Pictures. All Rights Reserved. (p. 173); Gary Hershorn/Reuters/Landov (p. 176).

Zach Hunter: Photo by Tom Sapp/courtesy Penny Hunter (p. 179); Ted Haddock/International Justice Mission® (pp. 182, 184); BE THE CHANGE: YOUR GUIDE TO FREEING SLAVES AND CHANGING THE WORLD (Zondervan Publishing) Copyright © 2007 by Zach Hunter. Cover Photography: The Visual Reserve. Cover Design: Burnkit. Creative Team: Doug Davidson, Rich Cairnes, Heather Haggerty, and David Conn. (p. 187).

Bindi Irwin: BINDI: THE JUNGLE GIRL on Discovery Kids Channel. Copyright © 2008 Discovery Communications, LLC (pp. 189, 194, 197); Myung Jung Kim/PA/Associated Press (p. 191).

Jonas Brothers: Kevin Parry/WireImage/Getty (p. 199); Frank Micelotta/Getty Images for Fox (p. 202); CD: JONAS BROTHERS © (p) 2007 Hollywood Records. All Rights Reserved. (p. 205); Mathew Imaging/FilmMagic/Getty (p. 207).

Lisa Ling: Alexandra Wyman/WireImage (p. 211); Michael Caulfield/Associated Press (p. 215); Stuart Ramson/Associated Press (p. 216); DVD: CHINA'S LOST GIRLS.

PHOTO AND ILLUSTRATION CREDITS

Copyright © 2005 NGHT, Inc. All rights reserved. (p. 218); WHO CARES ABOUT GIRLS? Oxygen Photo/via NBC Universal, Inc. (p. 221).

Eli Manning: Al Bello/Getty Images (p. 225); Courtesy of Ole Miss Athletics (pp. 227, 231); Ray Stubblebine/Reuters/Landov (p. 233); Andy Lyons/Getty Images (p. 236); Mike Groll/AP Photo (p. 238).

Kimmie Meissner: Kathy F. Atkinson, courtesy of University of Delaware (p. 241); Jonathan Ferrey/Getty Images (p. 245); Cool Kids Campaign/Mitch Stringer (pp. 246, 254); Jeff Haynes/AFP/Getty Images (p. 249); Matthew Stockman/Getty Images (p. 251).

Scott Niedermayer: Mike Cassese/Reuters/Landov (p. 257); Scott Levy/Getty Images (p. 259); Brian Clarkson/Associated Press (p. 262); Jeff Vinnick/Stringer/Getty Images (p. 264); Jim McIsaac/Getty Images (p. 267).

Christina Norman: Stan Honda/AFP/Getty Images (p. 271); DVD: BEAVIS AND BUTTHEAD: The Mike Judge Collection – Volume 2 © 2006 MTV Networks. All Rights Reserved. Beavis and Butthead created by Mike Judge. (p. 274); DVD: THE OSBOURNES: The 2nd Season. Copyright © Buena Vista Home Entertainment, Inc. © 2003 JOKS, LLC (p. 276); Jemal Countess/WireImage (p. 279); Frank Micelotta/Getty Images (p. 282).

Masi Oka/Photos: Chris Haston/NBC Photo. Copyright © 2007 NBC Universal, Inc. All Rights Reserved. (p. 285); DVD: THE PERFECT STORM copyright © 2000 Warner Bros. Entertainment, Inc. All Rights Reserved. (p. 289); Copyright © 2007 NBC Universal, Inc. All Rights Reserved. Paul Drinkwater/NBC Photo (pp. 292, 295 top, center), Michael Muller/NBC Photo (p. 295 bottom).

Tyler Perry: PRNewsFoto/Newscom (p. 301); DVD: TYLER PERRY'S DIARY OF A MAD BLACK WOMAN © Copyright 2006 Lions Gate Entertainment. Photo by Alfeo Dixon. (pp. 304, 309); DVD: TYLER PERRY'S MADEA'S FAMILY REUNION © Copyright 2006 Lions Gate Entertainment. Photo by Alfeo Dixon. (pp. 305, 311 top); DVD: TYLER PERRY'S WHY DID I GET MARRIED? © Copyright 2006 Lions Gate Entertainment. Photo by Alfeo Dixon. (p. 311 center); DVD: TYLER PERRY'S DADDY'S LITTLE GIRLS © Copyright 2006 Lions Gate Entertainment. Photo by Alfeo Dixon. (p. 311 bottom); HOUSE OF PAYNE, photo by Andrew Eccles, copyright © Turner Broadcasting System, Inc. (p. 313).

Morgan Pressel: Scott Halleran/Getty Images (p. 319); Photo courtesy South-Florida Sun-Sentinel (p. 323); Harry How/Getty Images (p. 325); Robert Laberge/Stringer/Getty Images (p. 327).

Rihanna: PRNewsFoto/Island Def Jam Music Group via Newscom (p. 331); MUSIC OF THE SUN Copyright © Island Def Jam/Universal Music Group (p. 334); GOOD GIRL GONE BAD Copyright © Island Def Jam/Universal Music Group (p. 337); Frank Micelotta/Getty Images for Universal Music (p. 339); Heidi Gutman/NBC Photo (p. 340).

John Roberts Jr.: Mark Wilson/Getty Images (p. 345); 1979 Harvard Law School Yearbook, Courtesy of Special Collections, Harvard Law School Library (p. 347); Shawn Thew/UPI/POOL/Landov (p. 351); Steve Petteway, Collection of the Supreme Court of the United States (pp. 353, 356).

J.K. Rowling: Richard Young/PRNewsFoto/Newscom (p. 361); Gareth Davies/Getty Images (p. 365); HARRY POTTER AND THE SORCERER'S STONE. Text copyright © 1997 by J.K. Rowling. Illustrations copyright © 1998 by Mary GrandPré. Jacket art by Mary GrandPré. Jacket Design by Mary GrandPré and David Saylor. All Rights Reserved. Published by Arthur A. Levine Books, an imprint of Scholastic Press by arrangement with Bloomsbury Publishing Plc (p. 368); Peter Mountain/copyright © 2001 Warner Bros. All Rights Reserved. (p. 371 top, bottom); Photograph by Murray Close/Warner Bros via KRT/Newscom (p. 371 center); HARRY POTTER AND THE GOBLET OF FIRE © 2005 Warner Bros. Entertainment. Harry Potter Publishing Rights © J.K.R. Harry Potter characters, names and related indicia are trademarks of and © Warner Bros. Entertainment. All Rights Reserved. Photo by Murray Close (p. 373 top, bottom); Photo ITAR-TASS/Karo-Film Press Service/Newscom (p. 373 center); HARRY POTTER AND THE DEATHLY HALLOWS. Text copyright © 2007 by J.K. Rowling. Jacket art/illustrations by Mary GrandPré copyright © 2007 by Warner Brothers. Jacket design by Mary GrandPré and David Saylor. HARRY POTTER & all related characters and elements are TM of and © WBEI. Harry Potter Publishing Rights © J.K. Rowling. All Rights Reserved. Published by Arthur A. Levine Books, an imprint of Scholastic Inc. (p. 376); Bill Haber/Associated Press (p. 379).

James Stewart Jr.: Brian Myrick/Associated Press (pp. 383, 385); Jeff Kardas/Getty Images (pp. 387, 390); Craig Durling/WireImage (p. 393).

Ichiro Suzuki: Orlin Wagner/Associated Press (p. 395); Koji Sasahara/Associated Press (p. 400); C.J. Gunther/AFP/Getty Images (p. 403); Robert Beck/MLB Photos via Getty Images (p. 404); Lisa Blumenfeld/Getty Images (p. 406); John Froschauer/Associated Press (p. 409).

Karen P. Tandy: Courtesy Drug Enforcement Administration (DEA/U.S. Department of Justice) (pp. 415, 421, 423, 426); Mike Theiler/Reuters/Landov (p. 418).

Marta Tienda: Courtesy of Marta Tienda (pp. 431, 441, 444); Photo by Marion Post Wolcott, FSA/OWI, Library of Congress Prints and Photographs, LC-DIG-fsac-1a34398u. (p. 433); THE HISPANIC POPULATION OF THE UNITED STATES by Frank D. Bean and Marta Tienda. Copyright © 1987 by Russell Sage Foundation. All rights reserved. Cover design by Whit Vye. (p. 437); Photo by Susan R. Geller, Office of Communications, Princeton University. (p. 439).

Justin Timberlake: © and TM MTV Networks. All rights reserved. (pp. 447, 457, 463); MICKEY MOUSE CLUB © Disney. All rights reserved. (p. 450); *NSYNC publicity photo © 2001 Zomba Recording LLC © SONY (p. 452); CD: *NSYNC/ 'N THE MIX © RCA Music © SONY BMG (p. 454); DVD: SHREK THE THIRD TM & © 2007 DreamWorks Animation LLC. All rights reserved. Photo by DreamWorks Animation LLC. (p. 459); CD: FUTURESEX/LOVESOUNDS © 2006 Zomba Recording LLC © SONY BMG (p. 461).

Lee Wardlaw: Courtesy of Lee Wardlaw (www.leewardlaw.com) (pp. 467, 469, 475, 478); COREY'S FIRE © Lee Wardlaw, 1989 and 2006. All rights reserved. An Authors Guild Backinprint.com edition, published by iUniverse, Inc. Originally published by Avon/Flare. (p. 472); 101 WAYS TO BUG YOUR PARENTS © Lee Wardlaw Jaffurs, 1996. All rights reserved. Published by Puffin Books. (p. 476); illustrations by Cathi Mingus, courtesy of Lee Wardlaw (pp. 481, 482).

Cumulative General Index

This cumulative index includes names, occupations, nationalities, and ethnic and minority origins that pertain to all individuals profiled in *Biography Today* since the debut of the series in 1992.

Aaliyah . . . . .Jan 02
Aaron, Hank . . . . .Sport V.1
Abbey, Edward . . . . .WorLdr V.1
Abdul, Paula . . . . .Jan 92; Update 02
Abdul-Jabbar, Kareem . . . . .Sport V.1
Aboriginal
   Freeman, Cathy . . . . .Jan 01
Abzug, Bella . . . . .Sep 98
activists
   Abzug, Bella . . . . .Sep 98
   Arafat, Yasir . . . . .Sep 94;
     Update 94; Update 95; Update 96;
     Update 97; Update 98; Update 00;
     Update 01; Update 02
   Ashe, Arthur . . . . .Sep 93
   Askins, Renee . . . . .WorLdr V.1
   Aung San Suu Kyi . . . . .Apr 96;
     Update 98; Update 01; Update 02
   Banda, Hastings Kamuzu . . . .WorLdr V.2
   Bates, Daisy .Apr 00
   Bellamy, Carol . . . . .Jan 06
   Benjamin, Regina . . . . .Science V.9
   Bono . . . . .Sep 06
   Brower, David . . . . .WorLdr V.1;
     Update 01
   Burnside, Aubyn . . . . .Sep 02
   Calderone, Mary S. . . . . .Science V.3
   Carter, Majora . . . . .Sep 08
   Chavez, Cesar . . . . .Sep 93
   Chavis, Benjamin . . . . . .Jan 94; Update 94
   Cronin, John . . . . .WorLdr V.3
   Dai Qing . . . . .WorLdr V.3
   Dalai Lama . . . . .Sep 98
   Douglas, Marjory
     Stoneman . . . . . .WorLdr V.1; Update 98
   Dworkin, Aaron . . . . .Apr 07
   Ebadi, Shirin . . . . .Apr 04
   Edelman, Marian Wright . . . . .Apr 93
   Fay, Michael . . . . .Science V.9

   Foreman, Dave . . . . .WorLdr V.1
   Forman, James . . . . .Apr 05
   Fuller, Millard . . . . .Apr 03
   Gibbs, Lois . . . . .WorLdr V.1
   Gore, Al . . . . .Sep 08
   Haddock, Doris (Granny D). . . . . . .Sep 00
   Huerta, Dolores . . . . .Sep 03
   Hunter, Zach . . . . .Jan 08
   Jackson, Jesse . . . . .Sep 95; Update 01
   Ka Hsaw Wa . . . . .WorLdr V.3
   Kaunda, Kenneth . . . . .WorLdr V.2
   Kenyatta, Jomo . . . . .WorLdr V.2
   Kielburger, Craig . . . . .Jan 00
   Kim Dae-jung . . . . .Sep 01
   King, Coretta Scott . . . . .Sep 06
   Kopp, Wendy . . . . .Sep 07
   LaDuke, Winona . . . . .WorLdr V.3;
     Update 00
   Lewis, John . . . . .Jan 03
   Love, Susan . . . . .Science V.3
   Maathai, Wangari . . . .WorLdr V.1; Sep 05
   Mandela, Nelson . . . . . .Jan 92; Update 94;
     Update 01
   Mandela, Winnie . . . . .WorLdr V.2
   Mankiller, Wilma . . . . .Apr 94
   Martin, Bernard . . . . .WorLdr V.3
   Masih, Iqbal .Jan 96
   Menchu, Rigoberta . . . . .Jan 93
   Mendes, Chico . . . . .WorLdr V.1
   Mugabe, Robert . . . . .WorLdr V.2
   Marshall, Thurgood . . . .Jan 92; Update 93
   Nakamura, Leanne . . . . .Apr 02
   Nhat Hanh (Thich) . . . . .Jan 04
   Nkrumah, Kwame . . . . .WorLdr V.2
   Nyerere, Julius Kambarage . . .WorLdr V.2;
     Update 99
   Oliver, Patsy Ruth . . . . .WorLdr V.1
   Parks, Rosa . . . .Apr 92; Update 94; Apr 06
   Pauling, Linus . . . . .Jan 95
   Poussaint, Alvin . . . . .Science V.9

CUMULATIVE GENERAL INDEX

Saro-Wiwa, Ken ....WorLdr V.1
Savimbi, Jonas ....WorLdr V.2
Spock, Benjamin ......Sep 95; Update 98
Steinem, Gloria ....Oct 92
Steingraber, Sandra ....Science V.9
Tenberken, Sabriye ....Sep 07
Teresa, Mother ....Apr 98
Watson, Paul ....WorLdr V.1
Werbach, Adam ....WorLdr V.1
Wolf, Hazel ....WorLdr V.3
Yunus, Muhammad ....Sep 07
Zamora, Pedro ....Apr 95

actors/actresses
Aaliyah ....Jan 02
Affleck, Ben ....Sep 99
Alba, Jessica ....Sep 01
Allen, Tim ....Apr 94; Update 99
Alley, Kirstie ....Jul 92
Aly & AJ ....Sep 08
Anderson, Gillian ....Jan 97
Aniston, Jennifer ....Apr 99
Arnold, Roseanne ....Oct 92
Banks, Tyra ....PerfArt V.2
Barrymore, Drew ....Jan 01
Bell, Drake.....................Jan 07
Bell, Kristen ....Sep 05
Bergen, Candice ....Sep 93
Berry, Halle ....Jan 95; Update 02
Bialik, Mayim ....Jan 94
Black, Jack ....Jan 05
Blanchard, Rachel ....Apr 97
Bledel, Alexis ....Jan 03
Bloom, Orlando ....Sep 04
Brandis, Jonathan ....Sep 95
Brandy ....Apr 96
Brody, Adam ....Sep 05
Brown, Chris ....Apr 07
Bryan, Zachery Ty ....Jan 97
Burke, Chris ....Sep 93
Bush, Sophia ....Apr 08
Bynes, Amanda ....Sep 03
Cameron, Candace ....Apr 95
Campbell, Neve ....Apr 98
Candy, John ....Sep 94
Carrey, Jim ....Apr 96
Carvey, Dana ....Jan 93
Chan, Jackie ....PerfArt V.1
Culkin, Macaulay ....Sep 93
Cyrus, Miley ....Sep 07
Danes, Claire ....Sep 97

Depp, Johnny ....Apr 05
Diaz, Cameron ....PerfArt V.3
DiCaprio, Leonardo ....Apr 98
Diesel, Vin ....Jan 03
Doherty, Shannen .....Apr 92; Update 94
Duchovny, David ....Apr 96
Duff, Hilary ....Sep 02
Dunst, Kirsten ....PerfArt V.1
Efron, Zac ....Apr 08
Eminem ....Apr 03
Eve ....Jan 05
Fanning, Dakota ....Jan 06
Ferrell, Will ....Apr 07
Ferrera, America ....Sep 07
Fey, Tina ....Author V.16
Foray, June ....Jan 07
Ford, Harrison ....Sep 97
Garth, Jennie ....Apr 96
Gellar, Sarah Michelle ....Jan 99
Gilbert, Sara ....Apr 93
Goldberg, Whoopi ....Apr 94
Gomez, Selena ....Sep 08
Goodman, John ....Sep 95
Hanks, Tom ....Jan 96
Hart, Melissa Joan ....Jan 94
Hartnett, Josh ....Sep 03
Hathaway, Anne ....Apr 05
Hewitt, Jennifer Love.............Sep 00
Highmore, Freddie ....Apr 06
Holmes, Katie ....Jan 00
Hudgens, Vanessa ....Jan 08
Hudson, Jennifer ....Jan 08
Jones, James Earl ....Jan 95
Knightley, Keira ....Apr 07
Kutcher, Ashton ....Apr 04
Lee, Spike ....Apr 92
Locklear, Heather ....Jan 95
Lohan, Lindsay ....Sep 04
López, George ....PerfArt V.2
Lopez, Jennifer ....Jan 02
Mac, Bernie ....PerfArt V.1
McAdams, Rachel ....Apr 06
Moore, Mandy ....Jan 04
Muniz, Frankie ....Jan 01
Murphy, Eddie ....PerfArt V.2
Myers, Mike ....PerfArt V.3
O'Donnell, Rosie ......Apr 97; Update 02
Oka, Masi ....Jan 08
Oleynik, Larisa ....Sep 96
Olsen, Ashley ....Sep 95

490

CUMULATIVE GENERAL INDEX

Olsen, Mary Kate .... Sep 95
Perry, Luke .... Jan 92
Perry, Tyler .... Sep 08
Phoenix, River .... Apr 94
Pitt, Brad .... Sep 98
Portman, Natalie .... Sep 99
Priestley, Jason .... Apr 92
Prinze, Freddie Jr. .... Apr 00
Radcliffe, Daniel .... Jan 02
Raven .... Apr 04
Reagan, Ronald .... Sep 04
Reeve, Christopher ..... Jan 97; Update 02
Reeves, Keanu .... Jan 04
Roberts, Julia .... Sep 01
Romeo, Lil' .... Jan 06
Ryder, Winona .... Jan 93
Sandler, Adam .... Jan 06
Shatner, William .... Apr 95
Simpson, Ashlee .... Sep 05
Sinatra, Frank .... Jan 99
Smith, Will .... Sep 94
Spears, Jamie Lynn .... Sep 06
Stewart, Jon .... Jan 06
Stewart, Patrick .... Jan 94
Stiles, Julia .... PerfArt V.2
Thiessen, Tiffani-Amber .... Jan 96
Thomas, Jonathan Taylor .... Apr 95
Tisdale, Ashley .... Jan 07
Tucker, Chris .... Jan 01
Usher .... PerfArt V.1
Vega, Alexa .... Jan 04
Vidal, Christina .... PerfArt V.1
Washington, Denzel ... Jan 93; Update 02
Watson, Barry .... Sep 02
Watson, Emma .... Apr 03
Wayans, Keenen Ivory .... Jan 93
Welling, Tom .... PerfArt V.3
White, Jaleel .... Jan 96
Williams, Robin .... Apr 92
Williams, Tyler James .... Sep 06
Wilson, Mara .... Jan 97
Winfrey, Oprah .... Apr 92; Update 00; Business V.1
Winslet, Kate .... Sep 98
Witherspoon, Reese .... Apr 03
Wood, Elijah .... Apr 02
Adams, Ansel .... Artist V.1
Adams, William (will.i.am)
see Black Eyed Peas .... Apr 06
Adams, Yolanda .... Apr 03

Adu, Freddy .... Sport V.12
Affleck, Ben .... Sep 99
African Americans
see blacks
Agassi, Andre .... Jul 92
Agosto, Ben .... Sport V.14
Aguilera, Christina .... Apr 00
Aidid, Mohammed Farah ..... WorLdr V.2
Aikman, Troy .... Apr 95; Update 01
Alba, Jessica .... Sep 01
Albanian
Teresa, Mother .... Apr 98
Albright, Madeleine .... Apr 97
Alcindor, Lew
see Abdul-Jabbar, Kareem ...... Sport V.1
Aldrich, George .... Science V.11
Alexander, Lloyd .... Author V.6
Alexander, Shaun .... Apr 07
Algerian
Boulmerka, Hassiba .... Sport V.1
Ali, Laila .... Sport V.11
Ali, Muhammad .... Sport V.2
Allen, Marcus .... Sep 97
Allen, Tim .... Apr 94; Update 99
Allen, Tori .... Sport V.9
Alley, Kirstie .... Jul 92
Almond, David .... Author V.10
Alvarez, Julia .... Author V.17
Alvarez, Luis W. .... Science V.3
Aly & AJ .... Sep 08
Amanpour, Christiane .... Jan 01
Amend, Bill .... Author V.18
Amin, Idi .... WorLdr V.2
Amman, Simon .... Sport V.8
An Na .... Author V.12
Anders, C.J.
see Bennett, Cherie .... Author V.9
Anderson, Brett (Donna A.)
see Donnas .... Apr 04
Anderson, Gillian .... Jan 97
Anderson, Laurie Halse ...... Author V.11
Anderson, Marian .... Jan 94
Anderson, Terry .... Apr 92
André 3000
see OutKast .... Sep 04
Andretti, Mario .... Sep 94

491

CUMULATIVE GENERAL INDEX

Andrews, Ned . . . . .Sep 94
Angelou, Maya . . . . .Apr 93
Angolan
    Savimbi, Jonas . . . . .WorLdr V.2
animators
    see also cartoonists
    Hillenburg, Stephen . . . . .Author V.14
    Jones, Chuck . . . . .Author V.12
    Lasseter, John. . . . . .Sep 00
    Park, Nick . . . . .Sep 06
    Tartakovsky, Genndy . . . . . . .Author V.11
Aniston, Jennifer . . . . .Apr 99
Annan, Kofi . . . . Jan 98; Update 01
Anthony, Carmelo . . . . .Sep 07
apl.de.ap (Alan Pineda Lindo)
    see Black Eyed Peas . . . . .Apr 06
Applegate, K.A. . . . . .Jan 00
Arab-American
    Nye, Naomi Shihab . . . . .Author V.8
Arafat, Yasir . . . . .Sep 94; Update 94;
    Update 95; Update 96; Update 97; Update
    98; Update 00; Update 01; Update 02
Arantes do Nascimento, Edson
    see Pelé . . . . .Sport V.1
architects
    Berger, Francie . . . . .Sep 04
    Juster, Norton . . . . .Author V.14
    Lin, Maya . . . . Sep 97
    Pei, I.M. . . . . .Artist V.1
    Wright, Frank Lloyd . . . . .Artist V.1
Aristide, Jean-Bertrand . . . . .Jan 95;
    Update 01
Armstrong, Billie Joe
    see Green Day . . . . .Apr 06
Armstrong, Lance. . . . . .Sep 00; Update 00;
    Update 01; Update 02
Armstrong, Robb . . . . .Author V.9
Armstrong, William H. . . . . . . .Author V.7
Arnesen, Liv . . . . .Author V.15
Arnold, Roseanne . . . . .Oct 92
artists
    Adams, Ansel . . . . .Artist V.1
    Barron, Robert . . . . .Science V.9
    Bearden, Romare . . . . .Artist V.1
    Bemelmans, Ludwig . . . . .Author V.16
    Bennett, Olivia . . . . .Sep 03
    Calder, Alexander . . . . .Artist V.1
    Chagall, Marc . . . . .Artist V.1

Chihuly, Dale . . . . .Jan 06
Christo . . . . .Sep 96
Feelings, Tom . . . . .Author V.16
Frankenthaler, Helen . . . . .Artist V.1
Gorey, Edward . . . . .Author V.13
GrandPré, Mary . . . . .Author V.14
Johns, Jasper . . . . .Artist V.1
Lawrence, Jacob . . . .Artist V.1; Update 01
Lin, Maya . . . . Sep 97
Lobel, Arnold . . . . .Author V.18
Moore, Henry . . . . .Artist V.1
Moses, Grandma . . . . .Artist V.1
Nechita, Alexandra . . . . .Jan 98
Nevelson, Louise . . . . .Artist V.1
O'Keeffe, Georgia . . . . .Artist V.1
Parks, Gordon . . . . .Artist V.1
Pinkney, Jerry . . . . .Author V.2
Ringgold, Faith . . . . .Author V.2
Rivera, Diego . . . . .Artist V.1
Rockwell, Norman . . . . .Artist V.1
Warhol, Andy . . . . .Artist V.1
Asbaty, Diandra . . . . .Sport V.14
Ashanti .PerfArt V.2
Ashe, Arthur . . . . .Sep 93
Ashley, Maurice . . . . .Sep 99
Asians
    An Na . . . . .Author V.12
    Aung San Suu Kyi . . . . .Apr 96;
    Update 98; Update 01; Update 02
    Chan, Jackie . . . . .PerfArt V.1
    Chung, Connie . . . . . . .Jan 94; Update 96
    Dai Qing . . . . .WorLdr V.3
    Fu Mingxia . . . . .Sport V.5
    Guey, Wendy . . . . .Sep 96
    Ho, David . . . . .Science V.6
    Ka Hsaw Wa . . . . .WorLdr V.3
    Kadohata, Cynthia . . . . .Sep 06
    Kim Dae-jung . . . . .Sep 01
    Kwan, Michelle . . . . .Sport V.3; Update 02
    Lee, Jeanette . . . . .Apr 03
    Lin, Maya .Sep 97
    Ling, Lisa .Apr 08
    Ma, Yo-Yo .Jul 92
    Ohno, Apolo . . . . .Sport V.8
    Oka, Masi .Jan 08
    Pak, Se Ri . . . . .Sport V.4
    Park, Linda Sue . . . . .Author V.12
    Pei, I.M. .Artist V.1
    Shinoda, Mike (Linkin Park) . . . . . . .Jan 04
    Suzuki, Ichiro . . . . .Apr 08

CUMULATIVE GENERAL INDEX

Tan, Amy . . . . .Author V.9
Wang, An . . . . .Science V.2
Wie, Michelle . . . . .Sep 04
Woods, Tiger . . . . . . .Sport V.1; Update 00
Yamaguchi, Kristi . . . . .Apr 92
Yao Ming . . . . .Sep 03
Yep, Laurence . . . . .Author V.5
Asimov, Isaac .Jul 92
Askins, Renee . . . . .WorLdr V.1
astronauts
   Collins, Eileen . . . . .Science V.4
   Glenn, John .Jan 99
   Harris, Bernard . . . . .Science V.3
   Jemison, Mae . . . . .Oct 92
   Lovell, Jim . . . . .Jan 96
   Lucid, Shannon . . . . .Science V.2
   Ochoa, Ellen . . . . .Apr 01; Update 02
   Ride, Sally . . . . .Jan 92
   Whitson, Peggy . . . . .Science V.9
athletes
   see sports
Attenborough, David . . . . .Science V.4
Atwater-Rhodes, Amelia . . . . . .Author V.8
Aung San Suu Kyi . . . . .Apr 96; Update 98; Update 01; Update 02
Australians
   Beachley, Layne . . . . .Sport V.9
   Freeman, Cathy . . . . .Jan 01
   Irwin, Bindi .Apr 08
   Irwin, Steve . . . . .Science V.7
   Norman, Greg . . . . .Jan 94
   Travers, P.L. . . . . .Author V.2
   Webb, Karrie . . . . . . .Sport V.5; Update 01; Update 02
Austrian
   Bemelmans, Ludwig . . . . .Author V.16
authors
   Abbey, Edward . . . . .WorLdr V.1
   Alexander, Lloyd . . . . .Author V.6
   Almond, David . . . . .Author V.10
   Alvarez, Julia . . . . .Author V.17
   An Na . . . . .Author V.12
   Anderson Laurie Halse . . . . . .Author V.11
   Angelou, Maya . . . . .Apr 93
   Applegate, K.A. . . . . .Jan 00
   Armstrong, Robb . . . . .Author V.9
   Armstrong, William H. . . . . . . .Author V.7
   Arnesen, Liv . . . . .Author V.15
   Asimov, Isaac .Jul 92

Attenborough, David . . . . .Science V.4
Atwater-Rhodes, Amelia . . . . .Author V.8
Avi . . . . .Jan 93
Babbitt, Natalie . . . . .Jan 04
Baldwin, James . . . . .Author V.2
Bauer, Joan . . . . .Author V.10
Bemelmans, Ludwig . . . . .Author V.16
Bennett, Cherie . . . . .Author V.9
Benson, Mildred . . . . .Jan 03
Berenstain, Jan . . . . .Author V.2
Berenstain, Stan . . . . .Author V.2
Bloor, Edward . . . . .Author V.15
Blum, Deborah . . . . .Science V.8
Blume, Judy .Jan 92
Boyd, Candy Dawson . . . . .Author V.3
Bradbury, Ray . . . . .Author V.3
Brashares, Ann . . . . .Author V.15
Brody, Jane . . . . .Science V.2
Brooks, Gwendolyn . . . . .Author V.3
Brower, David . . . .WorLdr V.1; Update 01
Brown, Claude . . . . .Author V.12
Bruchac, Joseph . . . . .Author V.18
Byars, Betsy . . . . .Author V.4
Cabot, Meg . . . . .Author V.12
Caplan, Arthur . . . . .Science V.6
Card, Orson Scott . . . . .Author V.14
Carle, Eric . . . . .Author V.1
Carson, Rachel . . . . .WorLdr V.1
Chambers, Veronica . . . . .Author V.15
Childress, Alice . . . . .Author V.1
Choldenko, Gennifer . . . . .Author V.18
Cleary, Beverly . . . . .Apr 94
Clements, Andrew . . . . .Author V.13
Colfer, Eoin . . . . .Author V.13
Collier, Bryan . . . . .Author V.11
Collins, Billy . . . . .Author V.16
Cooney, Barbara . . . . .Author V.8
Cooney, Caroline B. . . . . .Author V.4
Cooper, Floyd . . . . .Author V.17
Cooper, Susan . . . . .Author V.17
Cormier, Robert . . .Author V.1; Update 01
Cosby, Bill . . . . .Jan 92
Coville, Bruce . . . . .Author V.9
Creech, Sharon . . . . .Author V.5
Crichton, Michael . . . . .Author V.5
Crilley, Mark . . . . .Author V.15
Cronin, John . . . . .WorLdr V.3
Curtis, Christopher Paul . . . . .Author V.4; Update 00
Cushman, Karen . . . . .Author V.5

493

CUMULATIVE GENERAL INDEX

Dahl, Roald . . . . .Author V.1
Dai Qing . . . . .WorLdr V.3
Danziger, Paula . . . . .Author V.6
Delany, Bessie . . . . .Sep 99
Delany, Sadie . . . . .Sep 99
dePaola, Tomie . . . . .Author V.5
DiCamillo, Kate . . . . .Author V.10
Douglas, Marjory Stoneman .WorLdr V.1; Update 98
Dove, Rita .Jan 94
Draper, Sharon . . . . .Apr 99
Dunbar, Paul Lawrence . . . . . .Author V.8
Duncan, Lois . . . . .Sep 93
Ellison, Ralph . . . . .Author V.3
Farmer, Nancy . . . . .Author V.6
Feelings, Tom . . . . .Author V.16
Fey, Tina . . . . .Author V.16
Feynman, Richard P. . . . . .Science V.10
Filipovic, Zlata . . . . .Sep 94
Fitzhugh, Louise . . . . .Author V.3
Flake, Sharon . . . . .Author V.13
Forman, James . . . . .Apr 05
Fox, Paula . . . . .Author V.15
Frank, Anne . . . . .Author V.4
Freedman, Russell . . . . .Author V.14
Funke, Cornelia . . . . .Sep 05
Gantos, Jack . . . . .Author V.10
Gates, Henry Louis Jr. . . . . .Apr 00
George, Jean Craighead . . . . . .Author V.3
Giff, Patricia Reilly . . . . .Author V.7
Gorey, Edward . . . . .Author V.13
Gould, Stephen Jay . . . . .Science V.2; Update 02
Grandin, Temple . . . . .Science V.3
Greenburg, Dan . . . . .Author V.14
Grimes, Nikki . . . . .Author V.14
Grisham, John . . . . .Author V.1
Guy, Rosa . . . . .Author V.9
Gwaltney, John Langston . . . .Science V.3
Haddix, Margaret Peterson . . .Author V.11
Hakim, Joy . . . . .Author V.16
Hale, Shannon . . . . .Author V.18
Haley, Alex .Apr 92
Hamilton, Virginia . . . . .Author V.1; Author V.12
Handford, Martin . . . . .Jan 92
Hansberry, Lorraine . . . . .Author V.5
Heinlein, Robert . . . . .Author V.4
Henry, Marguerite . . . . .Author V.4
Herriot, James . . . . .Author V.1

Hesse, Karen . . . . . .Author V.5; Update 02
Hiaasen, Carl . . . . .Author V.18
Hillenbrand, Laura . . . . .Author V.14
Hinton, S.E. . . . . .Author V.1
Hobbs, Will . . . . .Author V.18
Horvath, Polly . . . . .Author V.16
Howe, James . . . . .Author V.17
Hughes, Langston . . . . .Author V.7
Hurston, Zora Neale . . . . .Author V.6
Jackson, Shirley . . . . .Author V.6
Jacques, Brian . . . . .Author V.5
Jenkins, Jerry B. . . . . .Author V.16
Jiménez, Francisco . . . . .Author V.13
Johnson, Angela . . . . .Author V.6
Jones, Diana Wynne . . . . .Author V.15
Juster, Norton . . . . .Author V.14
Kadohata, Cynthia . . . . .Sep 06
Kamler, Kenneth . . . . .Science V.6
Kerr, M.E. . . . . .Author V.1
King, Stephen . . . . .Author V.1; Update 00
Konigsburg, E.L. . . . . .Author V.3
Krakauer, Jon . . . . .Author V.6
Kübler-Ross, Elisabeth . . . . . .Science V.10
LaDuke, Winona . . . . .WorLdr V.3; Update 00
LaHaye, Tim . . . . .Author V.16
Lansky, Bruce . . . . .Author V.17
Lasky, Kathryn . . . . .Author V.18
Lee, Harper . . . . .Author V.9
Lee, Stan . . . . .Author V.7; Update 02
Le Guin, Ursula K. . . . . .Author V.8
L'Engle, Madeleine . . . . .Jan 92; Apr 01
Leopold, Aldo . . . . .WorLdr V.3
Lester, Julius . . . . .Author V.7
Levine, Gail Carson . . . . .Author V.17
Lewis, C.S. . . . . .Author V.3
Lindgren, Astrid . . . . .Author V.13
Lionni, Leo . . . . .Author V.6
Lipsyte, Robert . . . . .Author V.12
Lobel, Arnold . . . . .Author V.18
Love, Susan . . . . .Science V.3
Lowry, Lois . . . . .Author V.4
Lynch, Chris . . . . .Author V.13
Macaulay, David . . . . .Author V.2
MacLachlan, Patricia . . . . .Author V.2
Martin, Ann M. . . . . .Jan 92
Martinez, Victor . . . . .Author V.15
McCloskey, Robert . . . . .Author V.15
McCully, Emily Arnold . . . . .Jul 92; Update 93

494

CUMULATIVE GENERAL INDEX

McDaniel, Lurlene . . . . .Author V.14
McDonald, Janet . . . . .Author V.18
McKissack, Fredrick L. . . . . .Author V.3
McKissack, Patricia C. . . . . .Author V.3
Mead, Margaret . . . . .Science V.2
Meltzer, Milton . . . . .Author V.11
Morrison, Lillian . . . . .Author V.12
Morrison, Toni . . . . .Jan 94
Moss, Cynthia . . . . .WorLdr V.3
Mowat, Farley . . . . .Author V.8
Muir, John . . . . .WorLdr V.3
Murie, Margaret . . . . .WorLdr V.1
Murie, Olaus J. . . . . .WorLdr V.1
Murphy, Jim . . . . .Author V.17
Myers, Walter Dean . . . .Jan 93; Update 94
Napoli, Donna Jo . . . . .Author V.16
Naylor, Phyllis Reynolds . . . . .Apr 93
Nelson, Marilyn . . . . .Author V.13
Nhat Hanh (Thich) . . . . .Jan 04
Nielsen, Jerri . . . . .Science V.7
Nixon, Joan Lowery . . . . .Author V.1
Noor al Hussein, Queen of Jordan . .Jan 05
Nye, Naomi Shihab . . . . .Author V.8
O'Dell, Scott . . . . .Author V.2
Oliver, Jamie . . . . .Apr 07
Opdyke, Irene Gut . . . . .Author V.9
Paolini, Christopher . . . . .Author V.16
Park, Linda Sue . . . . .Author V.12
Pascal, Francine . . . . .Author V.6
Paterson, Katherine . . . . .Author V.3
Paulsen, Gary . . . . .Author V.1
Peck, Richard . . . . .Author V.10
Peet, Bill . . . . .Author V.4
Perry, Tyler .Sep 08
Peterson, Roger Tory . . . . .WorLdr V.1
Pierce, Tamora . . . . .Author V.13
Pike, Christopher . . . . .Sep 96
Pinkney, Andrea Davis . . . . . .Author V.10
Pinkwater, Daniel . . . . .Author V.8
Pinsky, Robert . . . . .Author V.7
Potter, Beatrix . . . . .Author V.8
Poussaint, Alvin . . . . .Science V.9
Prelutsky, Jack . . . . .Author V.2; Sep 07
Pullman, Philip . . . . .Author V.9
Reid Banks, Lynne . . . . .Author V.2
Rennison, Louise . . . . .Author V.10
Rice, Anne . . . . .Author V.3
Rinaldi, Ann . . . . .Author V.8
Ringgold, Faith . . . . .Author V.2
Rogers, Fred . . . . .PerfArt V.3
Rowan, Carl . . . . .Sep 01
Rowling, J.K. . . . . .Sep 99; Update 00;
    Update 01; Update 02; Jan 08
Russell, Charlie . . . . .Science V.11
Ryan, Pam Muñoz . . . . .Author V.12
Rylant, Cynthia . . . . .Author V.1
Sachar, Louis . . . . .Author V.6
Sacks, Oliver . . . . .Science V.3
Salinger, J.D. . . . . .Author V.2
Saro-Wiwa, Ken . . . . .WorLdr V.1
Scarry, Richard . . . . .Sep 94
Scieszka, Jon . . . . .Author V.9
Sendak, Maurice . . . . .Author V.2
Senghor, Léopold Sédar . . . . .WorLdr V.2
Seuss, Dr. . . . . .Jan 92
Silverstein, Shel . . . . .Author V.3;
    Update 99
Sleator, William . . . . .Author V.11
Small, David . . . . .Author V.10
Smith, Betty . . . . .Author V.17
Snicket, Lemony . . . . .Author V.12
Snyder, Zilpha Keatley . . . . . .Author V.17
Sones, Sonya . . . . .Author V.11
Soto, Gary . . . . .Author V.5
Speare, Elizabeth George . . . . .Sep 95
Spiegelman, Art . . . . .Author V.17
Spinelli, Jerry . . . . .Apr 93
Spock, Benjamin . . . . . .Sep 95; Update 98
Steingraber, Sandra . . . . .Science V.9
Stepanek, Mattie . . . . .Apr 02
Stine, R.L. .Apr 94
Strasser, Todd . . . . .Author V.7
Tan, Amy . . . . .Author V.9
Tarbox, Katie . . . . .Author V.10
Taylor, Mildred D. . . . . .Author V.1;
    Update 02
Thomas, Lewis . . . . .Apr 94
Thomas, Rob . . . . .Jan 07
Tolan, Stephanie S. . . . . .Author V.14
Tolkien, J.R.R. . . . . .Jan 02
Travers, P.L. . . . . .Author V.2
Tyson, Neil deGrasse . . . . . . .Science V.11
Van Allsburg, Chris . . . . .Apr 92
Van Draanen, Wendelin . . . . .Author V.11
Voigt, Cynthia . . . . .Oct 92
Vonnegut, Kurt Jr. . . . . .Author V.1
Wardlaw, Lee . . . . .Sep 08
White, E.B. . . . . .Author V.1
White, Ruth . . . . .Author V.11
Wilder, Laura Ingalls . . . . .Author V.3

495

CUMULATIVE GENERAL INDEX

Wiles, Deborah ....Author V.18
Williams, Garth ....Author V.2
Williams, Lori Aurelia ....Author V.16
Williamson, Kevin ....Author V.6
Wilson, August ....Author V.4
Wilson, Edward O. ....Science V.8
Wolff, Virginia Euwer ....Author V.13
Woodson, Jacqueline ....Author V.7;
 Update 01
Wrede, Patricia C. ....Author V.7
Wright, Richard ....Author V.5
Yep, Laurence ....Author V.5
Yolen, Jane ....Author V.7
Zindel, Paul ....Author V.1; Update 02
autobiographies
 Handford, Martin ....Jan 92
 Iacocca, Lee ....Jan 92
 L'Engle, Madeleine ....Jan 92
 Parkinson, Jennifer ....Apr 95
Avi ....Jan 93
Babbitt, Bruce ....Jan 94
Babbitt, Natalie ....Jan 04
Backstreet Boys ....Jan 00
Bahrke, Shannon ....Sport V.8
Bailey, Donovan ....Sport V.2
Baiul, Oksana ....Apr 95
Baker, James ....Oct 92
Baldwin, James ....Author V.2
Ballard, Robert ....Science V.4
ballet
 see dance
Banda, Hastings Kamuzu .....WorLdr V.2
Bangladeshi
 Yunus, Muhammad ....Sep 07
Banks, Tyra ....PerfArt V.2
Barbadian
 Rihanna ....Apr 08
Bardeen, John ....Science V.1
Barkley, Charles ....Apr 92; Update 02
Barr, Roseanne
 see Arnold, Roseanne ....Oct 92
Barron, Robert ....Science V.9
Barrymore, Drew ....Jan 01
Barton, Hazel ....Science V.6
baseball
 Aaron, Hank ....Sport V.1
 Beckett, Josh ....Sport V.11
 Bonds, Barry ....Jan 03

Fielder, Cecil ....Sep 93
Griffey, Ken Jr. ....Sport V.1
Hernandez, Livan ....Apr 98
Jackson, Bo ....Jan 92; Update 93
Jeter, Derek ....Sport V.4
Johnson, Randy ....Sport V.9
Jordan, Michael ....Jan 92; Update 93;
 Update 94; Update 95; Update 99;
 Update 01
Maddux, Greg ....Sport V.3
Mantle, Mickey ....Jan 96
Martinez, Pedro ....Sport V.5
McGwire, Mark ....Jan 99; Update 99
Moreno, Arturo R. ....Business V.1
Pujols, Albert ....Sport V.12
Ramirez, Manny ....Sport V.13
Ripken, Cal Jr. ......Sport V.1; Update 01
Robinson, Jackie ....Sport V.3
Rodriguez, Alex ....Sport V.6
Rodriguez, Ivan "Pudge" ....Jan 07
Rose, Pete ....Jan 92
Ryan, Nolan ....Oct 92; Update 93
Sanders, Deion ....Sport V.1
Schilling, Curt ....Sep 05
Soriano, Alfonso ....Sport V.10
Sosa, Sammy ....Jan 99; Update 99
Suzuki, Ichiro ....Apr 08
Williams, Ted ....Sport V.9
Winfield, Dave ....Jan 93
Basich, Tina ....Sport V.12
basketball
 Abdul-Jabbar, Kareem ....Sport V.1
 Anthony, Carmelo ....Sep 07
 Barkley, Charles ....Apr 92; Update 02
 Bird, Larry ....Jan 92; Update 98
 Bird, Sue ....Sport V.9
 Bryant, Kobe ....Apr 99
 Carter, Vince ....Sport V.5; Update 01
 Catchings, Tamika ....Sport V.14
 Chamberlain, Wilt ....Sport V.4
 Dumars, Joe ....Sport V.3; Update 99
 Duncan, Tim ....Apr 04
 Ewing, Patrick ....Jan 95; Update 02
 Ford, Cheryl ....Sport V.11
 Garnett, Kevin ....Sport V.6
 Hardaway, Anfernee "Penny" ..Sport V.2
 Hill, Grant ....Sport V.1
 Holdsclaw, Chamique. ....Sep 00
 Iverson, Allen ....Sport V.7
 Jackson, Phil ....Sport V.10

CUMULATIVE GENERAL INDEX

James, LeBron . . . . Sport V.12
Johnson, Magic . . . . Apr 92; Update 02
Jordan, Michael . . . . Jan 92; Update 93;
  Update 94; Update 95; Update 99;
  Update 01
Kidd, Jason . . . . Sport V.9
Lennox, Betty . . . . Sport V.13
Leslie, Lisa . . . . Jan 04
Lobo, Rebecca . . . . Sport V.3
McGrady, Tracy . . . . Sport V.11
Nash, Steve . . . . Jan 06
Olajuwon, Hakeem . . . . Sep 95
O'Neal, Shaquille . . . . Sep 93
Palmer, Violet . . . . Sep 05
Pippen, Scottie . . . . Oct 92
Robinson, David . . . . Sep 96
Rodman, Dennis . . . . . . Apr 96; Update 99
Stiles, Jackie . . . . Sport V.6
Stockton, John . . . . Sport V.3
Summitt, Pat . . . . Sport V.3
Swoopes, Sheryl . . . . Sport V.2
Taurasi, Diana . . . . Sport V.10
Wade, Dwyane . . . . Sport V.14
Wallace, Ben . . . . Jan 05
Ward, Charlie . . . . Apr 94
Weatherspoon, Teresa . . . . Sport V.12
Yao Ming . . . . Sep 03
Bass, Bill . . . . Apr 08
Bass, Lance
  see *N Sync . . . . Jan 01
Bates, Daisy . . . . Apr 00
Battle, Kathleen . . . . Jan 93
Bauer, Joan . . . . Author V.10
Beachley, Layne . . . . Sport V.9
Bearden, Romare . . . . Artist V.1
beauty pageants
  Lopez, Charlotte . . . . Apr 94
  Whitestone, Heather . . . . Apr 95;
    Update 02
Beckett, Josh . . . . Sport V.11
Beckham, David . . . . Jan 04
Belbin, Tanith . . . . Sport V.14
Belgian
  Clijsters, Kim . . . . Apr 04
Bell, Drake . . . . Jan 07
Bell, Kristen . . . . Sep 05
Bellamy, Carol . . . . Jan 06

Bemelmans, Ludwig . . . . Author V.16
Ben-Ari, Miri . . . . Jan 06
Benjamin, André
  see OutKast . . . . Sep 04
Benjamin, Regina . . . . Science V.9
Bennett, Cherie . . . . Author V.9
Bennett, Olivia . . . . Sep 03
Bennington, Chester
  see Linkin Park . . . . Jan 04
Benson, Mildred . . . . Jan 03
Berenstain, Jan . . . . Author V.2
Berenstain, Stan . . . . Author V.2
Bergen, Candice . . . . Sep 93
Berger, Francie . . . . Sep 04
Berners-Lee, Tim . . . . Science V.7
Berry, Halle . . . . Jan 95; Update 02
Bethe, Hans A. . . . . Science V.3
Bezos, Jeff . . . . Apr 01
Bhutto, Benazir . . . . Apr 95; Update 99;
  Update 02
Bialik, Mayim . . . . Jan 94
bicycle riding
  Armstrong, Lance. . . . . Sep 00;
    Update 00; Update 01; Update 02
  Dunlap, Alison . . . . Sport V.7
  LeMond, Greg . . . . Sport V.1
  Mirra, Dave . . . . Sep 02
Big Boi
  see OutKast . . . . Sep 04
billiards
  Lee, Jeanette . . . . Apr 03
Binford, Greta . . . . Jan 08
bin Laden, Osama . . . . Apr 02
Bird, Larry . . . . Jan 92; Update 98
Bird, Sue . . . . Sport V.9
Black, Jack . . . . Jan 05
Black, Thomas
  see Black, Jack . . . . Jan 05
Black Eyed Peas . . . . Apr 06
Blackmun, Harry . . . . Jan 00
blacks
  Aaliyah . . . . Jan 02
  Aaron, Hank . . . . Sport V.1
  Abdul-Jabbar, Kareem . . . . Sport V.1
  Adams, Yolanda . . . . Apr 03
  Adu, Freddy . . . . Sport V.12
  Aidid, Mohammed Farah . . . . WorLdr V.2

497

CUMULATIVE GENERAL INDEX

Alexander, Shaun . . . . .Apr 07
Ali, Laila .Sport V.11
Ali, Muhammad . . . . .Sport V.2
Allen, Marcus . . . . .Sep 97
Amin, Idi . . . . .WorLdr V.2
Anderson, Marian . . . . .Jan 94
Angelou, Maya . . . . .Apr 93
Annan, Kofi . . . . Jan 98; Update 01
Anthony, Carmelo . . . . .Sep 07
apl.de.ap (Alan Pineda Lindo) . . . . .Apr 06
Aristide, Jean-Bertrand . . . . .Jan 95;
  Update 01
Armstrong, Robb . . . . .Author V.9
Ashanti .PerfArt V.2
Ashe, Arthur . . . . .Sep 93
Ashley, Maurice . . . . .Sep 99
Bailey, Donovan . . . . .Sport V.2
Baldwin, James . . . . .Author V.2
Banda, Hastings Kamuzu . . . .WorLdr V.2
Banks, Tyra . . . . .PerfArt V.2
Bates, Daisy .Apr 00
Battle, Kathleen . . . . .Jan 93
Bearden, Romare . . . . .Artist V.1
Benjamin, Regina . . . . .Science V.9
Berry, Halle .Jan 95
Blake, James . . . . .Sport V.14
Blige, Mary J. . . . . .Apr 02
Bonds, Barry .Jan 03
Booker, Cory .Jan 08
Boyd, Candy Dawson . . . . .Author V.3
Boyz II Men .Jan 96
Bradley, Ed . . . . .Apr 94
Brandy . . . . .Apr 96
Brooks, Gwendolyn . . . . .Author V.3
Brooks, Vincent . . . . .Sep 03
Brown, Chris . . . . .Apr 07
Brown, Claude . . . . .Author V.12
Brown, Ron .Sep 96
Bryant, Kobe . . . . .Apr 99
Canady, Alexa . . . . .Science V.6
Carson, Ben . . . . .Science V.4
Carter, Majora . . . . .Sep 08
Carter, Regina . . . . .Sep 07
Carter, Vince . . . . . . .Sport V.5; Update 01
Catchings, Tamika . . . . .Sport V.14
Chamberlain, Wilt . . . . .Sport V.4
Chambers, Veronica . . . . .Author V.15
Champagne, Larry III . . . . .Apr 96
Chavis, Benjamin . . . . . .Jan 94; Update 94
Childress, Alice . . . . .Author V.1

Clemons, Kortney . . . . .Sep 07
Collier, Bryan . . . . .Author V.11
Combs, Sean (Puff Daddy) . . . . .Apr 98
Coolio . . . . .Sep 96
Cooper, Floyd . . . . .Author V.17
Cosby, Bill . . . . .Jan 92
Cruz, Celia . . . . .Apr 04
Culpepper, Daunte . . . . .Sport V.13
Curtis, Christopher Paul . . . . .Author V.4;
  Update 00
Dawson, Matel Jr. . . . . .Jan 04
Dayne, Ron .Apr 00
Delany, Bessie . . . . .Sep 99
Delany, Sadie . . . . .Sep 99
Destiny's Child . . . . .Apr 01
Devers, Gail . . . . .Sport V.2
Dove, Rita . . . . .Jan 94
Draper, Sharon . . . . .Apr 99
Dumars, Joe . . . . .Sport V.3; Update 99
Dunbar, Paul Lawrence . . . . . .Author V.8
Duncan, Tim . . . . .Apr 04
Dworkin, Aaron . . . . .Apr 07
Edelman, Marian Wright . . . . .Apr 93
Elliott, Missy . . . . .PerfArt V.3
Ellison, Ralph . . . . .Author V.3
Eve . . . . .Jan 05
Ewing, Patrick . . . . .Jan 95; Update 02
Farrakhan, Louis . . . . .Jan 97
Feelings, Tom . . . . .Author V.16
Felix, Allyson . . . . .Sport V.10
Fielder, Cecil . . . . .Sep 93
Fitzgerald, Ella . . . . .Jan 97
Flake, Sharon . . . . .Author V.13
Flowers, Vonetta . . . . .Sport V.8
Ford, Cheryl . . . . .Sport V.11
Forman, James . . . . .Apr 05
Franklin, Aretha . . . . .Apr 01
Freeman, Cathy . . . . .Jan 01
Garnett, Kevin . . . . .Sport V.6
Gates, Henry Louis Jr. . . . . .Apr 00
Gayle, Helene . . . . .Science V.8
George, Eddie . . . . .Sport V.6
Gillespie, Dizzy . . . . .Apr 93
Glover, Savion . . . . .Apr 99
Goldberg, Whoopi . . . . .Apr 94
Gonzalez, Tony . . . . .Sport V.11
Graves, Earl . . . . .Business V.1
Griffey, Ken Jr. . . . . .Sport V.1
Grimes, Nikki . . . . .Author V.14
Gumbel, Bryant . . . . .Apr 97

CUMULATIVE GENERAL INDEX

Guy, Jasmine . . . . .Sep 93
Guy, Rosa . . . . .Author V.9
Gwaltney, John Langston . . . .Science V.3
Haley, Alex . . . . .Apr 92
Hamilton, Virginia . . . . .Author V.1;
   Author V.12
Hammer . . . . .Jan 92
Hansberry, Lorraine . . . . .Author V.5
Hardaway, Anfernee "Penny" . .Sport V.2
Harris, Bernard . . . . .Science V.3
Hayden, Carla . . . . .Sep 04
Hayes, Tyrone . . . . .Science V.10
Hernandez, Livan . . . . .Apr 98
Hill, Anita . . . . .Jan 93
Hill, Grant . . . . .Sport V.1
Hill, Lauryn .Sep 99
Holdsclaw, Chamique. . . . . .Sep 00
Holmes, Priest . . . . .Apr 05
Honoré, Russel . . . . .Jan 06
Hoskins, Michele . . . . .Business V.1
Houston, Whitney . . . . .Sep 94
Howard, Tim . . . . .Apr 06
Hudson, Jennifer . . . . .Jan 08
Hughes, Langston . . . . .Author V.7
Hunter-Gault, Charlayne . . . . .Jan 00
Hurston, Zora Neale . . . . .Author V.6
Ice-T . . . . .Apr 93
Iverson, Allen . . . . .Sport V.7
Jackson, Bo . . . . .Jan 92; Update 93
Jackson, Jesse . . . . .Sep 95; Update 01
Jackson, Shirley Ann . . . . .Science V.2
Jakes, T.D. . . . . .Jan 05
James, LeBron . . . . .Sport V.12
Jamison, Judith . . . . .Jan 96
Jemison, Mae . . . . .Oct 92
Jeter, Derek . . . . .Sport V.4
Johnson, Angela . . . . .Author V.6
Johnson, John . . . . .Jan 97
Johnson, Keyshawn . . . . .Sport V.10
Johnson, Lonnie . . . . .Science V.4
Johnson, Magic . . . . . . .Apr 92; Update 02
Johnson, Michael . . . . .Jan 97; Update 00
Jones, James Earl . . . . .Jan 95
Jones, Marion . . . . .Sport V.5
Jones, Quincy . . . . .PerfArt V.2
Jordan, Barbara . . . . .Apr 96
Jordan, Michael . . . . . . .Jan 92; Update 93;
   Update 94; Update 95; Update 99;
   Update 01

Joyner-Kersee, Jackie . . . . .Oct 92;
   Update 96; Update 97; Update 98
Kaunda, Kenneth . . . . .WorLdr V.2
Kenyatta, Jomo . . . . .WorLdr V.2
Keys, Alicia . . . . .Jan 07
Kidd, Jason . . . . .Sport V.9
King, Coretta Scott . . . . .Sep 06
Koff, Clea . . . . .Science V.11
Lawrence, Jacob . . . .Artist V.1; Update 01
Lee, Spike . . . . .Apr 92
Lennox, Betty . . . . .Sport V.13
Leslie, Lisa . . . . .Jan 04
Lester, Julius . . . . .Author V.7
Lewis, Carl . . . . .Sep 96; Update 97
Lewis, John .Jan 03
Long, Irene D. . . . . .Jan 04
Maathai, Wangari . . . .WorLdr V.1; Sep 05
Mac, Bernie . . . . .PerfArt V.1
Mandela, Nelson . . . . . .Jan 92; Update 94;
   Update 01
Mandela, Winnie . . . . .WorLdr V.2
Marsalis, Wynton . . . . .Apr 92
Marshall, Thurgood . . . .Jan 92; Update 93
Martinez, Pedro . . . . .Sport V.5
Maxwell, Jody-Anne . . . . .Sep 98
McCarty, Oseola . . . . . . .Jan 99; Update 99
McDonald, Janet . . . . .Author V.18
McGrady, Tracy . . . . .Sport V.11
McGruder, Aaron . . . . .Author V.10
McKissack, Fredrick L. . . . . . . .Author V.3
McKissack, Patricia C. . . . . . . .Author V.3
McNabb, Donovan . . . . .Apr 03
McNair, Steve . . . . .Sport V.11
Mitchell-Raptakis, Karen . . . . .Jan 05
Mobutu Sese Seko . . . . .WorLdr V.2;
   Update 97
Morgan, Garrett . . . . .Science V.2
Morrison, Sam . . . . .Sep 97
Morrison, Toni . . . . .Jan 94
Moss, Randy . . . . .Sport V.4
Mugabe, Robert . . . . .WorLdr V.2
Murphy, Eddie . . . . .PerfArt V.2
Myers, Walter Dean . . . .Jan 93; Update 94
Ndeti, Cosmas . . . . .Sep 95
Nelly . . . . .Sep 03
Nelson, Marilyn . . . . .Author V.13
Nkrumah, Kwame . . . . .WorLdr V.2
Norman, Christina . . . . .Apr 08
Nyerere, Julius Kambarage . . .WorLdr V.2;
   Update 99

CUMULATIVE GENERAL INDEX

Obama, Barack . . . . Jan 07
O'Brien, Soledad . . . . Jan 07
Olajuwon, Hakeem . . . . Sep 95
Oliver, Patsy Ruth . . . . WorLdr V.1
O'Neal, Shaquille . . . . Sep 93
OutKast . . . . Sep 04
Palmer, Violet . . . . Sep 05
Parks, Gordon . . . . Artist V.1
Parks, Rosa . . . . Apr 92; Update 94; Apr 06
Payton, Walter . . . . Jan 00
Pelé . . . . Sport V.1
Perry, Tyler . . . . Sep 08
Pinkney, Andrea Davis . . . . . . Author V.10
Pinkney, Jerry . . . . Author V.2
Pippen, Scottie . . . . Oct 92
Poussaint, Alvin . . . . Science V.9
Powell, Colin . . . . Jan 92; Update 93; Update 95; Update 01
Queen Latifah . . . . Apr 92
Raven . . . . Apr 04
Rice, Condoleezza . . . . Apr 02
Rice, Jerry . . . . Apr 93
Rihanna . . . . Apr 08
Ringgold, Faith . . . . Author V.2
Roba, Fatuma . . . . Sport V.3
Robinson, David . . . . Sep 96
Robinson, Jackie . . . . Sport V.3
Rodman, Dennis . . . . . . Apr 96; Update 99
Romeo, Lil' . . . . Jan 06
Rowan, Carl . . . . Sep 01
Rudolph, Wilma . . . . Apr 95
Salt 'N' Pepa . . . . Apr 95
Sanders, Barry . . . . Sep 95; Update 99
Sanders, Deion . . . . Sport V.1
Sapp, Warren . . . . Sport V.5
Saro-Wiwa, Ken . . . . WorLdr V.1
Satcher, David . . . . Sep 98
Savimbi, Jonas . . . . WorLdr V.2
Schwikert, Tasha . . . . Sport V.7
Scurry, Briana . . . . Jan 00
Senghor, Léopold Sédar . . . . . WorLdr V.2
Shabazz, Betty . . . . Apr 98
Shakur, Tupac . . . . Apr 97
Simmons, Russell . . . . Apr 06
Simmons, Ruth . . . . Sep 02
Smith, Emmitt . . . . Sep 94
Smith, Will . . . . Sep 94
Soriano, Alfonso . . . . Sport V.10
Sosa, Sammy . . . . Jan 99; Update 99
Stanford, John . . . . Sep 99
Stewart, James Jr. . . . . Apr 08
Stewart, Kordell . . . . Sep 98
Strahan, Michael . . . . Sport V.12
Swoopes, Sheryl . . . . Sport V.2
Tarvin, Herbert . . . . Apr 97
Taylor, Mildred D. . . . . Author V.1; Update 02
Thomas, Clarence . . . . Jan 92
Tomlinson, LaDainian . . . . Sport V.14
Tubman, William V.S. . . . . WorLdr V.2
Tucker, Chris . . . . Jan 01
Tyson, Neil deGrasse . . . . Science V.11
Usher . . . . PerfArt V.1
Vick, Michael . . . . Sport V.9
Wade, Dwyane . . . . Sport V.14
Wallace, Ben . . . . Jan 05
Ward, Charlie . . . . Apr 94
Ward, Lloyd D. . . . . Jan 01
Washington, Denzel . . . Jan 93; Update 02
Watley, Natasha . . . . Sport V.11
Wayans, Keenen Ivory . . . . Jan 93
Weatherspoon, Teresa . . . . Sport V.12
White, Jaleel . . . . Jan 96
White, Reggie . . . . Jan 98
WilderBrathwaite, Gloria . . . . . Science V.7
will.i.am (William Adams) . . . . Apr 06
Williams, Lori Aurelia . . . . Author V.16
Williams, Serena . . . . Sport V.4; Update 00; Update 02
Williams, Tyler James . . . . Sep 06
Williams, Venus . . . . . . Jan 99; Update 00; Update 01; Update 02
Willingham, Tyrone . . . . Sep 02
Wilson, August . . . . Author V.4
Winans, CeCe . . . . Apr 00
Winfield, Dave . . . . Jan 93
Winfrey, Oprah . . . . Apr 92; Update 00; Business V.1
Woods, Tiger . . . . Sport V.1; Update 00; Sport V.6
Woodson, Jacqueline . . . . Author V.7; Update 01
Wright, Richard . . . . Author V.5
Blair, Bonnie . . . . Apr 94; Update 95
Blair, Tony . . . . Apr 04
Blake, James . . . . Sport V.14
Blanchard, Rachel . . . . Apr 97
Bledel, Alexis . . . . Jan 03

CUMULATIVE GENERAL INDEX

Bleiler, Gretchen . . . . Sport V.13
Blige, Mary J. Apr 02
Bloom, Orlando . . . . Sep 04
Bloor, Edward . . . . Author V.15
Blum, Deborah . . . . Science V.8
Blume, Judy . . . . Jan 92
BMX
   see bicycle riding
bobsledding
   Flowers, Vonetta . . . . Sport V.8
Bonds, Barry . . . . Jan 03
Bono . . . . Sep 06
Booker, Cory . . . . Jan 08
Borgman, Jim . . . . Author V.15
Bosnian
   Filipovic, Zlata . . . . Sep 94
Boulmerka, Hassiba . . . . Sport V.1
Bourdon, Rob
   see Linkin Park . . . . Jan 04
Bourke-White, Margaret . . . . Artist V.1
Boutros-Ghali, Boutros . . . . Apr 93;
   Update 98
bowling
   Asbaty, Diandra . . . . Sport V.14
boxing
   Ali, Laila . . . . Sport V.11
   Ali, Muhammad . . . . Sport V.2
Boyd, Candy Dawson . . . . Author V.3
Boyle, Ryan . . . . Sport V.10
Boyz II Men . . . . Jan 96
Bradbury, Ray . . . . Author V.3
Bradley, Ed . . . . Apr 94
Brady, Tom . . . . Sport V.7
Branch, Michelle . . . . PerfArt V.3
Brandis, Jonathan . . . . Sep 95
Brandy . . . . Apr 96
Brashares, Ann . . . . Author V.15
Brazilians
   da Silva, Fabiola . . . . Sport V.9
   Mendes, Chico . . . . WorLdr V.1
   Pelé . . . . Sport V.1
Breathed, Berke . . . . Jan 92
Brin, Sergey . . . . Sep 05
Brody, Adam . . . . Sep 05
Brody, Jane . . . . Science V.2
Brooks, Garth . . . . Oct 92
Brooks, Gwendolyn . . . . Author V.3

Brooks, Vincent . . . . Sep 03
Brower, David . . . . . WorLdr V.1; Update 01
Brown, Chris . . . . Apr 07
Brown, Claude . . . . Author V.12
Brown, Ron . . . . Sep 96
Bruchac, Joseph . . . . Author V.18
Brundtland, Gro Harlem . . . . . . Science V.3
Bryan, Zachery Ty . . . . Jan 97
Bryant, Kobe . . . . Apr 99
Buckley, Kelsie . . . . Sep 06
Buffett, Warren . . . . Business V.1
Bulgarian
   Christo . . . . Sep 96
Burger, Warren . . . . Sep 95
Burke, Chris . . . . Sep 93
Burmese
   Aung San Suu Kyi . . . . Apr 96;
     Update 98; Update 01; Update 02
   Ka Hsaw Wa . . . . WorLdr V.3
Burns, Ken . . . . Jan 95
Burnside, Aubyn . . . . Sep 02
Burrell, Stanley Kirk
   see Hammer . . . . Jan 92
Bush, Barbara . . . . Jan 92
Bush, George . . . . Jan 92
Bush, George W. . . . . Sep 00; Update 00;
   Update 01; Update 02
Bush, Laura . . . . Apr 03
Bush, Sophia . . . . Apr 08
business
   Barron, Robert . . . . Science V.9
   Berger, Francie . . . . Sep 04
   Bezos, Jeff . . . . Apr 01
   Brashares, Ann . . . . Author V.15
   Brin, Sergey . . . . Sep 05
   Brown, Ron . . . . Sep 96
   Buffett, Warren . . . . Business V.1
   Capolino, Peter . . . . Business V.1
   Case, Steve . . . . Science V.5
   Chavez, Julz . . . . Sep 02
   Cheney, Dick . . . . Jan 02
   Combs, Sean (Puff Daddy) . . . . Apr 98
   Crabtree, Taylor . . . . Jan 07
   Dell, Michael . . . . Business V.1
   Diemer, Walter . . . . Apr 98
   Fields, Debbi . . . . Jan 96
   Fiorina, Carly . . . . Sep 01; Update 01;
     Update 02

CUMULATIVE GENERAL INDEX

Fox, Vicente . . . . .Apr 03
Fuller, Millard . . . . .Apr 03
Gates, Bill . . . . .Apr 93; Update 98;
   Update 00; Science V.5; Update 01
Graves, Earl . . . . .Business V.1
Groppe, Laura . . . . .Science V.5
Handler, Ruth . . . . .Apr 98; Update 02
Hoskins, Michele . . . . .Business V.1
Iacocca, Lee A. . . . . .Jan 92
Jobs, Steven . . . . .Jan 92; Science V.5
Johnson, John . . . . .Jan 97
Johnson, Lonnie . . . . .Science V.4
Joy, Bill . . . . .Science V.10
Kamen, Dean . . . . .Science V.11
Kapell, Dave . . . . .Science V.8
Kurzweil, Raymond . . . . .Science V.2
Kwolek, Stephanie . . . . .Science V.10
Land, Edwin . . . . .Science V.1
Mars, Forrest Sr. . . . . .Science V.4
McGrath, Judy . . . . .Business V.1
Mitchell-Raptakis, Karen . . . . .Jan 05
Mohajer, Dineh . . . . .Jan 02
Moreno, Arturo R. . . . . .Business V.1
Morgan, Garrett . . . . .Science V.2
Morita, Akio . . . . .Science V.4
Norman, Christina . . . . .Apr 08
Oliver, Jamie . . . . .Apr 07
Page, Larry .Sep 05
Perot, H. Ross . . . . .Apr 92; Update 93
Rowland, Pleasant T. . . . . . . .Business V.1
Romero, John . . . . .Science V.8
Simmons, Russell . . . . .Apr 06
Spade, Kate .Apr 07
Stachowski, Richie . . . . .Science V.3
Stewart, Martha . . . . .Business V.1
Swanson, Janese . . . . .Science V.4
Tandy, Karen P. . . . . .Jan 08
Thomas, Dave . . . . .Apr 96; Update 02
Tompkins, Douglas . . . . .WorLdr V.3
Trump, Donald . . . . .Apr 05
Wang, An . . . . .Science V.2
Ward, Lloyd D. . . . . .Jan 01
Whitman, Meg . . . . .Sep 03
Winfrey, Oprah . . . . .Business V.1
Wright, Will .Apr 04
Butcher, Susan . . . . .Sport V.1
Byars, Betsy . . . . .Author V.4
Bynes, Amanda . . . . .Sep 03
Cabot, Meg . . . . .Author V.12

Caldecott Medal
   Cooney, Barbara . . . . .Author V.8
   Lobel, Arnold . . . . .Author V.18
   Macauley, David . . . . .Author V.2
   McCully, Emily Arnold . .Jul 92; Update 93
   Myers, Walter Dean . . . .Jan 93; Update 94
   Sendak, Maurice . . . . .Author V.2
   Small, David . . . . .Author V.10
   Van Allsburg, Chris . . . . .Apr 92
Calder, Alexander . . . . .Artist V.1
Calderone, Mary S. . . . . .Science V.3
Cameron, Candace . . . . .Apr 95
Campbell, Neve . . . . .Apr 98
Canadians
   Bailey, Donovan . . . . .Sport V.2
   Belbin, Tanith . . . . .Sport V.14
   Blanchard, Rachel . . . . .Apr 97
   Campbell, Neve . . . . .Apr 98
   Candy, John . . . . .Sep 94
   Carrey, Jim .Apr 96
   Crosby, Sidney . . . . .Sport V.14
   Dion, Celine . . . . .Sep 97
   Galdikas, Biruté . . . . .Science V.4
   Giguère, Jean-Sébastien . . . . . .Sport V.10
   Gretzky, Wayne . . . . . . .Jan 92; Update 93;
      Update 99
   Howe, Gordie . . . . .Sport V.2
   Jennings, Peter . . . . .Jul 92
   Johnston, Lynn . . . . .Jan 99
   Kielburger, Craig . . . . .Jan 00
   lang, k.d. . . . . .Sep 93
   Lavigne, Avril . . . . .PerfArt V.2
   Lemieux, Mario . . . . .Jul 92; Update 93
   Martin, Bernard . . . . .WorLdr V.3
   McAdams, Rachel . . . . .Apr 06
   Messier, Mark . . . . .Apr 96
   Morissette, Alanis . . . . .Apr 97
   Mowat, Farley . . . . .Author V.8
   Myers, Mike . . . . .PerfArt V.3
   Nash, Steve .Jan 06
   Niedermayer, Scott . . . . .Jan 08
   Priestley, Jason . . . . .Apr 92
   Reeves, Keanu . . . . .Jan 04
   Roy, Patrick . . . . .Sport V.7
   Russell, Charlie . . . . .Science V.11
   Sakic, Joe . . . . .Sport V.6
   Shatner, William . . . . .Apr 95
   Twain, Shania . . . . .Apr 99
   Vernon, Mike . . . . .Jan 98; Update 02
   Watson, Paul . . . . .WorLdr V.1

CUMULATIVE GENERAL INDEX

Wolf, Hazel . . . . .WorLdr V.3
Yzerman, Steve . . . . .Sport V.2
Canady, Alexa . . . . .Science V.6
Candy, John . . . . .Sep 94
Cantore, Jim . . . . .Science V.9
Caplan, Arthur . . . . .Science V.6
Capolino, Peter . . . . .Business V.1
Capriati, Jennifer . . . . .Sport V.6
car racing
    Andretti, Mario . . . . .Sep 94
    Earnhardt, Dale . . . . .Apr 01
    Earnhardt, Dale Jr. . . . . .Sport V.12
    Gordon, Jeff . . . . .Apr 99
    Muldowney, Shirley . . . . .Sport V.7
    Newman, Ryan . . . . .Sport V.11
    Patrick, Danica . . . . .Apr 06
    Petty, Richard . . . . .Sport V.2
    Stewart, Tony . . . . .Sport V.9
Card, Orson Scott . . . . .Author V.14
Carey, Mariah . . . . .Apr 96
Carle, Eric . . . . .Author V.1
Carmona, Richard . . . . .Science V.8
Carpenter, Mary Chapin . . . . .Sep 94
Carrabba, Chris . . . . .Apr 05
Carrey, Jim . . . . .Apr 96
Carson, Ben . . . . .Science V.4
Carson, Rachel . . . . .WorLdr V.1
Carter, Aaron . . . . .Sep 02
Carter, Chris . . . . .Author V.4
Carter, Jimmy . . . . .Apr 95; Update 02
Carter, Majora . . . . .Sep 08
Carter, Nick
    see Backstreet Boys . . . . .Jan 00
Carter, Regina . . . . .Sep 07
Carter, Vince . . . . . . .Sport V.5; Update 01
cartoonists
    see also animators
    Amend, Bill . . . . .Author V.18
    Armstrong, Robb . . . . .Author V.9
    Borgman, Jim . . . . .Author V.15
    Breathed, Berke . . . . .Jan 92
    Crilley, Mark . . . . .Author V.15
    Davis, Jim . . . . .Author V.1
    Groening, Matt . . . . .Jan 92
    Guisewite, Cathy . . . . .Sep 93
    Hillenburg, Stephen . . . . .Author V.14
    Johnston, Lynn . . . . .Jan 99
    Jones, Chuck . . . . .Author V.12

Larson, Gary . . . . .Author V.1
Lee, Stan . . . . .Author V.7; Update 02
McGruder, Aaron . . . . .Author V.10
Schulz, Charles . . . .Author V.2; Update 00
Scott, Jerry . . . . .Author V.15
Spiegelman, Art . . . . .Author V.17
Tartakovsky, Genndy . . . . .Author V.11
Watterson, Bill . . . . .Jan 92
Carvey, Dana . . . . .Jan 93
Case, Steve . . . . .Science V.5
Castellano, Torry (Donna C.)
    see Donnas . . . . .Apr 04
Castro, Fidel . . . . .Jul 92; Update 94
Catchings, Tamika . . . . .Sport V.14
Chagall, Marc . . . . .Artist V.1
Chamberlain, Wilt . . . . .Sport V.4
Chambers, Veronica . . . . . . .Author V.15
Champagne, Larry III . . . . .Apr 96
Chan, Jackie . . . . .PerfArt V.1
Chan Kwong Sang
    see Chan, Jackie . . . . .PerfArt V.1
Chasez, JC
    see *N Sync . . . . .Jan 01
Chastain, Brandi . . . . .Sport V.4; Update 00
Chavez, Cesar . . . . .Sep 93
Chavez, Julz . . . . .Sep 02
Chavis, Benjamin . . . . . . .Jan 94; Update 94
chef
    Oliver, Jamie . . . . .Apr 07
Cheney, Dick . . . . .Jan 02
chess
    Ashley, Maurice . . . . .Sep 99
Chihuly, Dale . . . . .Jan 06
Childress, Alice . . . . .Author V.1
Chinese
    Chan, Jackie . . . . .PerfArt V.1
    Dai Qing . . . . .WorLdr V.3
    Fu Mingxia . . . . .Sport V.5
    Pei, I.M. . . . . .Artist V.1
    Wang, An . . . . .Science V.2
    Yao Ming . . . . .Sep 03
    Yuen Wo-Ping . . . . .PerfArt V.3
Choldenko, Gennifer . . . . . . .Author V.18
choreography
    see dance
Christo . . . . .Sep 96
Chung, Connie . . . . .Jan 94; Update 95;
    Update 96

Cisneros, Henry ....Sep 93
civil rights movement
  Chavis, Benjamin ......Jan 94; Update 94
  Edelman, Marian Wright ....Apr 93
  Jackson, Jesse ....Sep 95; Update 01
  King, Coretta Scott ....Sep 06
  Lewis, John ....Jan 03
  Marshall, Thurgood ....Jan 92; Update 93
  Parks, Rosa ....Apr 92; Update 94; Apr 06
  Shabazz, Betty ....Apr 98
Clark, Kelly ....Sport V.8
Clarkson, Kelly ....Jan 03
Clay, Cassius Marcellus Jr.
  see Ali, Muhammad ....Sport V.2
Cleary, Beverly ....Apr 94
Clements, Andrew ....Author V.13
Clemons, Kortney ....Sep 07
Clijsters, Kim ....Apr 04
Clinton, Bill ....Jul 92; Update 94; Update 95; Update 96; Update 97; Update 98; Update 99; Update 00; Update 01
Clinton, Chelsea ....Apr 96; Update 97; Update 01
Clinton, Hillary Rodham ....Apr 93; Update 94; Update 95; Update 96; Update 99; Update 00; Update 01
Cobain, Kurt ....Sep 94
Cohen, Adam Ezra ....Apr 97
Cohen, Sasha ....Sport V.12
Colfer, Eoin ....Author V.13
Collier, Bryan ....Author V.11
Collins, Billy ....Author V.16
Collins, Eileen ....Science V.4
Collins, Francis ....Science V.6
Colombian
  Ocampo, Adriana C. ....Science V.8
  Shakira ....PerfArt V.1
Combs, Benji
  see Madden, Benji ....PerfArt V.3
Combs, Joel
  see Madden, Joel ....PerfArt V.3
Combs, Sean (Puff Daddy) ....Apr 98
comedians
  Allen, Tim ....Apr 94; Update 99
  Arnold, Roseanne ....Oct 92
  Candy, John ....Sep 94
  Carrey, Jim ....Apr 96
  Carvey, Dana ....Jan 93
  Cosby, Bill ....Jan 92
  Fey, Tina ....Author V.16
  Goldberg, Whoopi ....Apr 94
  Leno, Jay ....Jul 92
  Letterman, David ....Jan 95
  López, George ....PerfArt V.2
  Mac, Bernie.................PerfArt V.1
  Murphy, Eddie ....PerfArt V.2
  Myers, Mike ....PerfArt V.3
  O'Donnell, Rosie ......Apr 97; Update 02
  Sandler, Adam ....Jan 06
  Seinfeld, Jerry ....Oct 92; Update 98
  Stewart, Jon ....Jan 06
  Tucker, Chris...................Jan 01
  Wayans, Keenen Ivory ....Jan 93
  Williams, Robin ....Apr 92
comic strips
  see cartoonists
computers
  Berners-Lee, Tim ....Science V.7
  Bezos, Jeff ....Apr 01
  Case, Steve ....Science V.5
  Cray, Seymour ....Science V.2
  Dell, Michael ....Business V.1
  Engelbart, Douglas ....Science V.5
  Fanning, Shawn ....Science V.5; Update 02
  Fiorina, Carly ....Sep 01; Update 01; Update 02
  Flannery, Sarah ....Science V.5
  Gates, Bill ....Apr 93; Update 98; Update 00; Science V.5; Update 01
  Groppe, Laura ....Science V.5
  Hopper, Grace Murray ....Science V.5
  Jobs, Steven ....Jan 92; Science V.5
  Joy, Bill ....Science V.10
  Kurzweil, Raymond ....Science V.2
  Miller, Rand ....Science V.5
  Miller, Robyn ....Science V.5
  Miyamoto, Shigeru ....Science V.5
  Oka, Masi ....Jan 08
  Perot, H. Ross ....Apr 92
  Romero, John ....Science V.8
  Torvalds, Linus ....Science V.11
  Wang, An ....Science V.2
  Wozniak, Steve ....Science V.5

CUMULATIVE GENERAL INDEX

Wright, Will . . . . Apr 04
Congress
  see representatives
  see senators
conservationists
  see environmentalists
Cook, Alicia Augello
  see Alicia Keys . . . . Jan 07
Cool, Tré (Frank Edwin Wright III)
  see Green Day . . . . Apr 06
Coolio . . . . Sep 96
Cooney, Barbara . . . . Author V.8
Cooney, Caroline B. . . . . Author V.4
Cooper, Anderson . . . . Sep 08
Cooper, Floyd . . . . Author V.17
Cooper, Susan . . . . Author V.17
Córdova, France . . . . Science V.7
Cormier, Robert . . . . Author V.1; Update 01
Cosby, Bill . . . . Jan 92
Coughlin, Natalie . . . . Sport V.10
Cousteau, Jacques . . . . . . Jan 93; Update 97
Covel, Toby Keith
  see Keith, Toby . . . . Jan 05
Coville, Bruce . . . . Author V.9
Cox, Lynne . . . . Sport V.13
Crabtree, Taylor . . . . Jan 07
Crawford, Cindy . . . . Apr 93
Cray, Seymour . . . . Science V.2
Creech, Sharon . . . . Author V.5
Crichton, Michael . . . . Author V.5
Crilley, Mark . . . . Author V.15
Cronin, John . . . . WorLdr V.3
Crosby, Sidney . . . . Sport V.14
Cruz, Celia . . . . Apr 04
Cubans
  Castro, Fidel . . . . Jul 92; Update 94
  Cruz, Celia . . . . Apr 04
  Estefan, Gloria . . . . Jul 92
  Fuentes, Daisy . . . . Jan 94
  Hernandez, Livan . . . . Apr 98
  Zamora, Pedro . . . . Apr 95
Culkin, Macaulay . . . . Sep 93
Culpepper, Daunte . . . . Sport V.13
Curtis, Christopher Paul . . . . . . Author V.4;
  Update 00
Cushman, Karen . . . . Author V.5
Cyrus, Miley . . . . Sep 07

Czechoslovakians
  Hasek, Dominik . . . . Sport V.3
  Hingis, Martina . . . . Sport V.2
  Jagr, Jaromir . . . . Sport V.5
  Navratilova, Martina . . . Jan 93; Update 94
da Silva, Fabiola . . . . Sport V.9
Dae-jung, Kim
  see Kim Dae-jung . . . . Sep 01
Dahl, Roald . . . . Author V.1
Dai Qing . . . . WorLdr V.3
Dakides, Tara . . . . Sport V.7
Dalai Lama . . . . Sep 98
Daly, Carson . . . . Apr 00
dance
  Abdul, Paula . . . . Jan 92; Update 02
  de Mille, Agnes . . . . Jan 95
  Estefan, Gloria . . . . Jul 92
  Farrell, Suzanne . . . . PerfArt V.1
  Glover, Savion . . . . Apr 99
  Hammer . . . . Jan 92
  Jamison, Judith . . . . Jan 96
  Kistler, Darci . . . . Jan 93
  Nureyev, Rudolf . . . . Apr 93
  Tharp, Twyla . . . . PerfArt V.3
Danes, Claire . . . . Sep 97
Daniel, Beth . . . . Sport V.1
Danziger, Paula . . . . Author V.6
da Silva, Fabiola . . . . Sport V.9
Davenport, Lindsay . . . . Sport V.5
Davis, Jim . . . . Author V.1
Dawson, Matel Jr. . . . . Jan 04
Dayne, Ron . . . . Apr 00
de Klerk, F.W. . . . . Apr 94; Update 94
Delany, Bessie . . . . Sep 99
Delany, Sadie . . . . Sep 99
Dell, Michael . . . . Business V.1
Delson, Brad
  see Linkin Park . . . . Jan 04
DeMayo, Neda . . . . Apr 06
de Mille, Agnes . . . . Jan 95
Democratic Party
  Brown, Ron . . . . Sep 96
  Carter, Jimmy . . . . Apr 95; Update 02
  Clinton, Bill . . . . Jul 92; Update 94;
    Update 95; Update 96; Update 97;
    Update 98; Update 99; Update 00;
    Update 01

CUMULATIVE GENERAL INDEX

Gore, Al ....Jan 93; Update 96; Update 97; Update 98; Update 99; Update 00; Update 01; Sep 08
Lewis, John ....Jan 03
Obama, Barack ....Jan 07
Pelosi, Nancy ....Sep 07
dentist
Delany, Bessie ....Sep 99
Denton, Sandi
see Salt 'N' Pepa ....Apr 95
dePaola, Tomie ....Author V.5
Depp, Johnny ....Apr 05
Destiny's Child ....Apr 01
Devers, Gail ....Sport V.2
Diana, Princess of Wales ....Jul 92; Update 96; Update 97; Jan 98
Diaz, Cameron ....PerfArt V.3
DiCamillo, Kate ....Author V.10
DiCaprio, Leonardo ....Apr 98
Diemer, Walter ....Apr 98
Diesel, Vin ....Jan 03
Dion, Celine ....Sep 97
diplomats
Albright, Madeleine ....Apr 97
Annan, Kofi ....Jan 98; Update 01
Boutros-Ghali, Boutros ....Apr 93; Update 98
Rowan, Carl ....Sep 01
directors
Burns, Ken ....Jan 95
Carter, Chris ....Author V.4
Chan, Jackie ....PerfArt V.1
Crichton, Michael ....Author V.5
Farrell, Suzanne ....PerfArt V.1
Jackson, Peter ....PerfArt V.2
Jones, Chuck ....Author V.12
Lasseter, John. ....Sep 00
Lee, Spike ....Oct 92
Lucas, George ....Apr 97; Update 02
Park, Nick ....Sep 06
Parks, Gordon ....Artist V.1
Perry, Tyler ....Sep 08
Spielberg, Steven ......Jan 94; Update 94; Update 95
Taymor, Julie ....PerfArt V.1
Warhol, Andy ....Artist V.1
Wayans, Keenen Ivory ....Jan 93
Whedon, Joss ....Author V.9
Williamson, Kevin ....Author V.6

Yuen Wo-Ping ....PerfArt V.3
Dirnt, Mike (Michael Pritchard)
see Green Day ....Apr 06
disabled
Buckley, Kelsey ....Sep 06
Burke, Chris ....Sep 93
Chihuly, Dale ....Jan 06
Clemons, Kortney ....Sep 07
Dole, Bob ....Jan 96
Driscoll, Jean ....Sep 97
Glennie, Evelyn ....PerfArt V.3
Grandin, Temple ....Science V.3
Gwaltney, John Langston ....Science V.3
Hamilton, Bethany ....Apr 05
Hawking, Stephen ....Apr 92
Hillenbrand, Laura ....Author V.14
Howard, Tim ....Apr 06
Parkinson, Jennifer ....Apr 95
Perlman, Itzhak ....Jan 95
Reeve, Christopher .....Jan 97; Update 02
Runyan, Marla ....Apr 02
Stepanek, Mattie ....Apr 02
Whitestone, Heather ....Apr 95; Update 02
diving
Fu Mingxia ....Sport V.5
Streeter, Tanya ....Sport V.11
Dixie Chicks ....PerfArt V.1
doctors
Benjamin, Regina ....Science V.9
Brundtland, Gro Harlem .....Science V.3
Calderone, Mary S. ....Science V.3
Canady, Alexa ....Science V.6
Carmona, Richard ....Science V.8
Carson, Ben ....Science V.4
Collins, Francis ....Science V.6
Farmer, Paul Jr. ....Science V.11
Fauci, Anthony S. ....Science V.7
Gayle, Helene ....Science V.8
Gerberding, Julie ....Science V.10
Greer, Pedro José Jr. ....Science V.10
Harris, Bernard ....Science V.3
Healy, Bernadine ....Science V.1; Update 01
Heimlich, Henry ....Science V.6
Ho, David ....Science V.6
Jemison, Mae ....Oct 92
Kamler, Kenneth ....Science V.6
Kübler-Ross, Elisabeth .....Science V.10
Long, Irene D. ....Jan 04

506

Love, Susan . . . . .Science V.3
Nielsen, Jerri . . . . .Science V.7
Novello, Antonia . . . . Apr 92
Pippig, Uta .Sport V.1
Poussaint, Alvin . . . . .Science V.9
Richardson, Dot . . . .Sport V.2; Update 00
Sabin, Albert . . . . .Science V.1
Sacks, Oliver . . . . .Science V.3
Salk, Jonas . . . . Jan 94; Update 95
Satcher, David . . . . .Sep 98
Spelman, Lucy . . . . .Science V.6
Spock, Benjamin . . . . . .Sep 95; Update 98
WilderBrathwaite, Gloria . . . . .Science V.7
Doherty, Shannen . . . . . .Apr 92; Update 94
Dole, Bob . . . . .Jan 96; Update 96
Dole, Elizabeth . . . . .Jul 92; Update 96;
 Update 99
Domingo, Placido . . . . .Sep 95
Dominicans
 Alvarez, Julia . . . . .Author V.17
 Martinez, Pedro . . . . .Sport V.5
 Pujols, Albert . . . . .Sport V.12
 Ramirez, Manny . . . . .Sport V.13
 Soriano, Alfonso . . . . .Sport V.10
 Sosa, Sammy . . . . Jan 99; Update 99
Donnas . . . . .Apr 04
Donovan, Marion . . . . .Science V.9
Dorough, Howie
 see Backstreet Boys . . . . Jan 00
Douglas, Marjory Stoneman . .WorLdr V.1;
 Update 98
Dove, Rita . . . . Jan 94
Dragila, Stacy . . . . .Sport V.6
Draper, Sharon . . . . .Apr 99
Driscoll, Jean . . . . .Sep 97
Duchovny, David . . . . .Apr 96
Duff, Hilary . . . . .Sep 02
Duke, David . . . . .Apr 92
Dumars, Joe . . . . .Sport V.3; Update 99
Dumitriu, Ioana . . . . .Science V.3
Dunbar, Paul Lawrence . . . . . . .Author V.8
Duncan, Lois . . . . .Sep 93
Duncan, Tim . . . . .Apr 04
Dunlap, Alison . . . . .Sport V.7
Dunst, Kirsten . . . . .PerfArt V.1
Dutch
 Lionni, Leo . . . . .Author V.6
Dworkin, Aaron . . . . .Apr 07

Earle, Sylvia . . . . .Science V.1
Earnhardt, Dale . . . . .Apr 01
Earnhardt, Dale Jr. . . . . .Sport V.12
Ebadi, Shirin . . . . .Apr 04
economist
 Yunus, Muhammad . . . . .Sep 07
Edelman, Marian Wright . . . . .Apr 93
educators
 Armstrong, William H. . . . . . . .Author V.7
 Arnesen, Liv . . . . .Author V.15
 Calderone, Mary S. . . . . .Science V.3
 Córdova, France . . . . .Science V.7
 Delany, Sadie . . . . .Sep 99
 Draper, Sharon . . . . .Apr 99
 Forman, Michele . . . . .Jan 03
 Gates, Henry Louis Jr. . . . . .Apr 00
 Giff, Patricia Reilly . . . . .Author V.7
 Jiménez, Francisco . . . . Author V.13
 Napoli, Donna Jo . . . . .Author V.16
 Poussaint, Alvin . . . . .Science V.9
 Rodriguez, Gloria . . . . .Apr 05
 Simmons, Ruth . . . . .Sep 02
 Stanford, John . . . . .Sep 99
 Suzuki, Shinichi . . . . .Sep 98
 Tenberken, Sabriye . . . . Sep 07
Efron, Zac . . . . .Apr 08
Egyptians
 Boutros-Ghali, Boutros . . . . .Apr 93;
 Update 98
 Sadat, Anwar . . . . .WorLdr V.2
Elion, Getrude . . . . .Science V.6
Ellerbee, Linda . . . . .Apr 94
Elliott, Missy . . . . .PerfArt V.3
Ellison, Ralph . . . . .Author V.3
Elway, John . . . . .Sport V.2; Update 99
Eminem . . . . .Apr 03
Engelbart, Douglas . . . . .Science V.5
English
 Almond, David . . . . Author V.10
 Amanpour, Christiane . . . . Jan 01
 Attenborough, David . . . . .Science V.4
 Barton, Hazel . . . . .Science V.6
 Beckham, David . . . . .Jan 04
 Berners-Lee, Tim . . . . .Science V.7
 Blair, Tony . . . . .Apr 04
 Bloom, Orlando . . . . .Sep 04
 Cooper, Susan . . . . .Author V.17
 Dahl, Roald . . . . .Author V.1

507

CUMULATIVE GENERAL INDEX

Diana, Princess of Wales . . . . Jul 92;
   Update 96; Update 97; Jan 98
Goodall, Jane . . . . .Science V.1; Update 02
Handford, Martin . . . . Jan 92
Hargreaves, Alison . . . . Jan 96
Hawking, Stephen . . . . Apr 92
Herriot, James . . . . Author V.1
Highmore, Freddie . . . . Apr 06
Jacques, Brian . . . . Author V.5
Jones, Diana Wynne . . . . Author V.15
Knightley, Keira . . . . Apr 07
Koff, Clea . . . . Science V.11
Leakey, Louis . . . . Science V.1
Leakey, Mary . . . . Science V.1
Lewis, C.S. . . . . Author V.3
MacArthur, Ellen . . . . Sport V.11
Macaulay, David . . . . Author V.2
Moore, Henry . . . . Artist V.1
Oliver, Jamie . . . . Apr 07
Park, Nick . . . . Sep 06
Potter, Beatrix . . . . Author V.8
Pullman, Philip . . . . Author V.9
Radcliffe, Daniel . . . . Jan 02
Reid Banks, Lynne . . . . Author V.2
Rennison, Louise . . . . Author V.10
Rowling, J.K. . . . . .Sep 99; Update 00;
   Update 01; Update 02; Jan 08
Sacks, Oliver . . . . Science V.3
Stewart, Patrick . . . . Jan 94
Stone, Joss . . . . Jan 06
Streeter, Tanya . . . . Sport V.11
Tolkien, J.R.R. . . . . Jan 02
Watson, Emma . . . . Apr 03
Winslet, Kate . . . . Sep 98
environmentalists
   Abbey, Edward . . . . WorLdr V.1
   Adams, Ansel . . . . Artist V.1
   Askins, Renee . . . . WorLdr V.1
   Babbitt, Bruce . . . . Jan 94
   Brower, David . . . .WorLdr V.1; Update 01
   Brundtland, Gro Harlem . . . . .Science V.3
   Carson, Rachel . . . . WorLdr V.1
   Carter, Majora . . . . Sep 08
   Cousteau, Jacques . . . . Jan 93
   Cronin, John . . . . WorLdr V.3
   Dai Qing . . . . WorLdr V.3
   DeMayo, Neda . . . . Apr 06
   Douglas, Marjory Stoneman
      WorLdr V.1; Update 98
   Earle, Sylvia . . . . Science V.1

Fay, Michael . . . . Science V.9
Foreman, Dave . . . . WorLdr V.1
Gibbs, Lois . . . . WorLdr V.1
Gore, Al . . . . Sep 08
Irwin, Steve . . . . Science V.7
Ka Hsaw Wa . . . . WorLdr V.3
LaDuke, Winona . . . . WorLdr V.3;
   Update 00
Leopold, Aldo . . . . WorLdr V.3
Maathai, Wangari . . . . WorLdr V.1
Martin, Bernard . . . . WorLdr V.3
Mendes, Chico . . . . WorLdr V.1
Mittermeier, Russell A. . . . . . . WorLdr V.1
Moss, Cynthia . . . . WorLdr V.3
Mowat, Farley . . . . Author V.8
Muir, John . . . . WorLdr V.3
Murie, Margaret . . . . WorLdr V.1
Murie, Olaus J. . . . . WorLdr V.1
Nakamura, Leanne . . . . Apr 02
Nelson, Gaylord . . . . WorLdr V.3
Oliver, Patsy Ruth . . . . WorLdr V.1
Patrick, Ruth . . . . Science V.3
Peterson, Roger Tory . . . . WorLdr V.1
Saro-Wiwa, Ken . . . . WorLdr V.1
Steingraber, Sandra . . . . Science V.9
Tompkins, Douglas . . . . WorLdr V.3
Watson, Paul . . . . WorLdr V.1
Werbach, Adam . . . . WorLdr V.1
Wolf, Hazel . . . . WorLdr V.3
Erdös, Paul . . . . Science V.2
Estefan, Gloria . . . . Jul 92
Ethiopians
   Haile Selassie . . . . WorLdr V.2
   Roba, Fatuma . . . . Sport V.3
Evans, Janet . . . . Jan 95; Update 96
Eve . . . . Jan 05
Evert, Chris . . . . Sport V.1
Ewing, Patrick . . . . Jan 95; Update 02
Fall Out Boy . . . . Sep 07
Fanning, Dakota . . . . Jan 06
Fanning, Shawn . . . .Science V.5; Update 02
Farmer, Nancy . . . . Author V.6
Farmer, Paul Jr. . . . . Science V.11
Farrakhan, Louis . . . . Jan 97
Farrell, Dave
   see Linkin Park . . . . Jan 04
Farrell, Suzanne . . . . PerfArt V.1
fashion designer
   Spade, Kate . . . . Apr 07

CUMULATIVE GENERAL INDEX

Fatone, Joey
   see *N Sync .... Jan 01
Fauci, Anthony S. .... Science V.7
Favre, Brett .... Sport V.2
Fay, Michael .... Science V.9
Federer, Roger .... Jan 07
Fedorov, Sergei .... Apr 94; Update 94
Feelings, Tom .... Author V.16
Felix, Allyson .... Sport V.10
Fenty, Robyn Rihanna
   see Rihanna .... Apr 08
Fergie (Ferguson, Stacy)
   see Black Eyed Peas .... Apr 06
Ferguson, Stacy (Fergie)
   see Black Eyed Peas .... Apr 06
Fernandez, Lisa .... Sport V.5
Ferrell, Will .... Apr 07
Ferrera, America .... Sep 07
Fey, Tina .... Author V.16
Feynman, Richard P. .... Science V.10
Ficker, Roberta Sue
   see Farrell, Suzanne .... PerfArt V.1
Fielder, Cecil .... Sep 93
Fields, Debbi .... Jan 96
Fijian
   Singh, Vijay .... Sport V.13
Filipino
   apl.de.ap (Alan Pineda Lindo) .... Apr 06
Filipovic, Zlata .... Sep 94
film critic
   Siskel, Gene .... Sep 99
Finch, Jennie .... Jan 05
Finnish
   Torvalds, Linus .... Science V.11
Fiorina, Carly .... Sep 01; Update 01; Update 02
First Ladies of the United States
   Bush, Barbara .... Jan 92
   Bush, Laura .... Apr 03
   Clinton, Hillary Rodham .... Apr 93; Update 94; Update 95; Update 96; Update 99; Update 00; Update 01
fishing
   Yelas, Jay .... Sport V.9
Fitzgerald, Ella .... Jan 97
Fitzhugh, Louise .... Author V.3
Flake, Sharon .... Author V.13

Flannery, Sarah .... Science V.5
Flowers, Vonetta .... Sport V.8
football
   Aikman, Troy .... Apr 95; Update 01
   Alexander, Shaun .... Apr 07
   Allen, Marcus .... Sep 97
   Brady, Tom .... Sport V.7
   Culpepper, Daunte .... Sport V.13
   Dayne, Ron .... Apr 00
   Elway, John .... Sport V.2; Update 99
   Favre, Brett .... Sport V.2
   George, Eddie .... Sport V.6
   Gonzalez, Tony .... Sport V.11
   Griese, Brian .... Jan 02
   Harbaugh, Jim .... Sport V.3
   Holmes, Priest .... Apr 05
   Jackson, Bo .... Jan 92; Update 93
   Johnson, Jimmy .... Jan 98
   Johnson, Keyshawn .... Sport V.10
   Madden, John .... Sep 97
   Manning, Eli .... Sep 08
   Manning, Peyton. .... Sep 00
   Marino, Dan .... Apr 93; Update 00
   McNabb, Donovan .... Apr 03
   McNair, Steve .... Sport V.11
   Montana, Joe .... Jan 95; Update 95
   Moss, Randy .... Sport V.4
   Payton, Walter .... Jan 00
   Rice, Jerry .... Apr 93
   Roethlisberger, Ben .... Sep 06
   Sanders, Barry .... Sep 95; Update 99
   Sanders, Deion .... Sport V.1
   Sapp, Warren .... Sport V.5
   Shula, Don .... Apr 96
   Smith, Emmitt .... Sep 94
   Stewart, Kordell .... Sep 98
   Strahan, Michael .... Sport V.12
   Tomlinson, LaDainian .... Sport V.14
   Urlacher, Brian .... Sep 04
   Vick, Michael .... Sport V.9
   Ward, Charlie .... Apr 94
   Warner, Kurt .... Sport V.4
   Weinke, Chris .... Apr 01
   White, Reggie .... Jan 98
   Willingham, Tyrone .... Sep 02
   Young, Steve .... Jan 94; Update 00
Foray, June .... Jan 07
Ford, Cheryl .... Sport V.11
Ford, Harrison .... Sep 97

CUMULATIVE GENERAL INDEX

Ford, Maya (Donna F.)
see Donnas ....Apr 04
Foreman, Dave ....WorLdr V.1
Forman, James ....Apr 05
Forman, Michele ....Jan 03
Fossey, Dian ....Science V.1
Foudy, Julie ....Sport V.13
Fox, Paula ....Author V.15
Fox, Vicente ....Apr 03
Frank, Anne ....Author V.4
Frankenthaler, Helen ....Artist V.1
Franklin, Aretha ....Apr 01
Freedman, Russell ....Author V.14
Freeman, Cathy ....Jan 01
French
  Cousteau, Jacques .....Jan 93; Update 97
  Marceau, Marcel ....PerfArt V.2
Fresh Prince
  see Smith, Will ....Sep 94
Friday, Dallas ....Sport V.10
Fu Mingxia ....Sport V.5
Fuentes, Daisy ....Jan 94
Fuller, Millard ....Apr 03
Funk, Mary Wallace
  see Funk, Wally ....Jan 05
Funk, Wally ....Jan 05
Funke, Cornelia ....Sep 05
Galdikas, Biruté ....Science V.4
Galeczka, Chris ....Apr 96
Gantos, Jack ....Author V.10
Garcia, Jerry ....Jan 96
Garcia, Sergio ....Sport V.7
Garnett, Kevin ....Sport V.6
Garth, Jennie ....Apr 96
Gates, Bill ....Apr 93; Update 98;
  Update 00; Science V.5; Update 01
Gates, Henry Louis Jr. ....Apr 00
Gayle, Helene ....Science V.8
Geisel, Theodor Seuss
  see Seuss, Dr. ....Jan 92
Gellar, Sarah Michelle ....Jan 99
Geography Bee, National
  Galeczka, Chris ....Apr 96
George, Eddie ....Sport V.6
George, Jean Craighead ....Author V.3
Gerberding, Julie ....Science V.10

Germans
  Bethe, Hans A. ....Science V.3
  Frank, Anne ....Author V.4
  Funke, Cornelia ....Sep 05
  Graf, Steffi ....Jan 92; Update 01
  Otto, Sylke ....Sport V.8
  Pippig, Uta ....Sport V.1
  Tenberken, Sabriye ....Sep 07
Ghanaians
  Adu, Freddy ....Sport V.12
  Annan, Kofi ....Jan 98; Update 01
  Nkrumah, Kwame ....WorLdr V.2
Gibbs, Lois ....WorLdr V.1
Giddens, Rebecca ....Sport V.14
Giff, Patricia Reilly ....Author V.7
Giguère, Jean-Sébastien ....Sport V.10
Gilbert, Sara ....Apr 93
Gilbert, Walter ....Science V.2
Gillespie, Dizzy ....Apr 93
Gilman, Billy ....Apr 02
Gingrich, Newt ....Apr 95; Update 99
Ginsburg, Ruth Bader ....Jan 94
Giuliani, Rudolph ....Sep 02
Glenn, John ....Jan 99
Glennie, Evelyn ....PerfArt V.3
Glover, Savion ....Apr 99
Goldberg, Whoopi ....Apr 94
golf
  Daniel, Beth ....Sport V.1
  Garcia, Sergio ....Sport V.7
  Nicklaus, Jack ....Sport V.2
  Norman, Greg ....Jan 94
  Ochoa, Lorena ....Sport V.14
  Pak, Se Ri ....Sport V.4
  Pressel, Morgan ....Jan 08
  Singh, Vijay ....Sport V.13
  Sorenstam, Annika ....Sport V.6
  Webb, Karrie ....Sport V.5; Update 01;
    Update 02
  Wie, Michelle ....Sep 04
  Woods, Tiger ......Sport V.1; Update 00;
    Sport V.6
Gomez, Jamie (Taboo)
  see Black Eyed Peas ....Apr 06
Gomez, Selena ....Sep 08
Gonzalez, Tony ....Sport V.11

Good Charlotte
 see Madden, Benji and
    Madden, Joel . . . . .PerfArt V.3
Goodall, Jane . . . . . .Science V.1; Update 02
Goodman, John . . . . .Sep 95
Gorbachev, Mikhail . . . .Jan 92; Update 96
Gordon, Jeff .Apr 99
Gore, Al . . . . .Jan 93; Update 96;
    Update 97; Update 98; Update 99;
    Update 00; Update 01; Sep 08
Gorey, Edward . . . . .Author V.13
Gould, Stephen Jay . . . . .Science V.2;
    Update 02
governors
    Babbitt, Bruce . . . . .Jan 94
    Bush, George W. . . . . . .Sep 00; Update 00;
       Update 01; Update 02
    Carter, Jimmy . . . . .Apr 95; Update 02
    Clinton, Bill . . . . .Jul 92; Update 94;
       Update 95; Update 96; Update 97;
       Update 98; Update 99; Update 00;
       Update 01
    Nelson, Gaylord . . . . .WorLdr V.3
    Reagan, Ronald . . . . .Sep 04
    Ventura, Jesse . . . . .Apr 99; Update 02
Graf, Steffi . . . . .Jan 92; Update 01
Granato, Cammi . . . . .Sport V.8
Grandin, Temple . . . . .Science V.3
GrandPré, Mary . . . . .Author V.14
Granny D
 see Haddock, Doris. . . . . .Sep 00
Grant, Amy . . . . .Jan 95
Graves, Earl . . . . .Business V.1
Green Day . . . . .Apr 06
Greenburg, Dan . . . . .Author V.14
Greer, Pedro José Jr. . . . . .Science V.10
Gretzky, Wayne . . . . . . .Jan 92; Update 93;
    Update 99
Griese, Brian . . . . .Jan 02
Griffey, Ken Jr. . . . . .Sport V.1
Griffith Joyner, Florence . . . . . . .Sport V.1;
    Update 98
Grimes, Nikki . . . . .Author V.14
Grisham, John . . . . .Author V.1
Groening, Matt . . . . .Jan 92
Groppe, Laura . . . . .Science V.5

Guatemalan
    Menchu, Rigoberta . . . . .Jan 93
Guey, Wendy . . . . .Sep 96
Guisewite, Cathy . . . . .Sep 93
Gumbel, Bryant . . . . .Apr 97
Guy, Jasmine . . . . .Sep 93
Guy, Rosa . . . . .Author V.9
Gwaltney, John Langston . . . . .Science V.3
Gyatso, Tenzin
 see Dalai Lama . . . . .Sep 98
gymnastics
    Memmel, Chellsie . . . . .Sport V.14
    Miller, Shannon . . . . . . .Sep 94; Update 96
    Moceanu, Dominique . . . . .Jan 98
    Patterson, Carly . . . . .Sport V.12
    Schwikert, Tasha . . . . .Sport V.7
    Zmeskal, Kim . . . . .Jan 94
Haddix, Margaret Peterson . . .Author V.11
Haddock, Doris. . . . . .Sep 00
Hahn, Joe
 see Linkin Park . . . . .Jan 04
Haile Selassie . . . . .WorLdr V.2
Haitian
    Aristide, Jean-Bertrand . . . . .Jan 95;
       Update 01
Hakim, Joy . . . . .Author V.16
Halaby, Lisa
 see Noor al Hussein, Queen
    of Jordan .Jan 05
Hale, Shannon . . . . .Author V.18
Haley, Alex .Apr 92
Hamilton, Bethany . . . . .Apr 05
Hamilton, Laird . . . . .Sport V.13
Hamilton, Virginia . . . . .Author V.1;
    Author V.12
Hamm, Mia . . . . .Sport V.2; Update 00
Hammer . . . . .Jan 92
Hampton, David . . . . .Apr 99
Handford, Martin . . . . .Jan 92
Handler, Daniel
 see Snicket, Lemony . . . . .Author V.12
Handler, Ruth . . . . .Apr 98; Update 02
Hanh, Thich Nhat
 see Nhat Hanh (Thich) . . . . .Jan 04
Hanks, Tom .Jan 96
Hansberry, Lorraine . . . . .Author V.5
Hanson . . . . .Jan 98

511

CUMULATIVE GENERAL INDEX

Hanson, Ike
   see Hanson . . . . Jan 98
Hanson, Taylor
   see Hanson . . . . Jan 98
Hanson, Zac
   see Hanson . . . . Jan 98
Harbaugh, Jim . . . . Sport V.3
Hardaway, Anfernee "Penny" . . . Sport V.2
Harding, Tonya . . . . Sep 94
Hargreaves, Alison . . . . Jan 96
Harris, Bernard . . . . Science V.3
Hart, Melissa Joan . . . . Jan 94
Hartnett, Josh . . . . Sep 03
Hasek, Dominik . . . . Sport V.3
Hassan II . . . . WorLdr V.2; Update 99
Hathaway, Anne . . . . Apr 05
Haughton, Aaliyah Dana
   see Aaliyah . . . . Jan 02
Hawk, Tony . . . . Apr 01
Hawking, Stephen . . . . Apr 92
Hayden, Carla . . . . Sep 04
Hayes, Tyrone . . . . Science V.10
Haynes, Cornell Jr.
   see Nelly . . . . Sep 03
Healy, Bernadine . . . Science V.1; Update 01
Heimlich, Henry . . . . Science V.6
Heinlein, Robert . . . . Author V.4
Hendrickson, Sue . . . . Science V.7
Henry, Marguerite . . . . Author V.4
Hernandez, Livan . . . . Apr 98
Herriot, James . . . . Author V.1
Hesse, Karen . . . . Author V.5; Update 02
Hewitt, Jennifer Love . . . . Sep 00
Hewson, Paul
   see Bono . . . . Sep 06
Hiaasen, Carl . . . . Author V.18
Highmore, Freddie . . . . Apr 06
Hill, Anita . . . . Jan 93
Hill, Faith . . . . Sep 01
Hill, Grant . . . . Sport V.1
Hill, Lauryn . . . . Sep 99
Hillary, Sir Edmund . . . . Sep 96
Hillenbrand, Laura . . . . Author V.14
Hillenburg, Stephen . . . . Author V.14
Hingis, Martina . . . . Sport V.2
Hinton, S.E. . . . . Author V.1

Hispanics
   Agosto, Ben . . . . Sport V.14
   Aguilera, Christina . . . . Apr 00
   Alba, Jessica . . . . Sep 01
   Alvarez, Julia . . . . Author V.17
   Alvarez, Luis W. . . . . Science V.3
   Bledel, Alexis . . . . Jan 03
   Carmona, Richard . . . . Science V.8
   Castro, Fidel . . . . Jul 92; Update 94
   Chambers, Veronica . . . . Author V.15
   Chavez, Cesar . . . . Sep 93
   Chavez, Julz . . . . Sep 02
   Cisneros, Henry . . . . Sep 93
   Córdova, France . . . . Science V.7
   Cruz, Celia . . . . Apr 04
   Diaz, Cameron . . . . PerfArt V.3
   Domingo, Placido . . . . Sep 95
   Estefan, Gloria . . . . Jul 92
   Fernandez, Lisa . . . . Sport V.5
   Ferrera, America . . . . Sep 07
   Fox, Vicente . . . . Apr 03
   Fuentes, Daisy . . . . Jan 94
   Garcia, Sergio . . . . Sport V.7
   Gomez, Selena . . . . Sep 08
   Gonzalez, Tony . . . . Sport V.11
   Greer, Pedro José Jr. . . . . Science V.10
   Hernandez, Livan . . . . Sep 93
   Huerta, Dolores . . . . Sep 03
   Iglesias, Enrique . . . . Jan 03
   Jiménez, Francisco . . . . Author V.13
   Lopez, Charlotte . . . . Apr 94
   López, George . . . . PerfArt V.2
   Lopez, Jennifer . . . . Jan 02
   Martin, Ricky . . . . Jan 00
   Martinez, Pedro . . . . Sport V.5
   Martinez, Victor . . . . Author V.15
   Mendes, Chico . . . . WorLdr V.1
   Millan, Cesar . . . . Sep 06
   Moreno, Arturo R. . . . . Business V.1
   Muniz, Frankie . . . . Jan 01
   Norman, Christina . . . . Apr 08
   Novello, Antonia . . . . Apr 92
   O'Brien, Soledad . . . . Jan 07
   Ocampo, Adriana C. . . . . Science V.8
   Ochoa, Ellen . . . . Apr 01; Update 02
   Ochoa, Lorena . . . . Sport V.14
   Ochoa, Severo . . . . Jan 94
   Pele . . . . Sport V.1
   Prinze, Freddie Jr. . . . . Apr 00
   Pujols, Albert . . . . Sport V.12

Ramirez, Manny . . . . .Sport V.13
Ramos, Jorge . . . . .Apr 06
Rivera, Diego . . . . .Artist V.1
Rodriguez, Alex . . . . .Sport V.6
Rodriguez, Eloy . . . . .Science V.2
Rodriguez, Gloria . . . . .Apr 05
Rodriguez, Ivan "Pudge" . . . . .Jan 07
Ryan, Pam Muñoz . . . . .Author V.12
Sanchez, Ricardo . . . . .Sep 04
Sanchez Vicario, Arantxa . . . . . . .Sport V.1
Selena . . . . .Jan 96
Shakira . . . . .PerfArt V.1
Soriano, Alfonso . . . . .Sport V.10
Soto, Gary . . . . .Author V.5
Taboo (Jamie Gomez) . . . . .Apr 06
Tienda, Marta . . . . .Sep 08
Toro, Natalia . . . . .Sep 99
Vega, Alexa . . . . .Jan 04
Vidal, Christina . . . . .PerfArt V.1
Villa, Brenda . . . . .Jan 06
Villa-Komaroff, Lydia . . . . .Science V.6
Zamora, Pedro . . . . .Apr 95
Ho, David . . . . .Science V.6
Hobbs, Will . . . . .Author V.18
hockey
   Crosby, Sidney . . . . .Sport V.14
   Fedorov, Sergei . . . . . .Apr 94; Update 94
   Giguère, Jean-Sébastien . . . . . .Sport V.10
   Granato, Cammi . . . . .Sport V.8
   Gretzky, Wayne . . . . . . .Jan 92; Update 93;
    Update 99
   Hasek, Dominik . . . . .Sport V.3
   Howe, Gordie . . . . .Sport V.2
   Jagr, Jaromir . . . . .Sport V.5
   Lemieux, Mario . . . . .Jul 92; Update 93
   Lidstrom, Nicklas . . . . .Sep 03
   Messier, Mark . . . . .Apr 96
   Niedermayer, Scott . . . . .Jan 08
   Roy, Patrick . . . . .Sport V.7
   Sakic, Joe . . . . .Sport V.6
   Vernon, Mike . . . . .Jan 98; Update 02
   Yzerman, Steve . . . . .Sport V.2
Hogan, Hulk . . . . .Apr 92
Holdsclaw, Chamique. . . . . .Sep 00
Holmes, Katie . . . . .Jan 00
Holmes, Priest . . . . .Apr 05
Honoré, Russel . . . . .Jan 06
Hooper, Geoff . . . . .Jan 94
Hopper, Grace Murray . . . . .Science V.5

Horner, Jack . . . . .Science V.1
horse racing
   Krone, Julie . . . . .Jan 95; Update 00
Horvath, Polly . . . . .Author V.16
Hoskins, Michele . . . . .Business V.1
House, Donna . . . . .Science V.11
House of Representatives
   see representatives
Houston, Whitney . . . . .Sep 94
Howard, Tim . . . . .Apr 06
Howe, Gordie . . . . .Sport V.2
Howe, James . . . . .Author V.17
Hrdy, Sarah Blaffer . . . . .Apr 07
Hudgens, Vanessa . . . . .Jan 08
Hudson, Jennifer . . . . .Jan 08
Huerta, Dolores . . . . .Sep 03
Hughes, Langston . . . . .Author V.7
Hughes, Sarah . . . . .Jan 03
Hungarians
   Erdös, Paul . . . . .Science V.2
   Seles, Monica . . . . .Jan 96
   Teller, Edward . . . . .Science V.9
Hunter-Gault, Charlayne . . . . .Jan 00
Hunter, Zach . . . . .Jan 08
Hurley, Andy
   see Fall Out Boy . . . . .Sep 07
Hurston, Zora Neale . . . . .Author V.6
Hussein, King . . . . .Apr 99
Hussein, Saddam . . . . . . .Jul 92; Update 96;
   Update 01; Update 02
Iacocca, Lee A. . . . . .Jan 92
ice skating
   see skating (ice)
Ice-T . . . . .Apr 93
Ichiro
   see Suzuki, Ichiro . . . . .Apr 08
Iglesias, Enrique . . . . .Jan 03
illustrators
   Bemelmans, Ludwig . . . . .Author V.16
   Berenstain, Jan . . . . .Author V.2
   Berenstain, Stan . . . . .Author V.2
   Carle, Eric . . . . .Author V.1
   Collier, Bryan . . . . .Author V.11
   Cooney, Barbara . . . . .Author V.8
   Cooper, Floyd . . . . .Author V.17
   Crilley, Mark . . . . .Author V.15
   dePaola, Tomie . . . . .Author V.5

CUMULATIVE GENERAL INDEX

Feelings, Tom . . . . .Author V.16
Fitzhugh, Louise . . . . .Author V.3
George, Jean Craighead . . . . . .Author V.3
Gorey, Edward . . . . .Author V.13
GrandPré, Mary . . . . .Author V.14
Handford, Martin . . . . .Jan 92
Konigsburg, E.L. . . . . .Author V.3
Lionni, Leo . . . . .Author V.6
Lobel, Arnold . . . . .Author V.18
Macaulay, David . . . . .Author V.2
McCloskey, Robert . . . . .Author V.15
McCully, Emily Arnold . . . . .Apr 92; Update 93
Peet, Bill . . . . .Author V.4
Pinkney, Jerry . . . . .Author V.2
Pinkwater, Daniel . . . . .Author V.8
Potter, Beatrix . . . . .Author V.8
Ringgold, Faith . . . . .Author V.2
Rockwell, Norman . . . . .Artist V.1
Scarry, Richard . . . . .Sep 94
Sendak, Maurice . . . . .Author V.2
Seuss, Dr. . . . . .Jan 92
Silverstein, Shel . . . . .Author V.3; Update 99
Small, David . . . . .Author V.10
Van Allsburg, Chris . . . . .Apr 92
Williams, Garth . . . . .Author V.2
Indian
Wadhwa, Meenakshi . . . . . . .Science V.11
in-line skating
see skating (in-line)
Internet
Berners-Lee, Tim . . . . .Science V.7
Bezos, Jeff .Apr 01
Brin, Sergey . . . . .Sep 05
Case, Steve . . . . .Science V.5
Fanning, Shawn . . . . .Science V.5; Update 02
Flannery, Sarah . . . . .Science V.5
Groppe, Laura . . . . .Science V.5
Page, Larry .Sep 05
Tarbox, Katie . . . . .Author V.10
Whitman, Meg . . . . .Sep 03
inventors
Alvarez, Luis W. . . . . .Science V.3
Berners-Lee, Tim . . . . .Science V.7
Brin, Sergey . . . . .Sep 05
Cousteau, Jacques . . . . . .Jan 93; Update 97
Diemer, Walter . . . . .Apr 98
Donovan, Marion . . . . .Science V.9
Engelbart, Douglas . . . . .Science V.5
Fanning, Shawn . . . . .Science V.5; Update 02
Grandin, Temple . . . . .Science V.3
Hampton, David . . . . .Apr 99
Handler, Ruth . . . . . . .Apr 98; Update 02
Heimlich, Henry . . . . .Science V.6
Johnson, Lonnie . . . . .Science V.4
Kamen, Dean . . . . .Science V.11
Kapell, Dave . . . . .Science V.8
Kurzweil, Raymond . . . . .Science V.2
Kwolek, Stephanie . . . . .Science V.10
Land, Edwin . . . . .Science V.1
Lemelson, Jerome . . . . .Science V.3
Mars, Forrest Sr. . . . . .Science V.4
Morgan, Garrett . . . . .Science V.2
Ochoa, Ellen . . . . .Apr 01; Update 02
Page, Larry .Sep 05
Patterson, Ryan . . . . .Science V.7
Stachowski, Richie . . . . .Science V.3
Swanson, Janese . . . . .Science V.4
Wang, An . . . . .Science V.2
Warrick, Earl . . . . .Science V.8
Wozniak, Steve . . . . .Science V.5
Iranian
Ebadi, Shirin . . . . .Apr 04
Iraqi
Hussein, Saddam . . . . . .Jul 92; Update 96; Update 01; Update 02
Irish
Bono . . . . .Sep 06
Colfer, Eoin . . . . .Author V.13
Flannery, Sarah . . . . .Science V.5
Lewis, C.S. . . . . .Author V.3
Robinson, Mary . . . . .Sep 93
Irwin, Bindi . . . . .Apr 08
Irwin, Steve . . . . .Science V.7
Israelis
Ben-Ari, Miri . . . . .Jan 06
Perlman, Itzhak . . . . .Jan 95
Portman, Natalie . . . . .Sep 99
Rabin, Yitzhak . . . . . . .Oct 92; Update 93; Update 94; Update 95
Italians
Andretti, Mario . . . . .Sep 94
Krim, Mathilde . . . . .Science V.1
Levi-Montalcini, Rita . . . . . . .Science V.1
Iverson, Allen . . . . .Sport V.7

Ivey, Artis Jr.
　see Coolio .... Sep 96
Jackson, Bo .... Jan 92; Update 93
Jackson, Jesse .... Sep 95; Update 01
Jackson, Peter .... PerfArt V.2
Jackson, Phil .... Sport V.10
Jackson, Shirley .... Author V.6
Jackson, Shirley Ann .... Science V.2
Jacques, Brian .... Author V.5
Jagr, Jaromir .... Sport V.5
Jakes, T.D. .... Jan 05
Jamaicans
　Ashley, Maurice .... Sep 99
　Bailey, Donovan .... Sport V.2
　Denton, Sandi
　　see Salt 'N' Pepa .... Apr 95
　Ewing, Patrick .... Jan 95; Update 02
　Maxwell, Jody-Anne .... Sep 98
James, Cheryl
　see Salt 'N' Pepa .... Apr 95
James, LeBron .... Sport V.12
Jamison, Judith .... Jan 96
Jansen, Dan .... Apr 94
Japanese
　Miyamoto, Shigeru .... Science V.5
　Morita, Akio .... Science V.4
　Oka, Masi .... Jan 08
　Suzuki, Ichiro .... Apr 08
　Suzuki, Shinichi .... Sep 98
　Uchida, Mitsuko .... Apr 99
Javacheff, Christo V.
　see Christo .... Sep 96
Jeffers, Eve
　see Eve .... Jan 05
Jemison, Mae .... Oct 92
Jenkins, Jerry B. .... Author V.16
Jennings, Peter .... Jul 92
Jeter, Derek .... Sport V.4
Jewel .... Sep 98
Jiménez, Francisco .... Author V.13
Jobs, Steven .... Jan 92; Science V.5
jockey
　Krone, Julie .... Jan 95; Update 00
John Paul II .... Oct 92; Update 94;
　Update 95; Sep 05
Johns, Jasper .... Artist V.1
Johnson, Angela .... Author V.6

Johnson, Jimmy .... Jan 98
Johnson, Johanna .... Apr 00
Johnson, John .... Jan 97
Johnson, Keyshawn .... Sport V.10
Johnson, Lonnie .... Science V.4
Johnson, Magic .... Apr 92; Update 02
Johnson, Michael ...... Jan 97; Update 00
Johnson, Randy .... Sport V.9
Johnston, Lynn .... Jan 99
Jonas Brothers .... Jan 08
Jonas, Joseph
　see Jonas Brothers .... Jan 08
Jonas, Kevin
　see Jonas Brothers .... Jan 08
Jonas, Nick
　see Jonas Brothers .... Jan 08
Jones, Chuck .... Author V.12
Jones, Diana Wynne .... Author V.15
Jones, James Earl .... Jan 95
Jones, Marion .... Sport V.5
Jones, Norah .... PerfArt V.2
Jones, Quincy .... PerfArt V.2
Jordan, Barbara .... Apr 96
Jordan, Michael .... Jan 92;
　Update 93; Update 94; Update 95;
　Update 99; Update 01
Jordanian
　Hussein, King .... Apr 99
journalists
　Amanpour, Christiane .... Jan 01
　Anderson, Terry .... Apr 92
　Benson, Mildred .... Jan 03
　Blum, Deborah .... Science V.8
　Bradley, Ed .... Apr 94
　Brody, Jane .... Science V.2
　Chung, Connie .... Jan 94; Update 95;
　　Update 96
　Cooper, Anderson .... Sep 08
　Dai Qing .... WorLdr V.3
　Ellerbee, Linda .... Apr 94
　Hiaasen, Carl .... Author V.18
　Hunter-Gault, Charlayne .... Jan 00
　Jennings, Peter .... Jul 92
　Krakauer, Jon .... Author V.6
　Ling, Lisa .... Apr 08
　Lipsyte, Robert .... Author V.12
　O'Brien, Soledad .... Jan 07

515

CUMULATIVE GENERAL INDEX

Pauley, Jane . . . . .Oct 92
Ramos, Jorge . . . . .Apr 06
Roberts, Cokie . . . . .Apr 95
Rowan, Carl . . . . .Sep 01
Soren, Tabitha . . . . .Jan 97
Steinem, Gloria . . . . .Oct 92
Walters, Barbara . . . . .Sep 94
Joy, Bill .Science V.10
Joyner-Kersee, Jackie . . . . .Oct 92;
Update 96; Update 97; Update 98
Jung, Kim Dae
see Kim Dae-jung . . . . .Sep 01
Juster, Norton . . . . .Author V.14
Ka Hsaw Wa . . . . .WorLdr V.3
Kaddafi, Muammar
see Qaddafi, Muammar . . . . .Apr 97
Kadohata, Cynthia . . . . .Sep 06
Kamen, Dean . . . . .Science V.11
Kamler, Kenneth . . . . .Science V.6
Kapell, Dave . . . . .Science V.8
Kaunda, Kenneth . . . . .WorLdr V.2
kayaking
Giddens, Rebecca . . . . .Sport V.14
Keene, Carolyne
see Benson, Mildred . . . . .Jan 03
Keith, Toby .Jan 05
Kenyans
Kenyatta, Jomo . . . . .WorLdr V.2
Maathai, Wangari . . . .WorLdr V.1; Sep 05
Ndeti, Cosmas . . . . .Sep 95
Kenyatta, Jomo . . . . .WorLdr V.2
Kenyon, Cynthia . . . . .Science V.11
Kerr, M.E. .Author V.1
Kerrigan, Nancy . . . . .Apr 94
Keys, Alicia . . . . .Jan 07
Kidd, Jason . . . . .Sport V.9
Kielburger, Craig . . . . .Jan 00
Kiessling, Laura L. . . . . .Science V.9
Kilcher, Jewel
see Jewel . . . . .Sep 98
Kim Dae-jung . . . . .Sep 01
Kimball, Cheyenne . . . . .Jan 07
King, Coretta Scott . . . . .Sep 06
King, Mary-Claire . . . . .Science V.10
King, Stephen . . . . . .Author V.1; Update 00
Kiraly, Karch . . . . .Sport V.4

Kirkpatrick, Chris
see *N Sync .Jan 01
Kistler, Darci . . . . .Jan 93
Klug, Chris . . . . .Sport V.8
Knightley, Keira . . . . .Apr 07
Knowles, Beyoncé
see Destiny's Child . . . . .Apr 01
Koff, Clea . . . . .Science V.11
Konigsburg, E.L. . . . . .Author V.3
Kopp, Wendy . . . . .Sep 07
Korean
An Na . . . . .Author V.12
Kim Dae-jung . . . . .Sep 01
Pak, Se Ri . . . . .Sport V.4
Krakauer, Jon . . . . .Author V.6
Kratt, Chris . . . . .Science V.10
Kratt, Martin . . . . .Science V.10
Krauss, Alison . . . . .Apr 05
Krim, Mathilde . . . . .Science V.1
Krone, Julie . . . . .Jan 95; Update 00
Kübler-Ross, Elisabeth . . . . . .Science V.10
Kurzweil, Raymond . . . . .Science V.2
Kutcher, Ashton . . . . .Apr 04
Kwan, Michelle . . . . . .Sport V.3; Update 02
Kwolek, Stephanie . . . . .Science V.10
lacrosse
Boyle, Ryan . . . . .Sport V.10
Laden, Osama bin
see bin Laden, Osama . . . . .Apr 02
LaDuke, Winona . . .WorLdr V.3; Update 00
LaHaye, Tim . . . . .Author V.16
Lalas, Alexi .Sep 94
Lama, Dalai
see Dalai Lama . . . . .Sep 98
Land, Edwin . . . . .Science V.1
lang, k.d. . . . . .Sep 93
Lansky, Bruce . . . . .Author V.17
Larson, Gary . . . . .Author V.1
Lasky, Kathryn . . . . .Author V.18
Lasseter, John . . . . .Sep 00
Latino/Latina
see Hispanics
Lavigne, Avril . . . . .PerfArt V.2
Lawrence, Jacob . . . . .Artist V.1; Update 01
lawyers
Abzug, Bella . . . . .Sep 98
Babbitt, Bruce . . . . .Jan 94

CUMULATIVE GENERAL INDEX

Boutros-Ghali, Boutros .Apr 93; Update 98
Clinton, Hillary Rodham .... .Apr 93
Ebadi, Shirin .... .Apr 04
Giuliani, Rudolph .... .Sep 02
Grisham, John .... .Author V.1
Reno, Janet .... .Sep 93
Roberts, John Jr. .... .Apr 08
Schroeder, Pat .... .Jan 97
Leakey, Louis .... .Science V.1
Leakey, Mary .... .Science V.1
Lee, Harper .... .Author V.9
Lee, Jeanette .... .Apr 03
Lee, Spike .... .Apr 92
Lee, Stan .... .Author V.7; Update 02
Le Guin, Ursula K. .... .Author V.8
Leibovitz, Annie .... .Sep 96
Lemelson, Jerome .... .Science V.3
Lemieux, Mario .... .Jul 92; Update 93
LeMond, Greg .... .Sport V.1
L'Engle, Madeleine .... .Jan 92; Apr 01
Lennox, Betty .... .Sport V.13
Leno, Jay .... .Jul 92
Leopold, Aldo .... .WorLdr V.3
Leslie, Lisa .... .Jan 04
Lester, Julius .... .Author V.7
Letterman, David .... .Jan 95
Levi-Montalcini, Rita .... .Science V.1
Levine, Gail Carson .... .Author V.17
Lewis, C.S. .... .Author V.3
Lewis, Carl .... .Sep 96; Update 97
Lewis, John .... .Jan 03
Lewis, Shari .... .Jan 99
Liberian
   Tubman, William V.S. .... .WorLdr V.2
librarians
   Avi .... .Jan 93
   Bush, Laura .... .Apr 03
   Cleary, Beverly .... .Apr 94
   Hayden, Carla .... .Sep 04
   Morrison, Lillian .... .Author V.12
   Morrison, Sam .... .Sep 97
   Rylant, Cynthia .... .Author V.1
Libyan
   Qaddafi, Muammar .... .Apr 97
Lidstrom, Nicklas .... .Sep 03
Lil' Romeo
   see Romeo, Lil' .... .Jan 06
Limbaugh, Rush .... .Sep 95; Update 02

Lin, Maya .... .Sep 97
Lindgren, Astrid .... .Author V.13
Lindo, Alan Pineda (apl.de.ap)
   see Black Eyed Peas .... .Apr 06
Ling, Lisa .... .Apr 08
Linkin Park .... .Jan 04
Lionni, Leo .... .Author V.6
Lipinski, Tara .... .Apr 98
Lipsyte, Robert .... .Author V.12
Lisanti, Mariangela .... .Sep 01
Lithuanian
   Galdikas, Biruté .... .Science V.4
Littrell, Brian
   see Backstreet Boys .... .Jan 00
Lobel, Arnold .... .Author V.18
Lobo, Rebecca .... .Sport V.3
Locklear, Heather .... .Jan 95
Lohan, Lindsay .... .Sep 04
Long, Irene D. .... .Jan 04
Lopez, Charlotte .... .Apr 94
López, George .... .PerfArt V.2
Lopez, Jennifer .... .Jan 02
Love, Susan .... .Science V.3
Lovell, Jim .... .Jan 96
Lowe, Alex .... .Sport V.4
Lowman, Meg .... .Science V.4
Lowry, Lois .... .Author V.4
Lucas, George .... .Apr 97; Update 02
Lucid, Shannon .... .Science V.2
luge
   Otto, Sylke .... .Sport V.8
Lynch, Chris .... .Author V.13
Ma, Yo-Yo .... .Jul 92
Maathai, Wangari ..... .WorLdr V.1; Sep 05
Mac, Bernie .... .PerfArt V.1
MacArthur, Ellen .... .Sport V.11
Macaulay, David .... .Author V.2
MacLachlan, Patricia .... .Author V.2
Madden, Benji .... .PerfArt V.3
Madden, Joel .... .PerfArt V.3
Madden, John .... .Sep 97
Maddux, Greg .... .Sport V.3
Maguire, Martie
   see Dixie Chicks .... .PerfArt V.1
Maines, Natalie
   see Dixie Chicks .... .PerfArt V.1
Malawian
   Banda, Hastings Kamuzu ....WorLdr V.2

CUMULATIVE GENERAL INDEX

Mandela, Nelson . . . . . . .Jan 92; Update 94; Update 01
Mandela, Winnie . . . . .WorLdr V.2
Mangel, Marcel
 see Marceau, Marcel . . . . .PerfArt V.2
Mankiller, Wilma . . . . .Apr 94
Manning, Eli .Sep 08
Manning, Peyton . . . . .Sep 00
Mantle, Mickey . . . . .Jan 96
Marceau, Marcel . . . . .PerfArt V.2
Margulis, Lynn . . . . .Sep 96
Marino, Dan . . . . .Apr 93; Update 00
Marrow, Tracy
 see Ice-T . . . . .Apr 93
Mars, Forrest Sr. . . . . .Science V.4
Marsalis, Wynton . . . . .Apr 92
Marshall, Thurgood . . . . .Jan 92; Update 93
Martin, Ann M. . . . . .Jan 92
Martin, Bernard . . . . .WorLdr V.3
Martin, Ricky . . . . .Jan 00
Martinez, Pedro . . . . .Sport V.5
Martinez, Victor . . . . .Author V.15
Masih, Iqbal .Jan 96
mathematicians
 Dumitriu, Ioana . . . . .Science V.3
 Erdös, Paul . . . . .Science V.2
 Flannery, Sarah . . . . .Science V.5
 Hopper, Grace Murray . . . . . . .Science V.5
 Nash, John Forbes Jr. . . . . .Science V.7
Mathers, Marshall III
 see Eminem . . . . .Apr 03
Mathis, Clint .Apr 03
Mathison, Melissa . . . . .Author V.4
Maxwell, Jody-Anne . . . . .Sep 98
Mayer, John .Apr 04
McAdams, Rachel . . . . .Apr 06
McCain, John . . . . .Apr 00
McCarty, Oseola . . . . . . .Jan 99; Update 99
McCary, Michael
 see Boyz II Men . . . . .Jan 96
McClintock, Barbara . . . . .Oct 92
McCloskey, Robert . . . . .Author V.15
McCully, Emily Arnold . .Jul 92; Update 93
McDaniel, Lurlene . . . . .Author V.14
McDonald, Janet . . . . .Author V.18
McEntire, Reba . . . . .Sep 95
McGrady, Tracy . . . . .Sport V.11
McGrath, Judy . . . . .Business V.1
McGruder, Aaron . . . . .Author V.10
McGwire, Mark . . . . .Jan 99; Update 99
McKissack, Fredrick L.. . . . . . . .Author V.3
McKissack, Patricia C. . . . . .Author V.3
McLean, A.J.
 see Backstreet Boys . . . . .Jan 00
McNabb, Donovan . . . . .Apr 03
McNair, Steve . . . . .Sport V.11
McNutt, Marcia . . . . .Science V.11
Mead, Margaret . . . . .Science V.2
Meaker, Marijane
 see Kerr, M.E. . . . . .Author V.1
Mebarak Ripoll, Shakira Isabel
 see Shakira . . . . .PerfArt V.1
Meissner, Kimmie . . . . .Sep 08
Meltzer, Milton . . . . .Author V.11
Memmel, Chellsie . . . . .Sport V.14
Menchu, Rigoberta . . . . .Jan 93
Mendes, Chico . . . . .WorLdr V.1
Messier, Mark . . . . .Apr 96
Mexicans
 Fox, Vicente . . . . .Apr 03
 Jiménez, Francisco . . . . .Author V.13
 Millan, Cesar . . . . .Sep 06
 Ochoa, Lorena . . . . .Sport V.14
 Ramos, Jorge . . . . .Apr 06
 Rivera, Diego . . . . .Artist V.1
 Santana, Carlos . . . . .Sep 05
Michalka, Alyson Renae
 see Aly & AJ . . . . .Sep 08
Michalka, Amanda Joy
 see Aly & AJ . . . . .Sep 08
Milbrett, Tiffeny . . . . .Sport V.10
military service
 – Israel
  Rabin, Yitzhak . . . . .Oct 92
 – Libya
  Qaddafi, Muammar . . . . .Apr 97
 – Somalia
  Aidid, Mohammed Farah . . .WorLdr V.2
 – Uganda
  Amin, Idi . . . . .WorLdr V.2
 – United States
  Brooks, Vincent . . . . .Sep 03
  Clemons, Kortney . . . . .Sep 07
  Honoré, Russel . . . . .Jan 06
  Hopper, Grace Murray . . . . . .Science V.5
  McCain, John . . . . .Apr 00

518

CUMULATIVE GENERAL INDEX

Powell, Colin . . . . Jan 92; Update 93;
   Update 95; Update 01
   Sanchez, Ricardo . . . . Sep 04
   Schwarzkopf, H. Norman . . . . Jan 92
   Stanford, John . . . . Sep 99
– Zaire
   Mobutu Sese Seko . . . . WorLdr V.2
Millan, Cesar . . . . Sep 06
Miller, Percy Romeo
   see Romeo, Lil' . . . . Jan 06
Miller, Rand . . . . Science V.5
Miller, Robyn . . . . Science V.5
Miller, Shannon . . . . Sep 94; Update 96
Milosevic, Slobodan . . . Sep 99; Update 00;
   Update 01; Update 02
mime
   Marceau, Marcel . . . . PerfArt V.2
Mirra, Dave . . . . Sep 02
Mister Rogers
   see Rogers, Fred . . . . PerfArt V.3
Mitchell-Raptakis, Karen . . . . Jan 05
Mittermeier, Russell A. . . . . WorLdr V.1
Miyamoto, Shigeru . . . . Science V.5
Mobutu Sese Seko . . . . WorLdr V.2;
   Update 97
Moceanu, Dominique . . . . Jan 98
models
   Banks, Tyra . . . . PerfArt V.2
   Crawford, Cindy . . . . Apr 93
Mohajer, Dineh . . . . Jan 02
Monroe, Bill . . . . Sep 97
Montana, Joe . . . . Jan 95; Update 95
Moore, Henry . . . . Artist V.1
Moore, Mandy . . . . Jan 04
Moreno, Arturo R. . . . . Business V.1
Morgan, Garrett . . . . Science V.2
Morissette, Alanis . . . . Apr 97
Morita, Akio . . . . Science V.4
Moroccan
   Hassan II . . . . WorLdr V.2; Update 99
Morris, Nathan
   see Boyz II Men . . . . Jan 96
Morris, Wanya
   see Boyz II Men . . . . Jan 96
Morrison, Lillian . . . . Author V.12
Morrison, Samuel . . . . Sep 97
Morrison, Toni . . . . Jan 94

Moseley, Jonny . . . . Sport V.8
Moses, Grandma . . . . Artist V.1
Moss, Cynthia . . . . WorLdr V.3
Moss, Randy . . . . Sport V.4
motorcycle racing
   Stewart, James Jr. . . . . Apr 08
Mother Teresa
   see Teresa, Mother . . . . Apr 98
mountain climbing
   Hargreaves, Alison . . . . Jan 96
   Hillary, Sir Edmund . . . . Sep 96
   Kamler, Kenneth . . . . Science V.6
   Krakauer, Jon . . . . Author V.6
   Lowe, Alex . . . . Sport V.4
movies
   see actors/actresses
   see animators
   see directors
   see film critic
   see producers
   see screenwriters
Mowat, Farley . . . . Author V.8
Mugabe, Robert . . . . WorLdr V.2
Muir, John . . . . WorLdr V.3
Mulanovich, Sofia . . . . Apr 07
Muldowney, Shirley . . . . Sport V.7
Muniz, Frankie . . . . Jan 01
Murie, Margaret . . . . WorLdr V.1
Murie, Olaus J. . . . . WorLdr V.1
Murphy, Eddie . . . . PerfArt V.2
Murphy, Jim . . . . Author V.17
Murray, Ty . . . . Sport V.7
music
   Aaliyah . . . . Jan 02
   Abdul, Paula . . . . Jan 92; Update 02
   Adams, Yolanda . . . . Apr 03
   Aguilera, Christina . . . . Apr 00
   Aly & AJ . . . . Sep 08
   Anderson, Marian . . . . Jan 94
   Ashanti . . . . PerfArt V.2
   Backstreet Boys . . . . Jan 00
   Battle, Kathleen . . . . Jan 93
   Ben-Ari, Miri . . . . Jan 06
   Black, Jack . . . . Jan 05
   Black Eyed Peas . . . . Apr 06
   Blige, Mary J. . . . . Apr 02
   Bono . . . . Sep 06
   Boyz II Men . . . . Jan 96

519

CUMULATIVE GENERAL INDEX

Branch, Michelle ....PerfArt V.3
Brandy ....Apr 96
Brooks, Garth ....Oct 92
Brown, Chris ....Apr 07
Carey, Mariah ....Apr 96
Carpenter, Mary Chapin ....Sep 94
Carrabba, Chris ....Apr 05
Carter, Aaron ....Sep 02
Carter, Regina ....Sep 07
Clarkson, Kelly ....Jan 03
Cobain, Kurt ....Sep 94
Combs, Sean (Puff Daddy) ....Apr 98
Coolio ....Sep 96
Cruz, Celia ....Apr 04
Cyrus, Miley ....Sep 07
Destiny's Child ....Apr 01
Dion, Celine ....Sep 97
Dixie Chicks ....PerfArt V.1
Domingo, Placido ....Sep 95
Donnas ....Apr 04
Dworkin, Aaron ....Apr 07
Efron, Zac ....Apr 08
Elliott, Missy ....PerfArt V.3
Eminem ....Apr 03
Estefan, Gloria ....Jul 92
Eve ....Jan 05
Fall Out Boy ....Sep 07
Fitzgerald, Ella ....Jan 97
Franklin, Aretha ....Apr 01
Garcia, Jerry ....Jan 96
Gillespie, Dizzy ....Apr 93
Gilman, Billy ....Apr 02
Glennie, Evelyn ....PerfArt V.3
Grant, Amy ....Jan 95
Green Day ....Apr 06
Guy, Jasmine ....Sep 93
Hammer ....Jan 92
Hanson ....Jan 98
Hill, Faith ....Sep 01
Hill, Lauryn ....Sep 99
Houston, Whitney ....Sep 94
Hudgens, Vanessa ....Jan 08
Hudson, Jennifer ....Jan 08
Ice-T ....Apr 93
Iglesias, Enrique ....Jan 03
Jewel ....Sep 98
Johnson, Johanna ....Apr 00
Jonas Brothers ....Jan 08
Jones, Norah ....PerfArt V.2
Jones, Quincy ....PerfArt V.2
Keith, Toby ....Jan 05
Keys, Alicia ....Jan 07
Kimball, Cheyenne ....Jan 07
Krauss, Alison ....Apr 05
lang, k.d. ....Sep 93
Lavigne, Avril ....PerfArt V.2
Linkin Park ....Jan 04
Lopez, Jennifer ....Jan 02
Ma, Yo-Yo ....Jul 92
Madden, Benji ....PerfArt V.3
Madden, Joel ....PerfArt V.3
Marsalis, Wynton ....Apr 92
Martin, Ricky ....Jan 00
Mayer, John ....Apr 04
McGrath, Judy ....Business V.1
McEntire, Reba ....Sep 95
Monroe, Bill ....Sep 97
Moore, Mandy ....Jan 04
Morissette, Alanis ....Apr 97
*N Sync ....Jan 01
Nelly ....Sep 03
OutKast ....Sep 04
Perlman, Itzhak ....Jan 95
Queen Latifah ....Apr 92
Raven ....Apr 04
Rihanna ....Apr 08
Rimes, LeAnn ....Jan 98
Romeo, Lil' ....Jan 06
Salt 'N' Pepa ....Apr 95
Santana, Carlos ....Sep 05
Selena ....Jan 96
Shakira ....PerfArt V.1
Shakur, Tupac ....Apr 97
Simmons, Russell ....Apr 06
Simpson, Ashlee ....Sep 05
Sinatra, Frank ....Jan 99
Smith, Will ....Sep 94
Spears, Britney ....Jan 01
Stefani, Gwen ....Sep 03
Stern, Isaac ....PerfArt V.1
Stone, Joss ....Jan 06
Suzuki, Shinichi ....Sep 98
Timberlake, Justin ....Sep 08
Tisdale, Ashley ....Jan 07
Twain, Shania ....Apr 99
Uchida, Mitsuko ....Apr 99
Underwood, Carrie ....Apr 07
Usher ....PerfArt V.1
Vidal, Christina ....PerfArt V.1

CUMULATIVE GENERAL INDEX

Wilson, Gretchen .... Sep 06
Winans, CeCe .... Apr 00
Myers, Mike .... PerfArt V.3
Myers, Walter Dean ..... Jan 93; Update 94
***N Sync** .... Jan 01
Nakamura, Leanne .... Apr 02
Napoli, Donna Jo .... Author V.16
Nash, John Forbes Jr. .... Science V.7
Nash, Steve .... Jan 06
Native Americans
  Bruchac, Joseph .... Author V.18
  Fergie (Stacy Ferguson) .... Apr 06
  House, Donna .... Science V.11
  LaDuke, Winona .... WorLdr V.3;
    Update 00
  Mankiller, Wilma .... Apr 94
  Menchu, Rigoberta .... Jan 93
Navratilova, Martina .... Jan 93; Update 94
Naylor, Phyllis Reynolds .... Apr 93
Ndeti, Cosmas .... Sep 95
Nechita, Alexandra .... Jan 98
Nelly .... Sep 03
Nelson, Gaylord .... WorLdr V.3
Nelson, Marilyn .... Author V.13
Nevelson, Louise .... Artist V.1
New Zealanders
  Hillary, Sir Edmund .... Sep 96
  Jackson, Peter .... PerfArt V.2
Newbery Medal
  Alexander, Lloyd .... Author V.6
  Armstrong, William H. .... Author V.7
  Cleary, Beverly .... Apr 94
  Creech, Sharon .... Author V.5
  Curtis, Christopher Paul ..... Author V.4;
    Update 00
  Cushman, Karen .... Author V.5
  Freedman, Russell .... Author V.14
  George, Jean Craighead ..... Author V.3
  Hamilton, Virginia .... Author V.1;
    Author V.12
  Hesse, Karen ...... Author V.5; Update 02
  Kadohata, Cynthia .... Sep 06
  Konigsburg, E.L. .... Author V.3
  L'Engle, Madeleine .... Jan 92; Apr 01
  MacLachlan, Patricia .... Author V.2
  Naylor, Phyllis Reynolds .... Apr 93
  O'Dell, Scott .... Author V.2
  Paterson, Katherine .... Author V.3
  Peck, Richard .... Author V.10

Rylant, Cynthia .... Author V.1
Sachar, Louis .... Author V.6
Speare, Elizabeth George .... Sep 95
Spinelli, Jerry .... Apr 93
Taylor, Mildred D. .... Author V.1;
  Update 02
Voight, Cynthia .... Oct 92
Newman, Ryan .... Sport V.11
Newsom, Lee Ann .... Science V.11
Nhat Hanh (Thich) .... Jan 04
Nicklaus, Jack .... Sport V.2
Niedermayer, Scott .... Jan 08
Nielsen, Jerri .... Science V.7
Nigerians
  Olajuwon, Hakeem .... Sep 95
  Saro-Wiwa, Ken .... WorLdr V.1
Nixon, Joan Lowery .... Author V.1
Nixon, Richard .... Sep 94
Nkrumah, Kwame .... WorLdr V.2
Nobel Prize
  Alvarez, Luis W. .... Science V.3
  Aung San Suu Kyi .... Apr 96; Update 98;
    Update 01; Update 02
  Bardeen, John .... Science V.1
  Bethe, Hans A. .... Science V.3
  Carter, Jimmy .... Apr 95; Update 02
  Dalai Lama .... Sep 98
  de Klerk, F.W. .... Apr 94
  Ebadi, Shirin .... Apr 04
  Elion, Gertrude .... Science V.6
  Feynman, Richard P. .... Science V.10
  Gilbert, Walter .... Science V.2
  Gorbachev, Mikhail .... Jan 92
  Gore, Al .... Sep 08
  Kim Dae-jung .... Sep 01
  Levi-Montalcini, Rita .... Science V.1
  Maathai, Wangari .... Sep 05
  Mandela, Nelson ...... Jan 92; Update 94;
    Update 01
  McClintock, Barbara .... Oct 92
  Menchu, Rigoberta .... Jan 93
  Morrison, Toni .... Jan 94
  Nash, John Forbes Jr. .... Science V.7
  Ochoa, Severo .... Jan 94
  Pauling, Linus .... Jan 95
  Sadat, Anwar .... WorLdr V.2
  Teresa, Mother .... Apr 98
  Watson, James D. .... Science V.1
  Yunus, Muhammad .... Sep 07

CUMULATIVE GENERAL INDEX

Noor al Hussein, Queen of Jordan . . Jan 05
Norman, Christine . . . . Apr 08
Norman, Greg . . . . Jan 94
Norwegians
    Arnesen, Liv . . . . Author V.15
    Brundtland, Gro Harlem . . . . . Science V.3
Norwood, Brandy
    see Brandy . . . . Apr 96
Novello, Antonia . . . . Apr 92; Update 93
*N Sync . . . . Jan 01
Nureyev, Rudolf . . . . Apr 93
Nye, Bill . . . . Science V.2
Nye, Naomi Shihab . . . . Author V.8
Nyerere, Julius Kambarage . . . WorLdr V.2;
    Update 99
Obama, Barack . . . . Jan 07
O'Brien, Soledad . . . . Jan 07
Ocampo, Adriana C. . . . . Science V.8
Ochoa, Ellen . . . . Apr 01; Update 02
Ochoa, Lorena . . . . Sport V.14
Ochoa, Severo . . . . Jan 94
O'Connor, Sandra Day . . . . Jul 92
O'Dell, Scott . . . . Author V.2
O'Donnell, Rosie . . . . Apr 97; Update 02
Ohno, Apolo . . . . Sport V.8
Oka, Masi . . . . Jan 08
O'Keeffe, Georgia . . . . Artist V.1
Olajuwon, Hakeem . . . . Sep 95
Oleynik, Larisa . . . . Sep 96
Oliver, Jamie . . . . Apr 07
Oliver, Patsy Ruth . . . . WorLdr V.1
Olsen, Ashley . . . . Sep 95
Olsen, Mary Kate . . . . Sep 95
Olympics
    Agosto, Ben . . . . Sport V.14
    Ali, Muhammad . . . . Sport V.2
    Ammann, Simon . . . . Sport V.8
    Armstrong, Lance. . . . . Sep 00; Update 00;
        Update 01; Update 02
    Bahrke, Shannon . . . . Sport V.8
    Bailey, Donovan . . . . Sport V.2
    Baiul, Oksana . . . . Apr 95
    Belbin, Tanith . . . . Sport V.14
    Bird, Larry . . . . Jan 92; Update 98
    Blair, Bonnie . . . . Apr 94
    Boulmerka, Hassiba . . . . Sport V.1
    Capriati, Jennifer . . . . Sport V.6
    Carter, Vince . . . . Sport V.5; Update 01
    Catchings, Tamika . . . . Sport V.14
    Chastain, Brandi . . . . Sport V.4; Update 00
    Clark, Kelly . . . . Sport V.8
    Cohen, Sasha . . . . Sport V.12
    Davenport, Lindsay . . . . Sport V.5
    Devers, Gail . . . . Sport V.2
    Dragila, Stacy . . . . Sport V.6
    Dunlap, Alison . . . . Sport V.7
    Evans, Janet . . . . Jan 95; Update 96
    Ewing, Patrick . . . . Jan 95; Update 02
    Fernandez, Lisa . . . . Sport V.5
    Finch, Jennie . . . . Jan 05
    Flowers, Vonetta . . . . Sport V.8
    Foudy, Julie . . . . Sport V.13
    Freeman, Cathy . . . . Jan 01
    Fu Mingxia . . . . Sport V.5
    Garnett, Kevin . . . . Sport V.6
    Giddens, Rebecca . . . . Sport V.14
    Granato, Cammi . . . . Sport V.8
    Griffith Joyner, Florence . . . . Sport V.1;
        Update 98
    Hamm, Mia . . . . Sport V.2; Update 00
    Harding, Tonya . . . . Sep 94
    Hasek, Dominik . . . . Sport V.3
    Hill, Grant . . . . Sport V.1
    Hughes, Sarah . . . . Jan 03
    James, LeBron . . . . Sport V.12
    Jansen, Dan . . . . Apr 94
    Johnson, Michael . . . . . . Jan 97; Update 00
    Jones, Marion . . . . Sport V.5
    Joyner-Kersee, Jackie . . . . Oct 92;
        Update 96; Update 97; Update 98
    Kerrigan, Nancy . . . . Apr 94
    Klug, Chris . . . . Sport V.8
    Kwan, Michelle . . . . . Sport V.3; Update 02
    Leslie, Lisa . . . . Jan 04
    Lewis, Carl . . . . Sep 96
    Lipinski, Tara . . . . Apr 98
    Lobo, Rebecca . . . . Sport V.3
    Milbrett, Tiffeny . . . . Sport V.10
    Miller, Shannon . . . . Sep 94; Update 96
    Moceanu, Dominique . . . . Jan 98
    Moseley, Jonny . . . . Sport V.8
    Ohno, Apolo . . . . Sport V.8
    Otto, Sylke . . . . Sport V.8
    Patterson, Carly . . . . Sport V.12
    Phelps, Michael . . . . Sport V.13
    Pippig, Uta . . . . Sport V.1
    Richardson, Dot . . . . Sport V.2; Update 00

Roba, Fatuma .... Sport V.3
Robinson, David .... Sep 96
Roy, Patrick .... Sport V.7
Rudolph, Wilma .... Apr 95
Runyan, Marla .... Apr 02
Sakic, Joe .... Sport V.6
Sanborn, Ryne .... Sport V.8
Sanchez Vicario, Arantxa ...... Sport V.1
Schwikert, Tasha .... Sport V.7
Scurry, Briana .... Jan 00
Shea, Jim Jr. .... Sport V.8
Stockton, John .... Sport V.3
Street, Picabo .... Sport V.3
Summitt, Pat .... Sport V.3
Swoopes, Sheryl .... Sport V.2
Teter, Hannah .... Sep 06
Thompson, Jenny .... Sport V.5
Van Dyken, Amy .... Sport V.3; Update 00
Villa, Brenda .... Jan 06
Wade, Dwyane .... Sport V.14
Walsh, Kerri .... Sport V.13
Weatherspoon, Teresa .... Sport V.12
White, Shaun .... Sport V.14
Williams, Serena .... Sport V.4;
　Update 00; Update 02
Williams, Venus .... Jan 99;
　Update 00; Update 01; Update 02
Yamaguchi, Kristi .... Apr 92
Zmeskal, Kim .... Jan 94
O'Neal, Shaquille .... Sep 93
Opdyke, Irene Gut .... Author V.9
Oppenheimer, J. Robert ...... Science V.1
Otto, Sylke .... Sport V.8
OutKast .... Sep 04
Page, Larry .... Sep 05
painters
　see artists
Pak, Se Ri .... Sport V.4
Pakistanis
　Bhutto, Benazir .... Apr 95; Update 99
　Masih, Iqbal .... Jan 96
Palenik, Skip .... Jan 07
Palestinian
　Arafat, Yasir .... Sep 94; Update 94;
　Update 95; Update 96; Update 97;
　Update 98; Update 00; Update 01;
　Update 02
Palmer, Violet .... Sep 05

Panamanian
　Chambers, Veronica .... Author V.15
Paolini, Christopher .... Author V.16
Park, Linda Sue .... Author V.12
Park, Nick .... Sep 06
Parkinson, Jennifer .... Apr 95
Parks, Gordon .... Artist V.1
Parks, Rosa ..... Apr 92; Update 94; Apr 06
Pascal, Francine .... Author V.6
Paterson, Katherine .... Author V.3
Patrick, Danica .... Apr 06
Patrick, Ruth .... Science V.3
Patterson, Carly .... Sport V.12
Patterson, Ryan .... Science V.7
Patton, Antwan
　see OutKast .... Sep 04
Pauley, Jane .... Oct 92
Pauling, Linus .... Jan 95
Paulsen, Gary .... Author V.1
Payton, Walter .... Jan 00
Pearman, Raven-Symone
　see Raven .... Apr 04
Peck, Richard .... Author V.10
Peet, Bill .... Author V.4
Pei, I.M. .... Artist V.1
Pelé .... Sport V.1
Pelosi, Nancy .... Sep 07
Perlman, Itzhak .... Jan 95
Perot, H. Ross .... Apr 92; Update 93;
　Update 95; Update 96
Perry, Luke .... Jan 92
Perry, Tyler .... Sep 08
Peruvian
　Mulanovich, Sofia .... Apr 07
Peterson, Roger Tory .... WorLdr V.1
Petty, Richard .... Sport V.2
Phelps, Michael .... Sport V.13
philanthropists
　Dawson, Matel Jr. .... Jan 04
　McCarty, Oseola ...... Jan 99; Update 99
　Rowland, Pleasant T. .... Business V.1
philosopher
　Caplan, Arthur .... Science V.6
Phoenix, River .... Apr 94
photographers
　Adams, Ansel .... Artist V.1
　Bourke-White, Margaret .... Artist V.1

523

CUMULATIVE GENERAL INDEX

Land, Edwin .... Science V.1
Leibovitz, Annie .... Sep 96
Parks, Gordon .... Artist V.1
Pierce, Tamora .... Author V.13
Pike, Christopher .... Sep 96
pilots
   Funk, Wally .... Jan 05
   Van Meter, Vicki .... Jan 95
Pine, Elizabeth Michele .... Jan 94
Pinkney, Andrea Davis ...... Author V.10
Pinkney, Jerry .... Author V.2
Pinkwater, Daniel .... Author V.8
Pinsky, Robert .... Author V.7
Pippen, Scottie .... Oct 92
Pippig, Uta .... Sport V.1
Pitt, Brad .... Sep 98
playwrights
   Bennett, Cherie .... Author V.9
   Bruchac, Joseph .... Author V.18
   Hansberry, Lorraine .... Author V.5
   Hughes, Langston .... Author V.7
   Perry, Tyler .... Sep 08
   Smith, Betty .... Author V.17
   Wilson, August .... Author 98
poets
   Alvarez, Julia .... Author V.17
   Brooks, Gwendolyn .... Author V.3
   Bruchac, Joseph .... Author V.18
   Collins, Billy .... Author V.16
   Dove, Rita .... Jan 94
   Dunbar, Paul Lawrence ..... Author V.8
   Grimes, Nikki .... Author V.14
   Hughes, Langston .... Author V.7
   Jewel .... Sep 98
   Lansky, Bruce .... Author V.17
   Martinez, Victor .... Author V.15
   Morrison, Lillian .... Author V.12
   Nelson, Marilyn .... Author V.13
   Nye, Naomi Shihab .... Author V.8
   Pinsky, Robert .... Author V.7
   Prelutsky, Jack .... Author V.2; Sep 07
   Senghor, Léopold Sédar ..... WorLdr V.2
   Silverstein, Shel ... Author V.3; Update 99
   Sones, Sonya .... Author V.11
   Soto, Gary .... Author V.5
   Stepanek, Mattie .... Apr 02
Polish
   John Paul II .... Oct 92; Update 94;
      Update 95; Sep 05

Opdyke, Irene Gut .... Author V.9
political leaders
   Abzug, Bella .... Sep 98
   Amin, Idi .... WorLdr V.2
   Annan, Kofi .... Jan 98; Update 01
   Arafat, Yasir .... Sep 94; Update 94;
      Update 95; Update 96; Update 97;
      Update 98; Update 00; Update 01;
      Update 02
   Aristide, Jean-Bertrand .... Jan 95;
      Update 01
   Babbitt, Bruce .... Jan 94
   Baker, James .... Oct 92
   Banda, Hastings Kamuzu .... WorLdr V.2
   Bellamy, Carol .... Jan 06
   Booker, Cory .... Jan 08
   Bhutto, Benazir .... Apr 95; Update 99;
      Update 02
   Blair, Tony .... Apr 04
   Boutros-Ghali, Boutros .... Apr 93;
      Update 98
   Brundtland, Gro Harlem ..... Science V.3
   Bush, George .... Jan 92
   Bush, George W... ..... Sep 00; Update 00;
      Update 01; Update 02
   Carter, Jimmy .... Apr 95; Update 02
   Castro, Fidel .... Jul 92; Update 94
   Cheney, Dick .... Jan 02
   Cisneros, Henry .... Sep 93
   Clinton, Bill .... Jul 92; Update 94;
      Update 95; Update 96; Update 97;
      Update 98; Update 99; Update 00;
      Update 01
   Clinton, Hillary Rodham .... Apr 93;
      Update 94; Update 95; Update 96;
      Update 99; Update 00; Update 01
   de Klerk, F.W. .... Apr 94; Update 94
   Dole, Bob .... Jan 96; Update 96
   Duke, David .... Apr 92
   Fox, Vicente .... Apr 03
   Gingrich, Newt .... Apr 95; Update 99
   Giuliani, Rudolph .... Sep 02
   Glenn, John .... Jan 99
   Gorbachev, Mikhail ... Jan 92; Update 94;
      Update 96
   Gore, Al .... Jan 93; Update 96;
      Update 97; Update 98; Update 99;
      Update 00; Update 01; Sep 08
   Hussein, King .... Apr 99

CUMULATIVE GENERAL INDEX

Hussein, Saddam . . . . . .Jul 92; Update 96;
   Update 01; Update 02
Jackson, Jesse . . . . .Sep 95; Update 01
Jordan, Barbara . . . . .Apr 96
Kaunda, Kenneth . . . . .WorLdr V.2
Kenyatta, Jomo . . . . .WorLdr V.2
Kim Dae-jung . . . . .Sep 01
Lewis, John . . . . .Jan 03
Mandela, Nelson . . . . .Jan 92; Update 94;
   Update 01
McCain, John . . . . .Apr 00
Milosevic, Slobodan . . . . .Sep 99;
   Update 00; Update 01; Update 02
Mobutu Sese Seko . . . . .WorLdr V.2;
   Update 97
Mugabe, Robert . . . . .WorLdr V.2
Nelson, Gaylord . . . . .WorLdr V.3
Nixon, Richard . . . . .Sep 94
Nkrumah, Kwame . . . . .WorLdr V.2
Nyerere, Julius Kambarage . . .WorLdr V.2;
   Update 99
Obama, Barack . . . . .Jan 07
Pelosi, Nancy . . . . .Sep 07
Perot, H. Ross . . . . .Apr 92; Update 93;
   Update 95; Update 96
Powell, Colin . . . . .Jan 92; Update 93;
   Update 95; Update 01
Rabin, Yitzhak . . . . .Oct 92; Update 93;
   Update 94; Update 95
Reagan, Ronald . . . . .Sep 04
Rice, Condoleezza . . . . .Apr 02
Robinson, Mary . . . . .Sep 93
Sadat, Anwar . . . . .WorLdr V.2
Savimbi, Jonas . . . . .WorLdr V.2
Schroeder, Pat . . . . .Jan 97
Senghor, Léopold Sédar . . . . .WorLdr V.2
Sessions, Michael . . . . .Apr 07
Tubman, William V.S. . . . . . . .WorLdr V.2
Ventura, Jesse . . . . .Apr 99; Update 02
Yeltsin, Boris . . . . .Apr 92; Update 93;
   Update 95; Update 96; Update 98;
   Update 00

Pope of the Roman Catholic Church
John Paul II . . . . .Oct 92; Update 94;
   Update 95; Sep 05

Portman, Natalie . . . . .Sep 99
Potter, Beatrix . . . . .Author V.8
Poussaint, Alvin . . . . .Science V.9

Powell, Colin . . . . .Jan 92; Update 93;
   Update 95; Update 01
Prelutsky, Jack . . . . .Author V.2; Sep 07
presidents
 – **Cuba**
   Castro, Fidel . . . . .Jul 92; Update 94
 – **Egypt**
   Sadat, Anwar . . . . .WorLdr V.2
 – **Ghana**
   Nkrumah, Kwame . . . . .WorLdr V.2
 – **Haiti**
   Aristide, Jean-Bertrand . . . . .Jan 95;
   Update 01
 – **Iraq**
   Hussein, Saddam . . . . .Jul 92; Update 96;
   Update 01
 – **Ireland**
   Robinson, Mary . . . . .Sep 93
 – **Kenya**
   Kenyatta, Jomo . . . . .WorLdr V.2
 – **Liberia**
   Tubman, William V.S. . . . . . .WorLdr V.2
 – **Malawi**
   Banda, Hastings Kamuzu . . .WorLdr V.2
 – **Republic of South Africa**
   de Klerk, F.W. . . . . .Apr 94; Update 9
   Mandela, Nelson . . . . .Jan 92; Update 94;
   Update 01
 – **Republic of Tanzania**
   Nyerere, Julius
      Kambarage . . . . .WorLdr V.2;
   Update 99
 – **Russian Federation**
   Yeltsin, Boris . . . . .Apr 92; Update 93;
   Update 95; Update 96; Update 98;
   Update 00
 – **Senegal**
   Senghor, Léopold Sédar . . . .WorLdr V.2
 – **South Korea**
   Kim Dae-jung . . . . .Sep 01
 – **Soviet Union**
   Gorbachev, Mikhail . . . . .Jan 92
 – **Uganda**
   Amin, Idi . . . . .WorLdr V.2
 – **United States**
   Bush, George . . . . .Jan 92
   Bush, George W. . . . .Sep 00; Update 00;
   Update 01; Update 02
   Carter, Jimmy . . . . .Apr 95; Update 02

525

CUMULATIVE GENERAL INDEX

Clinton, Bill . . . . .Jul 92; Update 94;
   Update 95; Update 96; Update 97;
   Update 98; Update 99; Update 00;
   Update 01
Nixon, Richard . . . . .Sep 94
Reagan, Ronald . . . . .Sep 04
– **Yugoslavia**
   Milosevic, Slobodan . . . . .Sep 99;
   Update 00; Update 01; Update 02
– **Zaire**
   Mobutu Sese Seko . . . . .WorLdr V.2;
   Update 97
– **Zambia**
   Kaunda, Kenneth . . . . .WorLdr V.2
– **Zimbabwe**
   Mugabe, Robert . . . . .WorLdr V.2
Pressel, Morgan . . . . .Jan 08
Priestley, Jason . . . . .Apr 92
prime ministers
– **Israel**
   Rabin, Yitzhak . . . . . . .Oct 92; Update 93;
   Update 94; Update 95
– **Norway**
   Brundtland, Gro Harlem . . . .Science V.3
– **Pakistan**
   Bhutto, Benazir . . . . . .Apr 95; Update 99;
   Update 02
– **United Kingdom**
   Blair, Tony . . . . .Apr 04
Prinze, Freddie Jr. . . . . .Apr 00
Pritchard, Michael (Mike Dirnt)
see Green Day . . . . .Apr 06
Probst, Jeff . . . . .Jan 01
producers
Barrymore, Drew . . . . .Jan 01
Carter, Chris . . . . .Author V.4
Chan, Jackie . . . . .PerfArt V.1
Combs, Sean (Puff Daddy) . . . . .Apr 98
Cousteau, Jacques . . . . .Jan 93
Groppe, Laura . . . . .Science V.5
Hillenburg, Stephen . . . . .Author V.14
Jackson, Peter . . . . .PerfArt V.2
Jones, Chuck . . . . .Author V.12
Jones, Quincy . . . . .PerfArt V.2
Kutcher, Ashton . . . . .Apr 04
Lucas, George . . . . .Apr 97; Update 02
Park, Nick .Sep 06
Perry, Tyler . . . . .Sep 08
Rogers, Fred . . . . .PerfArt V.3

Spielberg, Steven . . . . .Jan 94
Thomas, Rob . . . . .Jan 07
Whedon, Joss . . . . .Author V.9
Williamson, Kevin . . . . .Author V.6
Winfrey, Oprah . . . . .Business V.1
Puerto Ricans
see also Hispanics
Lopez, Charlotte . . . . .Apr 94
Martin, Ricky . . . . .Jan 00
Novello, Antonia . . . . .Apr 92
Rodriguez, Ivan "Pudge" . . . . .Jan 07
Puff Daddy
see Combs, Sean (Puff Daddy) . . . . .Apr 98
Puffy
see Combs, Sean (Puff Daddy) . . . . .Apr 98
Pujols, Albert . . . . .Sport V.12
Pullman, Philip . . . . .Author V.9
Qaddafi, Muammar . . . . .Apr 97
Qing, Dai
see Dai Qing . . . . .WorLdr V.3
Queen Latifah . . . . .Apr 92
Quesada, Vicente Fox
see Fox, Vicente . . . . .Apr 03
Quintanilla, Selena
see Selena . . . . .Jan 96
Rabin, Yitzhak . .Oct 92; Update 93; Update 94; Update 95
Radcliffe, Daniel . . . . .Jan 02
radio
Hunter-Gault, Charlayne . . . . .Jan 00
Limbaugh, Rush . . . . . .Sep 95; Update 02
Roberts, Cokie . . . . .Apr 95
Ramirez, Manny . . . . .Sport V.13
Ramos, Jorge .Apr 06
rappers
see music
Raven . . . . .Apr 04
Raymond, Usher IV
see Usher . . . . .PerfArt V.1
Reagan, Ronald . . . . .Sep 04
Reeve, Christopher . . . . .Jan 97; Update 02
Reeves, Keanu . . . . .Jan 04
referee
Palmer, Violet . . . . .Sep 05
Reid Banks, Lynne . . . . .Author V.2
religious leaders
Aristide, Jean-Bertrand . . . . .Jan 95;
   Update 01

CUMULATIVE GENERAL INDEX

Chavis, Benjamin ...... Jan 94; Update 94
Dalai Lama .... Sep 98
Farrakhan, Louis .... Jan 97
Jackson, Jesse .... Sep 95; Update 01
Jakes, T.D. .... Jan 05
John Paul II .... Oct 92; Update 94;
 Update 95; Sep 05
Nhat Hanh (Thich) .... Jan 04
Teresa, Mother .... Apr 98
Rennison, Louise .... Author V.10
Reno, Janet .... Sep 93; Update 98
representatives
 Abzug, Bella .... Sep 98
 Cheney, Dick .... Jan 02
 Gingrich, Newt .... Apr 95; Update 99
 Jordan, Barbara .... Apr 96
 Lewis, John .... Jan 03
 Pelosi, Nancy .... Sep 07
 Schroeder, Pat .... Jan 97
Republican Party
 Baker, James .... Oct 92
 Bush, George .... Jan 92
 Bush, George W.. ..... Sep 00; Update 00;
  Update 01; Update 02
 Cheney, Dick .... Jan 02
 Gingrich, Newt .... Apr 95; Update 99
 Giuliani, Rudolph .... Sep 02
 McCain, John .... Apr 00
 Nixon, Richard .... Sep 94
 Reagan, Ronald .... Sep 04
Rice, Anne .... Author V.3
Rice, Condoleezza .... Apr 02
Rice, Jerry .... Apr 93
Richardson, Dot ..... Sport V.2; Update 00
Richardson, Kevin
 see Backstreet Boys .... Jan 00
Ride, Sally .... Jan 92
Rihanna .... Apr 08
Riley, Dawn .... Sport V.4
Rimes, LeAnn .... Jan 98
Rinaldi, Ann .... Author V.8
Ringgold, Faith .... Author V.2
Ripken, Cal Jr. .... Sport V.1; Update 01
Risca, Viviana .... Sep 00
Rivera, Diego .... Artist V.1
Roba, Fatuma .... Sport V.3
Roberts, Cokie .... Apr 95
Roberts, John Jr. .... Apr 08
Roberts, Julia .... Sep 01
Robertson, Allison (Donna R.)
 see Donnas .... Apr 04
Robinson, David .... Sep 96
Robinson, Jackie .... Sport V.3
Robinson, Mary .... Sep 93
Robison, Emily
 see Dixie Chicks .... PerfArt V.1
rock climbing
 Allen, Tori .... Sport V.9
Rockwell, Norman .... Artist V.1
Roddick, Andy .... Jan 03
rodeo
 Murray, Ty .... Sport V.7
Rodman, Dennis .... Apr 96; Update 99
Rodriguez, Alex .... Sport V.6
Rodriguez, Eloy .... Science V.2
Rodriguez, Gloria .... Apr 05
Rodriguez, Ivan "Pudge" .... Jan 07
Roethlisberger, Ben .... Sep 06
Rogers, Fred .... PerfArt V.3
Romanians
 Dumitriu, Ioana .... Science V.3
 Nechita, Alexandra .... Jan 98
 Risca, Viviana. .... Sep 00
Romeo, Lil' .... Jan 06
Romero, John .... Science V.8
Roper, Dee Dee
 see Salt 'N' Pepa .... Apr 95
Rosa, Emily .... Sep 98
Rose, Pete .... Jan 92
Rowan, Carl .... Sep 01
Rowland, Kelly
 see Destiny's Child .... Apr 01
Rowland, Pleasant T. .... Business V.1
Rowling, J.K. .... Sep 99; Update 00;
 Update 01; Update 02; Jan 08
Roy, Patrick .... Sport V.7
royalty
 Diana, Princess of Wales .... Jul 92;
  Update 96; Update 97; Jan 98
 Haile Selassie .... WorLdr V.2
 Hassan II .... WorLdr V.2; Update 99
 Hussein, King .... Apr 99
 Noor al Hussein, Queen of Jordan . Jan 05
Rubin, Jamie .... Science V.8
Rudolph, Wilma .... Apr 95

527

CUMULATIVE GENERAL INDEX

running
  Bailey, Donovan .... Sport V.2
  Boulmerka, Hassiba .... Sport V.1
  Felix, Allyson .... Sport V.10
  Freeman, Cathy .... Jan 01
  Griffith Joyner, Florence .... Sport V.1;
    Update 98
  Johnson, Michael ..... Jan 97; Update 00
  Jones, Marion .... Sport V.5
  Lewis, Carl .... Sep 96; Update 97
  Ndeti, Cosmas .... Sep 95
  Pippig, Uta .... Sport V.1
  Roba, Fatuma .... Sport V.3
  Rudolph, Wilma .... Apr 95
  Runyan, Marla .... Apr 02
  Webb, Alan .... Sep 01
Runyan, Marla .... Apr 02
Russell, Charlie .... Science V.11
Russians
  Brin, Sergey .... Sep 05
  Chagall, Marc .... Artist V.1
  Fedorov, Sergei .... Apr 94; Update 94
  Gorbachev, Mikhail ... Jan 92; Update 96
  Nevelson, Louise .... Artist V.1
  Sharapova, Maria .... Sep 05
  Tartakovsky, Genndy .... Author V.11
  Yeltsin, Boris .... Apr 92; Update 93;
    Update 95; Update 96; Update 98;
    Update 00
Ryan, Nolan .... Oct 92; Update 93
Ryan, Pam Muñoz .... Author V.12
Ryder, Winona .... Jan 93
Rylant, Cynthia .... Author V.1
Sabin, Albert .... Science V.1
Sachar, Louis .... Author V.6
Sacks, Oliver .... Science V.3
Sadat, Anwar .... WorLdr V.2
Sagan, Carl .... Science V.1
sailing
  MacArthur, Ellen .... Sport V.11
  Riley, Dawn .... Sport V.4
Sakic, Joe .... Sport V.6
Salinger, J.D. .... Author V.2
Salk, Jonas .... Jan 94; Update 95
Salt 'N' Pepa .... Apr 95
Sampras, Pete .... Jan 97; Update 02
Sanborn, Ryne .... Sport V.8
Sanchez, Ricardo .... Sep 04

Sanchez Vicario, Arantxa .... Sport V.1
Sanders, Barry .... Sep 95; Update 99
Sanders, Deion .... Sport V.1
Sandler, Adam .... Jan 06
Santana, Carlos .... Sep 05
Sapp, Warren .... Sport V.5
Saro-Wiwa, Ken .... WorLdr V.1
Satcher, David .... Sep 98
Saudi
  bin Laden, Osama .... Apr 02
Savimbi, Jonas .... WorLdr V.2
Scalia, Antonin .... Jan 05
Scarry, Richard .... Sep 94
Schilling, Curt .... Sep 05
Schroeder, Pat .... Jan 97
Schulz, Charles M .. Author V.2; Update 00
Schwarzkopf, H. Norman .... Jan 92
Schwikert, Tasha .... Sport V.7
science competitions
  Cohen, Adam Ezra .... Apr 97
  Lisanti, Mariangela .... Sep 01
  Patterson, Ryan .... Science V.7
  Pine, Elizabeth Michele .... Jan 94
  Risca, Viviana .... Sep 00
  Rosa, Emily .... Sep 98
  Rubin, Jamie .... Science V.8
  Toro, Natalia .... Sep 99
  Vasan, Nina .... Science V.7
scientists
  Alvarez, Luis W. .... Science V.3
  Asimov, Isaac .... Jul 92
  Askins, Renee .... WorLdr V.1
  Attenborough, David .... Science V.4
  Ballard, Robert .... Science V.4
  Bardeen, John .... Science V.1
  Barton, Hazel .... Science V.6
  Bass, Bill .... Apr 08
  Berners-Lee, Tim .... Science V.7
  Bethe, Hans A. .... Science V.3
  Binford, Greta .... Jan 08
  Brundtland, Gro Harlem ..... Science V.3
  Calderone, Mary S. .... Science V.3
  Carson, Ben .... Science V.4
  Carson, Rachel .... WorLdr V.1
  Collins, Francis .... Science V.6
  Córdova, France .... Science V.7
  Cray, Seymour .... Science V.2
  Earle, Sylvia .... Science V.1

Elion, Gertrude .... Science V.6
Engelbart, Douglas .... Science V.5
Farmer, Paul Jr. .... Science V.11
Fauci, Anthony S. .... Science V.7
Fay, Michael .... Science V.9
Feynman, Richard P. .... Science V.10
Fossey, Dian .... Science V.1
Galdikas, Birutė .... Science V.4
Gayle, Helene .... Science V.8
Gilbert, Walter .... Science V.2
Goodall, Jane ..... Science V.1; Update 02
Gould, Stephen Jay .... Science V.2; Update 02
Grandin, Temple .... Science V.3
Gwaltney, John Langston .... Science V.3
Harris, Bernard .... Science V.3
Hawking, Stephen .... Apr 92
Hayes, Tyrone .... Science V.10
Healy, Bernadine .... Science V.1; Update 01
Hendrickson, Sue .... Science V.7
Ho, David .... Science V.6
Horner, Jack .... Science V.1
House, Donna .... Science V.11
Hrdy, Sarah Blaffer .... Apr 07
Jackson, Shirley Ann .... Science V.2
Jemison, Mae .... Oct 92
Kenyon, Cynthia .... Science V.11
Kiessling, Laura L. .... Science V.9
King, Mary-Claire .... Science V.10
Koff, Clea .... Science V.11
Krim, Mathilde .... Science V.1
Kübler-Ross, Elisabeth ...... Science V.10
Kurzweil, Raymond .... Science V.2
Kwolek, Stephanie .... Science V.10
Leakey, Louis .... Science V.1
Leakey, Mary .... Science V.1
Levi-Montalcini, Rita .... Science V.1
Long, Irene D. .... Jan 04
Love, Susan .... Science V.3
Lowman, Meg .... Science V.4
Lucid, Shannon .... Science V.2
Margulis, Lynn .... Sep 96
McClintock, Barbara .... Oct 92
McNutt, Marcia .... Science V.11
Mead, Margaret .... Science V.2
Mittermeier, Russell A. ..... WorLdr V.1
Moss, Cynthia .... WorLdr V.3
Newsom, Lee Ann .... Science V.11
Ocampo, Adriana C. .... Science V.8
Ochoa, Severo .... Jan 94
Oppenheimer, J. Robert ...... Science V.1
Palenik, Skip .... Jan 07
Patrick, Ruth .... Science V.3
Pauling, Linus .... Jan 95
Ride, Sally .... Jan 92
Rodriguez, Eloy .... Science V.2
Sabin, Albert .... Science V.1
Sacks, Oliver .... Science V.3
Sagan, Carl .... Science V.1
Salk, Jonas .... Jan 94; Update 95
Satcher, David .... Sep 98
Spelke, Elizabeth .... Science V.10
Steingraber, Sandra .... Science V.9
Tarter, Jill .... Science V.8
Teller, Edward .... Science V.9
Thomas, Lewis .... Apr 94
Tuttle, Merlin .... Apr 97
Tyson, Neil deGrasse .... Science V.11
Villa-Komaroff, Lydia .... Science V.6
Wadhwa, Meenakshi .... Science V.11
Warrick, Earl .... Science V.8
Watson, James D. .... Science V.1
Whitson, Peggy .... Science V.9
Wilson, Edward O. .... Science V.8

Scieszka, Jon .... Author V.9
Scott, Jerry .... Author V.15
Scottish
  Glennie, Evelyn .... PerfArt V.3
  Muir, John .... WorLdr V.3
screenwriters
  Affleck, Ben .... Sep 99
  Carter, Chris .... Author V.4
  Crichton, Michael .... Author V.5
  Jackson, Peter .... PerfArt V.2
  Mathison, Melissa .... Author V.4
  Park, Nick .... Sep 06
  Peet, Bill .... Author V.4
  Thomas, Rob .... Jan 07
  Whedon, Joss .... Author V.9
  Williamson, Kevin .... Author V.6
sculptors
  see artists
Scurry, Briana .... Jan 00
Sealfon, Rebecca .... Sep 97
Seinfeld, Jerry .... Oct 92; Update 98
Selena .... Jan 96
Seles, Monica .... Jan 96

529

senators
  Clinton, Hillary Rodham . . . . .Apr 93;
    Update 94; Update 95; Update 96;
    Update 99; Update 00; Update 01
  Dole, Bob . . . . .Jan 96; Update 96
  Glenn, John .Jan 99
  Gore, Al . . . . .Jan 93; Update 96;
    Update 97; Update 98; Update 99;
    Update 00; Update 01; Apr 08
  McCain, John . . . . .Apr 00
  Nelson, Gaylord . . . . .WorLdr V.3
  Nixon, Richard . . . . .Sep 94
  Obama, Barack . . . . .Jan 07
Sendak, Maurice . . . . .Author V.2
Senegalese
  Senghor, Léopold Sédar . . . . .WorLdr V.2
Senghor, Léopold Sédar . . . . . .WorLdr V.2
Serbian
  Milosevic, Slobodan . . . . .Sep 99;
    Update 00; Update 01; Update 02
Sessions, Michael . . . . .Apr 07
Seuss, Dr. . . . . .Jan 92
Shabazz, Betty . . . . .Apr 98
Shakira . . . . .PerfArt V.1
Shakur, Tupac . . . . .Apr 97
Sharapova, Maria . . . . .Sep 05
Shatner, William . . . . .Apr 95
Shea, Jim Jr. . . . . .Sport V.8
Shinoda, Mike
  see Linkin Park . . . . .Jan 04
Shula, Don . . . . .Apr 96
Silva, Fabiola da
  see da Silva, Fabiola . . . . .Sport V.9
Silverstein, Shel . . . .Author V.3; Update 99
Simmons, Russell . . . . .Apr 06
Simmons, Ruth . . . . .Sep 02
Simpson, Ashlee . . . . .Sep 05
Sinatra, Frank . . . . .Jan 99
singers
  see music
Singh, Vijay . . . . .Sport V.13
Siskel, Gene .Sep 99
skateboarding
  Hawk, Tony . . . . .Apr 01
  White, Shaun . . . . .Sport V.14
skating (ice)
  Agosto, Ben . . . . .Sport V.14
  Baiul, Oksana . . . . .Apr 95

  Belbin, Tanith . . . . .Sport V.14
  Blair, Bonnie . . . . .Apr 94; Update 95
  Cohen, Sasha . . . . .Sport V.12
  Harding, Tonya . . . . .Sep 94
  Hughes, Sarah . . . . .Jan 03
  Jansen, Dan . . . . .Apr 94
  Kerrigan, Nancy . . . . .Apr 94
  Kwan, Michelle . . . . .Sport V.3; Update 02
  Lipinski, Tara . . . . .Apr 98
  Meissner, Kimmie . . . . .Sep 08
  Ohno, Apolo . . . . .Sport V.8
  Yamaguchi, Kristi . . . . .Apr 92
skating (in-line)
  da Silva, Fabiola . . . . .Sport V.9
skeleton
  Shea, Jim Jr. . . . . .Sport V.8
skiing
  Amman, Simon . . . . .Sport V.8
  Arnesen, Liv . . . . .Author V.15
  Bahrke, Shannon . . . . .Sport V.8
  Moseley, Jonny . . . . .Sport V.8
  Street, Picabo . . . . .Sport V.3
Sleator, William . . . . .Author V.11
sled-dog racing
  Butcher, Susan . . . . .Sport V.1
  Zirkle, Aliy . . . . .Sport V.6
Small, David . . . . .Author V.10
Smith, Betty . . . . .Author V.17
Smith, Emmitt . . . . .Sep 94
Smith, Will .Sep 94
Smyers, Karen . . . . .Sport V.4
Snicket, Lemony . . . . .Author V.12
snowboarding
  Basich, Tina . . . . .Sport V.12
  Bleiler, Gretchen . . . . .Sport V.13
  Clark, Kelly . . . . .Sport V.8
  Dakides, Tara . . . . .Sport V.7
  Klug, Chris . . . . .Sport V.8
  Teter, Hannah . . . . .Sep 06
  White, Shaun . . . . .Sport V.14
Snyder, Zilpha Keatley . . . . . .Author V.17
soccer
  Adu, Freddy . . . . .Sport V.12
  Beckham, David . . . . .Jan 04
  Chastain, Brandi . . . .Sport V.4; Update 00
  Foudy, Julie . . . . .Sport V.13
  Hamm, Mia . . . . .Sport V.2; Update 00
  Howard, Tim . . . . .Apr 06
  Lalas, Alexi . . . . .Sep 94

CUMULATIVE GENERAL INDEX

Mathis, Clint . . . . Apr 03
Milbrett, Tiffeny . . . . Sport V.10
Pelé . . . . Sport V.1
Scurry, Briana . . . . Jan 00
sociologist
    Tienda, Marta . . . . Sep 08
softball
    Fernandez, Lisa . . . . Sport V.5
    Finch, Jennie . . . . Jan 05
    Richardson, Dot . . . . Sport V.2; Update 00
    Watley, Natasha . . . . Sport V.11
Somalian
    Aidid, Mohammed Farah . . . . WorLdr V.2
Sones, Sonya . . . . Author V.11
Soren, Tabitha . . . . Jan 97
Sorenstam, Annika . . . . Sport V.6
Soriano, Alfonso . . . . Sport V.10
Sosa, Sammy . . . . Jan 99; Update 99
Soto, Gary . . . . Author V.5
South Africans
    de Klerk, F.W. . . . . Apr 94; Update 94
    Mandela, Nelson . . . . . Jan 92; Update 94;
        Update 01
    Mandela, Winnie . . . . WorLdr V.2
South Korean
    Pak, Se Ri . . . . Sport V.4
Spade, Kate . . . . Apr 07
Spaniards
    Domingo, Placido . . . . Sep 95
    Garcia, Sergio . . . . Sport V.7
    Iglesias, Enrique . . . . Jan 03
    Sanchez Vicario, Arantxa . . . . . . Sport V.1
Speare, Elizabeth George . . . . Sep 95
Spears, Britney . . . . Jan 01
Spears, Jamie Lynn . . . . Sep 06
Spelke, Elizabeth . . . . Science V.10
spelling bee competition
    Andrews, Ned . . . . Sep 94
    Guey, Wendy . . . . Sep 96
    Hooper, Geoff . . . . Jan 94
    Maxwell, Jody-Anne . . . . Sep 98
    Sealfon, Rebecca . . . . Sep 97
    Thampy, George. . . . . Sep 00
Spelman, Lucy . . . . Science V.6
Spencer, Diana
    see Diana, Princess of Wales . . . . Jul 92;
        Update 96; Update 97; Jan 98
Spiegelman, Art . . . . Author V.17

Spielberg, Steven . . . . . . Jan 94; Update 94;
    Update 95
Spinelli, Jerry . . . . Apr 93
Spock, Dr. Benjamin . . . Sep 95; Update 98
sports
    Aaron, Hank . . . . Sport V.1
    Abdul-Jabbar, Kareem . . . . Sport V.1
    Adu, Freddy . . . . Sport V.12
    Agassi, Andre . . . . Jul 92
    Agosto, Ben . . . . Sport V.14
    Aikman, Troy . . . . Apr 95; Update 01
    Alexander, Shaun . . . . Apr 07
    Ali, Laila . . . . Sport V.11
    Ali, Muhammad . . . . Sport V.2
    Allen, Marcus . . . . Sep 97
    Allen, Tori . . . . Sport V.9
    Ammann, Simon . . . . Sport V.8
    Andretti, Mario . . . . Sep 94
    Anthony, Carmelo . . . . Sep 07
    Armstrong, Lance. . . . . Sep 00; Update 00;
        Update 01; Update 02
    Asbaty, Diandra . . . . Sport V.14
    Ashe, Arthur . . . . Sep 93
    Bahrke, Shannon . . . . Sport V.8
    Bailey, Donovan . . . . Sport V.2
    Baiul, Oksana . . . . Apr 95
    Barkley, Charles . . . . Apr 92; Update 02
    Basich, Tina . . . . Sport V.12
    Beachley, Layne . . . . Sport V.9
    Beckett, Josh . . . . Sport V.11
    Beckham, David . . . . Jan 04
    Belbin, Tanith . . . . Sport V.14
    Bird, Larry . . . . Jan 92; Update 98
    Bird, Sue . . . . Sport V.9
    Blair, Bonnie. . . . . Apr 94
    Blake, James . . . . Sport V.14
    Bleiler, Gretchen . . . . Sport V.13
    Bonds, Barry . . . . Jan 03
    Boulmerka, Hassiba . . . . Sport V.1
    Boyle, Ryan . . . . Sport V.10
    Brady, Tom . . . . Sport V.7
    Bryant, Kobe . . . . Apr 99
    Butcher, Susan . . . . Sport V.1
    Capolino, Peter . . . . Business V.1
    Capriati, Jennifer . . . . Sport V.6
    Carter, Vince . . . . Sport V.5; Update 01
    Catchings, Tamika . . . . Sport V.14
    Chamberlain, Wilt . . . . Sport V.4
    Chastain, Brandi . . . . Sport V.4; Update 00
    Clark, Kelly . . . . Sport V.8

CUMULATIVE GENERAL INDEX

Clemons, Kortney . . . . Sep 07
Clijsters, Kim . . . . Apr 04
Cohen, Sasha . . . . Sport V.12
Coughlin, Natalie . . . . Sport V.10
Cox, Lynne . . . . Sport V.13
Crosby, Sidney . . . . Sport V.14
Culpepper, Daunte . . . . Sport V.13
Dakides, Tara . . . . Sport V.7
Daniel, Beth . . . . Sport V.1
da Silva, Fabiola . . . . Sport V.9
Davenport, Lindsay . . . . Sport V.5
Dayne, Ron . . . . Apr 00
Devers, Gail . . . . Sport V.2
Dragila, Stacy . . . . Sport V.6
Driscoll, Jean . . . . Sep 97
Dumars, Joe . . . . Sport V.3; Update 99
Duncan, Tim . . . . Apr 04
Dunlap, Alison . . . . Sport V.7
Earnhardt, Dale . . . . Apr 01
Earnhardt, Dale Jr. . . . . Sport V.12
Elway, John . . . . Sport V.2; Update 99
Evans, Janet . . . . Jan 95
Evert, Chris . . . . Sport V.1
Ewing, Patrick . . . . Jan 95; Update 02
Favre, Brett . . . . Sport V.2
Federer, Roger . . . . Jan 07
Fedorov, Sergei . . . . . . Apr 94; Update 94
Felix, Allyson . . . . Sport V.10
Fernandez, Lisa . . . . Sport V.5
Finch, Jennie . . . . Jan 05
Flowers, Vonetta . . . . Sport V.8
Ford, Cheryl . . . . Sport V.11
Foudy, Julie . . . . Sport V.13
Freeman, Cathy . . . . Jan 01
Friday, Dallas . . . . Sport V.10
Fu Mingxia . . . . Sport V.5
Garcia, Sergio . . . . Sport V.7
Garnett, Kevin . . . . Sport V.6
George, Eddie . . . . Sport V.6
Giddens, Rebecca . . . . Sport V.14
Giguère, Jean-Sébastien . . . . . . Sport V.10
Gonzalez, Tony . . . . Sport V.11
Gordon, Jeff . . . . Apr 99
Graf, Steffi . . . . Jan 92; Update 01
Granato, Cammi . . . . Sport V.8
Gretzky, Wayne . . . . . . Jan 92; Update 93;
    Update 99
Griese, Brian . . . . Jan 02
Griffey, Ken Jr. . . . . Sport V.1

Griffith Joyner, Florence . . . . Sport V.1;
    Update 98
Hamilton, Bethany . . . . Apr 05
Hamilton, Laird . . . . Sport V.13
Hamm, Mia . . . . Sport V.2; Update 00
Harbaugh, Jim . . . . Sport V.3
Hardaway, Anfernee "Penny" . . Sport V.2
Harding, Tonya . . . . Sep 94
Hasek, Dominik . . . . Sport V.3
Hawk, Tony . . . . Apr 01
Hernandez, Livan . . . . Apr 98
Hill, Grant . . . . Sport V.1
Hingis, Martina . . . . Sport V.2
Hogan, Hulk . . . . Apr 92
Holdsclaw, Chamique. . . . . Sep 00
Holmes, Priest . . . . Apr 05
Howard, Tim . . . . Apr 06
Howe, Gordie . . . . Sport V.2
Hughes, Sarah . . . . Jan 03
Iverson, Allen . . . . Sport V.7
Jackson, Bo . . . . Jan 92; Update 93
Jackson, Phil . . . . Sport V.10
Jagr, Jaromir . . . . Sport V.5
James, LeBron . . . . Sport V.12
Jansen, Dan . . . . Apr 94
Jeter, Derek . . . . Sport V.4
Johnson, Jimmy . . . . Jan 98
Johnson, Keyshawn . . . . Sport V.10
Johnson, Magic . . . . . . Apr 92; Update 02
Johnson, Michael . . . . . Jan 97; Update 00
Johnson, Randy . . . . Sport V.9
Jones, Marion . . . . Sport V.5
Jordan, Michael . . . . . . Jan 92; Update 93;
    Update 94; Update 95; Update 99;
    Update 01
Joyner-Kersee, Jackie . . . . Oct 92;
    Update 96; Update 97; Update 98
Kerrigan, Nancy . . . . Apr 94
Kidd, Jason . . . . Sport V.9
Kiraly, Karch . . . . Sport V.4
Klug, Chris . . . . Sport V.8
Kwan, Michelle . . . . . Sport V.3; Update 02
Lalas, Alexi . . . . Sep 94
Lee, Jeanette . . . . Apr 03
Lemieux, Mario . . . . Jul 92; Update 93
LeMond, Greg . . . . Sport V.1
Lennox, Betty . . . . Sport V.13
Leslie, Lisa . . . . Jan 04
Lewis, Carl . . . . Sep 96; Update 97
Lidstrom, Nicklas . . . . Sep 03

532

CUMULATIVE GENERAL INDEX

Lipinski, Tara .... Apr 98
Lobo, Rebecca .... Sport V.3
Lowe, Alex .... Sport V.4
MacArthur, Ellen .... Sport V.11
Madden, John .... Sep 97
Maddux, Greg .... Sport V.3
Manning, Eli .... Sep 08
Manning, Peyton .... Sep 00
Mantle, Mickey .... Jan 96
Marino, Dan .... Apr 93; Update 00
Martinez, Pedro .... Sport V.5
Mathis, Clint .... Apr 03
McGrady, Tracy .... Sport V.11
McGwire, Mark .... Jan 99; Update 99
McNabb, Donovan .... Apr 03
McNair, Steve .... Sport V.11
Meissner, Kimmie .... Sep 08
Memmel, Chellsie .... Sport V.14
Messier, Mark .... Apr 96
Milbrett, Tiffeny .... Sport V.10
Miller, Shannon .... Sep 94; Update 96
Mirra, Dave .... Sep 02
Moceanu, Dominique .... Jan 98
Montana, Joe .... Jan 95; Update 95
Moreno, Arturo R. .... Business V.1
Moseley, Jonny .... Sport V.8
Moss, Randy .... Sport V.4
Mulanovich, Sofia .... Apr 07
Muldowney, Shirley .... Sport V.7
Murray, Ty .... Sport V.7
Nash, Steve .... Jan 06
Navratilova, Martina .... Jan 93;
  Update 94
Niedermayer, Scott .... Jan 08
Newman, Ryan .... Sport V.11
Ndeti, Cosmas .... Sep 95
Nicklaus, Jack .... Sport V.2
Ochoa, Lorena .... Sport V.14
Ohno, Apolo .... Sport V.8
Olajuwon, Hakeem .... Sep 95
O'Neal, Shaquille .... Sep 93
Otto, Sylke .... Sport V.8
Pak, Se Ri .... Sport V.4
Palmer, Violet .... Sep 05
Patrick, Danica .... Apr 06
Patterson, Carly .... Sport V.12
Payton, Walter .... Jan 00
Pelé .... Sport V.1
Petty, Richard .... Sport V.2
Phelps, Michael .... Sport V.13

Pippen, Scottie .... Oct 92
Pippig, Uta .... Sport V.1
Pressel, Morgan .... Jan 08
Pujols, Albert .... Sport V.12
Ramirez, Manny .... Sport V.13
Rice, Jerry .... Apr 93
Richardson, Dot .... Sport V.2; Update 00
Riley, Dawn .... Sport V.4
Ripken, Cal Jr. ...... Sport V.1; Update 01
Roba, Fatuma .... Sport V.3
Robinson, David .... Sep 96
Robinson, Jackie .... Sport V.3
Roddick, Andy .... Jan 03
Rodman, Dennis .... Apr 96; Update 99
Rodriguez, Alex .... Sport V.6
Rodriguez, Ivan "Pudge" .... Jan 07
Roethlisberger, Ben .... Sep 06
Rose, Pete .... Jan 92
Roy, Patrick .... Sport V.7
Rudolph, Wilma .... Apr 95
Runyan, Marla .... Apr 02
Ryan, Nolan .... Oct 92; Update 93
Sakic, Joe .... Sport V.6
Sampras, Pete .... Jan 97; Update 02
Sanchez Vicario, Arantxa .... Sport V.1
Sanders, Barry .... Sep 95; Update 99
Sanders, Deion .... Sport V.1
Sapp, Warren .... Sport V.5
Schilling, Curt .... Sep 05
Schwikert, Tasha .... Sport V.7
Scurry, Briana .... Jan 00
Seles, Monica .... Jan 96
Sharapova, Maria .... Sep 05
Shea, Jim Jr. .... Sport V.8
Shula, Don .... Apr 96
Singh, Vijay .... Sport V.13
Smith, Emmitt .... Sep 94
Smyers, Karen .... Sport V.4
Sorenstam, Annika .... Sport V.6
Soriano, Alfonso .... Sport V.10
Sosa, Sammy .... Jan 99; Update 99
Stewart, James Jr. .... Apr 08
Stewart, Kordell .... Sep 98
Stewart, Tony .... Sport V.9
Stiles, Jackie .... Sport V.6
Stockton, John .... Sport V.3
Strahan, Michael .... Sport V.12
Street, Picabo .... Sport V.3
Streeter, Tanya .... Sport V.11
Summitt, Pat .... Sport V.3

533

CUMULATIVE GENERAL INDEX

Suzuki, Ichiro .... Apr 08
Swoopes, Sheryl .... Sport V.2
Taurasi, Diana .... Sport V.10
Teter, Hannah .... Sep 06
Thompson, Jenny .... Sport V.5
Tomlinson, LaDainian .... Sport V.14
Urlacher, Brian .... Sep 04
Van Dyken, Amy .... Sport V.3; Update 00
Ventura, Jesse .... Apr 99; Update 02
Vernon, Mike .... Jan 98; Update 02
Vick, Michael .... Sport V.9
Villa, Brenda .... Jan 06
Wade, Dwyane .... Sport V.14
Wallace, Ben .... Jan 05
Walsh, Kerri .... Sport V.13
Ward, Charlie .... Apr 94
Warner, Kurt .... Sport V.4
Watley, Natasha .... Sport V.11
Weathersoon, Teresa .... Sport V.12
Webb, Alan .... Sep 01
Webb, Karrie ...... Sport V.5; Update 01; Update 02
Weinke, Chris .... Apr 01
White, Reggie .... Jan 98
White, Shaun .... Sport V.14
Wie, Michelle .... Sep 04
Williams, Serena .... Sport V.4; Update 00; Update 02
Williams, Ted .... Sport V.9
Williams, Venus ...... Jan 99; Update 00; Update 01; Update 02
Willingham, Tyrone .... Sep 02
Winfield, Dave .... Jan 93
Woods, Tiger ...... Sport V.1; Update 00; Sport V.6
Yamaguchi, Kristi .... Apr 92
Yao Ming .... Sep 03
Yelas, Jay .... Sport V.9
Young, Steve .... Jan 94; Update 00
Yzerman, Steve .... Sport V.2
Zirkle, Aliy .... Sport V.6
Zmeskal, Kim .... Jan 94
Stachowski, Richie .... Science V.3
Stanford, John .... Sep 99
Stefani, Gwen .... Sep 03
Steinem, Gloria .... Oct 92
Steingraber, Sandra .... Science V.9
Stern, Isaac .... PerfArt V.1
Stewart, James Jr. .... Apr 08

Stewart, Jon .... Jan 06
Stewart, Kordell .... Sep 98
Stewart, Martha .... Business V.1
Stewart, Patrick .... Jan 94
Stewart, Tony .... Sport V.9
Stiles, Jackie .... Sport V.6
Stiles, Julia .... PerfArt V.2
Stine, R.L. .... Apr 94
Stockman, Shawn
  see Boyz II Men .... Jan 96
Stockton, John .... Sport V.3
Stoker, Joscelyn
  see Stone, Joss .... Jan 06
Stone, Joss .... Jan 06
Strahan, Michael .... Sport V.12
Strasser, Todd .... Author V.7
Street, Picabo .... Sport V.3
Streeter, Tanya .... Sport V.11
Strug, Kerri .... Sep 96
Stump, Patrick
  see Fall Out Boy .... Sep 07
Summitt, Pat .... Sport V.3
Supreme Court
  Blackmun, Harry .... Jan 00
  Burger, Warren .... Sep 95
  Ginsburg, Ruth Bader .... Jan 94
  Marshall, Thurgood .... Jan 92; Update 93
  O'Connor, Sandra Day .... Jul 92
  Scalia, Antonin .... Jan 05
  Thomas, Clarence .... Jan 92
surfing
  Beachley, Layne .... Sport V.9
  Hamilton, Bethany .... Apr 05
  Hamilton, Laird .... Sport V.13
  Mulanovich, Sofia .... Apr 07
Suzuki, Ichiro .... Apr 08
Suzuki, Shinichi .... Sep 98
Swanson, Janese .... Science V.4
Swedish
  Lidstrom, Nicklas .... Sep 03
  Lindgren, Astrid .... Author V.13
  Sorenstam, Annika .... Sport V.6
swimming
  Coughlin, Natalie .... Sport V.10
  Cox, Lynne .... Sport V.13
  Evans, Janet .... Jan 95; Update 96
  Phelps, Michael .... Sport V.13
  Thompson, Jenny .... Sport V.5
  Van Dyken, Amy .... Sport V.3; Update 00

CUMULATIVE GENERAL INDEX

Swiss
   Ammann, Simon . . . . .Sport V.8
   Federer, Roger . . . . .Jan 07
   Kübler-Ross, Elisabeth . . . . . .Science V.10
Swoopes, Sheryl . . . . .Sport V.2
Taboo (Jamie Gomez)
   see Black Eyed Peas . . . . .Apr 06
Taiwanese
   Ho, David . . . . .Science V.6
Tan, Amy .Author V.9
Tandy, Karen P. . . . . .Jan 08
Tanzanian
   Nyerere, Julius Kambarage . . .WorLdr V.2;
   Update 99
Tarbox, Katie . . . . .Author V.10
Tartakovsky, Genndy . . . . .Author V.11
Tartar
   Nureyev, Rudolph . . . . .Apr 93
Tarter, Jill . . . . .Science V.8
Tarvin, Herbert . . . . .Apr 97
Taurasi, Diana . . . . .Sport V.10
Taylor, Mildred D. . . . . .Author V.1;
   Update 02
Taymor, Julie . . . . .PerfArt V.1
teachers
   see educators
television
   Alba, Jessica . . . . .Sep 01
   Allen, Tim . . . . .Apr 94; Update 99
   Alley, Kirstie . . . . Jul 92
   Amanpour, Christiane . . . . .Jan 01
   Anderson, Gillian . . . . .Jan 97
   Aniston, Jennifer . . . . .Apr 99
   Arnold, Roseanne . . . . .Oct 92
   Attenborough, David . . . . . . .Science V.4
   Banks, Tyra . . . . .PerfArt V.2
   Bell, Drake . . . . .Jan 07
   Bell, Kristen . . . . .Sep 05
   Bergen, Candice . . . . .Sep 93
   Bialik, Mayim . . . . .Jan 94
   Blanchard, Rachel . . . . .Apr 97
   Bledel, Alexis . . . . .Jan 03
   Brandis, Jonathan . . . . .Sep 95
   Brandy . . . . .Apr 96
   Brody, Adam . . . . .Sep 05
   Bryan, Zachery Ty . . . . .Jan 97
   Burke, Chris . . . . .Sep 93
   Burns, Ken .Jan 95
   Bush, Sophia . . . . .Apr 08

Bynes, Amanda . . . . .Sep 03
Cameron, Candace . . . . .Apr 95
Campbell, Neve . . . . .Apr 98
Candy, John .Sep 94
Cantore, Jim . . . . .Science V.9
Carter, Chris . . . . .Author V.4
Carvey, Dana . . . . .Jan 93
Chung, Connie . . . . . . .Jan 94; Update 95;
   Update 96
Clarkson, Kelly . . . . .Jan 03
Cooper, Anderson . . . . .Sep 08
Cosby, Bill . . . . .Jan 92
Cousteau, Jacques . . . . .Jan 93
Crawford, Cindy . . . . .Apr 93
Crichton, Michael . . . . .Author V.5
Cyrus, Miley . . . . .Sep 07
Daly, Carson . . . . .Apr 00
Doherty, Shannen . . . . .Apr 92; Update 94
Duchovny, David . . . . .Apr 96
Duff, Hilary .Sep 02
Efron, Zac . . . . .Apr 08
Ellerbee, Linda . . . . .Apr 94
Eve . . . . .Jan 05
Ferrell, Will .Apr 07
Ferrera, America . . . . .Sep 07
Foray, June .Jan 07
Fuentes, Daisy . . . . .Jan 94
Garth, Jennie . . . . .Apr 96
Gellar, Sarah Michelle . . . . .Jan 99
Gilbert, Sara . . . . .Apr 93
Goldberg, Whoopi . . . . .Apr 94
Gomez, Selena . . . . .Sep 08
Goodman, John . . . . .Sep 95
Groening, Matt . . . . .Jan 92
Gumbel, Bryant . . . . .Apr 97
Guy, Jasmine . . . . .Sep 93
Hart, Melissa Joan . . . . .Jan 94
Hewitt, Jennifer Love . . . . .Sep 00
Holmes, Katie . . . . .Jan 00
Hudgens, Vanessa . . . . .Jan 08
Hudson, Jennifer . . . . .Jan 08
Hunter-Gault, Charlayne . . . . .Jan 00
Irwin, Bindi .Apr 08
Irwin, Steve . . . . .Science V.7
Jennings, Peter . . . . .Jul 92
Jones, Quincy . . . . .PerfArt V.2
Kimball, Cheyenne . . . . .Jan 07
Kratt, Chris . . . . .Science V.10
Kratt, Martin . . . . .Science V.10
Kutcher, Ashton . . . . .Apr 04

535

CUMULATIVE GENERAL INDEX

Leno, Jay . . . . Jul 92
Letterman, David . . . . Jan 95
Lewis, Shari . . . . Jan 99
Limbaugh, Rush . . . . . . Sep 95; Update 02
Ling, Lisa . . . . Apr 08
Locklear, Heather . . . . Jan 95
López, George . . . . PerfArt V.2
Mac, Bernie . . . . PerfArt V.1
Madden, John . . . . Sep 97
McGrath, Judy . . . . Business V.1
Millan, Cesar . . . . Sep 06
Muniz, Frankie . . . . Jan 01
Myers, Mike . . . . PerfArt V.3
Norman, Christina . . . . Apr 08
Nye, Bill . . . . Science V.2
O'Brien, Soledad . . . . Jan 07
O'Donnell, Rosie . . . . . . Apr 97; Update 02
Oka, Masi . . . . Jan 08
Oleynik, Larisa . . . . Sep 96
Oliver, Jamie . . . . Apr 07
Olsen, Ashley . . . . Sep 95
Olsen, Mary Kate . . . . Sep 95
Park, Nick . . . . Sep 06
Pauley, Jane . . . . Oct 92
Perry, Luke . . . . Jan 92
Perry, Tyler . . . . Sep 08
Priestley, Jason . . . . Apr 92
Probst, Jeff . . . . Jan 01
Ramos, Jorge . . . . Apr 06
Raven . . . . Apr 04
Roberts, Cokie . . . . Apr 95
Rogers, Fred . . . . PerfArt V.3
Romeo, Lil' . . . . Jan 06
Sagan, Carl . . . . Science V.1
Seinfeld, Jerry . . . . Oct 92; Update 98
Shatner, William . . . . Apr 95
Simpson, Ashlee . . . . Sep 05
Siskel, Gene . . . . Sep 99
Smith, Will . . . . Sep 94
Soren, Tabitha . . . . Jan 97
Spears, Jamie Lynn . . . . Sep 06
Stewart, Jon . . . . Jan 06
Stewart, Martha . . . . Business V.1
Stewart, Patrick . . . . Jan 94
Tartakovsky, Genndy . . . . Author V.11
Thiessen, Tiffani-Amber . . . . Jan 96
Thomas, Jonathan Taylor . . . . Apr 95
Thomas, Rob . . . . Jan 07
Tisdale, Ashley . . . . Jan 07
Trump, Donald . . . . Apr 05

Tyson, Neil deGrasse . . . . Science V.11
Underwood, Carrie . . . . Apr 07
Vidal, Christina . . . . PerfArt V.1
Walters, Barbara . . . . Sep 94
Watson, Barry . . . . Sep 02
Wayans, Keenen Ivory . . . . Jan 93
Welling, Tom . . . . PerfArt V.3
Whedon, Joss . . . . Author V.9
White, Jaleel . . . . Jan 96
Williams, Robin . . . . Apr 92
Williams, Tyler James . . . . Sep 06
Williamson, Kevin . . . . Author V.6
Winfrey, Oprah . . . . Apr 92;
   Update 00; Business V.1
Zamora, Pedro . . . . Apr 95
Teller, Edward . . . . Science V.9
Tenberken, Sabriye . . . . Sep 07
tennis
   Agassi, Andre . . . . Jul 92
   Ashe, Arthur . . . . Sep 93
   Blake, James . . . . Sport V.14
   Capriati, Jennifer . . . . Sport V.6
   Clijsters, Kim . . . . Apr 04
   Davenport, Lindsay . . . . Sport V.5
   Evert, Chris . . . . Sport V.1
   Federer, Roger . . . . Jan 07
   Graf, Steffi . . . . Jan 92; Update 01
   Hingis, Martina . . . . Sport V.2
   Navratilova, Martina . . . Jan 93; Update 94
   Roddick, Andy . . . . Jan 03
   Sampras, Pete . . . . Jan 97; Update 02
   Sanchez Vicario, Arantxa . . . . . . Sport V.1
   Seles, Monica . . . . Jan 96
   Sharapova, Maria . . . . Sep 05
   Williams, Serena . . . Sport V.4; Update 00;
      Update 02
   Williams, Venus . . . . . . Jan 99; Update 00;
      Update 01; Update 02
Tenzin Gyatso
   see Dalai Lama . . . . Sep 98
Teresa, Mother . . . . Apr 98
Teter, Hannah . . . . Sep 06
Thampy, George. . . . . Sep 00
Tharp, Twyla . . . . PerfArt V.3
Thich Nhat Hanh
   see Nhat Hanh (Thich) . . . . Jan 04
Thiessen, Tiffani-Amber . . . . Jan 96
Thomas, Clarence . . . . Jan 92
Thomas, Dave . . . . Apr 96; Update 02

CUMULATIVE GENERAL INDEX

Thomas, Jonathan Taylor .... Apr 95
Thomas, Lewis .... Apr 94
Thomas, Rob .... Jan 07
Thompson, Jenny .... Sport V.5
Tibetan
   Dalai Lama .... Sep 98
Tienda, Marta .... Sep 08
Timberlake, Justin .... Sep 08
   see also *N Sync .... Jan 01
Tisdale, Ashley .... Jan 07
Tolan, Stephanie S. .... Author V.14
Tolkien, J.R.R. .... Jan 02
Tomlinson, Wade .... Sport V.14
Tompkins, Douglas .... WorLdr V.3
Toro, Natalia .... Sep 99
Torvalds, Linus .... Science V.11
track
   Bailey, Donovan .... Sport V.2
   Clemons, Kortney .... Sep 07
   Devers, Gail .... Sport V.2
   Dragila, Stacy .... Sport V.6
   Griffith Joyner, Florence .... Sport V.1; Update 98
   Felix, Allyson .... Sport V.10
   Freeman, Cathy .... Jan 01
   Johnson, Michael ...... Jan 97; Update 00
   Jones, Marion .... Sport V.5
   Joyner-Kersee, Jackie .... Oct 92; Update 96; Update 97; Update 98
   Lewis, Carl .... Sep 96; Update 97
   Rudolph, Wilma .... Apr 95
   Runyan, Marla .... Apr 02
Travers, P.L. .... Author V.2
Tré Cool (Frank Edwin Wright III)
   see Black Eyed Peas .... Apr 06
triathlon
   Smyers, Karen .... Sport V.4
Trinidadian
   Guy, Rosa .... Author V.9
Trohman, Joe
   see Fall Out Boy .... Sep 07
Trump, Donald .... Apr 05
Tubman, William V.S. .... WorLdr V.2
Tucker, Chris .... Jan 01
Tuttle, Merlin .... Apr 97
Twain, Shania .... Apr 99
Tyson, Neil deGrasse .... Science V.11

Uchida, Mitsuko .... Apr 99
Ugandan
   Amin, Idi .... WorLdr V.2
Ukrainians
   Baiul, Oksana .... Apr 95
   Stern, Isaac .... PerfArt V.1
Underwood, Carrie .... Apr 07
United Nations
   – **Ambassadors to**
      Albright, Madeleine .... Apr 97
      Bush, George .... Jan 92
   – **Secretaries General**
      Annan, Kofi .... Jan 98; Update 01
      Boutros-Ghali, Boutros .... Apr 93; Update 98
United States
   – **Attorney General**
      Reno, Janet .... Sep 93; Update 98
   – **Centers for Disease Control**
      Gayle, Helene .... Science V.8
      Gerberding, Julie .... Science V.10
   – **Drug Enforcement Agency**
      Tandy, Karen P. .... Jan 08
   – **First Ladies**
      Bush, Barbara .... Jan 92
      Bush, Laura .... Apr 03
      Clinton, Hillary Rodham .... Apr 93; Update 94; Update 95; Update 96; Update 99; Update 00; Update 01
   – **Joint Chiefs of Staff, Chairman**
      Powell, Colin .... Jan 92; Update 93; Update 95; Update 01
   – **National Institutes of Health**
      Collins, Francis .... Science V.6
      Fauci, Anthony S. .... Science V.7
      Healy, Bernadine .... Science V.1; Update 01
   – **National Security Advisor**
      Rice, Condoleezza .... Apr 02
   – **Nuclear Regulatory Commission**
      Jackson, Shirley Ann .... Science V.2
   – **Poet Laureates**
      Collins, Billy .... Author V.16
      Dove, Rita .... Jan 94
      Pinsky, Robert .... Author V.7
      Prelutsky, Jack .... Sep 07
   – **Presidents**
      Bush, George .... Jan 92

CUMULATIVE GENERAL INDEX

Bush, George W. ....Sep 00; Update 00; Update 01; Update 02
Carter, Jimmy ....Apr 95; Update 02
Clinton, Bill ....Jul 92; Update 94; Update 95; Update 96; Update 97; Update 98; Update 99; Update 00; Update 01
Nixon, Richard ....Sep 94
Reagan, Ronald ....Sep 04
- **Secretary of Commerce**
  Brown, Ron ....Sep 96
- **Secretary of Defense**
  Cheney, Dick ....Jan 02
- **Secretary of Housing and Urban Development**
  Cisneros, Henry...............Sep 93
- **Secretary of the Interior**
  Babbitt, Bruce ....Jan 94
- **Secretary of Labor**
  Dole, Elizabeth Hanford ....Jul 92; Update 96; Update 99
- **Secretaries of State**
  Albright, Madeleine ....Apr 97
  Baker, James ....Oct 92
  Powell, Colin ....Jan 92; Update 93; Update 95; Update 01
- **Secretary of Transportation**
  Dole, Elizabeth ....Jul 92; Update 96; Update 99
- **Secretary of the Treasury**
  Baker, James ....Oct 92
- **Senate Majority Leader**
  Dole, Bob ....Jan 96; Update 96
- **Speaker of the House of Representatives**
  Gingrich, Newt ......Apr 95; Update 99
  Pelosi, Nancy ....Sep 07
- **Supreme Court Justices**
  Blackmun, Harry ....Jan 00
  Burger, Warren ....Sep 95
  Ginsburg, Ruth Bader ....Jan 94
  Marshall, Thurgood ..Jan 92; Update 93
  O'Connor, Sandra Day ....Jul 92
  Roberts, John Jr. ....Apr 08
  Scalia, Antonin ....Jan 05
  Thomas, Clarence ....Jan 92
- **Surgeons General**
  Carmona, Richard ....Science V.8
  Novello, Antonia ....Apr 92; Update 93

Satcher, David ....Sep 98
- **Vice-Presidents**
  Bush, George ....Jan 92
  Cheney, Dick ....Jan 02
  Gore, Al ....Jan 93; Update 96; Update 97; Update 98; Update 99; Update 00; Update 01; Sep 08
  Nixon, Richard ....Sep 94
Urlacher, Brian ....Sep 04
Usher ....PerfArt V.1
Van Allsburg, Chris ....Apr 92
Van Draanen, Wendelin .....Author V.11
Van Dyken, Amy ....Sport V.3; Update 00
Van Meter, Vicki ....Jan 95
Vasan, Nina ....Science V.7
Vega, Alexa ....Jan 04
Ventura, Jesse ....Apr 99; Update 02
Vernon, Mike ....Jan 98; Update 02
veterinarians
  Herriot, James ....Author V.1
  Spelman, Lucy ....Science V.6
Vice-Presidents
  Bush, George ....Jan 92
  Cheney, Dick ....Jan 02
  Gore, Al ....Jan 93; Update 96; Update 97; Update 98; Update 99; Update 00; Update 01; Sep 08
  Nixon, Richard ....Sep 94
Vick, Michael ....Sport V.9
Vidal, Christina ....PerfArt V.1
Vietnamese
  Nhat Hanh (Thich) ....Jan 04
Villa, Brenda ....Jan 06
Villa-Komaroff, Lydia ....Science V.6
Vincent, Mark
  see Diesel, Vin ....Jan 03
Voigt, Cynthia ....Oct 92
volleyball
  Kiraly, Karch ....Sport V.4
  Walsh, Kerri ....Sport V.13
Vonnegut, Kurt Jr. ....Author V.1
Wa, Ka Hsaw
  see Ka Hsaw Wa ....WorLdr V.3
Wade, Dwyane ....Sport V.14
Wadhwa, Meenakshi ....Science V.11
wakeboarder
  Friday, Dallas ....Sport V.10

538

CUMULATIVE GENERAL INDEX

Wallace, Ben ....Jan 05
Walsh, Kerri ....Sport V.13
Walters, Barbara ....Sep 94
Wang, An ....Science V.2
Ward, Charlie ....Apr 94
Ward, Lloyd D. ....Jan 01
Wardlaw, Lee ....Sep 08
Warhol, Andy ....Artist V.1
Warner, Kurt ....Sport V.4
Warrick, Earl ....Science V.8
Washington, Denzel ....Jan 93; Update 02
water polo
  Villa, Brenda ....Jan 06
Watley, Natasha ....Sport V.11
Watson, Barry ....Sep 02
Watson, Emma ....Apr 03
Watson, James D. ....Science V.1
Watson, Paul ....WorLdr V.1
Watterson, Bill ....Jan 92
Wayans, Keenen Ivory ....Jan 93
Weatherspoon, Teresa ....Sport V.12
Webb, Alan ....Sep 01
Webb, Karrie ....Sport V.5; Update 01; Update 02
Weinke, Chris ....Apr 01
Welling, Tom ....PerfArt V.3
Wentz, Pete
  see Fall Out Boy ....Sep 07
Werbach, Adam ....WorLdr V.1
Whedon, Joss ....Author V.9
White, E.B. ....Author V.1
White, Jaleel ....Jan 96
White, Reggie ....Jan 98
White, Ruth ....Author V.11
White, Shaun ....Sport V.14
Whitestone, Heather ....Apr 95; Update 02
Whitman, Meg ....Sep 03
Whitson, Peggy ....Science V.9
Wie, Michelle ....Sep 04
Wilder, Laura Ingalls ....Author V.3
WilderBrathwaite, Gloria .....Science V.7
Wiles, Deborah ....Author V.18
will.i.am (William Adams)
  see Black Eyed Peas ....Apr 06
Williams, Garth ....Author V.2
Williams, Lori Aurelia ......Author V.16

Williams, Michelle
  see Destiny's Child ....Apr 01
Williams, Robin ....Apr 92
Williams, Serena ....Sport V.4; Update 00; Update 02
Williams, Ted ....Sport V.9
Williams, Tyler James ....Sep 06
Williams, Venus ....Jan 99; Update 00; Update 01; Update 02
Williamson, Kevin ....Author V.6
Willingham, Tyrone ....Sep 02
Wilson, August ....Author V.4
Wilson, Edward O. ....Science V.8
Wilson, Gretchen ....Sep 06
Wilson, Mara ....Jan 97
Winans, CeCe ....Apr 00
Winfield, Dave ....Jan 93
Winfrey, Oprah ....Apr 92; Update 00; Business V.1
Winslet, Kate ....Sep 98
Witherspoon, Reese ....Apr 03
Wojtyla, Karol Josef
  see John Paul II ....Oct 92; Update 94; Update 95; Sep 05
Wolf, Hazel ....WorLdr V.3
Wolff, Virginia Euwer ....Author V.13
Wood, Elijah ....Apr 02
Woods, Tiger ....Sport V.1; Update 00; Sport V.6
Woodson, Jacqueline ....Author V.7; Update 01
Woo-Ping, Yuen
  see Yuen Wo-Ping ....PerfArt V.3
Wo-Ping, Yuen
  see Yuen Wo-Ping ....PerfArt V.3
World Wide Web
  see Internet
Wortis, Avi
  see Avi ....Jan 93
Wozniak, Steve ....Science V.5
Wrede, Patricia C. ....Author V.7
wrestling
  Hogan, Hulk ....Apr 92
  Ventura, Jesse ....Apr 99; Update 02
Wright, Frank Edwin III (Tré Cool)
  see Green Day ....Apr 06
Wright, Frank Lloyd ....Artist V.1

539

CUMULATIVE GENERAL INDEX

Wright, Richard . . . . .Author V.5
Wright, Will . . . . .Apr 04
Yamaguchi, Kristi . . . . .Apr 92
Yao Ming . . . . .Sep 03
Yelas, Jay . . . . .Sport V.9
Yeltsin, Boris . . . . .Apr 92; Update 93;
    Update 95; Update 96; Update 98;
    Update 00
Yep, Laurence . . . . .Author V.5
Yolen, Jane . . . . .Author V.7
Young, Steve . . . . .Jan 94; Update 00
Yuen Wo-Ping . . . . .PerfArt V.3
Yunus, Muhammad . . . . .Sep 07
Yzerman, Steve . . . . .Sport V.2
Zairian
    Mobutu Sese Seko . . . . .WorLdr V.2;
        Update 97
Zambian
    Kaunda, Kenneth . . . . .WorLdr V.2
Zamora, Pedro . . . . .Apr 95
Zimbabwean
    Mugabe, Robert . . . . .WorLdr V.2
Zindel, Paul . . . . .Author V.1; Update 02
Zirkle, Aliy . . . . .Sport V.6
Zmeskal, Kim . . . . .Jan 94

Places of Birth Index

The following index lists the places of birth for the individuals profiled in *Biography Today*. Places of birth are entered under state, province, and/or country.

Alabama
- Aaron, Hank – *Mobile* . . . . .Sport V.1
- Allen, Tori – *Auburn* . . . . .Sport V.9
- Barkley, Charles – *Leeds* . . . . .Apr 92
- Benjamin, Regina – *Mobile* . . . .Science V.9
- Flowers, Vonetta – *Birmingham* . .Sport V.8
- Fuller, Millard – *Lanett* . . . . .Apr 03
- Hamm, Mia – *Selma* . . . . .Sport V.2
- Hurston, Zora Neale
 – *Notasulga* . . . . Author V.6
- Jackson, Bo – *Bessemer* . . . . .Jan 92
- Jemison, Mae – *Decatur* . . . . .Oct 92
- Johnson, Angela – *Tuskegee* . . .Author V.6
- Johnson, Lonnie – *Mobile* . . . . .Science V.4
- King, Coretta Scott – *Heiberger* . . . .Sep 06
- Lee, Harper – *Monroeville* . . . . .Author V.9
- Lewis, Carl – *Birmingham* . . . . .Sep 96
- Lewis, John – *Pike County* . . . . .Jan 03
- Parks, Rosa – *Tuskegee* . . . . .Apr 92; Apr 06
- Rice, Condoleezza – *Birmingham* . . .Apr 02
- Satcher, David – *Anniston* . . . . .Sep 98
- Wallace, Ben – *White Hall* . . . . .Jan 05
- Whitestone, Heather – *Dothan* . . . .Apr 95
- Wiles, Deborah – *Mobile* . . . . .Author V.18
- Wilson, Edward O.
 – *Birmingham* . . . . .Science V.8

Alaska
- Brooks, Vincent – *Anchorage* . . . . . .Sep 03
- Schilling, Curt – *Anchorage* . . . . .Sep 05

Algeria
- Boulmerka, Hassiba
 – *Constantine* . . . . .Sport V.1

Angola
- Savimbi, Jonas – *Munhango* . . .WorLdr V.2

Arizona
- Bennington, Chester – *Phoenix* . . . . .Jan 04
- Branch, Michelle – *Flagstaff* . . .PerfArt V.3
- Chavez, Cesar – *Yuma* . . . . .Sep 93
- Chavez, Julz – *Yuma* . . . . .Sep 02
- Farmer, Nancy – *Phoenix* . . . . . .Author V.6

- Jonas, Joseph – *Casa Grande* . . . . . . .Jan 08
- Moreno, Arturo R. – *Tucson* . .Business V.1
- Morrison, Sam – *Flagstaff* . . . . .Sep 97
- Murray, Ty – *Phoenix* . . . . .Sport V.7
- Strug, Kerri – *Tucson* . . . . .Sep 96

Arkansas
- Bates, Daisy – *Huttig* . . . . .Apr 00
- Clinton, Bill – *Hope* . . . . .Jul 92
- Clinton, Chelsea – *Little Rock* . . . . . .Apr 96
- Grisham, John – *Jonesboro* . . . . .Author V.1
- Holmes, Priest – *Fort Smith* . . . . . . .Apr 05
- Johnson, John – *Arkansas City* . . . . .Jan 97
- Pippen, Scottie – *Hamburg* . . . . .Oct 92

Australia
- Beachley, Layne – *Sydney* . . . . . . .Sport V.9
- Freeman, Cathy – *Mackay,
 Queensland* . . . . .Jan 01
- Irwin, Bindi – *Queensland* . . . . .Apr 08
- Irwin, Steve – *Victoria* . . . . .Science V.7
- Norman, Greg – *Mt. Isa, Queensland* Jan 94
- Travers, P.L. – *Maryborough,
 Queensland* . . . . .Author V.2
- Webb, Karrie
 – *Ayr, Queensland* . . . . .Sport V.5

Austria
- Bemelmans, Ludwig – *Meran* . .Author V.16

Bangladesh
- Yunus, Muhammad – *Bathua,
 Eastern Bengal* . . . . .Sep 07

Barbados
- Rihanna – *St. Michael* . . . . .Apr 08

Belgium
- Clijsters, Kim – *Bilzen* . . . . .Apr 04

Bosnia-Herzogovina
- Filipovic, Zlata – *Sarajevo* . . . . .Sep 94

Brazil
- da Silva, Fabiola – *Sao Paulo* . . . .Sport V.9
- Mendes, Chico
 – *Xapuri, Acre* . . . . .WorLdr V.1

PLACES OF BIRTH INDEX

Pelé – *Tres Coracoes,*
   Minas Gerais . . . . .Sport V.1
Bulgaria
   Christo – *Gabrovo* . . . . .Sep 96
Burma
   Aung San Suu Kyi – *Rangoon* . . . . . .Apr 96
   Ka Hsaw Wa – *Rangoon* . . . . . .WorLdr V.3
California
   Abdul, Paula – *Van Nuys* . . . . .Jan 92
   Adams, Ansel – *San Francisco* . . .Artist V.1
   Affleck, Ben – *Berkeley* . . . . .Sep 99
   Aikman, Troy – *West Covina* . . . . . .Apr 95
   Alba, Jessica – *Pomona* . . . . .Sep 01
   Ali, Laila – *Los Angeles* . . . . .Sport V.11
   Allen, Marcus – *San Diego* . . . . .Sep 97
   Alvarez, Luis W.
     – *San Francisco* . . . . .Science V.3
   Aniston, Jennifer – *Sherman Oaks* . .Apr 99
   Armstrong, Billie Joe – *Rodeo* . . . . . .Apr 06
   Babbitt, Bruce – *Los Angeles* . . . . . . .Jan 94
   Bahrke, Shannon – *Tahoe City* . . .Sport V.8
   Banks, Tyra – *Los Angeles* . . . . .PerfArt V.2
   Barrymore, Drew – *Los Angeles* . . . . .Jan 01
   Basich, Tina – *Fair Oaks* . . . . .Sport V.12
   Bell, Drake – *Newport Beach* . . . . . . .Jan 07
   Bergen, Candice – *Beverly Hills* . . . .Sep 93
   Bialik, Mayim – *San Diego* . . . . .Jan 94
   Bonds, Barry – *Riverside* . . . . .Jan 03
   Bourdon, Rob – *Los Angeles* . . . . . . .Jan 04
   Brady, Tom – *San Mateo* . . . . .Sport V.7
   Breathed, Berke – *Encino* . . . . .Jan 92
   Brody, Adam – *San Diego* . . . . .Sep 05
   Brower, David – *Berkeley* . . . . .WorLdr V.1
   Bush, Sophia – *Pasadena* . . . . .Apr 08
   Bynes, Amanda – *Thousand Oaks* . .Sep 03
   Cameron, Candace . . . . .Apr 95
   Carter, Chris – *Bellflower* . . . . . .Author V.4
   Chastain, Brandi – *San Jose* . . . . .Sport V.4
   Choldenko, Gennifer
     – *Santa Monica* . . . . .Author V.18
   Cohen, Sasha – *Westwood* . . . . .Sport V.12
   Coolio – *Los Angeles* . . . . .Sep 96
   Coughlin, Natalie –*Vallejo* . . . . .Sport V.10
   Crabtree, Taylor – *San Diego* . . . . . . .Jan 07
   Dakides, Tara – *Mission Viejo* . . .Sport V.7
   Davenport, Lindsay
     – *Palos Verdes* . . . . .Sport V.5
   Delson, Brad – *Los Angeles* . . . . .Jan 04
   Diaz, Cameron – *San Diego* . . .PerfArt V.3
   DiCaprio, Leonardo – *Hollywood* . . .Apr 98

Dirnt, Mike – *Rodeo* . . . . .Apr 06
Dragila, Stacy – *Auburn* . . . . .Sport V.6
Efron, Zac – *San Luis Obispo* . . . . . .Apr 08
Evans, Janet – *Fullerton* . . . . .Jan 95
Felix, Allyson – *Los Angeles* . . . .Sport V.10
Fernandez, Lisa – *Long Beach* . . . .Sport V.5
Ferrell, Will – *Irvine* . . . . .Apr 07
Ferrera, America – *Los Angeles* . . . . .Sep 07
Fielder, Cecil – *Los Angeles* . . . . .Sep 93
Fields, Debbi – *East Oakland* . . . . . . .Jan 96
Finch, Jennie .Jan 05
Fossey, Dian – *San Francisco* . .Science V.1
Foudy, Julie – *San Diego* . . . . . . .Sport V.13
Freedman, Russell
  – *San Francisco* . . . . .Author V.14
Garcia, Jerry – *San Francisco* . . . . . . .Jan 96
Gilbert, Sara – *Santa Monica* . . . . . .Apr 93
Gonzalez, Tony – *Torrance* . . . . .Sport V.11
Gordon, Jeff – *Vallejo* . . . . .Apr 99
Griffith Joyner, Florence
  – *Los Angeles* . . . . .Sport V.1
Hahn, Joe – *Los Angeles* . . . . .Jan 04
Hamilton, Laird – *San Francisco* . .Sport V.13
Hammer – *Oakland* . . . . .Jan 92
Hanks, Tom – *Concord* . . . . .Jan 96
Hawk, Tony – *San Diego* . . . . .Apr 01
Hudgens, Vanessa – *Salinas* . . . . . . .Jan 08
Jackson, Shirley –
  San Francisco . . . . .Author V.6
Jobs, Steven – *San Francisco* . . . . . .Jan 92;
  Science V.5
Johnson, Johanna . . . . .Apr 00
Johnson, Keyshawn
  – *Los Angeles* . . . . .Sport V.10
Johnson, Randy – *Walnut Creek* .Sport V.9
Jones, Marion – *Los Angeles* . . . . .Sport V.5
Kidd, Jason – *San Francisco* . . . . .Sport V.9
Kistler, Darci – *Riverside* . . . . .Jan 93
Kwan, Michelle –*Torrance* . . . . . .Sport V.3
LaDuke, Winona – *Los Angeles* . .WorLdr V.3
Lasseter, John – *Hollywood* . . . . .Sep 00
Le Guin, Ursula K. – *Berkeley* . .Author V.8
LeMond, Greg – *Los Angeles* . . . .Sport V.1
Leslie, Lisa – *Los Angeles* . . . . .Jan 04
Ling, Lisa – *Sacramento* . . . . .Apr 08
Lobel, Arnold – *Los Angeles* . . .Author V.18
Locklear, Heather – *Los Angeles* . . . .Jan 95
López, George – *Mission Hills* .PerfArt V.2
Lucas, George – *Modesto* . . . . .Apr 97
Martinez, Victor – *Fresno* . . . . .Author V.15

PLACES OF BIRTH INDEX

Mathison, Melissa . . . . .Author V.4
McGwire, Mark – *Pomona* . . . . .Jan 99
Michalka, Alyson Renae (Aly)
 – *Torrance* . . . . .Sep 08
Michalka, Amanda Joy (AJ)
 – *Torrance* . . . . .Sep 08
Moceanu, Dominique – *Hollywood* . .Jan 98
Nixon, Joan Lowery
 – *Los Angeles* . . . . .Author V.1
Nixon, Richard – *Yorba Linda* . . . . . .Sep 94
Ochoa, Ellen – *Los Angeles* . . . . .Apr 01
O'Dell, Scott – *Terminal Island* . .Author V.2
Oleynik, Larisa – *San Francisco* . . . .Sep 96
Olsen, Ashley . . . . .Sep 95
Olsen, Mary Kate . . . . .Sep 95
Palmer, Violet – *Los Angeles* . . . . . . .Sep 05
Prinze, Freddie Jr. – *Los Angeles* . . . .Apr 00
Ride, Sally – *Encino* . . . . .Jan 92
Runyan, Marla – *Santa Maria* . . . . . .Apr 02
Ryan, Pam Muñoz
 – *Bakersfield* . . . . .Author V.12
Shinoda, Mike – *Los Angeles* . . . . . .Jan 04
Snicket, Lemony
 – *San Francisco* . . . . .Author V.12
Snyder, Zilpha Keatley
 – *Lemoore* . . . . .Author V.17
Soto, Gary – *Fresno* . . . . .Author V.5
Stachowski, Richie . . . . .Science V.3
Stefani, Gwen – *Fullerton* . . . . .Sep 03
Swanson, Janese – *San Diego* . .Science V.4
Tan, Amy – *Oakland* . . . . .Author V.9
Taurasi, Diana – *Los Angeles* . . .Sport V.10
Thiessen, Tiffani-Amber – *Modesto* . .Jan 96
Villa, Brenda – *Los Angeles* . . . . .Jan 06
Walsh, Kerri – *Santa Clara* . . . . .Sport V.13
Watley, Natasha – *Canoga Park* . .Sport V.11
Werbach, Adam – *Tarzana* . . . .WorLdr V.1
White, Jaleel – *Los Angeles* . . . . .Jan 96
White, Shaun – *San Diego* . . . . .Sport V.14
Williams, Ted – *San Diego* . . . . . .Sport V.9
Williams, Venus – *Lynwood* . . . . . . .Jan 99
Wilson, Mara – *Burbank* . . . . .Jan 97
Woods, Tiger – *Long Beach* . . . . .Sport V.1,
 Sport V.6
Wozniak, Steve – *San Jose* . . . . .Science V.5
Yamaguchi, Kristi – *Fremont* . . . . . . .Apr 92
Yep, Laurence
 – *San Francisco* . . . . .Author V.5

Canada
Belbin, Tanith – *Kingston,
 Ontario* . . . . .Sport V.14
Blanchard, Rachel – *Toronto,
 Ontario* . . . . .Apr 97
Campbell, Neve – *Toronto,
 Ontario* . . . . .Apr 98
Candy, John – *Newmarket,
 Ontario* . . . . .Sep 94
Carrey, Jim – *Newmarket,
 Ontario* . . . . .Apr 96
Crosby, Sidney – *Halifax,
 Nova Scotia* . . . . .Sport V.14
Dion, Celine – *Charlemagne,
 Quebec* . . . . .Sep 97
Giguère, Jean-Sébastien – *Montreal,
 Quebec* . . . . .Sport V.10
Gretzky, Wayne – *Brantford,
 Ontario* . . . . .Jan 92
Howe, Gordie – *Floral,
 Saskatchewan* . . . . .Sport V.2
Jennings, Peter – *Toronto, Ontario* . . .Jul 92
Johnston, Lynn – *Collingwood,
 Ontario* . . . . .Jan 99
Kielburger, Craig – *Toronto,
 Ontario* . . . . .Jan 00
lang, k.d. – *Edmonton, Alberta* . . . . .Sep 93
Lavigne, Avril – *Belleville,
 Ontario* . . . . .PerfArt V.2
Lemieux, Mario – *Montreal,
 Quebec* . . . . .Jul 92
Martin, Bernard – *Petty Harbor,
 Newfoundland* . . . . .WorLdr V.3
McAdams, Rachel – *London,
 Ontario* . . . . .Apr 06
Messier, Mark – *Edmonton,
 Alberta* . . . . .Apr 96
Morissette, Alanis – *Ottawa,
 Ontario* . . . . .Apr 97
Mowat, Farley – *Belleville,
 Ontario* . . . . .Author V.8
Myers, Mike – *Toronto,
 Ontario* . . . . .PerfArt V.3
Niedermayer, Scott – *Edmonton,
 Alberta* . . . . .Jan 08
Priestley, Jason – *Vancouver,
 British Columbia* . . . . .Apr 92
Roy, Patrick – *Quebec City,
 Quebec* .Sport V.7
Russell, Charlie – *Alberta* . . . .Science V.11

543

PLACES OF BIRTH INDEX

Sakic, Joe – *Burnbary,*
  British Columbia ....Sport V.6
Shatner, William – *Montreal,*
  Quebec ....Apr 95
Twain, Shania – *Windsor,*
  Ontario ....Apr 99
Vernon, Mike – *Calgary, Alberta* ....Jan 98
Watson, Paul – *Toronto,*
  Ontario ....WorLdr V.1
Wolf, Hazel – *Victoria,*
  British Columbia ....WorLdr V.3
Yzerman, Steve – *Cranbrook,*
  British Columbia ....Sport V.2

China
Chan, Jackie – *Hong Kong* .....PerfArt V.1
Dai Qing – *Chongqing* ....WorLdr V.3
Fu Mingxia – *Wuhan* ....Sport V.5
Lucid, Shannon – *Shanghai* ...Science V.2
Paterson, Katherine – *Qing Jiang,*
  Jiangsu ....Author 97
Pei, I.M. – *Canton* ....Artist V.1
Wang, An – *Shanghai* ....Science V.2
Yao Ming – *Shanghai* ....Sep 03
Yuen Wo-Ping – *Guangzhou* ...PerfArt V.3

Colombia
Ocampo, Adriana C.
  – *Barranquilla* ....Science V.8
Shakira – *Barranquilla* ....PerfArt V.1

Colorado
Allen, Tim – *Denver* ....Apr 94
Bryan, Zachery Ty – *Aurora* ....Jan 97
Dunlap, Alison – *Denver* ....Sport V.7
Handler, Ruth – *Denver* ....Apr 98
Klug, Chris – *Vail* ....Sport V.8
Patterson, Ryan
  – *Grand Junction* ....Science V.7
Romero, John
  – *Colorado Springs* ....Science V.8
Stachowski, Richie – *Denver* ..Science V.3
Toro, Natalia – *Boulder* ....Sep 99
Van Dyken, Amy – *Englewood* ...Sport V.3

Connecticut
Brandis, Jonathan – *Danbury* ......Sep 95
Bush, George W. – *New Haven* ....Sep 00
Cantore, Jim – *Waterbury* .....Science V.9
Carrabba, Chris – *Hartford* ....Apr 05
DeMayo, Neda – *New Haven* .....Apr 06
dePaola, Tomie – *Meriden* .....Author V.5
Land, Edwin – *Bridgeport* .....Science V.1
Leibovitz, Annie – *Waterbury* ......Sep 96

Lobo, Rebecca – *Hartford* ....Sport V.3
Mayer, John – *Bridgeport* ....Apr 04
McClintock, Barbara – *Hartford* ....Oct 92
Shea, Jim Jr. – *Hartford* ....Sport V.8
Spelman, Lucy – *Bridgeport* ...Science V.6
Spock, Benjamin – *New Haven* .....Sep 95
Tarbox, Katie – *New Canaan* ...Author V.10

Cuba
Castro, Fidel – *Mayari, Oriente* ......Jul 92
Cruz, Celia –*Havana* ....Apr 04
Estefan, Gloria – *Havana* ....Jul 92
Fuentes, Daisy – *Havana* ....Jan 94
Hernandez, Livan – *Villa Clara* ....Apr 98
Zamora, Pedro ....Apr 95

Czechoslovakia
Albright, Madeleine – *Prague* ......Apr 97
Hasek, Dominik – *Pardubice* ....Sport V.3
Hingis, Martina – *Kosice* ....Sport V.2
Jagr, Jaromir – *Kladno* ....Sport V.5
Navratilova, Martina – *Prague* .....Jan 93

Delaware
Heimlich, Henry – *Wilmington* ..Science V.6

Dominican Republic
Martinez, Pedro
  – *Manoguayabo* ....Sport V.5
Pujols, Albert
  – *Santo Domingo* ....Sport V.12
Ramirez, Manny
  – *Santo Domingo* ....Sport V.13
Soriano, Alfonso
  – *San Pedro de Macoris* ......Sport V.10
Sosa, Sammy
  –*San Pedro de Macoris* ....Jan 99

Egypt
Arafat, Yasir – *Cairo* ....Sep 94
Boutros-Ghali, Boutros – *Cairo* ....Apr 93
Sadat, Anwar
  – *Mit Abu al-Kum* ....WorLdr V.2

England
Almond, David – *Newcastle* ...Author V.10
Amanpour, Christiane – *London* ....Jan 01
Attenborough, David – *London* .Science V.4
Barton, Hazel – *Bristol* ....Science V.6
Beckham, David – *Leytonstone* .....Jan 04
Berners-Lee, Tim – *London* ....Science V.7
Bloom, Orlando – *Canterbury* .....Sep 04
Cooper, Susan – *Burnham* ....Author V.17
Diana, Princess of Wales
  – *Norfolk* ....Jul 92; Jan 98
Goodall, Jane – *London* ....Science V.1

Handford, Martin – *London* . . . . Jan 92
Hargreaves, Alison – *Belper* . . . . Jan 96
Hawking, Stephen – *Oxford* . . . . . . .Apr 92
Herriot, James – *Sunderland* . . .Author V.1
Highmore, Freddie – *London* . . . . . .Apr 06
Jacques, Brian – *Liverpool* . . . . .Author V.5
Jones, Diana Wynne
  – *London* . . . . .Author V.15
Knightley, Keira – *Teddington* . . . . .Apr 07
Koff, Clea – *London* . . . . .Science V.11
Leakey, Mary – *London* . . . . . . .Science V.1
MacArthur, Ellen
  – *Whatstandwell* . . . . .Sport V.11
Macaulay, David
  – *Burton-on-Trent* . . . . .Author V.2
Moore, Henry – *Castleford* . . . . . .Artist V.1
Oliver, Jamie – *Clavering* . . . . .Apr 07
Park, Nick – *Preston* . . . . .Sep 06
Potter, Beatrix – *London* . . . . . . .Author V.8
Pullman, Philip – *Norwich* . . . . .Author V.9
Radcliffe, Daniel – *London* . . . . .Jan 02
Reid Banks, Lynne – *London* . . .Author V.2
Rennison, Louise – *Leeds* . . . .Author V.10
Rowling, J.K. –
  Chipping Sodbury . . . . . .Sep 99 & Jan 08
Sacks, Oliver – *London* . . . . . . .Science V.3
Stewart, Patrick – *Mirfield* . . . . .Jan 94
Stone, Joss – *Dover* . . . . .Jan 06
Winslet, Kate – *Reading* . . . . .Sep 98

Ethiopia
Haile Selassie
  – *Ejarsa Goro, Harar* . . . . . . .WorLdr V.2
Roba, Fatuma – *Bokeji* . . . . .Sport V.3

Fiji
Singh, Vijay – *Lautoka* . . . . . . .Sport V.13

Finland
Torvalds, Linus – *Helsinki* . . . .Science V.11

Florida
Carter, Aaron – *Tampa* . . . . .Sep 02
Carter, Vince – *Daytona Beach* . . .Sport V.5
Culpepper, Daunte – *Miami* . . .Sport V.13
Dorough, Howie – *Orlando*. . . . . . .Jan 00
Evert, Chris – *Ft. Lauderdale* . . . . .Sport V.1
Friday, Dallas – *Orlando* . . . . . . .Sport V.10
Greer, Pedro José Jr.
  – *Miami*. . . . . .Science V.10
Griese, Brian – *Miami* . . . . .Jan 02
Hayden, Carla – *Tallahassee* . . . . . . .Sep 04
Hiaasen, Carl – *Plantation* . . . .Author V.18
McGrady, Tracy – *Bartow* . . . . . .Sport V.11

McLean, A.J. – *West Palm Beach* . . . .Jan 00
Napoli, Donna Jo – *Miami* . . . .Author V.16
Pressel, Morgan – *Tampa* . . . . .Jan 08
Reno, Janet – *Miami* . . . . .Sep 93
Richardson, Dot – *Orlando* . . . . . .Sport V.2
Robinson, David – *Key West* . . . . . . .Sep 96
Rubin, Jamie – *Ft. Myers* . . . . . .Science V.8
Sanders, Deion – *Ft. Myers* . . . . .Sport V.1
Sapp, Warren – *Plymouth* . . . . . . .Sport V.5
Smith, Emmitt – *Pensacola* . . . . .Sep 94
Stewart, James Jr. – *Bartow* . . . . . . .Apr 08
Tarvin, Herbert – *Miami* . . . . .Apr 97
Trohman, Joe – *Hollywood* . . . . .Sep 07
Vega, Alexa – *Miami* . . . . .Jan 04

France
Córdova, France – *Paris* . . . . . .Science V.7
Cousteau, Jacques
  – *St. Andre-de-Cubzac* . . . . .Jan 93
Ma, Yo-Yo – *Paris* . . . . .Jul 92
Marceau, Marcel
  – *Strasbourg* . . . . .PerfArt V.2

Georgia
Aldrich, George
  – *Fort Benning* . . . . .Science V.11
Benjamin, André – *Atlanta* . . . . .Sep 04
Carter, Jimmy – *Plains* . . . . .Apr 95
Fanning, Dakota – *Conyers* . . . . .Jan 06
Grant, Amy – *Augusta* . . . . .Jan 95
Hogan, Hulk – *Augusta* . . . . .Apr 92
Johns, Jasper – *Augusta* . . . . .Artist V.1
Lee, Spike – *Atlanta* . . . . .Apr 92
Mathis, Clint – *Conyers* . . . . .Apr 03
Patton, Antwan – *Savannah* . . . . . . .Sep 04
Raven – *Atlanta* . . . . .Apr 04
Roberts, Julia – *Atlanta* . . . . .Sep 01
Robinson, Jackie – *Cairo* . . . . .Sport V.3
Rowland, Kelly – *Atlanta* . . . . .Apr 01
Thomas, Clarence – *Pin Point* . . . . . .Jan 92
Tucker, Chris – *Decatur* . . . . .Jan 01
Ward, Charlie – *Thomasville* . . . . . .Apr 94
Wright, Will – *Atlanta* . . . . .Apr 04

Germany
Bethe, Hans A. – *Strassburg* . . .Science V.3
Frank, Anne – *Frankfort* . . . . . .Author V.4
Funke, Cornelia – *Dorsten,*
  Westphalia . . . . .Sep 05
Galdikas, Biruté – *Wiesbaden* . . .Science V.4
Graf, Steffi – *Mannheim* . . . . .Jan 92
Otto, Sylke – *Karl-Marx Stad*
  (Chemnitz) . . . . .Sport V.8
Pippig, Uta – *Berlin* . . . . .Sport V.1

PLACES OF BIRTH INDEX

Tenberken, Sabriye . . . . Sep 07
Ghana
Adu, Freddy – *Tema* . . . . Sport V.12
Annan, Kofi – *Kumasi* . . . . Jan 98
Nkrumah, Kwame – *Nkrofro* . . WorLdr V.2
Grand Cayman
Streeter, Tanya – *Georgetown* . . . Sport V.11
Guatemala
Menchu, Rigoberta – *Chimel,*
 El Quiche . . . . Jan 93
Haiti
Aristide, Jean-Bertrand – *Port-Salut* . . Jan 95
Hawaii
Case, Steve – *Honolulu* . . . . Science V.5
Hamilton, Bethany . . . . Apr 05
Lowry, Lois – *Honolulu* . . . . Author V.4
Nakamura, Leanne – *Honolulu* . . . . . Apr 02
Obama, Barack – *Honolulu* . . . . Jan 07
Tuttle, Merlin – *Honolulu* . . . . Apr 97
Wie, Michelle – *Honolulu* . . . . Sep 04
Yelas, Jay – *Honolulu* . . . . Sport V.9
Holland
Lionni, Leo
 – *Watergraafsmeer* . . . . Author V.6
Hungary
Erdös, Paul – *Budapest* . . . . Science V.2
Teller, Edward – *Budapest* . . . . . Science V.9
Idaho
Street, Picabo – *Triumph* . . . . Sport V.3
Illinois
Agosto, Ben – *Chicago* . . . . Sport V.14
Anderson, Gillian – *Chicago* . . . . Jan 97
Asbaty, Diandra – *Oak Lawn* . . . Sport V.14
Barron, Robert – *DuQuoin* . . . . Science V.9
Bauer, Joan – *River Forest* . . . . Author V.10
Blackmun, Harry – *Nashville* . . . . . . Jan 00
Blum, Deborah – *Urbana* . . . . . Science V.8
Boyd, Candy Dawson
 – *Chicago* . . . . Author V.3
Bradbury, Ray – *Waukegan* . . . . Author V.3
Clinton, Hillary Rodham
 – *Chicago* . . . . Apr 93
Crawford, Cindy – *DeKalb* . . . . Apr 93
Crichton, Michael – *Chicago* . . . Author V.5
Cushman, Karen – *Chicago* . . . . Author V.5
Ford, Harrison – *Chicago* . . . . Sep 97
Forman, James – *Chicago* . . . . Apr 05
Garth, Jennie – *Urbana* . . . . Apr 96
Gorey, Edward – *Chicago* . . . . Author V.13
Granato, Cammi
 – *Downers Grove* . . . . Sport V.8

Greenburg, Dan – *Chicago* . . . Author V.14
Hansberry, Lorraine
 – *Chicago* . . . . Author V.5
Hendrickson, Sue – *Chicago* . . . Science V.7
Hoskins, Michele – *Chicago* . . Business V.1
Hudson, Jennifer – *Chicago* . . . . Jan 08
Jones, Quincy – *Chicago* . . . . . . PerfArt V.2
Joyner-Kersee, Jackie
 – *East St. Louis* . . . . Oct 92
Kadohata, Cynthia – *Chicago* . . . . . Sep 06
Kenyon, Cynthia
 – *Chicago* . . . . Science V.11
King, Mary-Claire – *Evanston* . Science V.10
Krauss, Alison – *Decatur* . . . . Apr 05
Mac, Bernie – *Chicago* . . . . PerfArt V.1
Margulis, Lynn – *Chicago* . . . . Sep 96
McCully, Emily Arnold – *Galesburg* . . Jul 92
McGruder, Aaron
 – *Chicago* . . . . Author V.10
McNabb, Donovan – *Chicago* . . . . . Apr 03
Palenik, Skip – *Chicago* . . . . Jan 07
Park, Linda Sue – *Urbana* . . . . Author V.12
Peck, Richard – *Decatur* . . . . . . Author V.10
Reagan, Ronald – *Tampico* . . . . Sep 04
Rowland, Pleasant T.
 – *Chicago* . . . . Business V.1
Silverstein, Shel – *Chicago* . . . . . Author V.3
Siskel, Gene – *Chicago* . . . . Sep 99
Steingraber, Sandra
 – *Champaign* . . . . Science V.9
Stump, Patrick – *Glenview* . . . . Sep 07
Van Draanen, Wendelin
 – *Chicago* . . . . Author V.11
Wade, Dwyane – *Chicago* . . . . . . Sport V.14
Watson, James D. – *Chicago* . . . Science V.1
Williams, Michelle – *Rockford* . . . . . Apr 01
Wilson, Gretchen – *Granite City* . . . Sep 06
Wrede, Patricia C. – *Chicago* . . . Author V.7
India
Wadhwa, Meenakshi . . . . Science V.11
Yunus, Muhammad – *Bathua,*
 Eastern Bengal . . . . Sep 07
Indiana
Bird, Larry – *West Baden* . . . . Jan 92
Binford, Greta – *Crawfordsville* . . . . Jan 08
Cabot, Meg – *Bloomington* . . . . Author V.12
Crilley, Mark – *Hartford City* . . Author V.15
Davis, Jim – *Marion* . . . . Author V.1
Donovan, Marion – *South Bend* . . Science V.9
Lasky, Kathryn
 – *Indianapolis* . . . . Author V.18

546

PLACES OF BIRTH INDEX

Letterman, David – *Indianapolis* ....Jan 95
Naylor, Phyllis Reynolds
  – *Anderson* ....Apr 93
Newman, Ryan – *South Bend* ...Sport V.11
Pauley, Jane – *Indianapolis* ....Oct 92
Peet, Bill – *Grandview* ....Author V.4
Scott, Jerry – *Elkhart* ....Author V.15
Sessions, Michael – *Goshen* ....Apr 07
Stewart, Tony – *Rushville* ....Sport V.9
Tharp, Twyla – *Portland* ....PerfArt V.3
Vonnegut, Kurt – *Indianapolis* .Author V.1

Iowa
Benson, Mildred – *Ladora* ....Jan 03
Kutcher, Ashton – *Cedar Rapids* ...Apr 04
Leopold, Aldo – *Burlington* ...WorLdr V.3
Warner, Kurt – *Burlington* ......Sport V.4
Whitson, Peggy – *Mt. Ayr* ....Science V.9
Wood, Elijah – *Cedar Rapids* ....Apr 02

Iran
Ebadi, Shirin – *Hamadan* ....Apr 04

Iraq
Hussein, Saddam – *al-Auja* ....Jul 92

Ireland, Northern
Lewis, C.S. – *Belfast* ....Author V.3

Ireland, Republic of
Bono – *Dublin* ....Sep 06
Colfer, Eoin – *Wexford* ....Author V.13
Flannery, Sarah – *Blarney,*
  County Cork ....Science V.5
Robinson, Mary – *Ballina* ....Sep 93

Israel
Ben-Ari, Miri – *Ramat-Gan* ....Jan 06
Perlman, Itzhak – *Tel Aviv* ....Jan 95
Portman, Natalie – *Jerusalem* ......Sep 99
Rabin, Yitzhak – *Jerusalem* ....Oct 92

Italy
Andretti, Mario – *Montana* ....Sep 94
Krim, Mathilde – *Como* ......Science V.1
Levi-Montalcini, Rita – *Turin* .Science V.1

Jamaica
Ashley, Maurice – *St. Andrew* .....Sep 99
Bailey, Donovan – *Manchester* ..Sport V.2
Denton, Sandi – *Kingston* ....Apr 95
Ewing, Patrick – *Kingston* ....Jan 95
Maxwell, Jody-Anne – *St. Andrew* ..Sep 98

Japan
Miyamoto, Shigeru – *Sonobe* ..Science V.5
Morita, Akio – *Kasugaya* ......Science V.4
Oka, Masi – *Tokyo* ....Jan 08
Suzuki, Ichiro – *Kasugai* ....Apr 08
Suzuki, Shinichi – *Nagoya* ....Sep 98

Uchida, Mitsuko – *Tokyo* ....Apr 99

Jordan
Hussein, King – *Amman* ....Apr 99

Kansas
Alley, Kirstie – *Wichita* ....Jul 92
Ballard, Robert – *Wichita* ......Science V.4
Brooks, Gwendolyn – *Topeka* ..Author V.3
Dole, Bob – *Russell* ....Jan 96
Parks, Gordon – *Fort Scott* ......Artist V.1
Patrick, Ruth ....Science V.3
Probst, Jeff – *Wichita* ....Jan 01
Sanders, Barry – *Wichita* ....Sep 95
Stiles, Jackie – *Kansas City* .....Sport V.6
Wardlaw, Lee – *Salina* ....Sep 08

Kentucky
Alexander, Shaun – *Florence* ......Apr 07
Ali, Muhammad – *Louisville* ....Sport V.2
Depp, Johnny – *Owensboro* ....Apr 05
Littrell, Brian – *Lexington* ....Jan 00
Monroe, Bill – *Rosine* ....Sep 97
Morgan, Garrett – *Paris* ......Science V.2
Richardson, Kevin – *Lexington* .....Jan 00

Kenya
Kenyatta, Jomo – *Ngenda* ....WorLdr V.2
Leakey, Louis – *Nairobi* ......Science V.1
Maathai, Wangari – *Nyeri* ....WorLdr V.1;
  Sep 05
Ndeti, Cosmas – *Machakos* ....Sep 95

Lebanon
Reeves, Keanu – *Beirut* ....Jan 04

Liberia
Tubman, William V.S.
  – *Harper City* ....WorLdr V.2

Libya
Qaddafi, Muammar ....Apr 97

Louisiana
Dawson, Matel Jr. – *Shreveport* .....Jan 04
Dumars, Joe – *Natchitoches* .....Sport V.3
Ford, Cheryl – *Homer* ....Sport V.11
Gumbel, Bryant – *New Orleans* ....Apr 97
Honoré, Russel – *Lakeland* ....Jan 06
Kapell, Dave – *Leesville* ....Science V.8
Manning, Eli – *New Orleans* ....Sep 08
Manning, Peyton – *New Orleans* ...Sep 00
Marsalis, Wynton – *New Orleans* ...Apr 92
Patterson, Carly – *Baton Rouge* .Sport V.12
Perry, Tyler – *New Orleans* ....Sep 08
Rice, Anne – *New Orleans* .....Author V.3
Roberts, Cokie – *New Orleans* .....Apr 95
Romeo, Lil' – *New Orleans* ....Jan 06
Spears, Britney – *Kentwood* ....Jan 01

547

PLACES OF BIRTH INDEX

Stewart, Kordell – *Marrero* .... Sep 98
Witherspoon, Reese – *New Orleans* .. Apr 03

Macedonia
Teresa, Mother – *Skopje* .... Apr 98

Maine
King, Stephen – *Portland* ...... Author V.1

Malawi
Banda, Hastings Kamuzu
– *Chiwengo, Nyasaland* ..... WorLdr V.2

Maryland
Atwater-Rhodes, Amelia
– *Silver Spring* .... Author V.8
Boyle, Ryan – *Hunt Valley* ..... Sport V.10
Brashares, Ann – *Chevy Chase* .. Author V.15
Collier, Bryan – *Salisbury* .... Author V.11
Hesse, Karen – *Baltimore* ..... Author V.5
Madden, Benji – *Waldorf* ...... PerfArt V.3
Madden, Joel – *Waldorf* .... PerfArt V.3
Marshall, Thurgood – *Baltimore* .... Jan 92
Meissner, Kimmie – *Baltimore* ..... Sep 08
Pelosi, Nancy – *Baltimore* .... Sep 07
Phelps, Michael – *Baltimore* .... Sport V.13
Ripken, Cal Jr.
– *Havre de Grace* .... Sport V.1
Sleator, William
– *Havre de Grace* .... Author V.11
Stepanek, Mattie
– *Upper Marlboro* .... Apr 02

Massachusetts
Amend, Bill – *Northampton* ... Author V.18
Bush, George – *Milton* .... Jan 92
Butcher, Susan – *Cambridge* .... Sport V.1
Caplan, Arthur – *Boston* ..... Science V.6
Cormier, Robert – *Leoministre* .. Author V.1
Cox, Lynne – *Boston* .... Sport V.13
Fanning, Shawn – *Brockton* ... Science V.5
Farmer, Paul Jr.
– *North Adams* .... Science V.11
Farrell, David .... Jan 04
Foray, June – *Springfield* .... Jan 07
Gilbert, Walter – *Cambridge* ... Science V.2
Grandin, Temple – *Boston* .... Science V.3
Guey, Wendy – *Boston* .... Sep 96
Guy, Jasmine – *Boston* .... Sep 93
Kerrigan, Nancy – *Woburn* .... Apr 94
Krakauer, Jon – *Brookline* ..... Author V.6
Lynch, Chris – *Boston* .... Author V.13
Meltzer, Milton – *Worcester* .. Author V.11
Pine, Elizabeth Michele – *Boston* ... Jan 94
Robison, Emily – *Pittsfield* ..... PerfArt V.1
Scarry, Richard – *Boston* .... Sep 94

Seuss, Dr. – *Springfield* .... Jan 92
Sones, Sonya – *Boston* .... Author V.11
Speare, Elizabeth George
– *Melrose* .... Sep 95
Taymor, Julie – *Newton* ...... PerfArt V.1
Thompson, Jenny – *Georgetown* .. Sport V.5
Voigt, Cynthia – *Boston* .... Oct 92
Walters, Barbara – *Boston* .... Sep 94

Mexico
Fox, Vicente – *Mexico City* .... Apr 03
Jiménez, Francisco – *San Pedro,*
Tlaquepaque .... Author V.13
Millan, Cesar – *Culiacan* .... Sep 06
Ochoa, Lorena – *Guadalajara* .. Sport V.14
Ramos, Jorge – *Mexico City* .... Apr 06
Rivera, Diego – *Guanajuato* ..... Artist V.1
Santana, Carlos – *Autlan de*
Navarro, Jalisco .... Sep 05

Michigan
Applegate, K.A. .... Jan 00
Askins, Renee .... WorLdr V.1
Bell, Kristen – *Huntington Woods* .. Sep 05
Canady, Alexa – *Lansing* ...... Science V.6
Carson, Ben – *Detroit* .... Science V.4
Carter, Regina – *Detroit* .... Sep 07
Curtis, Christopher Paul
– *Flint* .... Author V.4
Galeczka, Chris – *Sterling Heights* .. Apr 96
Horvath, Polly – *Kalamazoo* ... Author V.16
Jenkins, Jerry B. – *Kalamazoo* .. Author V.16
Johnson, Magic – *Lansing* .... Apr 92
Joy, Bill – *Detroit* .... Science V.10
Kiraly, Karch – *Jackson* .... Sport V.4
Krone, Julie – *Benton Harbor* ...... Jan 95
LaHaye, Tim – *Detroit* .... Author V.16
Lalas, Alexi – *Royal Oak* .... Sep 94
Mohajer, Dineh – *Bloomfield Hills* .. Jan 02
Page, Larry – *East Lansing* .... Sep 05
Riley, Dawn – *Detroit* .... Sport V.4
Scieszka, Jon – *Flint* .... Author V.9
Shabazz, Betty – *Detroit* .... Apr 98
Small, David – *Detroit* .... Author V.10
Van Allsburg, Chris – *Grand Rapids* .Apr 92
Ward, Lloyd D. – *Romulus* .... Jan 01
Watson, Barry – *Traverse City* ..... Sep 02
Webb, Alan – *Ann Arbor* .... Sep 01
Williams, Serena – *Saginaw* ..... Sport V.4
Winans, CeCe – *Detroit* .... Apr 00

Minnesota
Burger, Warren – *St. Paul* .... Sep 95

PLACES OF BIRTH INDEX

Douglas, Marjory Stoneman
  – *Minneapolis* . . . . .WorLdr V.1
Hartnett, Josh – *St. Paul* . . . . .Sep 03
Madden, John – *Austin* . . . . .Sep 97
Mars, Forrest Sr.
  – *Minneapolis* . . . . .Science V.4
McNutt, Marcia
  – *Minneapolis* . . . . .Science V.11
Murie, Olaus J. . . . . .WorLdr V.1
Paulsen, Gary – *Minneapolis* . . .Author V.1
Ryder, Winona – *Winona* . . . . .Jan 93
Schulz, Charles
  – *Minneapolis* . . . . .Author V.2
Scurry, Briana – *Minneapolis* . . . . . .Jan 00
Ventura, Jesse – *Minneapolis* . . . . . .Apr 99
Weinke, Chris – *St. Paul* . . . . .Apr 01
Winfield, Dave – *St. Paul* . . . . .Jan 93

Mississippi
Bass, Lance – *Clinton* . . . . .Jan 01
Brandy – *McComb* . . . . .Apr 96
Clemons, Kortney – *Meridien* . . . . . .Sep 07
Favre, Brett – *Gulfport* . . . . .Sport V.2
Forman, Michele – *Biloxi* . . . . .Jan 03
Hill, Faith – *Jackson* . . . . .Sep 01
Jones, James Earl
  – *Arkabutla Township* . . . . .Jan 95
McCarty, Oseola
  – *Wayne County* . . . . .Jan 99
McNair, Steve – *Mount Olive* . . .Sport V.11
Payton, Walter – *Columbia* . . . . . . .Jan 00
Rice, Jerry – *Crawford* . . . . .Apr 93
Rimes, LeAnn – *Jackson* . . . . .Jan 98
Spears, Jamie Lynn – *McComb* . . . . .Sep 06
Taylor, Mildred D. – *Jackson* . . .Author V.1
Winfrey, Oprah – *Kosciusko* . . . . . . .Apr 92;
  Business V.1
Wright, Richard – *Natchez* . . . . .Author V.5

Missouri
Angelou, Maya – *St. Louis* . . . . .Apr 93
Champagne, Larry III – *St. Louis* . . .Apr 96
Eminem – *Kansas City* . . . . .Apr 03
Goodman, John – *Affton* . . . . .Sep 95
Heinlein, Robert – *Butler* . . . . . .Author V.4
Hughes, Langston – *Joplin* . . . .Author V.7
Lester, Julius – *St. Louis* . . . . . .Author V.7
Limbaugh, Rush – *Cape Girardeau* .Sep 95
Miller, Shannon – *Rolla* . . . . .Sep 94
Nye, Naomi Shihab – *St. Louis* . .Author V.8
Spade, Kate – *Kansas City* . . . . .Apr 07

Montana
Carvey, Dana – *Missoula* . . . . .Jan 93

Horner, Jack – *Shelby* . . . . .Science V.1
Jackson, Phil – *Deer Lodge* . . . . .Sport V.10
Lowe, Alex – *Missoula* . . . . .Sport V.4
Paolini, Christopher . . . . .Author V.16

Morocco
Hassan II – *Rabat* . . . . .WorLdr V.2
Newsom, Lee Ann . . . . .Science V.11

Myanmar
see Burma

Nebraska
Buffett, Warren – *Omaha* . . . .Business V.1
Cheney, Dick – *Lincoln* . . . . .Jan 02
Roddick, Andy – *Omaha* . . . . .Jan 03

Nevada
Agassi, Andre – *Las Vegas* . . . . .Jul 92
Schwikert, Tasha – *Las Vegas* . . . .Sport V.7

New Hampshire
Moore, Mandy – *Nashua* . . . . .Jan 04
Zirkle, Aliy – *Manchester* . . . . . . .Sport V.6

New Jersey
Bellamy, Carol – *Plainfield* . . . . .Jan 06
Bloor, Edward – *Trenton* . . . . .Author V.15
Blume, Judy . . . . .Jan 92
Carpenter, Mary Chapin
  – *Princeton* . . . . .Sep 94
Catchings, Tamika – *Stratford* . .Sport V.14
Clements, Andrew – *Camden* . .Author V.13
Dunst, Kirsten – *Point Pleasant* . .PerfArt V.1
Earle, Sylvia – *Gibbstown* . . . . .Science V.1
Fay, Michael – *Plainfield* . . . . . .Science V.9
Glover, Savion – *Newark* . . . . .Apr 99
Gwaltney, John Langston
  – *Orange* . . . . .Science V.3
Hill, Lauryn – *South Orange* . . . . . . .Sep 99
Houston, Whitney – *Newark* . . . . . .Sep 94
Howard, Tim – *North Brunswick* . . .Apr 06
Ice-T – *Newark* . . . . .Apr 93
Jeter, Derek – *Pequannock* . . . . . . .Sport V.4
Jonas, Kevin – *Teaneck* . . . . .Jan 08
Kratt, Chris
  – *Warren Township* . . . . .Science V.10
Kratt, Martin
  – *Warren Township* . . . . .Science V.10
Lawrence, Jacob – *Atlantic City* . .Artist V.1
Love, Susan – *Long Branch* . . . .Science V.3
Martin, Ann M. – *Princeton* . . . . .Jan 92
Morrison, Lillian – *Jersey City* .Author V.12
Muniz, Frankie – *Ridgewood* . . . . . . .Jan 01
Murphy, Jim – *Newark* . . . . . . .Author V.17
O'Neal, Shaquille – *Newark* . . . . . . .Sep 93
Pinsky, Robert – *Long Branch* . .Author V.7

549

PLACES OF BIRTH INDEX

Queen Latifah – *Newark* .... Apr 92
Rodman, Dennis – *Trenton* .... Apr 96
Scalia, Antonin – *Trenton* .... Jan 05
Schwarzkopf, H. Norman
 – *Trenton* .... Jan 92
Sinatra, Frank – *Hoboken* .... Jan 99
Stewart, Jon – *Lawrence* .... Jan 06
Stewart, Martha – *Jersey City* .. Business V.1
Thomas, Dave – *Atlantic City* ...... Apr 96
Tisdale, Ashley – *West Deal* .... Jan 07

New Mexico
Bezos, Jeff – *Albuquerque* .... Apr 01
Foreman, Dave – *Albuquerque* .. WorLdr V.1
Funk, Wally – *Taos* .... Jan 05
Huerta, Dolores – *Dawson* .... Sep 03
Villa-Komaroff, Lydia
 – *Las Vegas* .... Science V.6

New York State
Aaliyah – *Brooklyn* .... Jan 02
Abdul-Jabbar, Kareem
 – *New York City* .... Sport V.1
Abzug, Bella – *Bronx* .... Sep 98
Aguilera, Christina – *Staten Island* .. Apr 00
Alvarez, Julia – *New York City* .. Author V.17
Anderson, Laurie Halse
 – *Potsdam* .... Author V.11
Anthony, Carmelo – *Brooklyn* ..... Sep 07
Ashanti – *Glen Cove* .... PerfArt V.2
Avi – *New York City* .... Jan 93
Baldwin, James
 – *New York City* .... Author V.2
Bennett, Cherie – *Buffalo* ...... Author V.9
Berger, Francie – *Queens* .... Sep 04
Bird, Sue – *Syosset* .... Sport V.9
Blair, Bonnie – *Cornwall* .... Apr 94
Blake, James – *Yonkers* .... Sport V.14
Blige, Mary J. – *Yonkers* .... Apr 02
Bourke-White, Margaret
 – *New York City* .... Artist V.1
Brody, Jane – *Brooklyn* .... Science V.2
Brown, Claude
 – *New York City* .... Author V.12
Bruchac, Joseph
 – *Saratoga Springs* .... Author V.18
Burke, Chris – *New York City* ...... Sep 93
Burns, Ken – *Brooklyn* .... Jan 95
Bush, Barbara – *New York City* .... Jan 92
Calderone, Mary S.
 – *New York City* .... Science V.3
Capriati, Jennifer – *Long Island* .. Sport V.6
Carey, Mariah – *New York City* .... Apr 96

Carle, Eric – *Syracuse* .... Author V.1
Carmona, Richard
 – *New York City* .... Science V.8
Carter, Majora – *New York City* .... Sep 08
Carter, Nick – *Jamestown*. .... Jan 00
Cohen, Adam Ezra
 – *New York City* .... Apr 97
Collins, Billy – *New York City* .. Author V.16
Collins, Eileen – *Elmira* .... Science V.4
Combs, Sean (Puff Daddy)
 – *New York City* .... Apr 98
Cooney, Barbara – *Brooklyn* .... Author V.8
Cooney, Caroline B. – *Geneva* .. Author V.4
Cooper, Anderson – *New York City* .Sep 08
Coville, Bruce – *Syracuse* ...... Author V.9
Cronin, John – *Yonkers* .... WorLdr V.3
Culkin, Macaulay – *New York City* .. Sep 93
Danes, Claire – *New York City* ..... Sep 97
de Mille, Agnes – *New York City* .... Jan 95
Diesel, Vin – *New York City* .... Jan 03
Duchovny, David – *New York City* .. Apr 96
Dworkin, Aaron – *Monticello* ..... Apr 07
Elion, Gertrude
 – *New York City* .... Science V.6
Farrakhan, Louis – *Bronx* .... Jan 97
Fatone, Joey – *Brooklyn* .... Jan 01
Fauci, Anthony S. – *Brooklyn* .. Science V.7
Feelings, Tom – *Brooklyn* ..... Author V.16
Feynman, Richard P.
 – *Far Rockaway* .... Science V.10
Fox, Paula – *New York City* ... Author V.15
Frankenthaler, Helen
 – *New York City* .... Artist V.1
Gayle, Helene – *Buffalo* .... Science V.8
Gellar, Sarah Michelle
 – *New York City* .... Jan 99
Giff, Patricia Reilly – *Queens* .. Author V.7
Ginsburg, Ruth Bader – *Brooklyn* .. Jan 94
Giuliani, Rudolph – *Brooklyn* ...... Sep 02
Goldberg, Whoopi
 – *New York City* .... Apr 94
Gould, Stephen Jay
 – *New York City* .... Science V.2
Graves, Earl – *Brooklyn* ...... Business V.1
Grimes, Nikki
 – *New York City* .... Author V.14
Hakim, Joy – *Forest Hills* ..... Author V.16
Haley, Alex – *Ithaca* .... Apr 92
Hart, Melissa Joan – *Smithtown* .... Jan 94
Hathaway, Anne – *Brooklyn* .... Apr 05
Healy, Bernadine – *Queens* .... Science V.1

PLACES OF BIRTH INDEX

Holdsclaw, Chamique – *Queens* ....Sep 00
Hopper, Grace Murray
 – *New York City* ....Science V.5
Howe, James – *Oneida* ......Author V.17
Hughes, Sarah – *Great Neck* ......Jan 03
James, Cheryl – *New York City* .....Apr 95
Jones, Norah – *New York City* . .PerfArt V.2
Jordan, Michael – *Brooklyn* ....Jan 92
Juster, Norton – *Brooklyn* ....Author V.14
Kamen, Dean
 – *Rockville Centre* ....Science V.11
Kamler, Kenneth
 – *New York City* ....Science V.6
Kerr, M.E. – *Auburn* ....Author V.1
Keys, Alicia – *Manhattan* ....Jan 07
Konigsburg, E.L.
 – *New York City* ....Author V.3
Kurzweil, Raymond
 – *New York City* ....Science V.2
Lansky, Bruce
 – *New York City* ....Author V.17
Lee, Jeanette – *Brooklyn* ....Apr 03
Lee, Stan – *New York City* ....Author V.7
Lemelson, Jerome
 – *Staten Island* ....Science V.3
L'Engle, Madeleine
 – *New York City* ....Jan 92; Apr 01
Leno, Jay – *New Rochelle* ....Jul 92
Levine, Gail Carson
 – *New York City* ....Author V.17
Lewis, Shari – *New York City* .....Jan 99
Lipsyte, Robert
 – *New York City* ....Author V.12
Lisanti, Mariangela – *Bronx* ....Sep 01
Lohan, Lindsay
 – *Cold Spring Harbor* ....Sep 04
Lopez, Jennifer – *Bronx* ....Jan 02
Lowman, Meg – *Elmira* .....Science V.4
McDonald, Janet – *Brooklyn* . .Author V.18
Mirra, Dave – *Syracuse* ....Sep 02
Mitchell-Raptakis, Karen – *Brooklyn* . .Jan 05
Mittermeier, Russell A.
 – *New York City* ....WorLdr V.1
Moses, Grandma – *Greenwich* ...Artist V.1
Moss, Cynthia – *Ossining* .....WorLdr V.3
Murphy, Eddie – *Brooklyn* .....PerfArt V.2
Norman, Christina – *New York City* Apr 08
O'Donnell, Rosie – *Commack* ......Apr 97
Oppenheimer, J. Robert
 – *New York City* ....Science V.1

Pascal, Francine
 – *New York City* ....Author V.6
Peterson, Roger Tory
 – *Jamestown* ....WorLdr V.1
Pike, Christopher – *Brooklyn* ......Sep 96
Poussaint, Alvin
 – *New York City* ....Science V.9
Powell, Colin – *New York City* .....Jan 92
Prelutsky, Jack
 – *Brooklyn* ....Author V.2; Sep 07
Reeve, Christopher – *Manhattan* ...Jan 97
Rinaldi, Ann
 – *New York City* ....Author V.8
Ringgold, Faith
 – *New York City* ....Author V.2
Roberts, John Jr. – *Buffalo* ....Apr 08
Rockwell, Norman
 – *New York City* ....Artist V.1
Rodriguez, Alex – *New York City* . .Sport V.6
Roper, Dee Dee – *New York City* ...Apr 95
Sachar, Louis – *East Meadow* . .Author V.6
Sagan, Carl – *Brooklyn* ......Science V.1
Salinger, J.D. – *New York City* . .Author V.2
Salk, Jonas – *New York City* ....Jan 94
Sandler, Adam – *Brooklyn* ....Jan 06
Sealfon, Rebecca
 – *New York City* ....Sep 97
Seinfeld, Jerry – *Brooklyn* ....Oct 92
Sendak, Maurice – *Brooklyn* ...Author V.2
Shakur, Tupac – *Bronx* ....Apr 97
Simmons, Russell – *Queens* ......Apr 06
Smith, Betty – *Brooklyn* ......Author V.17
Spelke, Elizabeth – *New York* . .Science V.10
Stiles, Julia – *New York City* ...PerfArt V.2
Strasser, Todd – *New York City* . .Author V.7
Tarter, Jill – *Eastchester* ......Science V.8
Trump, Donald – *New York City* ...Apr 05
Tyson, Neil deGrasse
 – *Bronx* ....Science V.11
Vidal, Christina – *Queens* .....PerfArt V.1
Washington, Denzel – *Mount Vernon* . Jan 93
Wayans, Keenen Ivory
 – *New York City* ....Jan 93
Welling, Tom – *West Point* ....PerfArt V.3
White, E.B. – *Mount Vernon* ...Author V.1
Whitman, Meg
 – *Cold Spring Harbor* ....Sep 03
WilderBrathwaite, Gloria
 – *Brooklyn* ....Science V.7
Williams, Garth – *New York City* .Author V.2

551

PLACES OF BIRTH INDEX

Williams, Tyler James
 – *New York City* . . . . .Sep 06
Yolen, Jane – *New York City* . . .Author V.7
Zindel, Paul – *Staten Island* . . . .Author V.1

New Zealand
Hillary, Sir Edmund – *Auckland* . . . .Sep 96
Jackson, Peter – *Pukerua Bay* . .PerfArt V.2

Nigeria
Olajuwon, Hakeem – *Lagos* . . . . . . .Sep 95
Saro-Wiwa, Ken
 – *Bori, Rivers State* . . . . .WorLdr V.1

North Carolina
Bearden, Romare – *Charlotte* . . . .Artist V.1
Burnside, Aubyn – *Hickory* . . . . .Sep 02
Byars, Betsy – *Charlotte* . . . . . .Author V.4
Chavis, Benjamin – *Oxford* . . . . . . .Jan 94
Delany, Bessie – *Raleigh* . . . . .Sep 99
Dole, Elizabeth Hanford – *Salisbury* .Jul 92
Earnhardt, Dale – *Kannapolis* . . . . . .Apr 01
Earnhardt, Dale Jr.
 – *Kannapolis* . . . . .Sport V.12
Kimball, Cheyenne – *Jacksonville* . . .Jan 07
Petty, Richard – *Level Cross* . . . . .Sport V.2
Williamson, Kevin
 – *New Bern* . . . . .Author V.6
Willingham, Tyrone – *Kinston* . . . . .Sep 02

Norway
Arnesen, Liv – *Baerum* . . . . . . .Author V.15
Brundtland, Gro Harlem
 – *Baerum* . . . . .Science V.3

Ohio
Anderson, Terry – *Lorain* . . . . .Apr 92
Babbitt, Natalie – *Dayton* . . . . .Jan 04
Battle, Kathleen – *Portsmouth* . . . . .Jan 93
Berry, Halle – *Cleveland* . . . . .Jan 95
Bleiler, Gretchen – *Toledo* . . . . .Sport V.13
Borgman, Jim – *Cincinnati* . . . .Author V.15
Creech, Sharon
 – *Mayfield Heights* . . . . .Author V.5
Dove, Rita – *Akron* . . . . .Jan 94
Draper, Sharon – *Cleveland* . . . . . . .Apr 99
Dunbar, Paul Laurence
 – *Dayton* . . . . .Author V.8
Farrell, Suzanne – *Cincinnati* . .PerfArt V.1
Glenn, John – *Cambridge* . . . . .Jan 99
Guisewite, Cathy – *Dayton* . . . . . . .Sep 93
Haddix, Margaret Peterson
 – *Washington Court House* . .Author V.11
Hamilton, Virginia
 – *Yellow Springs* Author V.1, Author V.12
Hampton, David . . . . .Apr 99

Harbaugh, Jim – *Toledo* . . . . .Sport V.3
Holmes, Katie – *Toledo* . . . . .Jan 00
James, LeBron – *Akron* . . . . .Sport V.12
Lin, Maya – *Athens* . . . . .Sep 97
Long, Irene D. – *Cleveland* . . . . .Jan 04
Lovell, Jim – *Cleveland* . . . . .Jan 96
McCloskey, Robert
 – *Hamilton* . . . . .Author V.15
Morrison, Toni – *Lorain* . . . . .Jan 94
Nelson, Marilyn – *Cleveland* . .Author V.13
Nicklaus, Jack – *Columbus* . . . . .Sport V.2
Nielsen, Jerri – *Salem* . . . . .Science V.7
Perry, Luke – *Mansfield* . . . . .Jan 92
Roethlisberger, Ben – *Lima* . . . . .Sep 06
Rose, Pete – *Cincinnati* . . . . .Jan 92
Shula, Don – *Grand River* . . . . .Apr 96
Spielberg, Steven – *Cincinnati* . . . . .Jan 94
Steinem, Gloria – *Toledo* . . . . .Oct 92
Stine, R.L. – *Columbus* . . . . .Apr 94
Tolan, Stephanie S. – *Canton* . . .Author V.14
Tompkins, Douglas
 – *Conneaut* . . . . .WorLdr V.3
Woodson, Jacqueline
 – *Columbus* . . . . .Author V.7

Oklahoma
Brooks, Garth – *Tulsa* . . . . .Oct 92
Cooper, Floyd – *Tulsa* . . . . . . .Author V.17
Duke, David – *Tulsa* . . . . .Apr 92
Ellison, Ralph
 – *Oklahoma City* . . . . .Author V.3
Hanson, Ike – *Tulsa* . . . . .Jan 98
Hanson, Taylor – *Tulsa* . . . . .Jan 98
Hanson, Zac – *Tulsa* . . . . .Jan 98
Hill, Anita – *Morris* . . . . .Jan 93
Hillenburg, Stephen – *Fort Sill* .Author V.14
Hinton, S.E. – *Tulsa* . . . . .Author V.1
Keith, Toby – *Clinton* . . . . .Jan 05
Lennox, Betty – *Hugo* . . . . .Sport V.13
Mankiller, Wilma – *Tahlequah* . . . .Apr 94
Mantle, Mickey – *Spavinaw* . . . . . . .Jan 96
McEntire, Reba – *McAlester* . . . . . . .Sep 95
Pitt, Brad – *Shawnee* . . . . .Sep 98
Underwood, Carrie – *Muskogee* . . . .Apr 07

Oregon
Cleary, Beverly – *McMinnville* . . . . .Apr 94
Engelbart, Douglas
 – *Portland* . . . . .Science V.5
Groening, Matt – *Portland* . . . . .Jan 92
Harding, Tonya – *Portland* . . . . .Sep 94
Hooper, Geoff – *Salem* . . . . .Jan 94

PLACES OF BIRTH INDEX

Milbrett, Tiffeny – *Portland* ....Sport V.10
Pauling, Linus – *Portland* ....Jan 95
Phoenix, River – *Madras* ....Apr 94
Schroeder, Pat – *Portland* ....Jan 97
Wolff, Virginia Euwer
 – *Portland* ....Author V.13
Pakistan
Bhutto, Benazir – *Karachi* ....Apr 95
Masih, Iqbal ....Jan 96
Yunus, Muhammad – *Bathua,
 Eastern Bengal* ....Sep 07
Palestine
Perlman, Itzhak – *Tel Aviv* ......Jan 95
Rabin, Yitzhak – *Jerusalem* ....Oct 92
Panama
Chambers, Veronica ....Author V.15
McCain, John
 – *Panama Canal Zone* ....Apr 00
Pennsylvania
Abbey, Edward – *Indiana* .....WorLdr V.1
Alexander, Lloyd
 – *Philadelphia* ....Author V.6
Anderson, Marian – *Philadelphia* ...Jan 94
Armstrong, Robb
 – *Philadelphia* ....Author V.9
Berenstain, Jan – *Philadelphia* ..Author V.2
Berenstain, Stan
 – *Philadelphia* ....Author V.2
Bradley, Ed – *Philadelphia* ....Apr 94
Bryant, Kobe – *Philadelphia* ......Apr 99
Calder, Alexander – *Lawnton* ....Artist V.1
Capolino, Peter – *Philadelphia* .Business V.1
Carson, Rachel – *Springdale* ...WorLdr V.1
Chamberlain, Wilt
 – *Philadelphia* ....Sport V.4
Cosby, Bill ....Jan 92
DiCamillo, Kate – *Philadelphia* ..Author V.10
Diemer, Walter – *Philadelphia* .....Apr 98
Duncan, Lois – *Philadelphia* ....Sep 93
Eve – *Philadelphia* ....Jan 05
Fey, Tina – *Upper Darby* ......Author V.16
Flake, Sharon – *Philadelphia* ..Author V.13
Gantos, Jack
 – *Mount Pleasant* ....Author V.10
George, Eddie – *Philadelphia* ....Sport V.6
Gingrich, Newt – *Harrisburg* ......Apr 95
Griffey, Ken Jr. – *Donora* ....Sport V.1
Hobbs, Will – *Pittsburgh* ....Author V.18
Iacocca, Lee A. – *Allentown* ......Jan 92
Jamison, Judith – *Philadelphia* .....Jan 96
Kirkpatrick, Chris – *Clarion* ....Jan 01

Kwolek, Stephanie
 – *Kensington* ....Science V.10
Lipinski, Tara – *Philadelphia* ....Apr 98
Maguire, Martie – *York* ....PerfArt V.1
Marino, Dan – *Pittsburgh* ....Apr 93
McCary, Michael – *Philadelphia* ....Jan 96
McDaniel, Lurlene
 – *Philadelphia* ....Author V.14
McGrath, Judy – *Scranton* ....Business V.1
Mead, Margaret
 – *Philadelphia* ....Science V.2
Montana, Joe – *New Eagle* ....Jan 95
Morris, Nathan – *Philadelphia* ......Jan 96
Morris, Wanya – *Philadelphia* ......Jan 96
Pierce, Tamora
 – *Connellsville* ....Author V.13
Pinkney, Jerry – *Philadelphia* ...Author V.2
Rogers, Fred – *Latrobe* ....PerfArt V.3
Smith, Will – *Philadelphia* ....Sep 94
Smyers, Karen – *Corry* ....Sport V.4
Stanford, John – *Darby* ....Sep 99
Stockman, Shawn – *Philadelphia* ...Jan 96
Thomas, Jonathan Taylor
 – *Bethlehem* ....Apr 95
Van Meter, Vicki – *Meadville* ......Jan 95
Warhol, Andy ....Artist V.1
Warrick, Earl – *Butler* ....Science V.8
Wilson, August – *Pittsburgh* ...Author V.4
Peru
Mulanovich, Sofia – *Lima* ....Apr 07
Philippines
apl.de.ap –
 Sapang Bato, Pampanga ....Apr 06
Poland
John Paul II – *Wadowice* ...Oct 92; Sep 05
Opdyke, Irene Gut
 – *Kozienice* ....Author V.9
Sabin, Albert – *Bialystok* ......Science V.1
Puerto Rico
Lopez, Charlotte ....Apr 94
Martin, Ricky – *Santurce* ....Jan 00
Moseley, Jonny – *San Juan* .....Sport V.8
Novello, Antonia – *Fajardo* ....Apr 92
Rodriguez, Ivan "Pudge"
 – *Manati* ....Jan 07
Rhode Island
Clark, Kelly – *Newport* ....Sport V.8
Gilman, Billy – *Westerly* ....Apr 02
Romania
Dumitriu, Ioana – *Bucharest* ...Science V.3
Nechita, Alexandra – *Vaslui* ......Jan 98

553

PLACES OF BIRTH INDEX

Risca, Viviana – *Bucharest* ....Sep 00
Russia
  Asimov, Isaac – *Petrovichi* ....Jul 92
  Brin, Sergey – *Moscow* ....Sep 05
  Chagall, Marc – *Vitebsk* ....Artist V.1
  Fedorov, Sergei – *Pskov* ....Apr 94
  Gorbachev, Mikhail – *Privolnoye* ...Jan 92
  Nevelson, Louise – *Kiev* ....Artist V.1
  Nureyev, Rudolf ....Apr 93
  Sharapova, Maria – *Nyagan* ....Sep 05
  Tartakovsky, Genndy
    – *Moscow* ....Author V.11
  Yeltsin, Boris – *Butka* ....Apr 92
Saudi Arabia
  bin Laden, Osama – *Riyadh* ......Apr 02
Scotland
  Blair, Tony – *Edinburgh* ....Apr 04
  Glennie, Evelyn – *Aberdeen* ....PerfArt V.3
  Muir, John – *Dunbar* ....WorLdr V.3
Senegal
  Senghor, Léopold Sédar – *Joal* ..WorLdr V.2
Serbia
  Milosevic, Slobodan – *Pozarevac* ...Sep 99
  Seles, Monica – *Novi Sad* ....Jan 96
Somalia
  Aidid, Mohammed Farah ....WorLdr V.2
South Africa
  de Klerk, F.W. – *Mayfair*...........Apr 94
  Mandela, Nelson – *Umtata, Transkei* .Jan 92
  Mandela, Winnie
    – *Pondoland, Transkei* ....WorLdr V.2
  Nash, Steve – *Johannesburg* ....Jan 06
  Tolkien, J.R.R. – *Bloemfontein* .....Jan 02
South Carolina
  Childress, Alice – *Charleston* ...Author V.1
  Daniel, Beth – *Charleston* ....Sport V.1
  Edelman, Marian Wright
    – *Bennettsville* ....Apr 93
  Garnett, Kevin – *Greenville* .....Sport V.6
  Gillespie, Dizzy – *Cheraw* ....Apr 93
  Hayes, Tyrone – *Columbia* ....Science V.10
  Hunter-Gault, Charlayne
    – *Due West* ....Jan 00
  Jackson, Jesse – *Greenville* ....Sep 95
South Dakota
  Gerberding, Julie – *Estelline* ..Science V.10
  GrandPré, Mary – *Aberdeen* ...Author V.14
South Korea
  An Na ....Author V.12
  Kim Dae-jung – *Hugwang* ....Sep 01

Pak, Se Ri – *Daejeon* ....Sport V.4
Spain
  Domingo, Placido – *Madrid* ....Sep 95
  Garcia, Sergio – *Castellon* ....Sport V.7
  Iglesias, Enrique – *Madrid* ....Jan 03
  Ochoa, Severo – *Luarca* ....Jan 94
  Sanchez Vicario, Arantxa
    – *Barcelona* ....Sport V.1
Sweden
  Lidstrom, Nicklas – *Vasteras* ......Sep 03
  Lindgren, Astrid
    – *Vimmerby* ....Author V.13
  Sorenstam, Annika – *Stockholm* ..Sport V.6
  Spiegelman, Art – *Stockholm* ..Author V.17
Switzerland
  Federer, Roger – *Bern* ....Jan 07
  Kübler-Ross, Elisabeth
    – *Zurich* ....Science V.10
Taiwan
  Ho, David – *Taichung* ....Science V.6
Tanzania
  Nyerere, Julius Kambarage ...WorLdr V.2
Tennessee
  Andrews, Ned – *Oakridge* ....Sep 94
  Cyrus, Miley – *Franklin* ....Sep 07
  Doherty, Shannen – *Memphis* .....Apr 92
  Fitzhugh, Louise – *Memphis* ...Author V.3
  Franklin, Aretha – *Memphis* ....Apr 01
  Hardaway, Anfernee "Penny"
    – *Memphis* ....Sport V.2
  McKissack, Fredrick L.
    – *Nashville* ....Author V.3
  McKissack, Patricia C.
    – *Smyrna* ....Author V.3
  Pinkwater, Daniel – *Memphis* ..Author V.8
  Rowan, Carl T. – *Ravenscroft* ......Sep 01
  Rudolph, Wilma – *St. Bethlehem* ...Apr 95
  Summit, Pat – *Henrietta* ....Sport V.3
  Timberlake, Justin
    – *Memphis* ....Jan 01 & Sep 08
  White, Reggie – *Chattanooga* ....Jan 98
Texas
  Adams, Yolanda – *Houston* ....Apr 03
  Armstrong, Lance – *Plano* ....Sep 00
  Baker, James – *Houston* ....Oct 92
  Beckett, Josh – *Spring* ....Sport V.11
  Bledel, Alexis – *Houston* ....Jan 03
  Buckley, Kelsie – *Houston* ....Sep 06
  Bush, Laura – *Midland* ....Apr 03
  Cisneros, Henry – *San Antonio* .....Sep 93

PLACES OF BIRTH INDEX

Clarkson, Kelly – *Burleson* .... Jan 03
Dell, Michael – *Houston* .... Business V.1
Duff, Hilary – *Houston* .... Sep 02
Ellerbee, Linda – *Bryan* .... Apr 94
Fiorina, Carly – *Austin* .... Sep 01
Gomez, Selena – *Grand Prairie* ... Sep 08
Groppe, Laura – *Houston* ..... Science V.5
Harris, Bernard – *Temple* ..... Science V.3
Hewitt, Jennifer Love – *Waco*. .... Sep 00
Hill, Grant – *Dallas* .... Sport V.1
Hrdy, Sarah Blaffer – *Dallas* ...... Apr 07
Johnson, Jimmy – *Port Arthur* ..... Jan 98
Johnson, Michael – *Dallas* .... Jan 97
Jonas, Nick – *Dallas* .... Jan 08
Jordan, Barbara – *Houston* .... Apr 96
Knowles, Beyoncé – *Houston* ..... Apr 01
Kopp, Wendy – *Austin* .... Sep 07
Maddux, Greg – *San Angelo* ..... Sport V.3
Maines, Natalie – *Lubbock* ..... PerfArt V.1
Nelly – *Austin* .... Sep 03
O'Connor, Sandra Day – *El Paso* ... Jul 92
Oliver, Patsy Ruth
 – *Texarkana* .... WorLdr V.1
Perot, H. Ross – *Texarkana* .... Apr 92
Rodriguez, Eloy – *Edinburg* .... Science V.2
Rodriguez, Gloria – *San Antonio* .. Apr 05
Ryan, Nolan – *Refugio* .... Oct 92
Sanchez, Ricardo – *Rio Grande City* .. Sep 04
Selena – *Lake Jackson* .... Jan 96
Simmons, Ruth – *Grapeland* ...... Sep 02
Simpson, Ashlee – *Waco* .... Sep 05
Soren, Tabitha – *San Antonio* ..... Jan 97
Strahan, Michael – *Houston* .... Sport V.12
Swoopes, Sheryl – *Brownfield* ... Sport V.2
Tandy, Karen P. – *Fort Worth* ..... Jan 08
Thampy, George – *Houston* ...... Sep 00
Tienda, Marta – *Edcouch* .... Sep 08
Tomlinson, LaDainian
 – *Rosebud* .... Sport V.14
Usher – *Dallas* .... PerfArt V.1
Weatherspoon, Teresa
 – *Jasper* .... Sport V.12
Williams, Lori Aurelia
 – *Houston* .... Author V.16
Zmeskal, Kim – *Houston* .... Jan 94

Tibet
Dalai Lama – *Takster, Amdo* ..... Sep 98

Trinidad
Guy, Rosa – *Diego Martin* ..... Author V.9

Uganda
Amin, Idi – *Koboko* .... WorLdr V.2

Ukraine
Baiul, Oksana – *Dnepropetrovsk* .... Apr 95
Stern, Isaac – *Kreminiecz* ...... PerfArt V.1

USSR – Union of Soviet Socialist Republics
Asimov, Isaac – *Petrovichi, Russia* ... Jul 92
Baiul, Oksana – *Dnepropetrovsk, Ukraine* .... Apr 95
Fedorov, Sergei – *Pskov, Russia* .... Apr 94
Gorbachev, Mikhail – *Privolnoye, Russia* .... Jan 92
Nureyev, Rudolf – *Russia* .... Apr 93
Yeltsin, Boris – *Butka, Russia* ..... Apr 92

Utah
Arnold, Roseanne – *Salt Lake City* .. Oct 92
Bennett, Olivia – *Salt Lake City* .... Sep 03
Hale, Shannon
 – *Salt Lake City* .... Author V.18
Jewel – *Payson* .... Sep 98
Young, Steve – *Salt Lake City* ..... Jan 94

Vermont
Muldowney, Shirley – *Burlington* .. Sport V.7
Teter, Hannah – *Belmont* .... Sep 06

Vietnam
Nhat Hanh (Thich) .... Jan 04

Virgin Islands (U.S.)
Duncan, Tim – *St. Croix* .... Apr 04

Virginia
Armstrong, William H.
 – *Lexington* .... Author V.7
Ashe, Arthur – *Richmond* .... Sep 93
Bass, Bill – *Staunton* .... Apr 08
Brown, Chris – *Tappahannock* .... Apr 07
Collins, Francis – *Staunton* .... Science V.6
Dayne, Ron – *Blacksburg* .... Apr 00
Delany, Sadie – *Lynch's Station* .... Sep 99
Elliott, Missy – *Portsmouth* .... PerfArt V.3
Fitzgerald, Ella – *Newport News* ... Jan 97
Hillenbrand, Laura – *Fairfax* .. Author V.14
Iverson, Allen – *Hampton* .... Sport V.7
Rylant, Cynthia – *Hopewell* .... Author V.1
Vick, Michael – *Newport News* .. Sport V.9
White, Ruth – *Whitewood* .... Author V.11

Wales
Dahl, Roald – *Llandaff* .... Author V.1

Washington DC
Booker, Cory .... Jan 08
Brown, Ron .... Sep 96

555

PLACES OF BIRTH INDEX

Chasez, JC . . . . Jan 01
Chung, Connie . . . . Jan 94
Danziger, Paula . . . . Author V.6
George, Jean Craighead . . . . . . Author V.3
Gore, Al . . . . Jan 93 & Sep 08
House, Donna . . . . Science V.11
Jackson, Shirley Ann . . . . Science V.2
Noor al Hussein, Queen of Jordan . . . Jan 05
Nye, Bill . . . . Science V.2
Pinkney, Andrea Davis. . . . . . . Author V.10
Sampras, Pete . . . . Jan 97
Vasan, Nina . . . . Science V.7
Watterson, Bill . . . . Jan 92

Washington State
Card, Orson Scott
– *Richland* . . . . Author V.14
Chihuly, Dale – *Tacoma* . . . . Jan 06
Cobain, Kurt – *Aberdeen* . . . . Sep 94
Devers, Gail – *Seattle* . . . . Sport V.2
Elway, John – *Port Angeles* . . . . . . Sport V.2
Gates, Bill – *Seattle* . . . . Apr 93; Science V.5
Hunter, Zach . . . . Jan 08
Jones, Chuck – *Spokane* . . . . . . Author V.12
Larson, Gary – *Tacoma* . . . . Author V.1
Murie, Margaret – *Seattle* . . . . . WorLdr V.1
Ohno, Apolo – *Seattle* . . . . Sport V.8
Stockton, John – *Spokane* . . . . Sport V.3
Thomas, Rob – *Sunnyside* . . . . Jan 07
Urlacher, Brian – *Pasco* . . . . Sep 04

West Virginia
Gates, Henry Louis Jr. – *Keyser* . . . . Apr 00
Jakes, T.D. – *South Charleston* . . . . . . Jan 05
Moss, Randy – *Rand* . . . . Sport V.4
Myers, Walter Dean
– *Martinsburg* . . . . Jan 93
Nash, John Forbes Jr.
– *Bluefield* . . . . Science V.7

Wisconsin
Bardeen, John – *Madison* . . . . . Science V.1
Cray, Seymour
– *Chippewa Falls* . . . . Science V.2
Driscoll, Jean – *Milwaukee* . . . . Sep 97
Giddens, Rebecca – *Green Bay* . . Sport V.14
Henry, Marguerite
– *Milwaukee* . . . . Author V.4
Hurley, Andy – *Menominee Falls* . . . Sep 07
Jansen, Dan – *Milwaukee* . . . . Apr 94
Kiessling, Laura L.
– *Milwaukee* . . . . Science V.9
Memmel, Chellsie – *Milwaukee* . . Sport V.14
Nelson, Gaylord
– *Clear Lake* . . . . WorLdr V.3
O'Keeffe, Georgia
– *Sun Prairie* . . . . Artist V.1
Patrick, Danica – *Beloit* . . . . Apr 06
Wilder, Laura Ingalls
– *Pepin* . . . . Author V.3
Wright, Frank Lloyd
– *Richland Center* . . . . Artist V.1

Wyoming
MacLachlan, Patricia
– *Cheyenne* . . . . Author V.2

Yugoslavia
Filipovic, Zlata – *Sarajevo,
Bosnia-Herzogovina* . . . . Sep 94
Milosevic, Slobodan – *Pozarevac,
Serbia* . . . . Sep 99
Seles, Monica – *Novi Sad, Serbia* . . . . Jan 96

Zaire
Mobutu Sese Seko – *Lisala* . . . WorLdr V.2

Zambia
Kaunda, Kenneth – *Lubwa* . . . WorLdr V.2

Zimbabwe
Mugabe, Robert – *Kutama* . . . . WorLdr V.2

Birthday Index

January		Year
1	Salinger, J.D.	1919
2	Asimov, Isaac	1920
	Cox, Lynne	1957
3	Dawson, Matel Jr.	1921
	Fuller, Millard	1935
	Manning, Eli	1981
	Tolkien, J.R.R.	1892
4	Naylor, Phyllis Reynolds	1933
	Runyan, Marla	1969
	Shula, Don	1930
5	Ocampo, Adriana C.	1955
6	Van Draanen, Wendelin	?
7	Hurston, Zora Neale	?1891
	Rodriguez, Eloy	1947
	Soriano, Alfonso	1978
8	Castellano, Torry (Donna C.)	1979
	Cooper, Floyd	1956
	Ford, Maya (Donna F.)	1979
	Hawking, Stephen W.	1942
	Spelman, Lucy	1963
9	Garcia, Sergio	1980
	Graves, Earl	1935
	McLean, A.J	1978
	Menchu, Rigoberta	1959
	Nixon, Richard	1913
10	Streeter, Tanya	1973
11	Leopold, Aldo	1887
12	Amanpour, Christiane	1958
	Bezos, Jeff	1964
	Capolino, Peter	1945
	Lasseter, John	?1957
	Limbaugh, Rush	1951
13	Bloom, Orlando	1977
	Burnside, Aubyn	1985
	Webb, Alan	1983
14	Bellamy, Carol	1942
	Lucid, Shannon	1943
15	Agosto, Ben	1982
	Teller, Edward	1908

	Werbach, Adam	1973
16	Aaliyah	1979
	Fossey, Dian	1932
	Hakim, Joy	1931
	Lipsyte, Robert	1938
	Pujols, Albert	1980
	Tarter, Jill	1944
17	Carrey, Jim	1962
	Cormier, Robert	1925
	Jones, James Earl	1931
	Lewis, Shari	?1934
	Tartakovsky, Genndy	1970
	Wade, Dwyane	1982
18	Ali, Muhammad	1942
	Chavez, Julz	1962
	Messier, Mark	1961
19	Askins, Renee	1959
	Johnson, John	1918
20	Bourdon, Rob	1979
	DeMayo, Neda	1960
	Wright, Will	1960
21	Domingo, Placido	1941
	Nicklaus, Jack	1940
	Olajuwon, Hakeem	1963
22	Chavis, Benjamin	1948
	Ward, Lloyd D.	1949
23	Elion, Gertrude	1918
	Foudy, Julie	1971
	Thiessen, Tiffani-Amber	1974
24	Haddock, Doris (Granny D.)	1910
25	Alley, Kirstie	1955
	Keys, Alicia	1981
26	Carter, Vince	1977
	Hale, Shannon	1974
	Morita, Akio	1921
	Siskel, Gene	1946
	Tarbox, Katie	1982
27	Lester, Julius	1939
	Roberts, John Jr.	1955
	Teter, Hannah	1987

BIRTHDAY INDEX

January (continued)	Year
Vasan, Nina	1984
28 Carter, Nick	1980
Culpepper, Daunte	1977
Fatone, Joey	1977
Gretzky, Wayne	1961
Wood, Elijah	1981
29 Abbey, Edward	1927
Gilbert, Sara	1975
Hasek, Dominik	1965
Peet, Bill	1915
Winfrey, Oprah	1954
30 Alexander, Lloyd	1924
Cheney, Dick	1941
Engelbart, Douglas	1925
Horvath, Polly	1957
31 Collier, Bryan	1967
Flannery, Sarah	1982
Funk, Wally	1939
Robinson, Jackie	1919
Ryan, Nolan	1947
Timberlake, Justin	1981

February	Year
1 Cabot, Meg	1967
Hughes, Langston	1902
Patton, Antwan	1975
Spinelli, Jerry	1941
Yeltsin, Boris	1931
2 Shakira	1977
3 Heimlich, Henry	1920
Nixon, Joan Lowery	1927
Rockwell, Norman	1894
Sanborn, Ryne	1989
4 Parks, Rosa	1913
Patterson, Carly	1988
5 Aaron, Hank	1934
6 Leakey, Mary	1913
Reagan, Ronald	1911
Rosa, Emily	1987
Zmeskal, Kim	1976
7 Brooks, Garth	1962
Kutcher, Ashton	1978
Nash, Steve	1974
Wang, An	1920
Wilder, Laura Ingalls	1867
8 Farrell, David	1977
Grisham, John	1955
Hamilton, Bethany	1990
9 Love, Susan	1948

	Whitson, Peggy	1960
10	Konigsburg, E.L.	1930
	Norman, Greg	1955
11	Aniston, Jennifer	1969
	Brandy	1979
	Rowland, Kelly	1981
	Shinoda, Mike	1977
	Yolen, Jane	1939
12	Blume, Judy	1938
	Kurzweil, Raymond	1948
	Small, David	1945
	Woodson, Jacqueline	?1964
13	GrandPré, Mary	1954
	Moss, Randy	1977
	Sleator, William	1945
14	Highmore, Freddie	1992
	McNair, Steve	1973
15	Groening, Matt	1954
	Jagr, Jaromir	1972
	Sones, Sonya	1952
	Spiegelman, Art	1948
	Van Dyken, Amy	1973
16	Cantore, Jim	1964
	Freeman, Cathy	1973
17	Anderson, Marian	1897
	Armstrong, Billie Joe	1972
	Hargreaves, Alison	1962
	Jordan, Michael	1963
18	Kenyon, Cynthia	1954
	Morrison, Toni	1931
19	McNutt, Marcia	1952
	Tan, Amy	1952
20	Adams, Ansel	1902
	Barkley, Charles	1963
	Cobain, Kurt	1967
	Crawford, Cindy	1966
	Hernandez, Livan	1975
	Littrell, Brian	1975
	Rihanna	1988
21	Carpenter, Mary Chapin	1958
	Hewitt, Jennifer Love	1979
	Jordan, Barbara	1936
	Lewis, John	1940
	Mugabe, Robert	1924
22	Barrymore, Drew	1975
	Fernandez, Lisa	1971
	Gorey, Edward	1925
	Singh, Vijay	1963
23	Brown, Claude	1937
	Dell, Michael	1965

558

BIRTHDAY INDEX

February (continued)		Year
	Fanning, Dakota	1994
24	Borgman, Jim	1954
	Jobs, Steven	1955
	Vernon, Mike	1963
	Whitestone, Heather	1973
25	Voigt, Cynthia	1942
26	Thompson, Jenny	1973
27	Clinton, Chelsea	1980
	Gonzalez, Tony	1976
	Hunter-Gault, Charlayne	1942
	King, Mary-Claire	1946
28	Andretti, Mario	1940
	Napoli, Donna Jo	1948
	Pauling, Linus	1901

March		Year
1	Ellison, Ralph Waldo	1914
	Murie, Olaus J.	1889
	Nielsen, Jerri	1952
	Rabin, Yitzhak	1922
	Zamora, Pedro	1972
2	Gorbachev, Mikhail	1931
	Hamilton, Laird	1964
	Roethlisberger, Ben	1982
	Satcher, David	1941
	Seuss, Dr.	1904
3	Hooper, Geoff	1979
	Joyner-Kersee, Jackie	1962
	MacLachlan, Patricia	1938
4	Armstrong, Robb	1962
	Morgan, Garrett	1877
5	Margulis, Lynn	1938
6	Ashley, Maurice	1966
	Howard, Tim	1979
7	McCarty, Oseola	1908
8	Prinze, Freddie Jr.	1976
	Rowland, Pleasant T.	1941
10	Guy, Jasmine	1964
	Miller, Shannon	1977
	Underwood, Carrie	1983
	Wolf, Hazel	1898
11	Buckley, Kelsie	1995
	Madden, Benji	1979
	Madden, Joel	1979
	Scalia, Antonin	1936
12	Hamilton, Virginia	1936
	Hiaasen, Carl	1953
	Nye, Naomi Shihab	1952
13	Van Meter, Vicki	1982

14	Dayne, Ron	1977
	Hanson, Taylor	1983
	Jones, Quincy	1933
	Williamson, Kevin	1965
15	Ginsburg, Ruth Bader	1933
	Hahn, Joe	1977
	White, Ruth	1942
	will.i.am	1975
16	O'Neal, Shaquille	1972
	Ramos, Jorge	1958
17	Hamm, Mia	1972
	Nureyev, Rudolf	1938
18	Blair, Bonnie	1964
	de Klerk, F.W.	1936
	Griese, Brian	1975
	Queen Latifah	1970
19	Blanchard, Rachel	1976
	Brashares, Ann	1967
20	Bennington, Chester	1976
	Lee, Spike	1957
	Lowry, Lois	1937
	Rogers, Fred	1928
	Sachar, Louis	1954
21	Gilbert, Walter	1932
	O'Donnell, Rosie	1962
22	Collins, Billy	1941
	Marceau, Marcel	1923
	Shatner, William	1931
23	Kidd, Jason	1973
24	Manning, Peyton	1976
25	Aly (Alyson Renae Michalka)	1989
	Dragila, Stacy	1971
	Franklin, Aretha	1942
	Granato, Cammi	1971
	Lovell, Jim	1928
	Park, Linda Sue	1960
	Patrick, Danica	1982
	Steinem, Gloria	1934
	Swoopes, Sheryl	1971
26	Allen, Marcus	1960
	Erdös, Paul	1913
	Knightley, Keira	1985
	O'Connor, Sandra Day	1930
	Page, Larry	1973
	Pelosi, Nancy	1940
	Stockton, John	1962
	Witherspoon, Reese	1976
27	Alvarez, Julia	1950
	Carey, Mariah	1970
	Fergie	1975

559

BIRTHDAY INDEX

March (continued)		Year
	Wrede, Patricia C.	1953
28	James, Cheryl	?
	McEntire, Reba	1955
	Stiles, Julia	1981
	Tompkins, Douglas	1943
29	Capriati, Jennifer	1976
30	Dion, Celine	1968
	Hammer	1933
	Jones, Norah	1979
31	Caplan, Arthur	1950
	Chavez, Cesar	1927
	Gore, Al	1948
	Howe, Gordie	1928

April		Year
1	Maathai, Wangari	1940
2	Carvey, Dana	1955
3	Berger, Francie	1960
	Bynes, Amanda	1986
	Garth, Jennie	1972
	Goodall, Jane	1934
	Murphy, Eddie	1961
	Street, Picabo	1971
4	Angelou, Maya	1928
	Mirra, Dave	1974
	Spears, Jamie Lynn	1991
5	Kamen, Dean	1951
	McDaniel, Lurlene	1944
	Peck, Richard	1934
	Powell, Colin	1937
6	Watson, James D.	1928
7	Black, Jack	1969
	Chan, Jackie	1954
	Douglas, Marjory Stoneman	1890
	Forman, Michele	1946
8	Annan, Kofi	1938
	Brody, Adam	1980
9	Haddix, Margaret Peterson	1964
10	AJ (Amanda Joy Michalka)	1991
	Bleiler, Gretchen	1981
	Carrabba, Chris	1975
	Huerta, Dolores	1930
	Madden, John	1936
	Moore, Mandy	1984
11	Stone, Joss	1987
12	Cleary, Beverly	1916
	Danes, Claire	1979
	Doherty, Shannen	1971
	Hawk, Tony	1968

		Year
	Letterman, David	1947
	Soto, Gary	1952
13	Brandis, Jonathan	1976
	Henry, Marguerite	1902
14	Collins, Francis	1950
	Gellar, Sarah Michelle	1977
	Maddux, Greg	1966
	Rose, Pete	1941
15	Martin, Bernard	1954
	Watson, Emma	1990
16	Abdul-Jabbar, Kareem	1947
	Atwater-Rhodes, Amelia	1984
	Selena	1971
	Williams, Garth	1912
17	Champagne, Larry III	1985
18	Ferrera, America	1984
	Hart, Melissa Joan	1976
	Villa, Brenda	1980
19	Sharapova, Maria	1987
20	Brundtland, Gro Harlem	1939
21	Muir, John	1838
22	Fox, Paula	1923
	Levi-Montalcini, Rita	1909
	Oppenheimer, J. Robert	1904
23	López, George	1961
	Watson, Barry	1974
24	Clarkson, Kelly	1982
25	Duncan, Tim	1976
	Fitzgerald, Ella	1917
26	Giff, Patricia Reilly	1935
	Nelson, Marilyn	1946
	Pei, I.M.	1917
	Welling, Tom	1977
27	Bemelmans, Ludwig	1898
	Booker, Cory	1969
	King, Coretta Scott	1927
	LaHaye, Tim	1926
	Stump, Patrick	1984
	Wilson, August	1945
28	Alba, Jessica	1981
	Baker, James	1930
	Duncan, Lois	1934
	Hussein, Saddam	1937
	Kaunda, Kenneth	1924
	Lee, Harper	1926
	Leno, Jay	1950
	Lidstrom, Nicklas	1970
29	Agassi, Andre	1970
	Earnhardt, Dale	1951

BIRTHDAY INDEX

April (continued)		Year
	Seinfeld, Jerry	1954
30	Dunst, Kirsten	1982

May		Year
2	Beckham, David	1975
	Hughes, Sarah	1985
	Scott, Jerry	1955
	Spock, Benjamin	1903
4	Bass, Lance	1979
	Dirnt, Mike	1972
5	Brown, Chris	1989
	Lionni, Leo	1910
	Maxwell, Jody-Anne	1986
	Opdyke, Irene Gut	1922
	Strasser, Todd	1950
	WilderBrathwaite, Gloria	1964
6	Blair, Tony	1953
7	Land, Edwin	1909
	Wiles, Deborah	1953
8	Attenborough, David	1926
	Iglesias, Enrique	1975
	Meltzer, Milton	1915
9	Bergen, Candice	1946
	Yzerman, Steve	1965
10	Bono	1960
	Cooney, Caroline B.	1947
	Curtis, Christopher Paul	1953
	Galdikas, Biruté	1946
	Jamison, Judith	1944
	Ochoa, Ellen	1958
11	Farrakhan, Louis	1933
	Feynman, Richard P.	1918
	Snyder, Zilpha Keatley	1927
12	Mowat, Farley	1921
13	Pascal, Francine	1938
	Rodman, Dennis	1961
14	Kapell, Dave	1962
	Lucas, George	1944
	Smith, Emmitt	1969
15	Albright, Madeleine	1937
	Almond, David	1951
	Beckett, Josh	1980
	Hillenbrand, Laura	1967
	Johns, Jasper	1930
	Poussaint, Alvin	1934
	Zindel, Paul	1936
16	Coville, Bruce	1950
	Giguère, Jean-Sébastien	1977
17	Paulsen, Gary	1939
18	Fey, Tina	1970
	John Paul II	1920
19	Brody, Jane	1941
	Feelings, Tom	1933
	Garnett, Kevin	1976
	Hansberry, Lorraine	1930
20	Stewart, Tony	1971
21	Crilley, Mark	1966
	Robinson, Mary	1944
22	Lobel, Arnold	1933
	Ohno, Apolo	1982
23	Bardeen, John	1908
	Cooper, Susan	1935
	Jewel	1974
	O'Dell, Scott	1898
	Pressel, Morgan	1988
24	Beachley, Layne	1972
	Dumars, Joe	1963
	Gilman, Billy	1988
	McGrady, Tracy	1979
25	Myers, Mike	1963
	Urlacher, Brian	1978
26	Hill, Lauryn	1975
	Ride, Sally	1951
27	Benjamin, André	1975
	Carson, Rachel	1907
	Kerr, M.E.	1927
	Oliver, Jamie	1975
28	Giuliani, Rudolph	1944
	Johnston, Lynn	1947
	Shabazz, Betty	1936
	Spelke, Elizabeth	1949
29	Anthony, Carmelo	1984
	Clements, Andrew	1949
30	Anderson, Brett (Donna A.)	1979
	Cohen, Adam Ezra	1979
	Ramirez, Manny	1972
31	Hurley, Andy	1980

June		Year
1	Arnesen, Liv	1953
	Lalas, Alexi	1970
	Lansky, Bruce	1941
	Morissette, Alanis	1974
2	Adu, Freddy	1989
	Juster, Norton	1929
3	Cooper, Anderson	1967
4	Kistler, Darci	1964
	Nelson, Gaylord	1916
5	Scarry, Richard	1919

BIRTHDAY INDEX

June (continued)	Year
Wentz, Pete	1979
6 Ford, Cheryl	1981
Rylant, Cynthia	1954
7 Brooks, Gwendolyn	1917
Iverson, Allen	1975
Oleynik, Larisa	1981
8 Berners-Lee, Tim	1955
Bush, Barbara	1925
Clijsters, Kim	1983
Davenport, Lindsay	1976
Edelman, Marian Wright	1939
Wayans, Keenen Ivory	1958
Wright, Frank Lloyd	1869
9 Depp, Johnny	1963
Jakes, T.D.	1957
Portman, Natalie	1981
10 Frank, Anne	1929
Lipinski, Tara	1982
Sendak, Maurice	1928
Shea, Jim Jr.	1968
Wilson, Edward O.	1929
11 Cousteau, Jacques	1910
Montana, Joe	1956
Taurasi, Diana	1982
12 Bush, George	1924
Rubin, Jamie	1986
13 Allen, Tim	1953
Alvarez, Luis W.	1911
Christo	1935
Nash, John Forbes Jr.	1928
14 Bourke-White, Margaret	1904
Graf, Steffi	1969
Summitt, Pat	1952
Trump, Donald	1946
Yep, Laurence	1948
15 Greer, Pedro José Jr.	1956
Horner, Jack	1946
Jacques, Brian	1939
16 McClintock, Barbara	1902
Shakur, Tupac	1971
17 Gingrich, Newt	1943
Jansen, Dan	1965
Williams, Venus	1980
18 da Silva, Fabiola	1979
Johnson, Angela	1961
Morris, Nathan	1971
Van Allsburg, Chris	1949
19 Abdul, Paula	1962
Aung San Suu Kyi	1945

Muldowney, Shirley	1940
20 Goodman, John	1952
Greenburg, Dan	1936
21 Bhutto, Benazir	1953
Breathed, Berke	1957
22 Bradley, Ed	1941
Daly, Carson	1973
Warner, Kurt	1971
23 Clemons, Kortney	1980
Memmel, Chellsie	1988
Rudolph, Wilma	1940
Thomas, Clarence	1948
Tomlinson, LaDainian	1979
24 Lasky, Kathryn	1944
Mulanovich, Sofia	1983
25 Carle, Eric	1929
Gibbs, Lois	1951
26 Ammann, Simon	1981
Harris, Bernard	1956
Jeter, Derek	1974
LeMond, Greg	1961
Vick, Michael	1980
Wilson, Gretchen	1973
27 Babbitt, Bruce	1938
Bell, Drake	1986
Dunbar, Paul Laurence	1872
Perot, H. Ross	1930
28 Elway, John	1960
Yunus, Muhammad	1940
29 Basich, Tina	1969
Jiménez, Francisco	1943
Kopp, Wendy	1967
30 Ballard, Robert	1942
Phelps, Michael	1985

July	Year
1 Brower, David	1912
Calderone, Mary S.	1904
Diana, Princess of Wales	1961
Duke, David	1950
Elliott, Missy	1971
Lewis, Carl	1961
McCully, Emily Arnold	1939
Tharp, Twyla	1941
2 Bethe, Hans A.	1906
Branch, Michelle	1983
Fox, Vicente	1942
Gantos, Jack	1951
George, Jean Craighead	1919
Kadohata, Cynthia	1956

BIRTHDAY INDEX

July (continued)		Year
	Lohan, Lindsay	1986
	Lynch, Chris	1962
	Marshall, Thurgood	1908
	McGrath, Judy	1952
	Petty, Richard	1937
	Thomas, Dave	1932
	Tisdale, Ashley	1985
3	Simmons, Ruth	1945
5	Watterson, Bill	1958
6	Bush, George W.	1946
	Dalai Lama	1935
	Dumitriu, Ioana	1976
7	Chagall, Marc	1887
	Heinlein, Robert	1907
	Kwan, Michelle	1980
	Leslie, Lisa	1972
	Otto, Sylke	1969
	Sakic, Joe	1969
	Stachowski, Richie	1985
8	Bush, Sophia	1982
	Hardaway, Anfernee "Penny"	1971
	Keith, Toby	1961
	Kübler-Ross, Elisabeth	1926
	MacArthur, Ellen	1976
	Sealfon, Rebecca	1983
9	Farmer, Nancy	1941
	Hanks, Tom	1956
	Hassan II	1929
	Krim, Mathilde	1926
	Lee, Jeanette	1971
	Rodriguez, Gloria	1948
	Sacks, Oliver	1933
10	Ashe, Arthur	1943
	Benson, Mildred	1905
	Boulmerka, Hassiba	1969
11	Belbin, Tanith	1984
	Cisneros, Henry	1947
	Hrdy, Sarah Blaffer	1946
	White, E.B.	1899
12	Bauer, Joan	1951
	Cosby, Bill	1937
	Johnson, Johanna	1983
	Yamaguchi, Kristi	1972
13	Ford, Harrison	1942
	Stewart, Patrick	1940
14	Taboo	1975
15	Aristide, Jean-Bertrand	1953
	Ventura, Jesse	1951
16	Ferrell, Will	1967

	Johnson, Jimmy	1943
	Sanders, Barry	1968
17	An Na	1972
	Stepanek, Mattie	1990
18	Bell, Kristen	1980
	Diesel, Vin	1967
	Glenn, John	1921
	Lemelson, Jerome	1923
	Mandela, Nelson	1918
19	Glennie, Evelyn	1965
	Kratt, Chris	1969
	Tarvin, Herbert	1985
20	Hillary, Sir Edmund	1919
	Santana, Carlos	1947
21	Catchings, Tamika	1979
	Chastain, Brandi	1968
	Hartnett, Josh	1978
	Reno, Janet	1938
	Riley, Dawn	1964
	Stern, Isaac	1920
	Williams, Robin	1952
22	Calder, Alexander	1898
	Dole, Bob	1923
	Gomez, Selena	1992
	Hinton, S.E.	1948
	Johnson, Keyshawn	1972
23	Haile Selassie	1892
	Krauss, Alison	1971
	Williams, Michelle	1980
24	Abzug, Bella	1920
	Bonds, Barry	1964
	Irwin, Bindi	1998
	Krone, Julie	1963
	Lopez, Jennifer	1970
	Moss, Cynthia	1940
	Wilson, Mara	1987
25	Payton, Walter	1954
26	Berenstain, Jan	1923
	Clark, Kelly	1983
27	Dunlap, Alison	1969
	Kimball, Cheyenne	1990
	Rodriguez, Alex	1975
28	Babbitt, Natalie	1932
	Davis, Jim	1945
	Potter, Beatrix	1866
29	Burns, Ken	1953
	Creech, Sharon	1945
	Dole, Elizabeth Hanford	1936
	Hayes, Tyrone	1967
	Jennings, Peter	1938

BIRTHDAY INDEX

July (continued)	Year
Morris, Wanya	1973
30 Allen, Tori	1988
Hill, Anita	1956
Moore, Henry	1898
Norman, Christina	1963
Schroeder, Pat	1940
31 Cronin, John	1950
Kwolek, Stephanie	1923
Radcliffe, Daniel	1989
Reid Banks, Lynne	1929
Rowling, J.K.	1965
Weinke, Chris	1972

August	Year
1 Brown, Ron	1941
Coolio	1963
Garcia, Jerry	1942
2 Asbaty, Diandra	1980
Baldwin, James	1924
Healy, Bernadine	1944
Howe, James	1946
3 Brady, Tom	1977
Roper, Dee Dee	?
Savimbi, Jonas	1934
Stewart, Martha	1941
4 Gordon, Jeff	1971
Obama, Barack	1961
Whitman, Meg	1956
5 Córdova, France	1947
Ewing, Patrick	1962
Jackson, Shirley Ann	1946
6 Carter, Regina	?1963
Cooney, Barbara	1917
Robinson, David	1965
Warhol, Andy	?1928
7 Byars, Betsy	1928
Crosby, Sidney	1987
Duchovny, David	1960
Leakey, Louis	1903
Villa-Komaroff, Lydia	1947
8 Boyd, Candy Dawson	1946
Chasez, JC	1976
Federer, Roger	1981
9 Anderson, Gillian	1968
Holdsclaw, Chamique	1977
Houston, Whitney	1963
McKissack, Patricia C.	1944
Sanders, Deion	1967
Travers, P.L.	?1899

10	Hayden, Carla	1952
	Tienda, Marta	1950
11	Haley, Alex	1921
	Hogan, Hulk	1953
	Rowan, Carl T.	1925
	Wozniak, Steve	1950
12	Barton, Hazel	1971
	Martin, Ann M.	1955
	McKissack, Fredrick L.	1939
	Myers, Walter Dean	1937
	Sampras, Pete	1971
13	Aldrich, George	1955
	Battle, Kathleen	1948
	Castro, Fidel	1927
14	Berry, Halle	?1967
	Johnson, Magic	1959
	Larson, Gary	1950
	Mitchell-Raptakis, Karen	1956
15	Affleck, Benjamin	1972
	Ellerbee, Linda	1944
	Jonas, Joseph	1989
	Thomas, Rob	1965
	Walsh, Kerri	1978
16	Bennett, Olivia	1989
	Farrell, Suzanne	1945
	Fu Mingxia	1978
	Gayle, Helene	1955
	Jones, Diana Wynne	1934
	Robison, Emily	1972
	Thampy, George	1987
18	Danziger, Paula	1944
	Murie, Margaret	1902
19	Clinton, Bill	1946
	Romeo, Lil'	1989
	Soren, Tabitha	1967
20	Chung, Connie	1946
	Dakides, Tara	1975
	Milosevic, Slobodan	1941
21	Brin, Sergey	1973
	Chamberlain, Wilt	1936
	Draper, Sharon	1952
	Hillenburg, Stephen	1961
	Toro, Natalia	1984
22	Bradbury, Ray	1920
	Dorough, Howie	1973
	Gerberding, Julie	1955
	Hobbs, Will	1947
	Schwarzkopf, H. Norman	1934
23	Bryant, Kobe	1978
	Coughlin, Natalie	1982

BIRTHDAY INDEX

August (continued)

		Year
	Noor al Hussein, Queen of Jordan	1951
	Novello, Antonia	1944
	Phoenix, River	1970
24	Arafat, Yasir	1929
	Card, Orson Scott	1951
	Dai Qing	1941
	Ripken, Cal Jr.	1960
25	Case, Steve	1958
	Wolff, Virginia Euwer	1937
26	Burke, Christopher	1965
	Culkin, Macaulay	1980
	Robertson, Allison (Donna R.)	1979
	Sabin, Albert	1906
	Teresa, Mother	1910
	Tuttle, Merlin	1941
27	Adams, Yolanda	1961
	Moseley, Jonny	1975
	Nechita, Alexandra	1985
	Rinaldi, Ann	1934
	Steingraber, Sandra	1959
	Vega, Alexa	1988
28	Dove, Rita	1952
	Evans, Janet	1971
	Peterson, Roger Tory	1908
	Priestley, Jason	1969
	Rimes, LeAnn	1982
	Twain, Shania	1965
29	Grandin, Temple	1947
	Hesse, Karen	1952
	McCain, John	1936
30	Alexander, Shaun	1977
	Bass, Bill	1928
	Buffett, Warren	1930
	Diaz, Cameron	1972
	Earle, Sylvia	1935
	Ling, Lisa	1973
	Roddick, Andy	1982
	Williams, Ted	1918
31	Niedermayer, Scott	1973
	Perlman, Itzhak	1945

September

		Year
1	Estefan, Gloria	1958
	Guy, Rosa	1925
	Smyers, Karen	1961
	Trohman, Joe	1984
2	Bearden, Romare	?1912
	Galeczka, Chris	1981

	Lisanti, Mariangela	1983
	Mohajer, Dineh	1972
	Reeves, Keanu	1964
	Yelas, Jay	1965
3	Delany, Bessie	1891
	Finch, Jennie	1980
	White, Shaun	1986
4	Knowles, Beyoncé	1981
	Wright, Richard	1908
5	Guisewite, Cathy	1950
6	Fiorina, Carly	1954
	Friday, Dallas	1986
7	Lawrence, Jacob	1917
	Moses, Grandma	1860
	Pippig, Uta	1965
	Scurry, Briana	1971
8	Prelutsky, Jack	1940
	Scieszka, Jon	1954
	Thomas, Jonathan Taylor	1982
9	Sandler, Adam	1966
10	Gould, Stephen Jay	1941
	Johnson, Randy	1963
	Wallace, Ben	1974
11	Dworkin, Aaron	1970
12	Hudson, Jennifer	1981
	Yao Ming	1980
13	Johnson, Michael	1967
	Monroe, Bill	1911
	Perry, Tyler	1969
	Taylor, Mildred D.	1943
14	Armstrong, William H.	1914
	Koff, Clea	1972
	Stanford, John	1938
15	dePaola, Tomie	1934
	Marino, Dan	1961
	McCloskey, Robert	1914
16	Bledel, Alexis	1981
	Dahl, Roald	1916
	Gates, Henry Louis Jr.	1950
	Jonas, Nick	1992
17	Binford, Greta	1965
	Burger, Warren	1907
	Jackson, Phil	1945
	Levine, Gail Carson	1947
18	Armstrong, Lance	1971
	Carson, Ben	1951
	de Mille, Agnes	1905
	Fields, Debbi	1956
	Foray, June	1917
	Nakamura, Leanne	1982

BIRTHDAY INDEX

September (continued)	Year
19 Delany, Sadie	1889
Fay, Michael	1956
Giddens, Rebecca	1977
O'Brien, Soledad	1966
20 Chihuly, Dale	1941
Crabtree, Taylor	1990
21 Fielder, Cecil	1963
Hill, Faith	1967
Jones, Chuck	1912
Kiessling, Laura L.	1960
King, Stephen	1947
Nkrumah, Kwame	1909
22 Richardson, Dot	1961
Sessions, Michael	1987
23 Jenkins, Jerry B.	1949
Nevelson, Louise	1899
Warrick, Earl	1911
24 George, Eddie	1973
Ochoa, Severo	1905
25 Gwaltney, John Langston	1928
Locklear, Heather	1961
Lopez, Charlotte	1976
Murphy, Jim	1947
Pinkney, Andrea Davis	1963
Pippen, Scottie	1965
Reeve, Christopher	1952
Smith, Will	1968
Walters, Barbara	1931
26 Mandela, Winnie	1934
Stockman, Shawn	1972
Williams, Serena	1981
27 Handford, Martin	1956
Lavigne, Avril	1984
28 Blake, James	1979
Cray, Seymour	1925
Duff, Hilary	1987
Pak, Se Ri	1977
29 Berenstain, Stan	1923
Guey, Wendy	1983
Gumbel, Bryant	1948
30 Hingis, Martina	1980
Moceanu, Dominique	1981

October	Year
1 Carter, Jimmy	1924
McGwire, Mark	1963
2 Leibovitz, Annie	1949
3 Campbell, Neve	1973
Herriot, James	1916

	Richardson, Kevin	1972
	Simpson, Ashlee	1984
	Stefani, Gwen	1969
	Winfield, Dave	1951
4	Cushman, Karen	1941
	Forman, James	1928
	Kamler, Kenneth	1947
	Meissner, Kimmie	1989
	Rice, Anne	1941
	Simmons, Russell	1957
5	Fitzhugh, Louise	1928
	Hill, Grant	1972
	Lemieux, Mario	1965
	Lin, Maya	1959
	Roy, Patrick	1965
	Tyson, Neil deGrasse	1958
	Winslet, Kate	1975
6	Bennett, Cherie	1960
	Lobo, Rebecca	1973
7	Holmes, Priest	1973
	Ma, Yo-Yo	1955
	McAdams, Rachel	1976
8	Jackson, Jesse	1941
	Ringgold, Faith	1930
	Stine, R.L.	1943
	Winans, CeCe	1964
9	Bryan, Zachery Ty	1981
	Senghor, Léopold Sédar	1906
	Sorenstam, Annika	1970
	Williams, Tyler James	1992
10	Earnhardt, Dale Jr.	1974
	Favre, Brett	1969
	Saro-Wiwa, Ken	1941
11	Freedman, Russell	1929
	Murray, Ty	1969
	Perry, Luke	?1964
	Wie, Michelle	1989
	Young, Steve	1961
12	Bloor, Edward	1950
	Childress, Alice	?1920
	Jones, Marion	1975
	Maguire, Martie	1969
	Ward, Charlie	1970
13	Ashanti	1980
	Carter, Chris	1956
	Kerrigan, Nancy	1969
	Rice, Jerry	1962
14	Daniel, Beth	1956
	Maines, Natalie	1974
	Mobutu Sese Seko	1930

BIRTHDAY INDEX

October (continued)	Year
Usher	1978
15 Donovan, Marion	1917
Iacocca, Lee A.	1924
16 Bruchac, Joseph	1942
Mayer, John	1977
Stewart, Kordell	1972
17 Eminem	1972
Jemison, Mae	1956
Kirkpatrick, Chris	1971
18 Bird, Sue	1980
Efron, Zac	1987
Foreman, Dave	1946
Marsalis, Wynton	1961
Navratilova, Martina	1956
Suzuki, Shinichi	1898
19 Blum, Deborah	1954
Pullman, Philip	1946
20 Grimes, Nikki	1950
Kenyatta, Jomo	?1891
Mantle, Mickey	1931
Pinsky, Robert	1940
21 Cruz, Celia	?1924
Gillespie, Dizzy	1956
Le Guin, Ursula K.	1929
22 Hanson, Zac	1985
Suzuki, Ichiro	1973
23 Anderson, Laurie Halse	1961
Crichton, Michael	1942
Milbrett, Tiffeny	1972
Pelé	1940
24 Tandy, Karen P.	1953
25 Martinez, Pedro	1971
Tolan, Stephanie S.	1942
26 Clinton, Hillary Rodham	1947
Cohen, Sasha	1984
Farmer, Paul Jr.	1959
Newsom, Lee Ann	1956
27 Anderson, Terry	1947
Carter, Majora	1966
Morrison, Lillian	1917
28 Gates, Bill	1955
Roberts, Julia	1967
Romero, John	1967
Salk, Jonas	1914
29 Flowers, Vonetta	1973
Ryder, Winona	1971
31 Candy, John	1950
Jackson, Peter	1961
Paterson, Katherine	1932

	Year
Patterson, Ryan	1983
Pauley, Jane	1950
Tucker, Chris	1973

November	Year
2 lang, k.d.	1961
Nelly	1974
3 Arnold, Roseanne	1952
Ho, David	1952
Kiraly, Karch	1960
4 Bush, Laura	1946
Combs, Sean (Puff Daddy)	1969
Handler, Ruth	1916
5 Jonas, Kevin	1987
7 Bahrke, Shannon	1980
Canady, Alexa	1950
8 Joy, Bill	1954
Mittermeier, Russell A.	1949
9 Denton, Sandi	?
Sagan, Carl	1934
10 Bates, Daisy	?1914
Eve	1979
11 Blige, Mary J.	1971
DiCaprio, Leonardo	1974
Vonnegut, Kurt	1922
12 Andrews, Ned	1980
Blackmun, Harry	1908
Harding, Tonya	1970
Hathaway, Anne	1982
Sosa, Sammy	1968
13 Goldberg, Whoopi	1949
14 Boutros-Ghali, Boutros	1922
Hussein, King	1935
Lindgren, Astrid	1907
Rice, Condoleezza	1954
Schilling, Curt	1966
15 Long, Irene D.	1951
Miyamoto, Shigeru	1952
Ochoa, Lorena	1981
O'Keeffe, Georgia	1887
Pinkwater, Daniel	1941
16 Baiul, Oksana	1977
17 Fuentes, Daisy	1966
Hanson, Ike	1980
18 Driscoll, Jean	1966
Felix, Allyson	1985
Klug, Chris	1972
Mankiller, Wilma	1945
Vidal, Christina	1981
19 Collins, Eileen	1956
Devers, Gail	1966

BIRTHDAY INDEX

November (continued)   **Year**
    Glover, Savion 1973
    Strug, Kerri 1977
20 Wardlaw, Lee 1955
21 Aikman, Troy 1966
    Griffey, Ken Jr. 1969
    Schwikert, Tasha 1984
    Speare, Elizabeth George 1908
    Strahan, Michael 1971
22 Boyle, Ryan 1981
    Carmona, Richard 1949
    Cyrus, Miley 1992
24 Ndeti, Cosmas 1971
25 Grant, Amy 1960
    Mathis, Clint 1976
    McNabb, Donovan 1976
    Thomas, Lewis 1913
26 Patrick, Ruth 1907
    Pine, Elizabeth Michele 1975
    Schulz, Charles 1922
27 Nye, Bill 1955
    Watley, Natasha 1981
    White, Jaleel 1977
28 apl.de.ap 1974
    Stewart, Jon 1962
29 L'Engle, Madeleine 1918
    Lewis, C.S. 1898
    Tubman, William V.S. 1895
30 Jackson, Bo 1962
    Parks, Gordon 1912
    Rodriguez, Ivan "Pudge" 1971

December   **Year**
1 Delson, Brad 1977
2 Hendrickson, Sue 1949
    Macaulay, David 1946
    Seles, Monica 1973
    Spears, Britney 1981
    Watson, Paul 1950
3 Kim Dae-jung .... ?1925
    Filipovic, Zlata 1980
4 Banks, Tyra 1973
    Lennox, Betty 1976
5 Muniz, Frankie 1985
6 Park, Nick 1958
    Risca, Viviana 1982
7 Bird, Larry 1956
    Carter, Aaron 1987
8 Newman, Ryan 1977
    Rivera, Diego 1886

    Weatherspoon, Teresa 1965
    Williams, Lori Aurelia .... ?
9 Hopper, Grace Murray 1906
    Tré Cool 1972
10 Raven 1985
12 Bialik, Mayim 1975
    Frankenthaler, Helen 1928
    Sinatra, Frank 1915
13 Fedorov, Sergei 1969
    Pierce, Tamora 1954
14 Hudgens, Vanessa 1988
    Jackson, Shirley 1916
15 Aidid, Mohammed Farah 1934
    Mendes, Chico 1944
    Smith, Betty .... ?1896
    Taymor, Julie 1952
16 Bailey, Donovan 1967
    McCary, Michael 1971
    Mead, Margaret 1901
17 Kielburger, Craig 1982
18 Aguilera, Christina 1980
    Holmes, Katie 1978
    Pitt, Brad 1964
    Sanchez Vicario, Arantxa 1971
    Spielberg, Steven 1947
19 Morrison, Sam 1936
    Sapp, Warren 1972
    White, Reggie 1961
20 Uchida, Mitsuko 1948
    Zirkle, Aliy 1969
21 Evert, Chris 1954
    Griffith Joyner, Florence 1959
    Stewart, James Jr. 1985
    Stiles, Jackie 1978
    Webb, Karrie 1974
22 Pinkney, Jerry 1939
23 Avi 1937
    Kratt, Martin 1965
    Harbaugh, Jim 1963
    Lowman, Meg 1953
24 Fauci, Anthony S. 1940
    Flake, Sharon 1955
    Lowe, Alex 1958
    Martin, Ricky 1971
25 Ryan, Pam Muñoz 1951
    Sadat, Anwar 1918
26 Butcher, Susan 1954
27 Oka, Masi 1974
    Roberts, Cokie 1943
28 Lee, Stan 1922

BIRTHDAY INDEX

December (continued)   **Year**
       Torvalds, Linus 1969
       Washington, Denzel 1954
30 Ali, Laila 1977
       James, LeBron 1984
       Willingham, Tyrone 1953
       Woods, Tiger 1975

Biography Today

General Series

For ages 9 and above

Biography Today **General Series** includes a unique combination of current biographical profiles that teachers and librarians — and the readers themselves — tell us are most appealing. The **General Series** is available as a 3-issue subscription; hardcover annual cumulation; or subscription plus cumulation.

Within the **General Series**, your readers will find a variety of sketches about:
- Authors
- Musicians
- Political leaders
- Sports figures
- Movie actresses & actors
- Cartoonists
- Scientists
- Astronauts
- TV personalities
- and the movers & shakers in many other fields!

"*Biography Today* will be useful in elementary and middle school libraries and in public library children's collections where there is a need for biographies of current personalities. High schools serving reluctant readers may also want to consider a subscription."
— *Booklist,* American Library Association

"Highly recommended for the young adult audience. Readers will delight in the accessible, energetic, tell-all style; teachers, librarians, and parents will welcome the clever format [and] intelligent and informative text. It should prove especially useful in motivating 'reluctant' readers or literate nonreaders."
— *MultiCultural Review*

"Written in a friendly, almost chatty tone, the profiles offer quick, objective information. While coverage of current figures makes *Biography Today* a useful reference tool, an appealing format and wide scope make it a fun resource to browse." — *School Library Journal*

"The best source for current information at a level kids can understand."
— Kelly Bryant, School Librarian, Carlton, OR

"Easy for kids to read. We love it! Don't want to be without it."
— Lynn McWhirter, School Librarian, Rockford, IL

ONE-YEAR SUBSCRIPTION
- 3 softcover issues, 6" x 9"
- Published in January, April, and September
- 1-year subscription, list price $66. **School and library price $64**
- 150 pages per issue
- 10 profiles per issue
- Contact sources for additional information
- Cumulative Names Index

HARDBOUND ANNUAL CUMULATION
- Sturdy 6" x 9" hardbound volume
- Published in December
- List price $73. **School and library price $66 per volume**
- 450 pages per volume
- 30 profiles — includes all profiles found in softcover issues for that calendar year
- Cumulative General Index, Places of Birth Index, and Birthday Index

SUBSCRIPTION AND CUMULATION COMBINATION
- $110 for 3 softcover issues plus the hardbound volume

For Cumulative General, Places of Birth, and Birthday Indexes, please see www.biographytoday.com.

571

LOOK WHO'S APPEARED — GENERAL SERIES

1992
Paula Abdul
Andre Agassi
Kirstie Alley
Terry Anderson
Roseanne Arnold
Isaac Asimov
James Baker
Charles Barkley
Larry Bird
Judy Blume
Berke Breathed
Garth Brooks
Barbara Bush
George Bush
Fidel Castro
Bill Clinton
Bill Cosby
Diana, Princess of Wales
Shannen Doherty
Elizabeth Dole
David Duke
Gloria Estefan
Mikhail Gorbachev
Steffi Graf
Wayne Gretzky
Matt Groening
Alex Haley
Hammer
Martin Handford
Stephen Hawking
Hulk Hogan
Saddam Hussein
Lee Iacocca
Bo Jackson
Mae Jemison
Peter Jennings
Steven Jobs
John Paul II
Magic Johnson
Michael Jordon
Jackie Joyner-Kersee
Spike Lee
Mario Lemieux
Madeleine L'Engle
Jay Leno
Yo-Yo Ma
Nelson Mandela
Wynton Marsalis
Thurgood Marshall
Ann Martin
Barbara McClintock
Emily Arnold McCully
Antonia Novello
Sandra Day O'Connor
Rosa Parks
Jane Pauley
H. Ross Perot
Luke Perry
Scottie Pippen
Colin Powell
Jason Priestley
Queen Latifah
Yitzhak Rabin
Sally Ride
Pete Rose
Nolan Ryan
H. Norman Schwarzkopf
Jerry Seinfeld
Dr. Seuss
Gloria Steinem
Clarence Thomas
Chris Van Allsburg
Cynthia Voigt
Bill Watterson
Robin Williams
Oprah Winfrey
Kristi Yamaguchi
Boris Yeltsin

1993
Maya Angelou
Arthur Ashe
Avi
Kathleen Battle
Candice Bergen
Boutros Boutros-Ghali
Chris Burke
Dana Carvey
Cesar Chavez
Henry Cisneros
Hillary Rodham Clinton
Jacques Cousteau
Cindy Crawford
Macaulay Culkin
Lois Duncan
Marian Wright Edelman
Cecil Fielder
Bill Gates
Sara Gilbert
Dizzy Gillespie
Al Gore
Cathy Guisewite
Jasmine Guy
Anita Hill
Ice-T
Darci Kistler
k.d. lang
Dan Marino
Rigoberta Menchu
Walter Dean Myers
Martina Navratilova
Phyllis Reynolds Naylor
Rudolf Nureyev
Shaquille O'Neal
Janet Reno
Jerry Rice
Mary Robinson
Winona Ryder
Jerry Spinelli
Denzel Washington
Keenen Ivory Wayans
Dave Winfield

1994
Tim Allen
Marian Anderson
Mario Andretti
Ned Andrews
Yasir Arafat
Bruce Babbitt
Mayim Bialik
Bonnie Blair
Ed Bradley
John Candy
Mary Chapin Carpenter
Benjamin Chavis
Connie Chung
Beverly Cleary
Kurt Cobain
F.W. de Klerk
Rita Dove
Linda Ellerbee
Sergei Fedorov
Zlata Filipovic
Daisy Fuentes
Ruth Bader Ginsburg
Whoopi Goldberg
Tonya Harding
Melissa Joan Hart
Geoff Hooper
Whitney Houston
Dan Jansen
Nancy Kerrigan
Alexi Lalas
Charlotte Lopez
Wilma Mankiller
Shannon Miller
Toni Morrison
Richard Nixon
Greg Norman
Severo Ochoa
River Phoenix
Elizabeth Pine
Jonas Salk
Richard Scarry
Emmitt Smith
Will Smith
Steven Spielberg
Patrick Stewart
R.L. Stine
Lewis Thomas
Barbara Walters
Charlie Ward
Steve Young
Kim Zmeskal

1995
Troy Aikman
Jean-Bertrand Aristide
Oksana Baiul
Halle Berry
Benazir Bhutto
Jonathan Brandis
Warren E. Burger
Ken Burns
Candace Cameron
Jimmy Carter
Agnes de Mille
Placido Domingo
Janet Evans
Patrick Ewing
Newt Gingrich
John Goodman
Amy Grant
Jesse Jackson
James Earl Jones
Julie Krone
David Letterman
Rush Limbaugh
Heather Locklear
Reba McEntire
Joe Montana
Cosmas Ndeti
Hakeem Olajuwon
Ashley Olsen
Mary Kate Olsen
Jennifer Parkinson
Linus Pauling
Itzhak Perlman
Cokie Roberts
Wilma Rudolph
Salt 'N' Pepa
Barry Sanders
William Shatner

LOOK WHO'S APPEARED — GENERAL SERIES

Elizabeth George
 Speare
Dr. Benjamin Spock
Jonathan Taylor
 Thomas
Vicki Van Meter
Heather Whitestone
Pedro Zamora

1996

Aung San Suu Kyi
Boyz II Men
Brandy
Ron Brown
Mariah Carey
Jim Carrey
Larry Champagne III
Christo
Chelsea Clinton
Coolio
Bob Dole
David Duchovny
Debbi Fields
Chris Galeczka
Jerry Garcia
Jennie Garth
Wendy Guey
Tom Hanks
Alison Hargreaves
Sir Edmund Hillary
Judith Jamison
Barbara Jordan
Annie Leibovitz
Carl Lewis
Jim Lovell
Mickey Mantle
Lynn Margulis
Iqbal Masih
Mark Messier
Larisa Oleynik
Christopher Pike
David Robinson
Dennis Rodman
Selena
Monica Seles
Don Shula
Kerri Strug
Tiffani-Amber Thiessen
Dave Thomas
Jaleel White

1997

Madeleine Albright
Marcus Allen
Gillian Anderson
Rachel Blanchard
Zachery Ty Bryan
Adam Ezra Cohen
Claire Danes
Celine Dion
Jean Driscoll
Louis Farrakhan
Ella Fitzgerald
Harrison Ford
Bryant Gumbel
John Johnson
Michael Johnson
Maya Lin
George Lucas
John Madden
Bill Monroe
Alanis Morissette
Sam Morrison
Rosie O'Donnell
Muammar el-Qaddafi
Christopher Reeve
Pete Sampras
Pat Schroeder
Rebecca Sealfon
Tupac Shakur
Tabitha Soren
Herbert Tarvin
Merlin Tuttle
Mara Wilson

1998

Bella Abzug
Kofi Annan
Neve Campbell
Sean Combs (Puff
 Daddy)
Dalai Lama (Tenzin
 Gyatso)
Diana, Princess of
 Wales
Leonardo DiCaprio
Walter E. Diemer
Ruth Handler
Hanson
Livan Hernandez
Jewel
Jimmy Johnson
Tara Lipinski
Jody-Anne Maxwell
Dominique Moceanu
Alexandra Nechita
Brad Pitt
LeAnn Rimes
Emily Rosa
David Satcher
Betty Shabazz
Kordell Stewart
Shinichi Suzuki
Mother Teresa
Mike Vernon
Reggie White
Kate Winslet

1999

Ben Affleck
Jennifer Aniston
Maurice Ashley
Kobe Bryant
Bessie Delany
Sadie Delany
Sharon Draper
Sarah Michelle Gellar
John Glenn
Savion Glover
Jeff Gordon
David Hampton
Lauryn Hill
King Hussein
Lynn Johnston
Shari Lewis
Oseola McCarty
Mark McGwire
Slobodan Milosevic
Natalie Portman
J.K. Rowling
Frank Sinatra
Gene Siskel
Sammy Sosa
John Stanford
Natalia Toro
Shania Twain
Mitsuko Uchida
Jesse Ventura
Venus Williams

2000

Christina Aguilera
K.A. Applegate
Lance Armstrong
Backstreet Boys
Daisy Bates
Harry Blackmun
George W. Bush
Carson Daly
Ron Dayne
Henry Louis Gates, Jr.
Doris Haddock
 (Granny D)
Jennifer Love Hewitt
Chamique Holdsclaw
Katie Holmes
Charlayne Hunter-
 Gault
Johanna Johnson
Craig Kielburger
John Lasseter
Peyton Manning
Ricky Martin
John McCain
Walter Payton
Freddie Prinze, Jr.
Viviana Risca
Briana Scurry
George Thampy
CeCe Winans

2001

Jessica Alba
Christiane Amanpour
Drew Barrymore
Jeff Bezos
Destiny's Child
Dale Earnhardt
Carly Fiorina
Aretha Franklin
Cathy Freeman
Tony Hawk
Faith Hill
Kim Dae-jung
Madeleine L'Engle
Mariangela Lisanti
Frankie Muniz
*N Sync
Ellen Ochoa
Jeff Probst
Julia Roberts
Carl T. Rowan
Britney Spears
Chris Tucker
Lloyd D. Ward
Alan Webb
Chris Weinke

2002

Aaliyah
Osama bin Laden
Mary J. Blige
Aubyn Burnside
Aaron Carter
Julz Chavez
Dick Cheney
Hilary Duff

573

LOOK WHO'S APPEARED — GENERAL SERIES

Billy Gilman
Rudolph Giuliani
Brian Griese
Jennifer Lopez
Dave Mirra
Dineh Mohajer
Leanne Nakamura
Daniel Radcliffe
Condoleezza Rice
Marla Runyan
Ruth Simmons
Mattie Stepanek
J.R.R. Tolkien
Barry Watson
Tyrone Willingham
Elijah Wood

2003

Yolanda Adams
Olivia Bennett
Mildred Benson
Alexis Bledel
Barry Bonds
Vincent Brooks
Laura Bush
Amanda Bynes
Kelly Clarkson
Vin Diesel
Eminem
Michele Forman
Vicente Fox
Millard Fuller
Josh Hartnett
Dolores Huerta
Sarah Hughes
Enrique Iglesias
Jeanette Lee
John Lewis
Nicklas Lidstrom
Clint Mathis
Donovan McNabb
Nelly
Andy Roddick
Gwen Stefani
Emma Watson
Meg Whitman
Reese Witherspoon
Yao Ming

2004

Natalie Babbitt
David Beckham
Francie Berger
Tony Blair

Orlando Bloom
Kim Clijsters
Celia Cruz
Matel Dawson, Jr.
The Donnas
Tim Duncan
Shirin Ebadi
Carla Hayden
Ashton Kutcher
Lisa Leslie
Linkin Park
Lindsay Lohan
Irene D. Long
John Mayer
Mandy Moore
Thich Nhat Hanh
OutKast
Raven
Ronald Reagan
Keanu Reeves
Ricardo Sanchez
Brian Urlacher
Alexa Vega
Michelle Wie
Will Wright

2005

Kristen Bell
Jack Black
Sergey Brin & Larry Page
Adam Brody
Chris Carrabba
Johnny Depp
Eve
Jennie Finch
James Forman
Wally Funk
Cornelia Funke
Bethany Hamilton
Anne Hathaway
Priest Holmes
T.D. Jakes
John Paul II
Toby Keith
Alison Krauss
Wangari Maathai
Karen Mitchell-Raptakis
Queen Noor
Violet Palmer
Gloria Rodriguez
Carlos Santana
Antonin Scalia
Curtis Schilling

Maria Sharapova
Ashlee Simpson
Donald Trump
Ben Wallace

2006

Carol Bellamy
Miri Ben-Ari
Black Eyed Peas
Bono
Kelsie Buckley
Dale Chihuly
Neda DeMayo
Dakota Fanning
Green Day
Freddie Highmore
Russel Honoré
Tim Howard
Cynthia Kadohata
Coretta Scott King
Rachel McAdams
Cesar Millan
Steve Nash
Nick Park
Rosa Parks
Danica Patrick
Jorge Ramos
Ben Roethlisberger
Lil' Romeo
Adam Sandler
Russell Simmons
Jamie Lynn Spears
Jon Stewart
Joss Stone
Hannah Teter
Brenda Villa
Tyler James Williams
Gretchen Wilson

2007

Shaun Alexander
Carmelo Anthony
Drake Bell
Chris Brown
Regina Carter
Kortney Clemons
Taylor Crabtree
Miley Cyrus
Aaron Dworkin
Fall Out Boy
Roger Federer
Will Ferrell
America Ferrera
June Foray

Sarah Blaffer Hrdy
Alicia Keys
Cheyenne Kimball
Keira Knightley
Wendy Kopp
Sofia Mulanovich
Barack Obama
Soledad O'Brien
Jamie Oliver
Skip Palenik
Nancy Pelosi
Jack Prelutsky
Ivan "Pudge" Rodriguez
Michael Sessions
Kate Spade
Sabriye Tenberken
Rob Thomas
Ashley Tisdale
Carrie Underwood
Muhammad Yunus

2008

Aly & AJ
Bill Bass
Greta Binford
Cory Booker
Sophia Bush
Majora Carter
Anderson Cooper
Zac Efron
Selena Gomez
Al Gore
Vanessa Hudgens
Jennifer Hudson
Zach Hunter
Bindi Irwin
Jonas Brothers
Lisa Ling
Eli Manning
Kimmie Meissner
Scott Niedermayer
Christina Norman
Masi Oka
Tyler Perry
Morgan Pressel
Rihanna
John Roberts Jr.
J. K. Rowling
James Stewart Jr.
Ichiro Suzuki
Karen P. Tandy
Marta Tienda
Justin Timberlake
Lee Wardlaw